www.ingramcontent.com/pod-product-compliance
Lightning Source LLC
Chambersburg PA
CBHW071425070526
44578CB00001B/2

be the judge, jury, or objective assessor of the state of your own character! As proof, just think hard on and recollect just a couple of people whom *you* have in *any* way hurt or harmed and let someone ask *them* if you are so noble or righteous. They'll let it rip! If everyone were privy to your thoughts, would *all* of your thoughts be pure and selfless? Just put yourself in the back of the return line at Wal-Mart's Customer Service the day after Christmas, recall your attitude when you felt wronged in traffic, or think back on when you felt the sting of some injustice done to you or your family or at work. Yes, you and I most certainly *do* need Him if we are to have any hope of letting go of our egos and becoming an active participant in His blueprint of love. Speaking of which, the only way you can conduct yourself becomingly in an exasperating or crushing moment is to let Jesus within you interact with others; in other words, let the "good treasure in your heart bring forth what is good" (Luke 6:45). Sometimes a private and tender hug can jumpstart healing more than a thousand carefully-chosen words can. Ah, it takes time for love to become a habit. Not only this, but when one goes about a life focused on consuming or acquiring goods, people, and experiences, one cannot achieve *sustaining* fulfillment. Most are unaware that we unknowingly seek Him our whole life. You are not reading this by happenstance! He may very well have nudged me to write this book, so it could become a master key that would fit in and unlock your heart such that you might then become readied enough to receive Jesus when His Holy Spirit beckons *you*. *God does not hide when you seek*, and when you do find Him, you can't help but fall in love with His Son who died for you. Do you not realize that you, too, were "fearfully and wonderfully made"? (Psalm 139:14). Do you think all of this business about Jesus is just history from long ago? "Jesus Christ is the same yesterday and today and forever" (Heb. 13:8); He's both in and outside human chronology. I just can't seem to stop wanting to quote Scripture, so it's time to put down my pen. It is not by chance you have read this account; it's your turn now; you're up! Now go and seek Him for yourself. You will find Him *and* yourself anew. *Hallelujah!*

encouragement from my pastor and run for Him!

My purpose has been to show you what the early stage of my sanctification looks like and not just the rosy rainbow stuff of the afterglow of salvation, though that moment is the ultimate game-changer. Three years is the time on planet earth wherein Jesus preached and taught, and I've given you roughly four years of this follower of His early growth, including joys and pains. Have I covered a fraction of the questions *you* might have as relates to God? Not hardly. You will have your own areas of greater fascination or consternation as you come to seek to know Him more; questions may or may not be answered, but none is a deal-breaker as regards true faith. In being firm in my salvation, all else is small fry. By taking in my Bible daily, like some essential vitamin from Him, I, like millions of people, keep on being amazed at how countless details and lives throughout millennia fit together kit and glove in God's chronicle of redemption which culminated in Christ. Those who had faith in Him afterward risked their lives to pass on the flaming torch to you and me. Once you realize that this life is all you have, you can boldly start your date with destiny by approaching Him like a youngster. You've got everything to lose but even more to gain! If you don't yet believe, think of your encounter here with me as one with a close friend who wants to let you know that you've got your shirt on inside out and backward, even if you hadn't noticed it before, don't care, or kind of like it. As He did with me, God can also get our attention by bringing us to our knees through some calamity *or* by having us perchance upon Scripture that penetrates our soul. More often than not, you'll first encounter God through one of those who simply believe in Him. It happened to me, and I hope it's now happening to you. It's totally on you to claim Him.

You may say, "I am not one of those who *need* <u>Him</u> because I am basically okay and good-to-go; I pretty much do good anyway. After all, I *try* to practice the Golden Rule; I'm can't be all *that* bad." Doing good deeds, though good in and of itself, will not get you an eternal reward, whether or not you seek such; this is reason number one. Number two, though *you* may not consider it true, yes, you as well I really *are* "that bad." It's not a matter of degree for God; it's all the same, whether the wrongdoing is a peccadillo or an atrocity. One can lead to the other. Ben Franklin said, "A small leak sinks a great ship." Anyway, *you cannot* person. And the magnificent decision to love Him *and others* back is also personal and free. For many, accepting the free gift from Him is difficult, but once we do, we commence starting out on His "narrow" path. Our challenge becomes to love the unlovable or difficult ones in our lives. Oh, it's easy to love those who love you back, but what about those hurting people who are perhaps snarky, mean, dismissive, silent, or cynical? Are you one of these? I surely was. I *also* know it is the *seemingly* weak and meek, but, in reality, the kind and His un-blind, as it were, who are the ones that turn the world's values upside down, inside out, and on its head, for all they're worth in His namesake.

No, I will never complete perfect sanctification this side of Heaven (unless Jesus comes at the Rapture), and trials will always come about. God not only doesn't *cause* bad things to happen to good people; He doesn't even send folks to Hell. Anyway, hell was never intended for us; God didn't want us to perish. It's just that He can't maintain the absolute perfection of His divine and holy nature of being all-good to show occasional favoritism by making exceptions when He hears our pleas or excuses. When people choose to reject Him, *they* choose damnation for themselves. This aside, God our Savior "desires *all* men to be saved" (1 Tim. 2:3, emphasis mine). Mark would emphasize that this hope for us is "God's heartbeat"! God often inconveniences us and disrupts our lives to shake us out of our complacency so that we can do more for Him in ways unimagined. Maddeningly, Satan also never stops, but I am better at knowing what my blind spots are. If I could, I wish I could throw Satan into the lake of fire right now myself! I love my little church, and often when Mark preaches, my heart doesn't know whether to burst or break. I feel like I've been given rocket fuel! This man lives by Hebrew 3:13 and is one who readily "encourages day after day" by fusing the sacred into the secular. For example, something as simple and profound as taking communion becomes another opportunity to unite with Him. Why? Christ offers communion as a means for us to remember Him. It is a moment to think about His body being broken and blood being spilled to have made it possible to have a relationship with Him. That is exactly what *I* now have. I think so many people overthink things and get hung up. So, should *you* come to Him, *yes*, take communion! It is for all who believe and have a relationship with Jesus!!" I would take this mindlessly following each other, all but to jump off a cliff to their demise. Now I see seeking a sign that I am a normal person desiring an authentic and meaningful connection with her supreme maker. Most of us take a lot of wrong turns and look in so many directions for "it," in other words, some ultimate answer, bliss, or peace, etc., and not *Him*. It's also no great surprise that often, a more fervent search begins at the crossroads of middle age when we find ourselves standing and trying to attain balance, direction, and thrust for the *rest* of our lives. We look back but must press ahead, hopefully finding passion and purpose in and through Him. I used to think that God was so big and busy that I either couldn't count for Him or that I wasn't bad off enough to be helped, let alone noticed. The Bible assures me that since God knows the numbers of hairs on my head and even feeds sparrows (adapted from Luke 12:7), then, of *course*, He's got my back and wants me on His front line. To devalue or minimize myself in any way amounts to insulting God who made me just as I am — with and on purpose. How can I doubt Him? He alone possesses omniscience, omnipotence, and omnibenevolence, which translates into good intentions for me? I don't get to blame God for whatever I perceive at some moment as unfair, painful, or bad. It is "my bad," my *mea culpa*, to even think so! As God asked Job, "Where were *you* when I laid the foundation of the earth?" (Job 38:4, emphasis mine). Ha! That's a good one! I no longer trying to gauge God's intentions is not the same thing as accepting a wrong without trying to right it in the capacity I've been given!

And just how *personal* is all of this? Very. How did I come to understand that Jesus is who He said He is? Through the love of Christ demonstrated in real life by real and flawed people. Honestly, I used to think it a little odd that, upon occasion, Mark would end his texts with the brotherly-minded, "I love you," when it is more typical to hear and say the impersonal and generic, "*Love* you." Think about it though: the impact of taking yourself, the subject, out of the sentence depersonalizes the message. If there is no subject, how could you, the object, *not* feel less love, even if semantically? God, through His Son, would never say this! Can you imagine God merely saying to us, "Love you"??! The big "I am" came down here to demonstrate in the most potent and victorious way possible to tell and show that "I love" is not only possible but necessary. He did so for us in the flesh, in *first years were unfolding* because I want people — including *you* — to see what a new takeoff in post-salvation might look like. This book deals with many factors that led to my salvation; in the process, I feel like I have gone from telling my story to having a conversation with you! There are many valuable resources that can help you decipher words and concepts new to you to navigate the Bible. This book teaches you about matters of eternal consequence and values of lasting merit. You will have an encounter with Jesus Christ. Sweet encouragement abounds during times of trouble when you are struggling and hurting. You will leave feeling triumphant when you make the discovery of how *you* fit in the living construct God made, which has Christ as its "chief cornerstone" (Ephesians 2:20 NKJV); you are a piece therein. Through the Holy Spirit's guidance, I hope that in writing this, just as Paul shares about himself, it doesn't phase you that "I have become all things to all men, so that I may, by all means, save some" (1 Corinthians 9:22). I say to my fellow intellectuals that having faith doesn't mean I'm not rational, logical, and intellectually curious. I *am*, but there are spheres of knowledge, including the reason for our existence, that go above beyond whatever we think we may know. To those with an irreverent sense of humor, I can say that, yes, when I see "Jesus Saves" spray-painted on an overpass, I can recall back when, not so long ago, I might have asked myself, "Saves *what*? S & H Green Stamps? Whales?" But then, my reasoning unbeliever, my curious reader, or my fellow brother or sister in Christ, I took a few steps into Truth and came to realize the meaning behind the words Paul gave to the Corinthian Greeks, those which previously had been elusive: "When I was a child, I used to speak like a child, think like a child, reason like a child; when I became a man, I did away with childish things" (1 Corinthians 13:11). I *am* that adult now, even though I still come to Him daily as a child! I love contemplating what knowing "*fully*" (v. 12) will mean one day for me! I cherish the promise of seeing Him "face to face" (v. 12) after I am no more here.

What then has changed? Well, just everything. I know that I get stronger with every day I read and pray, no matter what life throws at or hands me on a platter. I used to think if the masses liked or believed something, then it just couldn't be or come to good, let alone be right. In my mind's eye, I would imagine the well-known myth of lemmings

AFTERWARD

"'For I know the plans that I have for you,' declares the LORD, 'plans for welfare and not for calamity to give you a future and a hope.'"
— Jeremiah 29:11

"We have this hope as an anchor for the soul, firm and secure..."
— Hebrew 6:19 NIV

Well, that's it. As Mark would say, "I'm not done; I'm just stopping here." A testimony of coming to Christ is hardly uncommon, though you may find mine unique. You may rightly say to yourself that you are hardly reading the book of an accomplished and seasoned Christian. Maybe not, but I don't pretend to be, yet there *is* merit in catching a glimpse of the life of one who is on her way to evolving more fully in Him. I hope with all I've you that may find something here with which *you* can identify! As I wrap up these final thoughts, there is none more important than for me

to tell you that though I may have penned this book, in a sense, I know good and well I did not pioneer it. I may be the writer, but Jesus Christ is the "author and perfecter of [my] faith" (Hebrews 12:2) such that what you hold even came to fruition. Do I feel used or expendable, like a vessel that performed what she *had* to? Far from it! I became inspired and moved such that I couldn't *not* write! If Jesus had not come to bestow His grace on us all *and* given me the capacity to have faith in Him, such that the same Holy Spirit who was in Him is also *in* me, there's no way I would have used any talent to have seen it through! In other words, though He chose me to share Himself in this manner, time, and place, I can't take credit for what I didn't generate. It all boils down to the fact that God gets all the glory for acts done in obedience and love given back to Him. No one ought to brag because, as I've heard Mark say many times, "no one can out-give God," and what a beautiful thing that is! In anticipation of some of the readership, it became vital for me to write this *as these* cue in the song, "Amazing Grace" now, bagpipes and all. First of all, that coming to Him even came to be is something I never saw coming, but in my curiosity, attraction, then outright and steady hunger for Him, it is obvious to me there is no turning back. He is already in my future, and the battle is won, even though we continue to undergo challenges in our daily life. Why? As the only eternal and living God — unlike any god which man makes for himself — He is always with me, and since He is for me, there's nothing that can happen to me to separate or sever what exists between Him and me (Romans 8:38–39). Does this mean I won't have conflict or problems? Goodness, no! As you have seen, this past year has been chock full of challenges, fears, and threats. Do I think that these are the worst that anyone has experienced? Not by a long shot. I'm just sharing with you this unlikely journey, one that starts where it did, led me to right here, right now. When it's all said and done, *all anybody wants in life is to know that they matter*; God gives us this love and validation. It is hard to find a place to stop because, quite frankly, gentle reader, though I have never met you, I hope you can tell I do care for you. I want to pour what I have of Him in me into you, yes, pass the baton to *you* and run in this relay for Him *together*.

more and more "progress, not perfection" here, too! And lest you think I think that I've somehow arrived, this all-over-the-map lady knows all too well she's got a long way to go, but even that is great: I'm just grateful I met Him and got started! Mark confided that he was proud of me and that he didn't know the answer to why God had to allow me to walk through these waters but that I was doing wonderfully at representing Him and His love. *We don't allow this world and others to shake our faith.* He assured me that *anybody that Jesus has ever used for anything had felt the way I did.* Battles in life can be so overwhelming at times. Then he ended by telling me, "You can't fix you, but Jesus can. There may be nothing at all to fix, that it's just that Jesus is allowing you to be melted down in refinement. Pure gold!! And remember that Paul would say, 'We are more than conquerors!'" (Romans 8:37 KJV). When I get beleaguered, drained, and spent because He is *in* me through His Holy Spirit, *beside* me as my Savior and Friend, and *above* me as my Father in Heaven, I can find no greater encouragement than this. He defeated death, and I am on my way to victory because the payment for *all* sins is done; "it *is* finished" (John 19:30). I will pass on to *you* what I, as a believer, have been called to do. It's called the Great Commission; the risen Jesus said, "Go and make disciples of all the nations" (from Matthew 28:19). On the way to school this morning, I cranked up "I Got Saved" on repeat. Looking up at a shaft of sunlight peeping through the clouds, I felt like my heart was going to explode! I know who is my "Alpha and Omega" (Rev. 1:8), and so I hit pause and thanked Jesus for what He did. I also want to thank *you* for having an open mind and ready heart to take a chance on me and read this book written for you. How can I not end my testimony with the most compelling and invitation to come to a richer life than ever imaginable? Like me, you are also a "whosoever"! I pray that you, too, a person vital to this world, will see the light and experience His vast love. Why? "For God so loved the world that He gave His only begotten Son, that whoever believes in Him should not perish but have everlasting life. For God did not send His Son into the world to condemn the world, but that the world through Him might be saved" (John 3:16–17 NKJV).

When I look back over what to date is just past the four-year mark into my relationship with Christ, I am amazed. In fact, go ahead and

"Why me?" Now when I reflected, I found myself more in the mindset of the Puritan historian, Cotton Mather, who asked himself, *"What improvement in godliness and usefulness does this affliction call me to?"* What "engine of good" may I yet become and how? This way of living takes me from victim to victor, a state of powerlessness to triumph through submission to Him alone and *not* to that of the world hostile to Him. Here's my takeaway: Through no fault of their own, students today cannot do what I expect and get results from like the students I'd had at the beginning of my career. Many simply have not been taught self-discipline, the need to show respect, and the value of perseverance, let alone, had instilled in them a sense of wonder (let alone a love for reading). You can ask Siri or Google absolutely anything and have the answer at your fingertips in a second or two, so why should the same not be true for achieving other types of gain? This is what we have come to expect in our brave new world of interconnected isolation. Secondly, who am I to think that in nine hours a week, I can successfully cover my curriculum to thirty students required to be there when the remainder of their busy week floods out His goodness I also attempt to instill. I don't have the luxury of being upset at that which is beyond any of my control, but I can maintain my steady walk with Him and share His way through me with them as I gently sway them through love and enthusiasm in my teaching. Changes abound everywhere, but I continue to seek biblical succor first. How could I have foreseen that by becoming humble and willing to grow, I would be honored with "Teacher of the Month" the following year and praised by our administrators for my flexibility and overall improvement? Even though I had done no wrong, there's no reason why I can't get better and be more in the right by Him! A couple of months after this, another administrator told me that the kids had been telling him I was their favorite teacher.

    I attribute any success and small victory to the fact that I'm starting to look a little bit more like Him when I devote my *whole* self and energy to Him. When I am at my wit's end, I try to remember that, just as was shown to me, *mercy triumphs over judgment.* Therefore, as they say in A.A., I will "seek to understand rather than be understood" and be the bigger man by trying to be the first to confess, apologize, or speak the truth, but do so with tact, consideration, and kindness. I seek

8.30 PASS IT FORWARD

For me thus far, I love what I do because I love people. How would my being a Christian shape my growth and glory for Him in and beyond the classroom? Is it that kids' needs that have fundamentally changed? No, they still seek and crave respect, loving affirmation, consistency, and guidance. I have come to realize that to remain influential, I need to adapt to the times without changing my core Christian values. Yes, such *is* possible! I began to read articles that confirmed that the environment I teach now is different from that I started, now over a quarter of a century ago. No joke! It has become imperative to educate myself on how to face my class as it currently stands, even if I see that kids still have some basic needs that have *not* changed!. Adapting myself to change gives me the chance to become an even stronger and more relevant Christian! What I take in from the world I transmute with what all there is to share of Him. It's a win-win, two-for-one way to share Him! After all, I am charged to "not be conformed to this world but be transformed by the renewing of [my] mind, so that I may prove what the will of God is, that which is good and acceptable and perfect" (Romans 12:2). Here I am, a public school teacher, seeking ways to share Him in a manner that *He gets in* without ruffling any feathers or any being aware of it. I am undercover and incognito, but I'm still me! I hope they notice that there's something about my manner that they can't quite put their finger on that resonates a better way, *His* way, to do *life*, let alone class requirements. I have come to learn the value, the imperative of respectfully entreating and including parents in our village effort to grow their child, my student. Providing new avenues for success and hope needs to be given more frequently and in a pleasing format. Has the world gone upside down? Maybe. Was I daft? Hardly. Was the world so different from the time I had started teaching? Vastly.

In this persistent path of seeking improvement, I began to ask myself difficult questions, which I would not have before becoming a Christian. In having undergone what I did at work just two months ago, my old thought process unquestioningly would have queried, careful that in my high standards and expectations, I might falter and inadvertently say something to dishearten someone. Oswald Chambers warns us that "an unguarded strength is a double weakness." More often than I would like, I get reminded that strengths can mask weaknesses, but it is in these my weaknesses where Jesus always shows out, so throughout all the highs, lows, and plateaus of my life, I keep running to Him; hopefully, others are taking note for themselves. Anyway, an hour and a half came and went like a flash. Not only did I not ask any of my questions, but also, I didn't even think of them. Over the past nearly four years, our time has grown from Mark's being our mentor and protector to that of an abiding brother and awesome friend. I'll now share with you a short poem I wrote in gratitude to this man who helped me find Him, and in so doing, brought the "God of hope [who] fills [me] with all joy and peace in believing" (Romans 15:13).

    Here's to a man who abounds in loyalty
    Affection and good cheer make for his royalty!
    He keeps it so real, yet sets his sights on the sky,
    'Cause he sees the big picture and knows the Big Guy.
    We love him for friendship, laughter, and, well, just because.
    So, in the midst of life's flurries, for him we do pause
    To say thanks for your heart, grit, wisdom, and wit;
    There's no one else like you, and it just had to be writ!

Later that same night, Bonnie asked me, like a child asks a parent, to tell her *how it's going to be*. Bonnie said, "Tell me about *Jesus*," which I took as my nudge to tell her just how much He loves her. This time, rather than repeating confirmations of her salvation, I took a thread from Mark's visit earlier in the day and suggested to her that whenever she got troubled about *anything*, to turn to Him

and read *her* favorite book in the New Testament; for Bonnie, this happened to be the Gospel of John. As far as she is concerned, John expresses Jesus' love more sweetly and supremely than any other person. I said that whenever we get down and out, this means we need Jesus just like a scuba diver needs an oxygen tank. When we get down and out in the world — in her case, most recently through having had cancer — we get oxygen-deprived, and that without breathing Him in *daily*, we will either get the bends or suffocate for lack of His love, His Word, and His Life in us.

8.29 Just Keepin' in Real

Yesterday when Mark came to visit, he came right on in, carrying in one hand a lovely cantilever lily for Bonnie, as it was her birthday, and a Starbucks iced coffee in the other. It had been three months since he visited, so I felt a tidal wave of relief to tell him in person and a condensed and animated fashion all the challenges I'd had at work. Talking to him is like flying with him, and he gets the way I communicate which, more often than not, is like scattered buckshot going a thousand miles an hour toward its target. We started out sitting on the back porch but returned to the kitchen for some hot wings I'd picked up for us to eat. Again, though months and miles spanned between our now quarterly visits, we were often on similar pages in life. He shared with us some things going on in his life as a coach, and I shared with him, for example, about speaking at that young man's funeral. I gave my opinion on how the children of the day were living in "a culture of losers," which, of course, is *not* to say that they *are* losers! Far from it!! It just means that children often expect everything to be given to them, and they do not know how to persevere and sacrifice to bring out the best in each other and in themselves. Expectations for success and achievement are now microwaved for both adult and child to be expected instantly. It is the *adult* who must tow the line and be a leader. He or she must share Jesus with his or her children through loving, protective, and consistent righteous actions to present a united front, a band of warriors who "fight the good fight of faith" (1 Timothy 6:12) against conceit promoted by the world. Anyway, nobody can go back in time and live in some cocoon or time bubble and reject this or that aspect of our Information Age. To do so would be like cutting off your nose to spite your face; you'd lose your chance to be most effective for Him out where it counts — yes, in the world! We all have room for improvement, which I now see as the means to serve Him better. For example, I had that recent cause to reevaluate my manner in the classroom, not because it was professionally imperative, but as an adult Christian, I did not want to be guilty of "provoking … children to anger" (Ephesians 6:4). I am a natural encourager, but I must *also* be

Connecting the Dots...

An Unanticipated Journey of Finding Faith

By
Dimitria Christakis

Connecting the Dots…

Copyright © 2021 by Dimitria Christakis

All rights reserved. No part of this publication may be reproduced, distributed, or transmitted in any form or by any means, including photocopying, recording, or other electronic or mechanical methods, without the prior written permission of the author, except in the case of brief quotations embodied in critical reviews and certain other non-commercial uses permitted by copyright law.

Any similarity to real persons, living or dead, is coincidental and not intended by the author.

Unless otherwise indicated, Scripture quotations are taken from the New American Standard Bible (NASB) from Bible Gateway.

Living Stones: 52 Love Letters is available as another work written by this author.

ISBN
978-1-954932-21-0 (Hardback)
978-1-954932-20-3 (Paperback)
978-1-954932-19-7 (eBook)

Dimitria Christakis

This book is dedicated to those who helped me come to *faith*, in the *hope* that those reading this might also come to believe in Him, and with *love* to My Lord and Savior Jesus Christ who lives.

"You shall not delay the offering from your harvest…"

Exodus 22:29

"Let your light shine before men in such a way that they may see your good works, and glorify your Father who is in heaven."

Matthew 5:16

BOOK 1: ME IN B.C.

Chapter 1: Growing up in S-P-G	2
Chapter 2: Mother Russia	48
Chapter 3: The Call to Teach	92
Chapter 4: Booze and "A Power Greater"	136

BOOK 2: D.C. IN A.D.

Chapter 5: Year 1, Salvation: Accepting the Invitation	189
Chapter 6: Year 2, Growing Pains	318
Chapter 7: Year 3, Becoming Fruitful	423
Chapter 8: Year 4, "Be Anxious for Nothing"	546

PREFACE

"You will seek Me and find Me when you search for Me with all your heart." (Jeremiah 29:13)

If you have ever wondered how a person comes to faith with scant spiritual nurturing or how God draws people to Himself, follow my story. You will discover through my childhood, my calling and vocation — teaching, travels, and through the faithful friendship of a pastor, how I became enthusiastically receptive to God's gift of grace! How did this come to be? In America, where everything at your beck and call and arm's reach to satisfy our every whim and wish, I craved pitch and purpose of lasting value; I was searching a sense of belonging in a manner and measure for which I had no words. Little did I know at the time that there was no person or place, let alone thought, action, or acquisition could provide the profound love I was seeking.

Let me also *thank you* for picking this book to read; you are in for a spiritual adventure of a lifetime! I hope that you will recognize the common thread running through my journey to salvation, that everything had been leading inexorably towards my coming to know Christ. When you start out reading this book, it might not initially seem like it. I'm going to look like a confused child who was interested in her heritage. Some may wonder why I spend so much time talking about theology or Russians or all things Greek, but in seeking the divine, my mind went about it through a convoluted process, possibly more common than not. There will be some who might appreciate this book because I am passionate about making a difference in a child's world through teaching. Others who read this may have a fascination with theology and various religious studies, and this book will pique their interest. There are those who have a passion for American literature; you will appreciate parts of this book. Lovers of travel will find merit in this book, particularly if you are interested in Russia or Greece. Perhaps you have been in charge of a group that had to be in the public eye. I have led many student trips abroad, and I always told them that they should consider themselves "ambassadors" for the United States. Little did I know then that I would come to consider myself a representative for Christ, and I have a message to convey on His behalf. Perhaps if I had chosen to write this book ten years later, it would be completely saturated with Scripture and my favorite Bible passages, but I'm nowhere near there yet, and I chose purposefully to write a book at this early stage of my Christian development. I wanted to convey the supernatural change within me *as it was transpiring* to be as authentic, accurate, and true to the experience as I could. Memories fade, and recollections collide and can get jumbled, and my acceptance of Christ was too vital not to record the transformation while it was occurring soon after the spark of conversion. As time passes by in this story, you will witness the mental switch's flip regarding my heart's desire. The cynic might quip to me, "Oh, your brain has fallen out, you are no longer rationally thinking about things, you have become 'one of them,' you decided to 'join them instead of beat them,'" and so on and so forth. Yet I know at my very core that is *not* the case, and the evolution within me has shaken my foundations and solidified the sense of what I am here for, and that is to share what I've come to know and love about Him with you.

When I was younger, I used to think that becoming a Christian sometimes occurred when people who were desperate to change their lifestyle went overboard the opposite way and adopted a set of values that put God in charge. Indeed, a full recovery would nearly necessitate the intervention of clinging to a higher power to empower them to let go of some horrid activity that was killing them. Such tales of deprivation, extreme suffering, or wrongdoing are not what you will find in this book. You might also wonder why she talks about Russian or American literature? Why would she probe the theology of Puritans, on the one hand, and the mindset of Unitarians, on the other? Or why is she exploring aspects of Greece and Greek culture? Never having put all the pieces together before, this has become my way of revealing what lay beneath the veil: all roads in my life, all my choices, passions, and life events have been leading me to Christ, and in so doing, have launched me into a destiny of serving the Lord in *this* manner. Why would I write this *now*, you may ask? I mean, it's not like I am about to rewrite Scripture or say anything new, but I can share the perspective of someone *as* she was undergoing a supernatural transformation, a regeneration, a bonafide metamorphosis into a Christian pilgrim. Such progress! I am well aware that you, my gentle reader, can easily access weighty and authoritative books by theologians or talk to seasoned pastors about the nuts and bolts and the finer points of Christianity. I heartily encourage you to do so! However, if you are curious about what it was like for an ignorant and stubborn rebel such as I not only to come to Him in the first place, but *stay* with Him, and if you want it straight from the horse's mouth, *this* is your book! For me, this is precisely the point: *how it all starts*. That I have become a Christian *and* am compelled to share my testimony *this* way reveals to me that the Holy Spirit is urging me to strike while the iron is hot. There's not a shadow of a doubt. I don't want to wait until I'm retired, or my memories have faded or become distorted to the point that I could not relate my experience. I am filled with a reverberating reverence; I am basking in the Holy Spirit's prompting to share this *while* these changes are going on inside me. I have almost a decade left before I retire, and so many times, I have daydreamed about writing *something* and *someday* after I retire. However, currently, I have a different perspective: there is not enough time to tarry and wait; nay, I cannot wait to convey the good news of my life. The time is *now*.

Writing this book while I'm still in the full throws of my career as a teacher proves that Christ is leading me to do what would seem impossible. Considering the workload of what an English and foreign language teacher has to do outside school hours, I never imagined I would start on a book now, let alone one with this subject matter. Further, that this book has seemed to write itself, which also defies logic, is surefire proof that He's behind the idea, inspiration, *and* me all the way. I would never have thought, let alone spoke of, let alone wanted to write you, a stranger, about Him! Some might think I have become obsessed or possessed. It's not that I have become overtaken by anything; I am *filled with the Holy Spirit*. I now use vocabulary that I never knew existed before, but such *has* to be used because it accurately conveys what I now know. The bare fact is that *it* could and did happen to me: I am a follower of Christ, and I answer to God and seek His wisdom for my life. One additional benefit in writing this is to help people who do not fully understand Christian-based terminology. I certainly do not want to reinvent the wheel by what I have to say, but I do have a strong desire to stir the hearts and minds of the people who have been turned off to Jesus because of the institution of the church.

Often, I feel like I am a modern-day Samaritan. Just as the Samaritans were looked down upon by some during Christ's day because they were not pure enough in their bloodline or belief system for the Jewish of that time, I had never been an accepted member of a so-called "real church." I didn't believe! For much of my life, I straddled the fence where faith is concerned, which, for some, might disqualify me right off the bat from being His. This is not the case. When doubt comes my way, I now know to keep my eye on Christ! I'm not really into dedicating books, but my reason for writing this, first of all, is to glorify God. This book would never have gotten off the ground had it not been for the desire to share what He put in me. This book is also written especially for those of you who, like me, might consider yourself an intellectual, a thinker, a doubter, a rationalist, a curious dabbler of various philosophies and religions. Maybe you have a droll sense of humor and finds yourself thinking irreverent thoughts when observing so-called spiritual people. Perhaps you never even searched for God or thought about your place in the world. I did. I have realized that the stakes are just too high to remain in pride or ignorance, which leaves you alone in a state of beguiled narcissism, self-justification, or a sense of superiority or entitlement, which, in turn, leads to a final cessation that was never intended. Am I trying to change you? Well, not exactly. As Walt Whitman would say, "You must travel this road before you for yourself." Anyway, that's not on me, and I don't possess that kind of power; however, the Spirit of God inside me *does*. All I can do is show you through what *I've* learned that somebody like *you* who thinks that religion is not for him, who thinks there are *many* different and equally valid paths to God, or who believes he is pretty good, very much need to reconsider.

There is an invisible battle out there to win you over, and it's not one of "flesh and blood, but spiritual forces of wickedness" (from Ephesians 6:12). I don't want you to be caught unaware in stubbornness, nonchalant disbelief, or blithe ignorance. You may rightfully ask how a person goes about determining and deciding which religion is the best, most suitable, or truest? You may think you should opt for none of the above. If so, this book is for you! And last but not least, to my fellow Christian brothers and sisters, I prayerfully, lovingly dedicate this book to you because you might find this tome another way to present His truth to someone. Yes, there are thousands upon thousands of testimonies, one each for every Christian. I suspect many who identify as Christians were raised or grew up in a Christian-identified household, even if nominal or quasi. It goes beyond my text's scope to discuss mission fields of peoples who have *never* been exposed to Christ. Maybe you are already a Christian, but I feel like you haven't done much lately. Maybe you feel stymied or in the doldrums. Do you desire to grow in your faith? Do you long to be more patient and loving and shed the familiar cloak of self-satisfaction that curbs this? Then join me, and, as Hebrews 12:1–2 says, "let us run with endurance the race that is set before us, fixing our eyes on Jesus"! Of course, we must dive deeply into the word of God, and we will. Hopefully, you'll never get your fill, and with God's help, we *both* can bear much fruit for Him. This journey is presented from the perspective of one who grew up in a household that was neutral, disinterested, or indifferent to Jesus at best, and ridiculing, critical, or rejecting of Christianity at worst. Ultimately, looking back and connecting the dots, what I know is that this lesson in perspective into the divine, to the Lord of lords, is available to *all* who are open to Him. Therefore, I present this kaleidoscope, this unique key that I hope will fit into a previously locked door, such that it can be opened and that you have the most mind-blowing and life-altering experience that you never thought was possible! I love you already!

BOOK 1:
Me in B.C.

Chapter 1:
Growing up in S-P-G

"I don't know how to love him…"
— from Jesus Christ Superstar (1973)

"They say that heaven is 10 zillion light years away, but if there is a God, we need Him now…
and I say it's taken Him so long 'cause we've got so far to come."
— from Stevie Wonder's "Heaven Is Ten Zillion Miles Away," from the album, *Fulfillingness' First Finale* (1974)

1.1 From Eden to the South

> I, Dimi Christakis, a follower of Jesus Christ, by the will of God and the Spirit of Jesus Christ,
> To both the church of my heart and to those curious and yearning for more than what you find in this beautiful world at large, Grace to you and peace from God, our Father and the Lord Jesus Christ.

The introduction above is, more or less, how all the epistles or letters start out in the New Testament, so I thought I'd humbly borrow from the best in this opening chapter of my life to you. My real name is Dimitria, a name I hated as a young girl just because it sounded weird; therefore, I just shortened it and went by Dimi. At that time, I didn't know that it originated from the Greek goddess Demeter, goddess of the harvest. Then later, Saint Dimitrios, a warrior, was credited for some miraculous defending of the Greek city, Thessaloniki. My last name, Christakis, though I was quite aware and proud is Greek, meant precious little else to me, the import of the first syllable of which was as unknown to me as I was lost to Him. It would not be until a month before I turned fifty that coming to Him got up close and personal. Exploring and discovering this my identity — from an inchoate, primordial, and amorphous albeit lovely and dying one to one that is unique, specific, and brightly everlasting — will crystallize before your eyes *now* and before I could have known *then*. And so, I wish for you that "the grace of the Lord Jesus Christ, and the love of God, and the fellowship of the Holy Spirit be with you all" (2 Cor. 13:14 NLV).

Before we moved to Spartanburg, South Carolina, the day before Labor Day in 1969, life for me was exhilaratingly free! I felt no restraint to do whatever joy and goodness my heart desired; I was a little girl who loved to climb trees, make forts, and dance; I walked to my school every day by myself, joyfully and safely in a world that wasn't fearful for its children. Pippi Longstocking would soon be my literary heroine. My dolls were all carefully put to bed permanently in shoeboxes like little coffins lining the baseboard of our guestroom. I loved my collection of stuffed monkeys. My mom, understanding my wanting for these pets of mine to have a home, spray-painted a tree branch gold and stood it in a base in the corner of my room so that I could put these little playmates on the smaller branches thereof. And speaking of branches, at five, I was quite the happy tree-climber, and a couple of years later, I lived to make forts, both inside and out-of-doors. I still recall imagining how I would survive storms if I could adequately fortify the semicircular teepee of a wooden tent made up of boards and branches leaning against a thick oak tree. It was like an eagle's glen for this girl-child. Soon after we moved to Spartanburg, there was one particular fort I erected at age eight that would be my masterpiece and a hideout from life's storms. Like many kids, I often got stopped in my tracks by things of rushing beauty I saw in Nature: I can still recall with such vividness seeing in wonderment my first rainbow reflected in a large puddle, created by the spray I had made with the garden hose, yes, the one with the metal nozzle from which I would gratefully drink. In the fall, my mother would have my younger sister and me making shish kebabs out of the burnt-orange fall leaves skewered on a stick in the front yard. On weekends or after work, my father would play his Greek records and sing along with them, probably trying to evoke a trace of a world then gone to him. I remember loving the sound of the bouzouki so much that I would try to replicate the notes on the piano in a made-up Greek song for my father, hoping to please him. My father and I had a favorite trick we did together: he would lay on his back, hold his legs straight up, and I would stand atop and on his feet, like a mirror image of himself four feet up. In the evenings, we would lie on the floor beside one another holding hands and just gaze at the fish in his saltwater tank; he also had sea horses, one of the few animals that have the father take care of his young. And at five, I would proudly proclaim to my mother that I would marry Mr. Rogers when I grew up. My favorite movies were *The Jungle Book* and *Mary Poppins*. My maternal grandparents once recorded on an old 8 mm movie camera free-spirited me dancing like King Louie. Numerous times, I attempted to launch into flight by jumping off the top of the jungle gym, umbrella in hand, high above my head. Even today, I remain convinced that all parents should interact with and instruct their children as Mary Poppins did. Later in life, I would subconsciously use her approach as a model for how this teacher should treat her students.

The move to the South from Akron, Ohio was quite a scary prospect as I thought that we would move into the side of a cave den and live as coyotes do. I was *so* unprepared for and unknowing of how southerners thought little girls were supposed to act, and I did not fit in at all. I remember in first and second grade, we had mandatory chapel service every Tuesday morning. We'd all file in the auditorium, not knowing if the minister de jour would be a young or older man, but it was always a serious or solemn occasion; now and again, one would get particularly flushed and frothy. At the end of this routine service, we were told to bow our heads, something that struck me as odd and pray along with the man who'd say words in a strange tone. I didn't know what either meant. I only bent my head slightly and, out of curiosity, kept my eyes open to furtively glance around the auditorium. Most of the time, we ended the service with something called the Lord's Prayer. My head tucked even lower so that my chin nearly touched my chest, I noticed everyone was chanting something in unison, and everyone knew it but me. I didn't know if I should feel embarrassed, but I did feel awkward and shy. So that nobody would know that I didn't know the words, I decided to move my mouth anyway, as if I, too, were speaking these mysterious utterances. I remember doing this more than once, and even then, it made me feel like a fake. At the same time, I must admit I was not so much curious about *what* they were saying as much as I was hyperaware that I felt very different. It's not that I wanted to join them or be a part of this whole affair.

In a similar vein, the move down south also introduced a mindset difficult for me to fathom: why were girls were supposed to act a certain way? Why did boys get to do cool stuff like play freeze tag, and I had to ask to join? Even though I was teased and mocked, I did so anyway. One teacher in particular made it her calling to teach me how a girl should act by punishing me to break me of everything I did to the contrary; this was my second-grade teacher, Miss Sally Fillmore. She looked like the bride of Frankenstein and had one streak of white hair traveling north by northeast through that helmet head of otherwise blackish hair. Before we'd go out in the world outside her little kingdom of a classroom, she took forever to powder her nose as there was that one humongous and irksome age spot that stubbornly resisted her efforts. Like most elementary school-aged children, I lived for the freedom of play period, and I was quite the daredevil. I was that one you'd have to worry about standing on the swings because I would intentionally go so high that catapulting myself off might either make me airborne for the next state or go splat on the unforgiving concrete beneath. I would hold hostage the smaller kids sitting at the upper end of the seesaw, or, like some chimpanzee, I would play leg war on the jungle gym set. One particular day, I climbed up the very tall, steel ladder of the slide designated for the big kids and noting the 200-degree surface of the slide that could have melted my hide, I elected to hurl my shoes off go down while standing ski-style. It was like flying! It was brilliant and fabulous! Miss Fillmore did not think so. The next thing you know, many of the kids imitated in like fashion; the instigator had to be stopped. The next day, I learned my sentence of losing my play period for an eternal week. Our P.E. teacher, a burly older woman named Miss Cox, had us play one sport and one sport only: killer kickball. Miss Cox combed back her graying and slick-backed hair, dyed a curious blue, and she possessed a constellation of dark freckles on her cheeks. She issued short, guttural commands to us, and while she watched us, fist on hip, she'd spit out the dark juice from her chewing tobacco. We dared not give it our all for her, and I'm sure I didn't disappoint. This same year, I lost my play period again for inadvertently taking an extra set of silverware in the cafeteria. I remember this because I got lost in thought staring at the framed picture of the blonde and rather girly-looking Jesus on the wall; I'd never seen a man look like that! The worst transgression I committed that led to a showcase showdown happened when Miss Fillmore, bound and determined to have me play with and behave like the other girls playing with their Barbie dolls, grouped me with them. Having just quit Brownies the week before for refusing to cut out dresses for Barbie dolls and now finding myself thrust into a pile of such girls, I retaliated in the way that would shock the class: I pulled off Barbie's head, yes, decapitated my assigned doll, and, in protest, flung said head across the room like a rocket. One girl cried. Another boy's jaw dropped. It was then that Miss Fillmore and I reached a sort of non-verbal truce. I would quit being an instigator, and she would leave me alone and happy to play with my Lincoln Logs, my clackers, or my slinky. I didn't even know how to jump rope; playing hopscotch seemed silly.

Trading Wacky Packages and wearing my favorite green poncho and camouflage hat for days on end was more to my liking as I did my time at what felt like a prison. I return to the Tuesday morning chapel service because one incident led to my mother extracting me from this school routine.

1.2 Mandatory Chapel Service

On Tuesday mornings, there were these men in stiff, dark suits who would come to talk to us in our school's auditorium. Each would tell us a story from a sizeable black book that was always brought along, and I didn't know one of these tales. One time in spring, we were told a particular story that alarmed me. I went home that afternoon and repeated it in an anxious and confused state to my mother: I warned her that she would have to paint the door red, or else I, as her eldest, would be killed! First of all, she didn't even know (nor could have imagined) that we had chapel service; she just kept repeating incredulously to us both, "You heard that *in school*?!?" The next thing you know, she swiftly had me pulled from this activity. After that, all I remember was having to sit in the main office's entry, right next to a tuba that was stored there, as the rest of my class walked to the auditorium. Looking out that open door, I stared out at all the rest of the school children who filed by on their way to chapel service, and many would point at me, whisper, and giggle among themselves. I would have preferred to go chapel and take my chances with impending death than feel the burn of shame of ostracism for what I didn't understand. In particular, I recall the Fanning brothers from our neighborhood who all three in unison would hiss that I was an *atheist*; I had no idea what this was, but I could tell it was terrible. Other kids caught on to their label, and I was called this over and over again mercilessly. It didn't make me feel sad, just bewildered and a little scared; their faces were filled with hatred. Another source of rejection I experienced was because I was a young tomboy, so I wasn't winning popularity contests in this department either. My bucked-toothed chum, Tom Jordan, would earnestly ask me, "Do you *really* think girls are as good as boys?"

It wasn't only in chapel that I came to know of the Bible. My first-grade teacher had us memorize Bible verses that she would neatly write in thick chalk up on the blackboard every day. Thanks to her, there are two verses I still can recall: The first is "This is the day which the LORD has made; Let us rejoice and be glad in it" (Psalm 188:24). And the second was "Make a joyful noise unto the LORD, all ye lands. Serve the

Lord with gladness: come before his presence with singing. Know ye that the Lord he is God: *it is He that hath made us, and not we ourselves*; we are his people, and *the sheep* of His pasture." I italicize those words in particular that struck me then. She had a soft heart and an essential goodness to her. She wasn't trying to push anything onto us; her faith came from a wellspring that gently overflowed from within. We were all *glad* to be her "little lambs," which she would call us; we made our own "joyful noise" in her classroom. Not all shepherds were as kind as she, as I would find out a few years later. Another memory came about when I was in the second or third grade, and our whole grade level went to the area's planetarium. Oh, it was spectacular and phenomenal to gaze up in wonderment at the re-created heavens while a deep voice pointed out and explained what all we were beholding! At the very end of the presentation, we were asked if there were any questions. I stood up and asked, "Where did all this come from? Who made it?" And the man looked back at me and queried, "Who do *you* think made everything?" All the kids around urged and prompted me to say what to them was the obvious, easy, and correct answer: "God!" Yet I, in good conscience, couldn't say this because I didn't know who or what God was, let alone who made *Him* for Him to have created the Milky Way, etc., to begin with! I was stumped; therefore, much to the kids' shock and disbelief, I replied not a word to him and sheepishly sat down. You could've heard a pin drop as my classmates were agog and bewildered by my apparent and vast ignorance. Later on, under the helm of our fifth-grade teacher, whose hair, lips, and toenails were all the same loud shade of coral and whose dragon breath reeked of Salem cigarette smoke, Miss Linda Sprint taped up an old poster depicting calm, majestic mountains that were *way* beyond the reach of her classroom. It had part of Psalm 121 (KJV) written in bold calligraphy beneath: "I will lift up mine eyes unto the hills, from whence cometh my help. My help cometh from the Lord, which made heaven and earth." We all looked to this Lord to liberate or preserve us from her reign of terror. There were no "joyful noises" here, and we were painfully aware that we were there to either serve her or, at the very least, not bother her. We knew she didn't care for us, and she let us know by her attitude that she would rather have been anywhere else but with us. Daily she transported herself to other vistas, all to the musical backdrop of Charlie Rich, who was played on the transistor radio behind her desk. He serenaded us as we did long division from a stale workbook, while in the meantime, she clipped grocery coupons from the newspaper. Once, we even tried to set fire to a tiny piece of paper in her cloakroom using a magnifying glass that someone excitedly snuck into class one day. I was right there with the instigator, busily working as the sun was streamed down on our project. Alas, these attempts were in vain. It was in this grade that our class advanced to Bible study every week. I didn't attend even one of these classes, so promptly did my mother again intervene and circumvent another misread Bible story. On her own, she re-separated church and state and whisked me to the library, where I completed a year's worth of spelling lessons in a month. I read a lot and daydreamed of being set free from "Washington Jail," as we called George Washington Elementary School. The following year, when I was in the sixth grade, we had a commencement ceremony for which we were all to memorize as a class the entirety of 1 Corinthians 13. It's just what we did, and I didn't question (or inform my mother) anymore. There was one line in particular that I didn't understand: "For now we see only a reflection as in a mirror; then we shall see face to face; then I shall know fully, even as I am fully known" (NIV). The prospect of being "known," something I certainly didn't feel at the time, compelled, excited, and mystified me. Though we memorized this chapter, we never discussed what it meant. I still hadn't even fully memorized the Lord's Prayer. It's important to remember my feelings during all of these experiences; none of these experiences made me particularly curious about God or Jesus; in fact, the whole affair made me feel different and somehow unlovable. To say I didn't have any traditional religious foundation would be an understatement. On Sunday mornings, my parents tuned the FM dial to fill our living room with classical music. In fact, that was the only station that even played music because most of the other AM stations were devoted to live church broadcasts where preachers would speak like no adult *I'd* ever heard. Their voices would either emit odd ululations, or else the tone would seem angry. Sometimes they spoke with such vim and vigor, and in such a strong southern accent, it became indecipherable to me! "*Jeeeeezzus Krahst daaahd on thuh cross fer yore see-uhnz, uh!*" The voice sounded like the Loony Tunes character, Foghorn Leghorn, only in a nasal pitch. I didn't understand what they were saying, let alone what all the fuss was about. I just knew it was very odd to be living in a land where everybody thought this type of speech was normal. The lone tri-cities Unitarian Church my mother took us to when I was little taught us about the existence of many *gods*, but not about *the* God everyone at school or in our community knew. My mother was on the warpath to protect us; my father was oddly mute.

1.3 Strangers in a Strange Land

Early on, it became evident that our family's values and priorities were radically different from those who lived around us: we lived in an affluent neighborhood with a golf course, but we never joined the country club. Indeed, my mother would brag that our family was more interested in art, culture, and travel than tennis lessons, brand-name clothes, and golf, all of which was dubbed "a waste of money." As a youngster, though, I was often jealous and would long to swim at the nearby Country Club swimming pool with all the other kids, who gleefully whizzed on their bikes just a short way past our house there. Our family had an opposite value construct: we were *anti*-elitist, cultured ones, if you will. I didn't remember feeling snobbish or superior, but I did recall feeling like an outcast in every way and all the time. Sometimes though, it was a good thing. For example, when I was six years old, I recall coming home from school one day playing the "air violin," and my mom responded swiftly by getting me started in violin lessons. Learning by the Suzuki method, I would initially learn to play by ear, memorizing the records I'd listened to over and over again. I would continue to take private lessons for the next sixteen years and play in our high school orchestra. Only my consuming passion for mastering the Russian language in graduate school would supplant the time and energy I had spent on music. Russian became like music to my ears, and, later, when I would come to teach Russian in high school, to hear it pronounced with a southern twang or valley girl monotone would grate my sensibilities. But back to my misfit maiden years: I remember for my eighth birthday, I had my first slumber party. It was my idea to have my girlfriends come to my solo violin recital, then come back home with me and dance to the Jackson Five or the Stevie Wonder albums I had gotten. This struck them odd. While all the other little girls swooned over and read about the latest about Donny Osmond and Keith Partridge in *Teen Beat*, I was smitten with Michael Jackson and his older brother, Tito. I loved dancing to the Jackson 5 songs. My absolute favorite song of Stevie Wonder's would come to be "Heaven Is Ten Zillion Miles Away"; it spoke to and reflected my deep longing for God to be closer to me and for humanity not to be so far in faith from Him.

These thoughts were embryonic then, but my latent desire to make Him *real* would make me seek Him in all sorts of places. Who or what He was, I surely didn't know. Perhaps seeking that which is richer, deeper, and different from us, I got from my mom. Maybe God was as an attractive force as was my father to me. I think half the reason why my mother married my father was to escape the stultifying, provincial outlook and add an exotic touch to the way too squeaky-clean, very white, and boring Midwest background. She also had a longing for more. Meanwhile, my father, ever the free-spirit, sought to escape the heavy restrictions and all-too clear expectations of his Byzantine background, wherein everything was known either by his mother at home or by God at church. The icon of the eye of God peered down on my dad from the cupola, high above the sanctuary. There was no escape. His whereabouts and activities were closely scrutinized and general Greek values and culture fervently guarded. At the end of the Greek Civil War, when my father was just eleven, his family moved to America, after which, his mother went on a mission of her own to shelter her sons from the many "evil" temptations in this country. At stake was the possibility of losing one's Greek identity, heritage, religion, and family; ultimately, his parents would lose this battle, and my father flew the coop. My father felt trapped and longed to escape such stultifying strictures. In short, *both* of my parents were renegades, rebels who ran toward each other but missed their mark in uniting. Every sensitive, inquisitive, and quietly spirited mother had her religious wings clipped at a tender age. I can imagine her pride at being the only one in her Sunday school class asked to read the nativity scene from Luke; nobody from home even showed up to watch her. Her father was an unabashed atheist. Later, I would wonder if she had committed apostasy in my journey by liking Jesus but rejecting His divinity. I was told that, no, she never even had any real chance to develop as a Christian. The world of art and architecture and being exposed to many international cultures— primarily South American Middle Eastern — captivated her attention and held her in wonder when she was in college. So many things to see, taste, and try! My mother said that upon getting serious about her relationship with my dad, when she probed and asked him to explain his religious beliefs, he turned away from her, cried, and got up and ran out of the room. I believe she misinterpreted his being unable to verbalize about matters of his faith to her. She erroneously took his inability to speak to mean that he was afraid of the imposing God who looked down on him from the Orthodox dome. I think that he was so stuck and in love that he felt like bolting with such a potentially game-changing question. He had to have realized the magnitude of what marrying her would mean: a severance from everything and everyone that had shaped who and what he was, and, religiously speaking, this went back centuries and connected him to generations before him. Was he concerned with the ramifications of abandoning his family and community, not to mention his faith and God? Did he consider that his mother tongue would not be spoken anymore, let alone to his yet unborn children? Was he thinking about the fact that no one would be preparing Greek food for him? Probably, but he had fallen head-over-heels in love with my mother, for better or for worse. As it turned out, it would turn out for the worse for both of them. One of the first things my father did after they got divorced was to come back attending to the Greek Orthodox Church.

Do know, however, that we had some *really* wonderful years as a family. My parents fostered a passion for that which was *not* the norm, and we had spice in *our* life. They loved and promoted music and world culture over sports and materialism. Whereas avid sports enthusiasts tend to look down on people who don't do sports, I was raised by parents who could have cared less about athletics. Later, when I was in college, I would announce that I would go to a football game when a university football player would attend a symphony concert. I thought sports fanatics were modern-day Neanderthals. My father clung to his own team, his tribe, and both of my parents would see the likes of golf and tennis and "keeping up with the Jones" as superficial, not enriching, and wastefully extravagant. When I saw men shout or cheer at their television sets and women happily huddle in the kitchen, I didn't see the attraction, let alone the point. And quite frankly, I didn't view there being much of a difference in the way most folks participated in church life from how they viewed sports: both to me seemed exclusive, excessive, and way too expressive. I even heard a minister half-jokingly once say that with a little imagination, the "T" from the University of Tennessee looked similar to the Christian cross! In short, like football and country clubs, we pooh-poohed religion and churches growing up. Our way of thinking heralded intellectualism, rationalism, science, and the power of the mind, but looking back, we were as snobbish and judgmental as the very ones we complained about. As a child, I was taught that religion could evoke strong feelings but that its ideas or beliefs — no matter to which version one subscribed — were not based on fact. My parents tended to look down on conventional churchgoers, but each for a different reason: dad because Protestantism wasn't part of his back-story and mom because she'd rejected anything smacking of inauthenticity or impossibility. Plus, neither of my parents fit in with people down here. My mom, a Midwesterner, wasn't like the other Southern women who coiffed their hair into a beehive and wore lots of makeup, and my short and very Greek dad in no way resembled the tall men who stood with legs wide apart, jingling their pocket change, and talking of sports. The likes of these were aliens to them.

In short, my parents' values and priorities were divested elsewhere. My mother, ever down-to-earth, practical, was at her core a social activist. She and my father were both frugal, and my father all the more so from having experienced the war first-hand. For my father, money should go to acquiring land, advancing one's education, and putting Mediterranean food on the table, which was nearly impossible. Once a year at Christmas, we would receive a CARE package from my Greek grandparents; it was bursting with Greek goodies! Living in South Carolina, they knew that we couldn't get the good stuff, meaning *real* Greek food, so they sent us Greek Easter bread, Greek pastries and cookies, olives, and the like. The package was always wrapped up in brown paper with strong twine and addressed in a belabored English script in capital letters; it seemed as if it had been sent from Africa. My mother created her own world culture for us, and in the rich nest of our home, each room was uniquely inviting; none was limited to its original purpose. Nothing ever matched, but everything went together; each of us got to decorate his room, and I slept under a psychedelic sky scene copied from a Peter Max mural that my mother painted on my ceiling for me. In the late afternoons when I got home from school,

I remember avidly reading one page in the newspaper without fail: it had my horoscope, the advice of Dear Abby, and a column of guidance from an older man named Billy Graham. Between the three of them, I always gleaned some piece of wisdom. My mom wanted us to feel special by making sure we had music, art, and other types of lessons, and as the oldest, I was the greatest beneficiary of this value construct. My father occasionally tried to fit in and would experimentally try to imitate what he *thought* was a southern accent, but we kids looked at him in shock, as if he'd turned into someone from outer space. Though we never talked about it in private, we all knew that what was normal outside our home made no sense to my dad and was rejected by my mother. This attitude took hold in me, too. In the summertime of my grade school years, we all would go to Camp Big Forge. It was a Christian-based camp, but one both my mother and grandmother went to as girls, so it was acceptable. Coming up the gravel driveway, the first thing you saw greeting you was an Indian totem pole (on a painted telephone pole), and every morning, here, too, we would have chapel service. This was not nearly the scary affair I had experienced in my elementary school in South Carolina. Teenage counselors with their long hair and wearing embroidered bib overalls would read a book called *The Way*, and they treated us kindly. The daily chapel service was held in a diminutive amphitheater at the shore of a lake, and it became both regular *and* special to start our day like this. In the evenings, we would all sit around a spectacular bonfire around which the counselors would passionately play their guitars and sing both camp tunes and popular songs from the '70s like Led Zeppelin's "Stairway to Heaven." Though I didn't really have a clear notion of who Jesus was or what He was all about, we would also sing a few Christian-based songs after lunch. For example, it was there I was first introduced to Noah, who "built him an arc-y arc-y, made of hic'ry bark-k-y bark-y." In my infantile seeking to make sense of the world around me, including matters of life and death, I would next turn with keen interest to an old and yet new-to-me figure on television: Dracula.

1.4 Dracula and the Undead

When I was in third grade, I was smitten with Dracula, as best enacted by Bela Lugosi and later by the intense Christopher Lee. Every week I looked forward to watching old horror movies on *Shock Theater*, a program that came on TV late Saturday mornings right after *Soul Train*. There were many creatures of fright to watch, but Dracula was in a league of his own. I was mesmerized by his power, his enigmatic ways, his intelligence, and his immortality, or, rather, his state of being "undead," as it was called. As legend had it, Count Vlad the Impaler was so upset over the fact that his wife died while he was in battle defending Christianity; out of spite and in anger, he made the fateful decision to worship the devil. In so doing, he turned from a righteous leader to an evil one and became infamous for impaling his victims and drinking their blood; this, in turn, allegedly gave him a quasi type of eternal life. My attraction to Dracula held me captive for several years; I felt like I understood him; anyway, his decision to turn away from good was motivated by disappointment and love. Plus, Count Dracula had such a keen mind and overt power over many; I was amazed at his ability to hypnotize. (I'm sure that Bela Lugosi's native Hungarian accent didn't hurt either.) I just wished my mind and will were as strong as Professor Van Helsing's because he could withstand Dracula's attempts to put him under his spell. I was impressed with Dracula's ability to bend the laws of physics and change at will his physical form into a wolf or bat; why, his image did not cast into a mirror! Dracula needed people to sustain his vitality, so he seduced women and took their lives to remain undead himself. It made sense to me, and I accepted it as gospel. I always rooted for Dracula and would lament when he was killed by having a stake driven through his heart. Looking back, I see this innocent fascination with Dracula as a misguided yearning to unite with that which possessed the power of life over death. Clearly, Dracula isn't Jesus, but, in retrospect, this particular attraction I had indicates I was seeking some lasting connection between love and death, fascinated by the concept of eternal life, and yearning for someone more powerful than anyone in this world could offer. The crucifix, in particular, proved repellant to Dracula; I was also fascinated but not so troubled by this symbol. When approached by some well-intended pastor at chapel service and asked if *I* had repented or if I were saved, I would recoil and turn away, much like Dracula did when he caught sight of the crucifix. I couldn't get away quick enough from such aggressive types. The words that came out of their mouths or stern countenance they held, I could not have fathomed was based on concern for my very soul.

Meanwhile, my parents created their refuge from a society in which we did not fit, and they never sought; neither Jesus nor God was a part of our world either. I was taught that the church was a source of most of man's wars and strife; I didn't disagree and could definitely and personally relate because if Christianity came up as a topic around me, I was the one treated like a witch. I cannot say there was no church impact or presence in my life; my mother was a Unitarian and my father defaulted to going with her to the one lone U.U. Church in the area; often though, he stayed at home in those early days, sulked until she and I got home. There was no Greek Church, let alone a handful of Greeks within thirty miles of where we lived. I attended Sunday school at the Unitarian Church off and on from age seven to eleven, when I began working in the nursery. I did take one trip to Boston when our high school youth group conjoined with the one from the next nearest church, ninety miles away. I now turn to why my parents chose to attend the Unitarian Church.

1.5 What Unitarianism Means to a Child

Defaulting to the *least* common denominator so they would not have to be confronted by a Christian minister who might question their discordant beliefs, my parents were married by a Unitarian minister. Unitarianism would be the faith of choice for my mother; my father defaulted to her decision as it was just easier to go along the path of least resistance. Unitarians were nonjudgmental, welcoming, and imposed no rules or regulations, and that may have included the Ten Commandments too! My mother had home-court advantage and the ultimate say about their place of worship. I do not think my dad thought this counted as "worship.". Therefore, my parents did not have a traditional, let alone a Christian ceremony. Their wedding was not based on a *holy* matrimony. Decades later, while obtaining my Greek citizenship, I learned my father did desire such. My mother confided that my father had also wanted to be married in the Orthodox Church as if to validate or sanction vows made in an unremarkable house by a minister that wasn't even Christian.

Why would this be important, you ask? I have since come to believe that the basis of such a hallowed commitment as marriage should compel one to have sacred vows taken. This foundation was never established with my parents. My father didn't even tell his parents about his getting married until sometime well after the fact! But I digress. Life was free and easy for us kids, and we never really even thought about going to church, but when we moved to South Carolina, we found the oasis in the desert, a Unitarian Church in a sea of Christian ones. My parents took us there. There they accepted everybody, celebrated differences, and didn't make a fuss over Jesus or anybody for that matter.

My early experiences in the Unitarian Church as a youth were gratifying, as they were concerned with cultivating our minds and imagination. There were many trips to nearby places that explored history and science, and other ways of life. As you can imagine, the Unitarian Church membership in this area was minuscule. Its members were well-educated, good-humored, liberal-minded, and tolerant folk and certainly unreligious in any conventional sense. Most had rejected the religious foundations of their youth, so there were ex-Catholics, former Jews, those who had no raising whatsoever, a few displaced Yankees, and then the garden variety disbelievers who chose to divest their energies elsewhere. I remember with fondness my Sunday school teacher, Miss Sylvia Tan, who took me under her wing. Our little clutch of youth was separated from the teenagers' side of the doublewide that served as our classroom. These teenagers cut out pictures from *Life* magazine to paste onto a wall that was to be covered by a mass mural, a collage of images that depicted their feelings about the Vietnam War. By and large, they were photos of demonstrations or gatherings of hippies promoting peace and free love; I thought it was so cool. Jesus, however, was not in the mix. Our class focused on Nature, like universalism plus pan-theism. Being in nature, learning about ecology, exploring how Indians (who were not yet "Native Americans") lived and what other (primarily non-Christian) religions espoused was their cup of tea. I just had no idea what *they* believed in other than choice. We took many field trips to nearby farms and went on short day hikes at popular trails in this mountainous region. In adolescence, I received several books on Native Americans, complete with impressive photographs of them in various stoic stances and explanations detailing their sad historic plight. I would peer into their stoic countenances and poured over the details of their way of life for hours on end. I became fascinated with their honoring spirits in sacred locales, their concept of life being cyclical, and I would love to draw pictures of them astride their horses. When my Great Aunt Carrie would come and visit us, she bought me books to encourage whatever passion I had; she also gave me many picture books on Native Americans, or "Indians," as we called them back then. I recall a commercial that showed an Indian with a single tear running down his cheek, expressing silent anguish over the damage we Americans had done to the land once we had taken it from them. That they saw all of life interconnected and that we don't really own anything, that we are here to borrow, protect, and preserve life, made total sense to me! Their conservationism and respect for life I adored and emulated as I innately knew that there *is* an order to things, and part of this order precludes we are to take care of the planet because *something even greater takes care of us.* I didn't know what or who this was, but the fact held, and the search was on.

As I grew older and moved to the next youth group, we investigated what *other* religions espoused. We were told repeatedly that whatever *we* ultimately came to believe would be what we decided upon for *ourselves*. This approach sounds good on paper, but it is not a particularly helpful or useful answer to a pondering youth not knowing what the adults around her believed. My younger sister latched onto a girlfriend of hers with a more conventional family; they went to a "regular" church, and she was taken in by the love and tender attention she felt when she attended a local Methodist Church with her friend's family. My mother bided her doing this because she understood that, more than anything, my sister's motivating force was just to fit in. She was too young to understand their beliefs. I was older, and my pursuit was more intent. In fact, at the time, had I gone to this church, I'm not sure I would have thought that Jesus loved *me* or that I had a friend in Him. After all, seeing as how He was dead and that the people I knew who went to His church weren't particularly fond of me reduced the chances of creating interest. Such a spark starts with one person caring, and I had no such person take me in and in this manner. Yes, I did have my uncle, who was also technically my godfather, but he lived nearly a thousand miles away, and he was more of a stranger than family to me. We had no other family or relatives down here. I would yearn for and subconsciously substitute other dear ones for lack of aunts, uncles, and cousins nearby. Little could I have known then that at midlife, I would come to gain a church family that would grow on me to the point that they became my brothers and sisters in Christ. In some sense, I felt closer to them than my flesh and blood siblings because we had the same foundational beliefs; the adults in my family avoided the topic of religion, *especially* Christianity. As far as visiting relatives went, we only saw only our maternal grandma and grandpa twice a year and my dad's parents every other year. We eagerly awaited my grandparents' big, blue Buick, full of Santa's presents at Christmas time, come up our driveway.

Christmas meant Santa Claus and gifts; we never mentioned baby Jesus in our house unless He happened to come up when we sang Christmas carols. My sister and I loved to sing "Silent Night" in harmony together, and I did have an oddly special and sweet feeling inside when I sang about "the little Lord Jesus." In general, though, He was not in my life. The second time we spent time with my grandparents was for a month during summer vacation. My parents packed up us kids along with our flowered suitcases in the Plymouth Fury station wagon. We drove for ten hours up to their cottage, which was situated on a small, pristine lake in northern Indiana, and there we'd hunt for turtles and frogs, swim daily, and generally romp about like children are meant to. Later, I would compare this place to our own Garden of Eden, as it represented our family's time of innocence. I turn back to the topic of my religious foundation again, however.

At our local Unitarian Church, not only did we have one black family and my Greek dad who attended, but there were also two Jewish members who no longer went to Temple. This couple gave our class an introduction to the history of the Jewish people. I remember nothing of this other than they were very animated about it. I wondered why they weren't still going to *their* church. Around this time, our family attended a Christmas Mass at the lone local cathedral because our parents' best friends had invited us there. We played with their kids, so it seemed okay. Upon entering the massive structure, I recall feeling frozen stiff inside, and terrified when I witnessed a life-sized Christ nailed up high on a cross, complete with a gash in His side and droplets of blood trickling from under the crown of thorns. Having only seen His portrait downstairs in our elementary school cafeteria, I was transfixed in horror at seeing Him up close and way too personal. Such brutality! I wanted to cry. I didn't understand what had happened to Him, and mom and dad never explained, let alone prepared us for this sight. Perhaps my way of processing what I saw up there in the Catholic Church was to start drawing pictures of this Christ being crucified, complete with His emaciated frame, punctured side, look of anguish, and all. I tried especially hard to render His pained expression and the particular slant of his head. And yet, I had no idea what He did or why He was up there. Nonetheless, there was *something* about Him I was drawn to that I couldn't explain. Perhaps an antidote to this visit, my parents also took us to a Protestant church on the black side of town.

What a switch! There was a group of brightly dressed, ready-to-laugh, and joyous women who hugged us children the minute we stepped foot inside; it made us feel sheepish and oddly welcome; this was a far cry from what I'd experienced in the Catholic Church. Here I saw the familiar Jesus, and His large, framed portrait was next to another one called *The Last Supper*, painted in hues that did not look like anything from this planet. We sat in pews before an impressive choir who were ready, swaying, and happy to sing for their Lord; in fact, they didn't want to stop. Based upon the summative responses of my observing these churches and probably because she was stumped as to how to broach the topic of religion, my mom bought me the most prized album of my early youth. More than anything else, this double-album gave me an idea of what Jesus might have been like as a real and living person. Okay, so it didn't deal with anything after His death, but at least it was something that made Him come to life for me. What was it? It was none other than the soundtrack to *Jesus Christ Superstar*. I eagerly memorized every word of every track, felt every emotion conveyed so powerfully, and I sang right along with every song and belted out with great feeling, seeing it all so clearly in my imagination. This Jesus seemed so smart, approachable, and one *I'd* certainly like to know! I was — and still am — most moved by the Jesus' Prayer in the Garden of Gethsemane (side three, track two), and rarely could I make it through the 39 lashes and His Crucifixion on side four. I would imagine Jesus' praying to His Father was lengthy, holy, and exhausting; I liked that He had to get away from everyone to do this. Regardless of how many blonde Jesuses I saw depicted out there, he looked more like Cat Stephens in my mind's eye. It seemed like He would have been a very patient man, one with a keen but quiet sense of humor, naturally friendly, and ready to talk to you in earnest. It was clear that He avoided pomp and circumstance, men with pride and rules and ego, and he had no desire to perform "magic tricks" for those who taunted him or demanded proof of identity. No amount of miracles would suffice. I remember thinking that His Apostles didn't seem so swift and that Mary Magdalene appeared to possess a keener understanding of Christ than did His own Disciples. It seemed to me that He genuinely felt sorry *for* us without looking down *on* us. Only later would I come to realize why Christians didn't like this album: this soundtrack ended at the moment of His dying on the cross, period, end of story. Decades later, I discovered the rest and most essential part of His life that came *after* He died. Meanwhile, there was a lot more in my own life than Jesus that impacted me, which included my Greek heritage.

1.6 My Greek Nature

For as long as I can remember, I have always been incredibly proud of my Greek background, so much so that when I was in fourth grade, I brought my father for show-and-tell. He taught our class a Greek dance and brought Greek sweets for us! Being proud that I am Greek is a recurring theme, and later it would compel and propel me to attain my dual citizenship! There is a flip side to being different: I never knew what it felt like to belong to one's immediate domain. And though I believe we all crave feeling a part of the pack, at the same time, we also desire to be unique and special. I might have had a disproportionate sense of feeling different in having a Yankee mom and a Greek dad. I saw that other children at school also had something called a church family, which I didn't comprehend any more than the man on the moon. My father's parents we saw even less than my mom's parents: not even a total of a dozen times growing up did we as a family visit them or they us. Their exotic and oily food, clickety-clack Greek accents, plastic-covered furniture, gilt-framed photos of dead relatives *we'd* never know, and many other oddities were other-worldly but captivating to me. They were loud, often anti-American, and rather uncivilized, and neither my mom nor they ever accepted one other. My mother was such an idealist. She didn't understand what melding cultures would entail in her immediate purview; there were jagged edges of the old country that could not be tamed to fit into the dream spun out by her imagination. My father didn't help matters either: for as exuberant and passionate a man as he was, he skirted around and never resolved problems dealing with matters of the heart or where cultures clashed, and he never was a good communicator. This matter, in turn, was accentuated by his humorous but far-from-perfect command of the English language. My father may very well have wanted to introduce his children to a church, but there simply wasn't a Greek Church in the area. I think my mother would rather have had a needle stuck in her eye than to have her children attend an odd, ancient church where its parishioners gesticulated in unison and repeated phrases by rote memory, all of which had *no* connection to modern life. Just as influential as was his Greek identity, my father was an organic chemist, and he was a man of science to his core. We were encouraged to ask "why" and "how" about *everything*. Both my parents would relish and promote a healthy intellectual curiosity within us. Unfortunately, we were also taught that such robust thinking was incongruous to having or believing in religion as if God was somehow the enemy. It would take many years to crack the code within me to revisit questions that we all come out asking, including "Why am I here?" and "Who made me?" We innately know but don't have the words to convey that our existence originates beyond our parents. My takeaway was that when two people from opposing religious backgrounds get married and don't come to a consensus as to what their basis of faith and value system will be and by which they will raise a family, the net result defaults to a nothingness, agnosticism, or a jumble of relativistic grey truths. Such was so for my parents. To have one's parents go their separate ways about something as primal as a religion while married can't help but lead to erosion, if not division later on unless each is mature enough to respect the other. Having children invariably brings this impasse to the forefront. I have given a glimpse into the crucible that was to help shape my identity and religious values, but I will now return to my overarching focus, the story heralding my coming to faith. Now for tales from the Greek side.

As a child, I do not remember having any religious discussions with my father. Yes, I had been baptized in the Greek Orthodox Church when I was but several weeks old, as were my two sisters and brother. When I was five, I remember watching my youngest sister getting baptized. Honestly, I thought that the priest was going to drown her in the baptismal bathwater, yet at the same time, I loved to look at his gentle face and full, resplendent beard. At the end of the ceremony, all were given a sachet of Jordanian almonds, soft pastel-colored bundles tied in delicate white crepe containing the colorful, sweet delights. I had no understanding of the Greek Church whatsoever, but at an early age, I loved the smell of the frankincense and the censor's sound, which when swung toward us by the other-worldly priest sounded like sleigh bells coming our way. The best was yet to come.

1.7 American Easter A La Greek Lite

Easter was a cause for celebration as it meant dying eggs with that Paas dye kit, and, like all American kids, we loved doing this! To carefully balance the egg over teacups full of bold colors and then add stickers or crayon designs to embellish was our creative little *tour de force*! And to get baskets filled with jelly beans and chocolate bunnies sitting atop haystacks of green grass was such the way to usher in spring! There was never any discussion of Christ dying or rising or whatever else He did, and God forbid the Resurrection to be mentioned. Nope, it was time to celebrate the renewal of life, learn of ritualistic pagan spring celebrations, see who found the most Easter eggs, and hope there'd be a nice spring outfit to wear. I remember distinctly in third grade that mom gave us beaded necklaces with Indian designs, and I wore mine with such satisfaction. Although we would go to the Unitarian Church, I don't remember their mentioning the names "Jesus" or "Christ," but you could count on the eclectic choice of music played and a potluck afterward.

On the other hand, for my father, Easter was a splendiferous celebration because, regardless of whether we went to the Greek Church, it gave him the opportunity to buy, slaughter, and roast a baby lamb for us. We never knew where or how he acquired the lamb because we never saw it alive, but, come break of Easter morn, we'd innocently peek outside. Instead of seeing our regular jungle gym set awaiting us in the back yard, we'd see a lifeless lamb hanging from it, splayed and gutted. The first time we beheld this, we were not a little horrified; then it became just another everyday thing our weird dad did. We couldn't be upset because dad was so happy, proud, and intent; in fact, we came not to think anything of it. I'm sure the neighbors and golfers passing by our house picked up the pace and trotted past our house when they spied it. Over the years, he accumulated a small collection of skins that were stiff as woolly boards, and he neatly stacked high them in the side closet in the garage. Now was time to prepare the feast: my dad would use a barrel soldered in half as a grill and half bury it in the ground. From it, he would set up a homemade rotisserie and rotate by hand the oregano-besprinkled lamb on the spit all morning. By early afternoon, his face was as swarthy as an Arab's, but later that evening, he would carve the succulent meat for us, and we would have that delicious lamb, grilled to perfection and falling off the bone. In early spring, we would receive our second CARE package from yiayia and papou. I always remembered the Greek Easter sweetbread and hoped to be the one who would get the slice that contained the coin inside. Even though he never explained its importance, religious significance, or that he had been doing this his whole life, to partake of this bread was as essential for my father as if we were taking part in communion.

To satisfy my father's impulse to go to church at Easter, our family would pile up in the station wagon and make the annual pilgrimage to the closest city to us with an Orthodox Church at Greek Easter. Easter was qualified by nationality because of the Greek's religious time zone, the date for Easter was based on the spring equinox, which was somehow connected to a full moon, and the hours were off. The Julian Calendar corrected this error, but the Greeks stubbornly refused. What's a day or two? The two Easters rarely coincided; this inconsistency became another symbol of how mismatched and out-of-sync my parents were. I remember that we'd let my little brother sleep in the pew, and once, my sister fainted for all the incense so thick in the air. While in the cathedral, my father got in the zone, and my mom would take the opportunity to quietly narrate the goings-on of this mystical place, especially to me, her oldest. These were her perceptions, but they were conveyed as if they were gospel. She would comment on icons and say, "Look at all those cartoon characters from the Bible up there floating in the sky." She would so often speak for my father and say, "Your father was always very fearful of God's eye looking down on him from up there like there was no escape from His gaze." I would glance over at dad to see if I could read this in his expression, but I could not. There was never any discussion of Christ, His purpose, or the significance of this extreme form of death, let alone any explanation of the traditions, art, or rituals taking place. My mother summated and proclaimed these were all forms of empty gestures. Meanwhile, my father explained nothing to us; he was full of quiet contentment and in the midst of taking part in the service along with the rest of his people. Looking back, I am sure he missed this and them. Though he usually never carried cash anywhere else, for this occasion, he was loaded. He gave us dollar bills like party favors so that we'd each have something to put in the offertory plate that came not once but twice; these heavy and shiny platters were collected by men that looked like they were members of the mafia. For the first time, I heard my father singing in unison with all these Greeks. He had memorized the hymns (or whatever they were called) long ago when he was a boy, and they had never left him. He'd cross himself and end with what I'd interpret as "closing the door," that is, a slight motion whereby *after* making the sign of the cross, he touched his heart with his fingertips. He did this instinctively, reflexively, and tenderly. I was in awe. A couple of minutes before midnight, all of the church's lights are turned off, and we all sat awaiting the stroke of midnight in total darkness and silence. Being in the dark made us extra aware of the significance of the three days when and right after Christ died, and in so doing, we imagined the punishment due us He took for *our* sin. He satisfied His Father's condition for expiation. Barely breathing, I waited with anticipation what came next. When the priest finally completed his list of preparatory work up there behind the iconostasis, and at the split-second the new day arrived, he turned and approached the church body, his sole taper lit, bright and mighty. He commenced lighting the candle of the first parishioner he came to. Then, down the row and one by one, candles were lit. In silence and reverence, we commenced lighting the candle of our neighbor, and before you knew it, the whole church was illuminated! Oh, what a magnificent moment this is. We were entranced. Meanwhile, since we were packed in the pews like sardines, all my mother could envision were the many chances for the whole church to go up in flames, what with these short, hairy Greeks in close proximity to one another. The women's hairdos of the day were piled high and shellacked with hairspray, so the likelihood for something to go up in flames seemed all the more likely. Then we all went outside *en masse* and sang the "Christ Has Risen" song. Like the "Lord's Prayer" I mouthed in elementary school chapel service, here, too, I would memorize the tune, and eke out a few, formulated Greek words I was sure were pretty close to the real deal. This time, I mimicked what I heard *not* to avoid the shame of not knowing what everyone else was saying but to take part in the specialness of this greater whole.

Rare was it that we would stay past this juncture to go back inside the church and finish out the service by participating in communion, and then afterward, to eat a lite meal with everyone. At the real conclusion of the service, one would receive or collect one of the crimson-colored dyed eggs on the way out of the sanctuary. They were so colored in order to symbolize the blood of Christ. Greeks then make a game of it and tap the tips with one another to see whose can outlast the other. My father always won this contest; his egg end never cracked, so he was evidently blessed with a year's worth of luck. Speaking in hushed tones, like some golf announcer giving blow-by-blow commentary during the actual service, my mother added, "Your father only comes here so he can get the free food afterward." For years I thought that this was the case, but we never stayed to partake. Most often, my father showed *us* mercy, and we left after the whole church crowd went outside to sing. Usually, we'd duck out and drive home to be in bed by 3:00 a.m. We weren't the only ones who did so, and some of the Greeks who left at the same time we did still had candles lit while they got inside their vehicle, so tired or talkative were they to notice. *Had* we have stayed, as I would later do with my father, and then annually as an adult on my own, this service would have lasted several hours more, and then, having prepared and purified their spirits by fasting, these Greeks then ate with particular gusto. I think my mother, a Protestant to her core, had no idea that fasting was something that still took place; it, too, seemed antiquated, formulaic, and absurd. In summation, for the unsuspecting child (or adult) attending the Orthodox Easter service, it becomes an endurance contest of an ongoing series of stand-up, sit-down, group responses, and crossing yourself. Yes, indeed, Lord, have mercy! However, you will *also* experience the power of participating in celebrating the life of Christ with other Orthodox believers, all of which have been ongoing in the same fashion for tens of centuries.

Later, much later, I would come to ponder what exactly Jesus did for us, and no duration of service, let alone hurt or offense caused by some member, would be reason enough for me *not* to attend. Hardly universal in the Orthodox Church's stance that Christ died for *all*, as not all will inherit the Kingdom of God, it becomes *imperative* for the Greek child to be baptized because the Orthodox person believes that so doing such gives proof or assurance of the child's salvation. Additionally, infant baptism provides a Christian foundation and network for later on in life. She or he becomes a fellow participant early on and has an automatic, built-in church community that is both Greek *and* Greek Orthodox. Belonging to such an unchanging, religious monolith seemed sacrosanct to me. I would not come to investigate all this until much later, but I can tell you that its impressive history, long-standing traditions, time-honored rites, and rituals do not compare to my ultimately developing a powerful and personal connection with Christ, something incomprehensible to me at this time. There were only a handful of such memories while we were growing up; we were not part of the Greek Orthodox community by any stretch. Greek Fest was as close as we got to hanging around Greeks outside of this, and I'm sure my father must have lived longing for more. I can only wonder what more he would have done for us kids had we lived closer to his church. I know he missed the community that church offers, and in the last decade or so of his life, he wouldn't stay away from his since-built small and local Orthodox Church. Even if he had to get a ride, he went to every function and loved keeping up with and being a part of this close-knit community, though his own family had long since scattered to the four winds. However, when I was a child, he was a crypt in matters regarding his faith. As is the case is for many, it was my mother who had the dominant influence on developing my religious outlook as a child. The freedom she allowed us ironically led me to that which and Whom she would *not* choose for herself; I do not take for granted this liberty she afforded us.

1.8 AMERICAN-STYLE X-MAS

I should like to move on to Christmas when my mother's parents came down to visit; they really made Christmas special for us, all the more so because 'tis also the season of my mother's depression. I suppose her doldrums were connected to the fact that year after year, my parents' wedding anniversary, also on Christmas Day, was often overlooked, dismissed, or forgotten by my father. My grandparents' Buick, larger than life and serving as Santa's sleigh, was filled to the brim with presents. There was absolutely nothing religious about this holiday; it was 100% sacredly secular. We didn't go to church, and we made fun of the ticky-tacky, hokey, plastic Nativity scenes in yards that were within the same proximity; you'd *also* spy bloated figurines of Rudolph, Frosty, or Santa. Don't get me wrong, it was a grand time of year as far as we children went, but Jesus was not a part of the picture for us. My father was always moody this time of year because he was outnumbered, as he would put it. I think he was jealous and suspicious of mom's parents because they looked at him like a Cretan caveman with no couth, culture, or manners. There was no going to church, but I have to tell you that our home was decorated with an array of international folk items. Along with decorating two live evergreens and baking a pineapple-covered ham, my mom prepared a few dishes foods from other parts of the world, and we were taught other customs. In fact, our home was like a living UNICEF card, complete with an Advent calendar from my dad's brother who lived in Germany and a decorative Jewish menorah, which was placed on a windowsill. Where some children would read about the birth of Christ, we would do craft projects, one of which was to make God's-eyes out of crossed sticks crisscrossed with multicolored yarn woven into a colorful design. There must have been thirty of them hanging from the rafter beams of our family room; they looked like birds suspended in flight. Our family's ritual on Christmas Eve was to play bingo. The reason for the season wasn't mentioned. As if she had some esoteric knowledge or was in on some clandestine secret, my mother would inform us that Jesus wasn't *really* born in December. Out of convenience or familiarity, those

Christians just replaced the winter solstice to use for Him. We felt like we were in some mystical grouping of our own and not one of the duped masses. The Unitarian Church did not focus on Jesus or Christ or anything of that nature at Christmas, but it *did* stress and demonstrate the importance of giving. It offered various and practical ways to do so. Although later in life, my mother would assure me that she "*did* like Jesus," I knew good and well that she meant Jesus the *man*, and the divine aspect of His identity was not as critical to her as His examples of fairness and compassion. As far as she was concerned, the jury was still hung on His being more than mere man, so we children came to view that such was either for the birds or the feeble-minded. We were given the imperative to figure out for ourselves what *we* believed in, and we ought not ever to let anybody *tell* us what to believe. It was Christmas more than any other time we got reminded of this. Mom shared the lighting of the Menorah candles with us, all to the backdrop of "It's a Charlie Brown Christmas," *The Ten Commandments*, or *How the Grinch Stole Christmas*. The implication was that we could mix and match this and that to suit our needs and wants when we got to be grownups. I suppose this could be quite liberating for one being raised in a conservative denomination wherein rules, tight structure, and threats to the contrary abound. As a child, all I remembered was asking my mom, "How are we supposed to know what *we* are to believe if you don't tell us what *you* believe? Do you believe in *anything*?" My mother's father was a confirmed atheist, and he certainly didn't shy away from telling me what he believed. He calmly informed me that there was no God and that a person made what he wanted himself to be in this life for himself, that only a "weak" person could not realize his full potential. His logic got turned sideways, and I saw his worldview was terribly skewed and even frightening. He would start asking me, his nine-year-old, half-Greek granddaughter, "Don't you wish that *you* had blonde hair? Don't you think that you need to practice smiling in the mirror?" He would tell me that he thought that Hitler had it right when people with "deficient" minds were "eliminated." They ought not even "reproduce." What adult tells this to a child?!? Little did he know that not even fifteen years later, he would become one of those whom he disdained: sedated and strapped into a geriatric chair-stroller, he suffered the effects of dementia. As a child though, I could not follow his line of reasoning. For being so smart, he sure seemed to be lacking in reason, and I saw little love in him. I thought it bizarre that an adult would even talk to me like this. Grandpa firmly believed that because he had a high intelligence, that we, too, were smart and thus "superior" to "common" people of mediocre aptitude. He lumped together people of average intelligence with those who "needed" to believe in God as being "weak" or that they hadn't the wherewithal to live staunchly and independently. They were to be "pitied" but not helped. I recount this here because it is the only time I remembered an adult talking so clearly, so adamantly about God and religion and people of faith. Not surprisingly, he subscribed to scientific theories; that was *his* religion. I never remember anybody else countering him; then again, these were private talks he had with me. No other grown-up talked about religion in my young world. Before he died, my grandfather requested that his ashes be spread onto his favorite green at the country club where he had spent much of his free time during retirement. I'm not kidding. The whole affair turned into a comedy of errors. After we said our awkward goodbyes and commenced scattering handfuls of his ashes into the air, suddenly a gust of blustery wind arrived, and we all ended up fighting ashes blown into our eyes as if we were in some desert storm. Other golfers were waiting on us in the near distance, but only my grandmother sat watching stone-faced as the whole disaster unfolded. Was this all there was to it? Were we but born to end up like this? I certainly hoped not!

1.9 Death Is the Ultimate Memory-Maker

My maternal grandmother was also not a Christian in the sense of *identifying* as such, although I knew she was a non-attending member of the Central Christian Church. Like the transcendentalists, my grandmother believed in the primacy of Nature; she never talked about Jesus or Christ; for her, God was experienced in Mother Nature, and the love of such is something that she promoted in all of us. Preferring the sounds and sites of Nature — especially birds — to the message of some minister, and from the comfort of her own home, she gave me my first subscription to *Ranger Rick*. She also provided all her grandchildren with art and drawing supplies of the best quality to capture on paper all the critters in Nature we liked, be it turtles, squirrels, or fish. I don't think that she put much stock in humankind because humans can be so cruel, as was evidenced by her own husband's attitude towards people in general. My grandmother was generous, thoughtful, and kind to us, her grandchildren, especially where fostering a love for reading and encouraging any latent talent in arts were concerned. Once, near death, my mother heard her reciting the end of a famous American poem by William Cullen Bryant, "Thanatopsis," which revealed her stance as to how we should face our expiration:

> To Him who in the love of Nature holds
> Communion with her visible forms…
> …live, that when thy summons comes to join
> The innumerable caravan which moves
> To that mysterious realm, … in the silent halls of death…
> Go … sustained and soothed
> By an unfaltering trust [and] approach thy grave
> Like one who wraps the drapery of his couch
> About him and lies down to pleasant dreams.

To learn of this touched me, as year in and year out, I taught this very poem to my juniors in American lit. I would never have imagined that reciting this as an anthem or requiem would be the backdrop by which one might choose to exit this life as if one was merely getting ready to take an extended nap of sorts. Her witty older sister and my ever-ready-to-jest Great Aunt Carrie would tell us that she believed the way people lived on after they died was *through people's memories*. This theory made sense to me if for no other reason than she was always quoting her then-deceased husband. She was a firm deist and fierce Democrat who showed open disdain for southerners, Catholics, and domineering men. Politics was her passion. Aunt Carrie introduced my mother to Unitarian Universalism and gave the final stamp of approval of my father becoming my mom's husband. After all, Greek culture and history were undeniably rich; plus, his intelligence would make him a good match for my mom, regardless of his being the wrong hue for her parents. Little did my mother know the depths to which her in-laws would think my father had sunk in marrying this American woman who had no history, culture, status, or money to speak of, let alone a dowry. She would remain without a name to them until she later produced a son for their son, a guaranteed little piece of eternity in this life for them.

Other than reacting negatively to what exposure to religion I had in grammar school, my mother did not talk very much about religion, let alone Christianity, with me. My father's faith was subsumed into a cocoon that wouldn't get resuscitated until they got divorced. I did know that, like her parents, she is a rationalist to her core and could not accept miracles or anything else reported in the Bible as actual and certifiable *facts*. I recall her saying that the Bible was full of love stories and history. The only time I ever recollect her reading the Bible to me as a little girl was when I was sick and had to lay still in bed. Then and only then would she occasionally read a story from the children's illustrated Bible. The one of Sampson was my favorite, or, I should say, the only story that I remember her reading. At best, my mom's keen mind helped us discern truths and appreciate art and music. At worst, these acute powers led her to become excessively critical-minded, elitist, and condescending. She looked down on and judged the very people she accused of being such themselves as if *she* was the authority of what a good Christian was. It didn't help their case one iota if she heard a pastor who preached with a southern drawl; she associated such with low breeding, if not a diminished IQ. How could those who couldn't even speak or pronounce English correctly be trusted to disseminate matters of faith? At least, this is how I came to consider what was going on in her brain. Again, my dad was audibly silent in these matters. I decided to believe in what was right in front of me: this big, beautiful world that was tangible and real. Who could believe in that which couldn't be seen, let alone, wasn't intelligible? Who would want to believe in a God that could be cruel as the one found in the Old Testament God? Who would want to believe in a God that lets boys be treated better than girls? Who would want to believe in a God represented by people who talked about Him with such vitriol and not one iota of love? All I had to do was reflect on those scarily intense chapel services to know I didn't want *that* God, let alone His Son, now long dead and gone. Later on, when I was in high school, I became curious about and enamored by Buddhism and transcendentalism. In the summer of my sixteenth year at my grandparents' cottage at what we called "the lake," I would blissfully read Emerson and Thoreau while sitting up in a gigantic tree on a small island. I liked the idea that we were all interconnected, that we all came from the same spirit, that we all owe each other some semblance of goodness; feeling joined, even if on the cosmic level, was very appealing to me. I had never experienced love or genuine interest from any preacher or anyone religious, but, then again, I'd never had the right opportunity to meet such a one who would demonstrate real love toward me. That would come much later. I appreciated transcendentalism, and I read everything I could get my hands on it before I taught it. However, the Bible, which I had yet to read and had only heard snatches and snippets of, couldn't have resonated with me because I'd never really been introduced to it. My mother's King James Version Bible she'd been given back a hundred years ago in her childhood stood next to our collected set of brand new *Encyclopedia Britannica*, and there it remained, dense, dust-bound, inaccessible, and unread. Thus, it was Emerson's "Oversoul" and essays from Thoreau's *Walden Pond* that would inspire and enthrall me. Yet, no matter how much philosophy and religion I would read and be fascinated by, there was *still* a yearning inside me for something that I could not quite put my finger on; unlike the books I read, I never spoke of this. And the more and harder I studied, the more I continued to search.

1.10 My First Trip to Greece and the Desire to Belong

Though I adored my father and ate up his passion and energy, my father was an enigma to me where fathoming one's inner-core and religious pulse were concerned. Still, something about him resonated with me; I'm told that in many ways, I am like him. That you are reading this, though, I attribute more to my mother because she, too, is a kind of wordsmith. I love laughing with her when we've simultaneously been stricken by something worded uniquely or which reveals some absurdity. In crossing over and colliding with each other's respective cultures when they got married, my parents exposed us to their world of hodge-podge cultures combined, and I became filled with wanderlust and desire to see the other countries. After turning over a new leaf from a flurry of social experimentation in my derelict middle school years, I decided to herald the Greek side of me. When I was a sophomore, I initiated an annual road trip with my father to Brooklyn to see his parents at Thanksgiving. It wasn't about the Greek food; I desperately wanted to get acquainted with my Greek grandparents, and even more, I desired to share my growing attraction towards my Greek heritage. I tried to speak the few Greek words I knew and absorbed everything I could about their lives in those seventy-two hours. I asked as many questions as I could to make up for lost time. These private talks with my yiayia, papou, and Uncle Kolya were golden to me, and I would make this trek for the next four years. At sixteen, I took my first trip abroad through an organization called People-to-People. Three of the six weeks were spent in weeklong homestays with families in different countries. One of these was Greece, and I was placed with a lively family on Salamina Island, not too far from Athens. Undoubtedly, a pinnacle moment for me was when my host family took me on a ferryboat back to the mainland with the sole purpose of having me visit my father's relatives in a suburb of Athens for a full afternoon. Right off the bat, these foreign relatives of mine were gracious, affectionate, and warm to me. Though I spoke no Greek, I was giddy to the point of being euphoric, and, though I had never met them and it had been decades since they saw my father, I was pleasantly surprised that they recognized my father in me. For the first time, I felt the rush of the sense of belonging to something vaster than just my life in the States. This experience would launch an even greater sense of pride in my Greek heritage, and later yet, of a profound wonderment when, as a Christian, I would travel to the parts of Greece where the Apostle Paul went on his missionary journeys. Paul was tri-lingual; he spoke Greek, Aramaic, and some Latin. The desire to speak Greek fluently still hasn't left me. Though my mother and I *had* taken a few Greek lessons at the Greek Church in Boston back when I was only four years old, this came to naught, as conversing in Greek wasn't fostered by my father. Even in high school, I wanted my father to teach me Greek, so much so that I begged him. Other than speaking a dozen or so words, he never followed through for any length of time. I suppose there was nothing about the culture he'd chosen for himself that motivated him to cultivate the language of his origin within us; therefore, speaking Greek was Greek to us. Perhaps another factor is because he didn't have a *formal* mastery of Greek, so, other than partaking in Greek food or music, this world was placed on the back shelf; he had a new life now. When I got to high school, I took matters into my own hands and visited an old Greek lady on Center Street once a week so that I could at least start to learn to read and write Greek. Six years later, after my parents split in 1985, the vault of my father's memories cracked open, and he would share story after story from his boyhood that he had carried in dormant silence since childhood. Some were precious, some horrific, and all captivating. A decade later, my brother and I accompanied my father on his first trip back to Greece since he left as a boy. Making our way back to the village in the mountain he'd hidden in during the war was like traveling with someone into the far recesses of a dream. Oh, the Greek came tumbling out when he reunited with these distant relatives there. Eventually, when I got interested in Russian culture, my dad would have my Uncle Kolya take me to every Russian Orthodox Church within a twenty-mile radius of their apartment in Brooklyn.

1.11 My Takeaway before I Left Home

I believe it is no coincidence that as a little girl, my favorite story that I asked to be read to me repeatedly was, *Are You My Mother?* The gist of this story was that a baby bird got separated from its mother, and it proceeded to look for and ask various entities if he, she, or it (including a bulldozer) was its mother. Only at the end of the story does the mother return with food to her child and save the day. It wasn't so much that, like the baby bird in the story, I wondered if I had or could find my mother; somehow though, I felt her mental absence. And although my mother was devoted to me, even at a tender age, I sensed she was discontent about *something* and might've flown the coop (and left her husband) long before she did. Oh, I knew there were distinct differences between my parents, and I felt more like the frenetic bundle of energy that was my father, but my mother poured a tremendous amount of time into me in my earliest years, and we have a special bond, too. When I reflect on my childhood, I acknowledge that it was she who made sure I had violin lessons. Looking back, I am filled with admiration for my mother because she gave back to her community and promoted those less well-off, including the elderly *and* children, Indians, or other marginalized groups in society. She may not claim to be one that Jesus preached about at the Sermon on the Mount, but she is one who naturally "hungers and thirsts for righteousness" (Matthew 5:6 NIV). Though I can be critical of certain aspects of my upbringing, I am grateful to my mother in particular for trying to inculcate in me freedom of thought, wonderment in Nature, and appreciation of the value of beauty in our lives. I do not blame her for her personal choice of what and how to instill God in my life, and I love her more than she will ever know. I *say* I would have introduced religion differently if I had been in her shoes, but I'm not in her skin, and I don't truly *know*; all I've got is now and this life of my own. I long to share with her (and all of my family) that which I have come to have faith in, but that is a topic for later. As an adult, I would learn to *give* to her what I wanted to *get* from her. Not receiving hardly any affection as a little girl herself, I now realize just how difficult it was for my shy mother to be warm and demonstrative toward us. Compared to her, my father was like a slurping, adoring puppy dog. Like my father, I am buoyant, exuberant, life-loving, and optimistic by nature; without thought or plan, I encourage others. Therefore, he and I often fed off one another's joy at the best of times, and at the worst of times, we could explode. Like my mother, I know the power and impact of wielding words just so. Often, I would tell my students that I wished I could be their life coach and crafted words of encouragement custom-suited for them. I didn't know then what I do know now: I find encouragement, strength, and correction for myself in reading Scripture daily. At some point in our lives, we are each compelled to look beyond the here and now and to seek a vaster source of power and love. At the time, we may not know what or who this is. Before I could even think about a place of worship where I might experience such a love, I would have to think beyond the present, the literal and concrete, to wonder what *else* there is to life. I did. I am hardly unique in these speculations, but eventually, I would come to believe in and be special to Jesus. Long before I came to Him, at least I had an openness and certainty that this life wasn't the end: I deduced that if physical matter can neither be created nor destroyed, then neither can *energy*. Then I made an analogy such that though I knew I would *physically* die one day, my *spirit* would continue in *some* capacity. At the time, I did not believe in Heaven or Hell's reality, but early on, I did at least acknowledge that life was eternal. To bolster my base of realizing there's more to reality than what meets the eye, I compared our inability to apprehend all phenomena in both the visible and audible spectrums to our capacity to comprehend the entirety of time and of life itself. We are incapable of understanding all of that which is around us no matter how intelligent we are! This circumstance doesn't mean that we ought not to figure things out and understand how the world around us functions! After all, God did give us a brain. Discernment is a slowly evolving puzzle, and we get to put the pieces together moment by moment as they are presented to us. I continued to search for that larger purpose in college.

1.12 Deconstructing My Freshman Year

My college freshman year is flooded with vivid memories that I crave to share. I started out majoring in pre-med, but I was discontent because I had always hoped to go to an out-of-state school. That year, my interests couldn't be more diverse: I would try my hand at women's rugby, and I continued playing my violin and played in the university's orchestra. Throughout this year of exploration and encountering all sorts of people, there was one bright star I met that year who, at the time, didn't seem all that significant to me. Her name was Barbara Styron, and she lived on the same floor as I did in Reese Hall. The roommate of a rugger friend of mine came to know me indirectly, but it wasn't too long before she wanted to talk to me about the Gospel. It was impossible to hate or want to avoid her; her approach to talking to me about Jesus was gentle, genuine, and positive. Instead of the quickie approach I'd experienced when I was younger, she did *not* seek my attention only to ask me in one breath, "Did-I-know-Jesus Christ-as-my-Lord-and-Savior?" or, the clincher, "Had I been *born again*?" She took a shining to me and realized I was blind and a blank-slate of a religious canvas; she was patient and loving toward me as well as curious about my thoughts on religion. That was a rarity! She did more than witness to me; she became my steadfast friend and stuck by me through all the turbulent changes I underwent that first year. She wasn't what I'd call a close friend by any stretch of the imagination, but she was never far off and always available should I need to talk. She asked nothing of me for herself, something I would note much later. At that time, my religious leanings were transcendental and out there enough to infuse aspects of Taoism from the readings I'd had in a college-level lit. class. I was curious about the historical Jesus. I had recently bought a book called *The Quest of the Historical Jesus*, by Albert Schweitzer. Barbara listened and then quietly told me about Jesus, as if He were still alive and someone she knew on a first-name basis, something that seemed impossible and outlandish to me. Yet, I was receptive to her and interested in Him because of our friendship. At the end of my freshman year, Barbara gave me my first Bible, and inside it, she dedicated it to me, quoting the renowned John 3:16. I kept it and used it for academic purposes, looking up allusions in my future Russian Lit. classes, but I never really read it as a source of growing my faith; that was nowhere near formulated within me! As soon as I came back to school that following fall, naturally, I sought out Barbara, but, in horror, I came to learn that she had died in a terrible car accident earlier that summer. I was in total shock, dismayed that it could have happened in the first place and to *her*, of all people! I was also stunned at just how hard her death hit me; after all, we weren't best friends, and I'd only known her a year. I didn't understand how this could've happened or why it happened. I didn't know whether to believe that God was proving the adage that "only the good die young" or that there was no rhyme or reason to anything. I kept the Bible with me during the next seven years of school, and it lays on my bedside stand to this day, ready for me to read a verse each night before I close my eyes and "lay me down to sleep and pray the Lord my soul to keep."

I must mention that during my freshman year, my two best friends from high school, Allan and Tim, and I decided to church swap and check out other views. We decided we'd try the other's church of origin. The following Sunday, they both came with me to the Unitarian Church, and I the following to a Baptist Church. After listening to a Unitarian sermon, where neither Jesus nor God was mentioned once, they remarked that it was more like attending one of their college lectures than a so-called "real" church. We heard the Beatles played at the offertory and a Baroque selection at the end. The minister introduced an attorney who spoke to the congregation about both a local environmental issue as well as what was going on with Apartheid in Africa. It was anticlimactic and rather curious for Allan and Tim in that there felt nothing vaguely religious there. That said, they did like the informal and easy manner among people whose politics and high education level were aligned. On the other hand, my experience was much more emotional, or, should I say, agitating and disturbing. When we three arrived at Calvary Baptist Church, the first thing that struck me was that there were so many people there; it seemed like an event. Everybody was dressed to the nines. What struck me most powerfully about the sermon was that nobody even flinched or did a double-take when the pastor settled in to proclaim something to the effect that you had to "die to yourself" to have Jesus. I felt panic-y and started trembling in my seat. I would have bolted out if I weren't trapped in among a sea of people. Nobody else batted an eye! Evidently, these specters had already died. It seemed no less drastic than if he'd asked us to commit suicide from self-loathing. He tried to clean things up by assuring us that one day we would be united with our loved ones. I also felt like this powerful pastor was trying to induce guilty in us over the fact that people like *us* had killed Jesus. Indeed, He had allowed this to happen because He was doing so *for* us. It made no sense. The whole topic seemed morbid, and he kept preaching on and on like it was no big deal to walk around "dead to self." Could he be real?!? I left spent and had difficulty even driving. I confessed to my chums that I never wanted to go back there again. They just smiled at me like I was a child, laughed a little, and helped me turn the page by getting something to eat nearby. For them, this was rote, a worn-out message that didn't plague them. This experience stuck with me and would be one I referenced decades later when I came to fathom and appreciate the paradox of this truth.

Throughout my freshman year at college, I became less and less interested in my studies at school, and I played rugby and my violin more and more. I took an introduction to philosophy course as my elective and discovered that I was very attracted to others' ideas regarding overall purpose, ultimate meaning, and personal improvement. This was no surprise to me, as the year before, I became enthralled with the ideas I'd learned from reading Ernest Becker's *The Denial of Death*. In early May and the end of my freshman year, my Greek grandfather died, and after finals were over, my father and I flew out to his memorial service. My father was particularly and uncharacteristically clingy to me, pledging just how much he wanted to teach me Greek. I still had the ancient grammar book my papou had given me about five years earlier when my dad and I began our trips up to Brooklyn. My papou, a gentle soul, encouraged me to learn Greek, too, and I promised him I would one day.

Meanwhile, life went on. I knew things had to change as far as my major went because I was discontent with my choice of major in pre-med. Like many at nineteen, I was young and healthy, confident but clueless. I felt blissfully free and lived too much for and in the moment to have noticed I had no real direction.

1.13 Our Paradise Lost

I would soon take a college course that would change my life, but in the meanwhile, it felt like my whole family was dissolving because my parents were getting divorced; the process was long-standing, protracted, messy, and complicated. Anyone who has been through this knows the toll it takes on everyone. Our way of dealing involved isolation, and there was so much support to be found anywhere. In this time of trouble, my mother, desperate for validation and respect that never came from her husband, sought therapy and psychoanalysis. Decades later, I would differentiate *worldly* wisdom from *godly* wisdom, and I have come to believe that living by the world's ever-changing standards was undoubtedly a contributing factor to the demise of my parents' marriage. My father retreated into his own private island of resentment and bewilderment. How could this be?!? My very Greek father did not appreciate who my mother was as an individual; she had real needs and wants, and for her, there was more to her than being wife and mother. Though she admired my father's energy, optimism, and confidence, my mother married him because the timing was right and other options had not panned out as she'd hoped. Neither understood nor knew how best to love the other. This was their Greek tragedy. That they went to a church that offered tolerance and inclusion, but no remote focus on, let alone redemption in *Him*, I reflect and conclude that the chances of such a mismatched and bittersweet union lasting had always been low. One score and four children later, this modern fairy tale was doomed to fail for its *not* being based on a Christian foundation, whereby both husband and wife join in subordination to Jesus Christ and His way. Of course, my father did not continue attending the Unitarian Church where all his ex-wife's friends were; in fact, it took no time for him to come back to the local Greek Church, which had since been founded.

On the other hand, I saw my mother bloom and come to life in a way I never knew possible. As you know, the focus of the 1970s in American society was based on the *individual*. After all, it was dubbed the "Me Generation." Such a concept would have been incomprehensible to a Greek, whose whole world revolved around the family unit, and this would have been extended to the church family in one's village. Later I would learn that this focus on and the importance of collective fellowship and group cohesion, called *koinonia*, originated in his church of origin and was embedded in his psyche. As my mom got fed up with him in the final years of their marital demise and swept up in self-actualization, my father held on fiercely to what they once had. He was lost in her maze. When it's all said and done, I don't think they ever really knew each other. As one now grounded in a Christian foundation, when I look back on my childhood with new clarity, it is no wonder that so many marriages end in divorce. How can a foundation endure when either there is no vow made or when one or both do not believe in something more significant than the two of them? If there is no foundation based upon eternal and unchanging principles, how can the union *not* but likely end in dissolution? If one relies upon the steadiness, good intentions, or perfection of the *human* heart to endure and stay true, one's own heart will be broken before you know it. I'm not at all saying there aren't divorces in Christian marriages! It seems likely the chances for success are greater when the union is based on more than feelings, vague hopes, and attraction. Why would I spend time telling you about my folks' divorce? Their fork in the road sparked something within me: a desire to seek something of better virtue and a more significant and longer-lasting value. My search next took me to a place where I found myself, my calling, and God all wrapped up in one country's culture.

CHAPTER 2:
Mother Russia

"I didn't choose Russia, but Russia chose me. I had been fascinated from an early age by the culture, the language, the literature and the history to the place."

— Ellen Dunmore

"The mystery of human existence lies not in just staying alive, but in finding something to live for."
— Fyodor Dostoyevsky, *The Brothers Karamazov* (1880)

2.1 Why Russian?

As does every underclassman in the college of liberal arts, I had to choose a required general civilization or culture course. I intentionally avoided the course everyone and his brother took, which was Western Civilization. Instead, after calling and conversing with several professors from various departments, I, like Goldilocks, found one that was "juuust right" for me. The particular professor who answered my phone call by identifying himself as "Daniel speaking." He had no problem telling me about a course called "Russian Culture." In fact, he had trouble stopping describing it. Plus, he had a dry sense of humor, and in his telling me about all about Russia, he often spoke with irony. I loved it! Bingo, I landed upon what I'd take! So, in the fall quarter of 1982, when the Cold War still very much in effect, I signed up for Russian Culture. General Secretary Leonid Brezhnev was in office at the time, but he would die that November. I still remember watching his funeral on television and Chopin's *Funeral March* being played so heavily and somberly, yet all the while, I felt like this was a time of new beginning for me. Taking this particular course and being under the tutelage of this professor would change my life forever; in fact, I would often describe this experience as being akin to somebody that has been "born again." I began to make my way through all the required classes for the Russian major at the University of South Carolina, looking through the course selections with the same thrill and anticipation of a child looking through the old Sears and Penney's Christmas catalogs. I would be remiss if I didn't spend time telling you more about this Dr. Theodore Daniel, the professor I came to love as we *both* "loved with a love that was more than a love" for all things Russian. My relationship with him was another pivotal force that altered the direction my academics and personal life would take. Eventually, I would teach Russian and take many trips abroad with students, and later yet, I would embark on a spiritual journey that led me to be born again. In the meanwhile, I began to explore every facet of Russian culture because, as Winston Churchill said, "Russia is a riddle wrapped in a mystery inside an enigma." I was hooked!

2.2 The Party and Man That Changed My Life's Direction

I gobbled up the five books we had to read concurrently in this course; in fact, I felt like I was plowing with a team of five horses, urging me on. I'd never read about such a compelling, tragic, and magnificent culture that was caught in the crossroads between east and west. I could so relate! My favorite of these books was James Billington's *The Icon and the Axe*, but we also read about Russian history, Russian art and architecture, as well as the then famous book on Russian culture, *The Russians*, by Hedrick Smith. After ingesting so much deliciously gratifying information about their tragic history and profound spirituality sustaining them through it all, a culminating moment for me in that course was when I wrote my capstone research paper. I entitled it "The Quasi-Religious Conscience of Russia." I researched this topic with zeal, relish, and intensity; I typed and retyped it on my new electric typewriter until it was perfect. Who knew that this religious focus of mine would predicate that which was later to transpire within me?

I was initially enamored by Russian culture because it fulfilled my desire to learn about Greek culture. My professor and our class even visited the Greek Orthodox Church one weekday evening. At our private lecture, the priest explained the significance of the Greek Orthodox Church's architecture, including its shape and eastward direction. The dome of the Orthodox Church was to represent Heaven above the earth; the significance of the incense was that it was like the prayers of the parishioners wafting up to God; and the unique music of the cantors, thoroughly Eastern in its tonality, accompanied these saints singing. And the clincher above all for me was that, regardless of the language used or icons depicted, the Orthodox Church in its basic structure and liturgy was *identical*, whether or not the actual cathedral was in Russia or Greece! *Eureka*! A connection! The priest next defined the architectural divisions of the structure (e.g., the narthex, nave, and sanctuary), described the classic features of the iconostasis, and elucidated the order of icons and some of the primary themes and figures depicted. Russians loved these iconostases so much they made them five tiers high! Dr. Daniel interpreted the colors and positionality of the Byzantine icons' figures, and I became even more thrilled because I'd long been saving the weekly Orthodox Church bulletins that were mailed to our home. For years I adored gazing at these otherworldly but very human saints; they were so different than the pink or white chubby cherubs holding little harps of their Western counterparts! I could go on and on. And the fact that Russians chose to go back to Constantinople, Greece, the capital of the Byzantine Empire, to determine if Orthodoxy was suitable (or advantageous) for them — this after they eventually researched via envoys investigating other religions, finding them all unacceptable for one reason or another — I related to my *own* quest for my heritage. All of this seeking was located somewhere in the subterranean recesses of my heart. So, as Eastern Orthodoxy became the church and religion of the Russians' choice, Russian became the language and culture for this half-Greek girl, starved for that underfed ancestral appetite. Dr. Daniel deciphered the Byzantine and early Russian icons for me and explained how their two-dimensional aspect symbolized humankind's dual nature. I loved the rich but somehow muted hues; they were just impressively vibrant. And though I had not yet learned the Russian alphabet, I knew that studying the Russian language could and would, in some sense, satisfy the longing in me, which had yearned to learn Greek. Further, this major would lead me to the world of Russian writers, which, I knew, contained some of the best in the world. It was the biggies, the giants of nineteenth-century Russian literature, who were concerned with the "eternal questions," that is, what is the meaning of life, why are we here, what underlies the struggles of the human heart, and what happens to us after we die, and so on. Russians instinctively know from their collective historical conscious the meaning of "laughter through the tears." Like me, Russia suffered its own identity crisis: it did not know its proper place in history. This country, straddled between the east and west, was neither the one nor the other. I could relate! I was a half-Greek, half-American, a strong-willed woman loving living in the south but indeed no southerner. I didn't know where, how, or if I'd *ever* fit in anywhere; therefore, I chose to steep myself in Russian culture, and it more than satiated me. As an aside, I feel compelled to comment that if this zeal for Russian were merely a replacement for what I craved in Greek culture, it is improbable that it would have lasted so long and become such an integral part of my life and career, now for pushing thirty years. I now return to the period when I changed my major and, consequently, my life's direction.

At the very end of the first semester of my taking Russian Culture, Dr. Daniel held a Christmas party at his house for all those studying or teaching Russian. I had never been to a professor's house before; it seemed so grown up. When I went walked up the steps to his home that Christmas of 1982, Dr. Daniel, slightly inebriated, answered the door, still wearing his suit and tie from school. Donning a ball cap with "Tolstoy" written on the front, he seemed glad to see me and grinned sheepishly as he never did in class. Although there were at least fifty people already inside milling about, laughing, eating homemade Russian appetizers or "zakooski," drinking, listening to Russian music, or engaging in deep conversation while standing around the keg of beer in his backyard, Dr. Daniel was intent on showing me his office. His study was a floor-to-ceiling library stacked with books categorized by subject, areas that were all of importance to him, including chemistry, biology, and American literature, in addition to hundreds of Russian books, also inventoried. They each had a smell all their own. In every window frame, he'd installed glass shelves to display his impressive insulator collection; they came from all over the world. I'd never noticed, let alone known what one was. Lined neatly in a row, from afar, they looked like stained glass, and I loved their aquamarine hues. He pointed out this and that book as if he were introducing me to old friends. In fact, it seemed as if nobody else were there, yet when I heard strains of balalaika music in the background and laughter just beyond, I was gladdened and aware that I was in a house full of folks that had the same interest in Russia like I did. Without saying it, Dr. Daniel knew this half-Greek girl in his class had been overtaken with the passion for all things Russian, too. Several drinks later, hearing a lively folk song, he and I were moved to break into folk dancing together spontaneously. Sensing the moment, the people in his living room cleared the tables and chairs to the corners of the room and formed a circle around us. I did a spirited rendition of something Greek while he did a form of

Russian dance. We were exuberant and got lost in this moment of united Russian and Greek dancing; unknowingly, we held captive an audience that was clapping us on. This was no crush; it was a love for something bigger than us. We had that same powerful attraction inside us, and we both knew and understood *this* was why we were drawn to one another. Once in a literature course I also took under him, Dr. Daniel challenged everyone to summarize in one sentence what the behemoth novel, *War and Peace*, was all about. After the class of twenty read aloud their sentences, most of them long and gangly, I read mine. I remember feeling odd that Dr. Daniel peered at me rather quaintly until he had another student in class read aloud what *he* had written. It was precisely the same as what I'd penned, down to the last word! I would begin to mark those serendipitous occurrences of goodness as signs that I was on the right track in life. Much later, I also view the circumstance as gifts of divine approval when they led me to Him and pointed back to the Cross. I would continue to go to Dr. Daniel's house and talk with him about Russian literature, about Russia, about life in general. He would tell me about pertinent things that had happened to him when he had visited Russia. In short, although very different people, we were kindred spirits. I took every course that man had to offer, and some twenty years later, I decided to visit him and thank him for what he had done for me and how much I'd learned from him. There was often a melancholy and haunted side to him, but upon my arrival, though by then a feeble older man, his eyes would sparkle as though he were coming back to life. I decided then and there to speak exclusively in Russian to him. This brought him an evident and tender joy. He didn't have much to say at that time in his life, but his eyes were so alive just *hearing* Russian. It can bring me to tears even now to remember him, and I still thank him. The difference one person can make in one's life is amazing. A couple of years later, I learned that he had died, but the love for Russian he infused me would eventually lead me to a gate with a whole new direction and meaning more than I could ever have fathomed.

In my final quarter, I took advanced language and literature classes with Dr. Isaac, another professor in the Germanic and Slavic Languages Dept. whom I came to admire. He had the visage of the Russian composer, Modest Mussorgsky, complete with blood-shot, sky-blue eyes, rubicund complexion, deep lines etched across his forehead, and the voice of Moses, so deep and rich that it mesmerized me. I would be hard-pressed to meet another person who lived and breathed to translate Russian poetry into English. It pleased me that my pronunciation of the language was good enough that he had me read aloud a Russian poem by Pushkin, *The Bronze Horseman*, for a foreign language function of the university. Speaking of having a keen ear for Russian, I must return for a moment to my violin playing, orchestra, and music. By the time I graduated high school, I had gotten pretty good and was proud to have received a small scholarship at the university to play in its orchestra. All but one year, I would also take violin lessons from a little Ukrainian man named Boris Chopinsky with whom I would keep in contact for over thirty years. Like my father, he, too, had known the atrocities of war, and though kind, he maintained a somewhat sardonic mindset. Leaning back in his diminutive chair, Benson & Hedges cigarette in hand, looking out an open window, he would play both the sublime and the secular on his violin, soulful and fanciful, with equal ease. He recognized the Greekness of my nature and would take delight in encouraging this part of me, be it talking about baklava or encouraging traveling. He would handpick out pieces that suited my personality, and these would always be ones in a minor key and those that were both sweeping and subtle, containing many moving and melancholic moments. Though I can still play by heart many baroque pieces, especially those of Vivaldi and Bach, which I'd learned as a youngster in the Suzuki violin program, as I grew older, I was drawn to the Slavic composers for their poignancy and pathos. Life's absurdities often amused Mr. Chopinsky, and underneath his mantle of humor and mirth, there was a sadness about him stemming from his life's disappointments. We complemented one other, and it was violin music that "soothed the savage beast" for us both.

2.3 Switching My Major to Russian and Finding Myself

The Monday following Dr. Daniel's Christmas party, I dropped my pre-med major for which I had been preparing nearly twelve years and switched it to Russian. The entirety of my life changed when I switched my major. I remember making that phone call home to inform my parents. My mom was happy and nonplussed; she was proud of her daughter for studying such an exotic language. My father, on the other hand, nearly dropped the phone. His initial response of chagrin, shock, and disappointment was rage. Where would I get a *job*?! What would I *do*? How long would this thing *last*? My attitude was like that of Scarlet O'Hara: "I'll think about that tomorrow." With job prospects plummeting from attaining a bachelor's degree with such a major, graduate school would become an imperative. To truly excel at the Russian language and grammar and complete those hefty reading assignments, I cloistered myself like a monk in my safe womb of a dorm room, far away from the confusing world of parental woes and personal ambiguities that proved too complicated for me. I sought to eliminate distractions, and this, also, would become a life habit. That semester, I started to skip meals and drank a lot of water, and much to my amazement, for the first time in my life, my pants started to fit loosely. I lost thirty-five pounds that quarter. I no longer played rugby, no longer fanaticized about leaving the University of South Carolina; I just couldn't get enough of absorbing everything associated with Russian. The world and all its alluring, seductive, yet troubling aspects distressed me greatly. I might as well have been Dostoevsky's "underground man" from nineteenth-century Russia for how I, too, chose to withdraw as an ascetic of sorts, vexed by the world's ways. Later, much later, I would see withdrawal as a form of retreat and *not* a way to purify myself, let alone improve the world.

Was I having romanticized notions about Russia? Did ingesting it serve multiple sub-conscious purposes? Beyond a doubt, the answer is "yes." Not too many months later, I would travel to the Soviet Union and bring my studies to life.

2.4 Fitting Pieces Together with the Russian Language

The quarter following the two-part course on Russian Culture, I began my first class in Russian Language. I memorized dialogue after dialogue and did not get to grammar, writing, and vocabulary until the second level. Then we took off at lightning speed, making up for lost time. Much to my delight, as with the Latin alphabet used by English-speakers, I discovered that the Russian alphabet also had as its basis the Greek alphabet for the vast majority of its letters! That it was two Greek monks from Thessaloniki, Cyril and Methodius, who went to what is now Ukraine around 860 to serve as missionaries to the pagan Slavs was music to my ears! They became known as the "Apostles to the Slavs," and Cyril's name was used to identify its descendant script, Cyrillic, afterward. To more fully share the Gospel with these illiterate Russian peoples, it became necessary to introduce an alphabet, and the language they initially used was called Glagolitic. These monks were sage enough to have fused alongside their native Greek alphabet new letters, which they devised for the uniquely Slavic sounds they were hearing from these people around them. Thus, this new alphabet that was an amalgam of modified Greek letters *and* novel Slavic ones was synthesized to create the Old Church Slavonic language that was to be used liturgically. For the masses that could not yet read, let alone make out God's Word, saints and biblical figures were visually introduced by way of icons; they soon became immediately recognizable by certain characteristic features. There was even an icon depicting Jesus the "Redeemer with the Moist Beard." And though these figures might have looked like dark and sinister villains to other westerners, the Dormition and Pantocrator icons proved powerful to my sensibilities. My favorite such personage was John the Baptist, who looked like a scraggly and possessed homeless man; it was apparent that he lived on locusts and wild honey from the desert. By and large, these icons depicted real and everyday people who achieved saintly status; optimally, they would inspire and motivate contemporary persons to be righteous and Godly improvement, all based on faith. If they could do it, so could we! Additionally, the saints' images from one's own country could then be added to the list of Biblical figures, thus expanding the connection between the Old Testament and New Testament to include one's contemporary and local martyrs. What inspiration! Russian just kept getting better and better for me! That I became taken by how these monks converted the Slavs, that is, patiently biding with them until it took, is no wonder, as decades later, patience and tender loving care were just what it took to massage His message of love into me. Standing at the precipice and ready to learn Greek, I instead jumped into mastering Russian. Later on, I would return and try to learn contemporary Greek, and I even dabbled with New Testament Greek. It led to a full circle completed. I came to crave not just words in Russian or Greek, but I would crave the Word itself. *This* is the crux. I also came to look upon icons as treasured art, not windows to aid in my sanctification or a vehicle to render the living God and His early promoters. Nowadays, His Word reverberates within me; His truth resonates within my soul, but it would take many more trips to Russia and much more to arrive where I am now.

2.5 A Change of Plans and My First Trip to Russia

In the early eighties, there were precious few options open as far as finding a career related to Russian went; pursuing this avenue involved a leap of faith in its own right. I had disappointed my father, bewildered my mother, and derailed my plans. I could either become a professor, try to find a job in the government, or get an undergraduate degree that would lead to nothing. Therefore, at that point, it looked like it was academia or bust for me; so, I took every Russian course offered. June of 1984, I and about fifteen other students and community members would go on a two-week tour to the Soviet Union lead by my favorite professor, Dr. Theodore Daniel. That first incandescent evening in Moscow, my fellow Russian students and I made a beeline for Red Square, and we kissed those not-so-red brick squares right in front of St. Basil's Cathedral. We were grateful just to be there and behold this enchanting and wondrous building that surpassed all the pictures that I had seen of it. In addition to many museums and Soviet landmarks, we went to a humongous bookstore where I found the heftiest book that I could on Russian icons. The reason for this purchase is that we had just come from the Tretyakovsky Museum, and it was there I was awestruck by the most incredible icon I'd ever seen. The Holy Trinity icon was painted by the famous Russian iconographer, Andrey Rublëv, who himself had been trained by a Greek artist. This depiction of the Holy Trinity, the Father, Son, and Holy Spirit renders them indistinguishable from the other. The figures are sitting in perfect, harmonious communion with one another around a small table with a chalice on it. If you didn't know the symbolism of their robes' colors and a few other details, you couldn't tell them apart. I was captivated by it and would later share it with my students, and finally, some thirty years later, I would give a small icon of this to the man who shared and explained the actual meaning of each of the members united in the trinity to me.

But back to my first trip to Mother Russia in 1984. At the time, as I said, Russia was still the Soviet Union. Of course, not only would we visit Moscow and what was then Leningrad, but we also rode the trans-Siberian Railway all the way out to Irkutsk and Lake Baikal. This 3 ½ -day sojourn traversed the length of the United States, and there is more territory yet to this country spanning nine time zones! While I was on this train ride, I remember wanting to try out my Russian, so I said, "Hello!" in Russian to a random Russian man in a jogger's suit who passed me in the narrow hallway in front of the berths. He stopped, smiled, and introduced me to everyone in his birth. I was on display — a real American! Even my speaking the most rudimentary of words in Russian caused them to beam at my attempt, and then sensing my innocence or trustworthiness, they began to pepper me with questions. They were hungry for information. Before I knew it, there were ten more faces jammed in that doorway, eager to learn what I had to reveal about America. They wanted to know how many bathrooms my house had; did I own a gun; and was I, as a woman, afraid to walk the streets in the university campus alone, and other such questions as that. They even wanted to know if we still hung blacks from trees in the south. Wow! These Russians, so ignorant, were also in a way insulated from the dangers of freedom like violence, rampant materialism, and the insecurity experienced if one can't find a job or pay for healthcare. Nearly a decade later, when the Soviet Union collapsed in 1991, I would, in shame and disappointment, watch as the worst of the west — drugs, guns, and prostitution — make its way to Russia. But back to the train ride and my being made welcome on the train by real Russians. Later still, I would wonder if I had what it took to approach a stranger and start a conversation about *Christ*. Discussing Him would mean broaching another about a new way of living centered on Him. No, I would not *lose* my Greek culture or knowledge of Russia but supersede this favored worldly knowledge and *gain* Godly wisdom and focus. The following summer of 1985 was when I truly became fluent in Russian. I went to an eight-week course at the Intensive Slavic Language Workshop in the Russian and East European Institute in Muncie, Indiana. I had never studied Russian so intently, so intensely before. My brain hurt from hearing Russian all morning; I thought I'd never been able to comprehend what was said! The few constituent words I did understand would increase to clusters of words. Then, little by slowly, I understood full sentences so that by the end of that workshop, I was even *dreaming* in Russian! The intent absorption and intense focus demonstrated above, I would later use to take in His Word. It not only riveted my attention, but it moved me to want to be more like Him. The following summer, I took another trip to study the Russian language in the Soviet Union, this time for six weeks at the Pushkin Institute in Moscow. Because of my previous summer's immersion program, this experience went exceptionally well. Studies went beyond the academic, and language came to life. After four years and two quarters, I completed my bachelor's degree at the University of South Carolina in March of 1986. I still did not know, let alone think about Christ except for what I came to learn of Him tangentially through Russian literature.

2.6 My Passion for Russian Literature

I must linger a moment and elaborate on how and why Russian literature, arguably some of the world's best, fulfilled my hungry heart, which craved depth and truth to satisfy my soul. The first class that I took in Russian literature was a survey of 20th-century Russian literature. I was dismayed to find that more often than not, I stayed after the dismissal bell, even longer than the Russian majors did, to finish my in-class essays. There was so much to say! Regardless of the plot, it seemed as if all of the topics touched upon the meaning of life or our faith in God. This literature course, in turn, led to my diving whole-hog into the world of nineteenth-century Russian literature, which I'd only dipped my toe in when I read Dostoevsky's *Crime and Punishment* as a senior back in high school. I re-read this novel with new eyes, getting into Raskolnikov's critical mind like never before as if I were with him on his journey of dynamic growth. To progress to *The Brothers Karamazov* was life-altering: sweet Alyosha's spiritual quest; the probing atheist brother, Ivan; the passionate sensualist brother, Dmitri; and the feeble-minded copycat of a half-brother, Svidrigailov, demonstrated the full spiritual spectrum and delved into knowing our place in life which I, too, sought. The prideful and intellectual Ivan rejected God and, in so doing, negatively impacted his younger and impressionable brother. I loved Father Zosima for telling Alyosha to "go out in the world," much in the same way as Maria was instructed to go back to the Von Trap family in *The Sound of Music*. A quarter of a century later, I would hear the call to live in a frame-of-mind of ready preparedness to "make disciples of all the nations" (Matthew 28:19). In short, I was attracted to all three brothers for different reasons: like Alyosha, I sought a better understanding of God's will for me. Like Ivan, I had vexing doubts and conflicting speculations about God and what faith in Him meant, and like the eldest son, Misha, I was often a victim of wild passions at this time of my life. Plus, the boys' father in this novel, an opportunistic hedonist to his core and one who also craftily played the fool to get his way, was so much like my father. My passion and quest for seeking and attaining some nebulous *more* out there in life got into a laser-like focus when later I, too, the leap of faith into the arms of our perfect Father, Who gave us love incarnate. In the meanwhile, it was the atheistic brother, Ivan, by whom I was most captivated. He probed into the reason behind Christ's perhaps failed mission through his own fictionalized Grand Inquisitor informing Christ that all people needed was "miracle, mystery, and authority." He was implying that humanity at large is incapable of believing through faith alone, let alone living as He asked. I could see from what I had recalled that ordinary people *then and now* insist that Jesus perform miracles. That Jesus was reluctant to do so and certainly didn't on command I admired and applauded; He was no magician, honcho, or messiah to merely one group. Ivan was suggesting that if the masses needed marvels or proofs to believe, how could Christianity ever become a success without such? In Ivan's subtext, it is the Church then that provides the proofs and razzmatazz for the masses, which, time and again, show they are looking for an affirmation of this fact. The fictitious Jesus kisses this Grand Inquisitor to indicate that he is right, that it is the *Church* and not He that satisfies this need in humanity. In so doing, the promise of freedom Jesus gave us is gone; the Grand Inquisitor implies that we gladly sacrifice freedom for a false assuredness and reduced responsibility. Perish the thought, I thought! Another problem Ivan suffered over was that if one asserts there is no God, there must also be no Devil, but this was far from the case. Ivan's hallucination of having a conversation with the Devil forces him to contend with the reality of *God's* existence. Double indemnity! In anguish, Ivan contended that they were *both* a figment of his creation, but he ended up losing his sanity, getting stuck in his convoluted syllogism. The thrust of his argument is that if there is no immortality and no divine retribution, then anything is permissible, including murder or suicide, both of which occur in this novel. Alas, Dostoevsky never completed what he intended to be a trilogy for these brothers' spiritual paths to work out, which would have proclaimed the triumphant righteousness of Christ worked out down here. That I share my take on this novel is ultimately to reveal that I spent a great deal of time and energy puzzling over what it meant to have *faith*. Had I not turned to Russian, a culture deeply imbued with Christian influence,

I might have continued to dismiss Christ, but this was not the case. I had no spiritual mentor, only the convolutions of my seeking self as I made my way through Russian classes. Alyosha was living proof that one could be a real person *and* a Christian; he became a model of such a type to me. Re-reading Dostoevsky's novel, *Crime and Punishment*, a second then a third time, I was brought into closer proximity to Christ by numerous allusions to Him and through the veiled warning of what happens if one tries to live above and without Him, as the protagonist, Raskolnikov, would try. I would later teach my students later that the root of his very surname in Russian translates to "schism." Where faith is concerned and at some point in our lives, we all stand at the crossroads.

Let me count the ways with which I identified with the protagonist, Raskolnikov: I, too, loved the life of the student and read voraciously; I was vaguely and smugly anti-western in my disdain for conspicuous consumption, rampant materialism, and the hyper-focus on the individual; I had a desire for purity within and parity in the world. Like Raskolnikov, I, too, experienced an inner duality — and not just the typical dialectic between good and evil, but what is involved in desiring to feel genuinely *whole*, acceptable, lovable, and worthy. I, too, had a sense of superiority, yet I knew that I lacked generosity of heart. I showed off my intellect to hide feelings of inadequacy and insecurity in other areas. But when Raskolnikov took the plunge and committed not only the justified murder of ridding society of a human "cockroach," but by accident, he had committed a second murder; he was now a common man, after all! I saw the danger of such a "superman theory" and nihilistic mentality. *No one is perfect*! No one is better than another, no matter what! We must all take responsibility for the wrong we do to others and change our wicked ways through obedience and suffering. At the time of reading, I had no idea what repentance was, but I would get a dose of what it involved in this novel. Another major moral takeaway that demonstrates hope for everyone with Christ and nothing but loss without Him is shown by two characters on the opposite ends of the social spectrum: Sonya, the prostitute, is the one with compassion. She becomes a savior of sorts and models what real forgiveness and steadfastness can bring one and others in life. She never abandons her friend, Raskolnikov, even when he is exiled to Siberia. On the other end of the spectrum is Svidrigailov, who is the greater success for all intents and purposes: he is both incredibly wealthy *and* a philanthropist. Sonya, a devout Christian, prostituted herself for her family's welfare; Svidrigailov, in reality, was a pedophile. And in the depraved but impressive world of his own fabrication, this atheist ended up taking his own miserable life. In the end, Raskolnikov was *not* caught: he *confesses* his crime. He accepts his punishment as necessary and vital to reconciling himself with humanity *and* purifying his soul. I came to believe that this passion, suffering, endurance, and perseverance is how one improves and grows one's character for God. (And I don't mean through some willing martyrdom.) Confession can help expunge moral guilt and proves a superior means to purify the soul; you become an active agent in learning the life lesson of our inter-connectedness, not remain a passive victim who must serve time. What was missing in this equation would take me decades to find that Christ and Christ alone washes away the stain of guilt. *Confession must be preceded by faith in Him.* I did not yet have this, so the search continued. At least Raskolnikov rejected the false notion of being above others and saw himself as a part of humanity in a way he'd never recognized before. Why did God seem so far away for me when He was so prevalent and immediate in these Russian novels? I would relish these books for the spiritual proximity that they would bring me to Christ, though at the time, I was only aware of the academic attraction.

Where Dostoevsky pricked my conscience and mind, Tolstoy moved my heart and soul. What I felt had expired regarding our family's intimacies and unique whole, which was now scattering to the four winds, was resuscitated in characters so fully developed in *War and Peace* and *Anna Karenina*. These novels became my friends and extended family. The summer I worked at my father's plant was the summer I read both a biography of Tolstoy and a first reading of the 1500-page novel, *War and Peace*. I would weep for joy when Natasha welcomed her brother back from the war and danced a Russian dance, would imagine that I was in the thick forest as Andrei contemplated the meaning of his life, and would feel contentment when the couples that *should* have been together at the beginning did so by the novel's end. Though I was not yet a Christian, it pleased me much that Tolstoy's didacticism of Christian values was sewn seamlessly into the fabric of his characters.

That summer, an older woman from work who became my sole friend reminded me of a character from a Russian novel. She sacrificed her paycheck to provide for her gypsy-existing, poor, and dissolute family of her brother. She read the Bible daily, knew the Old Testament like the back of her hand, walked miles every day, and was the epitome of kindness. She never judged anyone and always had a willingness to talk with me about things that mattered in life and quietly laugh over that which we found absurd or ironic. She seemed like a living saint to me. Another character from a short story by Tolstoy that I would be fascinated by was "Father Sergius." He had been a playboy and a dandy of a soldier before he decided to devote himself to Christ fully; he renounced the world and was renowned for his spiritual prowess. Though a monk living away from the world, upon seeing a beautiful widow seeking his advice, came to visit him in his small hermitage, he nonetheless felt a physical attraction toward her. His way of dispensing with his weakness was to go to his bedroom and cut off one of his fingers so that he might distract himself with pain and not succumb to the desire of his flesh. The moral of the story is that sin never leaves one, and temptations always persist. Never having read the Bible, I was unfamiliar with Jesus instructing us to remove completely whatever brings about such seduction; plus, I was fascinated by this radical approach of ridding oneself of that which could lead to a moral decline. I wasn't thinking or considering any literal or figurative approach to this; I just knew it made sense. I began to try to desist from drinking alcohol, recognizing in secret that more often than not, I over-indulged. I failed in this and many other attempts to do so. At the same time, I tried hard to find a fulfilling relationship or lasting intimacy, but I kept missing the mark. I still felt out of place in the south, out of kilter from my parents' divorce, and unsettled about where my education and life were heading. I didn't know who I was or where I fit in. It was in Russia itself that I found the first real and righteous friends I had been seeking; in fact, I had the impression that they would even die for me. With less material affluence to interfere or impede a relationship, I attained that soulful connection with others I wanted so desperately. You may rightly ask, well, aren't these just romanticized ideals? That very well may have been the case, but only if you look back in hindsight; in those moments, the friendships were genuine and satisfied something in me for which I had been yearning such a long time. All this seeking was leading me inexorably and compellingly to something more incredible that I could not have imagined. The six-month period between when I graduated from U.S.C. in the spring and when I entered Purdue that following fall, I existed in a giant vat of murky uncertainty; nothing was clear, no direction known. For just a few months, I lived with a troubled and troubling man who was going nowhere fast, and I knew I had to escape. Just a few months after the nuclear explosion occurred in Chernobyl, I got accepted to a summer program in Moscow, and the following fall, I would enter graduate school. Life lurched forward, and I was propelled.

2.7 Gradually on to Graduate School

When I got to Purdue University in the fall of 1986, I was immediately impressed with the size of the Russian Dept. there. It wasn't comprised of just four rooms, as was U.S.C.'s Germanic and Slavic Languages Dept. Rather, it had two full wings of offices for these professors of various Russian courses. When it's all said and done, I did not acquire the close-knit sense of family and camaraderie that I did at U.S.C., and this both surprised and disappointed me. During graduate school, I made the momentous decision to study for a full semester in the Soviet Union, which was a big deal because it meant being cut off from my world back home (unless you sent a telegram). This would be less than two years before the collapse of the Soviet Union, that failed experiment of communism. It is with pleasure that I now share with you some moments of the five-month winter term I spent in Moscow in 1988 because it will help you understand more of why I was attracted to this country and these people. Even more fundamentally, I was nurturing an inner religious zeal that was nascent and gestating to bring about what I then could not have anticipated would later occur.

2.8 Five Months in Moscow

Many people do not understand Russians: they think that they are an unhappy lot because they do not smile. This is *so* not so. That said, Russians have a duality to them: on the one hand, they are extremely private and do not readily or openly share their feelings with just anyone. Often, during their turbulent history, it was not safe for them to express their opinions with those other than immediate family members. And so, when I see Americans thinking that all Russians are dour or sour, I know by experience that in the intimacy of their own homes with their family members, they would do more for one another than the average American family does. Don't get me wrong, Russians can be total swine, and they will cheat the system if they can without missing a heartbeat. Also, there is no such thing as standing politely or orderly in line, the likes of which we have come to expect in our New England of America. Queues there amount to throngs morphing and moving like an amoeba: they do not have any linear sense of orderliness or apparent purpose; waiting with others can feel like madness. This situation would drive the normal American insane, and it did me many a time. Why do I mention this? I learned many a lesson in perspective there. What may be materially inefficient, antiquated, and nonsensical to me is superseded or overshadowed by the moral morass and chaos regarding values and priorities I see *here*. We stand in line here, but they stand in rapt attention to God there, regardless of what form of government is in place or type of leader is ruling. We Americans are proud to be independent and self-sufficient, but Russians as a whole recognize we are not as in control as we would like to think, and they evaluate in terms of the bigger picture, not the moment. As it turns out, God *does* see all. And just when you think you can't get much more exasperated from something simple not working out as it would have in the States, you experience something akin to divine intervention in Russia. In short, it is a truth that the Russian religious spirit is a deep one, and I came to love it so very much.

That semester, I would make several close friends, one of whom was my teacher in Russian conversation. She became a very dear friend and one whom I would visit over twenty-five years. During this semester, her mother died, and she ended up sharing her feelings about it with us. She even invited a few of us to accompany her to a monastery in Zagorsk, situated on the outskirts of Moscow, a place to which I would later take my students. This day trip required taking a train far into Moscow's outskirts; here, one can breathe in the lush, green earth coming to life. The reason she gave for going to this monastery was that she wanted to pray both for her mother and herself. I asked her why she had to leave home to do so. She told me that she *needed* to worship in church. This was no "celebration of life" that Americans fashion for their dead. In the Russian Orthodox Church, you can feel and hear the quiet recesses of souls in supplication. There may perhaps be the sound of shuffling feet moving toward some healing icon or in the background, an unseen but audible chorus can be detected, like angels serenading you from heaven; everyone there is united in prayers of petition, but privately so. I'd never witnessed the interconnectedness of *centuries* of history as I did then and there among these people. This cathedral was nothing like the austere or unadorned Protestant church, yet it was less grandiose than Catholic cathedrals. Here again, I found a connection to the Greek Church. Yet, Russians themselves are very different because Greeks do not have the servile, humble, and base readiness to suffer as does the Russian. The general temperament of a group always affects its nation's spiritual climate. Greeks love freedom more than anything! Regardless, when you are in an Orthodox Church, you feel connected to history and the rich offering it makes; here, Christ envelops and enfolds you still. When approaching the front to pray, I would stand among and watch the throng of other women there. There are *so* many Russian women are in these churches. There are no pews, no benches, and no carpet for comfort; even the oldest of women will get down prostrate on her knees, with her forehead touching the cool marble floor in reverential posture made in fervent prayer to God. I had never seen anything the likes of this in America! For a long, I was dismayed, even somewhat incensed, to think that evangelical missionaries would try to proselytize Russians as if they were nonbelievers! I had never witnessed a more believing Christian nation in all my life! I had such a dire need for that kind of contact with the divine that I cannot explain it adequately to you, yet at the time, I mistakenly looked for this comfort in the Church and not personally with Christ. *There's* the rub! In truth and faith, admittedly or not, every person seeks God in some way. What I didn't know then was that God was in pursuit of me! At the time, I did not understand how such a personal relationship was possible, let alone necessary, as I had come to see Protestants fixating on. All I knew was that I relished being a part of a group united in prayer in a church that hadn't changed in all of Christendom. Little did I fathom or distinguish *then* that such adherence to *form*, including the veneration of icons, reciting prayers from memory, lighting candles, and participation in ritualistic sacraments, was still not the deal. That you may be aware that He is Lord is not the same thing as fixing your focus and hope on *Christ alone* for your salvation. I was not there yet.

Being far away from home in the depths of winter in Russia, you'd think I'd get depressed. I did not. Like Russians who go outside to see the brightness of the white around them, I did the same. I loved to take long walks in the nearby birch forests, which led to moments, overtly communicated or not, where I was aware of God's presence. Once when I was strolling in a dense birch forest and while the snow was falling thick and silent, I stopped in my tracks, leaned back, and looked up through the tall, silver-gray of those birch trees up to the deep and dusky blue sky above and heard the crunch of the snow from people walking in the distance. I then looked back down at the indigo of the sky somehow reflected in the silver of the bark of these birch trees and then such as well in the snow itself, and I was in awe. God was so there. A couple of years after I finished graduate school and started teaching, I sought to share the tremendously valuable experience of traveling by taking students to Russia with me. From church to the circus to the countryside we went, by train and bus and plane.

Do not think that I was so spiritual as to have found my faith, but neither had I had any religion to lose. That time had not come. While in Russia that semester, I also got close to another Russian graduate student, Oleg, and we would become as close as brother and sister. I came back and visited him on my own in 1990, and he would eventually leave the Soviet Union right after its collapse and finally move to Australia. His roommate, Drake, played the guitar and knew dozens of songs and all of the verses of those many songs. On any given occasion to be celebrated, be it a birthday or holiday, he played his guitar mightily for our tightly-knit pack of friends, and we would all sing with such gusto in the privacy of their dorm room. Don't get me wrong; there was drinking in the evenings. A lot of drinking. I also learned a Russian tradition that once a bottle was open for a guest, it was considered impolite if he didn't finish help drink it with his host. His nose was still toasted if one didn't drink, while other toasts were made and shots glasses chinked together. This is how Russians are; they do not separate into little corners or clusters of individuals, they are a very *group*-oriented kind of people, and I had never experienced anything like this before as an adult. Since my family's fragmentation, I suppose I clung to this family that I had created in Russia all the more.

Many years later, I would find a church family with whom I shared more than I would or could with my blood relatives. That was and still is an oddity to me. Later that spring, I would work in a small capacity with NBC to show some of the photojournalists where to find places where interviews would be conducted in Moscow. President Reagan was coming to visit the head of the so-called "Evil Empire," President Gorbachev. It happened to be during the same year Russia was commemorating its *millennium* of Christianity founded and grounded in Russia. I was so proud of this country for that fact! Later on, and looking back, I would wonder how I, of all people, would come to put my faith in one man, in Christ alone. All along the way and "*from afar*, the Lord [was] *saying*, [to me], 'I have loved you with an everlasting love; therefore, *I have drawn you with loving-kindness*'" (Jeremiah 31:3, emphasis mine). It is no wonder that I was well on my way to Him even though I wasn't aware of it. When I returned from this trip to Russia, I would commence completing my graduate studies program at Purdue.

2.9 THE END OF MY EDUCATION AND THE DECISION TO BEGIN TEACHING

During my eighteen months at graduate school, I would move twice more, living in a bedroom of one house with four other graduate students and then dwelling in another such house with two fellow graduate students in Russian. The entirety of my earthly possessions could fit in my car. My sole focus was completing my dissertation, which required an oral defense of the thesis to satisfy the requirements of this terminating master's program. I had since switched from the Ph.D. track of Russian Linguistics to the Russian and East Europeans Studies Dept., from which select branches of the U.S. government solicited those who were eligible to work in military intelligence. My dissertation's title would be a mouthful to say and equally unappetizing to read: "The Connection between the Soviet Military-Industrial Complex and the Agricultural Sector." Every page I wrote confirmed the voice inside me that said working for the government would *not* be to my liking, but I'd come too far to give up on attaining my degree. Meanwhile, to survive, I needed more than the money that was allotted to me from student loans. I scraped by through doing several part-time jobs. At this time, I cleaned houses, once even for a Russian family, the grandmother of which would follow me furtively around the house either to make sure I did it right or to ensure I wouldn't steal something. As a personal favor but for no payment, I also visited one of my Russian professor's nonagenarian mother. She had been a physician for forty years in Leningrad and was born there when it was called Petrograd. I also made pocket money by working in the cafeteria, or, if extra hard-pressed, I even sold my plasma for ready cash. And although it hardly seemed anything like work, another job I undertook was tutoring. Teaching came quickly and naturally to me. Finally, the last semester arrived. I was so ready to be out in the so-called "real" world, but I didn't know where or how I was to live, let alone find a job. Nothing was lining up. I did not do well enough on the entrance exam required by the CIA, but I was called for a second interview with the NSA. In the end, I declined, and with my degree in hand, I turned away from this direction altogether. Another factor influencing my decision *not* to work for the government was based on an inevitable and irrevocable status change. As one no longer be a civilian, I would be disallowed to visit my Soviet chums freely. More to the point, I wanted no curtailments on my personal life or to my freedom. Both of these reasons were factual, but truth be told, there was yet another inchoate need, an unformulated plan brewing inside me which was eventually to come to fruition, and that was the call to teach. So, having completed all my required courses as well as a few extra coveted ones, including one on Byzantine Art and Architecture that I'd waited two years to be offered, I wrote my thesis, defended it to a panel of three professors, and attained my MA in January of 1989. Just as I would be getting my life together, the Soviet Union was falling apart.

When I reflect on those early days in the university, I must admit to you another motif or behavior that streamed alongside my years of studying Russian and continued right into my working years with increasing energy and impact. After all, as Socrates said, "The unexamined life is not worth living." And I'm telling you that I had a love affair with alcohol that would *have* to be terminated. When I switched my major to Russian, I half-jokingly used to say that deciding to do this was because I liked to drink, though I know that is certainly not the case. Like many, I started drinking in high school, and it was made easier to do so with my father's sweet strawberry wine, homemade and readily available by the dozens of bottles. Going to so many Russian parties and then traveling to Russia itself, I came to drink vast quantities of vodka; in fact, my freezer was never without a bottle of Stoli. I was even proud that I could drink as much as I did; somehow, it made me more "Russian." Mysteriously, somewhere around the age of thirty-five — after about twenty years of drinking *not* like your average person, that is, like one who could stop halfway through a glass of wine, or one who could limit himself to a couple of drinks, or one who did not need to hide his *actual* drinking habits — I picked up my first white chip, the white flag of surrender. Such submission would eventually lead to a vaster personal abandonment *and* empowerment than I could ever have anticipated. Ceasing to consume alcohol brought me a new life. Approaching fifty years of age, I would become like the infant who takes a big gulp of air into his lungs the moment he enters the world; my reality would change, expand, and improve to such a degree and fashion. I was not there yet, but you will see this topic brought up later on.

Meanwhile, with my M.A. diploma in hand and no job in sight, I would make the momentous decision to get certified to teach. So, back to U.S.C. I went, as I would have in-state status down there; plus, I decided that I most certainly did not want to live in the Midwest. I was fully aware that I would never be able to get a job solely teaching Russian. It occurred to me that teaching English would be a natural choice for me, so I began my program to attain dual certification in secondary education. Communicating in general and explaining the meaning of literature has always been a forté of mine, but I already knew that my *real* passion for teaching stemmed from my desire to connect with people about the things that are important and essential in life. Plus, I cared for people. Ever the eldest child, a person desirous to learn and share, and perhaps because I was a woman without children, teaching high school made total sense. I gave it my all. I like to tell my students that back as a freshman at U.S.C., I once took an interest survey test that helped give me an idea of which vocations I would find most fulfilling in life. When the results came in, mine lined up like this: a psychiatrist, a college professor, and — drumroll — a truck driver! Only when I got a job teaching and had my own classroom, the walls of which I would cover from floor to ceiling with colorful Soviet propaganda placards, maps, and dozens of the best posters from students' Russian culture and American literature projects over the years, did I realize that my classroom had become my own "big rig" I drove. One must be savvy in observing and respecting the myriad expressions, moods, and needs of children in one's class, and one must love sharing ideas, wisdom, not to mention one's own heart, to *really* make a difference. I sought not only to teach but to *inspire*. The results of this test all made sense now! Little could I have ever imagined that over twenty-five years later, the call to teach would blossom into a desire to share His Word, though *how* or even *if* this could transpire remained an unknown at the time. In the meanwhile, learning Russian now led to my teaching Russian, as I will soon relate.

2.10 An Introduction to Teaching Russian and a New Identity

I feel very fortunate, yes, *blessed*, to be able to teach both English *and* Russian, and on the first day of class, when I write my surname, CHRISTAKIS, on the board, students usually ask me if I am Russian; I suppose it only makes sense. Every year I answer, no, that my father was born in Greece. And then, invariably, kids next ask, "Why did you decide to take *Russian*?" If I had a nickel (or should I say kopeck) for every time I have been asked this, I would be a wealthy woman! I tell them that though my father was a Greek man, he never *taught* me Greek, and I had an overwhelming desire to learn the language because I was so proud of my Greek heritage. Greek food I could make, Greek music I took a shining to, and this country I had traveled to, but they don't call it the "*mother* tongue" for nothing. In other words, it is typically from one's mother — not one's father — that we learn the language we predominantly speak. I said that, in part, because I never got the side of me which *so* desired to learn and understand Greek satisfied, and then in college, because I elected *not* to take Western Civilization like everyone else, I chose a course in Russian culture. What I learned in this class came to satisfy me and take on a life of its own. Russian not only piqued my curiosity, but I also knew that there were linguistic and religious affiliations between Russia and Greece. The connection between these worlds was made! I became more than enamored with and fascinated by Russian culture: I changed my major from pre-med to Russian after completing the first part of this course, the experience so moving for me that I would describe it as similar to being "born again," not that I knew what this meant, mind you. I recounted to my students that although I had been preparing for a pre-med major since grade school, after taking that Russian culture class with Dr. Daniel, I dropped everything else like a hot potato to pursue my study of Russian. In a way, I haven't stopped yet. I wanted my students to know that things can change midstream and evolve towards what is meant to be right for you, no matter what one may have planned for his life. Little did I know that some twenty-five years later, I really would be born again in the religious sense! After I dispensed with my background, I eagerly turned to the posters on my classroom walls and took my students on a slow journey as I narrated a bit about each. To date, there is hardly any space on my walls, and even on the ceiling, I have the American flag, the Russian flag, and the Soviet flag! Thus, even my new students already feel themselves to be a part of the fold on day one. It pleases me for them to sense being a part of something vaster than themselves, even if it involves dealing with Russian culture or geography at school. To be a portion of something greater than one's individual life is a matter of vital importance! Then I make sure I congratulate my students for even selecting Russian, as our high school is only one of four high schools in South Carolina that offers this language. It is important to feel the power of free choice. Next, I tell these first-year students that their very first assignment is to pick a Russian name for themselves. Choosing from a list I provide, they are to select one and then copy it in large block letters onto a folded piece of paper placed on their desks, which is the first thing I'll see on day two. Oh, the look of eager anticipation on their faces as they try to read my expression on discovering which name they have decided to take. Often, I don't even know them by their American first names. Selecting their new identity excites them: it signifies both a fresh start in this new class and a connection with an ancient culture they are now a part of indirectly through this means. Many years later, I, too, would come to have a new identity and label for myself that would transcend mere familial and national ancestry. Upon becoming Christian, the earliest Russian leaders changed their given names to those from the Bible. This was in keeping with figures in the Bible who did the like when they'd undergone a significant change in their religious life such that they no longer felt they had the same identity. From Russian history, we have Vladimir I, who changed his name to Basil, and from the Bible, we have Jacob to Israel, Cephas to Peter, and Saul to Paul! So, when my students take on this new name, they become connected to prominent figures that have done the like in the past as well to our Russian class's "family." My next task is to quell the anxiety in everyone's mind: "Isn't Russian so hard to learn?" And I tell them, "Heavens, no! Look at what you already know." Then, I show the already familiar letters common to both English and Russian; these are the letters that look like Latin (e.g., A, K, M, O, and T), and then we add on to they know. As with anything new, it is prudent to start with manageable and familiar chunks of information and build from there. Much later on, the same would hold true for me as I built onto what minuscule exposure I'd had of the Gospel to catapult myself to higher vistas.

2.11 The Connection between Religion and Language

One of my favorite lectures is to relate the origins of the Russian alphabet, that is, how two Greek monks, Cyril and Methodius, made their way over to Russia to convert the heathen Slavs. They were not aggressively insistent of these people. Instead, they observed and lived among them and listened to the language already in use before introducing a newly adapted *written* version of the Greek alphabet so that the Slavs could read and study the Gospel these monks had been teaching. Many years from this, such a method of care, respect, and invested time would be just what it took to have my heart melted to be open to accepting Christ and His language of love. Meanwhile, I found I needed to give a backdrop to Christianity to go any further in my explanation of how the Russian alphabet came to be. Not dissimilar to my initial lecture in American lit. regarding what gave rise to the Reformation Movement, I start at the historical point of fracture that split the once unified Christian Church and took it from there and headed east instead of west. The fateful split of Christendom occurred in 1054 and ever since then, Christianity *has* exploded in scope and impact, the fork in the road, this bifurcation, gave rise to a resultant dichotomy, a discrepancy in worldview within the base of Christianity. I could certainly relate; my parents came from the opposite ends of the spectrum of Christian expression, and it took me *decades* to reconcile the two into one. Christ had gotten lost in the shuffle because these two ended up in a truce and disengaged from trinitarianism. It is no wonder that a full-throttle concentration of Christianity expressed by what these Russians chose, that is, Eastern Orthodoxy would command my attention. It is also not surprising that another favorite topic I covered pertains to how Russia came to select the *Orthodox* branch of Christianity as its national religion. This quest to find what religion was just right for the Russians would make sense to me; I could identify. At that time in my life, it's not that I was set on choosing from among various religions, but it brought me no small satisfaction to share with my students that Russia purposefully chose *Christianity* for its moral foundation, and, in particular, the Eastern Orthodox branch, for this burgeoning nation. Catholicism was rejected, and centuries later, Protestantism would be another new-fangled approach or declension that would have been dismissed as insufficient or even misguided, further bolstering the sense of reverence and righteousness in the still-standing Byzantine Orthodoxy. It would take what seemed like centuries within *me* to see the light and recognize that conformity to tradition and ritual, the very framework of which helped this ancient institution to survive, impeded my reckoning and dealing directly with and loving Christ for Himself. All that said, I did not have any personal agenda; at the time, I wasn't aware of what would become interlacing threads or impulses between my career and my yet-to-be choice of faith. I just knew that I respected the fact that Russians didn't merely accept the first religion that was expedient or politically advantageous to them. Prince Vladimir made his decision in 988 both for himself *and* for his subjects. King Basil, the Byzantine emperor, sparked his attention by inviting Vladimir to visit him in Constantinople for a détente. Basil's motive was for the Russians to quit marauding the Greek merchants as they made their way all the way down and through Russia to the Black Sea, which ended up in Constantinople. Prince Vladimir listened to the emperor's plea, but in so visiting, met and fell in love with this Greek Emperor's daughter. She refused his hand in marriage because Vladimir was still very much a pagan. To be exact, he was a follower of the Slavic god, Perun. Even for love, Vladimir would not convert to Christianity without researching to discern that which would be the best match for himself as well as for his country. He sent out emissaries far and wide to investigate the various major world religions of the time and report back to him which one seemed the best and most suitable. I have only touched upon this here, but I believe I was promoting the need for them to do the like for themselves in sharing this with my student*s*. I would later do so myself.

What does this have to do with the broader purpose of this testimonial memoir? I see everything fitting together in my perspective of hindsight. The two monks from Thessaloniki came to Russia to spread the Gospel, but they didn't just introduce the Bible and leave; they spend time with the Slavs, taught them, and provided a Gospel that they could read so that their faith could grow loyal and more mature. I would have a similar experience. Twenty years later, I shifted gears and came to Christ. In the early years, I was like a toddler in the faith, feeding, growing, and having some misunderstandings, not to mention falling prey to the schemes of one who would want me knocked off-center. As would these young Slavic believers, I needed much encouragement. Just as Paul sent Timothy from Ephesus to Corinth to deliver his letters of instruction and encouragement to those immature believers set awry by continued hedonism and misguided leaders, I came to befriend a man — a pastor — who would become a teacher and mentoring guide to me. He at first came weekly, then nearly monthly, for almost two years. He would visit for up to an hour and a half each time to help me in my understanding of Christ; all the while, we developed an honest friendship. As I step forward and glance back, I keep making connections between people and circumstances in my life and completing the circle that led me to a faith yet unimagined.

2.12 Russian Orthodoxy

As I indicated, I also gave a quick primer to my students on Christianity's history, which led to the critical split of 1054. This first year in Russian 1 is my launching point for explaining the reasons for the Church's rupture even though I know that there existed other points of contention before this date. I explain that the one unchanging and original church became known as the Eastern Orthodox branch. The Church in Rome would become the Catholic Church, and it ensured the inculcation of plebeians through the practical guidance of a human intermediary in the form of the Pope. To me, it seemed as though for them, Christ wasn't enough. No Russian tsar would share with power such a one who would, in effect, equivocate himself with the Godhead. This meant subsequently for Russia in the late tenth century that after they decided upon adopting the Orthodox version of Christianity, they would be forever tied to Byzantine culture and, to a great degree, to the Greek spiritual history as well. I would explain the following differences between the eastern and western branches' outlook on Christianity that also affected their worldview. First, in contrast to the singular voice of the Pope making decisions for the entirety of the Catholic Church, there exists an Ecumenical Council of twelve equals in the Orthodox Church such that there would never be any one voice dominant over another. Secondly, the perception of the nature of Christ also differs: the Catholics focus on His humanity and exquisite suffering, whereas for the Orthodox Church, it is the mystery, ineffability, and indivisibility of the Trinity; its constituent members form a synergetic and synthesized whole.

Christ is uniquely and fully man *and* God. No one aspect of the Trinity is any more prominent than another. Speaking of the Trinity, I didn't spend much time contemplating (or explaining) the triune nature of God, the Holy Spirit, Christ the Son all rolled into one because I wasn't a Christian; it was not my focus. This fascinating topic was academic for me, yet somehow, I knew there was more to this topic, and it was pushed back into the recesses of my mind for some undetermined "later." It would be another two decades before

I experienced the beckoning of the Holy Spirit to come to faith for myself. In the Orthodox faith, which the Russians adopted, the whole of God should be experienced within the Church body itself. I found this allegiance to unity and the perspective that the whole or group is greater than the sum of the constituent parts compelling. Next, I explained the notion of what it means to be a "holy fool," an individual living so intently for Christ that nothing he does makes sense to the world. Russian history is full of such characters! The holy fools in Russia scoffed at any attempt to modernize the church. I imparted this cultural phenomenon with my Russian class for two reasons. These explanations made possible an indirect means of speaking to them about God. First off, peer pressure and values promulgated by the students' contemporary world, including consumerism, self-indulgence, and extreme individualism, do not deliver what the soul craves, and a body *needs* to live a life of spiritual abundance, meaning, and satisfaction. Secondly, if my students follow a higher calling, they should expect to be called "foolish" because *what we are called to do may often not make sense to the world*. I told them not to take offense but to work hard at achieving their dreams. Such a vision must accord and conform to that at which they are naturally adept. Later, I, too, would become such a holy fool for God by my family's secular standards, and you hold the fruit of my labor. I also love that Russian culture sees value and merit in suffering — not for suffering's sake, but to imitate Christ — even if it meant seeming the simpleton if need be. Later on, and in my early steps of faith, I came to learn that suffering would be God's way of refining, purifying, and growing me, during which time one can't know for sure its future worth. You may ask, how can I verbalize these topics in a secular high school? I never proselytized or evangelized; that would have implied intentionality on my part. Instead, I taught intuitively, naturally, and with a passion that I now know was a God-given means that He would use to draw us *all* to Him through the concepts I taught.

2.13 Travels to Russia with Students

Now I will go on to the topic of taking students to Russia. It's one thing to teach Russian class and gets close to my students, and quite another matter to take students abroad. You get to know each other on a different level than possible within the school's formal and vertical hierarchy. Though it is an incredible responsibility and an honor and privilege for parents to entrust me with their sons and daughters, I feel free to be myself with them even while I am in charge. It boils down to trust, respect, and common courtesy. Two weeks translates to fourteen sixteen-hour days. Teaching is at once exhilarating and exhausting, stimulating and overwhelming, educational and beyond academic.

After the collapse of the Soviet Union in 1991, I decided to take a chance and begin this venture of traveling with students, even if I initially recruited just a handful. I could never have imagined that this first trip would be the first of sixteen tours abroad I'd lead, spanning over twenty-five years and traveling to twelve countries with close to a total of two hundred students. I absolutely love showing students life first-hand elsewhere; observing them see for their first time how another part of the world lives is probably one of the most gratifying things I have ever done in my life. They learn not only how the country they've studied looks, feels, tastes, and smells, but they learn a lot about themselves, about what it means to be an American, and about how and where history and geography intersect. Looking at life from another angle makes them reevaluate their own stance or position, often held as gospel. I impress upon my students to be the very best ambassadors they can. Who would know that such trips abroad would also have such a spiritual dimension? Who could have imagined that encouraging such a state of readiness could lead to my own personal and childlike curiosity, eagerness, and enthusiasm to come to Him? I didn't understand then what I would come to know later, which is that "whoever does not receive the kingdom of God *like a child* will not enter it at all" (Mark 10:15, emphasis mine). I fostered such a mindset in my students because it existed within me, and that, in turn, later served me well when I acceded to His invitation to come to Him by being open-minded. I will now tell you about some of my travels to Russia with students insofar as it relates to Christianity. Discussing religion was never my express intent, yet somehow such experiences were present on nearly every trip.

My first trip with students to Russia was 1992, and on this trip, we also had the opportunity to go and see Ukraine, the very year it gained its independence from Soviet Russia. Russians were elated to be able to return to their Christian roots and worship openly, and everywhere I saw people proudly wearing crosses on their necklaces. They did not take this freedom for granted, and they flocked to their churches, reopened up ones long closed, renovated others, and erected many a new Orthodox cathedral. This wasn't some fad, just a picking-up where they'd left off. I was also thrilled with the opportunity to visit Hagia Sophia in Kiev, the cathedral that was modeled after the original Hagia Sophia in Constantinople, now Istanbul. I would show my students the actual statue of Vladimir I, the Russian leader who officially Christianized his nation in 988. Some might say that to proclaim his country Christian by necessitating that his populace jump in the river in a mass baptism does not mean they were converted to Christianity. Their pagan mentality did not cease or desist overnight. I would ask the same thing of those people who came to be born again by responding to missionaries' invitation offering material aid or medical help. My analogy was imperfect: Vladimir *ordered* his citizenry to go into the Dnieper River; this was not of their own accord, although it did initiate a momentous change of a radical nature for Russia. On the other hand, when a missionary successfully brings about a conversion in a native elsewhere, there is no such forcing. Ultimately, even if there are three hundred testimonies of faith but only three that prove authentic and lasting, well, *that's three more than existed before*, three more than would have come about had a doubter or skeptic been in such a place! Praise God! To become a Christian *is* as simple as saying "Yes," to Him in faith. Of course, growth and maturation take time; it's a process that cannot be completed overnight by an ordeal or through being dunked, but *it has to start somewhere*. That said, baptism is a marker of salvation launched, if but only to symbolize what the individual has already chosen freely for him or herself. That I was baptized as an infant in the Greek Orthodox Church satisfied me on some technical level, but I still secretly doubted its veracity because, at the time, I was far from faith. My own baptism had been no different than those in ancient Russia who had been ordered into a river; I had yet to come to Him on my own.

Another tour I led in 1996 was fantastic in that my group was permitted to go and see things that I had not gone to on the previous tour. For example, I took my group on a picnic — complete with a backpack containing a couple of loaves of Russian black bread, cheese, salami, and a liter of carbonated apple juice — on the thousand-acre grounds of Kolomenskoe, founded in the thirteenth century alongside which ran the Moscow River. The most famous cathedral here is the Church of the Ascension, a gem to Russia; it is unique in architecture, height, and coloring, being all white. And all along the banks sit many art students painting the river, which casts in its reflection the various multi-colored and gold-domed churches across the river. There were many people quietly strolling on these grounds, and some swam, too. There is also a park within these grounds where you can visit the huts where Peter the Great went camping as a youngster. The main focal point here is the impressive, massive, yet relatively unadorned cathedral within it. As my small group made its way towards it, but before it came actually into our sight, we could hear the refrain of a small choir emanating from within it. Our curiosity was piqued. Deep bass voices counterpointed by others in a harmonious and ethereal union transported us before we'd even arrived. We quickened our pace as if we were being drawn there. The students had never heard Orthodox liturgical singing, and the *a cappella* voices got louder, fuller, and clearer. Some were bass, rich and penetrating, and others ethereal, soaring, and heavenly. Suddenly, one voice floated above and beyond the rest; it must have been a dove! Only a seraph's voice could have soared as such and reached Heaven! This concert was for the benefit of none other than God Himself. We felt lucky and blessed and a little stricken, as if we had intruded upon some sacred spot and moment. I told them, no, this was a *gift* to us! My students and I stared at each other in wonderment, knowing we had witnessed a miracle. I would be overjoyed for my students to have experienced just a little of that which

I found to be like heaven on earth! We all sat on a nearby bench and ate our bread and cheese as if we were taking communion. This experience best captured for them the reverential and spiritual consciousness that is within the Russian soul. This was not the last time I would hear such singing with students; in fact, I never led a trip that didn't leave at least a couple of students deeply moved by coming upon a small Russian choir singing the sacred hymns in the ethereal regions of the cathedral.

Another rapturous moment of a religious nature occurred with a student who was particularly strong in her Christian faith. I never got personal in my discussions of religion at school by going so far as to engage and outright ask them what their affiliations were (or permit them to inquire of me). On another trip, a student wanted to share her testimony with me; therefore, thousands of miles safely away from the classroom, I agreed to listen. The student with whom I had my first genuine talk about Christianity was a beautiful and pure-minded young lady named Flora. Raised Southern Baptist but having fallen in love with Russian culture, she was distraught that Russians might be going to Hell because they did not "know" Christ. Her sincere concern and earnest curiosity about what exactly Russians *did* believe as Christians drew me to her. In the culture presentation she'd given just two months before, she chose as her topic to explore the similarities and differences between these two branches of Christianity, that is, Southern Baptist and Russian Orthodox. Particularly troubling to her and bewildering to me was her angst over the fact that they hadn't personally asked Jesus Christ into their hearts. I remarked, "Look at these people. They don't even have pews. These women bow low and often touch their foreheads to the ground. They light candles for loved ones and pray without ceasing. What more could you ask for?" Christianity has helped keep the people of this country united for over a millennium. I believe we were both moved by each other's intentness, concern for, and admiration of Russians. Still yet, I felt we had come to an impasse because all the things that *I* listed did not make a person a Christian, even if she was demonstrably spirited in her profession of faith. All the while, Flora she looked at me with the affect of a saint; she was full of hope, and I sensed it was for me as much as for those Russians. It would be twenty years hence before I understood the personal nature of this relationship she'd mentioned. At the time, the Russians' devotion, humility, and reverence just bowled me away. How the Orthodox Christian worshiped was an admirable characteristic I subconsciously attached myself to by association or proxy. Unbeknownst to her, Flora became a source of inspiration for me. It was the first time I had had an in-depth conversation with a student about faith and Christianity, but I was only sharing what *Russians* at large believed. I hadn't yet articulated or deeply thought about such for myself.

The next time I went to Russia, I took a group to an active cathedral near a famous cemetery that contained the graves of Dostoevsky, Tchaikovsky, Borodin, and numerous other artists, writers, and the like. I love old cemeteries anyway, and this was a treasure chest of who's who. That warm Sunday in early June, the forest of trees was so tall and dense they seemed to lord over the graves. Their canopy made the sky scarcely visible. The Russians there happened to be celebrating some commemorative religious day, and it overlapped or concurred with a pagan festival which they'd never abandoned. This pagan holiday was juxtaposed with a Christian one, a two-for-one that made sense to the Russian. I had my students hemmed around me as we made our way inside. They were going to get to be a part of an active Russian Orthodox service, and it was incredibly crowded inside; the air was warm, still, and stifling. The priests wore majestic green vestments, and supple young branches with tender leaves adorned the church's sidewalls. There were so many people in the church that it would take some time before we could enter. The whole of this Russian crowd, an amoeboid mass, slowly swayed toward the priest, and my students and I were smack dab in the middle of this crowd, packed altogether as tight as sardines. Incense wafted thickly and permeated our pores as well as the air above. Somewhere in the far-off front, the lone cantor sang in Byzantine tones, otherworldly, minor, and ethereal. Suddenly I felt a palpable pressure against me: it was an older woman who had fainted and could not even make it to the ground for it being so crowded inside. Russians are not alarmists. Swiftly, I heard in Russian, "Men! Men!" And men nearby firmly but gently put their arms under hers, supporting her from beside and behind, and they pulled her out backward, her heels dragging on the floor and her chin tucked to her chest as they carefully managed to keep her somewhat upright. She was completely out. My students stared at me, somehow intuiting not to say a word. After we made our way all around the interior, just moving along forward with everyone else, we made our way back outside and were grateful for fresh air. Who should we see out there but that same woman, now awake and alert, having been resuscitated by taking a drink of cool water? In fact, as we were leaving, she was making her way back inside the church! Such an unforgettable experience this was for my students. I doubted that they had ever seen this type of mass reverence, chivalry, devotion, and spirited perseverance.

Many years later, I told my students another of the many stories from my travels to Soviet Russia. One in particular that struck them was about something that had happened on my first trip to the Soviet Union in 1984. A fellow student and one who happened to be Christian decided to secretly bring into the country several Bibles just to give away. He told no one. It was common knowledge to us Russian majors that despite the Soviet government being atheistic, Russian themselves had not abandoned their faith, even if they had to worship privately in homes or some clandestine meeting place. It's still ironic to me that in places hostile to Christianity, believers there are all the more fervent, courageous, and indomitable in their worship of Christ. This young man understood that what he was doing was illegal — Bibles were *not* for sale there — yet he was compelled to help his fellow brothers and sisters in Christ. Soon after we got our belongings stored on the train, the Soviet military or official guards searched the berths of us Americans, and, lo and behold, when this young Christian boy's suitcase was opened, there they were, all of those Bibles of his. There must have been ten or so. With the discovery made by these soldiers, the rest of us were petrified with fear, and we held our breath, not knowing if one or all of us would get in trouble. On the other hand, the young man who'd snuck in the contraband Bibles stood calmly and faced the guards unabashed and unashamed; in the end, they swiftly confiscated all but one that they generously left with and for him. Later that week, he gave this remaining one away, too, to some random, grateful soul. At the time, I thought this guy was crazy or just a Jesus fanatic. I had no idea of the power of the Gospel, let alone the imperative to *share* it.

At the collapse of the Soviet Union in 1991, there would be such a resurgence of Christianity in Russia that the world would recognize it. I was elated for them! Even today, Putin heralds Orthodox Christianity and chauvinistically touts Russia's spiritual supremacy over the west. By 2013, Christianity had returned to the social forefront in such a prominent way that Bibles couldn't be published quickly enough. Several of my Russian students with me on that particular trip were visiting an immense cathedral and had wanted to purchase a Bible in Russian, but the priest working at the register was reluctant to sell any to them. He said these Bibles were intended for Russian believers who desired and *needed* to read the Gospel; therefore, he was averse to sell what few remaining he had to wealthy western students he assumed had more money than faith. As I have said before, so many simple things in Russia don't turn out right, but when they do, one becomes aware that God Himself intervenes. These students bought the Bibles anyway and, minutes later, *gave* them all away to Russians. I didn't see it coming yet wasn't surprised when I did. I was incredibly proud of them and told them so.

When I reflect on the years that I planned on and prepared for becoming a doctor, then changing my focus to Russian, I finally reorganized the pieces as they were intended by becoming a teacher. I see the common denominator between teaching and healing: both actions *help* people. I would still serve. Russian satisfied my own need for a type of heritage fulfillment. But unbeknownst to me at the time, my interest in my Greek identity would later return to me fully when I found myself in the position of being a parent to my father. Over the next twenty-five years, I would bring my zest for Russian to life beyond the classroom and lead eight trips there on two-week tours with my students: 1992, 1994, 1996, 1998, 2006, 2009, 2013, and, God willing, a final trip in 2018. As it turned out, God was *not* willing for this last trip to take place; our trip was canceled because of an increased level of security threat. The world seems to be changing at a frenetic pace, and for all the splendor in Nature and precious moments we collect in our lives, much seems to be *not* for the best; that, too, however, is not surprising to a Christian whose joy is based elsewhere. In the meantime, each Russian class I taught and every trip I took became part of an extraordinary odyssey that my students and I shared collectively and individually.

Little did I know just how much I would love teaching English and, through it, adore American literature. Some of these American thinkers and writers, too, contributed to my coming to Him.

CHAPTER 3:
The Call To Teach

"Educating the mind without educating the heart is no education at all."

— Aristotle

"In the faces of men and women I see God, and in my own face in the glass, I find letters from God dropped in the street, and everyone is signed by God's name...."

— Walt Whitman

3.1 From Student to Teacher:
Culture Shock

As fortune would have it, there was a high school in Mullivanville that offered Russian, had had it for five years already, and so I would be placed there during my intern year at Admiral High School. And this wasn't any rural school either; it boasted a matriculation rate of the upper ninetieth percentile. One of its calling cards was that more A.P. courses and foreign languages were offered at this school than at any other school in the county. Whoopee!! When I got placed there, I was paired with the Russian teacher as one of my mentors, and she gave me the *least* successful students from both her Russian 1 and Russian 2 courses. It was trial by fire! We had six classes a day back then, and, not having a classroom of my own, I would have to travel my first three years, moving like a gypsy from wing to wing. In the first two centuries, Christians also had no proper building and worshiped in each other's homes before the first stone was laid to build a church. I loved being with my new students so much, it didn't even seem like I was teaching them. I didn't consider it a burden to move all over the school and teach in rooms with obstacles like sewing tables for desks or having a paper-thin wall to separate us from the typing room, which sounded like machine guns were being used when the class was at it. My mentoring teacher in English was transitioning to administration, so I was left to fend for myself. This situation was also for the best; I became learned and self-assured.

During those early days of teaching American literature that I knew precious little about, I felt insecure enough. I was devouring and double-reading the Norton Anthology of American Literature and what I had to for class. This was during the days before computer technology and the widespread use of the Internet; therefore, all my research was accomplished via scouring books. I poured over these annals and synthesized vast amounts of information in handouts that took hours upon hours to make. I came to fall in love with American literature, which included a zeal for learning about its earliest philosophical and religious ideas. In case you're wondering how American lit. relates to my coming to faith, I will share in this chapter how American literature became like an inanimate spiritual mentor to me. Through the writers I came in contact with, I would glean and collect their ideas to formulate a basis of my own belief. Yes, of course, I was teaching, but I was also holding on to some ideas more than others and subconsciously shaping a religion for myself. More than anything, I want to convey that though I was zealous in my search and passionate about teaching, the composite I came up with was intellectual; I had not experienced the holistic conversion of the total self faith generates. Not yet. And remember that I didn't have that momma or some Sunday School teacher to jump-start my faith as a child. As you read this chapter, it may seem like a condensed version of my lectures, but it is not. I'll tell you why: *we teach what we need to learn*. And so, I'll not focus on giving literary analyses, but rather on making known to you certain philosophical and religious concepts that helped keep me on the alert to possess a readiness for faith, and I didn't even know it! The choice of what I'm sharing with you is specific and intimate. Two years after I started teaching, I was thrust into the AP program to replace the former 11th grade AP teacher who was forced to resign. One day he was there; the next day, he was gone. Early lessons I learned include never to argue with a teenager and to realize that more than any segment of the population, teens are on high alert to note anything or anyone that isn't fair or one who smacks of double-mindedness. I would never be a syrupy-sweet teacher, but I always tried to be fair and respectful, use humor, and speak passionately about matters that mattered. They could count on my being authentic, encouraging, and as real as rain with them. When I was drawn to religious ideals within the literature from the early Puritan period, my students were right there with me and ready to investigate the values within that spoke to a greater purpose and godly intent. Later, I viewed my whole *modus operandi*, the choice to teach and where I found a job, not as some accident or chance, but a convolution of circumstances orchestrated by Him. I could teach to my heart's content stories and ideas that moved me to make students want the same.

3.2 American Literature and Calvinism Launches a Voyage into Studying Christianity

Little did I know that right off the bat, teaching American literature would necessitate my learning political history and Protestant theology to gain a complete context of the early literature. Truly American literary fiction didn't take off until the early nineteenth century. I could never have imagined my attention being held in rapt wonderment for hours reading about Calvinism and early Puritan theology! I even had my students memorize the famous acronym, T.U.L.I.P plus one. Getting kids stirred to understand the logic, purpose, and reason behind breaking away from the Church of England, now some three hundred years out, was a challenge, but I saw that the principles and moral challenges were no less complex, applicable, and timely than ever before. The obstacles may have looked different, but in spirit, they were precisely what these kids wrangle and grapple with today. That said, a couple of Calvinist terms, in particular, were nonsensical and seemed flat-out wrong to the optimistic and confidant teenage brain. These included the concepts of "total depravity" and "unconditional predestination." My students considered themselves fine and dandy and able to do whatever they wanted to in life! I will return to the pillars of this acronym in a moment.

After dispensing with the syllabus and class expectations, etc., I hit the ground running. I launched into my first lecture in the Puritan Pd. by asking my students the following question: "Assuming that Heaven and Hell *do* exist, do you believe *you* have control or any say over determining where you will end up after you die? Do you know your cosmic destiny?" After getting over the momentary shock of being asked such a serious question and when they could tell I was eager to know their thoughts, hands shot up left and right, usually to indicate the affirmative. I knew those who thought they could choose Heaven over Hell were my Baptists and Methodists. Catholics and some Presbyterians believed in predestiny and the <u>un</u>knowability of one's salvation. You may ask how I was able to do this in a public school. Quite easily: I was not proselytizing, and this type of thought process was what our distant descendants were contemplating. American literature's earliest foundation is not fiction; it is comprised of journals, observations, and religious speculations. (The pendulum later swung in the opposite direction during the Revolutionary period, and instead of religious thought, we find political philosophy explored.) After I heard all their responses, I knew they were prepared for my background lecture on Colonial literature; this necessitated I provide a condensed and simplified version of Christian history. It took less than fifteen minutes. Touching upon the Reformation set the table for explaining our Puritans' and Pilgrims' desire for and pursuit of religious freedom here. It is the same lecture I start with for my Russian 1 course, whereby I give the critical background to show how in choosing the *Eastern* branch, Russians would be forever culturally, politically, and religiously distinct from the rest of Europe. The Western branch ended up participating in the Renaissance and experiencing the wide-range effects of the Enlightenment. In short, for American literature, I took one path; for my Russian 1 class, I took another. Starting at the top of the board, I write "J.C., 0 – 33" with a straight line halfway down the board to the year 1054. Yes, there were many theological squabbles among prominent theologians in the Church Council in between, but this was the year that proved to be the "line-in-the-sand" as far as how the church was to stand on several pressing issues. It was the year the Christian Church was cleft in twain. I listed characteristics that differentiated these two dividing branches to my students, and little did they know that *I was learning as much as they*. For my American lit. class, I focused on the western branch, that is, Catholicism and quickly made my way to Protestantism. First came the introduction of a Pope as an intermediary between humankind and Christ. There also exists a pronounced focus on the suffering of Christ; doing such highlights Christ's humanity and facilitates a sense of accessibility to the Son of man *and* a quasi indebtedness to Him as our Savior. Adhering to dogma and abiding by what those at the top of the hierarchy deemed imperative to one's indoctrination became hallmarks of the Catholic Church. Compliance was compulsory. I made an analogy to what my students were experiencing to mandatory public education. Economic reasons aside, the mindset advanced is that one can't or won't learn if left to one's own devices. In other words, without the chastening effects of Christian virtues taught by the Church, the populace at large would have remained barbaric, unrestrained in its violence, and, generally speaking, an inconsiderate and uncontrollable people. Just as one could become a successful and contributing citizen through becoming educated, one could become a compliant Christian; both were accomplished through a system of training. Like public education, moral instruction in the Catholic Church was disseminated from the top down. Yet what had vertical alignment to do with the integrity of one's faith? Everything yet nothing, and therein laid the problem for the Protestant. The basic premise for both institutions is that left to their own inclinations, most people would not make an effort to become Christian or educated. Both became expected for residing in a civilized and advancing nation. To drive the point home, When I point-blank asked my students if they would attend school if they didn't *have* to by law, how many would be there? Unsurprisingly, hardly any raised their hands. (Of course, the AP students always eagerly asserted that *they* would attend.) Without knowing it, I would lead them to the Reformation Period by asking them if they could buy an "A" from class and walk out today, would they do so? Again, hands popped up, but when they heard my made-up going price of ten grand, the arms came down slowly, ashamedly even. I had them where I needed them to be to let them *feel* what it's like being on the short end of the stick when bribery, corruption, and privilege were beyond their reach to save them from the agony of school. To complete the transition to Protestantism, I stressed that though I had exaggerated, the situation was parallel and gave rise to the Reformation Movement. Regardless of how a person conducted himself morally, people of wealth and class could buy their so-called ticket to Heaven and secure their salvation, as if faith in particular and a fraction of goodness had nothing to do with it! One had no such guarantee if one were of average means, let alone destitute.

Furthermore, the excesses and corruption of the Church led to the dark epoch of the Bloody or Holy Roman Crusades, whereby heinous crimes and ethnic cleansing were committed against Jews, Muslims, and those deemed heretical. Being outraged at the abuses of the Church is what gave rise to the Protestant Reformation.

I would later experience a revolution within my own heart that was in a state of dismay, disarray, and disjointedness. Martin Luther and the theologian, John Calvin, wanted to streamline church affairs and dogma whereby one would have a *direct* relationship with God. I dubbed this connection between man and God as a person's making a "direct deposit" with God and Christ, whereby no middleman was necessary. No more mechanically observing the seven sacraments, no more crossing oneself, no more ostentation, and distracting regalia in church. It was time to get back to the basics! Yet, our earliest English settlers *did* fervently believe in predestiny because it was pleasing to them to know that *no one had any greater advantage over another regarding one's ability to "attain" salvation.* The king and a pauper had the same chances of making it to Heaven! On the other hand, they also had no abiding assurance of salvation either; that thought would come later. As an aside, I must say that I have no idea why so many English teachers dislike teaching the Puritan period. I find it rich, fascinating, and incredibly pertinent, and not at all dry or erudite. I also noted that most students, many themselves Christians, are not the least bit knowledgeable on Christian history, let alone Scripture. Therefore, I needed to teach much so that they could reap the full reward of their literary heritage; this necessitated explaining religious values imbued within the readings. What could be better?!

The people who came to this country that remained and resided here would be our Puritans and Pilgrims. Can you imagine the tremendous grit, courage, and perseverance that one would have to have possessed to go about the business of surviving, as there was no infrastructure here whatsoever? They had to start from scratch, and none were used to the kind of arduous labor necessary to survive. It would take incredible faith to have believed that they were destined and empowered to come to such a wild place, albeit one where they could worship freely, to have given them the oomph they needed to do all they had to. The Protestant man's direct access to God fortified a robust interaction with other believers. This illustrated another ideal that would shape the American religious identity: Martin Luther's *priesthood of all believers*. He maintained that every Christian has equal potential to minister on behalf of God. Such a concept completely countered the spiritual rank and file system within Catholicism. In other words, one does not have to be a clergyman, a bishop, or any higher position to have a meaningful impact on other Christians' lives. I found this notion to be thrillingly liberating! And I told the kids that each of them had that same power within them, too! It might seem odd to encourage students with a religious slant, but I saw this as pertinent, applicable, and justifiable. That democracy was selected as our form of government is in great part owed to our Protestant roots, which promote the individual's equal access to God. Though America did everything it could to avoid becoming a theocracy, these early Protestants' high standards imbued their every thought, act, and deed, making the religious and secular aspects of their lives overlap to the point of being united. This idea behind such belongs to John Calvin.

Now I return to what I taught the students (and myself): John Calvin's theology, T.U.L.I.P plus one. T stands for **t**otal depravity, of course. The idea of total depravity was irksome to students. When I would quiz them on these terms by giving them the definition and having them identify the term, many of them would say total depri̱vation, as if that the Puritans and Pilgrims had been deprived of food. To help them understand this necessitated going back to asserting that since Adam and Eve messed up, the effects of their sin were still present in us. I used the analogy that just like a large positive number multiplied by a negative one, even one as small as -0.00001 is always negative, so, too, are we who are thousands of generations past the Original Pair. Because we are the distant progeny of Adam and Eve, being morally stained would be our inherited destiny. This displeased them about as much as if I'd said I would keep the whole class after the bell because one kid was disobedient. It wasn't fair. The next tenet, **u**nconditional predestination, also made absolutely zero sense to them. What kind of God would preselect some folks for Hell? How could you know where you were headed? Could one change one's course through valiant efforts? In the end, such a stance would lead to the overwhelming question, "Why bother at all?" Typically, when students would hear about predestiny, the first question they logically come up with is if everybody is already predestined to Heaven or Hell, what is the motive to do good? If a person thinks he is doing wrong, has done a wrong, or has somehow displeased God such that he's going to wind up in hell anyway, why even try? To help them, I would ask if they had ever experienced something difficult in life, which later turned out to be for the best, yet at the time, it seemed either horrific or nonsensical. After all, God is not only omnipotent and omniscient, but He is omnipresent and omnibenevolent and can only have a perfect purpose for everything in life, regardless of whether *we* get to see how things pan out. He's already there; we're stuck in the present puzzlement. This predicament still didn't help my students understand what was accepted by the Puritans as divine parity; all they saw was that there would be no incentive to do good or act right if one might be headed to Hell anyway. On the other hand, for the Puritans, such a stance was refreshing and assuring that both kings and paupers had the same chance of attaining salvation. When it comes right down to it, in one's soul of souls, no one would know for sure if one were going to land in Heaven or Hell, so there is some fairness in that. Therefore, being a Protestant necessitated a greater mental rigor and moral fortitude to stay the course than it did for that of the Catholic who could rely on ritualistic vehicles to set right his course with God. For the Protestants, good behavior ought to be a natural by-product of one's faith, effort, and intent — not on exterior actions performed as prescribed by the Church. I commented that if the "U" tenet seems problematic, then the student could be assured that his particular denominational branch of Protestantism arose *after* this period. Though this concept may have pacified believers in *England*, once the Puritans got to America, I can't imagine that this would have made sense because they were all in the same boat, literally and figuratively, especially socio-economically. America's new heretics would be those individualistic Anne Hutchinsons who didn't feel the needed to worship corporately in church. I move onto the remaining Calvinist concepts.

The third tenet focuses on **l**imited atonement, which means that Christ died only for chosen those to be saved. Like its partner, unconditional predestination, this theory stated that getting to Heaven was for members only, only now it was Christ who picks and chooses. What felt equitable and fair to the Puritans proved unjust and repugnant to modern Americans. Limited atonement made provision for an equal opportunity to attain salvation (or damnation) in that *no one* had any control or say in the matter of determining where one spent eternity. There would be no bargaining with God based on one's financial or social status, and the Church certainly oughtn't to have clout in this matter. Before one lost all sense of hope for a merciful God to exist, the next tenet of Calvin's, **I**rresistible grace was, understandably, the favorite tenet of all. Grace boasted that there was nothing you could do to make God love you more and nothing you could do to compel God to refuse or withdraw His love. He was constant! What a welcome breath of fresh air! The fifth tenet, the **p**erseverance of the saints, acknowledged that being a Christian, a Protestant, would not be easy, and there *is* a relief in accepting this. To think and act at all times as if one was going to Heaven would have required great faith, dedication, fortitude, self-discipline, obedience, and pluck to keep on toeing the line for Him, not knowing for a fact if one's salvation was secured. To do otherwise would indicate both to yourself and your community that you were *not* Heaven-bound. Such a way of thinking had to have been distressing! What pressure and anxiety they must've felt believing that every deed, word, thought, and secret were not only known *to* God but that such would reveal to the believer himself an indication of God's pleasure or displeasure. This doesn't mean that they assumed they could influence Him with works, but it was God that was revealing His will to us through the scroll of life's events. If things weren't going well, they looked to *evil* causes rather than to what we today might see as a natural or logical reason for x, y, or z occurring. That said, the struggles we endure for His namesake pale in comparison to the suffering He did for us; therefore, the early Puritans were not complainers. Such a taking in, an internalizing of one's wrongful thoughts and acts gave rise to the infamous Puritan guilt trip. The Pilgrims undoubtedly held their tongue in check and kept whatever doubts, unseen misdeeds, or impure thoughts they had to themselves because to expose such might indicate to others as well as to themselves to that they were hell-bound. So, one would feel the pang of sin within, but there was no longer any formal means, let alone imperative, to expunge one's guilt then and there other than what one *chose* to confess to God. And who would naturally want to do that?!? If one doesn't strike while the iron is hot, one may dismiss (or forget) the wrongful act over time. The sense of guilt over what one was thinking or doing that which would *not* have been considered holy and righteous must have been constant. If one doesn't pray for forgiveness from God in a timely fashion, guilt can accrue and build up to the point of needing to come out. There *had* to have arisen either a sense of utter futility or a choice of reckless abandonment if one decided he was beyond all hope of relieving or keeping himself in check. Therefore, to persevere and keep on even though one might not understand what was happening in a trying moment is undoubtedly a hallmark of these stalwart and fallible people. As a humorous aside, I found that students rarely spelled this term correctly and would instead write "<u>preservation</u>" of the saints, as if these Puritans and Pilgrim were somehow embalmed. I could only laugh at both them and myself because I could remember back when I didn't know the Lord's Prayer, and I would utter phonetically what I thought I had heard: "h<u>o</u>llow be Thy name." There is one more stem added onto the Calvinist T.U.L.I P. to which they subscribed and which I would later pore over with gusto.

The last Calvinist tenet is an add-on: the dubbed "plus one" refers to God's Will is revealed solely in the Bible. You'd have to know that other texts had been used and/or were required in conjunction or instead of the Bible to appreciate this seeming stark simplicity or single-mindedness. In effect, they dispensed with all that the early church elders had contributed, that is, clarifying scholarship, much dogma, and many rules. To the Catholics, this would have been tantamount to heresy;, however, the case was just the opposite! The Puritans were enthusiastic and fixedly resolved in their adherence to and worshiping of the Bible alone. Consequently, ironically, and tragically, they became just as intolerant, rigid, and unloving as the very ones from whom they broke away. Only one such book is necessary for the Protestant then and now to understand God's will; no other authors need apply. The Bible by itself provides the inerrant guidebook for life and faith; resultantly, there are no discrepancies or conflicts of interest. Such a singular, laser-like focus on the Bible justifies and unifies the preceding five Calvinist pillars into a whole that made sense. When I became a Christian, I, too, put all my other religious texts aside, and, coming to understood that the Bible was reliable and accurate as a source of truth, *I read intently as God spoke to me in a way that I'd never experienced before*. Our Christian forefathers were so orthodox that they took the content of the Bible *literally* and interpreted events in life *symbolically*. Suppose one takes what is written in the Bible literally and interprets events in actual life as a matrix of God's signs of approval or disapproval regarding how one is living. In that case, one is under the constant scrutiny of self and others to figure out if one is passable or copacetic with God. For example, if things *appeared* dire or vile to others, this might indicate God's disapproval. How thought, deed, and circumstance were deciphered depended on an individual's frame of mind and temperament, as well as the capacity to deduce or hypothesize rationally. At the time, our powers of deduction or induction were not so sound. Such subjectivity can lead some to interpret a person is going Heaven, while someone else might declare wrongdoing was surely an indication of his being hell-bound.

The same mindset exists among some Christians today. For example, a man searching for the reason why even though he's got two jobs, he is barely eking by or why his mother, not even sixty, is stricken with cancer. This proves no different than the Puritan man who wonders why his crops are failing or his wife has had three miscarriages. He would *erroneously* deduce that God is mad at him or that he must have done something wrong to endure the suffering he does. He is likely to look with envy and malice towards his neighbor who has more possessions and seemingly fewer problems than he, and he wonders why God doesn't answer his prayers. We cannot say that God *causes* evil to happen; that would go against His perfect and benevolent nature. Trying to interpret God's mind is hubristic of us, and it leads to a downward spiral and slippery slope. When confronted with inexplicable pain or challenges, a person might grow bitter and dispirited. Do you know what can happen then? Such a person is likely to quit going to church because he feels weak, dejected, and hopeless. What is my point? Over time, the need for relying on our brethren to survive waned as we were becoming better able to do more for ourselves. It was natural to look to a more and independent relationship with God; the result over the centuries has been a waning of church attendance and a reduction in corporate worship. We become less likely to do good to neighbors we no longer see regularly. Our view of our fellow man becomes slanted such that one will judge his neighbor based on his prejudices and preferences and use the Bible to justify his cause or argument. When we reduce God to man, that's where God becomes problematic for people. Anthropomorphized depictions of God can sometimes make him as jolly as Santa Claus, whose reward for us is based on His naughty or nice list. At other times, when God is depicted as stern, we view Him as vengeful, furious, or even revolted by us. A theologian might describe God as the inscrutable, supreme judge. I'll just stick to God being love. Meanwhile, studying Calvinism was stirring something deep within me, and I found myself reading and closely studying these texts and sharing them with my students more and more. Yes, I kept to the appropriate designated period and the readings in our text. I felt forlorn because the more I read, the more I realized I was *so* ignorant about Christianity.

At the time, I didn't understand that becoming a Christian did not mean acquiring more knowledge! Faith involves a letting go to Let Him in, but I was not there yet. God's smiling upon me seemed a remote, if not unlikely, possibility. I was certainly not steeped in the old-time religion, and often I felt more like a foreigner in the pockets of Georgia and South Carolina than I ever did in Russia. I didn't know the code, the lingo, or the expectations. I'd heard it said, "not to wait to let the hearse take you to church," but that seemed ridiculous and hokey. Yet there was a special joy in many a Christian face that provided a subtle proof that they are moved and guided by the Spirit whom I didn't yet know. I was envious of reverent, faithful people, who, more often than not, had come to the Lord during their youth. I didn't feel like I had a chance, let alone a prayer, but I would continue to long for what I thought they had. Now flashback to the seventeenth century, to the commencement of the Puritan Period, the likes of which ended with the Salem Witch Trials where nineteen people who didn't abide by their community's standards condemned to death. I would announce to my students, thank goodness for the Scientific Revolution and Age of Enlightenment for shining facts and truths about our world! I have yet to share a few authors from the Puritan period whose ideas will connect to concepts I would grapple with when I became a Christian.

In my quest to select the most meaningful moments, I would be remiss if I neglected specific authors whose ideas shaped my religious outlook and upcoming faith. Though I was unaware, an evangelical approach to Christianity was brewing within me, and writer after Puritan writer piqued my interest and attraction to their angle. One of the first that comes to mind is Edward Taylor. He was a metaphysical poet from the Puritan Pd. whose poetry abounds in remarkable analogies connecting the spiritual realm to the physical. One of the poems that both my students and I found most intriguing and captivating was "Upon a Spider Catching a Fly." I began this lecture by writing the so-called seven deadly sins up on the board and tallying under each sin by taking a silent vote of a show of hands as to which ones were the most problematic: those that Satan used to target and trip us up. No, this list is not biblical, but all the kids are familiar with it, making it easier to teach this particular poem. More importantly, I hoped to make them aware that they are being barraged continually with advertising so that they buy into a system that wants them to become consumers of goods, not believers in God. Resultantly, gluttony, envy, and pride run amok; the evil of pride reigns unchecked in individual lives and thrives in the world. I always got a charge out when it came to any acknowledgment of "lust"; the boys would sheepishly grin and giggle, and the girls would roll their eyes. Sloth was also a big winner, too! Where we are weak, vulnerable, and susceptible to succumbing to sin is when we are "flies" to the "spider," Satan, who, with a home-court advantage here on planet earth as "prince of the power of air" (Eph. 2:2), spins his net to catch us. It was like a giant cartoon in our collective imagination! The goal is to be more like the "wasp" that stays spiritually fit and is alert to the "stratagems" of the devil. Most vitally — as it still is not enough for us to be smart enough, alert enough, or good enough — is that grace is "communicated" to Adam's race by God. It's such a game-changer to realize an invisible war is going on within our souls! Once you become aware of this, then you'll realize the truth of how Taylor can end his poem by indicating we must rely on and pray to Christ to *"communicate [His] Grace to break the cord* [of Satan's "net"]. Only then do we have a fighting chance; neither you nor I can do this for ourselves! We won't become completely safe until we are in Heaven, or, as Taylor called it, "Glory's cage." Our job here is to become a fit "wasp," a spiritual warrior ready to avoid temptation. We ought not to live obliviously as a "fly" and succumb to seductive forces of iniquity. I discussed these ideas years before the day of my salvation, and this is how I spoke to my students. At the time, the missing link for me faith in Him; my approach to Him was still academic, even if passionately so. A revival was yet to come.

    The Great Awakening and its most famous spokesman, Jonathan

Edwards, with his "Sinners in the Hands of an Angry God" was so over-the-top frothy to the kids, he could now have been written off as a zealous fanatic, but I took a shining to him. The background I gave on America's waning religiosity as the impetus for his intentness didn't faze my students. What that we might have such an awakening today; the times bespeak a need a hundred-fold what it did then. I empathized with Edwards' sense of urgency in desiring to jolt his society out of spiritual complacency and self-satisfaction. I, too, sought to motivate kids to do better in school and life and to rise above their circumstances, be it apathy in school or preoccupation with social media. I tried to show life's happenings from God's perspective. Once I asked the students to imagine their pet had disobeyed and left the yard, only to get hit in the road. Upon seeing one's beloved pet, one would be stuck between wanting to fix it and love on it and concurrently sickened by its blood, excrement, etc., resulting from its disobedience which got it killed in the first place. They sure got *that*! God is in a quandary of feeling overwhelming love and pity for us *and* for sickened as He can't look on sin! It's impossible for Him to do so in His pure and holy state. It's not that He disdains us; quite to the contrary! He shows restraint and infinite patience, that is, forbearance, to keep from giving us our just dues or punishment for running out in the road. Proverbs 26:11 tells us that "as a dog returns to its vomit, so fools repeat their folly" (NIV). I then ask my students which motivational strategy works better for them: the carrot method or the stick method, that is, a positive or negative reinforcement. Should the incentive be internal and intangible — like the sweet inner glow of knowing you have done a job well — or external and tangible, like getting money for grades? And I said it's not so much what you *prefer*, but what gets the results best *accomplished*. That is precisely what Jonathan Edwards tried to do in getting people to re-center their lives on Jesus Christ. Unfortunately, Edwards waited until the very end of his essay to mention God's magnificent grace because, throughout the bulk of this essay, his anthropomorphic descriptions of God show Him as perpetually miffed, full of wrath, and ready to drop one into the fiery pit of Hell.

    Another aspect of Jonathan Edward's preaching during the Great Awakening was his insistence that unregenerate and unrepentant congregants acknowledge the necessity of coming out of their "natural" state and *publicly* affirm their faith in God. It is not enough to attend church and sit on one's assumed laurels. For two decades, I thought it was Jonathan Edwards who made up this notion called being "born again." So, *this* was the guy that started this, I thought to myself! Five years into being a Christian, I came to read that it was Jesus Who coined this expression and which we still use today. Having the subsequent *spiritual* rebirth in Him *after* your physical entry into this world was paramount. To the bright but not comprehending Nicodemus, Jesus announced, "Truly, truly, I say to you, unless one is born of water *and the Spirit*, he cannot enter into the kingdom of God. That which is born of the flesh is flesh, and that which is born of the Spirit is spirit. Do not be amazed that I said to you, 'You must be *born again*' (John 3:1-5–7, emphasis mine). At the time, it seemed ironic that the Protestants who were *not* works-based would now re-introduce this one, that it wasn't enough to *say* one was Christian or merely *go* to Church or *do* nice things, but that there was now an imperative to proclaim and testify one's faith before others. No, this wasn't a sacrament, but it did re-introduce *tangible* proof that one believed. What I couldn't have comprehended at the time was that then, as today, *identifying* as a Christian is not necessarily indicative of concertedly placing your faith in Christ alone. Jonathan Edwards said that if you were an "unregenerate" Christian, that is, not "born again," there was an imperative for you to do so. It was not enough just to *think* it; one had to *proclaim* it. At the time, did I think there was anything deficient or insufficient about my being baptized as an infant? No. Did I think I was going to Hell if I didn't accept Christ? No. Did I think that these were Protestants just trying to re-add some rules? Yes. I became so taken by Jonathan Edwards, that I invited a Presbyterian minister to guest lecture to my class so that the students could understand Edwards' urgency and that his message has application for our lives today. All this I did *before* I became a Christian, and, no, there's no way I could've been able to have invited such guest some twenty years into my career; it would have crossed that secular line. And though *The Scarlet Letter*, published in 1850, is not technically from this period, it brings to life the Puritan mindset and lifestyle in a particularly vivid and real way. Trials and tribulations, double standards, and forgiveness are all depicted through this unforgettable love story, and many a connection could be witnessed in modern American society, too. I admired Hester Prynne who wore her badge of shame that led to a purification and improvement in her character, but I identified more with Reverend Dimmesdale, who, because he didn't want to set a bad example to his congregants and therefore kept his sins to himself, felt the particular burden of hypocrisy. I ached for Dimmesdale through a commiseration or identification I felt for him as I was of a similar mindset and position, and, like him, "by the constitution of his nature, he loved the truth, and loathed the lie, as few men ever did. Therefore, above all things else, he loathed his miserable self!" I tried to be a shining beacon and good example to my students in all I did and said, but in my early years, off the clock, I sought fast relief and restoration from things that not always beneficial. For all my grading, preparing, and evaluating at school, I had not yet turned the powers of critical observation on myself.

It surprised me to find that most kids who would call themselves Christian were unfamiliar with so many Biblical allusions. For example, Job was pronounced as like "job," and they had no idea what Patrick Henry meant when he warned his fellow Americans about the British and said, "Suffer not yourselves to be betrayed with a kiss." I'll end this section by telling you my favorite aspect of Puritan society. They placed the group's primal importance, which precluded the individual's indebtedness to such within a larger frame. The premise behind was based on stance Martin Luther promoted, which he called the "priesthood of all believers." Luther concluded that, ordained or not, *all* Christians have direct access to God and thereby full authority to aid their fellow brother in matters of faith and to encourage good behavior. He said something to the effect that "all baptized believers are called to be priests, but not all are called to be pastors." I was quite attracted to the idea of being personally empowered before and by God because it gave me a right and duty to divest righteous values to my students to grow *their* character. I felt a special privilege and calling to help make the world a better place through my small role in school. I recently read something by a man named Paul Althaus, an interpreter of Luther's theology, that best explains the original meaning of his term: "Luther emphasizes the Christian's evangelical authority to come before God on behalf of the brethren and also of the world. The universal priesthood expresses not *religious individualism*, but its exact opposite: the reality of the congregation *as a community*" (emphasis mine). Did I vocalize this to anyone? No, but I did lament to my students that the sense of personal accountability to the greater good in society appears to have declined to the point of near disappearance, what with the many liberties we enjoy which became heralded in the next period.

3.3 The 180-Degree Flip to Deism

The advent of the Revolutionary period would usher in democratic ideals. The importance of the individual's direct relationship with God and the imperative to show charity to one's neighbor would be supplanted by secular values evidenced in the immediate political realm: as we gained independence from Britain, the focus shifted the liberties with which we were endowed. I could relate: freedom meant the world to me, too! Christianity might be beneficial for growing faith and improving one's morals, but it didn't seem to have a place in the real world. Oh, woe be I for thinking this way! Like the men of this period, I, too, was attracted to the Enlightenment ideals, including neo-classical political philosophies and contributions made during the scientific revolution, as represented by the intellectual giants like Copernicus, Galileo, Descartes, and Newton, to name a few. Ironically, many of these men found *no conflict of interest between science and religion* and were ridiculed or worse by men of the Church. Meanwhile, my students got mental whiplash from our taking a 180-degree turn-about from the Puritan sense of religiosity to the liberation of the Revolutionary period's focus on socio-political progress. As I made my way through these periods with my students, I became very aware that on a personal and private level, I, too, was picking and choosing those ideas that were pleasing to me. I will continue to focus on those particular thoughts preparing me for a state of readiness to meet Christ.

The Revolutionary period started with a lecture on Deism. In my early days of teaching, deism appealed to me a great deal: this philosophy wasn't wishy-washy like agnosticism; it wasn't extremist or nihilistic like atheism which denied the existence of the divine, yet it wasn't as presumptuous, prescriptive, and prohibitive as Christianity. It seemed obvious that some*thing* far vaster than we set into being and motion creation itself and launched systems of physics, functions of biology, operations of chemistry into play such that *life started*. Notice I did not yet say "some*one*." Creation went on autopilot. In the Age of Reason, humankind could reap the benefits of living in an era dominated by reason and logic; no more superstitions, no more religious zealots full of blind hate, and no more burning people at the stake! Even in a carefully chosen political system like ours, wrongs committed against our fellow man persisted. Our nation's original sin would be slavery, which was allowed to co-exist within the paradigm of democracy. Within each lecture of this period, I often played the devil's advocate and attempted to get Christian kids to stretch their minds and question the veracity of the Bible, including its full authority and accuracy. I was an equal opportunity provoker: I also mildly taunted those who were so smug to think that there was nothing out there other than some spontaneous Big Bang; after all, it, too, had to be preceded by something! I even attempted to explain the root of evil in the world without blaming God, as so many non-believers are apt to do. These were back in my "Saul" days before the scales had fallen from my eyes to give way to a new perspective. For example, to show that mistakes and misinterpretations were sure to arise in the early recording of the Bible, I would whisper a short phrase to the first student in the first row and ask him to pass it on to the next and so on. By the time I checked in with the last person in the farthest row, my phrase would have been transformed into a radically different (and often absurd) sentence. My point was that there could be no way that the Bible could have been correctly translated or conveyed with complete accuracy from when it was first transcribed from the original Aramaic or ancient Greek. It was easy to see how I, a foreign language teacher myself, could get hung up on how incorrectly or insufficiently certain words — especially those that deal with the abstract — could be translated. Anyone who reads the Bible in English should know that it is likely translated from Latin, too. That's too much remixing! Plus, I couldn't see how today's audience should expect people from biblical times to report or record seemingly inexplicable events with accuracy if they couldn't understand phenomena or circumstances that *we* can now prove through science. Little did I know then that actual historical events could factually substantiate New Testament accounts. Never did I consider that multiple sources speaking to some singular event, like, for example, circumstances in the life of Jesus, including miracles performed, parables spoken, and His resurrection witnessed, could corroborate one another by their similitude. Differences over minutia do not alter or negate the primary occurrence's reality from being actual and factual. Later, I would tell my class that if I were the editor of a book to which each of my students contributed a chapter, there would be various narrations, but one central, undeniable account of how our class conducted itself. In the early days, however, still blind myself, I would excitedly bring in my *Jefferson Bible* to show my class that educated men like Thomas Jefferson admired and even touted the words of the wisdom of Jesus. However, it didn't mean one believed in Jesus as the Messiah or that He was somehow divine. To that end, Jefferson took it upon himself to cut out only those words (in red) that Jesus spoke and pasted them into his own reader's condensed version. In other words, Jefferson included only passages from the four Gospels and omitted anything dealing with miracles or alleged happenings *after* His being crucified. In fact, for Jefferson and many revolutionary leaders who were raised Christian, as learned adults, many rejected the resurrection. When Jesus died, that was the end of the story. Mine, however, had not yet begun to know this was incorrect. When that time came such that I became receptive enough to consider Jesus as the Christ, I experienced a true-blue miracle for myself: I could not have manufactured for myself a faith into being. There was no way I was capable of redeeming myself. For me, faith became my miracle and a gift of love, the likes of which I could never adequately explain, but neither could I ever deny. This was yet to be, but I was on my way.

About halfway through my years of teaching American lit., I would become unconvinced of what I had been saying about deism being the catchall for those who knew there was much more to life but didn't want to stake a specific claim. I would lean increasingly towards acknowledging man's inability to know everything and that there was only so far logic and reasoning could go. I would say, "The more you know, the more you know you don't know," and let that sink in. That said, I will be the first to tell you, proudly even, that I *am* a rationalist and one primarily left-brained. Despite my passion, imagination, and energy, you're reading a tome of one who is logical-minded with a type-A personality. My opener for the Revolutionary Period was to ask my classes how they would feel if a Moment of *Prayer* (not silence) became introduced as part of the school day. This topic always brought about a lively discussion. I was aware that there were and still are well-intended adults who lament that our nation's ruination occurred when we took prayer out of school. "Such simple-minded and errant people," I would say to myself. How could people blame the woes of society on the institution of school? Why, such peoples ought to take a few steps beyond and confess that the ills of American society started when we took prayer out of our *homes*; the alleged downfall occurred when Americans quit praying together at home as *families*! If I could, I would shout from the rooftops that one reason our country is as unique and free as it is, is *because* our Puritan forefathers opposed a formal theocracy that would have formalized a religious agenda from a church-sanctioned *state*. Ever self-disciplined, our pilgrims took it upon *themselves* to live prayerfully, reverently, and devotedly, 24-7. The original scores for our country's political life bears witness to the supremacy of the *individual*. Gone were the days of the Puritan individual's devotion to moral purity to ensure the *community's* sound spiritual health.

The Revolutionary anthem of "let freedom ring" became our curse *and* our blessing; freedom without accountability at every level leads to bedlam and chaos. Democratic ideals not equitably applied birthed hypocrisy and friction on multiple levels. Such remains. Ask any African-American or woman just how long and arduous has been the struggle to have liberty apply to *all*. Even today, I admit that it's still tempting for me to end the Pledge saying, "…with liberty and justice *for most*." I'll save my best and most personally inspiring fact for last. In response to a religious conversion he experienced as a captain of a slave ship headed for America, John Newton returned his ship to Africa and freed his human cargo. In 1779 he wrote the lyrics to the beloved hymn, "Amazing Grace." At the time, it would have been astonishing to think one would choose grace over gain, and it goes to show that change starts with one person at a time. Thankfully, it's never too late to see the light, no matter how little faith you think you possess! I would have loved to be on that ship to have witnessed Newton's moment of sweet salvation! I would experience and receive that same grace myself a relative few years later. As concerned both this country's and my religiosity, the pendulum swung first full right, then back left, and now it would arc out another 90 degrees when

America would celebrate itself with high emotion and patriotism. This epoch would be the Romantic era, and within it, the all-important Transcendental period, which will now be my primary focus insofar as it reveals my spiritual growth.

3.4 TRANSCENDING TO WHO-KNOWS-WHAT:
from Unitarianism to Transcendentalism

At this point in American lit., having explained many a religious viewpoint, I would be asked by curious students about what *I* believed. You may think this inappropriate or odd, but students *are* interested, and if they trust you, they invariably will want to know what *you* think. Of course, I must be professional and discreet, but I cannot be false either. I would start my lecture on Transcendentalism by saying when I was their age at sixteen, I would announce that "my father is Greek Orthodox, my mother is Unitarian, and I am *Confused*." The kids would always chuckle at this, probably because they knew these to be polar opposites, or, perhaps, because they could identify with me. I think what else made discussions dealing with religion fascinating for them was that I was genuinely interested in who *they* were, where they came from, and what *their* purpose was in life. I told them that there are no chances, no accidents, or random occurrences. The fact of the matter is that each of them didn't *have* to exist; they were conceived with intentionality *far* beyond their parents' will. It very well could have turned out that another spermatozoon could have united with their mother's ovum, but *it didn't happen that way*. It was precisely *each* of them in *particular* who was brought to be! Even if your parents tell you that you weren't "planned" *or* that they did all they could so that you *could* be conceived is an answer that misses the mark. We exist in God's design because He wills it and wants us; our parents are the vehicles to make us come about. I stop at this point in my lecture and leave them feeling somehow positively purposed about their existence, which, for some, might have been a first. Later on, when I became a Christian, I would come to know the rest of the account from God's perspective. I was on the right track, but I didn't take it far enough. It became a shoo-in for me to conceive that an infinite God could proclaim, "Before I formed you in the womb, I knew you" (Jer. 1:5 NIV). Revealing my *mother's* religion led to defining Unitarianism which then segued to my lecture on Transcendentalism. I cut to the chase and had them look at the root of this term, "unit," which could never be misconstrued as one who is a "Trinitarian," that is, Christian. At least these early Unitarians acknowledged that since the miracles were recorded, there was *something* unique about this Jesus. At the time, they didn't commit to defining what that was. They make no such claim now. As a teenager, I rejected Unitarianism because it left me high and dry, but I did not disagree with their assessment of who Jesus was, or, should I say, was not. I still didn't understand what miracles were, let alone what it meant for Jesus to be both the Son of God *and* God in the flesh. Surely, He was misunderstood and misrepresented by the writers and people of His day. Maybe they weren't ready for Him. I wasn't yet either. As Emily Dickinson wrote, "*The truth must dazzle gradually or every man be blind.*" It turned out that it wasn't that the early scribes and Disciples who had it wrong or that they were in errancy, but it was I who would have the rug pulled out from under me such that I was left face-to-face with Him. How could I have known then that it was I who was undiscerning and, in this state, prevented from seeing the truth? For me to have come to believe and have faith *in Him alone* was a modern-day wonder. Meanwhile, I elaborated on Transcendentalism because it possessed a religious mysticism and polyglot approach I found appealing. In short, at the time, this lecture became a personal testimony in its own right.

Transcendentalism was the first real American philosophy to synthesize eastern and western thought, much like our hippies from the sixties, and later New Age followers emulated. In preparing my A.P. students for Emerson and Thoreau, I would cross-compare Transcendentalism with Christianity and Unitarianism as well as Hinduism and Buddhism. This was so fascinating to me! Through this investigation, I discovered that neither Hinduism nor Buddhism acknowledges the existence of a God and that their ultimate goal in life is to remove oneself from desires, as desire ultimately leads to loss and suffering. If one can reach this state of personal withdrawal or renunciation, one might attain a state of nirvana. Hardly Heaven, this release into the void, this moksha, this blissful state of nothingness, becomes the zenith of one's personal realization. How disappointing, let alone impossible to want to un-be! There's no love, no joy, no sense of purpose or hope but to catapult oneself off the mad cycle of life's eternal suffering. Thankfully, Transcendentalism didn't absorb or promote *that* route. Still, it did foster spiritual growth, and that to become elevated, one ought to discard extraneous or superfluous material things that impeded one's spiritual maturation. "*Simplify! Simplify!*" Thoreau would herald. This made such sense to me! This aspect of Transcendentalism was more eastern than western, and, frankly, I found it appealing. I listed the top ten quotable quotes of Emerson and Thoreau for my students to memorize verbatim to earn extra credit, and, even more, I hoped that they might desire such wisdom for themselves. How could I have known then that it would be Scripture I later would crave to memorize for myself? More than any other time period, Transcendentalism concerned itself with the meaning of our existence. Like Thoreau, I also "wished to live *deliberately*, to front only the *essential* facts of life, and see if I could not learn what it had to teach, and *not, when I came to die, discover that I had not lived*… I wanted to *live deep* and suck out all the marrow of life, to live so sturdily and *Spartan-like* as to put to rout all that was not life" (emphasis mine). Everything in me screams that I should not waste a moment, that I should live life to the fullest, yet, paradoxically, the life we are given here isn't a drop in the bucket compared to eternal life, which many do not yet know was offered by a man not really dead. Why? The man is God who lives because He is not bound by time, place, or matter. Think about it: every philosophy is founded by a person just the same as I, who is racing the clock. Today I serve Jesus Christ who *transcended* death! He has not only taught me how to live with intentionality, intensity, and purpose but in reading His Word daily, I'm hopefully growing wiser and improving my character in terms of what I do for Him *and* others. He gets the credit and glory! In short, becoming a Christian involves more than the acquisition of knowledge or some path to self-improvement. I look back and see so clearly that many of the ideas I learned about in American lit. were pleasing but not life-altering, and that I kept searching indicated I had not yet found peace.

 I admired the transcendentalists because they believed they experienced God most closely when they were in Nature and that there is excellent value to spiritual contemplation while in solitude. I would ask my students to share what or where was *their* "Walden." I assured them that this could even include a silent drive home alone from school, that just mulling over one's thoughts without others around is, indeed, time well spent. The brain needs to process and percolate and contemplate what's going on in one's life without the background noise of vapid or alluring messages. Having gone on a Unitarian youth group road trip to Boston when I was sixteen, I was able to get a first-hand account of what Walden Pond (and the site of Thoreau's cabin) looked like. Nearby we walked on the ample acreage of Emerson's property, where he held gatherings for the Transcendentalist Club. It was still thick with tall pine trees and the air smelled of sap. If the transcendentalists thought we could experience the divine in nature more than anywhere else, my students immediately would propose for us to hold class outside. In my early years, I indulged them. It pleased me to no end to watch some boy spontaneously run free and break into a somersault or notice a pile of girls clustered together, picking flowers, and break into a chorus of unified laughter for no particular reason.

Even the contemporary non-fiction piece, *Into the Wild*, shows the transcendental spirit is alive and well today. Therefore, the do-your-own-thing value promotes a spirit of rebellion, liberation, *and* entitlement; therefore, though freedom dazzles the youth, risk and self-centeredness hover, ready to take over. What becomes more apparent and accurate as we make our way through life is that, as John Donne stated, "no man is an island." We can't gain a little piece of the world all by and for ourselves without losing a part of ourselves. Spiritually, we become desiccated and lifeless in such a mausoleum of self-containment. Anyway, deep beneath the islands and continents are tectonic plates that connect all such visible regions. They, too, are held in joint place through the pull of such forces like energy, convection currents, and gravity. No matter how disillusioned, disappointed, or disgusted one may get with the world, no matter how special, superior, or self-sufficient we may perceive ourselves to be, we become lost and trivialized when we divorce ourselves from our fellow man. Life is more extraordinary and richer and more meaningful when we give and serve in *some* capacity, even if we aren't particularly fond of the other guy. That's the circle of life, not the cycle of life. At one time, I was told that scientists had discovered a "God gene" that predisposes humans towards spiritual or mystical experiences. The person who told me such was pleased to let me know that man's mind had created God, not the other way around. Even more recently, a physicist has proposed the existence of a "God particle." Can the infinite be quantified? If so, that implies that God has causation prior to Himself, which would render Him somehow finite. This goes entirely against His nature. Neither my mind nor my faith can generate "it," the cosmos, let alone the origins of an infinite God; He's beyond quantification! To sum up, transcendentalism is the non-theistic expression I taught and tried to use for myself to supersede this life of sound, sight, and sense to unite with the ineffable. This vague and impersonal higher spirit did not satisfy until later my own spirit was joined with His in an intensely intimate encounter that held eternal significance.

3.5 THE REALISM OF EMILY AND WALT

In my transition to realism, I would teach a sub-unit devoted entirely to Walt Whitman and Emily Dickinson because they would cross over and have traits of transcendentalism juxtaposed with aspects of realism. I now continue being selective and choose only those aspects of the time periods and a few select writers that possess elements of my burgeoning religiosity and quest for truth that would lead to my becoming a Christian. In particular, I cannot adequately convey just how dear these two poets were to me; I loved them so. In class, I was on a first-name basis with them, and I would have enjoyed taking or teaching a course entirely devoted to them. Though opposite in temperament, focus, and style, each possessed an outlook and vision that made sense to my soul; I'll share it now with you. I didn't know then that when I became a Christian, I would turn to writing poetry to capture moments of my heart's murmuring or fluttering when the Holy Spirit took hold of me. I'll start with Emily, who, at her core, was so intensely focused, independent, selective, and private that, at first, I felt a little intrusive in reading her poetry. Then, I discovered I had a similar outlook as she, specifically with regards to her take on the church, God, and faith. I sympathized with her notion that one didn't have to be in a physical building to celebrate and worship God. Note in the following excerpt Emily's dryly-ironic tone and subtle disdain for long-winded and probable pompous preachers as compared to the perfection and adequacy of God rendering Himself in Nature. Plus, it made sense to me that she needn't feel compelled to fulfill *man's* requirements for attaining salvation when she'd already made a heaven on earth for herself here:

>Some keep the Sabbath going to Church –
>I keep it, staying at Home. . .
>God preaches, a noted Clergyman –
>And the sermon is never long,
>So instead of getting to Heaven, at last –

I'm going, all along.

Though a full quarter of Emily's poems deal with death and immortality, at the time, my focus was drawn to God and just where to find Him. That He was in another dimension or so distant as to render Him seemingly non-existent, Emily also grappled with and found analogies that brought Him closer and more real in a way one could apprehend. The poem below assures me I don't have to see it to believe it and to know with certainty that *He* exists:

I never saw a moor;
I never saw the sea,
Yet know I how the heather looks
And what a billow be.

I never spoke with God,
Nor visited in heaven.
Yet certain am I of the spot
As if the checks were given.

And one other poem that satisfied me is one in which Emily dared to say that it is in our brains we encounter God, that He isn't *out there* so much as *in us*. God as Creator is beyond our comprehension, but in creating us in His image, even if we have a scintilla of mental capacity compared to Him, we still have the wherewithal to be able to fathom Him. We are not powerless though we are finite; our imagination, curiosity, and inner vision *can* bring Him *to* mind *in* our mind all the while He is *beyond* our reach.

The Brain—is wider than the Sky—
For—put them side by side—
The one the other will contain
With ease—and You—beside—

The Brain is deeper than the sea—
For—hold them—Blue to Blue—
The one the other will absorb—
As Sponges—Buckets—do—

The Brain is just the weight of God—
For—Heft them—Pound for Pound—

> And they will differ—if they do—
> As Syllable from Sound—

And finally, like Emily, I had learned to embrace and even celebrate doubt within the broader scope of coming to faith. I did not view doubt as incongruous or insulting to God while I was trying to seek Him in a state of wonderment over Him. Any uncertainty or ambivalence I displayed showed my humanness; I just had an earnest desire to get it right. Anyway, in this one sphere, I didn't doubt *Him* as much as I lacked assuredness of my ability to attain and sustain faith. Another poem of hers I would relish is one that deals with one's grappling with immortality. She, too, would waver in her certainty of everlasting life. It's impossible to explain how or why a dimensionless and endless eternity "beckons and baffles" us in our finite and mortal state. We rationalize and try to figure just what that something more or else is and if we will be there. No wonder we seek miracles and proof. Regardless, neither she nor I can see into the future, let alone fathom or articulate what happens to us after we die, try though we might. She just knew that death was not the end of life; the termination point was perforated. Two decades later, I would come to have a relationship with the only one who could provide us the satiating answer to "*What's next?*" or "*Is that all there is?*" because *He lived to tell it*. I admired Dickinson's intense honesty and scrutiny: she vacillated between faith and doubt about *what*, not *if*, something happens to us after we die. Dickinson went past deducing what we have here and now and concluded that this here is *not* all there is. In the poem below, she implies that no one can define or describe what happens after death; all of man's attempts are mere speculation.

> This World is not Conclusion
> A Species stands beyond—
> Invisible, as Music—
> But positive, as Sound—
> It beckons, and it baffles—
> Philosophy—don't know—
> And through a Riddle, at the last—
> Sagacity, must go—
> To guess it, puzzles scholars—
> To gain it, Men have borne

> Contempt of Generations
> And Crucifixion, shown—
> Faith slips—and laughs, and rallies—
> Blushes, if any see—
> Plucks at a twig of *Evidence*—
> And asks a Vane, the way—
> Much Gesture, from the Pulpit—
> Strong Hallelujahs roll—
> Narcotics cannot still the Tooth
> That *nibbles* at the soul—

What "nibbles" is a disquieting misgiving that anyone can possess certitude or authority. Later, I thought that if one *requires* comprehensible or plausible evidence, then one bypasses faith. Moreover, evidence that proves He existed *and* visited us after He died indicates immortality is a sure thing. We lack the capacity to understand the mode of incorporeal life He possesses and which has no end. My acceding to such would arise from reading Isaiah 55:8. Here the Lord declares, "For My thoughts are not your thoughts, nor are your ways My ways." To say this is not a concession or a copout; it is just stating a fact. In some incomprehensible capacity, we return to the source which gave rise to our existence to begin with, which is why immortality is so hard for us to quantify or grasp. Emily tried her whole life to do so, and, may I add, with finesse.

Even though Emily Dickinson intrigued me with her riddles leading to truths, Walt Whitman matches me, moves me, and made me happy. I get him! He is broad, expansive, and curious about humanity. He loved to meet new people, see new places, and experience new things! He had an unbridled enthusiasm for life! I feel like this, too! There was no room or time for doubts and speculations about death or salvation for Walt Whitman. Oh, no! *There was too much life and inner energy to enjoy the here and now.* Unlike Emily, who, like the microscope she loved to peer through, was the type to look up close and personal at the intangibles of our existence, Whitman observed us from afar, as if he was a human telescope. He peered into human nature and noted the variations of expression while loving people and enjoying life. He not only *doesn't* complain about life's vicissitudes with guilt, shame, and fear, but he wryly says he'd rather live with the animals because people's

priorities are skewed regarding how we *ought* to live life. I agreed!
> They [animals] do not sweat and whine about their condition;
> They do not lie awake in the dark and weep for their sins;
> They do not make me sick discussing their duty to God;
> Not one is dissatisfied — not one is demented with the mania of owning things;

To me, there could be no better representative of America — *or me* — than Whitman because at the very least, he lists our various ones by state, tries to empathize with disenfranchised Americans like slaves, and even trumpets the awesomeness of women. I can think of no other man that would think to write, let alone proclaim, just how spectacular it is to be a woman. We are used to silence or scorn. Look how he celebrates us:

> I am the poet of the woman the same as the man,
> And I say it is as great to be a woman as to be a man,
> And I say there is nothing greater than the mother of men.

This democratic spirit of his I would find matched later on in the New Testament by a man named Paul who would attest to the *indistinguishable unity we have in Christ*. I mention the last few lines in the poem above because I found a similar posture of equality, empowerment, and hope in Christ through Paul's words in his earliest letter. Paul wrote to the Galatians that "there is neither Jew nor Greek, there is neither slave nor free man, there is neither male nor female; for you are all one in Christ Jesus" (Galatians 3:28). I had much more to look forward to!

Whitman resonated within me because my quest for God was not merely some *intellectual* exercise. I wasn't overtly trying to make some greatest hits package of beliefs of my own about what to believe, but throughout this time, *the search was on*. That's the best way I can tell you, and it involved *the totality* of me. We are more than our minds, and it is what's deep in our emotions and souls that gets us stirred and searching throughout life. In case you are wondering why I'm spending so much time on American literature and its authors and their ideas, it is because by sharing selections from this canon, I can demonstrate that I was hungry for that which I was teaching: divine direction. I can tell you that people reject Christianity not due to curiosity but because of *pride*. The final answer to what we seek is not intellectual but *moral*. Later, when God readied me, I could see that "the Gospel of Christ condemns what we like and commands what we hate" (Martyn Lloyd-Jones). In the meanwhile, I was enamored by Whitman's wit and wisdom. Who knew I might have an openness and readiness to be moved to the point of accepting His gift of grace? I didn't see it coming! It would be another decade before I'd love the Son of God, this man who spoke in parables, cared for the unfortunate and scorned, and ultimately died for all of us. I wasn't ready just yet, but all roads were heading inexorably there. I'm showing these to you now. I was creating a pathway that was leading to God, and in the meanwhile, I was figuring out who I was and who I was not. And what of God, you ask? Where is He in all of this? I first had to come to believe in God; His divine Son would come a bit later for me, but He did. They're a package deal; plus, you get His Spirit to boot. I *needed* to see that God was not distant, nebulous, or deistic, yet such a personal and intimate relationship that I desired would come later. For me, I found inspiration in the fact that *Whitman found God in everything and everyone he saw*, and it compelled me to look deeper and a little longer. Not only that, but the proof of God's existence is in His pudding: in *us*, His creation!

> And I say to mankind,
> Be not curious about God,
> For I who am curious about each am not curious about God…
> I hear and behold God in every object, yet understand God not in the least…

Whitman's final point that provided the stepping stone leading me to God was the realization that I am connected to *everyone*; I am no better or worse than anyone. We are each and all on a journey and therefore have an imperative to communicate and connect with one another. We aren't going it alone! Here is that excerpt about which I will comment more:

> I celebrate myself, and sing myself,
> And what I assume you shall assume,
> For every atom belonging to me as good belongs to you…
> I, now thirty-seven years old in perfect health begin,
> Hoping to cease not till death. . .
> I harbor for good or bad; I permit to speak at every hazard,

Nature without check with original energy.

Whitman's style of focusing on self can make him seem egotistical, but, in essence, this poet's voice points to the One Who fashioned us. Though Whitman didn't explicitly acknowledge God's creativity, I already believed He made me uniquely and especially, and I, too, felt like singing *His* praises for this in the same way Whitman "celebrated" his existence. Surely, I was on my way to loving the Lord with all my "heart, soul and mind" (Matt. 22:37 NKJV). My little mind was trying to with all its might. Whitman's asked us to "assume" of each other *because* we are made of "atoms," this is, the same stuff. When I became a Christian, I recognized Whitman's sentiment in the divine imperative. In what has been called the second greatest commandment, Jesus told us to "love your neighbor as yourself" (Matt. 22:39 NKJV). We are all the same at the foot of the cross! When I started teaching at *twenty*-seven, I didn't understand the line about "beginning at *thirty*-seven" until a decade later; having arrived at this age, I would quit drinking and begin life anew sober. It's hard to find God when you find yourself in a blind stupor. Thus, approaching middle age brought me back to square one and ultimately led me to a place where I *could* be a child of God and not merely one of what Whitman dubbed as "children of Adam." No, I didn't want to waste any more minutes of life; I, too, didn't even want to "cease" at death! My writing this now is my "harboring" for *God* because He is this "original energy" of which Whitman spoke. We see God through the person of Christ.

At the time, I also found a part of a poem I thought I would want to read at my funeral, should I die an untimely death. It is a portion taken from "When Lilacs Last in the Dooryard Bloom'd," In it, Whitman writes for the assassinated President Lincoln in such a lyrical and tender way that he presents death as comforting and far from horrid.

Come lovely and soothing death,
Undulate round the world, serenely arriving, arriving,
In the day, in the night, to all, to each,
Sooner or later delicate death.

Death may be a physical certainty, but that doesn't mean life itself ceases. No, life doesn't change form via reincarnation or transmigration; there is no proof or sense in this. Later, I would come to terms with death through the One who took away its "sting" altogether (1 Cor.

15:55 KJV). How could I have known then in my childlike Marco Polo attempts to find God, that my bounding toward all the "Polos" I liked would cease when I heard the name "Jesus"? I have no fear of death, just a desire to express love in what life I'm given. Of course, at times, it is just as much of a challenge to show love for me as it is for others! In short, what I loved about Whitman was that, at our core, I felt like he and I are similar in being rich, complex, and diverse persons who seek to affirm others in any way we can. Now I also *know* I had nothing to do with how God "created my inmost being... and knit me together in my mother's womb" (Psalm 139:13), that is, how I was created and designed. Whitman wrote, "I am large, I contain multitudes. . . I, too, am untranslatable ... and am not contained between my hat and boots..." I feel the same way about myself but take no credit for how God shaped me to be. Later, I would explore unique ways to serve and glorify Him.

This is not intended to be a survey, but *I need to show you certain ideas that I was drawn to* while seeking God. I am intentionally limiting and take care in what I choose to share with you. For this reason, I do not need to delve into the Realism Period because, by and large, it doesn't concern itself with matters of the heart, let alone the divine. Its scope is on the here and the now; their writers pointed out what needed to be done to solve problems. Realism involves us treating life on life's terms, or, to use a phrase of today, that we see that "it is what it is." We are the architects of our own woe, but there is still hope that exists beyond, even, for example, when you watch the evening news and feel despair. Though it's real and in some respects accurate, the bad that's depicted is still vastly incomplete as a representation of who we are and what our purpose is, individually and collectively, even if we are imperfect. I would come to learn that Satan wants to keep us discouraged and stuck in the moment; he wants to destroy our hopes, and if you only look at what's under your nose, you will succumb to his ploys. Realism came to be not so real for me in that such an "ism" is vastly incomplete; realism is hardly the representation of the grander picture to which we are *not* privy. At his core, Mark Twain, the literary titan from this period, was a cynical man. Though full of wit and humor, he took glee in exposing the hypocrisy and false piety of Christians, but, like so many others, he threw away the baby with the proverbial bathwater; that is, he abandoned Christ when he got disappointed by Christians. Nowhere is this more vivid than in a particular scene in *Adventures of Huckleberry Finn* where Twain depicts two feuding families. They briefly put their fighting on hold to attend church, but the men kept their guns standing up between their knees as they listened to the "pretty ornery preaching — all about brotherly love, and such-like tiredsomeness." No, the process of loving one's neighbor as oneself doesn't come naturally or easily; it runs counter-intuitively to our selfish natures, but it is the one thing that can make all the difference in the world where peace and love are concerned. And isn't that all we all really crave anyway? It seems only logical that we must look to One who is the apex of perfect love and peace; otherwise, we spin our wheels in futility and judgment, going nowhere fast. I will move past problems of America's political heritage from this period and head straight into Modernism because in it, I explored existentialism, and within this, the call to come to the "leap of faith," a phrase coined by the Christian existentialist, Søren *Kierkegaard*. I was intrigued, to say the least. This man wrote a book called *Fear and Trembling*. At the time, I had no idea he was alluding to Philippians 2:12, in which we are ordered to work out our salvation "with fear and trembling."

3.6 THE ASH HEAP OF MODERNISM

Despite its seeming bleakness, I love teaching modernism because it reveals the accepted socio-political structures, morals, and belief systems that advanced societies revere as being a sham. Indeed, it was the supposed most civilized nations which became involved in two world wars. Something *had* to be better than a way of living which, although historically rich in art and philosophy, ended up promoting the likes of self-indulgence, entitlement, and self-gain. Where was the personal responsibility or accountability to one's fellow man? The end result reveals a mindset or state of the soul in literary personalities which still resonate with people today. Modern characters are replete with a sense of alienation, anguish, loneliness, longing, and even absurdity. I give you this backdrop because *this* is such the state in which I found myself: I had that anguished heart, and my soul groaned in aching for that which I couldn't put my finger on, and every year, after winding up all I'd taught, I'd still be left silently wanting more. I got really good at stuffing my feelings and carrying on, yet I was only fooling myself. Just because I am an extrovert and happy by nature doesn't mean that the inner stirrings of my heart weren't quietly crying from a lacking His sustenance. It is no wonder that I was drawn to the melancholic; I hadn't yet turned to trust in Him. The common maxim, "No God, no peace; know God, know peace" would ring true for me. And though this condition may seem grim, I *was* that post-modern reader who fervently, if not desperately, searched for meaning in a world that just gets evermore bellicose, chaotic, senseless, and profane. School shootings had just started with the advent of Columbine. Yes, there *are* moments of beauty to be found in the madness, but just beyond the horizon of our front door is a world in such desperate need of love, of *Him*. What I would come to see was that without God, man, spiritually speaking, is dead. He lives a life of *take* and not *give*; and when you get right down to it, man ineptly tries to become his own god. This is also not new. Delving into this idea was yet to be, so I'll share the tenets

I conceived at the time to explain existentialism. Existentialism states that we're born alone and will ultimately die alone, too. This precept terrified me, so I mentally fled before it could stick to my innards. Morally, we are the sum total of all our actions; there is no absolute right or wrong, rather a moral relativism. Instinctively and reflexively, I felt like I was telling the students a lie in teaching this last idea because what kind of life can you have when *anything goes*? It can't be true that everything is correct depending on some subjective standpoint; in no other area of life is this valid, so why do we think it's applicable in matters of morality and God? Two plus two is always four; this fact is not dependent on an individual's perspective or experience! At the time, I couldn't realize that our impure natures seek self-justification at any cost, even truth. Such an existential state arising from when we deny and take God's place cannot but help but lead to disappointment and moral despair. In the wanderings of my restless soul, I was dissatisfied to leave matters there. I came up with my own bullet-point antidotes for overcoming existential anguish, which I hoped both my students and I could apply as truth and serve as a salve. I wanted to gain a sense of empowerment through the freedom we possess so that I would choose to do the *right* thing, yet time and again, I would prove that I was a slave to self. Before I became a Christian, here are those methods I would teach to conquer such angst: (1) We must be true to ourselves and face all problems responsibly and directly. *It would take a personal disaster or two for me to put this into gear.* (2) We should try to find new meaning through personal and fulfilling acts of creativity and make authentic, positive connections with others. *I would only scratch at the surface of this until I became a Christian and started to really consider other's feelings, which, in turn, took me out of self.* (3) We are to show "spontaneous compassion" for others. *At the time, I had no sense of this other than an academic one.* (4) Ultimately, we should consider taking the "leap of faith" and believe in a higher power even if there's no rational proof for such. *It would be this last axiom that I would come to try for myself. I knew that activating or coming to have faith was through no ability of my own, so when coming to faith in Him happened and took, it's no surprise that I was bowled away.* This was yet to be, but, looking back on certain literary characters to whom I was drawn who were *also* searching, it is no surprise that He was steering me towards Himself.

Following are the final few such ones from the modern period that, in hindsight, were preparing for becoming a Christian.

F. Scott Fitzgerald's novel, *The Great Gatsby*, is familiar to all, but I will share with you a part which really got to me: like some bizarre icon of God looking down on and watching us did I perceive Fitzgerald's billboard of the humongous eyes of Dr. T.J. Eckleburg. The billboard ostensibly was advertising for an optometrist in Queens, but in actuality, it pointed to the loss of spiritual values and growing commercialism in America. Later, disgusted with the vapidity and "carelessness" of those he knew in the East, the novel's narrator, Nick Carraway, returns home to the more centered Midwest; we assume this is because there he will continue to live by values that are righteous, thoughtful, and caring. Nick ironically and indirectly learned this life lesson through the romantic but misguided Gatsby who gave of himself to all that's wrong due to a lack of discernment and his naive love. Another bittersweet moment of human fragility and needfulness is shown in Tennessee Williams' play, *A Streetcar Named Desire*, a play I can just about quote all the way through. The central character, Blanche DuBois, haunted by guilt, tormented by transgressions, and overwrought by having single-handedly dealt with the deaths and dying of relatives, finds hope in her boyfriend, Mitch. Grateful that she has discovered in him a respite, Blanche remarks in one tender moment of particular vulnerability, "Sometimes—there's God—so quickly!" When we bank all of our hope on one *person*, we invariably get disappointed, but if both people united in love put their hope in *God*, they *can* become a refuge for each other in life's travails. This doesn't mean you always get what you want, but what He knows you need. There are many novels I've taught, but one of the best novels which captures the essence of the angst and longing to know one's true identity is Toni Morrison's *Song of Solomon*! Like the central character, Milkman, who made his way down south to explore his roots, I, too, would investigate parts of my own identity and heritage. In the climactic scene where Milkman is hunting with some of his southern male relatives, Milkman gets injured, scared, and stripped of all he'd used to give him a sense of assuredness. He gained much when he felt he'd lost himself. Milkman forgave his parents for, as he put it, "dumping" on him, and he learned how to *give* instead of take when it came to his intimate relations. These would serve as life lessons for me as well. At the very end of this novel, Milkman jumps off a cliff believing he can fly. Although the students and I would debate what this meant or if he actually died, I would experience a similar moment later in my own life. When I jumped off the fence of doubt and disbelief, I would feel like I was soaring and experiencing new life when I came to Jesus. I was in a state of euphoria when I leaped out to Him and subsequently sensed that His Holy Spirit had flown into me, and at that moment, I went from being a creation to a true child of God! This moment, however, would come way past the time of teaching this novel.

3.7 Confessions of a Teacher

Back then, in the late '90s, my teaching was on fire, and I was awarded Teacher of the Year in 1998. I'll never forget when I heard my name announced at graduation: I had to walk all the way up to the podium, and for the first time in my life, I was speechless. I just put my hand to my chest out of sincere gratitude to my students I loved. Only after I had walked all the way back to my seat did I realize I'd left that check for a thousand dollars up there! I held my crystal apple close to my heart and could hardly contain my joy. Two years before that, I had won the Presidential Award of Distinguished Teacher and would be one of many who were invited to visit President Clinton at the White House, but at that time, I was in Russia on a tour with students. These were some of the best days of my career because I got close to my students. Yet in the end, I know we are remembered for *who we are* and not *what* we do. I would proclaim that what counted in life is not how you show or use the intelligence with which you were born, but you must *grow your character*. Be kind! The rest will work out for itself. I asked them intently, when it is all said and done, what would *they* like to be remembered for? Would it be for their things and accomplishments? Possessions? Accolades? Status? Income? No, indeed, it would not! I said *the* most important thing they could develop would be *relationships* with people and respect and trust from loved ones. Later, emboldened and assured, I would even come right out and tell my secular-minded, public-school students that one's real success would hinge on whether or not one had a personal connection with God. I told all my students to imagine reflecting throughout their lives as if they were on their deathbed. Would they want to be surrounded by loved ones or things? Life is all about trying your best to treat others well. At the time, I did not go so far as to say anything about Jesus. How could I have? I hope that God knew I was on the right track and soon to be on His side.

In its own way, each class for me becomes like a family, and all the more so my Russian classes as these students choose to take this elective course. Regardless, all my students sought my *heart* and needed to know that they *mattered* to me, and though I told them that they were not so very unique, each student was special. The best and brightest possess the advantage and benefit of having someone pour assurance into them and develop their potential early, but there are *so* many that are just birthed and practically live like feral children, with no one to inculcate in them the things that matter most in life. Alas, modern American society can be morally flaccid, soulfully malnourished, and short-sited; we are easily distracted by the shiny things. Oh, I'm one to talk! Diversions almost lead to an undoing in me! Yes, I know we Americans are the envy of the world, what with our optimism, energy, freedoms, bounty, and vast opportunities, but so much is squandered, misspent, or misdirected. I see this every day in class with kids who are overindulged, overmedicated, ignored, or spoiled by entitlement. I sought to do more than to teach; I wanted to inspire and develop their essential selves. This is not an easy task because the teenager's job is to challenge, question, and test the boundaries to determine if the rules are foundationally sound and applicable to all. They will expose all that fraudulent, faulty, and not consistently applied. This occurs daily. Sometimes hourly. It can be maddening. And as a bonus, their ability to listen is often inverse proportion to how much their hormones have kicked in, which tells you a lot. Their brains have not yet cooled in the final stages of completing their frontal lobes' development, so their logic is awry, and emotions run high. But still, they have many moments of clarity, humor, profundity, wonder, and an openness such that I'm in awe of them. It's the readiness in this and all that changes everything in life.

All teachers behind closed doors think that they're changing the world in their precious little kingdoms. There is a deep desire to instill within all students, great and small, a sense of righteousness, life preparedness, and common sense. Sure, we chose our subject matter based upon our major which we fell in love with in college. My approach to teaching is to seamlessly make as many connections between the subject matter and their reality that they aren't even aware they're learning. An effective teacher must be energetic, enthusiastic, and brisk, but at her core, she must *show she cares*. After all, God does *us*. I use humor to arouse, keep, or harness their attention and keep the mood or climate positive. Almost effortlessly, I come up with concrete analogies to illustrate ideas. A good teacher must herself possess a desire to learn! My students always ask me which I like teaching better, Russian or English? And I would answer them that English satisfies my mind, and Russian fills my soul. It was the students who gratified my heart. Years later, I would come to be the student of a teacher the likes of which I never saw coming, one whom I would come to befriend, respect, and love. As a friend, he taught me about Godly wisdom and helped me with matters of the heart that deal with life and death.

By now, it is no surprise to you that I am moved by writers and thinkers who look beyond the surface of things and make profound observations about the human heart's interior workings. But for me, right here and now, to be inspired to write a book during the full throws of my career necessitates something *monumental,* something *magnificent* to have happened. And something did. I wasn't just impressed by something or someplace to have launched me into writing: *someone* changed me: Jesus. I never saw it coming, but looking back, I see it as plain as day. I am not knocking *carpe diem* or avoiding stopping to smell the proverbial roses. I am all too aware that life can be snuffed out in a moment, so there's precious little time to do something of significance, but how could one *not* try for Him? He died for me! Do I write merely to share my favorite writers and literary ideas or to disseminate facts about Russian culture and language? No! The urgency I feel is akin to what George Bailey experiences at the end of *It's a Wonderful Life* when he's been given the gift of seeing what life would have been like without him. Dreams of spending eternity with Him move me, which compels me to write about Him to you. I hope you also can see that all that's gestated in your life can propel you to a glory-drenched future should *you* choose to come to Christ. However, I get ahead of myself. I don't want to sound all fake like I've got it all figured out. Continue walking with me as I get real and vulnerable with you and reveal some things in my personal life that would eventually and inevitably lead me to my leap of faith.

Ch. 4. Booze and "A Power Greater"

"If we are painstaking about this phase of our development, we will be amazed before we are halfway through. We are going to know a new freedom and a new happiness. We will not regret the past nor wish to shut the door on it. We will comprehend the word 'serenity,' and we will know peace. No matter how far down the scale we have gone, we will see how our experience can benefit others. That feeling of uselessness and self-pity will disappear. We will lose interest in selfish things and gain interest in our fellows. Self-seeking will slip away. Our whole attitude and outlook upon life will change. Fear of people and economic insecurity will leave us. We will intuitively know how to handle situations which used to baffle us. We will suddenly realize that God is doing for us what we could not do for ourselves.

Are these extravagant promises? We think not. They are being fulfilled among us—sometimes quickly, sometimes slowly. They will always materialize if we work for them."
— "The Promises," from *Alcoholics Anonymous*

"…Where the Spirit of the Lord is, there is freedom."
— 2 Corinthians 3:17 (NIV)

4.1 A Brief History of My Drinking:
Predictable Unpredictability

Thus far, this quirky memoir may seem like an account of my life leading to a career or teaching as if I had no personal experiences outside of school and like I lived for Russian or teaching my students. This is not the case. I will weave in another strand that had been recurrent throughout much of my life, though at the time, I did not see it as a badge of shame, an impediment, let alone a hurdle. That I fell in love with drinking seemed natural, inevitable, and harmless. What was different about my drinking is that over time, somewhere in my early thirties, my drinking habits changed, and I wasn't aware of the fact. I couldn't anticipate how much I would drink, and I began to drink before some social event commenced so that it didn't seem as if I was drinking all that much when I was there, and I would leave early to continue with my own more intense drinking afterward. I also started to prefer to drink in private and loved isolating. I had blackouts with greater frequency, and I would begin to drink and drive regularly. I was what one friend called a "power drinker," and with those closest to me, I might order *two* drinks for my first drink. I could never have foreseen problems happening; no one ever does. The only difference between someone who has been in trouble with the law and me is that I quit before it happened, and it almost did the last time I got wasted. In some form or fashion, having problems with the law becomes an eventuality if you drink too much. One of the many A.A. sayings or go-to platitudes I'd come to know is that you'll either get "locked up or covered up if you don't sober up." But for the grace of God, there go I. I didn't kill or bodily injure anyone while driving; just the words, "not *yet*," were all I needed to add to any given statement about some horrific calamity or misfortune happening. No, I had not lost my job, my home, my family, my very life, no, "not *yet*." These things do happen, though! Did I want to deny that I had a problem and that my drinking had started to get out of hand? You'd better believe it! I was pleased with myself that I drank with such gusto. I particularly liked to drink right after I'd worked out because the rush of the cold beer coursing through my system cooled the electrical fire, verbiage I would use to describe my normal inner state. Alcohol quelled the super-charged energy I felt built up inside me. When I drank, I was more of a lover than a fighter, and I also liked to cook while drinking and be with friends with whom I could horselaugh. Ah, if only *a* drink could have sufficed. In high school, I would inform others that I drank upon occasion "like Europeans," that it was no big deal. This was a lie because I drank to excess from day one, be it at home, abroad, on my own, or with friends. I drank for any occasion and for no reason. It's a fact that when you begin drinking as I did, your emotional growth stops; therefore, no matter how educated I'd gotten or ostensibly mature I'd become, I was still about eighteen.

When I got to college, I met another girl like myself down the dorm room hall, and we immediately hit it off. I joined the U.S.C. Women's Rugby Club that year, and though I played poorly, there was something so attractive about this rough-and-tumble game and the hearty camaraderie among ruggers, that I was in a trance and stupor for much of my freshman year. As I became increasingly discontent with my pre-med major, I found myself drinking more and more; my grades were plummeting. I recall that the experience of playing in the Women's Rugby Festival in Athens, GA was like visiting another planet. The world had flipped upside down in that the stars were all warrior women! (Keep in mind that I had played a team sport only once during high school.) Our team rented a van to go to Athens, and half a dozen of us sat on a pile of cases of Miller Lite inside this seatless vehicle, swilling down beer all the way there; a few of them even made course gestures at a church van we passed by. After the game, what seemed like hundreds of women were partying in a nearby and decorated barn. I felt bewildered, fascinated, and repulsed all at the same time. That year, I skipped my German class, piled up in a sick-green Datsun B-210 with my rugger friends, and got drunk on the way to the South Carolina School of Beauty to get my haircut. The stylist-in-training lifted up my thick, shoulder-length hair to show me my future length of loss as I, in turn, looked back at myself in the mirror, my rugger friends — many with their mullet coif of the day — standing around me like a halo and egging me on. After the fateful shearing, my hair stood straight up like I'd been electrocuted or like I was donning a dandelion puff. I loved it. That year, I also smoked a pipe for tobacco, rode my 10-speed like it was some vehicle for flight, my long coat from Guatemala sailing behind me, and primarily lived for orchestra and rugby, the two worlds blurring and overlapping through drink. Once when I was intoxicated enough, I switched my B-52s cassette to a tape I'd had of an orchestral piece that another girl and I soloed in during high school, and my rugger friends bellowed cheeringly for that, too. At 10:00 every night, I'd quit my studying and go to a bar up on "The Hill" right off campus so I could watch the fireworks that the World's Fair put on every night. Though I loved and was used to the more cultured world of orchestra and academia, I could not deny I had something in common with these rugger women. What chaos! What pandemonium!

4.2 Identity Crisis

I hadn't yet the confidence in knowing who I was, how I was put together, and what purpose I was to serve; these things didn't even occur to me at the time. I suppose most college freshmen feel discombobulated in one way or another. The girl I'd met in my dorm, the one who'd played the music of Bob Dylan such that I listened and ferreted out the room from which it came, became a special friend to me. Those first few friends outside one's earliest youth you make in college reveal, reflect, and relish aspects of yourself that you hadn't known existed or could be found. I couldn't get enough of her; she was generous, magnanimous, and exuberant; I'd not met the likes of her elsewhere. She bought me my first drinks at a local dive, and we enjoyed each other's energy and company immensely. She and I did not possess the coveted American prototype of the Barbie-esque form. Hers was more Amazonian, and mine was the sinewy, athletic form of the ancient Greeks. Alcohol quelled the confusion, numbed my pain, and made it easier to go along with activities I usually would not have; I so wanted to be accepted. I wasn't seeking God or anything other than earthly things. I loved the effect alcohol gave me immediately: euphoria, an aliveness, and concurrently a balm to match the super-charged, zippy state I usually felt. I don't pretend to have ever been a good or even a regular rugby player. Oh, no! But I loved the camaraderie, conviviality, and raucousness we shared singing raunchy rugger songs at bars or around bonfires. I had not experienced what it was like to participate in a sports team, and I loved being a part of something bigger and more zestful than I ever could have been or done on my own. This sense of being intensely involved wasn't new to me; after all, I'd played the violin in the orchestra throughout high school and college; fellow musicians were like my family. Little did I know at the time that almost thirty years later, in my quest to do better things for Him, I would tap into and join a family of brothers and sisters bound for eternal glory. As I said, I had never gone all out for sports, but this year was new in that I was involved in both sports and music concurrently, and it was mind-altering but not life-changing. With laces tied together at the ends, I would sling my cleats around my neck, shoulder my violin strapped across my back, hop on my bright blue, ten-speed Schwinn, and then weave in and out of traffic on the main drag at school, dashing from orchestra to rugby practice. It was awesome, all except for the fact that my pre-med major was becoming less and less attractive to me, and I would not discover Russian until that next fall. In the meanwhile, my grades were declining. That summer, I got a job at a Cloudy State Park, and I loved working outdoors doing physical labor; I would do this again the following summer. My mother announced she wanted to get a divorce; this was news only to my father. For quite a few years and not without reason, she had been discontented, disappointed, and distraught over the state of her marriage. She made an analogy that stuck with and struck me: when two people get married, they are joined in a three-legged race; should one put a foot down to run on his own, the other person would surely fall. I wondered to myself, is this how marriage is designed, doomed but to fail if one of the partners changes? Our whole family's collective and individual worlds fell apart: first, my grandfather left my grandmother, my mom left my dad, and not even a year later, my uncle walked out on my aunt. This brokenness was symbolically rendered by the three connected nameplates atop one another which hung on the light pole by the entrance to our grandmother's lake house; that very summer, the unit had somehow broken off at one corner, leaving it dangling by a fleck of metal. I am not blaming my excessive drinking or my family's disintegration for my woes and wanderings, nor do I intend to justify self-pity and over-indulgence. Indeed, Tolstoy's famous opening line from *Anna Karenina* comes to mind: "All happy families are alike; each unhappy family is unhappy in its own way." It happened to be that this was the way it was for ours, too. In the meanwhile, I was far from the center point as I floundered with intention towards my future.

That summer, the summer of my sophomore year in college after I'd declared my major in Russian, I got a job in yarns at Westman, a job where I'd earn more money than I ever had before. I would also experience reverse discrimination from haughty and hardened blue-color women towards this college girl. I was also blessed with the friendship of an older woman named Terry Trent; she would be my guardian angel that summer and next. Unfortunately, and in the meanwhile, I learned to make sangria by the pitchers-full and had discovered Southern Comfort — long before I even knew the likes of the literary character Blanche Dubois. Oh, what comfort booze brought me, that and listening to *lots* of George Jones. If I knew I wasn't working the next day, I started to drink to the point of passing out. Terry Trent lived with her extended family, and like gypsies, they moved about every six months. Part Cherokee, Terry possessed a silent fortitude and capacity for endurance I'd not witnessed in my life. Little did I know that such strength came from her faith and not from her Native-American heritage. She was brown as a berry and crowned on the top with vigorous gray hair, and nearly daily, she would walk for hours on end just to have her own time to pray. It was hard to keep up with her whereabouts, but her wisdom, wry sense of humor, care for me, and essential groundedness were a balm, and I think that she was happy to have someone to talk to who took her seriously, valued her steadfastness, and respected her. I loved the mischievous look in her eye as she waited expectantly to see if I'd get the mirthful or ironic comment she'd just made. She taught the Old Testament in her church's Sunday School, and I found this rather awe-inspiring, so foreign was this realm to me. Often, she'd share stories about figures from the Bible with me as if she were talking about her relatives. No matter what else we might be doing, I'd be enrapt listening to her at such times. And as odd as it sounds, we also discovered in each other another who loved to visit graveyards. We'd find some unassuming marker and imagine the lives in the dash between the birth and death dates. When I'd come to pick her up to go for a ride, be it to an old graveyard, Cloudy State Park, or some used bookstore, her cigar-chomping brother would peer at me gruffly, as if to ask where I was taking her. Though a deeply devout woman, looking back, she never tried to evangelize to me; her life was a living testimony. She left my life as mysteriously as she came into it; her family moved once while I was away at school, and I never knew what became of her.

The quagmire of my parents' divorce, my floundering at school, and having no one I could turn to led to a whole host of poor choices on my part, though at the time, they seemed justified and not unacceptable. As I said, my drinking escalated during these summers. Phase one of my drinking had been during the typical teenage years of sneaking and experimenting, advancing next to more regular usage before intimacies, parties, or solo violin concerts. In college, phase two, my drinking graduated and got amped up because by then, I loved partying with others as a celebratory release that matched my energy within, be it with ruggers or fellow Russian majors. But in the summers in between school, home as I knew it no longer existed, and I was suspended in a limbo land of some blue funk. I watched my grieving father nearly lose his mind (and the rest of his hair) as my mother, in relief, found her life; therefore, I drank to quell my own pain and escape these turning tides. There was no longer such thing as one drink. Oh, how cluttered was my path, let alone unclear my future. What was I to do?

4.3 DAZED AND CONFUSED

As I flip back in my earlier years' annals, memories get jarred and then come back with haunting clarity. Referring to "the big D" of their divorce, my father would often crassly announce, "Your mother wants to quit at peak production," whereas my mother would say nearly nothing; her silence pregnant with meaning was deafening to me. It seemed that everyone but my dad could sense her loneliness and her current resolve to move on from that which, in her mind, couldn't be rectified or healed. Their divorce overlapped with the time I began my coming-of-age and legal drinking. But I digress. I have no intention of giving an account of my parents' failed marriage, so I will continue with where I ended up, which was majoring in Russian, and this would introduce me to the world of vodka. *This* would be my drink of choice. Like many, I loved drinking for how it made me feel inside, how it simultaneously calmed and enervated me, matching the rush of intensity within, but now, I had a new layer to add to its being pleasing to me. Surely, one of the better bonding experiences among us Russian students was to meet weekly at a local pub and hang out together informally at the university's sole Russian table. Here we would try our hand at speaking in Russian together and, in the process, build a warm camaraderie with one another. Upon occasion, even a professor or two would meet with us there. Many a Russian major was proud of his level of copious drinking that aligned with the vision of how we imagined "real Russians" might drink. Early on, I was already secretly aware that I had difficulty finding the off switch to my drinking, and once I began, more often than not, I lost the capacity to know when to quit or how to pace myself steadily. Majoring in Russian only added fuel to the fires in this respect. I'd get my studies done, and at my appointed times of the week, drinking would commence.

To begin with, I did not drink with abandon to oblivion. No one does. If I didn't mix too much and kept to beer and vodka only, I'd usually get to and maintain that happy drunk place. But that was a big *if*, and there was no counting on me. Like many a freshman, I tried all the pretty mixed drinks my freshman year, along with about 2,000 gallons of Miller Lite. I had already had several blackouts those first two years when I imbibed to complete saturation. Most of the time, thank goodness, I was in a safe place like my dorm or at a friend's home, but there were times I'd wake up in a stranger's house or another dorm and could only imagine or recoil at what might have happened the night before. I didn't know, and I didn't ask. Life proceeded as usual, with successes in school and satisfaction with both my academic and social choices. Yet I would unknowingly begin to lead a double life on several levels. Drinking made it easy to slip into a subterranean world of apparent glee and relief, but really, I was cutting myself off from both the world and my essential self. I felt split in two as I separated my public and private spheres: I held one set of values for my outer public self, utilizing all my energies toward achieving academic success and working toward attaining professional goals. On the other hand, my private sphere was chaotic and conflicted, and I was on lockdown and half unaware. I didn't know what the purpose of my life was. I lived freely, willfully, vibrantly, and oh, so carelessly. I didn't know what to make of God. That said, I had no deep, dark secrets, so I didn't feel like I was living a sham by not knowing what "it" was all about, as the "Hokey Pokey" song announces. I thought that once you declared your major, completed that goal, got a job pertaining to it, maybe had a family, that this was it: period, end of the story.

1Meanwhile, there persisted a driving pulse even deeper within me — one which I'm sure *every* person has — that repeatedly asked, "*Is this all there is?*" We shove that thought back for fear that either this might be the case, or worse, that we are more or less impotent, that we can't truly impact *our* world, let alone *the* world, and that in the end, cosmic entropy will swallow us up. Did I really ponder these things when I drank? No, not directly, but I ached from a desire to love, *be* loved, and to attain right *and* might. Honestly, my little world revolved around poor, poor pitiful me, and drinking got me stuck in whatever track of an album I put the needle on. And because I was able to keep up my double life while maintaining excellent grades and the self-discipline for working out, I thought I was able to do it all and have it all. And yet, there was undeniably *something* inside me, a something I just can't explain; it was similar to the static charge I would often feel running through me, but it was a *yearning for* <u>more</u>. I am sure this feeling I had is universal; it must be His light tap on our soul to get us out of and beyond ourselves. At the time, I never thought about drinking as a temptation or the means by which evil could get me maimed, incapacitated, or killed. It was just alcohol. And I took to drinking with the same intensity that I approached anything important to me; unbeknownst to me, the difference was that it only prolonged identity problems, promoted secrecy, and eroded my character. But more on that girl who got lost later on. I didn't know what "conviction" was or how I could make a full commitment to something, *someone* who'd I'd only imagined as being real.

I need to delve into the fragmented and disconnected parts of myself before I can eventually show how I came to myself unified and ready to serve the greater good and God. Some people drink so that they can lower their inhibitions; for me, it was to take a little bit of the edge off because I sometimes felt anxious inside to the point of being almost jittery with excess energy. I would attempt to channel, combat, or even enflame this intensity; in reality, drinking would just drown it and me. While I was in school, I justified my over-indulgence as my deserved and just reward for studying or working hard. Many do. I believed I would need an antidote just as vital to bring me down from my seriousness, too.

Drinking, of course, would also lead me to do all sorts of things I would not usually have done, not to mention prevented me from discerning aspects of myself I might have thought were ugly or in need of review, let alone desisting. I resisted claiming any one aspect of or singular identity from the many parts that I possessed because no one facet seemed sufficient or adequate in and of itself: I never felt whole, full, or complete, be it a *Greek* because I was only a so-called "half-breed," a typical *girl* because I certainly was not the type made of "sugar and spice and all that's nice," an *American* because I prided myself in having a healthy dose of ethnicity, or a *Christian* because, though a card-carrying, legitimized Greek Orthodox from infancy, I honestly believed that people of faith were at least partially delusional. The long and short of it was I didn't want to be pigeonholed, trapped, constrained, reduced, or labeled purely this *or* that! What has all this to do with drinking, you may ask? Well, as is the case with many, deep within, there were things about life and myself that I found perplexing with which I didn't know how to deal. I began drinking to fill in an emptiness I couldn't name. Not sure of anything, let alone myself, I tried to boost my sense of self-worth in my early high school years by latching onto my Greek heritage; I was confident that this part of me was something worth getting swept away by or involved in! In my early college days, like so many young women, I did *way* too much to feel loved, lovable, or desirable, all while under the influence. Oh, sure, I knew I was bright enough, studious, and talented in music, but most of the time, I felt like a weirdo, and I wasn't sure what to do with my uniqueness. I never fit in, and this sense of being different, or "terminal uniqueness," as I later heard it called, would lead me either to feeling prideful and self-centered or lonely and futile. I naturally gravitated toward the Greek in me. My father, a crypt where his own haunted and war-beleaguered past was concerned, didn't teach me Greek or take me to Greece, tearfully though I begged him. At least I persuaded him to take me on what would become our annual road trips around Thanksgiving to Brooklyn to see *his* parents and brother. Such concentrated Greekness I enthusiastically partook of there, and I sensed I was more like my paternal grandmother than I would ever come to know. I continued to seek pleasure and avoid pain; I had no moral compass of any integrity because north was never due north; I did what I thought was right for me. My experience is hardly unique! I am a reflection of our multi-faceted culture that condones and promotes myriad ways of looking at what is good, true, right, and fine. America says the individual is free to pick and choose anything, as long as no one gets (really) hurt; in short, *anything goes*. There is no sense of any standard, or if there is, it is often established on a superficial level such that it doesn't become a principle of lasting value or merit; the virtue becomes a sound byte. Later, I would contend with what I'd never done before: grapple with what *Scripture* bears as our foundation. Like not a few, I have felt hurt and rejected by being perceived as odd man out by church folks. I'm just grateful I never felt rejected by a hostile gavel-God. Later, coming to God would launch me into a new sense of wholeness and fullness of expanded self, all my parts and pieces integrated, unified, and filled with a Spirit I didn't even know existed. I'm jumping ahead too much. At the moment, thus far, I was proud of my charisma and accomplishments, never imagining there could be so much more.

As an adult, still possessing and not wanting to contend with all the fractured aspects within myself, I sought to quell what felt like electrical forces built up in me. Sometimes I drank because I didn't want to feel different. Sometimes I drank because I liked the feeling of fall in the air. I usually drank more for celebratory reasons than to drown my sorrows. As they say in A.A., I drank *"for every reason or no reason."* Though in the early years of my drinking, I was usually amusing and pleasant enough to be around, over some gray period, I got to be unpredictable in how I'd behave when intoxicated; I could get aggressive or volatile as quickly as syrupy sweet. My morals went out the window when I drank, but that's no shocker. With inhibitions lowered, I would, as the song says, "look for love in all the wrong places," hoping to find that right person out there who might love me for *me*. Again, this is unremarkable, but my drinking habits transformed over fifteen years from what they were in college days. My drinking went from starting up during the end of finals to indulging every weekend. Then I started drinking and driving after work on Fridays (putting a cooler with a six-pack of my favorite beer in the back seat with mournful classic country music cranked up), to then drinking when I had nothing pressing to do for the next weekday. I got to where I methodically planned my pre-drinking routine *before* regular social drinking commenced. I drank a couple of drinks beforehand, and then I would leave early to continue unhampered at home to where I would pass-out. Was I still working out, paying bills, and functioning at school? You betcha. Was I miserable deep inside? Undeniably. And for this, I take full responsibility. Drinking was slowly but surely altering, destroying the awesomeness of this unique person God created me to be, and I was utterly blind to it. When you love to drink, you always measure yourself by the person at the next rung or lower level you haven't stooped to yet, be it drinking in the morning, while at work, under a bridge, or whatever. This kind of self-justification is just the sort of lie that will get you to that low point and worse. Your friends know you're heading south fast and your family doubly so, but *life* has to have its way with you. I changed from being a social drinker to one who enjoyed and preferred drinking alone, where nobody could see me. Did this mean that I was not able to function? Absolutely not!

Work was still rewarding and going great, my passion for my students still strong. For health benefits and cheap therapy to decompress, I worked out like a fiend at least three days a week for a good block of time. Over a decade or so, my body started to speak to me in a way I hadn't experienced since earlier drinking days in Russia: the pit of my stomach began to burn from drinking too much; I secretly thought I might have an ulcer.

Somewhere about ten years into my career, when I was on autopilot at work, I met a new friend who became a drinking buddy. I'd drive through the mountains every weekend to visit this person, recklessly drinking the whole winding way and then nearly falling out of my car when I opened the door upon my arrival, music still blaring out of the speaker in the door. This friend, who initially drank more than I, got concerned about my drinking and driving. And though in the beginning, he was attentive, protective, and compassionate, little by little, I came to know a darker side to him. Now when we drank, instead of listening to and getting lost in some pleasing nostalgia of seventies soul music, we'd invariably nearly come to blows over nothing. It was a mystery to us how drinking took us to the edge of demise or bleakness of despair; we didn't even realize that alcohol was but the symptom of our problem. I'd always swear never again would I drink so much, only to break my promise to myself, get defeated and enraged at myself when it happened yet again, often later the same day! When we'd go past the point of no return in some alcohol-induced argument, his intense rage was met with my mockery and sarcasm, and the result was tears and embittered battles. Then the fun really began: the effects of my drinking didn't stay contained in my household. I was bouncing checks, I got pulled for passing a super slow car while driving with a beer buzz, I kept a wastebasket in the back floorboard of my back seat to toss my empty beer cans in, and perhaps the most damaging, I became the topic of scorn and shame among my family. They witnessed me go to drinking twice what I usually did — which was already a lot — so much so that when I came to visit my dad, he told me that he was in shock to see what he called such a "metamorphosis" in me and that I couldn't drink in his house anymore.

Additionally, after leaving from a visit with my second sister with whom I had gotten into yet another one of our catfights, she sent me a letter. In it, she informed me that though no one in the family felt like they could say anything directly to me because it was like walking on eggshells, she was going to tell it like it was: I drank too much, and I had become *"an extremist in thought and action."* I was so out of kilter; I resented her for trying or daring to correct me. That my drinking was getting out of control hadn't escaped my notice. I couldn't predict how much I would drink, but I could guarantee you I'd be drinking every weekend. If I hadn't essays to grade or a lesson to prepare, I began to drink *to get drunk* during the week, something that I swore that I would never do. Most times the next day, I'd be filled with remorse, self-loathing, and, again, a thousand promises to myself I wouldn't let it happen again, all but to break in a matter of days or hours and then feel all the worse. I sought relief from that elusive happiness and intense vigor which the first drink or two provides, and then I just kept at it, even when I didn't want to. Why, I might as well go ahead and finish that six-pack, might as well get another, might as well finish the bottle, I'd say to myself. Meanwhile, I was on fire in the classroom, so I thought things weren't really so bad. Come late Sunday afternoon, a time every teacher dreads, I was beginning to count loose change, even down to the penny, to be able to drink the remaining hours of my weekend away. I just didn't know what to do with my boredom, loneliness, inertia, and listlessness — I didn't know what to do with *myself*, and I couldn't face the void without my crutch. As I hadn't gotten in any trouble with the law or any institution, hadn't been forced to go to rehab or be hospitalized, didn't drink at work, and had maintained my responsibilities, I didn't think I could be a real alcoholic. I came to know only later, through others telling me subsequently, that I was now *regularly* having blackouts. I would often have *zero* recollection of what I'd said or done and even where I'd gone or been after about three drinks, and this was a *terrifying* reality to ponder. I became obsessed over making up my own private rules for drinking, including what kind, where, and when, and all sorts of methods for curtailing or stopping, all to no avail. This, in turn, would lead to demoralization, resignation, and utter despair. Something had to change, or I'd be a soon be a goner.

4.4 My Unmanageable Life and a First Step

Though I often felt helpless and hopeless, I was still in denial about my *real* problem because I hadn't lost my job or home or health. It can't be *that* bad, right? One Saturday morning, after about my hundredth time waking up nauseated and feeling surreal, out-of-the-blue, I up and decided to try an A.A. meeting. Nothing I'd done had worked before, so it couldn't hurt just to go and sit in a meeting; I was expecting it to be a cult of sorts, but I'd nothing to lose. I hadn't showered from being at some bar the night before, and I had two watches on. Don't ask me how this happened. I knew I needed to stop, and I came to realize that *I couldn't do it by myself*. With nothing but failures in my corner, I somehow drove myself to my first meeting, still bleary from the night before. Anyway, I knew it was a safe place in these rooms, and hot coffee awaited me. So, in January of 1996, I picked up my first white chip and started to go to A.A. regularly. I was surprised at how much my mind had gotten used to turning to the elixir of alcohol and instant relief after a week of school. Until *you* stand all day in front of a large group of expectant young faces — some eager and expectant, some bored and detached, some ornery, some mentally a thousand miles away — day in and day out, you cannot appreciate the *need* to physically decompress *and* restore after you have expended your soul's energy. If you do it right, teaching is exhausting and all-consuming, yet you cannot imagine or desire any other way for doing so, results evidential and measurable or not. My career was more than a job; teaching *is* my life's calling, compelling and gratifying. I am vexed that I ever used to my want to unwind to justify and provide an excuse to keep up my habit and desire to drink. I sought to reward myself with something tangible, even though we serve the greater good for the intrinsic gain of (hopefully) positively impacting lives. I know I'm called to do it; it comes naturally, joyfully, and meaningfully, but at this particular time in my life, my way of restoring myself was through flooding myself with a liquid panacea, like an alkaline to my acid. Parenthood is the marathon of raising your one or two or five offspring; teaching is the 50-yard dash, after dash, after dash of leading twenty or thirty kids *not* related to you.

Not to drink on the weekends wasn't a thought or consideration; I didn't know what to do with myself in the state I'd invariably find myself in by Friday: *spent*. I remember when I first started going to A.A. meetings on Friday evening *directly after I worked out*. I would stay there until the 8:00 meeting started because I knew I wasn't safe with myself: left to my own devices, I knew I would drink otherwise. I always tried to sit next to an old lady who went by "Alice" and would say with a twinkle in her eye, "I'm a *real* alcoholic." I even remember once holding her hand tightly through a whole Friday night meeting because I was shaking, knowing that alcohol was out there a few steps away, just waiting for me, and I knew I'd head straight for it if I left. I was afraid of myself. It took me about six *months* to even get to thirty days of continuous sobriety. I would pick up white chips at different locales because I was ashamed to keep picking up a white chip in front of my homegroup. I just kept messing up. Even though I had enough white chips to string together to make a necklace, no one ever gave me a look of scorn; no one ever chided me. In fact, there and only there at these meetings was the first place I didn't get judgment. I was relieved and amazed to find warmth, laughter, acceptance, earnestness, and singleness of purpose; we all knew the stakes we were dealing with, and condemnation and self-loathing were not the means to success in sustaining sobriety. Every meeting ended with a vocalized note of encouragement through the simple secret to abstinence: it's a one-day-at-a-time affair. Though we opened with the well-known Serenity Prayer, we closed with the Lord's Prayer, and then, eyes closed and hands extended and holding those of my neighbors, I'd actually imagine I was talking to *Him*. This was a first. Our mantra was "keep comin' back; it works if you work it, but you gotta work it every day." You'd always see people staying longer to chat together in pairs; heads were bent together in confidential and candid talk. When I *finally* made it to thirty days and picked up my yellow chip, it seemed ridiculous, but the "thirty days and a thousand nights" of *not* drinking were as real and vital to me as any accomplishment or accolade I'd earned thus far. Who knew that I was on my way to receiving a gift *not* of my own doing?

Many clichés, phrases, and pearls of wisdom come from people in A.A. that help one make it through difficult and tempting moments in life. Initially, I thought these were blasé platitudes, just sayings for people who were too weak or incapable of holding or getting it together for themselves independently. But I soon came to realize that *I was such a person*. And though I couldn't wrap my mind around why I drank too much, it was an undeniable reality. I *needed* to contend with it. And though I didn't know what makes one person an alcoholic and another person *not*, I did know that alcoholism, whenever or however or *if* ever it commences, invariably leads to other health afflictions, including the terrifying prospect of cutting short one's life. I had reached that white-flag moment where I *knew* that I couldn't continue in this way because there just was no controlling my drinking no matter how hard I tried, no matter what method I'd adopted, or no matter which self-help book I'd read to make it go away; in fact, the thing only got worse. Little did I know at the time that once I quit drinking, not only would my thinking get cleared up, but sobriety would pave the way for my core self to mature in a way that I never imagined possible. I didn't realize how self-centered I'd become! I think many people have no idea about the capacity for growth within them if they could only rid themselves of impediments and mental fixtures. Initially, I went to probably two, maybe three A.A. meetings a week. The love I felt in these rooms echoed in my heart when I was away from them, and I began to smile more easily as I listened more intently to the "experience, strength, and hope" I heard from my fellow anonymous friends of Bill W.

Soon after I began attending A.A. meetings with some regularity and picking up my six-month and "piece of the sky" blue chip, I met a woman, or should I say, she came up and introduced herself to me. She would forever change my life. Sensing a kinship in our personality and background, Rebecca Nelson, took a vested interest, tucked me under her wing, and became my sponsor. Like me, she adored her father, but we were not the sons our fathers had wanted. Like me, she was ethnic in a W.A.S.P.-y sea; only she was Jewish. Like me, she could be larger-than-life and was passionate about much. All these underlying factors contributed to her becoming an alcoholic, but we were dissimilar in that she now knew better than to waste one precious minute of life. We recognized that we were kindred spirits, that we had that same thing in our cores that made us tick the way we did. She reminded me of Liza Minnelli. She chose to focus on our love for our fathers, and she said to accept and let go of the facts that kept me stuck, which included believing that I couldn't fulfill my dad's old-world dreams or measure up to my mother's perfectionistic standards. Trying to perform well enough produced an audible incantation within me that drummed over and over: "Whatever I do, it's *not enough*. Nothing's enough. It's *never* enough. I'm not *good* enough. Nothing matters. *I* don't matter." This is the secret tape I play inside my head.

Over time, Rebecca got under my skin, made her into my heart, and gently prodded me to evaluate my *character*. Once we had arranged to meet at TCBY, I got there about 10-15 minutes late. No excuses, I was just plain old late. Without missing a beat or losing her cool, she called me out on it. She told me that when I'm late, I lose my credibility because my word of saying I'd be there wasn't good. In effect, I was implying that her time isn't valuable. She wasn't nit-picky or hateful, just lovingly instructive. She never brought this up to me again, and she never again had to. This and many other seemingly trivial moments I began to address and correct, such that over time, I started to gain back some trust and respect I hadn't even realized I'd lost with my family, let alone within myself. We would go out to eat after meetings, and I would share with her, for example, my early lusting after the wine that people at some nearby table were drinking. Without batting one of her very mascaraed eyes, she'd just calmly say, "Play it through, Dimi, all the way through," and I'd play that tape in my mind fast forward to the part where my drinking hurt me. Then all the "whys" began: Why couldn't I drink like ordinary people? Why did I have to finish not one, but all I'd bought? Why couldn't a hangover teach me? Why was I able to drink in a controlled fashion one day and with complete abandon the next? And then came all the "hows." How would I spend my free time, celebrate, wind down, or deal with and face boredom or pain? How was I going to fill that hole, that void, that longing? How would I conduct myself with that aspect of me now a near ghost? Thank goodness that the only criterion for attending an A.A. meeting is the *desire* to stop drinking!

Further, I certainly didn't want to admit I was an alcoholic or buy into the theory that this was some disease I had. I certainly didn't want to add *that* to the list of different identities that I possessed. I could drive myself crazy trying to psychoanalyze the genetic factors, developmental choices, and family dynamics. Rebecca told me that ultimately, none of this was essential because I had already repeatedly proven that "one drink was too many and a thousand were never enough" for me. I knew she was right, and to focus on anything but my own sobriety would derail me. The fact that it had become abundantly clear that there was something not right or normal about how I drank became enough for me to get started quitting before I inadvertently finished myself off too soon. Labels didn't matter to me as much as my life did. I didn't want to die for squabbling over semantics. The only brass fact I could state about my drinking was that it had progressed — seemingly of its own accord — throughout my adulthood, and Rebecca gingerly, yet firmly helped me realize that *there was a better way to live*. I started to read *Alcoholics Anonymous: The Big Book,* and she urged me to read out loud, over and over again "The Promises" for hope's sake, which I can still say nearly verbatim now. Later, I would learn of promises that were to be found in the "*big* Big Book," A.A.'s way of referencing the Bible.

Next, Rebecca had me start my fourth step, where I was "to make a list of the people that I had harmed" with my drinking. This particular step makes it obvious you aren't so disconnected or independent in your drinking; what you do *does* matter as you *do* impact others. To help me get started, I listened to her account, her story on a cassette tape, which she had presented earlier at a speaker meeting. Doing a fourth step is opposite the approach that psychiatrists and therapists typically take. The conventional wisdom of such trained professionals is to scour your past and find incidents where other people had done things hurtful *to* you, so for me to take ownership and focus on what wrongs *I* had done to *others* was brand new. Sure, she said, acknowledge the deleterious incident, but do not linger. There is no time or place for the debilitating indulgence of self-pity, let alone finger-pointing; otherwise, I'd never have stopped drinking for all the remaining reasons *to* drink. Oh, no, the buck stopped here with me. Once I completed this process, one that also involved my confessing or revealing the transgressions on my list to another person, I could go from victim to victor. Rebecca also then showed me that there are other things to do to have fun besides drink. That was a shocker. She invited me to come over to her house to paint plates, and she'd later fire them up and give them to me. Sometimes there would be several women at her kitchen table talking it up, drinking iced tea, listening to the radio, and jamming to painting our plates. All of us were getting lost in an activity outside ourselves, yet very much taking care of ourselves. Little did I know at the time that this initiation of clearing my head and my *body* of the poisons would help purify my *inner* sanctum to ready myself to invite a King into my life. She also taught me that when I sit in meetings and listen to strangers' stories, I should look for *similarities*, not differences among people. Despite my professional accomplishments and worldly successes, there remained unexplored galaxies within me which I needed to explore to be enabled to become all of what I still yet could be, hopefully, a wiser, sober, and better version of myself. This meta-cognition or self-examination coupled with A.A.'s maxim of "letting go and letting God" got me out of my own way such that I became enabled and ready to meet face-to-face to "the Man" that made and saved me.

4.5 Relapse and More

The longer I attended A.A. meetings and stayed sober, the more I began to retrain my brain to treat people and handle life situations in a different manner than I had before. Oh, where had the time gone for it to have come to this? For all how I kept to myself, I couldn't have noticed the decline in my ethics and values, but over time, the bad seeps out in all we do: our finances, our relations with loved ones, our work, and how we view God if we even do at all. At its core, drinking is a spiritual affliction, and even behind closed doors, there's no escape from yourself doing what you think no one knows what you're doing. *You are everywhere you go*, and if you have developed a problem with drinking, the relief you gulp down is illusory and transitory. You can never go back to the glory days of your first high; oh, it's a lie. All of what I tell you now is how it went down with me. Change doesn't happen overnight. I began searching, seeking, and finding nuggets of wisdom more precious than gold in these meetings. One old-timer told me out in the parking lot of my home group A.A. meeting place, "*It takes what it takes, but it doesn't have to!*" I didn't *have* to get to the point in my career of drinking where such and such *might* happen so that I would be *forced* to stop. All I knew was that if I didn't get sobered up, I'd get "locked up or covered up," plain and simple. Now *that's* a stark and sobering fact. There were many other firsts that initial year of sobriety: going to family holidays and even a trip to Russia I'd planned with students that summer of '96. How in the world was I going to go to Russia and not drink? Rebecca entrusted me with her Big Book to keep as a sort of security blanket. Though I had my own by that time, she wanted me to know that she'd be there with me and *believed in me* and that this was proof of her love and faith in me. That was huge for me! So, there I was in Moscow, carrying her well-worn *Big Book* in a faux leopard-skin cover that was *so* not me, reading it on the plane and every night before I went to sleep. Rebecca Nelson really loved me, and I could sense her affection. I think it was her belief in me that I could become better in a way I'd never imagined before, which tilted my direction back on course. And though she was hilarious and one of the most generous people I've ever met, her TLC and my valiant efforts did *not* keep me sober. No person ever can. And there's the whole crux and paradox of surrender: you become empowered when you relinquish the control you never had. After fourteen months of sobriety, a good friend, Kimberly, and I were at my father's place, and we were playing tennis in the sweltering heat and had gotten very thirsty, so she simply issued the fateful words, "You're a grown *adult*! You can have <u>a</u> drink anytime you want! What's the worst that could happen?" So, I had that drink, a nice, cold, big-as-I-could-find bottle of Heineken, and, sure enough, nothing happened. Then. That day. I began to stop going to meetings and avoided Rebecca, but she would call and tell me it didn't matter if I was drinking. She didn't want me not to phone her, and would I please check in? Did I do that? No, I was so ashamed of myself that I withdrew again, this time even more. I did not stop drinking then or anytime soon, but it took less than a year for me to know I needed to come back, and it was for good when I did so then.

Meanwhile, in the fall preceding the new millennium, Kimberly started losing weight, and she had a stubborn sore throat that just wouldn't get better, no matter that she went to the Instant Clinic three times seeking treatment. The last time I remembered looking down the back of her throat, it looked like she'd swallow a quart of maraschino cherries! That New Year's Eve, she came in stumbling drunk as I'd never seen her, but she just kept saying she'd shared only one bottle of wine. Now I will flash-forward to March 6, 2000, the day Kimberly, 39, was diagnosed with acute myelogenous leukemia. The day her oncologist told her this jolting fact, she wasn't permitted to go home. He'd already checked her into for treatment that evening in the hospital across the street. We sat stuck in our seats and frozen in that moment; it seemed like forever, and his voice going from clear and clinical to a blur of noise in the background as this death knell news settled in us. The regimen of her first treatment of chemotherapy began right away that day. She and our friend, Faye, and I left his office and plopped down on a bench in front of the hospital where Kimberly would spend the next three months. In a mind-bending torpor, each of us said we wanted the relief our vice might bring us: Faye wanted chocolate, Kimberly was dying for a cigarette, and I just wanted a beer. Not a week after she was finally released from there, one season later, even sicker than before, she was admitted to a hospital in another state and would receive a bone marrow transplant.

From that March until June, I'd make a bee-line from work to the hospital to spend every afternoon with Kimberly, who would end up undergoing three chemotherapy regimens, each one successively more rigorous than the last and each time producing no positive results. Every night, just before I'd arrive home, spent and empty, I'd buy myself some beers. That June of 2000, I canceled my tour with students to Russia because, at this time, she was scheduled to receive a bone marrow transplant from her sister, the one whose blood, as her oncologist put it, "looked to be a good match." During this entire crisis, I drank almost daily, feeling empty and powerless inside, like I was in a non-stop daze of some sort. Though I had relapsed, I did revisit reading Chapter 4 of *Alcoholics Anonymous*, the one specifically entitled "We Agnostics." I couldn't believe that there could be such a chapter in there for *me*. I don't even think I was an agnostic, but I did not nor could not claim or be pigeonholed into accepting any particular religion.

I've always had some idealized version of what it meant to be Greek Orthodox, but I didn't pretend to say I knew what all was entailed in this belief system. I went to the Greek Easter service, which I was always moved by, but that was about it. A.A. would address my "terminal sense of uniqueness," and I came to like and continued to use the slogans and phrases that I'd heard A.A. meeting. When I first got there, A.A. seemed like some old cult, which focused on ideals from yesteryear. I then realized that I had no such simple, let alone *any* sound framework by which *I* was living, one that was authentic, practical, *and* good for life. The easy laughter and amiability among people with whom I would never have had reason to interact in my everyday life conversed with one another earnestly, openly, and intently. Somewhere deep down, they each and all know that their very life depended upon it. I just hadn't hit my bottom before; fortunately, I was not that "low bottom" drunk. Going to A.A. will mess up your drinking if you go back "out there," and this was indeed (and thankfully) the case for me. Looking back on my first successful take of not drinking, I also stewed over remembering how I was unwilling to talk about *anything* dealing with religion! In fact, I resented those times in A.A. when people had so-called gratitude meetings. I certainly did not feel grateful; I felt out of control and plain ol' resentful that I couldn't drink like other people! I couldn't imagine, for example, walking away from half of a glass of wine still left. If I were drunk enough, I might even finish someone's unfinished drink on my way out. It's not something that I'm proud of — and that is hardly a drop in the bucket of what wrongs I'd done, but later, I did become grateful that I hadn't killed another or myself, let alone declined any further. I realized that I could not attribute sobriety to just my own doing; I could not take credit for what was enabled or made possible from something beyond me.

4.6 "God as We Understood Him"

Once you have accepted that you can't manage your drinking, the second two steps of A.A. are life-altering. They are the ones that get you outside of yourself. I come back to these early steps even while I'm telling you about the interrupted months of relapse to show you that these principles got under my skin and didn't leave me. They continued to silently goad me all the while I was swilling down liquor until that time that I finally returned, and it's these principles I'll continue to share with you as they remained in me. Steps two and three of A.A. combined say that we "came to believe that *a Power greater than ourselves* [emphasis mine] could restore us to sanity and that we made a decision to turn our will and our lives over to the care of God as we understood Him." That we "came to believe" permitted me to process this on my own and in my own good time and fashion; nobody was telling or forcing me what or in whom to believe! Their whole notion of a "higher power" was alluring to me because it was positive and real but unimposing. This approach to God by recording and *underlined* "God as we understand Him" in their literature certainly was one of *the* most significant contributing factors to my *continuing* to go to A.A. This brought a great deal of freedom *and* safety that was vital to me. And nobody was going to shove Jesus down my throat *here*! Nobody was going to tell me that I was going to Hell and that I was on some wrong path.

One time during the first month of my first fourteen months of being sober, back when I was white-knuckling it, there was a meeting during which a man used "Jesus Christ" to describe his God. I nearly threw a fit! What was *Jesus* doing here!? I walked out of that meeting because I didn't want to have *anything* that smacked of Christianity or any organized religion there. I wanted a trustworthy place where it was okay to talk about *anything* without the fear that someone might pipe up and even imply that I was heading south fast or that they had the only solution to going about the business of living life. I was so *en garde*! How little I appreciated A.A.! How little I knew about God! Most people in A.A. will tell you that they are "spiritual" and not "religious." I would come to learn later on that many people felt betrayed or damaged by the church. My hostile reaction to this man had nothing to do with God or even Christ; it had to do with being afraid of contending with people's judgment, scorn, and what seemed like a self-contented presumptuousness of being in the right. As time went on, I began to have my favorite people whom I could listen to or gain wisdom from in those meetings, and I would surely share as well. The first go around, I didn't think I had anything of merit to share, let alone the right to talk, but this isn't how things work there. Everyone knows he's just one drink away from being a newcomer again. We *all* needed reminding so that the holocaust might not repeat itself. Therefore, I knew that I needed to share my feelings because if I did, it might help *me* not to drink. After all, my drinking nearly always meant doing so to excess, and by doing so, I would put myself and others in jeopardy more and more. The bottom line is that *I didn't want to die*, and I certainly didn't want to kill anybody either.

Meanwhile, back in mid-September, during my near.y year-long relapse, I was driving back from eating a homemade meal at my brother's. He had just moved to Mullivanville a month before to pursue his MBA, and I had gotten toasted with him. This wasn't out of the ordinary. Driving home that night, it began to rain hard and steady. No biggie. The next thing I knew, less than two miles from my house, I lost control of my car going around a bend, and it flipped and careened upside-down in a ravine. A large branch punctured the top of my car straight through the sunroof, and the end of it thrust through. I found myself staring at it in shock, as it was just inches away from my head. I managed to open my car door while upside down and snaked my way up the ravine to find a man standing there who asked me if I was all right. I said that I thought so. Minutes later, I saw the dreaded blue flashing lights arrive, and the cop, a young man, asked me the fateful question, *"Have you been drinking?"* I didn't lie or even quantify the stock reply of "two beers"; I focused on being over-the-top respectful to him. Now I was *really* scared. When he asked me to step over to the side of the road, walk in a straight line, recite the alphabet backward, then lean back with my arms extended out to the side and touch my nose alternately with the fingertip of each hand. I felt like I was doing circus tricks in a mind-boggling dream. When he learned that I was a teacher, I recall him saying he would *give me a break* in hopes that I would learn my lesson. Grateful, I nodded with my whole head, soul, and body! Before he took me to my house, I shimmied on my belly in the mud back into my car to retrieve my school things and briefcase; I couldn't forget *that*! It wouldn't be until a month later that I would quit for good. That final night of drinking, I knew it would be my last, and I purposefully bought a six-pack of my favorite beer along with a package of clove cigarettes. Standing out on my back porch, the air around me thick in smoke and silent stars twinkling brightly above, an ice-cold lager saturating my blood and being, I knew beyond any doubt that this was my last lap. The next day I picked up (yet another) white chip, but for me, this was different than before, when I'd pick up white chips at various meetings for not staying sober thirty straight days. Now, none of that mattered; my pride had proven vain and deadly. I was welcomed back with open arms and that knowing look of compassion with *no judgment* from these steadfast men and women, these strangers who somehow knew me. I'd *now* have to reestablish credibility within *myself* before this return could be made known to my family and friends. During the first eighteen months of sobriety, I realized in stark frankness that I'd only been holding my breath, or "white-knuckling it," as they say. Sponsorship did and does help, but I still hadn't reached my white flag moment of total abandon. A rebellious and prideful streak in me didn't like the idea that my freedom would be taken away, but I had just proven again that *controlled drinking didn't work*. What good is freedom if it leads to bondage? I was a broken woman in need of healing.

In the meanwhile, during that epoch of relapse, while Kimberly was getting her treatments, I became acquainted with a friend of hers whowould come with steadfast devotion every week to visit her in the hospital. Her name was Bonnie, and once while she was visiting, I recalled overhearing her tell a friend on the phone in private that I was a two-fisted power drinker. What had become of me? Where and who was my higher power anyway? Was I finally ready "to turn my will and my life over to God"? My sources *then* had said, "unlikely," and I paid the price as I just described above, but I *was* given another chance, both by that young cop and apparently by God. Returning to A.A. with my tail tucked between my legs, I started again, only with a readiness and bare determination unlike before. There was no shame in surrender.

4.7 A Death and Rebirth

I want to linger and focus on Bonnie, whom I would grow to love and with whom I would spend a significant part of my life. It is during my friendship with her that I would come to find Christ. At the time, we were taking care of Kimberly. Our closeness came about slowly, unexpectedly, but surely; our bond was founded on mutual respect and single-mindedness in how we each saw about caring for Kimberly. I also marveled at Bonnie's love of nature, her capacity for endurance, her readiness for humble serving, her wisdom about human nature and motives, her always looking at the bigger picture, her kind nature and genuineness, and her gift of healing. In short, she is a giver and a lover. Bonnie suffered from clinical depression, and this depression was a discernable reality. I came to accept that this melancholic match for my sanguine and choleric nature was a natural yin-yang fit. For her to drive three hours and look after Kimberly was a miracle in and of itself, but her loyalty was stronger than her affliction. We were to begin a journey of companionship, the likes of which I had never known before and one that would know no end.

Long before she'd envisioned arriving with a knapsack on her back and standing on the front stoop of my front door, circumstances came to be that Bonnie made her way up my steep driveway, having moved to South Carolina for good. This little dream would be the first act of faith made in years on her part, and such a change was to be transformative for me as well. Who knew that establishing our friendship here and now would pan out to an infinitesimally more meaningful path in that we would become sisters in Christ? Not only that but in Bonnie's support of my not drinking, she, too, decided to join me in sober living, never realizing that this would not be as easy as she thought because it involves a radical change in mindset, not to mention lifestyle. In fact, it was only after a few months of not picking up a single drink that she realized she, too, had a problem with not relying on the crutch of mind-altering substances when in an emotional pinch or some psychic lurch. She would be just a week shy of getting her own 1-year chip when she relapsed, but after this, she, like I, realized the vital importance of keeping vigilant in sobriety; our lives depended on it, and we came not to want to miss a second of life for muddying the waters. As would become evident to us later, through choosing to maintain the way of a teetotaler and with a clear-headed presence of mind, we were unknowingly preparing ourselves for the readiness it takes to accept love and purpose the likes of which we'd never known.

It isn't hard to guess, and there's no sense in being coy or evasive here: we would come to know Jesus. Getting to that point may offer a token of commonality or familiarity to someone else out there who also may be subconsciously seeking Him. By bolstering ourselves at the core, we enabled ourselves to sense or to hear the prompting of the Spirit. When drunk, high, or in an altered frame-of-mind, you've debilitated yourself and impeded your capacity for connectedness, value, purpose, and a love you never fathomed possible before. Oh, I suppose it would seem like a shoo-in to some: first, I got sobered up, then, all of a sudden, I got religion. Only the wry cynic would quip such a reductive deduction; such a stance would expose how limited his powers of perception, yet all the while, he'd think he'd had it all figured out. I should like to add that Bonnie had always been reluctant to talk about anything dealing with church or God, a puzzlement to me since I loved to discuss theological matters. The two were not the same. I had a cerebral attraction to religion, but Bonnie's early experiences in the church were not warm and fuzzy. She'd later come to describe how talking about church, and God evoked a kind of P.T.S.D. in her. So as not to push God out completely, when no one else was present, every now and again, we would enter the local Greek Orthodox sanctuary, first, because it was always open for people to worship, and secondly, because it felt like an acceptable compromise in that this church was distant enough from her roots to be a safe place of private worship for her; for me, I felt a primal connection to this church though I really didn't know Jesus. Here we came to a truce and a commitment; it was the perfect place for us to start a friendship.

After school let out, Bonnie and I would attend to Kimberly, who by this time had been released from her recovery period after her bone marrow transplant, but she had had *so* many complications that she was placed back in the hospital. She wasn't doing well at all. By then,

Bonnie and I were each accustomed to finding and sleeping in hospital chairs that reclined into narrow beds. We lived like gypsies inside those hospital halls, scavenging for towels, blankets, pillows, and such, but we knew that this final stay would be the last; here would commence a death vigil. All of Kimberly's relatives were there except for Veronica, her eldest sister. When she flew in from California and stepped into Kimberly's hospital room, her siblings and parents made a ring around her bedside like an icon of Jesus surrounded by His Disciples at the Last Supper. Her family emanated from around her head like a holy crown. Even as measures were started to make her feel comfortable, she miraculously arose from joy in seeing her sister walk into her crowded room. The only words Kimberly spoke after that were to her father: "*Take me home*, daddy. Please, *I just want to go home.*" There was not a dry eye in the room, for we all knew where her "home" would soon be. We buried Kimberly on a clear, bright, and bitterly cold day in February. We spotted a lone hawk flying overhead during the funeral, observing us in the family cemetery her father had worked tirelessly to complete just the summer before. Despite the pain and loss, everyone was prayerful and hopeful; death was the end. Later, I would see that my time spent with Bonnie would lead both of us to our Heavenly Father. But first, slowly, but surely, we would need to till the soil, clear the weeds, and realize who we were and what we were not. And so, we began going to A.A. meetings *together*, something that would shift the direction of our identity and purpose.

4.8 SHIFTING SANDS WHILST UNAWARE

With taking care of Kimberly finished for good and with Bonnie now living in the same town as I, we almost didn't know what to do with ourselves in this open vista of time stretching out before us. What ended up drawing us closer together was that in choosing a life of sobriety, we put ourselves in a different standing with our friends who didn't know how to relate to us as sober. Admittedly, it was odd and new for us too. Having been given a second chance at sobriety, I took following the steps of A.A. with all due gravity this time. Fear became my teacher as I realized I could not only lose my job and home but my very life. At the time, what was to become of my eternal soul wasn't even a thought for me. I had no idea that re-taking this first step would lead some thirteen years later to a very different path. I couldn't have anticipated that the physical action of ceasing drinking would so impact the totality of my values. I just didn't want to hurt or to feel demoralized anymore. Little did I know that this round, I would experience a seismic change in how I viewed the world. And like Henry David Thoreau said in his cabin stay at Walden, I wanted to "put to rout all that was *not* life. I wanted to live deeply and suck the marrow out of *life*." I did not want to choke on the bone or die.

This second time of getting sober, I would get a *new* sponsor, and she and I would take long walks together in a beautiful and wooded park. She recommended that, along with *The Big Book*, I read other books, one of which was called *Conversations with God*. I did a fifth step with her after the completion of my fourth step that I did with Rebecca. The fourth step of taking a moral inventory puts the burden of accountability square on that individual's shoulders, but one without guilt or shame. In the fifth step, things got real for me because I had to *confess* and *rid* myself of ills by "admitting to God, to ourselves, and to another human being the exact nature of our wrongs." I began to live with the mindset of trying to maintain a "rigorous honesty." How else could I get better? I took this to mean being on-call for self-examination, scrutiny, and self-assessment; it was not a chance to blast or license to blame others for my so-called woes. All this translated to the fact that I was slowly but surely beginning to change spiritually and foundationally. Again, at that time, I was still resistant to ingesting anything related to religion in terms of staking some claim *for myself*, but I did have a burgeoning curiosity and a fascination about it more than in the usual academic sense. It's as if the A.A. program itself was just another first step. In wonderment, in that second go-round of sobriety, I had heard that my first sponsor, Rebecca, Jewish by birth, heritage, and faith, had since begun to attend a Christian church. Then, not even six months later, on her way to a Bible study class, she suffered a massive heart attack and died! In shock over this sucker-punch loss, I also marveled at her shifting allegiance to the church, and yet I somehow also knew that this could not just be some accident. That she converted to *Christianity* and pretty much stopped going to A.A. meetings struck me powerfully. What she'd learned in A.A. never left her; she was want for more is all. How I loved her. As I said, my next sponsor took on a different role in my life; she nurtured me less but came to expect more from me. With gentle care, she delicately probed and asked me all sorts of questions dealing with my motive, intent, and purpose for doing this and that. She was to my mind what Rebecca was to my heart.

Thankfully, one month after my car wreck, I stopped drinking for good the October before Bonnie moved to South Carolina that following January. I *had* to stop because to lie to others is one thing; it gets real when you lie to oneself *and know it*, and I hadn't even factored in God taking note, let alone caring. Some months after this, though it didn't take, I suggested to Bonnie that *instead* of going to our A.A. meeting, perhaps we could consider trying out some mutually agreed-upon church. She wouldn't even consider doing this because it brought to her mind fear and trepidation. Listening to more than two gospel music songs in a row made her want to change the station. Religion was such a mixed bag because Bonnie's granny, a beacon in her life and source of goodness and Christian love, prayed for Bonnie until her dying day, and when she died, Bonnie said she recalled and wondered to herself, "*Who would pray for her now?*" Yet, the rest of the topic of Christianity led to a dark place for her, so I let it go. Case closed.

In the meanwhile, we kept on going to A.A. every week. Some of the sayings in A.A. — and there are so many — became stays for me, lifelines to crossing over planks which led me further away from dissolution, danger, and dereliction. I often said them that I knew them like Scripture: "One drink is too much because a thousand are never enough" was a favorite. Another one that helped me not to take even one drink was to "play the tape all the way through to the end" so that I wouldn't just romanticize that first alluring drink. Even this second time back, I wasn't convinced I was a so-called *real* alcoholic. I only seemed to see the differences that convinced me I *wasn't* an alcoholic: I still hadn't been arrested; I hadn't lost my job, family, or home; and I hadn't been to rehab. I wasn't some old man living under a bridge! I didn't drink in the morning or at work! *These* are the types of lies we tell ourselves that entrench a mindset of denial, self-pity, and self-justification.

Regardless, I was still dubious over the disease concept: there was no way to verify or prove you were such until the effects of drinking had wreaked enough havoc on your body to the point that it was impacted. Does one cause or activate one's own disease, or is it just a predisposition playing itself out before one becomes aware? All these were mind games I didn't know I'd been playing with myself, which kept me from soaring to higher vistas and achieving a deeper personal growth. In short, it doesn't matter which comes first, the chicken or the egg; it was time to quit drinking, and ultimately, labels or diagnoses didn't matter. I didn't want to die for arguing over wording! So, I got over myself and finally put on blinders such that these inner-debates didn't dissuade me or hamper me from reaching the last two steps of the program. These two proclaim we are to "improve our conscious contact with God" to the point of having "a spiritual awakening." There is no graduating, but I finally got to a point where I wanted to help others! Finally, I was living my way out of the swamp of self-pity I'd been moping about in. But by far, *the* most profound bi-product of my going to A.A. was my *"coming to believe"* in a higher power. The gerund, "coming," is a verbal, which implies an active and ongoing process necessary for the cessation of drinking to take a firm and lasting hold. At the time, I hadn't any thought of the devil or wicked, evil forces swaying me, but I was introduced to alcohol described as *"cunning, baffling, and powerful."* Later, as a Christian, I heard the devil described as a "thief" whose whole job was to *"steal, and kill, and destroy"* my very life (John 10:10). I would put two and two together and realize that imbibing in any enticing drink was taking the devil's bait to lead me to my demise so that I would neither find nor look for Jesus. The devil wants me dead, in any shape, fashion, or form. His enticing logic worked before, but no more. The fact that someone like me could stop drinking showed me that it took a "power" greater than myself to accomplish *lasting* sobriety. To do so through the sheer efforts of willpower and self-discipline, herculean as I thought them to be, was not sustainable. The Promises of A.A., cited at the beginning of this chapter and etched in my memory forever, became my anthem of hope. I wanted more than anything to be "happy, joyous, and free" for *life*, and over a decade of attending A.A., I began to see these promises come to fruition.

4.9 A New Millennium

Bonnie and I innocently began on this path of sobriety and righteousness with discoveries and challenges yet in store. I'm grateful that this would be both an individual *and* joint venture as we could bolster each other when the goings weren't easy. There are *so* many things that I respect about Bonnie. In spite of the fact that she had had a mental break *and* a heart attack, despite her tenderness and sensitive nature, she would be one of the strongest women I would ever come to know; her wisdom seemed without bounds. So, I can *talk* — big whoopee. I would always reassure her that I may know *words*, but she spoke *truth*. And there's nothing she couldn't do or hadn't done vocationally, proving herself a perfect complement to my being more academically focused. I would joke that we ought to have a 14-month calendar highlighting all the different things that she had been or done to illustrate the various jobs she'd held. She was or had been a guitar player, a labor and delivery LPN, a roofer, a carpenter's helper, a waitress, a worker in the state park, and many others that I can't recall right now. She designed and built her own house, for heaven's sake! However, the greatest of her innate talents is that she is a healer. And unlike me, who often can't find my way back to my hotel room from the lobby or know which way to turn after getting off the interstate to get gas, Bonnie was born with an internal grid and never got lost. She was always that one at Christmas who could and would assemble the toys that needed such. This sense of centeredness about her I would come to value inestimably and depend upon greatly. She is eternally patient, kinder than anybody I know, and possesses a genuine love for the poor and the scorned. She is a rocker of babies.

Bonnie's way of thinking would be what I would call a "slow baker," the one who would always come up with the right or sage answer after careful consideration. An astute observer of human behavior, she often refers to herself as having an "emotional barometer" for what's *really* going on between people in the room. I must say I find it ironic and humbling that here I am a teacher of literature, yet more often than not, I would ask Bonnie to explain some complex human tangle we'd seen in the movies. I am in awe of her uncanny ability to read people and assess the social landscape with such accuracy, all of which she can mask under a sweet, southern, and poker face of a smile. There's much I may miss, and I usually view a situation optimistically at best or decline judgment at worst. I am more of a social butterfly by day and a recluse by night. My *modus operandi* is such that I possess charisma, encourage, show care, and abound in positive energy, but the flip side to my charm or lightness is that I can squickly become choleric, moody, acerbic, impatient, and defensive, the latter of which can be accompanied by a slathering of righteous indignation. Though I work in, for, and with the public, I prefer to restore my core in privacy or solitude. Though shy and reserved, Bonnie needs only a few steadfast friends who become like family to her. She expects them to be like she is, that is, ready to do life and be there for each other through thick and thin. To be alone for Bonnie is to face the abyss. Bonnie is a classic romantic, and the music that she loves or plays is tender; on the other hand, I prefer that which is melancholic, intense, and moving. In this sense, she is the major to my minor. Where I can be sharp, brusque, and abrupt, Bonnie is soft, gentle, and loving. Where I am detailed, she is broadminded; where I stand from the vantage point of the hawk way up high, she can live in and appreciate the moments of the mundane. I think we are unique in that we both possess a balanced mindset that concurrently blends scientific reasoning, realism, and pragmatism with our souls' craving music, poetry, and beauty. Though far from perfect, in terms of how she treats people, Bonnie's character is sterling. In terms of dealing with people at large and through her example, Bonnie taught me that it is better to be kind and peaceful than right but alienated; I *still* struggle with this. After all, I am the bossy eldest child, a natural leader, and a teacher to my core, to boot. To be with a high school teacher, let alone an *English* teacher, puts one in an unenviable position to be in intimate contact with one whose profession cultivates critical-mindedness. Yes, I do correct and try to grow others, but my ultimate aim is to inspire, improve, and uplift. It takes scores of hours to prepare and practice to be at ease enough in front of a large group of often resistant youth for this to come naturally, let alone effectively. Bonnie looked at the back of my head *many* a night while I was grading or sat working on the computer. We used to speculate why an educated intellectual befriended one who was a jack-of-all-trades with a core of common sense, why one who is a passionate logophile ended up with someone who struggles with words yet finds just the right one. The answer came through life joining our worlds to bring about a unified caretaker unit, first with Kimberly, then with my father, then with Bonnie's mother. As we grew closer together through dealing with deaths and dying and then just going through life, we somehow became inspired to seek a new life united in Him.

In caring go Kimberly, that first year, the hospital was our home away from home. We were way too familiar with the scent of hand sanitizer that masks sickness and death. Hospital rooms that maintain their eerie glow of fluorescent lights, irritating beeps of life-monitoring machines, nurses whispering, and patients moaning would be the setting in which we cultivated our burgeoning friendship. The summer after Kimberly died, we went to the beach and let the ocean wash over and cleanse us; I read books aloud to Bonnie while she fished. We also trekked to my mother's lake cottage and did projects and spent good, uninterrupted time just healing, breathing without worry, and building time and goodness together. It was Bonnie who made my orderly house a warm and loving home. It is she who is made the backyard into a veritable Garden of Eden, complete with fountain and numerous beds of varying perennials leaping out, planned as such for that time when she might not be able to tend to them. I am ever grateful for her and still rely on her more than she will ever know. The world is always right when we could laugh together and dream of things we hadn't done yet.

Not too long after Kimberly died, I would have to face that my father was not well and would need tending until his untimely death. But we are not there yet. Speaking of him and around the period of Kimberly's dying, I was having a particularly trying time with my father because I was struggling financially. My student load had just ballooned, and I was felt like I was drowning. At the time, I was having difficulty maintaining a calm tone with my father whom I loved *so* much because he had reneged on his word to pay my hefty student loan off. Bonnie taught me to try approaching my aging and cantankerous father with respect and to show him that I still needed him. My typical way of requesting anything from him as an adult was done from the presumption that he would and ought to accommodate me. In showing my father true kindness and the rush of love that I *really* felt for him, he of his own accord paid off this student loan I'd been saddled with and struggling to pay for thirteen years. In short, by changing how I approached him, my father made good on his initial promise to pay for me to "go as far as I could go" in my education. Yes, Bonnie taught me that deference, gentleness, and a spirit of humility would lead to righteousness in all manifestations. Being demanding and exacting of anyone, regardless of how right I may think I am, is *never* productive, helpful, or useful. Indeed, at my first attempt at getting vulnerable with my father, pleading with him and exposing my weaknesses, his ire melted, and we began mending our relationship. It would continue to grow by leaps and bounds until the day he died, less than a decade later. It was easy for us to bump heads because I was so much like him. Life experiences and background aside, we were like the same person inside. He was *my* Zorba the Greek. I now look back and can clearly see that the restoration of the relationship I, the child, had with my father was preparing me to become *his* parent as he underwent a decline of his own, one unanticipated, until the moment he died. To care for, respect, and love my *earthly* father the way I did and the reciprocation of him to me, in a child-like state, then made it more readily possible for me to experience the drenching and reckless love of and for my *Heavenly Father*. I just didn't know it then.

4.10 ROLES REVERSED: CARING FOR MY FATHER

In the fall of 2002, just ten months after Kimberly died, my father would have the first of two collisions where he totaled his car. Everything was like a fast-motion, hectic blur after that, starting with the diagnosis of his having Huntington's disease to the progress and termination of his slow-motion spiraling unto death, seven very full years later. I could write another book about the herculean challenges I faced and obstacles surmounted while I doggedly worked to care for my one-of-a-kind, stubborn, Spartan father who was diagnosed with this rare and degenerative neurological disease. In a way, I'm grateful he died from cancer rather than be ravaged by this other peculiar affliction. As I have said, there are a great many differences between Bonnie and me, but for the first time in my adult life, I'd met a person with whom core values were squarely aligned. When the time would come to pass such that we each would embark upon our journey to (or back to) salvation, that is, have an understanding and readiness to become a Christian, our experiences and perceptions couldn't have been more different as well. The theme of dealing with sickness and death — whether it was when we were caring for Kimberly, my father, or her mother, who was stricken with pancreatic cancer, or five months later, when we were facing *both* of our maternal grandmothers' deaths, and then handling Bonnie's host of health problems — would spur within us an urgent sense to *live life to the fullest*. We wouldn't postpone or hold off what we could do today. There was no time to waste! Bonnie suggested that I rev up my trips abroad with students again and start to make extended visits to Greece. I want to give Bonnie full credit for nurturing the passion for traveling, which we both had.

Though I had not yet fully returned and imbued myself with my Greek heritage, in 1995, I took a very memorable and influential trip to Greece with my father and brother. Ten years later, the spark for loving all things Greek was rekindled within me. With Bonnie's encouragement, sense of wonder and curiosity, and my pride in my

Greek background, I launched back up my international travels abroad with students. Beginning in 2005 to this date, we would take more ten-day tours abroad annually with literally dozens of students. The included three more trips to Russia; four to Italy and Greece; one to NYC, London, and Paris; one to Spain, Portugal, Morocco, and the French Riviera; a tour to Germany, Austria, and Switzerland, then even one to Japan. Impressions of all these travels, especially to Greece and Russia, merit their own time and attention, but I march forward on this particular chosen and destined path that I desire to share with you. That I was able to do and see so much in this period of my life was made possible by more than through my sheer effort and desire alone. God fashioned this in me thusly; soon I would venture forth on a path I'd never taken and which was headed for beyond places I'd ever been.

4.11 Searching Beyond A.A.: Christianity, Take 1

Though Bonnie and I continued to go to weekly A.A. meetings, it no longer felt necessary or obligatory; it was a part of our life. Afterward, whether we were at lunch or taking a long walk, we would talk about what was said in the meeting and how this or that could apply to us. In fact, we were changing, just not before our own eyes; we also realized what the relevant and consequential things in our lives were and how grateful we were that what we had squandered already would not be further lost. For whatever reason and beyond our knowledge, we were tilling the grounds of our minds and hearts; there arose flutterings, yearnings, and increased talk — even if only upon occasion — of going to church. In short, *we wanted more*. A few years after I first started going back to A.A., I began to desire something more definite, specific, and focused, like I imagined a church could offer, but I didn't know how to go about choosing one. I didn't understand that though I wasn't even talking about Him, Jesus through His Holy Spirit was already beginning to work on me such that I was being drawn to the church even though it was *Him* I was craving. Although I love the Easter service, I knew it couldn't be the Greek Church I'd go to with regularity, and I pretty much dismissed considering other "normal" churches. Where then could or ought I attend? With this thought expressed, Bonnie started asking me about things like being "born again" and wondering I'd be "getting saved" if I intended to go to church. These terms sounded like she was fishing to see if I had some badge of membership or a box to be checked off in the "I'm-a-*real*-southerner" list. I told her about my being baptized as an infant in the Greek Orthodox Church. She said *that didn't count* because that was done *to* me and that faith is something chosen *by* me. Claiming Orthodoxy does not indicate my condition of faith!

Meanwhile, I started inexplicably and increasingly drawn to God in a way I never had before, and in a manner I couldn't verbalize. *Not* being able to talk should have been my clue that I was onto something of significance. So, we started seriously discussing this. I just wanted more than A.A. could provide. Plus, I'd seen my first sponsor, born and raised Jewish, converted to Christianity. Now, *that* was something! I wondered what could have made this change occur. I was ready to claim with greater specificity and assuredness that I believed *more* than just in God "<u>as I understood Him</u>." I wanted to *know* Him *and* identify Him. The impetus to do so was due to my coming belief that John 3:16 was both truth and fact. I know this may seem like a no-brainer to most of you, but for me, if something is popular, I tend to doubt it all the more or to avoid it like the plague, but two thousand years' worth of believers surely points to an enduring reality. Later on, I would come to know of authenticating research and scholarship that backed up faith with fact, but my faith came *first*; the evidence clinched it. Honestly, I just read the words to this particular Bible verse repeatedly, transfixed, as if the words came off the page and entered into me. I took in these words for the first time even though I'd heard this passage for what seemed like forever. I realized that these words were both timeless and relevant. How can I not copy it now and emphasize the parts that did it for me? "God *so* loved <u>*the world*</u>, that He gave His only begotten Son, that *whosoever* believeth in him should *not* perish, but have *everlasting life*" (KJV, emphasis mine). Wow! At the time, I didn't know what all came before or after this particular verse, but I thought to myself, surely, this verse applies to me, too! Could it be? Deducing that this must be so, my attention and life riveted toward Him. You need to know that I was close, but I hadn't fully grasped and clasped the measure of His love. I thought I was just a part of the *masses* He came for, and I was hanging on to its coattails.

I hyper-focused on and clung to the fact that *I <u>am</u> a part of "the <u>world</u>,"* and I trusted that God was loving enough to want to connect with us His creation in ways beyond the immediate of the here and now. How? Why? I understood *so* little! At the time, my thought was that with Jesus being the epitome of the best nice guy ever *and* His saying on the cross His mission was "finished," only to come back in three days to show He wasn't mere man, how could I not I readily and easily say, "yes," to this, to *Him*? What *then* did I do? Bonnie informed and instructed me that I needed to get baptized to confirm my being saved. I remember she even excitedly called her mother; I didn't see what the fuss was all about. Bonnie explained how this confirmation of mine would mean I would go to Heaven. I sure wasn't thinking about *that*! Leave it also to Bonnie to have thought of a place out in the boonies of Murphy, Kentucky, a place called Field in the Forest (which I kept mistakenly kept calling "Field and Stream"), where I could get baptized to confirm that I had accepted Jesus as my Savior. Why there? We had no church or pastor, and, if it was at all possible, I wanted it to take place *outside*, directly under His dome and in full immersion. I hardly envisioned something of such magnitude as having a new lease on eternal life being marked in this small swimming pool. I put in a phone call there and made my request, and a date was set with a preacher who had never laid eyes on me. When we got there, I didn't know whether to laugh or cry. I looked at Bonnie to check for a look of affirmation from her to match the thought I had in my head, which was, "Whoa, this is crazy!" but, noooo, she didn't bat an eye or raise an eyebrow. After all, this locale was a place she'd taken a field trip to as a young girl. To me, it looked like one of the seven weird wonders of the world. There in the middle of a football field of a place, flanked on either side by 45-degree hills, one with the Ten Commandments in gargantuan-sized lettering on the lawn, and the other, with Jesus' Top Two rules, was a motel-sized, small swimming pool — the "baptismal," I was told. The rather elderly pastor on duty wore a fixed smile and donned the standard polyester suit; he instantly reminded me of one of those reverends who came to my elementary school. We made our introductions, and he told me how it would go down. He asked me three make-it-or-break-it questions that would indicate if I'd passed and could be baptized. After all, this was *not* about the baptism. Here they were: had I *repented* of my sins, had I acknowledged that I *needed* a Savior, and had I *put my faith in Jesus alone* as my Lord and Savior. These questions all blurred into one for me, and in being so moved, I looked him square in the eyes and quietly but assuredly whispered, "Yes," to him. On that bright and sun-drenched morning, only God and Bonnie attended and witnessed. I agreed to it *all*, though I had no idea what "repentance" meant. He pushed me gently backward as I held my nose, and down I went in the cool water. Bonnie was overjoyed for me in a way I didn't appreciate at the time; unbeknownst to me, she even took pictures. This was my first awkward step into faith; I didn't know what I was doing; I just knew I wanted in with Him.

Afterward, feeling proud and accomplished, I bravely sent some of these pictures she took to my family. I got no reply or acknowledgment whatsoever, so I realized that they thought that either I had become some Jesus groupie or that I had just transferred my A.A. obsession over to Christianity. Yep, I'd joined the masses. Perhaps they thought if I couldn't beat 'em, I'd join them. Maybe they thought that I had become so entrenched in southern culture that it had seeped into my pores and turned me into one of "them." I also selected one picture to email to others who were important to me, including one dear old friend. She had left the area and since earned her Ph.D. in theology and New Testament studies, but she had lost her faith in the process. She alone sent me back a three-word reply to the baptismal photo I'd sent: "*Are you kidding*!??" My written response to her was, "Are you blind?" I found all these reactions (that is, the lack thereof) disappointing, but I also gave myself a talking to and said, "Far be it for me to say or expect anything from them, of all people." I probably would have responded the same way! Not being Christian, I can appreciate that my family members didn't understand what or why I did what I did, you know, needing to make it all formal and such, especially since I'd been baptized as a baby. At the time, I thought that I was just barely a Christian, as if there were degrees to become a real one. All I could hang my hat on was that I had accepted Him for myself. I knew that He died — got Himself maliciously murdered — for the *world*, and I was one such person living in "the world."

To tell you the truth, I had no idea what this so-called "personal relationship" with Him was all about. I thought this was Baptist mumbo-jumbo. When Bonnie told me that her mother had told her to congratulate me because now I would make it to Heaven, I was reluctant to be so confident. How could salvation be so easy? Was becoming a Christian just like being an instant pop tart, that after I went down and popped up from the toaster, and now I was golden brown and good to go? Was it going to be as sweet as all that? With one word, I got the prize? When I took Jesus for His word, I never considered the benefits of what would happen to me after I died! After all, like many, I knew plenty of people who *called* themselves Christians and were hypocrites; they seemed to love to hate on people and condemn those around them who didn't fit in their cookie-cutter mold. Though I don't consider myself necessarily *judgmental*, I *can* be harsh, exacting, and critical. Anyway, it's all the same to God because, as I would come to learn, "*all* have sinned and fall short of the glory of God" (Romans 3:23, emphasis mine). Would these negative associations with Christians go away just because I jumped into a pool of water? Why, no! I had *such* a long way to go, but at least I was willing and happy to accept this first statement as *fact*. In a way, even though I was submerged completely — I, clothed in a white, short-sleeved sweater, pink trousers, and all — looking back on it, I was merely sticking my foot in the water to test the waters, finding it pleasing to the touch. Reflecting on where I came from to now, my, how big a step was this! This now also accomplished, I would continue to go to A.A. meetings because I'd found no local church of interest, let alone one to attend regularly. Frankly, I didn't see the need. It would have been nice, but, hey, I was okay. If it happened or one was somehow found, that'd be fine; the chances of finding some such sweet spot seemed rather low to me, so I just trucked on and commenced reading a paraphrased version of the Bible, a page a night right, before my head hit the pillow. There was no way of knowing then that some eight years from then, it would be the sister of a former student of mine who invited me to her church to see her son get baptized, and this church would be the very one which would become my new church home. In the meanwhile, much of my time and energy would be spent looking after my father! This is the time in my life when I restarted my trips abroad with students. I had a growing and palpable desire inside me to travel to Greece; I'm sure this longing was related to my taking care of my father. After he died, I took steps such that I would be able to do more than just visit Greece. That, too, would come later.

4.12 Changes in Education

Meanwhile, life in my safe world carried on as before, meaning Bonnie and I continued to go to A.A. meetings on Sunday mornings, and school, grading, and working out absorbed most of my waking hours during the school year. After my baptism of 2004, we did not immediately or actively seek a church. I was saddled with and consumed by another matter. My father's caretaking began less than six months after Kimberly died, that is, from 2002 until he died in 2009, with the last three years being *incredibly* intense and multi-faceted as far as my responsibilities went. He passed at 73, a "spring chicken," as he dubbed himself at this age. After my father died, there would be no rest for the weary, as soon I would have to teach a class that I had not taught in eighteen years, and both the curriculum as well as the text had changed. Not only that, with the advent of Common Core, there would be a new approach (and, of course, new jargon and acronyms) to an old problem of how to raise students' academic performance. We were now expected to collect *data* on our students; it was as if we didn't know them, let alone what we were doing. Now an even greater onus and burden were placed on teachers. Add onto that a new and convoluted instrument for teacher evaluation was also implemented. Student performance indicators on lengthy standardized tests were being used in part to evaluate teachers. Our fates were in the hands of students who were being tested on skills, not content. For us, they were indivisible. It was madness, I tell you. For the next two and a half years, I felt as overwhelmed as a first-year teacher with new texts and new classes. It's a good thing I was sober! Further, after not having taught seniors for some fifteen years, here I was back at it again. After teaching American lit. for twenty years, I was hardly excited at the prospect of more preparation, but there was no choice in it. And though I was still weary from dealing with *years* of my father's declining health and all that became necessary to accomplish for the handling of his mighty affairs, in the bigger and current scheme, I still loved teaching and got charged by it, so it didn't really matter what level or this and that new criterion I was given. The bottom line is they all still need "the medicine to go down" through the sugar of encouragement, genuine support, and a reliable platform by which a teacher operates.

Conquering the demon of alcoholism, caring for my father, and most movingly, becoming a Christian affected my outlook on the whole of my life and everything I did, including my job and my perception of the state of education in our country. I viewed its plight in a new light. Believe you me, I could also write another volume as to why the state of education and American youth, by and large, seem to have lost their intellectual vigor and moral compass. The long and the short of it is that education has shifted from beginning *at home* to being tinkered with by people at higher levels than teachers *at school*. They have little expertise of whom — not what — they're dealing with. Education is not a business; students will never be products. Teachers deal with minds and souls; those who seek to improve scores and standing deal with data and other tangible criteria. Is it working? No. What has this to do with my being a Christian? Everything. As a Christian, I now easily spot those children who have no idea who Jesus is other than knowing He founded Christianity; they think He's dead and gone. That history runs in cycles is inevitable, but He is outside this realm and so is in the position to offer a unique hope not found elsewhere. Of course, teens are particularly vulnerable to the incessant sounds of the sirens of commercialism that alluringly captivate them with promises of being loved, lovable, cool, or complete, if they will only buy this or look like that. They're so used to these not-so-subtle messages that they don't even notice. In today's world, where kids live in the surreal digital world provided by their phones or video games, there arises a deep desire for something, anything that's *real to* them. They can't get satisfaction. I am not knocking Smartphones!

All this leads me to say that, without Christ, there's a reduced chance for a child to know who he is, how he fits into the vast scheme of things, and that he's loved beyond all measure that the world can offer. If this sense is missing, how can one expect a child to do well in school? His or her essential self *craves* validation and the knowledge that he *matters*, that he is loved *unconditionally*, and everything he does counts. No one person can provide this kind of love! Kids will not give their best and quickly become isolated or distracted. They will more readily succumb to peer pressures and the world's hedonistic values if both of their parents aren't secure as a united front, and what better base than one founded on His sacrificial love. I'm certainly not saying that if one isn't Christian, one won't succeed. Of course, there will be successes! I'm referring to the child's spiritual care that involves promoting him to become a contributing part of a loving world family, created by one *beyond his parents* who has brought him or her into being with such love and intent that the sky's the limit! Education is not about jumping through hoops but about learning to ask the right questions, figuring out how to problem-solve, and knowing one is made to think, seek, *and* find his maker Who is beyond all shooting stars. Such a student will come to see that he has something unique and of merit to give, that he has some way to shine for the Him who also saved him! How can such come solely from a formal education? It can't. The immature, lonely, and desperate young adult who brandishes a gun in school doesn't do so because of "the state of our schools." He is seeking a quick-fix approach to provide instant relief for himself because of the need for what gives his soul sense and satisfaction; love is not microwavable, and it isn't a commodity!

As a Christian *and* a teacher, I try hard to provide and show *His* care they *need* every day by having them toe the line and hold them accountable to high standards beyond the academic. I ache for wanting students to know Him *as* I praise them for doing their best with what they have. Other Americans are frustrated and realize that something is wrong. Still, many simplify the situation that gives rise to school shootings and the like by saying or posting that the minute we took prayer out of the schools, everything changed for the worse. Unfortunately, this is inaccurate. To me, attractive as it may seem, this is a simplistic response. Many Americans conveniently (or out of ignorance) do not recall our First Amendment established in 1802, which states, *"Congress shall make no law respecting an establishment of religion, or prohibiting the free exercise thereof..."* This amendment was provided for us never again to operate under a theocracy, not because our founding fathers anticipated a religiously pluralistic society. The theocracy we left in England was an autocratic one, not a democratic system. I came to learn that Thomas Jefferson borrowed his rhetoric from the Puritan minister and founder of the first Baptist church in America, Roger Williams, who in 1644 promoted that there should be "a hedge or wall of separation between the garden of the church and the wilderness of the world." Why would I say this if I am such a passionate Christian? It's basic: one's walk in life as a Christian begins *at home*. The Christian home presents the hierarchy of life in proper order, where the buck stops with Christ and the child sees that his parents bow their knees to God; they live for more than the here and now of today and come to care for more than themselves. I have no problem with and may one day even be a part of some private Christian school, but I represent Him as best I can through my actions in public school today. That said, as I grow stronger in my faith and the whole of my life becomes further transformed, being a Christian is not something I can just turn on and off at school. My faith would be of particular value to me in my professional life when I experienced challenges there that impacted my livelihood. Who would have suspected that my professional reputation would be challenged, that I would be called upon the carpet not too long after I became a Christian? Certainly not I. It drove me to Him even more, but you will see that later. Perhaps the advent of my not-too-distant retirement will be akin to Frost's poem, "I Am Done with Apple Picking," that I will be done with "the harvest," but I suspect not: leaving this classroom may be a segue that leads me afresh to something new. In the meanwhile, I return to briefly to wrap up loose ends in telling you how my identity was shifting in ways I couldn't have anticipated.

4:13 DUAL CITIZENSHIP AND THE READINESS

In 2011, just two years after my father died, my brother, Stephen, my sister, Persephone, and I attained our dual Greek citizenship, a feat that took eighteen months to accomplish, but one which we can enjoy and be proud of for a lifetime. What did this mean? I could technically live in Greece for as long as I want and not have to leave after the designated ninety days! Little could I have known that only a couple of years after this, when I became Christian, I would surpass my Greek identity in coming to realize that in a still vaster sense, that my "*citizenship is in heaven*" (Philippians 3:20). This reality is still mind-boggling to me. The summer after we attained our dual citizenship, Stephen, Persephone, and her kids met Bonnie and me in Greece for a very fulfilling two-week sojourn, one which we were keenly aware would probably not happen again. Again, recounting my travels merit more stories for another time and space. What happens next is the beginning of a new journey, one that I could never have imagined happening, one that would change my life forever. Many books have been written about faith by theologians, scholars, and clergy, all with experience, scholarship, and profound wisdom, but I want to share with you the nuts-and-bolts process, the nitty-gritty searching, and the *real* story of coming to full-on faith in Christ. It is perhaps one that was a long time coming, but becoming a Christian certainly has been a tender story for me as, hopefully, you will see. As I conclude this first section, I want you to know that there is no way I could have known what was getting ready to happen just around the bend of my spiritual life. It is *so* true that at this time, I "now saw in a mirror *dimly*, …but *then* I *will* know *fully*…" (1 Cor. 13:12, emphasis mine). Clearly, I haven't reached the second half of that quote, but I already anticipate this expansion of knowledge of and contact with Him where all will be made clear. In the meanwhile, my direct encounter with Christ awaited me right around the bend before I knew it. He was right on time, waiting for my divine appointment with Him.

BOOK 2:
D.C. in A.D.

CHAPTER 5:
Year 1, Salvation: Accepting the Invitation

"If you confess with your mouth Jesus as Lord and believe in your heart that God raised Him from the dead, you will be saved."

— Romans 10:9

"And I, brethren, could not speak to you as to spiritual men, but as to men of flesh, as to infants in Christ. ² I gave you milk to drink, not solid food; for you were not yet able to receive it. Indeed, even now you are not yet able, ³ for you are still fleshly."

— 1 Corinthians 3:1–3

5.1 GOLDILOCKS SHOPS FOR A CHURCH

As you now know, I *did* get baptized in 2004, but what occurred was not *experiential*; I didn't possess that vital yet elusive *personal* relationship to which Christians in general and Baptists in particular refer. I should now relate to you my pre-conceived notions of the denomination of Baptists. There were so many of this type of Christians where I grew up that I became familiar with their ways. I'd heard of something they believed in called the "Second Coming," which sounded like a movie's re-release. They expected there to be "Antichrist," too (which reminded me of the physics term "antipode"). Was the *Anti*christ the means of nullifying their religious founder to make Him all the more popular as a leader? Why? All the nonsensical deductions I arrived at came about through the many happenstance encounters I'd had with them in my youth. There is so much more that I gleaned that I became nonplussed about the whole lot of them and their notions. They, not God, rained down wrath, fury, and condemnation on me; these people were certainly no beacons of love or representatives of a God I would like to meet. Baptist churches of many a hue, including First Baptist, Central, Liberty, Free Will, Reformed, Missionary, Evangelical, Southern, and, my favorite, Primitive, graced nearly every street corner. Their claim to fame seemed to be the unique and enviable position of providing full immersion baptism. I heard many in private wag their heads and gently chide the less-enthused Methodists' mere sprinkling. Give me a break. This is all I knew about Baptists, and their pride and simplicity seemed a farce and a travesty compared with the majesty and historicity of the Greek Orthodox Church. Even as an adult, I noticed what seemed like intentional small-mindedness and anti-rationalism. Why *wouldn't* one want to be able to defend his faith with sound logic that held water? It was like we were from two different species! I could never have imagined that I would one day be *attending* a Baptist church! It didn't seem like one, but it surely was, and I hated to miss even one service! God puts a spin on things of this nature all the time.

In the meantime, as a result of our growing desire to become a part of a church body, Bonnie and I *did* try visiting a few churches. We even ventured to go to a local Unitarian Church. To prepare her for the service, I told Bonnie this would not be like any church she'd ever attended. She might expect to hear the music of Beethoven, the Beatles, or an Indian sitar, not a hymn, and the actual so-called sermon would have had more in common with a lecture than what she'd ever heard from the "*pull*-pit," as I'd heard southerners pronounce "pulpit." They would probably discuss social woes or world events. "Think global; act local" was their creed. I told her not even to expect one word of "Jesus" to come out of their mouths; after all, this was *not* a Trinitarian church. When we entered, their greeting committee was welcoming, and all the people were warm and convivial. We proceeded to make our way into the bright sanctuary, which felt more like sitting in a spacious gallery in a modern art museum. That morning, a one-act play was to be put on; it was written and performed by several of its church members. In this story of a fractured family, there was quite a lot of cursing; I suppose this was to add realism. I'm not sure exactly why it rubbed me the wrong way — after all, my vocabulary could be peppered with profanity. For both this reason and the fact that there seemed no elevated purpose to what we'd heard, the whole affair left us disappointed and uninspired, to say the least. I also couldn't dismiss the flood of displeasing memories of the anything-goes mentality I had witnessed as a child among the adults at that Unitarian Church. We were craving more than a generic spirituality to which many of our friends gravitated. Many in A.A. had long left the church, too; they found their safe haven or spiritual refuge "in those rooms." It was often the case that their church of origin turned them off, turned them away, or damaged them to the point that to return might mean endangering their sobriety. In short, they did not come to the church for restoration of body and spirit. We also tried out an Episcopalian Church once, but, honestly, I remember so little about the service that this should tell you something. Rejecting the Unitarian Church and feeling like something was missing at A.A. had us again entertain the thought of attending the Greek Church, even if upon occasion. Certain critical events in our life also pressed upon us to have us speculate what more there was to life.

5.2 THE GREEK CHURCH?

After all that we had gone through in taking care of my dad and Bonnie's mom in their time of sickness and dying and death, the occurrences of which spanned forty days, and, not six months later, that both of us lost a grandmother within a month of each other, we were left reeling. Death seemed inescapable. Dealing with the human condition became *way* too real; I wasn't just explaining the definition to students. It got up close and personal, and we were in pain. The subject of death had been one of the easier topics to teach because of its thematic frequency in literature, and, truthfully, I was always glad for the opportunity to tell my students not to squander their life; it could be snuffed out like a candle. However, I found myself wanting, no, *needing* more than man's philosophy to make sense of this. Is life all for naught? Are we merely here today and gone tomorrow? Are we born but to die? Another repercussion from these deaths was that I gained a new appreciation and gratitude for what and whom I had remaining in my life. I started looking at my loved ones — even my students — as if I were going through a moment in life in slow-mo, whereby I saw them as if for the first time. I relished every moment I had with them — the good, the bad, and the ugly. In my mind, I chose to accentuate their positive and imagined what I would want to tell them if I had only one day left with them. Oh, such an exercise will change your perspective! It sure beat the alternative of *not* having them in my life! I also began to stew over Christianity more concertedly, namely, its dealing with death. Their claim to defeating death was the clincher if, indeed, it was true. Religion involves much more than a means to finding comfort in life's travails. Karl Marx once famously said that "religion is the opiate of the people." I now disagreed with him. How presumptuous, arrogant, and foolish this stance now seemed to me. I had long heard many non-Christens say superciliously of Christians that their notion of eternal life is a delusional fantasy created to placate or assuage weak minds that can't handle the truth of our inevitable, stark cessation. I now became <u>unconvinced</u> of this at every level. Since his beginnings, man's search for *more* and peering into the great void points to something more than we can know or ascertain. As an aside, did you know that Friedrich Nietzsche, fatherless at an early age and the one who claimed that "God is dead," died alone in an insane asylum?

Returning to one of my prescriptions for alleviating existential anguish, I had never taken upon myself to say what happened *after* one took the leap of faith. Faith *in* what? Faith *that* what? Faith in *whom*? All I had was faith in God, and I was holding on by a thread; evidently, that was enough. Dealing with death brought the moment of faith to a crisis within me. How exactly was I to approach God? How might He guide my life? Who was I to access God for myself when so many others had already done so before, but in a manner foreign or dissatisfying to me? Who am I to say that another's approach is invalid? In fact, who am I to say *anything* about God at all? Is there is an absolute right and wrong? If not, then why do people continually fight over their versions and rendition of such? This then probably meant that there is *a* right way and many wrong paths to God. Everybody can't be right, and to ask, "Why can't we all get along?" seemed sophomoric to me. Everything is great until it's not. Was believing in God like ordering a pizza, that it didn't matter what was on your pizza as long as you ordered one? I don't think so, yet I never wanted to be presumptuous, narrow-minded, or know-it-all in my stance to have settled on *one* version that staked *it* had all the answers, let alone *the* truth; therefore, I chose *none*. Nonetheless, I was aware that I was being drawn to worshipping God; an undeniable and longing for Him was growing. A friend would rationalize that my ongoing "fascination" with God was proof that since man seeks God, our brain conceives God, not the other way around, that God created *us*. She said that man makes God out of his need for assuredness that *his life has lasting meaning*; therefore, *we* fabricate something or someone out there which lasts beyond our brief and fleeting life. Even when I first got acquainted with the man-makes-God theory, it didn't sit right with me. This angle sounded inverted; after all, we didn't make ourselves!

The fact that that I'd been safely sober for some time and that A.A. was not as fulfilling as it used to be, coupled with the recent stack of deaths in the past year, gave rise to my own existential crisis. Perhaps the contributing or mitigating factors I just mentioned centrifuged with my background had spun out to seeking God in an increasingly compelling way. I really can't explain why I kept searching. Later, as a Christian, I would recognize that looking back, the Holy Spirit was working on me and in me, massaging, pricking, readying, agitating, moving, and I was definitely responding. I just didn't know how Jesus fit in the mix. I already believed in God, and I had started to enjoy sharing the fact that I was a believer. I had a situation arise that brought me trouble doing just that. When my youngest nephew at five innocently asked me about the icon of Christ I kept in my wallet, I tried to explain that it was a little picture of God's Son. Knowing he had no idea who God was and having the best of intentions, I made the executive decision to give him a colorful children's book on creation and animals; it wasn't at all what you'd call "religious-y." On the last page was written, "God created them all." I was told in no uncertain terms never to discuss religion, that this was the parents' job; I didn't disagree, but I found myself driving away with hot tears welling up in my eyes for feeling ashamed about something that I knew was good and pure and right. I did not go straight home, and two hours later, I found myself driving directly to the local Greek Church. A fellow teacher and Greek from school saw me weeping quietly at a back pew; she asked me what was wrong. I told her that there was nothing that she could do for me, that I had been told not to talk about God or Jesus in any form or fashion with my nephew, no matter what he asked. She listened intently and then walked away. A few minutes later, the priest came up to me while I was praying. He gently put his arm around me and caringly placed a small icon in my hands. He told me that it didn't matter what I'd been told, that *God sees all and loves what I was trying to do*. I should never stop sharing and never be ashamed of being a believer. That's all he said, but it moved me, and I still have that icon in my car. I adored icons, but more from an aesthetic and spiritual appeal than religious usefulness; this one, however, became a symbolic reminder for me to *never give up on God*.

The spring after Bonnie's mother died, we went a couple of times to the church cemetery where her family is buried. One Easter, we attended church there, and for the first time, I got to witness a real ol' timey preacher preach. I found the whole affair rather bizarre and disconcerting, not to mention distracting; he started speaking in a regular fashion, then his pitch and tone changed into in a manner that seemed very guttural and strangely primal. I suppose this is what is meant by being "in the Spirit." However, I wasn't moved, just annoyed. I describe all of my Goldilocks attempts at finding the right church to demonstrate my actively seeking. Bonnie began scouring the computer online and found some moderate Methodist churches we visited once, but there was nothing particularly inspiring or compelling about that church for me either. In the end, and at that time, we did not wind up attending any particular church and would default and continue going to A.A. meetings, as per norm.

5.3 Something New and Different

Another crucial component to my heading toward God occurred in the late 2000s. Bonnie's networks of friends in Georgia were dwindling for various and sundry reasons, namely, in a nutshell, due to the fact that their profligate way of living caught up with them health-wise. For one who has but a few select friends she holds all the closer, Bonnie found herself increasingly alone, lonely, and disconnected. A constant source of family in Mullivanville was the Townsends, and the oldest daughter, Catherine, had been a favorite student of mine and became a very dear friend. At that time, Catherine and her growing family lived two states away; on the other hand, her two sisters and mother lived nearby me. Slowly but surely, Bonnie and I became more and more involved in *their* lives. With her own family several hours away and a couple of her friends having deceased or become unavailable, Bonnie sought new family, that is, her own little village of people with whom she could sit around and watch football, break bread, cry, laugh, and bottom line, where she could be herself and be loved. My family had been like lone wolves, distant from and unlike those around us, so I didn't understand this seeking of others. Nonetheless, all of the Townsends became our family, and we did life with them. I don't know if we adopted them or they adopted us, but we became family for one another. One Sunday, we were asked to go with them to church to attend one of their children's baptisms, so, of course, we agreed to do so and with enthusiasm! Little did I know that we would be going to a *Baptist* church, a place I was reluctant to enter. There was nothing extraordinary about this simple, steepled church, but I must admit its idyllic country setting was quite charming.

After the singing of a few contemporary Christian songs — thankfully, *not* the more familiar, traditional gospel tunes and hymns of Bonnie's youth that could put her in a tizzy — the minister, a younger man with jet-black, slick-backed hair and a handsome appearance, practically jogged up to the stage. It was obvious that he was eager to get to the podium and begin preaching, as if he could hardly wait to talk to us. With an open, smiling face and dressed in an informal but hip fashion, he began. Dubious and skeptical, I made a conscious decision to look *away* from this preacher because, after all, he was a charismatic man, and I certainly did not want to be drawn in by the force of his personality, let alone succumb to the lure of personal charm. But the more he spoke, the more truth flowed out, and the more I listened intently and was engaged and enthralled. I had not ever experienced this before, and I was quite unprepared for being drawn into what this stranger was saying. He made endless analogies and referred to us all being "jacked up," including himself. This pastor focused on the usual problems people had (e.g., health, money, and various losses and hurts) and yet was quick to point to the fact there was real hope for all. He spoke to us intelligently, quickly, intently, sensitively, and somehow intimately, all rolled together; plus, he seemed earnest, genuine, and all the while fully joyful in what he felt compelled to share. In short, it was apparent that this man loved people and loved life. Who wouldn't want what he had? What he had happened to be Jesus. There was no wrath, condescension, condemnation, insinuations, or underlying agenda; it all seemed as real as rain. As absurd as it sounds, I hadn't even minded his talking about Christ. I still look back on this visit, and I'm quite moved by how I was so engaged, stirred, and ultimately became changed in less than an hour. It was as if he was a vehicle or medium for truths that so desperately needed to be said, truths I knew deep inside were valid, right, correct, and true, and I was silently inhaling what he said, veritably drinking it in for all I was worth! *Finally*! Before the sermon, we did see the baptism where our friend's child got dunked in their baptismal pool. It looked to me some big bathtub-of-a-pond up and behind the stage for our viewing ease and pleasure. Suspended above the pool on a façade above was a dove that looked like it could take a nosedive on those below if it wanted to. The baptism went as expected, but it was this sermon that would change the trajectory of my life forever. Do I remember precisely what he all said? No, but I knew that I wanted to hear more of what this man had to say, and I was curious about how this was going to transpire, seeing as how I didn't plan on going back to church. Try as I might, I couldn't get this man's words and ways off my mind, and I dared to think and to question of myself, "*What if I wrote him? What if I contacted him? Was he really who he said he was?*" I called my friend whose nephew had been baptized and asked her what she thought about my getting in touch with him. Enthusiastically, she said she didn't think he really would mind if I contacted him, and she gave me his email address. I will now share the letter that I wrote him in which I blurted out my past experiences with the church, my suspicions of *him*, and my general curiosity about it. I didn't want to jeopardize Bonnie's serenity by cracking open the vault that might as well have been Pandora's box by starting up something that might bring her angst. I didn't know what in the world possessed me to reach out and pursue this, but it was something relentless and driving within. Please know that I was not looking for an argument or seeking to challenge him in my desire to write him; I just felt like delving into this man's mind to see what he was made of. So, I approached with caution, ready to be defensive, reluctant, yet still all the more driven. Something was leading me forward to look into whatever this force of good just might be.

5.4 A QUERY…

I will share with you the letter I wrote to that pastor and thus launch my journey. I am abundantly aware that there are many books about theology written by scholars and clergy and not a few testimonies penned by people from sordid backgrounds that happened to have acquired faith, but I wanted to share the metamorphosis of this uncommon yet all-American woman who came to find and take hold of faith. It is also of vital importance to me not to stop with my being added to some scoreboard of saved souls. I wanted to get into the core workings of how Christianity went from being an abstract religion or platform I'd seen people use to scorn derelicts and renegades to one way of life that became incredibly personal, authentic, engaging, inspiring, and challenging. I want to, no, need to share this journey with you. Therefore, I invite you to watch me transform as I share this epoch in my life. Why stop at three years? Because it not only took, but it took off, and I see new developments branching off of this one pivotal move that will undoubtedly change the remainder of my life. Here is that fateful email I sent on Sunday, March 03, 2013, after attending one more service of his, like part 2 of my experiment. Writing it felt like taking such a risk! That he responded to me at all — and positively and with affirmation at that — changed the arc of my life forever. Here was the proverbial pebble that made the ripple, the tidal wave in my life and on into eternity:

Dear Mr. Jackson (Mark),
I know I put the cart before the horse when I inadvertently CC-ed you my baptism pictures I'd sent to my friends earlier today and hadn't even written you. Because I have had a twenty-plus year friendship with the Townsend family, which started with my teaching and then befriending their eldest daughter, Catherine, I have now been twice to your Baptist Church. Somehow, I inexplicably and unexpectedly found myself in unison of belief with the content of your sermon of last week. In fact, I'm *still* mulling over and talking about anecdotes you brought up and deeply believing you spoke

the capital T-Truth. Therefore, I decided to write you and *see if you were for real*, or, if you were, deep inside, like every other Baptist preacher I've come across in my life, that is, judgmental and believing they know who gets to Heaven and who doesn't and invoking guilt and shame as a means to an end. To get to the point, before I invest more time in going to your church, which I *am* interested in doing, and before I get my heart broke to find out yours is just another church where I am not welcome, I need to know if you are the type to condemn.

My father was a Greek man, baptized Greek Orthodox, as was I as an infant; he married a white girl from Indiana, who is a Unitarian. My joke as a teenager was when asked what *my* religion was, I would answer that I was "Confused." For a long time, I searched for faith, but it did not come intellectually or through intentional effort (though I did appreciate all your references to Jonathan Edwards and the Great Awakening). I have been in a 12-step program since the year 2000; I go there on Sunday mornings, and, honestly, I attribute its expression of "God <u>as we understood Him</u>" to my coming to believe in God, and then also, slowly but surely, to recognize the fact that He evidently loved us so much, that He chose to penetrate the Cosmos and come down in Person through Christ to show us His love. He made it possible to enter another mysterious dimension for eternity after we expire from our physical life. I'm not telling you anything you don't already know. I love and am very proud of being baptized Greek Orthodox and going to the Easter service there a big once a year; most W.A.S.P. sermons and what I see of their spiritual life leave me high and dry. Neither do theatrics impress me. In fact, your words spoke to me so keenly that I chose *not* to look at you so that I could completely focus on the spirit of your *words*. The Greek Church considers me somehow "deficient." Christ never said a word or made a point of labeling, and I'm banking on this. I think Paul's purpose was just to show us even a hard-core Jewish person can come to believe, so I don't pay attention to

his predilection for rules. My friend and I read the Bible every night; she would die rather than speak directly to you because she was raised Baptist and has all this internalized hooey about going to Hell. I could go on, but that's enough for now. I wanted to say again, if I may, Mark, I believe you have a gift of speaking truths in deep and profound ways. I know my purpose, both large and small-scale, and I just couldn't *not* write you because I hope my journey includes you and your church in some capacity someday. I need to know if you think that I am not only just another sinner, which I am, just another dust speck in the universe, but *one you reject*. I hope you take no offense at what I have written; I mean no disrespect. I just wanted to speak from the heart...
Respectfully,
Dimi Christakis

The long and the short of it is that Mark not only responded to my email positively and with sensitivity, but he also agreed to meet with us! Little did we know the adventure of growing pains and deep joys we would come to experience in our burgeoning faith, thanks to a blossoming friendship with this man, he who came to epitomize what a real follower of Jesus might look like.

5.5 Breaking the Ice

Arrangements were made, and it turned out that we would *not* to meet out in the world for coffee, but this pastor — this stranger — I decided to invite to my home. It was a rather scary prospect for Bonnie, but I was both excited and yet anxious, scared, and a little mad all at the same time. We were both a bundle of nerves. I'm pretty sure this pastor had no idea what he was getting into. Bonnie told me in private that she was prepared to either walk away from the table or walk him to the front door if she got a bad vibe from him. Knowing this also contributed to my feeling frozen inside, curious yet cautiously optimistic, and *en guard* all at the same time. The doorbell rang, and with a shout for him to "Come in," in the front door he came and up the stairs he went, again, at once energetic and unassuming. "It's just little ol' me!" he would shout up and smile at us. Sitting down together at our kitchen table, we took the first careful steps of getting to know each other, becoming vulnerable, each telling our story about what brought us where we were, both religiously and in life; Mark went last. He would describe the first time he went to a professor who said, "I want you to write down everything that you think you know about Christ and Christianity." After he had contentedly finished his essay, the professor waited until the end of class and told his students to *throw their essays in the trash* on their way out. Mark told us he said, "I want you to get rid of all your preconceived notions of Christ that you came with when you entered my class." Mark said at the time, he was flabbergasted, but he came to know the man to be correct. He hadn't known who Jesus was, just what he'd been taught. Mark proceeded to tell us that the church had hurt him, too, only professionally. He took a time out and experienced a dark period before cautiously returning to his calling. Although Bonnie and I had spoken about religion before, only that afternoon did it become clear to me that she and I were not only miles apart in terms of who we thought *Jesus* was, but we were on opposite ends of the spectrum as to how we thought God viewed us. Bonnie was concerned for her soul's salvation. The last time I believe she dealt with her destination was on her way to the hospital, when, just hours before suffering a heart attack, her mother looked square into her face and asked her, "*Are you prepared?* Do you *know* if you're going to Heaven?" Bonnie took that to mean that her mom was implying that she was *not* ready for Heaven, that her mother fully expected her to go to Hell! Thankfully, I had had no such experience like that! And so, to talk to Mark about, yet again, about the possibility of her *not* having salvation and experiencing the rejection she felt as a fifteen-year-old run-away, the prospect of where this conversation might lead was terrifying for her. I had none of these fears, none of this toxic baggage. After all, God had made me just the way He wanted to; it was as simple as that. I had no doubt that there was a God, and I knew that Jesus was somehow special, but despite all the reading that I had done, I didn't have a full grasp of His divinity. Yes, I know, I accepted Christ as my Savior back in 2004, but at the time, I was focusing on the point of the required standing found in John 3:16, which I'd fulfilled.

All that to say, within the hour, I knew we three had the beginnings of the making of an extraordinary friendship. Before he left, Mark prayed with us, and he said that he didn't know where this was leading, but he was in it for all he was worth. "Wow!" was what I thought to myself. Bonnie would have a lot of time at home during the day to think about this meeting, and the whole topic of the church brought about such a masked but still-apparent anxiety that I really got worried about her, but not enough to keep me from asking Mark to visit us again. Let me stress that he never pushed anything upon us, never called us, never initiated anything. Still, he was always quick to respond to texts and would be willing to meet with us whenever was convenient for both of our schedules, which would often be hard to work around, but we did. I was amazed. Here was a man, practically a stranger, giving of his own free time to us with no expectation of getting anything back in return, not even attending his church! At the time, Bonnie and I decided that we would still go to A.A., but we might try attending his church maybe every third weekend or so. After all, I was an alcoholic; therefore, we believed we could not afford the luxury of neglecting to attend these maintenance meetings. Yet all the while, there was something that just kept nipping and beckoning me to hear him preach again. I was unaware that a spirit welling up inside me kept getting more potent, a need for realness and assuredness. That for which I'd been searching for was right around the bend. I didn't know what was happening to me! I still get overwhelmed when I think about it.

When Mark came back to visit the next time, perhaps three weeks later, Bonnie meanwhile had herself written him a long letter, and she read it aloud to him right then and there before we even got started. What she read in a calm, cool, and collected manner to him was, in effect, a warning of giving him his "walking papers" if he came with the ulterior motive or intention to criticize. Condemnation was something that Bonnie could not face because the thought might be presented to her, that not only might she have to leave South Carolina, but that she might indeed end up in Hell. "Who *was* this woman?" I asked myself. I had no idea that she felt this way to her core. I didn't know whether to laugh, cry, shake her, or scream at the gods above for allowing such a blast of acid rain to fall on her. And yet I understood; Bonnie had grown up in a time and place where scrutiny was ongoing and routine, and the odds of getting to Heaven never looked good or in your favor, no matter who you were! I experienced such scorn second- or third-hand and indirectly, which was irritating enough, but a condemnation of self was not a part of the core of my foundation. So, who was this Mark, and why would our meeting of minds develop into a lasting friendship? There could have been no man more perfectly suited for Bonnie and me: Mark is a southern boy to his core and one who grew up very close to his mother; he understands women better than many a man. He is intimately familiar with the Baptist Church's machinations, its institution's traditions, and the bylaws of its association. And though Mark *is* charismatic and passionate and expressive, deep inside, he is an intellectual, seeking and yearning for the truth, and always aiming to be a more sympathetic and kinder person. It was *so* clear he loved Christ! I'd never seen the likes of such a man; at the same time, he was still an average guy, one ready to laugh and cut up. Mark was not the type content to take things at face value. From some keen sense he possessed, Mark understood exactly what we were feeling, and he was ready, willing, and open to help both us and others work through their pain. The chances of us meeting a Southern Baptist pastor who was not some fair Caspar Milquetoast type and us being willing to befriend him, I'd wager the odds to be about a million to one. This dark, slick-haired man with keen insight, energy, sensitivity, wit, and fierce intelligence, seemed not only receptive to the idea, but he actually *wanted* to meet us. That our meeting came to pass had me thinking later on that it was a divinely-ordained appointment, though I wouldn't have worded it like that at the time. We three became aware of our unique friendship. Little did I know then that the spark of interest I had in Him would gestate to a full birth within a relatively short period. It was to be followed by an immense processing that would take place first deep inside me, and then the new thoughts would start manifesting themselves into questions and actions. What was going on? I'll tell you. Jesus was working through life experiences and specific people to draw me to Him, and He'd set His Holy Spirit to work inside me. Before I knew it, my life's direction was changing, so much so that it was becoming evident to others.

5.6 WHO IS GOD TO ME?

When I talked to Mark in those early days, I told him how that I thought that God was unfathomable, unimaginable, and inaccessible, a mystical being that impacted the world when and how He wanted to, but, for the most part, He pretty much left us to our own devices. Yes, I hadn't thought of myself as a deist, but as far as God went, He was that removed once He'd got things started. Mark remarked that this "was an unfortunate state of affairs to contemplate." Did I believe in Jesus, meaning did I believe that such the man lived and was crucified? Of course, I did. Did I accept that Christ was the Son of God, different than any other man? Yes, I did. By now, I wanted to know how it could be that God could love me, Jesus could love me, and yet, God's creation, Man, could be so full of hate? Not being imbued with a swath of fear, guilt, shame, and self-loathing, I was left floating in the void, seeking union with the divine but not knowing how it could happen. I added that there are so many ways of approaching or contemplating the divine, including how one even refers to Him/It. I often felt frustrated in not knowing where to start. I hadn't done anything regarding growth after my lukewarm baptism at Field in the Forest. I was coming to realize that I was most certainly still in the dark and not out of the woods. I asked Mark what did it even mean to *know* Christ? Why is there such a fixation on this *personal* relationship with Jesus I keep hearing about? I mean, after all, the human part of Himself is no longer with us! I told Mark that though I *do* believe in God and that I *am* in-the-know that God *is* love, I didn't measure up, didn't stack up, didn't even come close to be able to get His attention. It wasn't so much that I was imperfect: that's obvious! I thought that there were so many more in real need or dire straits ahead of me, so many desperate people, so many abandoned or sick children in, say, Africa and Appalachia, in *genuine* need of His attention and help, that I just didn't qualify for or merit His attention. I *knew* I had it better than I deserved! He had *much* and many more to attend to. After all, I hadn't ever even suffered in life. I had come to have enough knowledge of what my father had gone through firsthand in WWII and the Greek

Civil War to always feel like, as Dorothy Parker would put it, "little lady bountiful. The prize sow." My friend, Kimberly, more succinctly put it and would often say I was "spoiled rotten." Therefore, to my way of thinking, when compared to the masses, I had no right to access, communicate with, let alone bother God with my little affairs. In being abundantly aware of having been richly blessed and that I lived the good life, why in the world would God want to bother with me? How could God possibly have time for me? I saw God as infinitely vast and distant and that I was minuscule. Bonnie's perception of God was just the opposite: for her, He was far too big and way too close for comfort. At the end of this first visit, when our two hours together flew by, Mark ended up looking at both of us and, chuckling, remarked, "If we could put your two views together, each of your understanding of Him would be complete." This would not be his last visit with us.

5.7 Why We Clicked

As it would turn out, for the next six months, we would meet nearly every other week — sometimes more — and most often, for almost two hours at a stretch. I had never experienced anything like this before! I had never had a complete stranger give his time to me with such earnestness, dedication, and care; I was overwhelmed. I think he got a kick out of us because we spoke to him as a real guy and friend first, rather than as a pastor and all that that entails, you know, thinking you have to act all spiritual and all. I don't know when or how, but how we were when we were together just grew on us. Mark and Bonnie had much in common regarding their care and compassion for the underdog and downtrodden. Both of them were intuitive and acutely observant of others. On the other hand, Mark and I had seemed to be cut from the same cloth in that we had a similar energy, passion, and innate optimism. So, this bond we had grew strong quickly. There was something special in the air when we got together, no matter what the topic. Hearing the wind rustle the leaves in the near distance from where we sat out on the back porch, Mark smiled and reminded us that "where two or three are gathered together in God's name, He is there in the midst" (Matthew 18:20 KJV). I also could not get over the fact that this stranger kept coming to see us to answer our many questions about God, to listen to our life's travails, and just to laugh and get to know one together. If I think about all the times that I've tutored students and charged $50 an hour, that alone would add up too many hundreds of dollars, and yet here he was coming to see us *pro bono*. I kept thinking he had a motive, and because past hurts had led to a wariness her, Bonnie was worried that at any time "the real him" was going to come out, and he'd just fall away from us or commence condemning. I was just more and more drawn to what he was telling us about Jesus, which, however, was not news to Bonnie. I was feeling myself the recipient of the generosity of an extraordinary man, yet very much an ordinary person who just happened to be living out his faith in authenticity *and* who had a real pulse on who Jesus really is. When he visited us, he told us with intention and in all seriousness that he came to be our *friend*. Mark hadn't known how these visits would go any more than we; he, too, was going with the flow and seeing where this would lead.

He clarified that he did *not* come to our home to save, evangelize, or proselytize to us, let alone to get us to join his church. He would rather that we remain friends first. He had nothing to gain or get by coming to visit or befriend us. I think that in dealing with demons in his own past — just like anyone does at some point — Mark's prior experiences of pain and hurt made it possible for him to recognize such a state in us, and he felt compelled to help us work through the hurt. He told us that from where he stood today, *he was a changed man*. This golden boy had come to grow through betrayal and loss, and he came out on the other side closer to who and what God evidently would have him be. The last topic of this particular visit we broached was predestiny, and in this area, Mark and I disagreed: I thought, yes; he said, no, but it was no biggie for us to agree to disagree on this point. Not getting my fill of talking to him and taking in more of what we would discuss as it related to God and just life, I would then begin to write him, first about predestiny and then about many more theological topics. This was not a correspondence; I just had these thoughts in my head that I spoke to him about and would put pen to paper so that they wouldn't just twirl up there. Anyway, I came to know it wasn't a matter of if but when we could get together so that I'd get some of these things cleared up. That said, our meeting was ever so much more than some mere Q-A session. Recondite conversations with the right people are priceless, and this was such a match. In short, we came to care about what was going on in each other's lives more than words can say.

5.8 Revealing More, Risking More

The next morning, Bonnie woke up saying that "for the first time, she felt she could be connected to God again." Although it would take time to shed layers of bad history, I was grateful for these visits with Mark, if for nothing else but to help her chip away at the fortress of self-protection. This could be frustrating to witness, too. Naturally, the teacher in me thought that perhaps we could take turns bringing up a topic, issue, or some Scripture for us to center on during our get-togethers, whenever they might turn out to be. Bonnie told me, "No," that she would like it to be "like we did yesterday," where the time together and our conversations just flowed. This was cool by me. That Mark would even consider coming again perhaps partially stemmed from the fact that he knew it would take more than a single meeting to heal and make God's love feel real. Probably, however, he was just intrigued by what looked to be the cusp of a good friendship blossoming. In the meantime, I shared with him why predestination appealed to me, including the reasons behind its coming to be a topic in early Protestant history. Looking back, I'm certain he already knew the material I spouted forth. Long story short, I told him that I believed that God *knows* but does not *cause* that which He fathomed from the start. I also thought that the notion of predestiny could be valid insofar as it expresses a predetermining or shaping of a person for tendencies. Anyway, God would not *intentionally* hurt someone — even after death — and "make" them hell-bound in how He originally constructed them. That God is fully aware of our ultimate destiny is a result of His detailed *foreknowledge* of us, all of which originated at creation. At the time, I disagreed that through exercising our free will *now*, we could be masters of our afterlife *then*.

Mark rejected predestiny for two reasons. The first, of course, was that God doesn't "send" anyone to hell. In a sermon several years later, Mark asserted that we send ourselves there if we reject Him! Secondly, he said predestiny is often used as a copout or excuse *not* to help those in need. Folks with the bucks may conveniently decline by saying "*it's God's will* [that they are poor, etc.]," and the converse is also true: one could use providence as an excuse for not trying to get out of a situation — good or bad — by saying, "*It was meant to be.*" I countered Mark by saying that I didn't think that anything in my life, including where I would wind up afterward, is *fixed* so much it is *God's prerogative* to use me or anyone in any fashion He wants to get the job done and fulfill His purpose. That would include whether or not I went to Heaven or Hell; it wasn't my call. I suppose this is where my not taking Him <u>im</u>personally came in handy. A particular line from *The Godfather*, comes to my mind: "It's not personal; it's just business." If the bigger picture is all about His transference of love by whatever means possible, who are we, we who possess such a limited faculty relative to His, to say something like, "It's not fair"? From our perspective, there is much in life that is not. God may have more lessons in store for us that we cannot comprehend now but serve as the means to bring about something more important or better later. Don't get me wrong — I don't like that people suffer senselessly, and I don't want to die today. I just think that God provides us with what He knows we need to demonstrate His love in general. Free will is a part of our pre-packaged deal; otherwise, we would be mere marionettes. I don't think the two — free will and predestiny — are incompatible. God already knows our thoughts and moves, yet we each have the potential to choose Him freely. At the time, I just thought that there were far more pressing issues with individuals' misfortunes at large than with me. Though He saw fit to die for us all, including little ol' me, I instinctively knew I deserved nothing. Therefore, in my way of thinking back then, I chose to take a back seat, to go to the end of the line so that He could deal with those who I perceived truly needed Him. Clearly, I didn't get the omnipotent and omnipresent aspect of God's character, that He of all could multi-task and that I could *both* be of use to Him *and* receive His care right here and now, yes, right alongside those suffering! I look back on this and see just how far I've come because I would go to Him even if I thought my life didn't depend on it, and I was told that He would save me even if I were the only one on the planet. In terms of intimacy with Christ, I would first have to listen more and talk less.

Connecting the Dots...

There were many ideas in Christianity that would not be cleared up for me until I'd marinated over them, some for months on end, as you will see. I hope that reading this will keep you from stumbling or stalling.

5.9 Christ in My Heart?!?

One month after our first visit, Mark came again, and right off the bat, we hit the ground running: I asked Mark to clarify for me what I did not understand and about which I was so ignorant: the Holy Spirit. All this time, I thought that the Holy *Spirit* was Jesus' [Holy] *Ghost* literally ascending to Heaven. Mark also tried his best to tie up loose ends from his last visit, so by the time he left, I was still not sure what the Holy Spirit does. Nonetheless, something about having Mark explaining the Trinity to me made something click. After he left, I didn't move from the kitchen table where we'd chatted. I just sat in my chair where we'd all three been together and didn't get up for a full two hours in my stewing over what all Mark had explained. How could I understand the Holy Spirit if I didn't really know what Jesus was capable of doing and did for me, too? I thought as hard as I ever had in my life, concentrating with all my might on what I can now look back and identify as my first real attempts at prayer. People who do not believe in God look at prayer as a form of silly and wishful thinking, and they roll their eyes at what appears to be a futile talking-to-oneself because there's nothing, let alone no one out there listening. Conversely, those who do believe can feel the promise and the power of God in prayer. I was experiencing this. Avidly, and with all my soul engaged, I mentally *poured* over our conversation, and, in particular, Mark's explanation (and drawing) of not only what the Trinity was, but more pointedly, explaining *who* the Holy Spirit is.

First things first, however. I backed up and took a good, long look at Jesus and what He wanted *for* me, Dimi. I experienced a euphoria at the moment of epiphany: I was finally getting it! The very second I got saved occurred when, in my mind's eye, I actually saw Christ beckon me to come to Him, and I accepted His invitation to do so. In fact, I couldn't contain myself, and I *ran* to Him! No wonder I felt elated! I got that *He had been waiting for me.* How could I not rush in joy to Him?!? This union with Him then simultaneously brought about the roaring rush of His Spirit into me! In that flash, I understood that, *too*! The Holy Spirit was not Jesus' Ghost floating up at the Ascension!

Good grief!! He is the Great Connector within the Trinity *and* between us and the whole of God. I now turned my attention to Who this was who took up invisible and yet real residence within me. I had had *so* much confusion in me that was further made cloudy by not knowing how to *talk* about these things. The next point (of many) we started to deal with had to do with the wording or diction Christians used so familiarly. In a way, for me, this involved learning a new language because words I had previously used and had associations with were being turned upside down and inside out. For example, when one talked about believing in Christ, the standard verbiage was "*Have you accepted Jesus Christ in your heart?*" Are you kidding me?! Why would I want Jesus in my heart? I am often moody and can be such a roller coaster and basket case of emotions. Why in the world would I want to place Him or to make my decision about Him in such an unstable part of myself? Bonnie kept using this wording, and I thought it was just jargon she used by rote, so I fought it all the more, but something kept leading me on, compelling me, and I was so close to it, my acceptance of Him, it actually hurt. I knew it was insufficient, let alone ridiculous to say that I accepted Jesus with "all my brain," even though this is obviously where all thought and feeling originate. I was reluctant and resistant to verbally claim that "He dwells in my heart" because, from my estimation, the heart is not a safe place for Him, especially in an emotional girl like me. I wanted for the place where He resides to be a setting of greater solidity, but Bonnie gently brought to my mind that the heart is not only an organ pumping blood with every beat, but it is a *metaphor* for the pulse of one's very life. I could accept that. Though I would walk up the red-carpeted aisle to the altar in front of our church that very next Sunday, *this* was to be the time of my salvation, the very moment where I would be born again regardless of whether I fully understood these words. Here is the conversation I recorded that Bonnie and I had as related to how my heart was involved in accepting Him. The story of my salvation is worth your hearing the original transcript.

> After Mark left, Bonnie and I remained sitting at the kitchen table and talked for nearly two hours about Jesus, the Holy Spirit, and the involvement of one's heart. We hadn't even thought about dinner, though the sun had already set. This

was the first of many such conversations to follow for us. It's as though once we made the turn, the tenor and substance of our conversations changed, too. Jesus became a regular part of our daily conversations, so much so that it became weird for us to be around people for whom Jesus wasn't even a thought. Now pushing 9:30, feeling stuck and frustrated, I felt I was beginning to make traction. I knew I was on the verge of penetrating this greatest mystery known to so many: Jesus sending His Holy Spirit upon my accepting Him, the very instant I said, "Yes," to Him with all my might and heart. What clicked and started the ball rolling for things to all fit together was the moment I realized that, just as Bonnie said, the heart is more than a just beating organ, more than just the seat of emotions that people talk about, but it is the life source, the symbolic center and core of all intentness and involvement of one's being. And if it expresses my core's desires, identity, and purpose, then, *of course*, this is where and with what I could accept Christ! And then I had this utterly distinct inner vision of Christ waiting outside on my front porch underneath the gutter, with heavy drops of cold rain dripping on His head as He waited for me *for years* to open the front door. When Jesus sensed my readiness through His Holy Spirit who had been hovering over and encouraging me from the sidelines as I mentally pressed on toward Him in the kitchen, He pursued me from a different angle. Rather than remain where He was, He then moved and went to the back of my house for me to witness Him at the kitchen window, right across from where I was sitting at the kitchen table in position to have been able to have seen Him! Without cause or provocation, I turned around and looked at the window above the kitchen sink. *There He was, arms outstretched, His whole face smiling, yes, beaming at me*!! I realized then and there that Christ had been waiting for me the whole time — not just for the world, but even and actually for me. Though Emily Dickinson wrote the following lines, I could now imagine *Christ* saying them to *me*: "I've known you from an ample nation, and I choose *you*, Dimi." Then, in a reciprocal manner, I would "close the valves of [my] attention – like stone" to anyone *but* Him. The search was over. Done. Mission impossible. Accomplished. I couldn't wait to accept Christ and invite Him into my heart *and make my heart the home for the Holy Spirit.* Come on in!! Jesus wasn't going to love me and leave me! He gives us a parting gift that is both proof of my salvation sealed and the means by which He can be in and with me: it is the very same conduit *He* had while He was alive on planet earth! Jesus' gift of love is His Spirit, a spirit kind of like mine, yet immeasurably *so* much more; it is one within the Trinity, thank you very much. I would come to understand this better over time. The fact that the Holy Spirit *could* dwell in me sounds so bizarre, so exciting, so amazing, and so inspiring that I became overwhelmed. At the moment when I started telling Bonnie that *it was happening*, that I was accepting Christ for what He did for me and Who He is, I started crying and laughing at the same time when I told her, "I got it!!" I also had the strangest sense that *it wasn't I who was talking*, that it was the Holy Spirit in me talking. I cannot express the feeling of all my past rationalizations vaporizing in that instant; I accepted as fact that Jesus *does* love me, and nothing else mattered. And all this happened in the quiet of a beautiful spring evening with just Bonnie and me at home. At the time, I was surprised how easily it took, but when I consider my decades-long journey and endless searching, I had been being made ready such that when the key notches were properly scored, He fit in the keyhole, and the mystery was revealed. And *that* this happened was of no one else's accord or doing other than God's. He knew and had me prepared for the particular moment I became ready, willing, and able to have and express my faith. God created me on purpose and just the way I was, and therefore, my salvation story reflects and is true to who I am. This unique and purposeful fashioning of His reminds me of the paper snowflakes we made in first grade. The craft project demonstrates that while everyone pretty much looks the same, on further inspection, each is unique. Therefore, when salvation occurs, though the same phenomenon exists, each occurrence will look different in form. That's how particular God is! Much to my surprise, my vocabulary started to change and align with what I formerly would have dubbed as "theirs," but now it was mine too. My life's purpose and direction were becoming transformed through the beginnings of my domain with Him. I didn't just wake up and consciously dictate that my vocabulary change to Christian-speak; it just started coming out that way, and it hasn't stopped. Indeed, it takes effort *not* to speak in a manner reflecting my faith. I had to learn to adjust how I spoke with consideration to my audience so I would not come off as off-putting to a potential future brother or sister has been a learning process. I have inadvertently burnt myself (and undoubtedly irritated others) in my zeal. In short, I would start to fathom just Who the Holy Spirit is and what His dwelling in me entailed. I was moved, grateful, overwhelmed, and full of joy from His love.

At this critical juncture, I want to share with you that I was in a place in my life to have enough wisdom to know that the harder you fall for something, the more likely it is to experience burnout. I realized that real and lasting change takes years of practice, practice, practice. Perfection, however, is not possible. Though the spark of love was hot to the touch, I wanted to be able to settle into a lower gear, steady my energies, and pace myself for the marathon of a life well-lived for Him. No, I couldn't prove anything to anyone, but I also knew that I would be moved from within to live differently. Did I slip and curse, judge, gossip, lose my temper, or participate in conversations I oughtn't to have, etc.? Of course, I did. Did they become less frequent? I think so. Does my salvation story sound fantastical or imaginary to you, as if I were possessed? Perhaps. Anyway, I *was* possessed insofar as I chose Him alone as my Lord. The burden of proof is on the person who hasn't been saved; his argument will remain two-dimensional and fall flat. Meanwhile, knowing full-well that I had become supernaturally changed, I steadied myself for the business of transforming my life so my life would testify that I love the Lord "with all [my] heart, soul, mind, and strength" (Mark 12:30). His love covers the totality of us; therefore, He wants *our* all because He gave *His* all. I also got another piece of the heart understood when I viewed man's heart from God's perspective. How did I do this, you ask? I found it in my Bible. Here it is: "You are those who justify yourselves in the sight of men, but *God knows your hearts*; for that which is alluring to man is detestable in the sight of God" (Luke 16:15, emphasis mine.) I found instruction for how I am to center the gravity of my existence and my core values quite by accident. The lens through which I evaluate the world is the opposite of what the unbeliever uses to make his deductions and conclusions. It's not the brain, but the heart, not the thought, but the soul that makes the call, and yet this doesn't abnegate intelligence! God judges me by *my inner motive* — my "*heart*" — that is, how true and into or obedient I am to Him and His righteous ways. The lies that the devil tells us, that we are not good enough or that none of this is real, over time, would become like cigarette smoke to the ex-smoker: enticing for a second, but disgusting in the end. Over time, you get better at recognizing that any silent, but real internalized self-talk that spits forth cruel words at you is scoffing that comes from Satan, and his ploys have the stench of death. Having technically repented at my salvation didn't mean I wouldn't continue to contend with sin, let alone this term; that was to follow.

5.10 A Point on the Map, a New Beginning

When I accepted Jesus as my Messiah earlier in 2004 — including getting baptized — my growth stopped, or rather, I should say, it didn't even get started. Why? I didn't have any real connection to Christ other than believing in His divinity and agreeing that He did what He said He came to do. I certainly had no accurate notion of who the Holy Spirit was. At that time, I was just joining the rank and file of folks who believed that Jesus came to save the world. Period, end of story. I readily acceded to that. There was nothing personal about this. I just knew I needed to differentiate my adult choice from that which occurred at my infant baptism in the Greek Orthodox Church because this time, I freely entered into the identity as Christian with intentionality. I didn't feel compelled to deal with the so-called personal aspect which so many people seemed fixated on. Only later would that be vital for me, too. And I thought that predestiny was God's way of evening out the playing field, regardless of what we humans construed for ourselves. Predestiny also helped me to feel that I was wanted. Why? Early on, my mother told us that we were all "accidents"; none of us was planned. Her birth control methods had failed her. And upon the birth of his last child, a son, my father exclaimed to his three daughters, "I finally, got it right!", like we were three failed experiments. Entering into a covenant with God through Jesus, even if by His coattails, I knew beyond a shadow of a doubt that I was *not* some "accident" to my Heavenly Father. I very much *do* matter to Him as a person *and* a woman He brought in this world with specificity and purposefulness. As far as I was concerned, He could do whatever He wants with me, yes, including sending me to Hell, if it helped bring about something greater in His plan. People just stared or laughed at me if I added this postscript. I didn't want anybody to think that I accepted Christ for the "get-out-of-jail-free card" or "fire insurance policy," as I'd heard tell. Mark kept assuring me that my salvation was "sealed," that God proved it "when He gave [me] the Spirit in [my] heart as a pledge" (2 Cor. 1:22). I couldn't undo this or inform God He could change His mind if He felt like it. It would take a while for this reality to meld in my soul as truth. This would be a process.

In the meanwhile, I focused on what I knew I had! When I said to Him, "Yes, thank you, I see that you took *my* sins away, too," my own "window" not only became crystal clear, sparkling, pristine-clean, and fixed, it began to emanate a light shining through me because He lives within me. Oh, my soul and body! My heart is beating fast again. I keep replaying the memory of my salvation afresh: I could hardly wait not only to open the window but tear it off the jambs to get to Him! When I look back over past decades, I recognize that Jesus *has* been with me; He had been waiting for just the right moment of my readiness to reach for Him. Such a gentleman He has been, not forcing or imposing Himself upon me and having His Spirit test the waters, perhaps stirring them up a bit for such a moment when I would be ready to partake of Him. And that moment was pure and sweet, not hyped-up, sensationalized, or remotely affected. To no one else's house did He come to fetch me but mine. In short, this direct meeting and my enthusiastic acceptance of Jesus was as personal and intimate and unique as it got. I felt like a little girl, like a safe child, yet I am now both Daughter *and* Sister as co-heir. This identity was so foreign to me! Could this really be?!

When you grow up having no formal exposure to God, your parents' views come to shape who you think you are and what your worth is on a very primal level. With no introduction to God, an unbeliever has no other center than self, so while feeling exhilarated and basking in seeming freedom and power, this person inevitably ends up confronting his fallibilities and limitations. The paradigm shift occurred in me when I recognized that not only is there a God, but Jesus is the Son of God, and I moved from seeing God the Creator to saying God my *Father*! Yes, I also came to accept that Jesus is the Son of God and our Messiah and that He freely accepted His Father's plan to sacrifice His life and taking on our sin, which had kept us from union with God. What all Jesus did still needed further clarifying; that would come in time, too, especially as I got acquainted with His Word. I just had heard that God could not "look upon sin" even though He made us. It was also apparent to me that God needs no one or nothing, but

He still *is* love. That said, He also conceived us with purpose — and one which we can't always divine — both to experience His love and to live out a life of love for His glory. Once saved, it may take some time to figure out what we are to do with our new selves, but He is a good and patient Father. Anyway, it would seem He might have me do something that would be in keeping with my character and passions so that I will not only *do* His work but do it well *and* readily! At the time of salvation, there was so much I didn't think about, you know, like, for example, Christ's "victory" over the "sting" of death (1 Cor. 15:55). Is a full understanding of Scripture or Jesus a prerequisite or qualification to come to Him? No, absolutely not! Thank heavens! In the meanwhile, I just kept wanting to thank God for giving me a chance! Though middle-aged, I had this new life ahead of me, one which gushed a spilling-over of love for and from Jesus, all of which I'd never known before! I couldn't stop telling anyone who would listen that I *believed* and that the Holy Spirit is the *best* present evaaaaah!! With this new knowledge that my life belongs to Christ, it begged the question, *now what?* I felt naked in a way, like, how am I exactly supposed to go around acting normally when this life-altering event has taken place? My life had been irrevocably and profoundly changed, yet I know salvation is only the first step, and Satan would not be pleased with such progress. I got scared that Satan would taint me with cynicism and self-centeredness, so I would try to be on the lookout because I knew I am meant to do so much more. I didn't want to get stuck or burn out or be lulled into complacency. It came to me that perhaps He could use me to be a unique key that can fit into the hearts and minds of those as blocked as I was. I am *so* born again! My public self would soon catch up with my private encounter with Jesus the following Sunday at church. When Marks checked and asked at the end of his sermon, "*Is there anyone of you today who would like to accept Jesus...,*" I felt my heart pound through my chest like it had grown to the size of a giant and didn't have room in me. How it went down follows.

5.11 SALVATION, TAKE 3:
I Finally Got It Right

On Sunday, April 28, 2013, just one month before I turned fifty and a few days after Mark visited us and clarified who the Holy Spirit is so that a little later that evening, I accepted Christ as my personal Savior, I knew within a few minutes of being in church that I would go down to the front when he gave what is called "altar call." I quietly double-checked with Bonnie to make sure I knew what "invitation" meant. Now that I had come to understand the heart's role, who the Holy Spirit is, and zooming up to Christ to stake a claim on Him in private, I felt compelled to make it public. It was the right thing to do. I'd already emailed Mark and told him what had happened later that evening after he left, so he knew. Still, my heart would not be stilled. With every minute that passed, my heart was beating harder and louder; even the sun's golden rays shone brighter and broader through the enormous windows of our church than I'd recalled before. The more Mark talked, the less I could hear because of the roar in my ears. With my heart pounding, seemingly right through my chest, I was aware that the Holy Spirit was moving me, and I knew that I needed to, *had* to go down to the front of the church, even if I'd gotten up close and personal with Jesus just a few days ago. As Mark was winding down and approached the closing of his sermon, he then gave "the invitation" for folks to come up to the altar. We were to put aside our former life, confess and lay our sins at the cross, and take up our new life with Christ. These words were coming out of his mouth as tears were welling up in my eyes, and I could not make them quit, so I tried not to blink. I felt like a caged animal standing among people in the pew, and I knew I had to walk down that red-carpeted aisle all the way up there by the altar, right near to where he preached, so making my way past people in the row, down I went. Though I tried to be cool, I probably looked possessed; I guess I was. Other people were also approaching the altar to kneel and pray in clusters or individually, but when I got down there as composed, but hurriedly as I could, I started pacing like a panther, a short back-and-forth, not knowing exactly where to plant myself and get down on my knees. I wasn't sure what was supposed to happen, let alone *do* with myself. Mark calmly came down those few steps directly to me and put his arm around my shoulder. We knelt together in our own private huddle. I was trembling, sweating, elated, and amazed all at the same time. He prayed over me and said that *I was like him*, sometimes *too smart for my own good*. He then quietly asked me if *I had asked Jesus to forgive me of my sins, had I repented, and had I accepted Jesus Christ as my Lord and Savior*. I nodded with my whole self while saying, "Yes," to it all. Then he smiled and told me that he was proud of me, and that was it! I wept quietly as I somehow made my way back to my seat, face beaming, head still nodding, and smile radiant; I hurt for joy. To be honest, though accepting Christ was the best part, I would later need guidance in contending with what all was involved with repenting. Part of me thought, well, I ought to just camp down there at the foot of the cross for all the repenting I needed to do, enumerating everything I could remember, all the while knowing that there would still be much more I'd forgotten or not even realized was sin. God surely didn't want a list, did He? And then my next thought was, well, He knows everything anyway, so just a blanket acknowledgment and declaration that "I *am* sorry, I know I've done wrong, and I'll try for the rest of my life to change and do better" would be a good place to start, and I *had* done this. The specifics of what repentance looks like would come up of their own accord later as life unfolded in this new chapter. I really can't tell you why I even went down to the altar when I'd already accepted Christ a few days before in my home, but I now know that I was experiencing the Holy Spirit beckoning me, leading me to confirm publicly just *to Whom I now belonged*. Though the deal was now sealed — thus, the phrase, "born again," which Evangelical Protestants use — this decision was just the beginning. Soon the questions would come. There was so much I didn't know about this new life. Over this next year, my journey of growth would be rich, full, involving, and, yes, even causing pain at times. Little did I know how long the process of sanctification would take; indeed, it involves one's lifetime. You don't graduate or arrive or attain perfection. Somehow though, I didn't feel defeated or discouraged; in fact, I felt victorious and free and privileged! Not knowing what sanctification really meant, let alone entailed, was all right by me though. At that moment, it was enough just to know and celebrate that I had been born again — this time, I got it right! The third time was the charm. Soon enough, I would contend with new terminology, phrasing, and concepts, and poor Mark would soon be flooded with emails and questions I had. Before that could happen, one more gift would become vital to and necessary for me.

5.12 The Afterglow

That week I was high as a kite, I was so full of the Spirit, yet I could see that Bonnie, though very happy for me, was a bit jealous. She had never had what she called that "lightning-bolt" moment; therefore, she sometimes doubted her salvation. I told her that I was halfway through my life should make it such that one not ought to be surprised that it took something bold to jolt me on the right path, and my heart matched the moment. Surely, every person's salvation looked different; it wasn't a one-size-fits-all formulaic experience. After all, wasn't salvation supposed to be personal? Bonnie informed me that though she had responded to the altar call at age thirteen-ish, she thought she might not truly be saved because "there were no bells and whistles," let alone stars or trumpets. When she quietly answered, "Yes," in response to the elderly but energetic pastor's asking if she had accepted Jesus, she didn't get the *feeling* she was expecting. Therefore, Bonnie doubted whether her salvation occurred, as if it could be co-based on emotional feedback rather than her decision. She had heard tell of and had anticipated a dramatic sensation to occur along with her public testimony, so when it did not happen, the doubts set in. She carried around the weight of that wrongful conclusion for *decades*. At the time, I was incredulous and not a little miffed that she could have thought that the one experience compelled the other. Anyway, she is so tenderhearted; Jesus probably knew better than to have the Holy Spirit jostle her young heartstrings. It wasn't called for. Learning about her incident re-confirmed my misgivings towards that so-called old-time religion, and it was difficult to hear about her disappointment because, quite frankly, I didn't want anything to rain on my parade. In my new frame of mind, I couldn't bear to think about such experiences in church as being contrived or inauthentic. I liked our little church! In fact, I enjoyed those old hymns and gospel tunes; they were new to me! On the other hand, Bonnie knew all the lyrics to most of those songs, many with such haunting or beautiful lyrics to simple tunes. After listening to just a couple of them, Bonnie had some internal buzzer that went off because it took only about that long for negative associations from her youth to get stirred up, and she knew she needed to turn the page.

As spring rounded the corner to summer, our visits with Mark would become more sporadic, but the Sunday before my actual birthday, two weeks after salvation, Mark hurried down the aisle before the service started to give each of us a brand-new, still-in-the-box Study Bible. No one even noticed because folks were milling about and still making their way in. He said to me, "*You're going to need this now*," smiled, turned, and left. This would be the *second*-best gift I received. It and only it could help me continue in my love story with God. I fell in love with Him anew as I began to read, and then *reread* His Word. I started to understand why it is said that God is a *living* God and that this book contains His living word. Once you're saved (or on your way to being saved), the Bible generates such a keen interest that it metaphysically brings about the reader's *whole* involvement. It is a moving affair, I tell you. Sure, a good book can be re-read and appreciated anew, but such an experience isn't life-changing! I surely didn't see this coming either! It's true that every night before I went to sleep, I was in the habit of reading one page from a paraphrased version of the Bible and one page from *One Day at a Time*, A.A. literature. But was it a study? No, and half the time, I was about half asleep anyway. I have no regrets; it was just right for ending the day all those years. To be precise, the version of the Bible Mark gave us each was the *MacArthur Study Bible*, and over that following year, Bonnie would read this Bible from cover to cover, including all its commentary. I, too, would read daily and study. Would getting this study Bible and my partaking of it jump-start me into prayer? No, not automatically, but I *soon began* to pray with regularity, even though I didn't feel like I knew what I was doing; prayer was so alien to me. Mark kept assuring and affirming us that we *would* mature and grow in our faith, that this would happen, in part, *while* we would read and studied His Word. Before too long, however, something happened inside both of us such that we couldn't *not* read the Bible daily and missed it terribly, longingly if we did. The first time I stumbled upon it, the following quote proved prophetic for me. 1 Peter 2 was spot-on accurate: like those before and after me, I was that eager child, who, "like [a] newborn baby, longs for the pure milk of the word, so that by it [she] may grow in respect to salvation"

(1 Peter 2).

Initially, soon after Mark gave us our Bibles, as I held and stared at that dense, daunting, and already dear book, I asked him, "Where should I start?" I'm so glad he didn't just automatically say with double-meaning intended, "In the beginning"! He thought about it and got back to us and answered with assuredness, "Start with the Letter to the Philippians; it's short and sweet, and it is essentially a love letter." And so, we did, and I was hooked. I then reread it before I then I went back and commenced reading the whole New Testament. After that first suggestion, Mark never assigned us specific Scripture to study. As I said, the ebb and flow of our getting together was natural, and our conversations meandered surely and freely. Nonetheless, as a caveat to misinterpreting something we might come upon, Mark would tell us that we needed to consider two things as we read: number one, the target audience, and number two, the context. We would not want to be guilty of cherry-picking, that is, selecting excerpts from the Bible to justify some perspective or corroborate our own viewpoint. Instead, we would examine certain passages closely to see if we couldn't appreciate each of them in the context in which it was written to discern what principles transcended the moment and would become universally applicable for all time's sake. On many occasions, something would strike me, and I would want to look something up or ask myself, "Why?" and "in what context was such-and-such written?" I had to take the same advice I gave to my students: always consider the source you are looking up. What is *the author's* angle and purpose? Be careful! Sometimes though, there were such moments of holiness or wisdom, I was struck mute in reverence. At other times, the timing of a message or passage was so uncanny with how it matched up or corresponded to an event in my life, and I came to be certain it wasn't chance at all that I came to read it. In between visits, after we had read a lot, questions built up in me to the point where I was about ready to burst. Mark always tried to find the time to work in a visit. For all of Mark's high spirits, joyful ways, and readiness to cut-up, he had a keen mind, quick wit, laser-focus, and a lawyer's logic. Even though he was about twenty years younger than us, his discernment of human nature was preternaturally keen, and his ability to cut to the chase and read people's motives with accuracy and tenderness was uncanny. Bonnie and I innocently asked why Christians had the reputation of being judgmental; we certainly didn't want to be like that. Mark said, in general, people focus on sins that are not their own, making it easier for them to feel in the right or better than another because such-and-such is not a difficulty or sacrifice that *they* have to make or to contend with.

Time and again, Mark told us he agreed with *the whole* of the Bible. He never went against Scripture or justified or rationalized any topic of the *world* by using the Bible to promote a socio-political agenda. Unlike other pastors I'd heard, Mark took pains to set the stage and get into the author's mindset. He sure made sure he knew the context, author's purpose, intended audience, and setting for any given piece of Scripture to understand better and explain any given message, not to mention the broader implication it held. This was old hat for him by now. A simple case in point, for example, would be for one to have to deal with numerous references in the N.T. to circumcision. He asked us, "Who might be those 'of the circumcision' *today?*" If we still didn't understand something, Mark illustrated by using some perfect analogy or specific example from his or our life; this was exactly how Christ explained things. The accuracy of our understanding of the Bible was of great importance to Mark; he is a teacher to his core, too. He didn't get upset if we got off-point; he was just protective of us. He explained with intentness and showed us in so many ways how Christ was valid, worthy, and necessary to go through life and that He would add new meaning and purpose to our lives. On the other hand, many passages stand alone with no need for research because the truth is already apparent and stunning and hits you square between the eyes. As the saying goes, the more things change, the more they remain the same, and the primitive and cruel tendencies of those in the days of Noah seemed upon us again. Mark seemed both appalled yet not surprised to see the degradations and ugliness of modern society, which promotes worldliness, greed, and self-centeredness. No matter what happens, Mark is still a man of hope; encouragement comes naturally to him. What I have come to appreciate over the months and years is that he is the most Biblically savvy man I'd ever met, and to the point, I really think he got Jesus.

That said, he certainly wasn't Jesus! No matter how hard Mark tried to reassure Bonnie that "once saved, always saved," that her salvation *was* sealed even though she hadn't had the strong emotional marker at salvation and because she thought she was undeserving, she remained dubious.

5.13 Bonnie's Stumbling Block

For the next year or more, though *not* an issue for me, it took Bonnie a long time to deal with her doubting her salvation. Bonnie and I each have unique paths in our walks, but it is also true we impact and affect one another by sharing our joys and pains in our close Christian friendship. One particular visit early in our meeting with Mark, Bonnie shared a poignant memory that enabled Mark to help her see that she *was* saved. It was useful to me in that it demonstrated not only the Holy Spirit's power, but it showed me just how limited Satan is, not that one should seek combat with him, mind you. Four years ago, when Bonnie's mother was in the last days before she died from pancreatic cancer, Bonnie took a short break from tending to her mother in the hospital. She was back for the final time after having hospice care provided in her mother's apartment, which happened to be up above a local funeral parlor. Her mother's preacher had insisted Bonnie leave for how exhausted she'd grown, but before she left, he asked her if there was anything he could do or prepare because her mother's death was imminent. Bonnie knew her mother had at one time told her the name of a particular song she wanted to be sung at her funeral, but for the life of her, she couldn't recall it. While busying herself doing yard work, then searching her house for the slip of paper she had jotted down the name of this hymn on, Bonnie suddenly recalled in horror and agony that she had stuck it in the glove box of her car she had sold months ago! What to do? Having exhausted all efforts to find it and failing to recall its title, she returned to her mother, who lay asleep but was in obvious pain. Kneeling at her mother's bedside in feeling utterly helpless for neither being able to ease her mother's suffering nor remembering the name of that song, she prayed silently, "Please, Lord, *please* help me remember." As she started to stand, suddenly the name of the song came to her: "It Is Well with My Soul." A wash of relief flooded Bonnie, and she looked up in wonder, tears, and gratitude. She would say that *this* was the moment she knew Jesus heard her even though initially, she thought the memory had been for her mother, not for her. At the time, she did use this occurrence as a confirmation that she was saved. Bonnie's brother disagreed and told her that *Satan can't read her mind*; therefore, it was *not* he who delivered this song to her as some hoax or practical joke to make her think she was saved. Mark also told Bonnie she wrong: *that* she remembered there and then was a gift for them both. Taking this a step further, *the Holy Spirit can't bring to mind a memory if He isn't already present* in the person; for this to be so, one *has* to have been saved, regardless if there occurred a lightning bolt sensation or even if she had left the church. At that moment, Mark told Bonnie to *claim her salvation*. That song was for her too, and not solely for her mother. After all, her mother had already slipped into unconsciousness. "Claim it!" meant accept that the Holy Spirit, the Comforter, was *in* her and that *He* brought to recollection the song for her so that she could do what she needed to for her mother. How can the Holy Spirit be working in a person if she hasn't already accepted Jesus? He can't because the Holy Spirit is gifted at the moment of salvation; therefore, *the Holy Spirit was and is in Bonnie; she most assuredly is saved*! You may say, oh, that was just her memory jogged, but I ask you, what are the chances that this would have occurred after having lost that slip of paper and the need for it arose at that particular time and place for one so distraught that she couldn't think straight? Later, she would again misconstrue this and say that Satan, who knows Scripture well, evoked this memory to trick her. Mark quickly said, "Satan cannot read your thoughts!" He then again reminded her to "claim it" during moments when she doubted her salvation, to hold onto this moment as if it were a lifebuoy in the ocean. This then became her life's motto, a truth on which she could count that she was saved. Several years later, Mark preached a sermon on the spirit's needs and revealed the stirring back story to this song, an anthem to charge our soul to keep the faith when our world is falling apart.

Why do I focus so much on Bonnie? Because, much to my astonishment, for well over a year, one of the topics that we would discuss almost every time we met was that she felt undeserving of Christ's love. The preachers back in the days of her youth were full of ire, vim, and vigor, and as a sensitive little girl, she got spooked easily. No grown-up batted an eye or gave assurance of His love for her. Mark stressed that neither she nor anyone could *earn* salvation. In spite of the many errors made in her life before and since then, *Christ never let go of her* because she *had* invited Him in her heart all those many years ago, regardless of what she did or did not feel. It was *she* who strayed from the church in her teenage years of rebellion. I came to see that the purpose of my witnessing her angst and hope was to add a level of gravitas, a level of seriousness that hadn't penetrated my Christian identity before. Though not at the forefront of my mind, Bonnie knew very well the eternal ramifications of *not* getting this right. Why would this matter to me? Over time, it didn't take much effort for me to notice that I knew so many who didn't know Him. What had Mark to do with Bonnie's grappling with salvation and with my learning who Jesus was? It became apparent that he was our go-to guy for theological questions and real-life stuff that came up. I would have tons of questions about new vocabulary and topics, like, for example, why in the world would Protestants want to evangelize and do missionary work in *Russia*? I would return to this topic later. In those early days, much of our time revolved around growing our understanding of Christ and building our friendship. When Mark came for a visit, whatever we came to discuss was of our choosing; Mark didn't come with a plan of his own. In fact, he often took a step back and paused to remind us that he was there first and foremost *as our friend*. In our own time, Bonnie and I independently poured over our Bibles, and then she and I spent hours upon hours talking about topics that we had never before broached or discussed with any appreciable depth. The more we got to know Jesus, the more the tenor and content of our conversations were being transformed. Mark saw this when he'd observe us talking to each other as we made our way to some point we had wanted to share with him. After he left, and by the time we finished mulling over this and that which Mark had said, we'd sometimes not eat dinner until well after 10 o'clock. And just when we had made a breakthrough in some topic, one of us would say something anew, and we would then hash *that* out. I would consider this to be one of the most rigorous, soul-wrenching, and yet fulfilling times of my life.

5.14 Here Come the Questions...

As I said, after I got saved, questions over particular words and biblical topics started to flood my brain seemingly of their own accord. I will always be grateful to Mark for his openness to asking him about them and not growing impatient with me or responding to them with some stock reply. He was always super considerate of my thought process and respectful in how he chose to answer me such that I could understand from my vantage point of an adult child in the faith. Like Jesus, Mark used analogies and illustrations to explain biblical concepts. As soon as he sat down and had a cup of coffee or some goodie, Bonnie always gave him a scratchpad on which to draw his diagrams. (Ironically, making analogies is how I clarified philosophic ideas or abstract concepts as expressed in literature for my students.) So, *how* he explained matters worked for me. Mark's and my acumen and mental speed matched each other, too; we made seemingly unrelated connections between this and that in a nanosecond. People joked that he had A.D.D. As I filled my mind and my heart with Him, I found myself early on being drawn to a discipline called *apologetics* that would facilitate my learning *and* growth. On the most primal level, I think I was just getting started at coming to understand *who God is*, which, of course, necessitates one also saying in the same breath, *just who Jesus is*. From this point, all begins and ends. Apologetics helped my mind unravel and put together that which my heart already knew.

When I went to the beach that summer after my salvation, I ordered online a couple of books on apologetics, and I was hooked! I couldn't get enough! These are not exactly your light and fun summer reads with pink and purple covers, but I was enthralled and lapped them up. They were compelling, factually based, truth-focused, full in scope, and justified my faith in both a rational and soulful way. Suffice it to say, what I read in these apologetics books supported what I was concurrently reading or had already read in the Bible. It's not that the Bible needed validation, but it sure was nice for my early and earthly

Christian self to have such authentication, especially considering my background. For example, what was the likelihood that force, matter, and energy spontaneously or randomly came together to create our planets, life, and then human life at that? Probability and statistics would confirm that is virtually impossible. *Something can't come from nothing.* The fact that the finite and tangible springs forth from that which is eternal and intangible proves to me that the latter is the prime mover. That the Earth came to exist indicates it has been created. *It didn't make itself!* Everything which is material is the *effect*, and the *cause* is a *creator* of some kind, which necessitates a *will*. And for me, this is proof that there is a God. God *is*. In the Bible, He identifies Himself as "I AM WHO I AM" (Exodus 3:14). He more than *exists*; otherwise, He would be bound to time and space. God Himself can't be created because He *is* the Creator; there is no beginning or end with Him. It's not lost on any Christian scholar that the Apostle John records that Jesus *also* identifies Himself seven times with "*I Am*" identifying statements, making an obvious parallel between Father and Son. What about matter from the other end of the spectrum? What about the incredible precision and accuracy needed in forming the strands of DNA, for example, which determine every cell's function? This, too, shows proof of planning outside the realm of the physical and finite. I would next consider Christ's unique ability to perform miracles. These no longer even seem like miracles, let alone a big deal when you consider He has access to the power of His Father, He Who created everything. He is God, so there's nothing He can't do! Anything is possible, is a piece of cake! Even as a man, He was still God, though He was choosy when He used His powers. Jesus didn't perform miracles gratuitously to promote Himself, let alone to impress or manipulate others. He did so with the intent to *point people to God*, and what better way than for Him to do so than to suspend the laws of physics God brought about anyway? Nothing is done in a happenstance fashion, let alone for our convenience or entertainment. The miracles are not for naught, even if they are incomprehensible. Neither God nor Jesus is not a genie in a bottle here to make our wish His command! In the Old Testament, God spoke through inanimate media, the occurrences of which would have been astonishing, as was the case when Moses encountered God Who communicated to him through a burning bush. In the New Testament, we graduate to God coming in the flesh, and Jesus provided drops of evidence of proof hither and yon as He saw necessary and fit to use. My favorite example is when Peter trusts that Jesus and can walk on water based on Jesus' enabling encouragement. I can just imagine being in Peter's sandals! Only God can suspend the laws of physics He created! And finally, the one fact that separates Christianity from every other religion is God's unique ability to *create life*, which *also* includes His power to bring someone *back to life* from the dead. Who knew? That Jesus did so for Lazarus is a sneak preview of what God did for Jesus. Jesus' resurrection is the zenith, the apex, the acme of human history, the game-changer for all time: it provides the proof of authenticity of His being divine, and, for the first time, through His resurrection, we are given the means to be forever reconciled to God. Only *He* could have provided this. This was no miracle for God; look at everything He accomplished beforehand! Phenomena and circumstances that *we* can't explain *still* serve to illuminate Him; in fact, there's always a possibility that some justification might not occur in your lifetime. All the same, if your eyes and heart are open, *miracles still abound today.*

I return to God and to see how *we* fit in His scheme. One of the very first questions Mark had for me was *what or who did I think God was*, and I immediately answered, albeit formulaically, "*Love.*" All of life had to originate from an intelligent being (and *not* by some inanimate design or Big Bang theory) that loves us. His love's essence or expression is *relational*; He can't *not* share and extend the love He self-possesses. It's uncontainable, boundless, and yet specific and intentional. There's no mistaking His love. Just take a look at yourself or any creation. Creation is a positive, outward, and manifest act; *it is not neutral*; it does not take away or negate us into the blissful nothingness of nirvana or moksha! That's when the Trinity first entered Mark's and my conversation: God, Jesus, and the Holy Spirit have always been in a *relationship*, and when we by faith receive that love, we share in that love and come into a relationship with God. He wants us to pay it forward and share it, His love, with others. God is not an *it* because an *it* doesn't love! Why would an *it* make anything *for no reason*? Only *someone* with enough care could have been behind something as magnificent, majestic, and comprehensive as Creation. Then, having set the stage, He made people in His image, which means we, too, are given the capacity for love and to love also. To turn this love into a genuine and authentic two-way street, He built into us the freedom to choose, but then He stacked the deck against Himself by permitting temptation to exist to make doubly certain our love for Him was real. We would have to resist evil and, most importantly, to reach for Him. And as if that weren't enough, to model the perfect form of love for us to see with our own two eyes, He came of His own accord and as Himself, both to show us perfect love *and* to enable us to reset our moral nature through His taking on our wrongs at the Cross. There's no way one can accept Christ for Who He is unless one first reckons with Who *God* is and all He is capable of. When you take in Christ, he gives you His Spirit. Each one points to the other. Every miracle that earlier I would have chalked up to man not having the language or knowledge to explain, say, the Virgin Birth or His Resurrection, I now saw as evidence that God had always been preparing the conditions for our upcoming restoration through His gift of grace. The miracles are just how His job gets done; the Resurrection completed it. I believe that deep down, we instinctively *know* that the Christian's claim to God is the only one because He covers *everything*: creation, ever-lasting love, grace, goodness, hope, and peace. That we can't fathom His ways or explain all miracles is proof of His being beyond human; the rest of the Bible's events *can* be historically verified and corroborated with other respected historical documents. Only a rookie would disagree; therefore, when we choose not to believe God is who He says he is, cynicism begins to grip us and choke the life out of us. You've seen this in young and old alike. Meanwhile, I came to see that Jesus is God's love letter to us — to *me*, and I just learned to read!

5.15 A Look Back to Look Ahead and Bonnie's Reclaiming Faith

In addition to the ideas put forth in apologetics, I became intrigued by the different ways that the devil tries to trip us up. In some ways, this harkened back to what I taught in American literature in the Puritan period, only now it wasn't academic; it was incredibly personal. To be honest, I had never seriously contemplated about Satan or Lucifer as even *existing*, let alone considered the impact he makes in this world and our daily lives. I guess I just dismissed him as the anthropomorphized source of or excuse for all our terrifying fears and wrongdoings, a personage created for effect in horror movies or used in backward churches with the underlying purpose of manipulating or cajoling people through terroristic methods. And though I had taught about him within the framework of literature, as in "Sinners in the Hands of an Angry God," I was now coming to learn who he truly was, including why he was expelled from Heaven and how he fits into God's master plan. The more I read, the more the Old and New Testament puzzle pieces fit together, and as I saw a vaster picture or a scroll unfolding before my eyes, time was becoming compressed. I also came to view the mythologies of the world as a sort of training ground for faith to go from a fascination with a multiplicity of gods reflecting us to just one God from whom we came. I also used to think that Christians must not have been aware that Christianity itself was just the latest in a religious continuum, that they were supplanting one set of beliefs, rituals, holidays, symbols, and art and architecture for their own. This is readily apparent in Greece, especially when you find an ancient church built atop the foundation of an even older temple or shrine to a pagan god. We are not one-up on God! It is God Who readied *us* across the millennia until all of the conditions were just right for the arrival of Jesus. I shared my theory with Bonnie that, just like it has taken us millennia to be able to accurately explain the biophysical phenomena around us (and we still have miles to go), religious occurrences also ought to be viewed on a continuum. Just as people *used* to believe that the world was flat or that the planets revolved around the Earth until, little by little, we came to know better, the same holds true concerning man's being prepared for a Savior entering the world. Man's looking *out* as expressed in paganism and pantheism was a preparatory baby step to be able to look even *further* than this, and at that moment, God *spoke* to us. He had let us go through this phase of curiosity whereby we concocted various mythologies that had us peering out before He could come to us in the flesh. Remember, time is a creation, too, and not a constraint or modality of which God is a part. For Him, the here-and-now as well as the then-and-there are all the same! Can you imagine if Jesus had arrived on the scene in the Garden to save the day the moment that Adam and Eve realized what wrong they had done and recognized the vastness of their folly? They would have been blown away! We as a people were not ready for Him. This free-fall they launched had to spin out to such a level of desperation to sufficiently ready humankind. Furthermore, the language had to be developed to make communication easier, roads needed to be built so people could travel longer distances more easily, and a host of other factors that only *He* knew about had to be set in place to make conditions ripe for His Son to come to us *and* for us to be able to get His word out. In short, God readies and develops us in His own timing. We cannot be impatient with that which we have no control over; therefore, we march forward in love and hope every day. I fumblingly wrote a remix of Emily Dickinson's poem, "Tell all the truth," to fit the analogy I'm trying to make:

> God's "in the beginning" launched all on a vast and brand-new start,
> He knew success would come to be, though people from Him'd soon part.
> It'd be too much for the two to meet Christ in Eden then so early on.
> They wouldn't see the need at all: to sin they were happ'ly drawn.
> As the burning bush would be a way for Moses Yahweh to see,
> And Commands were etched in stone to show His Will for all mankind,

God's truths must dazzle gradually,
Or every man be blind.

People of faith do not always subscribe to what the world says is logical or correct, and because of this, they are often lumped together with those who reject *any* sort of scientific or technological advancements. This is how the media often depicts us and, ironically, how <u>un</u>critically-thinking intellectuals often reduce Christians. This was no longer the case with me. As a new believer, my mind was on fire, and my heart was overcharged with faith. I possessed a new inner strength and such a sense of regeneration that I was continually feeling giddy and overwhelmed like I wanted to pinch myself to see if I were still me! Life *was* changing. And though Bonnie had been listening to a Christian radio station, now she would look up the music online and begin to take up playing her guitar again. That my journey was closely, albeit inversely related to Bonnie's, I firmly believe was also by design to help each other with what the other was weak in. More often than not, in those early days, it was Mark who had to unravel us and set us aright. He said that my God was too big and vast and indifferent, hers too small, nit-picky, and condemning. As we continued to steep ourselves in His Word, new topics came up.

5.16 What Does It Mean to "Turn Away"? What to Trust?

As I indicated, little by slowly, I started to ponder more deeply about what it meant for me to repent. It just kept coming back to me. It's like when I got saved, I took a turn down a new road, and I didn't know where I was going or where this road would lead me. Bonnie kept asking me about when I went up to the altar in response to the inner call to my salvation, didn't I repent? And I said, quite honestly, all I did was rush to Christ and turn all else aside! You can't believe how much this topic came up this first year, and, truthfully, I kept wanting to skirt away from it as it did not seem essential to me or my salvation. I mean, should I have stayed up there at the altar the rest of the day and enumerated all I'd done? Should I have read my fourth step from A.A., that is, where I had "made a list of all the people I had harmed"? Doesn't God already know what all I've done and will do? Well, of course, He does. Even before I became a Christian, I'd vaguely heard tell that "He "knitted me together in my mother's womb" (Psalm 139:13 ESV) and knows that "the very hairs of [my] head are all numbered (Luke 12:7). Yes, He can read my mind, but *His knowing and my confessing are two different things*. When I was a little girl and had done something wrong, my parents used to make me apologize, even though they already knew what it was! This time, however, the apology was to be *voluntary*. Though it was necessary, for realness' sake; it could not be made under compulsion, and the outcome ideally ought to be that I do not return to the way I was. I wondered if my one broad and sweeping apology for all of it did it? Would that get it? And did I really mean it? I know I can't fully or perfectly do so, yet at least this time, I've got God with me to hold my hand through all these next times. I have so many weaknesses and faults, but I know I am certainly not unique in this regard! Before I became a Christian, I would never have thought about focusing on *sin*; it sounded so antiquated and almost barbaric. Then I applied the "rigorous honesty" I'd learned in A.A. and let go of getting tripped up on the word to see the truth. I also never really considered that *all* my transgressions could be blotted out with *one* divine act, but to say this now would be to insinuate that what Jesus did was not adequate, and I surely knew that it was.

In short, it is still me here, only now, my *raison d'être* has shifted outward and beyond self to Him. I tried to bolster and strengthen my faith as a Christian as quickly as I could because I knew I would soon probably rub the wrong way those closest to me when they got a whiff of my being one of *them*, a Christian. Invariably and inevitably, they would soon enough wonder what in the world had come over me. Had I succumbed to the pressure of living in the south? Had this preacher seduced me with false promises? Had my brain fallen out? And what exactly *is* the denomination of this pastor? Baptist, you say?!? "You *have* lost your mind!" was the clear-as-a-bell mental shout from my family and certain friends and colleagues that I could already hear. In anticipation of their dubiousness, I unapologetically became enamored by apologetics so I could shore up my arguments. After all, isn't the best offense a good defense? In reality, however, with most folks, no such disputes ever arose, just a vague mental distance and sense of their watching me with curiosity, cautiousness, or some new neutrality. Regardless, such delving wasn't a waste or loss; apologetics only bolstered my faith in my process of trying to get a handle on how I could speak to those like I had been. What I didn't know then was that arguing effectively still didn't lead one to Christ. You can't prove Him into the heart of another! At the time, I didn't care that my family couldn't understand what had happened to me. Anyway, this subject helped me to understand God more, including the fulness of the Trinity. I'd take turns studying each of the three contained in the one Trinity, but for the time, I stuck with Jesus. No, Jesus wasn't just another super nice guy who, like many a religious leader, promoted His version of the Golden Rule. I set out to learn about His divinity, really taking in that Christ was who He said He was. Now, decades later, I would be able to complete the rest of the story that began with my being drawn to the superhero in *Jesus Christ Superstar*; I would know what happened *after* He died! I finished the story by reading *His* story!

So, what about all that is in the Bible? Can I *really* count on it? I can't say I seriously thought about taking the Bible literally before becoming a Christian, but I did at least recognize that some absolute truths are revealed in it. Now I *did* believe in its infallibility or inerrancy, but I owed it to God and to myself to read the Bible and some commentary and explanatory material. Perhaps this is not the norm for many who read the Bible; I don't know. Two of my pastors also told me that when a word is abstract, I should try and go back to the word in its *original* form. How perfect! As a foreign language teacher, I appreciated this advice! In this case, I well knew the imperative for investigating the original ancient Greek, or, at the very least, finding a version of the N.T. that gets as close as possible to the *spirit* of the word chosen by the author. No, as appealing as it sounded, I didn't take up learning ancient Greek. I found online support through something called Blue Line Bible Commentary that helped me with that. There are other things people object to other than hyper-focusing on just words. For people to say that the Bible is flawed and full of discrepancies or inconsistencies is to miss the whole story's flow, to miss the forest for the leaf of a tree. Any discrepancies are *minor*, not major, and they are hardly deal-breakers in disseminating the more significant facts. Slight differences of a statement or recorded testimony actually strengthen and fill in the gaps of history; uniformity would point to collusion. And it's not that I had it wrong before about Jesus' *life*; I just never really understood what happened *after* He died. Ah, those critical three days of His being good and dead which led to the Big Reveal *and* His remaining yet another forty days among us clinched it! The Resurrection is for real! How did word really get out? The *fact* of His Resurrection, which is recorded in Scripture by the detail-oriented researcher and physician, Luke, is substantiated by other primary sources and numerous eyewitnesses — some 500 people — who corroborate *seeing* the resurrected Jesus *and* witnessing His subsequent ascension. We also can't leave out Saul, the staunchly conservative *Pharisee* that spoke *Greek* and who was a *Roman* citizen that actively condemned the early followers of Christ. Like many today, he was an incredibly <u>un</u>likely candidate to come to Christ, but when he *encountered* Christ in such a dramatic and challenging way, it led to a startling conversion and to his becoming arguably the greatest missionary that ever lived. (Plus, he possessed a trifecta of perfect qualifications for evangelizing.) For me to learn that *all* of the apostles, though in cowardice and sadness went about their normal affairs right after He died, did a complete turnabout to became powerful advocates of and for Him. That all but one of them died defending Him is proof positive that Jesus was who He said he was. Who would die for a lie? Only John made it to a ripe old age, but he was exiled. They saw Him alive again with their own eyes and believed in this risen and living Christ. All of this spoke volumes to me. I woke up because it all added up. I am a doubting Thomas no more! And as if these accounts weren't enough, to comprehend the significance that Jesus sent the Holy Spirit coming to dwell in *them* at Pentecost the same as He now did in *me*, blew me away and finished me off, or rather, brought *me* to life.

5.17 Repentance, Continued

I return to the topic of repentance because, at the time, I was too overwhelmed by the magnetic force of attraction to Christ to really have had the presence of mind to do more than verbally agree to repent at my moment of salvation. Now that I'd returned to some normalcy, I had no intention or thought of taking it back, but I knew I needed help — and lots of it — regarding this topic. Where and when did I first really start stewing about and chewing on this word, "repentance"? At the beach. On summer vacation. And let me tell you, this brought no barrel of laughs. Looking out at the ocean, the sound of the waves cleansing the barnacles of my brain, I closed my eyes and considered deeply about just what it means to repent, and the first thing that occurred to me was that *it is not the same thing as regret*. What exactly does it mean to "turn away"? I know that, at times, I still have an old *tendency* to want to take things that aren't mine and to lie for self-preservation or self-promotion. For an adult, lying isn't usually big, bold, and outright, but subtle, as in embellishing or shading certain aspects or consciously omitting critical details, all to paint yourself in a more favorable light. Though you may not *technically* be lying, deception of any kind is still dishonesty. I would now look more at the spirit of things rather than take them at face value or the literal level. So much lies in the space between. Thankfully, I did not give up or feel defeated or even overwhelmed. I just kept persevering; over and over and through it all, I kept on reading and studying my Bible. Mark probably saw us changing or at least developing before his eyes. Sometimes when he would come over to the house, he would watch Bonnie and me go at it and discuss what Christ might have meant by this or that or some other biblical passage, as if he weren't even there. Mark should shake his head, pleased, it seemed to me. We had never talked like this before! And resultantly, we three in our friendship became fuller in Him. As I told you, I started writing Mark long emails about specific passages in the Bible that didn't make sense to me or about what may have been going on in life. He never wrote me back, but I would not have expected this of him.

On the other hand, he was swift to reply via text and say that he would read them but that these topics would be for us to discuss in person. I was still overwhelmed with his generosity of self; he spent many dozens of hours with us. He said that, as a pastor, he often saw that people were reluctant to be honest, authentic, or natural with him for fear of judgment, reprisal, or correction, but that he knew that this was not how we were with him; we did, indeed, have a real friendship. To tell you the truth, I was more honest with him than with my own family. I held nothing back, and much spilled out of my brain and heart. There was no weirdness either; just realness, a childlike curiosity, and an eager readiness to learn. Questions, jokes, revelations, and opinions flowed and blurred. Mark helped me get settled on so much, including repentance. He wasn't surprised, troubled, or in chagrin that I was still mulling over it. He leaned back, crossed his legs, put his hands behind and cradled his head, and calmly said, "Repentance means that from the point of salvation onward, each day I turn away as best I can a from anything that keeps me from being my best for Christ." He told me that I am a work in progress and that I am simply to lay all at the cross and humbly ask Jesus to have His way with me. He told me I should pray for the openness and readiness to be available and open to do *as* He wanted and *when* He wanted. Mark explained that believing in Jesus means *trusting my faith will grow* and that God will ready me for this growth through life's circumstances. Repentance simply involves a *letting-go* of that which makes me *less* like Him; as long as I remain in Him, such *will* happen. Quantifying the rate thereof, I mentally added the words from the Promises of A.A.: "*sometimes quickly, sometimes slowly.*" Such gold, such wisdom from this man, our friend! I was and remain incredibly grateful to him. And this was just another day for him! A life lived for Him on planet earth is both beautiful and challenging. It's that vast and simple.

5.18 Settling into Church and a Moving from Apologetics into Spiritual Warfare

After salvatcdidn't have so much to do with Jesus as it did with the church and what it might mean for me to be a church member. In the Greek Church, you can only become a member if you can commit financially and officially tithe to that church. It was a lot more loose and informal at this church; there were no requirements, just attending a new members class after verbally expressing to the pastors your desire to join. I suppose they could choose whether or not for this to be, but, in the end, being an official member turned out not to be so important to me. I got fed there and served in my own time and way, and there was also something inside me that didn't know where I'd be a decade from then. So, in the meantime, I was content to get to know people there a few at a time. I would keep an ever-growing list in my phone to keep up and call people by name. Some I came to be quite close to, and I whom I readily called church *family*. All this was *so* new to me! By now, Bonnie and I had gone from alternating going to church one weekend and an A.A. meeting the next, to now almost exclusively going to church. I can't express the hunger that both of us had for both Jesus and the Word of God, whether it be through reading, praying, or what I came to learn as *corporate* worship. After this, I'm told, the next step is to take all we gain or learn in church and share and promote Jesus out in the world, wherever we were. I was nowhere near ready yet. I confess that in those early days, at times, we vacillated over even continuing to attend church. It often felt like we had whiplash. Could this be? I knew I'd been searching for more, but did I mean to get involved whole-hog and in this way? I also wondered what in the world was I doing at this little church in the middle of nowhere. And why in heaven's name was I attending a church, the denomination of which was the same as the overly-zealous preachers of my youth, who were so concerned with my soul that they neglected to love on the little girl attached. Bonnie experienced what appeared to be the Second Flood, that is, a wash of guilt, doubts, and fear from dark days gone by. Unfortunately, opening up the floodgates of the past also brought about greater vulnerability, so when she got anxious, I felt protective of her, that is if I hadn't lost my patience about her unsureness. What a mess we were! Through it all, *we never stopped loving Jesus*, so this trouble, too, passed. Later, Bonnie would say that the Holy Spirit is not a silent partner to Jesus, so I also thanked the Spirit for helping me stay planted in Jesus, come what may. This habit would come to serve me well a little later on when some pushes came to shoves.

As I mentioned before, I became drawn to apologetics before I even really knew what it meant. For those of you that are not Christians, apologetics does not mean that I'm apologizing for what I believe; this term originates from the Greek word for "defense," ἀπολογία, and I can't lie that the fact that it was Greek in origin was just a bonus for me. Peter tells us it is crucial to be able to justify our faith! He said, "Always being ready to *make a defense* to everyone who asks you to give an account for the hope that is in you, *yet with gentleness and reverence*" (1 Peter 3:15, emphasis mine). Plus, that's mainly what the Apostle Paul does, left and right in his evangelizing during his mission trips and letter-writing. Being able to form a solid defense for *why* I believed in Him appealed to me; I wanted to prepare myself for nonChristian like I was, who might also be interested in Jesus or have other questions. It certainly didn't hurt me to read this type of material because learning the facts only further solidified my faith. That said, I was *hardly* in the position to defend when I was immature had so many questions! For example, I didn't understand the Holy Spirit's involvement and role in drawing a person to Christ. I do know salvation isn't *on* me or *about* me! I can get defensive if attacked; therefore, not wanting to *offend* anyone so that I wouldn't make myself vulnerable to attack, I sought knowledge to argue calmly, coolly, and collectedly. It turned out these defenses were *not* what was needed. I was not called to battle with anyone, but reading books on apologetics did serve to strengthen, condition, and bolster my faith for future challenges in life. Jesus just wanted me to show up and be ready, and that did not involve any disputes. That the occasion to question my faith never arose in those early days was a good thing because I was still too green not to get red hot if I heard smirks or saw eyes rolling. Through the Holy Spirit's invisible help, I re-trained myself to go from a stance of believing that I could count on no one and nothing in this world to make a conscious decision to trust, obey, and rely on Jesus. No, I wasn't going through life solo, and little by slowly, He softened my edges while making me stronger. Even if someone rubbed me the wrong way at church (as I'm sure I might have another), I knew what to do. After all, as A.A. introduced me to the precept that it's about "principles, not personalities." I recognized that though I was not strong enough to ever take Satan on, I had a fighting chance to stay strong in my faith with Jesus by my side. I read that though conflicts and problems came in the *appearance* of persons, but I realized my "struggle is *not* against flesh and blood, but against the world forces of this darkness [and] the spiritual forces of wickedness…" (from Ephesians 6:12, emphasis mine).

Apologetics readily lead to the next topic called "spiritual warfare." In a sense, this had me hopping from one form of defense to another. Though I would not seek it, the *mindset* one gets into after discovering the need for being "battle-ready" came naturally for me, so determined I was to be a private warrior for Him. From apologetics to spiritual warfare was a natural; they were so complimentary! Spiritual warfare introduced another realm, complete with vocabulary, tone, and mood I'd never experienced before but one that made total sense to me now. Without giving him any extra due or unnecessary attention or credit, I would begin to see the world in a war at the spiritual level with Satan. I had never even given him a thought before, let alone discussed him by name. He still was having his way, a field day, with *so* many people. If you read the Bible, it's no spoiler to announce that he will be finally and ultimately defeated. If you are not a Christian, get ready for jargon you may never have encountered in your everyday life. I want to lay down the gauntlet for what's going on in the world that has caught you unaware. Such a mindset will change the way you view events in the world and compel you to toe the line for Him as best you can all the more. Here I go.

The Devil charms, beguiles, and seduces us with the alluring promise of a moment's satisfaction in exchange for our ultimate demise. In case you didn't know, that's code for ending up in Hell, which is every bit as real as Heaven. I won't get into the different levels because I'm no expert, but suffice it to say, there are. I have come to learn that Satan, formerly Lucifer, actually fell from Heaven because God's banished him for his pride, so stunning it was that he wanted to take God's place! (Now *that's* chutzpah!) As John Donne wrote in his epic poem, *Paradise Lost*, Satan announced that it is "better to reign in Hell than serve in Heaven." It's weird to have these words come out of my mouth, as, not too many years ago, such sounded like something coming from fairytales, myths, or primitivistic Christians. When I consider that God created everything, including Satan, it seems problematic that He kicked him out, yet he still has the ability to toy with *us* in this world. It's no wonder that it is difficult for some to view God as omnibenevolent! What's up with that? God *allows* periods of pain to occur, sometimes by permitting Satan to tempt us, taunt us, or torture us. Satan will use any play in the book or trick up his sleeve, including diversions, distractions, and destructions, so that we might turn away from our Lord. When I look back over my life, though I am successful by western standards, that is, I have a career, financial independence, and relative sound health and happiness, I see myself as having been like a water bug. I used this comparison when I first got into A.A. to describe how, when contending with boredom or loneliness, I would go about filling up blank time with drinking. Other than figuring out when I could safely throwback my next drink, and now that I'd already found my job and calling, I had no vaster goal, dream, or purpose. Alcoholism is really about an emptiness within, so even sobered up, yet still not having found Christ and believing that I had it all figured out, I continued to flit about here and there, looking to and fro. My inner self quietly but persistently still *wondered what my life was all about.*

When I first got saved is when I was particularly vulnerable and susceptible to Satan's lies. I had switched camps, and he was not a happy camper! His favorite ploy with me was and is to tell me that all is futile, that *this was all there is*. Sobriety brought me a clear head, but Satan would have liked to have kept me there stuck. *A life without alcohol is not a life with Christ*, not to mention salvation. I know that now. I became acquainted with Satan's power first-hand, and I knew it as such even when I sent Mark that first email. I experienced a rush of cynical assumptions scorching my brain as to why this and that wasn't going to happen, that this was the most preposterous idea ever. The second time I became aware that Satan was trying to derail and incapacitate me was when I caught on to an easy and tried and true method for him. He made a mockery of my faith through old voices pushing doubt like drugs into my head. Of course, bad things happen, and sometimes *it's just life*, and they're not due to anything evil in and of itself. You know when dejection comes from Satan when your spirits become not only downcast, but there is an element of evil or a tinge of wrongfulness to the circumstance that's independent of your mood or the situation. Starting on my path with Christ put Satan on double-duty, and sometimes I felt like I was being attacked by a flock of pterodactyls on a vast desert. He would do *anything* in his power to get my attention off Him, but, as I said, over time, his methods do get more predictable. He'll always go for your weak spots, so you should have some awareness about this. He goes for the easy pickin' areas of your life, especially those which involve people who know you best and can get you riled. For me, unfortunately, these tended to be family members, the very ones I sought to know Christ! How dare he pit me against my family! And yet, more often than I'd like to admit, my disposition could quickly turn sour around them if I judged some aspect of their life off-the-mark by Him! Agh, shame on me! Another general method he uses to maim is to divide and conquer. He likes to get us isolated to pick us off; he can more easily corner us into a mindset trap of despair. What I taught in the Puritan period of American lit. in dealing with the ways the devil traps us, I was now experiencing first-hand in his attempts to get my goat or prick my pride. He frequently tried to pit Bonnie and me against one other because we were the very ones who could provide the best and most immediate support for each other in our respective walks with Him. Thank goodness for the peace He provides!

Even though I am now a believer, it is sometimes hard to understand how or why faith took in me. Why *me*? *How* me? Why not my [fill in the blank of some friend or family member]? Satan will try his best to tell you that you *aren't* saved and that this isn't even possible. And yet, the fullness and richness of God's love *rushes* into our souls like a welcomed breeze or warn wind and *blows him away* as King Jesus fills us with peace and hope. God speaks to us in *so* many ways in ordinary life. Sometimes He contacts us through natural phenomena, like a friend's hand on your shoulder delivering a touch of unexpected support, a glorious sunset at the beach, the perfect operation of any one of our body's systems, a hearty laugh, or the smile of a child. God also speaks through words, so let's begin with *His Word*. I don't have enough space or time to tell you how life-changing and mysteriously interactive reading the Bible is; you'll have to discover this for yourself! In like vein, I have experienced saying things or writing when *the words come out of their own accord* as if He were using me to speak to others. This has happened when I feel both still and invisible, like a vessel ready for His speech, and when I am out of the way so He can make use of me. On both occasions, if He is in the way to have His way, the words seem to come of their own (i.e., His) volition, as if they were provided on the spot; I'm utterly aware that *I* didn't think of the words to say. The right words flow when I am obedient and try not to overthink matters I have no control over or those of greater significance than meets the eye. Time and again, God provides and keeps His promises, especially when I'm anxious about an unknown or some harrowing moment. Mark reminded me not to fret because "it will be given you in that hour what you are to say. For *it is not you who speak, but it is* the Spirit of your Father who speaks in you" (Matthew 10:19–20, emphasis mine). His truths and wisdom can come forth through me. I am one in a very long line of inspired people who have been driven by His will to share His wisdom and ways with my own words and experience. Do you see? By the way, He told me to say this, too.

As I make my way forward, at times, I stop to reflect and to catch my breath. It's incredible for me to think that I may be halfway through my life, but just an infant in Christ. Just like in A.A., there is freedom in surrender and submission, both the freedom *from* choosing the enticing or harmful and the freedom *to* do the things in life I am fashioned to; I'm certain mine is to be a beating heart of communication. It's really so awesome to think about that! Why do you think I'm writing this book? It's for *you* who are reading this, and, ultimately, it is my gift to Him! At this writing, I am now almost eight years away from retirement, and I realize that time is of the essence, that I can't afford to waste time to do the things that I can and want to do to glorify God. I'm not waiting for retirement to do this or that! Am I such a different person now? You'd better believe it! Am I also still the person that has all the flaws, defects, experiences that have gone into making me who I am today? Of course, I am. Did my brain fall out when I decided to believe in God? No, in fact, it has opened up even more, and I have so much more that He compels me to do, and as I accomplish them, more will be revealed. Though certain circumstances may not make sense at the moment, I have faith in the plans to which He calls me. Maybe all my teaching has been leading to this need to share with *you*, gentle reader. Perhaps my traveling has been goading me to do *this* type of service for those to encounter Him in my print. Maybe this book will be translated into another language. Only God knows! He may use me in this fashion to reach someone out there to come to know Him. My service to Him is my love note back to Him! I may be but "a vapor" (James 4:14), but I hope to be a dense one! It is overwhelming to think that He can read my mind and knows my every thought and deed that I have ever had or will have; there are zero secrets from Him. It's also both awesome and terrifying to think that God examines my underlying motives, plans, and desires, as well as bolsters the gifts and talents with which He endowed me. Considering His intimate knowledge of me and my searching for that which pleases Him enables me to say that I have a *personal* relationship with Him; in fact, it would be an understatement extraordinaire.

Honestly, I feel like I'm only just getting to know Him! At the onset of my salvation and throughout these early years of sanctification, I haven't appreciated how tantamount a *personal* connection with Him is. Initially, I thought it meant that as a follower of God, I was to be *personally available* to serve Him in a way that He shaped me from my inception. Later, as I would take a look at the differences and similarities between Eastern Orthodox Christianity and Protestantism, I would see evolving within me an appreciation of *both* perspectives, which, in turn, brought a sense of harmony in me; that, too, was a blessing from God. Like the old skin sloughing off which was being replaced by new, I am undergoing a metamorphosis as He continues to have His way with me. It is still my skin in that it isn't unfamiliar, but part of my nature is new to me. When I glance back at the moment in college when I attended that Baptist Church and didn't understand what it meant to "die to self," let alone to be "crucified with Him" (Romans 6:6), it is no wonder I tore out of there, terrified and distraught to the point that I swore I'd never go back. That was the flesh speaking *with no spirit*, just as a soulful person can *seem* animated but is dead inside. Now that the Holy Spirit has been housed in me, it would take me some time to fully appreciate Who the Holy Spirit was, and that process is forthcoming. Suffice it to say, I realized that I had had some profound misunderstandings about the Trinity. Again, Mark would help steady me as I went from using training wheels to riding two-wheeled and hands-free.

5.19 First Steps into Exploring the Trinity and God's Part

In Mark's introduction to the Trinity, he made the analogy that he was a father, a son, and a pastor all at the same time. Which role he was engaged in was dependent on the context and what he was doing at the time; he could only be one of these identities at a time. All the while, these parts of himself were within the one man of Mark. A year or so later, this comparison, which was initially relatively easy to understand, I would want to know where and how I fit in the matrix with my Creator and Savior; after all, I was now connected to God *and* Christ through the Holy Spirit. Even if I knew I wasn't in *Their* whole midst, the Trinity certainly wasn't exterior to me anymore. What was my positioning relative to God? In digging deeper and wanting to know just *how* the Holy Spirit resided in me, I would roll this over and over in my mind by reading as much as I could on Him. I even drew pictures for myself to better visualize the Trinity. How was I to fit into this mix? Could I? Then, I'd flip it around. I would ponder about God within *His* trio as He dealt with man: though I had no problem acknowledging His omnipotence, which is manifested throughout time, material, and space in ways obvious and not yet known, I possessed a flawed concept about where He stood in relation to us, His creation. Like an old Russian proverb which says that "God is high above, and the tsar is far away," I viewed God as too distant or even busy to be even remotely, let alone intimately concerned with me! Unlike some churches which depict Him as a "gotcha" God," that is, One Who is *so* nearby that He's ready to pounce on a person or use guilt, shame, and fear to scorch his esteem, I didn't really think He could be *bothered* with me. I've already told you that I believed that there are millions in far greater need than I. I suppose this thought stems from the fact that I am acutely aware of how good I have it compared with survivors of war, atrocity, or deprivation, and much of the time, I feel spoiled, prideful, and wealthy (though I'm not rich). Very early on, Mark asked me what or who I thought God was, and I answered correctly, almost formulaically: "love." It would take some time before the word and His love would grow in me. God isn't on autopilot, and His love isn't to be just dismissed as just another given. One has to get *engaged* to experience His love beyond knowing the fact of the matter. Once I began to cling to Him, it pleased me to hear that He is a "jealous" God (Exodus 3:14); I could relate to that! Not too much later, I initially sought to resist this so-called gift of love because I didn't want to feel obligated to or guilty over someone's dying for me when I hadn't even asked for such a thing! All the while, my being drawn closer to Christ would have a collateral impact on my fellowship with friends and challenge me in ways I couldn't have anticipated.

5.20 CHALLENGES OF BEING NEW IN THE FAITH

The summer after I got saved, I remember I had quite an in-depth argument with my former student and now close friend, Catherine. To my discredit, my head-strong insistence on my view cost me not to speak to her for almost three months. Why? In that early period, I thought I could convince or effectively argue with one dear to me such that she or he might see the light. Oh, how wrong I was, and how off-putting this mentality is! Of all people, how could I not have known this?!? While Catherine *had* been a practicing Christian some fifteen years ago, at the present report, she had come to reject the Church — not God — altogether. Catherine challenged the church's authority on how it chose to speak for God because in so doing, invariably, some church members or leadership would publicly pick, point, and deem who was or was not eligible for salvation, like some bad Duck Duck Goose game. If she had to fear for one moment that anyone *she* loved turned out to be the odd-man-out in some cosmic version of a maniacal musical chairs practical joke, well, she'd have no part of that. Just how "narrow" *is* His way anyway (Matthew 7:14)?!? Is it a slender thread or dotted line such that you are doomed before you even start to make your way through life, all the while walking on His tightrope, teetering over the flames of Hell? She bravely concluded, "I think not," only with much more colorful language. This I see and get now, but at the time, I was only affronted at her throwing the baby, Christ, away with the dirty bathwater, the Church. In fact, she went from rejecting the Church's authority to questioning the whole of Christianity, including its exclusive claim to God, the Bible's authority, and the various views or interpretations of points Jesus made. What to do and whom to trust? She opted for (d) none of the above and stayed at home, stewing over the obvious errancy of man's mistake depicting Jesus as a snob and getting farther away from Him in the meanwhile. No matter how hard I tried to convince or prove to her that there is *only one way to God* in spite of the many different types of religions out there, she would come back and retort that there *are* many paths to God, all equally valid! What religion a person is likely to choose has *so* much to do with what culture she is born into and the people to whom she has been exposed. For the first time in our lives, we were not communicating, and it was I who was speaking *at* her. At the time, being around people I loved, yet wanting to talk about Christianity and feel regular, was like driving with the brake and accelerator on at the same time. My innate conscience Mark once described as the "governor" of my system, but when I sensed God not being appreciated or respected, I pushed the accelerator of my zeal past what I knew was right, and I produced hurt. Satan probably said, "Chalk one up for me." It would take me time to realize that this mystical coming to Jesus or seeing the proverbial light occurs in *God's timing*. For the conversation that she and I had to have to turn out in *His* favor, the power of the Holy Spirit would have had to have been involved in Catherine's will and state of life readiness. That said, I could have been a better draw for Christ, but *I, too, wasn't ready*. And for the record, when you hear a Christian say that the Holy Spirit must be involved in the process leading to salvation, this is not passive resignation or waiting for seeming random forces to be aligned. I only mean even if a person is exposed to His love and comes to have a suppleness of spirit such that he or she *is* receptive to eating this "bread of life" (John 6:35), that's not enough, but it *is* a start. We do not come to Christ through any impressive efforts of our own *or* another's doing. It's an inside job done by a loving Outsider. There's a verse that hit the bullseye which speaks to this: "For by grace you have been through faith; and that not of yourselves, it is the gift of God; not as a result of works, so that no one may boast" (Ephesians 2:8–9). Having the capacity to know Jesus is a gift in itself, but it doesn't mean I take no part in choosing to affirm my faith in Him. I am not passive. It just means I can't manufacture the potential for salvation or self-generate a faith activated any more than I can create a star. With this in mind, I finally understood the delicate interplay between God's creative forces, the Holy Spirit's orchestration, and my (or any person's) participation. The believer has a responsibility to be on-call and ready to provide a blanket of love if reception or curiosity is to be sparked in the nonbeliever. He or she must be an encourager, a cheerleader, or a shoulder to cry on. Yes, this would include those like Catherine, who had hit pause and tapped out of doing life as a Christian because some referee made a bad play on her court. All this churning, deliberating, and stewing over this and that at times brought me to a state of weariness. Fretting gets you nowhere. Sometimes there was something inside me that said, "This is all just a *lot*!" Now I understand why it is optimal for a person to be introduced to Jesus when he or she is a child. As soon as we can talk and walk, begins our search for meaning. Then and there come all the "*whys?*" and "*how comes?*"! If we ignore or dismiss this or tell the child "he can decide for himself when he's an *adult*," we rob the child of the opportunity to wear shoes when he is ready! When that child becomes an adult and the desire has long been squelched, callouses likely cover his soles *and* soul. It becomes much harder, if not impossible, for him to wear footgear. Quite frankly, this is why I feel like I'm a walking miracle!

5.21 AN INVITATION TO CHURCH STARTED A WILDFIRE

How did the miracle come about? The mundane occurrence of *a friend simply inviting me to church and my agreeing to go* is what got the ball rolling. I cannot overstate the magnitude of this simple act! I want to be that friend! From going to church to not wanting to stop pursuing God, I attribute to God and give *Him* the glory and credit, but I will forever be indebted to my friends who invited me there in the first place! I'm so glad the Holy Spirit stirred *their* hearts even to consider asking me there! It all goes back to *Him*, don't you see?! What a sense of irony, patience, and humor God has! My becoming a Christian could only have sprung from God. What are the chances that the daughter of a Unitarian mother, a social activist and rebel to her core, and of a Greek Orthodox father, an organic chemist with a free-thinking spirit, would become a Christian? The chances are slim-to-none. Neither parent practiced the faith or attended the church of his upbringing, and I grew up a rationalist and intellectual, pitying or scoffing at Christians. Now I was one of them! Though faith came to me relatively swiftly, absorption of what my change meant came slowly, and with that, an insatiable desire to understand much more.

For starters, the notion of Christ's substitution was problematic for me. How could *one* man absorb or propitiate *all* of the sins of the world? When I finally realized that this man was one of the Trinity, having the same aspect or attributes as God, all of this became possible and made sense. Jesus is not just some man, but *God in the flesh* — the *only* incarnate part of the Trinity who presented Himself to us through a normal-looking human life but who had the infinite capacity to take on *all* sin unto Himself. He and only He has the power to do a once-and-for-all cleansing. That said, though the potential to be saved is universal and for all-time's-sake, this does *not* mean that everyone is *automatically* saved; otherwise, faith would play no part! As mind-boggling as God is, when I think about what Jesus had to do, that is, to limit Himself and suffer the way He did for us, it sometimes occurs that doing this seems more arduous than creating the world, etc., no disrespect intended! What Jesus accomplished is beyond epic! And how Jesus taught folks of His day, for me as an educator, is breathtaking. Plus, *I* could take in what He had to say too. He knew His target audience and used analogies and imagery already familiar to *them*! He didn't come right out with harsh and sharp commands in delivering His message; people then *and* now get turned off and don't listen. Though peaceful, polite, and patient as He shared lessons through parables, He also knew when to be bold, direct, and forceful. With perfect timing, Jesus used irony to point out hypocrisy in prideful ones that leaves you shaking your head. I was captivated by and in love with Him, staggered by the impact He was having on me compared to how I *used* to think and be. I would sometimes ask myself, "Who was I to bring up Jesus with some other person? It's neither my job nor my place." Yet, at the same time, I had this inexplicable desire to share my faith as I've never wanted to share anything before. What did this look like for this teacher at work in school? Well, I'll tell you. Gradually and in subtle ways, my teaching began to change subtlety. Whereas before, I might have only perfunctorily mentioned or in passing explained some allusion made to the Bible, but now I used that reference as an opportunity to more fully describe the biblical context and relate it to the passage at hand. I would linger on select passages in British literature, starting with Milton's *Paradise Lost*, the purpose of which was to "explain the ways of God to man." Shakespeare's tragic play, *Hamlet*, compelled me to dive deep and get to the heart of the *why* of complex matters, like Hamlet contemplating suicide. In John Donne's Holy Sonnet, "Death, Be Not Proud," we learn how death is "defeated." These examples and many more gave me fresh opportunities to gently, indirectly, and yet lovingly point them to the power of God and Christ. The same held true for my Russian students whenever religion was brought up in a culture project. His light touch became fused in my teaching. I also became aware that instead of trying to do something awesome for God, God could do something extraordinary *through me*: there is a huge difference!

Little did I know then that making Jesus a part of my life not only impacted how I approached certain points in the classroom, but I would come to rely on Him as I underwent a test of strength and character at work. Speaking of school, I want to share with you just what my early education involved in getting better acquainted with Jesus.

5.22 A Shift in Reading

By now, Bonnie and I completed Henry Blackaby's daily workbook study, the cover of which had depicted on it the Charlton Heston-like Moses (whom I took for God). Bonnie's brother gave us this to jumpstart our faith into a more in-depth understanding, but even more importantly, into *action*. As a direct result of going through this workbook, we knew we needed to *do* for Him as well, but what would that look like? It soon became apparent that Bonnie had the spiritual gift of being a servant; she was the type to be the hands and feet of God. She pledged to say "Yes" and do anything and everything within her power that came her way if the church asked for volunteers. I was in awe of her. We also finished reading another book that summer called *The Purpose Driven Life*, by Rick Warren. Three years later, we would do a small-group study called "Forty Days in the Word," also by Warren, which taught us how to read and study the Bible, including several useful approaches. This would be just the beginning of my reading Christian-themed non-fiction or theological material. For someone who appreciates fiction and loves rich literature, it was novel for me to seek out hefty studies on more esoteric topics, but I was compelled. It's not that I loved literature less, but I sought His truths more. Anyway, how could I *not* read the Bible *and* study about it, especially now? To be honest, for years now, every time I'd frequent a bookstore, I'd go up and down the aisles, searching for a title to rivet my attention, hoping that something would catch my eye and move me. Reading the latest or greatest for entertainment's sake, especially if the selection contained no pith, beauty, depth, or hope, would leave me discontent. My standard for excellence in fiction remained classic nineteenth-century Russian literature or twentieth-century American Southern literature. It makes sense to me now because these authors typically dealt with weightier matters concerning our purpose, life's ironies, as well as conflict over core values.

Dimitria Christakis

As a Christian, my focus became singular and intent on reading that which would deepen the contours of my Christian thinking and ingest that which was biblical in focus, germane, and yet practicable, too. What better way to start than to participate in a focused study of the oldest book in the New Testament, the Book of James?

5.23 THE BOOK OF JAMES AND HOW I CAME TO READ THE BIBLE

In addition to using the *MacArthur Study Bible*, we would soon take up a focused study through Mark's teaching us all about the Book of James, written by Jesus' half-brother. Mark got it into his mind that he was going to lead a no-nonsense study of the Epistle of James every evening in our church for the full month of February; this ambitious study was phenomenal in that I got to see with my own eyes how a pastor read his Bible. It looked more like massaging than reading, slowly pouring over phrase by phrase, working in the previous one with the following one, then commenting on the whole of the passage upon its completion and taking heed of certain nuances or shades of meaning of words that the original language conveyed. Then add to that any references made to the Old Testament embedded within the passage at hand. Such a rich and rewarding process! To witness how he studied the word was like watching a farmer plow a field with a blade that was four shares deep! Plus, in the process of filling myself with a fuller sense of Who He is, I was falling deeper in love with Him! One evening, Mark stressed the need *to let go* of hurtful events, people, as well as one's own past actions, all of which could weigh a person down and prevent his or her growth in Christ. Part of this process necessitated forgiving others as well as oneself. I challenged Mark by telling him that I didn't think it was my place to forgive *myself*. He gently replied, "You have never been loved by anyone the way that God loves you, and when you let go of that pain or wrong-doing, you are, in effect, *freeing yourself for the goodness and service God has in store for you.*" He also taught us about the power of speech and to be wise in this, that, contrary to the child's rhyme, words most certainly can and do hurt. He also focused on the benefit of trials and pains endured for Him and stressed the necessity to "be doers of the word and not merely hearers" (James 1:22), in effect, to put your money where your mouth was; talk is cheap. Mark stressed that we don't have the luxury of holding onto some trophy of hurt; anyway, Jesus already eradicated it. I *only* have the rest of my life to be useful to Him, and who knows how short that may be? I must press on and reach forward. I am not going to rehash all of what we learned in the book of James, but I can tell you that reading and studying were not for the sake of merely acquiring new information. For me, this was a trembling *heart knowledge* I was coming by. Plus, I didn't want to be like some Pharisee who had clout but missed the boat!

Over time, I hoped I would become softer and more compassionate, all the while maintaining my edge and putting His Word into effect in a manner that mattered. I was just an eager beaver at this early stage and knew I had a long way to go. It may seem petty, but for that month, I joined another gym nearer my house so that I could still work out and make it to this study every evening. In short, my dedication to go to church more than on just Sundays (and now, Wednesdays) kept growing, and my desire to be with these people I'd come to know, one at a time, even if just through a friendly face and a name, increased. What in the world was happening to me? The answer is that I was getting a new family, a family of brothers and sisters whom I'd know for eternity. About a year and a half later, our church would add a new campus which was only five minutes from the house. Before this connectedness, I would have judged those people as small-minded, fake, or provincial, the operative word being "judged," the very word I was poised and ready to accuse *them* of being towards *me*! Then who would have been the hypocrite?! Now, here I was consorting with, looking forward to seeing, and, yes, coming to love them. Wow!

My morning time with God was growing and developing too. After I read my Bible, I also started to read two daily devotionals. One was by Oswald Chambers called *My Utmost for His Highest*; it is hardcore in its intensity because of how he challenges us. The other was *Jesus Calling*, and it is written from a first-person perspective as if Jesus ire speaking to us. I used these to help propel me to more meaningful prayer. At first, I set my alarm clock back just ten minutes, realizing that this was not enough time, I tried twenty minutes. Even that was not long enough, so I backed it up to thirty minutes so that I could read and study all I set out to do. This was just year one. My approach to reading the Bible was initially three-pronged: I started out simply making my way, one chapter at a time through the Old Testament, and then I alternated by months a chapter or page per day each from

Proverbs and the Psalms. I would end with a chapter from a Book or Letter in the New Testament. For the next lap, I'd do a chronological approach to the New Testament. Later, I'd read less and find additional studies or commentary to help me go more in-depth. In these early days, however, since I had never read, let alone studied the Bible for its own sake, I approached doing so like one of those super-wide combine harvesters, trying to cover a lot to make up for lost time. It was not an in-depth study, just a broad, steady manner. Despite my being middle-aged, I felt like someone who'd just learned to read for feeling so moved or amazed by this and that in the quiet of the early morning hours; it was like Christmas every day! I had difficulty not wanting to stay right where I was and just keep on reading. Anyway, you get the idea; this was to be a habit of love and one never to be finished. Not only did I find myself needing to get up earlier to study and to pray, but I became hyper-aware of the preciousness of prayer, yet here, too, I didn't feel like I knew what was doing! I saved the best for last, this conversation with Him, and I hoped that just talking would be good enough. I always started with a pile of gratitudes that came to mind, and then I moved on to a request or two; after all, I didn't want to seem too demanding. (This was before I more fully understood His power.) After my offers of gratitude were uttered, I didn't always feel like He was listening to me, but when I stopped talking so much and became more at ease with quietly and expectantly listening, there was a special envelopment that I could sense, especially if I had a concluding thought that He acceded to some prayer of mine which was on-point. Did this happen every time? No, but that it could, and when it did always move me, no less than if He'd touched my cheek with His hand. Plus, I should add that there's something powerful about getting on one's knees to pray that is very fulfilling. So many other thoughts came to me that I'd never considered before, for example, in reciting the Lord's Prayer, the part that says, "Give us this day our daily bread," refers not merely to physical provision but to the soul-filling sustenance of His Word. I would also come to experience His Word as not only something essential and elemental to me but *mighty*; after all, Paul dubbed it "the sword of the Spirit" (Ephesians 6:17).

I continue with the topic of biblical growth and faith with a dash of apologetics. Did I understand all that I then read in the Bible with clarity and accuracy? Hardly! I did not — not by a long shot. I was patient with myself here because I knew He was okay with me just where and as I was. One's attempt to better fathom Him is not as important as coming *to* Him; depth of discernment and biblical literacy will grow with time and loving effort. If comprehension of this supreme Judeo-Christian text were a prerequisite to being saved, we'd all be done for! Speaking of having faith, this particular study of James meant more to me than I confessed because I felt like I had something in common with both James and the doubting Apostle Thomas. My capacity for faith in Him had been as rife with doubt as theirs! I certainly wouldn't believe my brother if he claimed divinity for himself, and I can totally imagine asking to feel the hole in Jesus' palm! That adds credibility to the story of Jesus' life. Now I don't *have* to doubt, fret, or wonder because James and Thomas already went there and did that. I can learn from *their* lessons and say with assuredness that Jesus is Who He said He is. Soon after learning more about James, I was bowled over to discover that hundreds of people actually saw a different but altogether living Christ *after* He was crucified. This account was carefully researched and documented by the good doctor Luke, who conducted interviews with eyewitnesses. How could I, too, not see that this was not just some ordinary man? Who but God incarnate could come back from death to show us, prove to us, that through a connection of faith in Him, the Son, life *is* everlasting and eternal, even if in a capacity that *we* cannot fathom or appreciate *here and now*? No one! I was no longer Doubting Dimi!

Before, in all my worldly wisdom and ignorance, I took no small glee in pointing out discrepancies, inconsistencies, or apparent contractions that were scattered throughout the Bible. When I came to believe and started reading the Bible, I was certainly not looking for, let alone discovering the fulfillment of so many promises, prophesy, gems of wisdom, and pearls of truths contained therein. You can research for yourself the wealth of available historical data and documents that corroborate, validate, authenticate, and thereby prove that the timeline and personages contained in the Bible are, in fact, accurate. Discrepancies, inconsistencies, and the like can be explained either as minimal. They do not alter the essential, central truth, or they point to a difference in standards of measurement used (e.g., the recording of time and storytelling techniques). There are plenty of dependable eyewitnesses who have no reason to gain from Jesus' story being shared; indeed, the wealth and variety of accounts given only serve to strengthen the claims of His Resurrection and Ascension. In short, I would come to take into account *the spirit of the whole* of the Bible and not try to make mincemeat of the sum of its parts. And though we may not be able to adequately or accurately account for the terms of time given, let alone myriad details that may not make sense to *us*, does that mean the whole Bible is invalid? No! To illustrate, I told Bonnie once that I could recognize Mark by the drawing his eight-year-old son drew of him as well as any photograph. Was it entirely accurate? No. Was it unmistakably and undeniably Mark? Yes. What about whether or not I am to take certain points literally or figuratively? I think the answer is not either/or, but *both/and*. I'm not so extreme or stubborn to say everything in the Gospel is meant to be taken literally, with no interpretation of or pondering over this or that permissible. Events and words beyond their surface often unfold to convey greater truths! Just look at Jesus with His parables! There is so much beautifully, symbolically, and even hauntingly written; this can be no ordinary storybook of historical fiction. Now, as far as claiming any identity with any particular denomination, I would come just to want to call myself a *Christian*. Period. There were too many roadblocks that might come up if I labeled myself this or that. This included both Greek Orthodox and Baptist, the former with its greater focus on heritage and history by which I had been so enamored, and the latter still held negative associations for those I might be able to reach in the future (yes, through the help of the Holy Spirit). I may have been baptized Greek Orthodox as an infant, but what of it now? What to do? What good came of my being baptized as an infant now looking back, some fifty years later? Not much more than pride in my heritage. I had become familiar with some foundational truths, but the devil is in the details. I was now coming to see that I was, for sure, *Protestant* in my interpretation of the Gospel. In short, I am a joyful pilgrim of not-such constant sorrow, making slow-but-steady progress, and I would claim no particular denominational identity within Protestantism.

Meanwhile, I would take a good and hard look at the differences between the enduring Orthodoxy and my new-fangled and precious Protestantism.

5.24 ORTHODOXY VERSUS PROTESTANTISM:
A Closer Look

The dynamics would change regarding the discussion of religious matters between my family and me. It wasn't so easy. They *all* believe in *God* in *some* capacity, but Jesus was a topic off the table where His divinity was concerned; therefore, religion, in general, was usually avoided altogether. We tacitly agreed to disagree, and I wasn't around them enough to be any sort of beacon for Him to them. On the other hand, tremendous and joyful progress occurred regarding Bonnie's relationship with her brother, Josh, and his wife; it was fantastic and more than I could have dreamed of for her. While we were new in the faith, Bonnie and I went and visited her brother and sister-in-law like so many times before, but this time was different. We shared what we'd learned, felt, and experienced in our falling in love with Christ, and I didn't hesitate to discuss Scripture and ask questions I had at the moment. In short, there were no brakes, no hesitations, or no attempt to avoid, curtail, or cut short our flow of conversation on Jesus. It couldn't have been more opposite than what I experienced with my family. This unique and gratifying interaction would become the norm for us four, even if we only saw each other seasonally, and we heartily enjoyed a full fellowship that led to a burgeoning and robust friendship. Perhaps it was invigorating for them to have befriended those with a fresh or unique perspective, and without a doubt, for me, it was like meeting them anew, too, this time as a brother and sister in Christ. This type of camaraderie would only increase with time. We even broached the topic of mission work, which led to my re-examining Russian religiosity anew. Having done mission work in both Romania and Georgia, where the predominant amount of the populace is Orthodox Christian, I finally got to ask Bonnie's brother and sister-in-law, this time out of concern and curiosity, why they tried to convert a people who were already Christian and in a place where Christianity had survived for centuries and remained the dominant religion. Why go *there*? Why save *them*? They answered me gently and with ease that these people knew *of* Jesus, but they didn't know *Him*. I felt free to give them a bit of a religious backdrop on Russia to justify why I had asked them this.

Compared to many American churchgoers I had observed, I thought Russians were as earnest, devout, and longsuffering of Christian believers as they came. There was such a profound reverence and respect for the utter holiness and sanctity of God that seemed in due order in contrast to the all-too-familiar, informal, if not unintentionally flippant regard I saw many younger Protestants take towards Christ. It seemed to me that Catholics were overly obsessed with the agony of this Man's final hours; indeed, the Crucifixion is *the* prominent focal point in every cathedral. I readily concede that such an uninformed opinion coming from me before becoming a "real" Christian is highly ironic; I should have disqualified myself. Bonnie's brother and his wife both remarked about the Orthodox use of icons and their cult-like focus on Mary; the focus *should* be solely on Jesus. Years ago, at our first conversation about this, I slipped into a defensive posture and focused on the *institution* of Christianity being present for centuries in Russia and its orbital countries. At the time, I was in a different mental paradigm and did not consider probing the nature of *faith*, let alone what (or who) all was included in their worshipping Him. A little later on, conducting my own research brought me to a state of a readiness to assent that, in addition to Christ, there was so much more that *they* considered obligatory or essential to worshipping Him. In fact, however, there is *not*. We would continue this discussion more as time went by, but at least we'd made a start! Further, seeing as how we had a Romanian visitor getting ready to visit our little church, I next took the opportunity to survey Mark on this matter. His statement was simple: he just said they [Orthodox Christians] were "hung up on traditions." This, too, wasn't adequate for me only to concede they weren't true-blue Christian. I wanted to know if there were other theological or significant differences because, at their fundamental core, Protestants and Orthodox and Catholics *all* believe in the Trinity! Why evangelize to people who are not only already Christians but ones who have lived where Christianity has survived for *centuries*? Even the recent hiccup of seventy-ish years of atheistic Soviet totalitarianism couldn't eradicate it!

What could these well-intended American Protestants possibly know or feel or understand about this place I'd been studying and visiting with some regularity since 1982? I was flooded with fond memories of ethereal and somber Byzantine icons (not the chubby, pink, or meek ones of the west), of their richly ornate churches (that weren't so vast and impersonal as cathedrals or practically stark-naked as Protestant churches), the interior walls which were so full of these images or quasi-family portraits, that one would be hard-pressed to find any bare space remaining. As an Orthodox Christian, in addition to the obvious stars of Christianity, who are in proper and predictable order right up front, you are surrounded by icons depicting real and flawed persons who in faith had done extraordinary things for Christ in their lives. What inspiration! These images were right alongside icons of bold church elders and bishops, without whom Christianity as a religion might not have survived past the second century, so outcast, persecuted, disenfranchised, and unsolidified as a movement were the zealous followers of His Way. Thank goodness for Emperor Constantine! In any event, Bonnie's brother and sister-in-law continued to let me share my perspective because as a new Christian with the background I did, they knew I would not be willing to make a contrary call as to the nature of faith for Orthodox Christians. I would have to get out of my own way to come to appreciate both perspectives, and even later, know that it was not my place to condemn, but I did have an ardent desire to explain what I'd come to know one-on-one about Jesus. That would come later.

As I continued to study, I reflected on things I'd taught in school and previously known only from an *academic* stance. I was still drawn to my religious heritage, yet I began to be open to evaluating Orthodoxy with new eyes since there was no denying that I'd adopted the Protestant stance toward God, direct and unveiled, as it were. My new identity cracked the chink of my protective armor, that is, my umbrage toward what I formerly considered superficial and lightweight American Protestantism, even though, admittedly, I was smitten with the likes of both Jonathan Edwards and Cotton Mather from the Puritan era. They are hardly jejune. Before my salvation, I didn't see what the big deal was to be able to say one knew Him, but now having experienced this for myself, I knew beyond a shadow of a doubt that there most certainly *was* something of profound significance in being united with Jesus rather than being *associated* with Him, albeit along with the cherished customs, valued traditions, and symbolic art and architecture, existent longer in Orthodoxy than in any other Christian denomination. The longevity of the church's survival doesn't point to *Him*, however. My coming to Christ aside, I had trouble contending with what I saw as their missing the mark, and I didn't want to criticize my spiritual heritage, not to mention my passion! How could I say Orthodox Christians are not saved, that they don't know Jesus? Are you kidding me?!? And so, about eight months after I got saved, I decided to deconstruct and unpack Orthodox theology for myself. I found and ingested several books on this matter — some I read twice— to accurately understand the differences between Orthodoxy and Protestantism. Other than the obvious rejection of the Pope and the more mystical approach to the Godhead in Orthodoxy, there was a distinct difference in whether salvation was perceived as sealed for good *or* one hoped for and worked towards. This distinction gave me pause. My fascination with and pride of Orthodox consistency got infused with a more direct, streamlined, and intensely concentrated Protestant mindset. Being born again — this time for real and not by proxy as one soul in the world He saved — I confess to you has led to my privately and excitedly starting to imagine that maybe I could be a living bridge between east and west, be it in Russia or Greece!

I would come to them *not* with the expressed intent to correct or fix a centuries-old mentality, even if I now considered it just off-center, but to share my own expanded and intensified experience of what it means to partake of Jesus directly. I wanted to testify its being so. Yes, I fully appreciate and respect the Orthodox Church's unwavering consistency in this mad world, spinning like a top, yet I also undeniably came to believe the doctrines of grace alone, faith alone, and Christ alone that are posited in Protestantism. How did this happen? What were these differences? What got me to look beyond the prayers, candles, icons, and centuries of Christianity's deep presence existing there? It boils down to the Orthodox Christian's attitude towards Jesus. I mean, of *course*, they knew Him to be the Savior and Son of God! That's a no-brainer! It struck me that the experience or encounter *I* had with Jesus, which has led to this ongoing hunger for Him and desire to steep myself in accurate discernment of His Word, compelled me to want to *be more like Him*. In a way, this is akin to "progress, not perfection," I heard myself recite from A.A. This state of mind is *not* the same for the Orthodox Christian. Their reverential awe for and faith in Him is expressed by methodically and formulaically (perhaps mechanically) participating in various soothing and familiar rituals, rites, and sacraments. These are learned by all children and remain with them until the day they die. I saw this to be the case with my father. Participation in a church life centuries-old had inadvertently pushed Jesus into a broader backdrop; He seemed not in the singular forefront of the focal point of the operating believer. There were others to be recognized and have respects paid to in this history of His. Protestants didn't concern themselves with the host of helpers or extras responsible for getting the Church where it was; the Greeks did. Protestants didn't look to other folks as role models who'd done extraordinary things in the name of Jesus, just to Christ alone, our "cornerstone" (Ephesians 2:20 NKJV). Please note that Jesus *is* the centerpiece of both Orthodox and Protestant Christianity and *both* emphatically reject the potent figure of the Pope as the go-between for man to God. However, there still remains a whole list of helpers or in-between priests and saints available to aid you on your earthly journey, hopefully, to end up with Him. Orthodox Christians live, not ever knowing if they're saved and heaven-bound. It's a game of hope and chance, whereas I can and do shout from the rooftops, "*Yes, I am saved!*" I began to have one ah-ha moment after another when I chose Christ alone.

It is not the purpose of this book to detail how east and west differ, but I will detail the two central primary points of divergence. First, for the Protestant, salvation — knowing you will spend eternity in Heaven — is at hand the very moment when one repents, that is, when one declares an intentional shift in behavior to follow Him, *and* accepts that Jesus died for his or her transgressions (past *and* future). This decision and experience hits the reset button, such that *now* you start to live your life in and for Him. This is how your *spirit* gets "born again" at some point after the initial *physical* birth. One's salvation is "sealed" from that moment on; our life belongs to Him. We are charged with relinquishing ego and self-centeredness as we take on more of *His* attributes; this lifelong process is called sanctification. Conversely, for the Orthodox Christian, one is baptized as an infant, and this ceremony officially introduces him into the family of his church. From that moment on, he is to be in a lifelong process of something called *apotheosis*, which is an attempt to become more and more like Him to the point of being *in union with* God. Thus, the Protestant knows that his salvation has been realized; the Orthodox Christian does not. The Orthodox Christian would say that salvation can't be known or determined until the moment of death as we do not know the mind of God. Orthodox Christians criticize Protestants for thinking that once Jesus waves His magic wand and takes away sin — poof — that that person is good-to-go and technically doesn't *have* to improve or do anything for Him subsequently. I suppose some Christians *do* accept Christ to get the get-out-of-Hell ticket, and perhaps this is why I, for one, went around telling folks that this was *not* my motivation for coming to Christ. Instead, it is the "fruit" of our lives that bears witness to what kind of Christians we've evolved or matured into (John 15:5). The Orthodox Christian has the impossible task of trying to achieve perfection or union with God in his lifetime. As I stated above, this is called apotheosis or *deification*. Secondly, the Orthodox Church pays considerable attention to the liturgical writings of bishops and early church elders. I suspect this is done out of respect for their vital role in the church's history. In other words, the Bible isn't the *only* book to be read for one's religious edification. On the other hand, Protestants look to the Bible alone as their sole authority of God. In Protestantism, other than the Bible, no book carries that kind of authority or can stake claim in facilitating our Christian growth. None. In so doing, that is, rejecting other sourcebooks, this also increases the intensified focus of a one-on-one relationship with Jesus as opposed to the whole-group mentality of the Orthodox Christian. Yes, it does take a village to raise a Christian, but *I ought to follow no one else's lead but Christ's*. The sense of community in the Orthodox Church as compared to some mega Protestant churches is incomparable. You never leave your church of origin because there is no other from which to choose when you're a grown-up. You do *not* go shopping for churches to find the right "fit" for *you*! Good grief! The Orthodox Cathedral is the same everywhere in what it does and offers, be you in Atlanta, Georgia or Athens, Greece or Moscow, Russia. She, the cross-shaped cathedral, is open 24-7 for spiritual reflection, refreshment, or refuge, and you get a godparent who takes a formal and real interest in your spiritual development. Plus, there are saints and other church figures to fill or inspire you with encouragement and sense that *if they can do it, so can I*! Do you see why it is not so easy for me to ditch or dismiss Orthodoxy? And yet, I do not attend church there. That should tell you everything you need to know: all the good above notwithstanding, it is the direct deposit approach of Protestantism and the singular and eternal lifeline I *know* have in Christ that clinched this course for me.

5.25 East Versus West, Final Takeaways

So how do you get a group of people to shed their traditions and focus intently just on Jesus? Such a project is not an easy task. By the way, the answer is that you don't fix the group; change happens *one person at a time*. To get a better idea of what it's like to change lanes, let's look at change from the perspective of trying to alter something time-honored to you. I'll get up close and personal for the American: let's say, for instance, that you love football and you have a favorite team. What would you think if I came and told you that this team or university of yours would have to change its team's colors or its mascot or its official song? I mean, it's still all about football, isn't it? Okay, you still can have your traditional tailgating party, but what would happen if you no longer had, say, "Rocky Top" to sing? Up in arms, the Tennessee Vols would be! Does it mean that if they engage in all those fun rituals that give them a little sense of eternity that they partake in year after year, they *truly* understand how football is played? Yes, of course, many do. Now consider how many people actually can and do *play* football? There's the rub! In Christianity, we are called to *play* football, and our quarterback is Jesus. We must be in shape for and ready for every pass and move that comes our way, including being prepared to defend our teammates and eager to get back up even when the enemy has tackled us. Regardless, no one is too out-of-shape, untrained, or ill-equipped to join Team Jesus! Oh, and just so you know, never in a million years would I have ever imagined using such an analogy as I am no sports fanatic. Now we are getting to my original analogy. Through no doing of their own, Orthodox Christians are in the choice box seats, so far removed that they need jumbotrons to make out the plays; Protestants are closer up in the stands and are those who get all painted up and roar with gusto for their team. I'm trying to relate two things: first, it is hard to change traditions for *anyone*, so don't judge or be impatient with reluctance or suspicion when change is suggested. I mean, some people get bent out of shape if a visitor sits in their seat at church, for pity's sake! And secondly, when it comes right down to it, a lot of people don't invest the time or energy to get personally involved (that is, really ready to play in my football analogy), so they watch and critique from the ease of their pleather armchair.

But, hey, wait a minute! Back to Jesus! Where did He go? Though I have been baptized Greek Orthodox, from my limited experience of attending the Greek Church, it appears that Jesus gets lost in the shuffle of a crowded room full of frankincense incense, bearded elders, beautiful icons, Mother Mary, and even one's relatives. I had a Russian friend who once remarked that he thought American churches looked like simple "barns" compared to Orthodox cathedrals, which are designed to make one feel as if he were in a little microcosm of the earth under the dome of heaven! (And he hadn't even gone *inside* a Protestant church to see just how unembellished they were!) All of that withstanding, it is *He* who is the one who makes it possible to live forever in glory; it is *He* Who came here to live in the flesh perfectly, all but to die for those that would believe. It is *He* Who is one with God, *is* God. I am one of those who ran straight to Him, and I don't ever want to lose this focus. Therefore, this one-on-one experience and streamlined approach that Protestants take, which cuts to the chase, is the stance I choose. There are other strengths, weaknesses, and differences, but these that I have shared are the most important.

The Protestant viewpoint may seem simplistic at first, but there's such raw honesty, vulnerability, and yet power in being positioned (figuratively) to face God directly; it's no wonder that they (and I) want to evangelize! In Protestantism, to be saved means you have an encounter with the divine, and that you *can* and *do* is not based on history, heritage, effort, or association. You cannot receive the Holy Spirit via infant baptism; it can't work like that, noble or well-intended though the action performed may seem. I'll explain. Whereas the Protestant believes that the moment of salvation begins when you personally accept Christ and that the Holy Spirit then dwells within you, the Orthodox believes that at the moment of chrismation, at infancy, one is *gifted* the Holy Spirit, and baptism marks this moment. At that point, one begins the journey of deification, which would sound blasphemous to the Westerner, as if you could actually think you could come close to approaching Christ's perfect state. Performing church sacraments in the church family's group context facilitates one becoming more Christ-like, such that one tries to work towards perfecting compassionate behaviors and a righteous mindset within oneself. It is not expected for one to be able to fully 100% achieve, mind you. Life is a lifelong, uphill battle whereby one makes strides through acts of kindness and sacrifices as defined by the church. Yes, there is a greater focus on works than faith, but I must admit, though I am to live like Christ as best I can in the real world, I *am* attracted to the Orthodoxy's overt rejection of idolatrous aspects of modern secular life. This stance is not as strong or vigorous in most Protestant Churches, but when it does come into play, the Protestant focus is on spiritual warfare rather than a rejection of the world. That is huge for me because asceticism and monasticism and the like may involve self-discipline and impressive obedience, but you aren't necessarily living a loving life as Christ would have you to do. You're in your own little fish tank, and not many are any better off for it, though from a distance, you may be admired. Ultimately, it is *not* known during the Orthodox Christian's life whether or not he attains salvation, that is, whether he "gets to" Heaven. I can't imagine living my whole life wondering, worrying, and praying without ceasing that I'll "make it" to Gloryland! If Jesus is who He says He is, then my sincere and straightforward response of "Yes" to Him ought to suffice. Anyway, there are no take-backs with Jesus! If there were, that would make Him a liar! I'd have to shun Him. Should I disregard the Holy Spirit's massaging and gently nudging me to turn to Jesus, I would disappoint and *grieve* Him. Plus, with my rejection, I also disrespect God, and then, I disqualify myself of receiving a royal inheritance and life worth living in Him. *That's* why the stakes are so high, and the imperative to share or witness burns inside. Finding God and choosing Christ are *not* accomplished by me through prescribed, piecemeal, or mystical methods. God Himself invited me unto Him! And now, through the Holy Spirit's help, I grunt my unintelligible pangs and sweet prayers straight to the Father and His Son. Oh, this new life with and in Him is life-altering!

As a Protestant, I do *not* believe that one can "do good" one's way to salvation or Heaven. God did not provide a platform for coming to Him through any way other than through Him, Jesus; there is true beauty in such simplicity. It's perfect and complete in that I have direct access to the Trinity itself. That is staggering! I cannot help but revel in the nature of the Trinity, which, I suspect, is not a regular exercise or thought process one typically engages in as an Orthodox Christian. Faith is handed to you on a silver platter. To choose Protestantism is to choose unity and union with Christ here and now. This choice, in turn, brings to my mind the fact that the Trinity is *also* a seamless unity of three different aspects that possess one *essence*. The pre-existent Son of God voluntarily came down; though born of a woman, He did not just morph into a man. Jesus is not half-God, half-man, like some Greek demigod! He is uniquely and fully *both*. This means He is still every bit the holy and perfect one, except while He was here, He got to feel as fragile, vulnerable, weak, and as emotional as we regular humans do. How else could He feel for us but through experiencing life *as* we do?! That said, He wasn't what you'd call happy, yet it was obvious He was full of joy, regardless of what His circumstances were. (The former is in flux, the latter a permanent inner state when you're in allegiance with God.) There is no one else but Jesus who could've gone up against Satan while fasting in the desert for forty days and no one else but Christ Who voluntarily took the punishment for *our* sin and eliminated the final "sting" of death (1 Cor. 15:55). How could I *not* place all my stock and store and faith in Him? Fascinating ideas, revered institutions, and the beautiful things of the world do not point to Him first; these are all temptations, too! By now, I well know I am not to go up against Satan because if I argue with and try to outwit him, I will surely lose. I see this happen around me all the time; it seems to be the tragic norm. Again, I say, the stakes are terrifyingly high. If I had listened to the taunts, jeers, or brilliant arguments from Satan, saying, for example, that this book of love you hold in your hands will come to nothing, then I would never have finished it. The various songs of the siren in Satan I now recognize are the heckles, jeers, and offensive jokes from the peanut gallery; *they and he do not matter*. Satan will try to convince me that my life counts for nothing, or he will try to derail me into squandering precious time on things, busyness, and activities that make me *think* I'm effective or estimable, but I know otherwise. It is Jesus Who lives in me and loves me, and nothing else compares. Anyway, the Apostle John reminds me that "the world is passing away" (1 John 2:17), so how can I not put first things first, and Jesus is my number one! Now I truly feel, as an A.A. saying goes, *"happy, joyous, and free"*!

What is my final takeaway about these two denominations of Christianity? First off, I respect the Orthodox Christian's ability to embrace and acknowledge that there is intrinsic value in the suffering that occurs along one's path. Growth *is* arduous and requires conscious and continual effort. It's not that God is cruel, fallible, negligent, unfair, or lacking in power or goodness such that He refuses or can't make your life smooth-sailing and problem-free. This is a typical western non-believer's misconception. God can interrupt or intercede as He wills insofar as the action serves to fulfill His greater purpose for His glory. If you don't stress or challenge your muscles when you do anaerobic exercises, they will not get stronger. Challenges endured can add grit and lead to wisdom gained. That said, no one seeks or welcomes pain: I am no exception. My father's mantra in life was "patience and persistence"; this phrase that rhymes in Greek expressed his pledge to a life of endurance for the good, no matter what, through thick and through thin. I also appreciate the fact that all Orthodox Christians consider God to be in a community within Himself, just like we should be in a community corporately within our church and family. In other words, though I may have an intimate and personal relationship with Christ, that's just a starting point! Many an American believer is content to have a private affair with Jesus, so much so that he is self-satisfied to go rogue, go *solo* through life, never but once or twice a year entering a house of worship. Contrapuntally, to think that because I have been bestowed with the Holy Spirit at birth or that I can perform sacraments and venerate icons as a means of perfecting myself is ludicrous!

Another aspect of Orthodoxy that I hadn't thought of before is that this denomination of Christianity becomes fused with the nationality and heritage of the country. After all, it's Eastern Orthodoxy that is the particular branch, *not* Greek Orthodox or Russian Orthodox, as one is likely to hear! Can you imagine hearing someone say that she is a Mississippi Methodist or a Pennsylvania Presbyterian?! I bristle over the sense of egotism and entitlement when I hear "God Bless America"! Excuse me, but He blesses *all* of His believers! Is America *really* more "blessed" more than any other country, or is it that she seems more richly endowed?! God doesn't place His stamp of approval on any one particular *country*; we are all in His creation, and we all have the potential to be His children, too! (That withstanding, I *do* intend to pilgrimage to Jerusalem and behold the Holy Land one day!) The icons which previously I found so captivating, hauntingly beautiful, and moving and which are used in conjunction within corporate worship, I now see as a detraction. They miss the mark. Previously I had no idea that they were created as visual aids for people that couldn't read; they became necessary graphics for God's storybook! Centuries later, Orthodox believers still venerate these and ask for the saints and church elders to pray for them because they think they need all the outside help they can get — from friends, family, saints, you name it! It's a group effort to help the individual in his quest for the grail of perfection that our Savior attained. On the other hand, the Protestant comes to Christ naked, bare, knowingly flawed, and alone, soul bared and readied for the gestalt moment for *the ultimate change.* This was *my* experience, and a visceral one it was, indeed! Jesus has forever altered my life! Salvation is not just a hyped-up, pressured-cooker moment of sentimentality or a document inserted alongside my birth certificate as is done in the Greek community as if my baptism serves as a stamp of God's proof of authenticity. It doesn't work like that! Although I am assured that my name has been written in the Book of Life, I will continue to work on my building for all my livelong days. To be sure, sanctification brings new tension with unsaved friends as well as my family of origin. In some ways, I am now a foreigner. If everything and anything I say or do is not done in genuine love, my attempts to share Him will be vain, fruitless, and futile. In the meanwhile, I'll keep putting one foot in front of the other and pray I will represent Him well. There's no time to waste. Looking back, I'll savor and nurture my Greek heritage *and* follow Christ's way through the way of the Protestant. Direct contact is best.

5.26 Growing Faith Leads to More Questions

Three months into starting to read and study Scripture, the questions started coming daily, one right after another, so I began to prepare more for visits with Mark by having my questions ready for him. No one could've predicted how our visits would go or what we would talk about. This was a very fluid and organic process; more often than not, we unearthed other topics of mutual interest to us, including real-life happenings, world events, or just things that struck each other as silly or absurd. In short, we visited as friends always first and foremost, and if the way and time were right to broach my questions within our dynamic conversation, Mark would take on and answer as many as possible. Whatever words or ways he had used to answer me, I'd try to recall and quickly jot down within a day or so after he left from some much-anticipated visit. I wanted to make sure they'd be locked in my mind should that question again arise or some spin-off question come about that could be resolved with whatever he'd already told me. What follows is but the first of many such sets of questions I'd email to Mark. I'll share some of them with you, but please know that it is not my intent to merely provide you with answers in this book. While faith, when it came, was swift, complete, and overcoming, though it was *accomplished*, the whole of it was not *finished* within me. Some questions would take weeks to settle through my inner-wrangling and mulling; other points would converge with my life and be made manifest there; many a puzzlement Mark would find a way to answer, like a master locksmith with a light touch and discerning mind which opens the safe to present the diamonds; other questions I came just to let go, trusting that, in time, God would reveal truths to me in His own way and time. Here's the first batch I wrote to Mark:

1. Has the Holy Spirit always been in me, or did He enter when my heart was moved, and I then fully accepted Christ and what He did for me? If the Holy Spirit didn't enter until *afterward*, what was the source of that tug, that

desire to unite with Christ, that pull leading me towards Him in the first place? Does everyone have the Holy Spirit dormant nearby until God sees fit to deem it time to start the draw, the need, the want to unite with Him? Is He hovering nearby like a hummingbird, now you see Him, now you don't? I *know* it was the Holy Spirit that was making my heart pound that Sunday, April 28th, to come to the foot of the cross to have you usher me to being saved, but as you know, my epiphany actually occurred on the evening after you left me in a state of readiness from that *previous* Tuesday's visit. So, have I had the Holy Spirit in me the whole time since this past Tuesday, or was my salvation activated by going public and coming to the cross to repent and declare my faith and allegiance to Him this Sunday? I know it probably doesn't matter, but I was just curious considering that I felt moved to tears of joy on Tuesday night and then felt on the verge of having a heart attack Sunday morning, *both* times so full and moved.

2. I know that born-again Christians are free from the law as far as salvation goes, yet I also know good and well that our free will does not give us permission or license to sin. Is it so that if one has no discernable change in *outward* behavior and continues to do what some label as habitual, ongoing sin, all the while *professing* to be a Christian, has salvation ever really taken place? I thought it was sealed when you say, "I do." And I *know* He did His part! This situation feels like a conundrum. How can it be that Jesus gives us the two greatest commandments as corequisites with salvation, yet one finds sins that ostensibly negate this? I thought Christ bore the punishment for the curse of all of us believers. Plus, just how do I go about continuing to give up self so that the Holy Spirit (and God) can have His righteous way with me?

3. If the Holy Spirit and the Word must work together for you to hear God speaking, what happens if I am ignorant about some contextual clue or background of an author

or historical moment? Will I miss His point or possibly make an error of judgment or interpretation? I really don't want to get this wrong! I may be saved — and joyfully so — but I still feel like a wretch!

4. Just how am I to address scoffers, cynics, and critics of the Church? Some of my relatives have little regard for the Bible as the so-called word of God compared to other religious texts. They note with disdain the inconsistencies, mock the fairytale miracles, and wryly note that it promotes patriarchy. How can I counter, defend, or show its truth without losing my cool, especially with those I care so much? Am I to mind my own business and appear neutral, uninvolved, or blasé? It feels like I don't care if I play it safe and say nothing. James says Scripture testifies itself about Him, but timing and attitude are critical if I point folks to it gently.

5. The Holy Spirit isn't the same thing as conscience, is it? How do I know when the Holy Spirit is tugging at me to do (or *not* to do) something and not some other subconscious voice in my head?

6. I don't understand what it means to have a missionary spirit. I don't follow how churches choose to do mission work in their countries, especially if *other* churches have already been established there. More often than not, at the moment, I am timid about imposing myself on others, even to testify or witness about Him. That said, I sure hope one day to help lead others wavering or doubting to Him by following my example. I do so want to produce fruit, but I'm not sure what this will look like in the future. I wonder if it might include teaching. All I know is that now that I know and love Christ with all I've got, and in the meanwhile, these questions that arise and pile up inside me sometimes make it feel like I'm producing bitter vinegar, not wine or sweet fruit that I desire. I wanted to have salt, not brine, for Him.

7. I also have a confession and problem for which I don't see a solution: I currently serve two masters, and my idol

is security. The second Commandment deals with false idols, which for me personally takes the form of self-reliance and financial security, and yet I know full well that "No one can serve two masters; for either he will hate the one and love the other, or he will be devoted to one and despise the other. You cannot serve God and wealth" (Matthew 6:24). What does that even mean or look like in the course of everyday life? How exactly does one drop everything, or, conversely, pour God into everything one does? Is there help for this? How will Jesus guide me? I feel doomed here. Not only that, but I feel like my heart daily manufactures new idols. How can this ever be remedied? I feel like I am the manager Jesus referred to who buried his money in the ground.

8. John 17:9 reports Jesus saying to God, "I do *not* ask on behalf *of the world*, but of *those whom You have given Me*; for they are Yours" (emphasis mine). Am I one of these? Just who are God's Elect? And what exactly does it mean to have one's name written in the "Lamb's book of life" (Rev. 21:27)? All I know is that I want my name in that book! Why are so many references to fulfilling OT Scripture and numerous references described as "foreordained"? What part of free will, if any, even truly matters?

In short, I think I'm asking just *how I am to love Jesus*. Maybe it is because I have searched so hard for so long that He still seems far away at times. I can't go a day without God's Word in my head or on my lips. I continue to seek His love. I am clinging to Jesus. When I pray to Jesus, I am overwhelmed when I contemplate just what He did for little ol' nothing me. It is good that what Jesus did for me leaves me awestruck. Most go the opposite way and end up forgetting how awesome it is. The good news is that He isn't a stranger anymore! He lives inside me!

5.27 To Be Saved from There and Spiritual Hiccups

Gentle reader, you *need* to know that all of this questioning, probing, and wondering of mine is *not* because I just signed up for some New Testament class or that I want to please my professor. I am not so cavalier, frivolous, glib, or complacent as to think this journey is some phase or short-lived episode. I am acutely aware that the stakes are profoundly high for me, for you, for *all* of us. We need to *get this right* because what I choose now has *eternal* consequences. I did not want to have a shadow of a doubt about my salvation, and I did not want to give ground to new regrets, offenses, or recriminations. I am told that "without faith, it is impossible to please [God]" (Hebrews 11:6). If I don't have faith in Him, the consequences are simple and unmistakably clear: I will be eternally separated from Him and live on in ongoing anguish, torment, and misery, the likes of which I can't imagine. To be in the immediate presence of God Almighty the second after I die, only to be sentenced to hell for rejecting Him in life, would be worse than the worst I can imagine. To be banished with sudden swiftness, harshness, and finality would be like being shot from a missile straight into an inferno! And from there, it is only downhill to the finale of the lake of fire (Rev. 20:15)! I do not want this for my loved ones or myself! Hell is not like Hollywood depicts it. Why do you think when people get saved, yes, saved *from Hell*, that they have such an urge to evangelize and share His love? Hell was not designed for us, and He never even wanted us to perish to begin with, so why would one want to put oneself right in harm's way by driving on the wrong side of the road? I feel old-school in mentioning this in my testament, but if I didn't, I would be remiss. Perish the thought! Thank my Lord and Savior, Jesus Christ, I will *not* befall this calamity. Why? I believe and know that "as far as the east is from the west, so far He has removed our transgressions from us" (Psalm 103:12).

I would continue to deliberate on the nature of His love. Since God is eternal and non-substantial, how can He or *His* love be *personal*?

How could His love be felt and known to be *from* Him before Jesus arrived on the scene? It is *so* hard to accept Christ's gift as *free* because there is a price for everything in this life, and He paid with His life — hardly a free act! We evaluate our core selves based on the merit and purity of intent, word, and deed. God knows we try, but there's still a ghost in the machine. Can I possibly measure up for Him *after* I'm saved? I do glorify God, but I feel so cheap and undeserving as to accept the very blood of Christ. Sometimes I feel like I won the lottery, and I ask, "Why me?" I did *nothing* but *believe*, and I now have received Christ's indwelling Holy Spirit; I guess that "nothing" meant *everything* to Him. Eyes opened, I have been blown away by the many seeming miracles in my life. Though God made *this* "common clay pot" (2 Cor. 7) precisely as He wanted, does He love and accept *me* in the *same* way when He concluded, "It is good," after Creation? It is so hard to accept Jesus' free sacrifice because if *I'd* have been there at His crucifixion, I'd probably be just another one of the rabble who was duped and forsook Him. No doubt, the media lies of the day stirred the pot and confused folks). Plus, I am *still* loaded with sin, character defects, mistakes, and flaws; therefore, sometimes it hurts to accept the gift that cost Him His life! Who wants the guilt of taking a gift from the guy *you* helped murder, though it was and is for you?!? At the time, I didn't get it, didn't yet fully see how it all comes back full circle to God's love and *His wanting me to want Him*, which, by equivocation and equivalence, necessitates *loving His Son*; they are one and the same. For His giving His life for *me*, how can I not try to avoid sin and I give myself and my life to *Him*? I am His; He is tattooed in my heart. That said, I still love and relish the life He gives us; it's just second place to Him. I must prioritize daily. Next, I'll go from acrobatics in semantics by day to telling you about my dreams of Him at night.

5.28 Girding My Loins with Truth while Sifting through Images

About a week ago, I woke up with a dreadful image that I just couldn't shake and which seemed to rock my young foundations; this, in turn, led to a whole host of other doubts, troubling visions, and unanswered speculations. Though Ephesians reassured me that I have the means of protecting myself during spiritual warfare, I couldn't rid myself of certain troubling images that diverted my attention and distracted me from growing my faith. Here they are and how God helped me overcome them. Back in late April, Christ appeared triumphantly in my mind's eye at my kitchen window such that I couldn't wait to tear the jambs off of the window to get to Him and then feel the whoosh of the Holy Spirit fill me. Inexplicably, unexpectedly, and woefully, only one week later, I then saw as plain as day Jesus' pale, lifeless, marble body, heavy and limp on my kitchen table, just lying there. He looked exactly like the lifeless Jesus in Michelangelo's *Pietà*, which I've beheld five times in my life. It occurred to me again that if I had been alive and at His trial and Crucifixion two thousand years ago, I could just as well have been one of those who said to kill Him! Therefore, not only did I *not* deserve His grace or sacrifice, I was partly responsible, guilty, and culpable for the murder of this perfect man! I had blood on *me*; *I* committed murder! What the Devil kept me from following through in that moment of agony was to realize that He was resurrected three days later, that He wasn't mad at me or anyone, that here and now, I can know and do appreciate the necessity of Christ's Sacrifice. I weep for Him whenever I imagine Him in the Garden praying, probably shaking hard and knowing all the while what excruciations awaited Him in the upcoming, horrific Crucifixion which He was about to undergo for humanity, even (and especially) for those who despised Him. Though that pinnacle moment is past, I have faith that He is *not* dead, that He is radiantly alive and that He *chose* to die in the flesh for us and even for me, here and now. His Spirit is proof positive He lives in and animates me. *Thank you, Jesus!*

A second co-related and troubling image that I just couldn't shake was that of the actual blood of Christ covering me, this in addition to my belief that I was another Christ-killer. I'll describe what I imagined to you here and now, though, suffice it to say, my earliest floundering *did* settle into a more mature perspective. As in some time-warp of chronological distortion, like a scene from a bad movie, I next imagined myself looking up at Jesus from the foot of the cross *as* He was being crucified, His blood coming right down *on* me, and I felt *sick* with guilt. Why did He have to make such a sacrifice? Isn't that our job to do this for Him? Need God's punishment to be so severe? Why did He *have* to die? And in *that* way? For anyone? Everyone? For me? And anyway, can't God can see through His blood on me to the wretchedness underneath? I can't fool God; why hide under blood when imperfections and sins, still thick and apparent, are coursing through my veins? It seemed to me that there's no fig leaf big enough to cover *any* of us. And then this line of thought invariably led to recognizing that it was not just a man, any man, but The Christ, that is, God Who came to take it all away down here to make it possible to start anew. He *is* the *Crème de la Crème*, the quintessential, the nonpareil, the one and only, man in God, God in man, Son of God. There is no one *but* He who could, would, or did make it possible to make such a clean and complete break from sin and death. It is *on me* to obey Him and walk *His* way and *in* His way, slowly but surely undergoing a metamorphosis from the outside in to a more restored core.

Another question that came to me was why God Himself (through His Son) felt He *had* to come down and make such a sacrifice? That sounds rather conceited. Over 2000 years of Jewish history proves that, except for a dozen or so extraordinary ordinary men, people *couldn't* keep the Law; they became litigious, misguided, and arrogant. And let's not forget the Deceiver's role: Satan's arrows barrage us — crafted specially and uniquely for each of us — which zing us off the path of righteousness. I suppose God wanted to make it abundantly clear that we couldn't sacrifice our way to purification. Suppose every one of us sacrificed not just a ram, a goat, a lamb, or a beloved son, but also all of our worldly goods in a giant firey pyre. That we have free will and <u>un</u>knowingly sin on *top* of our volitional sinning renders eliminating them impossible. Then add to our disobedience our succumbing to Satan's master manipulations and machinations. Were it not for Jesus' generosity, we would be done-for. I am grateful! Not so fast! There's more *Because* God made this beautiful world ideally suited for us to live and love in, why *wouldn't* He want acknowledgment for the awesomeness of the gift of Life and His Perfect Love? That's the least we could do!! And Who more perfectly suited to take eradicate *all* of our sins *forevermore* in one fell swoop than He? Why would He create us but to terminate us forever, especially when He is aware just how like infants or buffoons we are in our disobedience? Since in our finiteness and imperfect state we *can't* do that one thing which would bring ourselves square back to Him *and* because He loves us enough to come down here in person to demonstrate how perfectly to live *and* to make that sacrifice for us in one big ka-pow moment, He would and did do it. That's a *lot* of love! And patience. A sacrifice of this magnitude of coverage *had* to be through the singularly perfect man. It was introduced in a manner the Israelites were already familiar with and had been practicing for over 2000 years. They and we should complete the circle of love by obeying and loving Him and giving our best to Him — regardless of our limitations. God gave His all for us; He still does.

At times, both here and later, I'd think to myself, "I'm not fooling God. He still knows I'm sinful by nature and that Satan still tries to work against me." In my enthusiastic acceptance of what Christ did for me, I came to realize that this would necessitate and lead to me sacrificing myself and my life to God, even if by steps and stages. I must confess: though I rationally know I can only give what much or little I have, this doesn't feel sufficient. I sometimes think that God got gypped by putting Christ in my stead, as if He'd bought a mongrel for top dollar. What did I have to give back to Him? Such the answer, the perfect offering I could offer Him, I found, of course, in the Bible. Here it is that famous Pauline verse from Romans 12:1–2 that proclaims what I am to give: "Therefore, I urge you, brethren, by the mercies of God, to present your bodies *a living and holy sacrifice*, acceptable to God, which is your *spiritual service* of worship. And do not be conformed to this world, but *be transformed* by the *renewing of your mind…*" (emphasis mine). I'd never thought of me, the total self, my very life, as a form of a "sacrifice." What does this actually *mean*? I think it involves a willingness to suffer for His sake, as in when I feel and accept scorn when I take His side. It can mean that I accept suffering when I choose to do something for Him that involves me taking the heat for Him in some fashion. And who doesn't recognize the need for "renewal" in making his way through the chaos, sin, and miasma of life? How could I *not* read my Bible and pray?

5.29 The Transitive Property of Christianity

Somewhere back in grade school, I learned a math theorem on the transitive property, stating, "If A = B, and B = C, then A = C." I plugged in Jesus (and God *knows* I mean no disrespect) and got something like this: If Jesus died for *me*, and this sacrifice is acceptable to *God*, then I am forgiven by God. God forgives *and* forgets, which is something we down here never do! I admit that I *still* had trouble fathoming this whole substitutionary notion, so the teacher in me came up with a classroom analogy (actually, several of them). Knowing that the entire class couldn't pass His course, God permitted the very best student who *could* pass to let the other students cheat off him. The arrangement in my imaginings was that God would leave the room — as He cannot technically tolerate cheating, and during that period, the student of *Jesus* would complete the rest of the students' tests. When God came back in the room, there were all of the tests, *voila*, completed and perfect. This scenario seemed like a game, like a farce, like God pre-determined for me not only to fail but to resort to cheating! And though Jesus wouldn't mind taking the hit by getting punished for taking the test on our behalf, in the meantime, I not only felt foolish, but it was as if I were in a bad set-up. I not only *didn't* rate enough to pass the course and leave school to walk in freedom, but I knew that I deserved to stay and die here in this windowless classroom. It was like I had gotten a false diploma based on a pretense of cheating by my letting Jesus take the test for me! And God knew it! Here's what finally broke this glacier in my brain: if in my analogy God is the teacher, then He also takes into consideration the conditions in which I take the test, as in here on earth where Satan has home-court advantage. The wily one tempts some people to daydream, some to sleep, some to forget, some to be anxiety-ridden, some to be preoccupied with self, and others to come without supplies to even take the test. Do I, as a teacher, wish for students to remain in my classroom forever, without being able to enjoy this wonderful world and living a meaningful life of service because of this imperfect lab of a classroom that can make it difficult even to take a test? *No!* And like an essay that can't be written anywhere near perfectly by some sophomore, it is not within my mental or spiritual capacity to make a perfect score on God's test. So, what if we were to change the grading scale to just a Pass-Fail system, thereby creating a way for the students to recognize it is through God's generosity and mercy that we *can* graduate to a life of service? The student's part in this equation is accepting the gift of God's recording the perfect score taken by their perfect classmate. No one is fooling anyone; this is how He intended it to be! Only when I am liberated, do I have the chance and power to become who I was created to be!

Meanwhile, out in the tumultuous world, Jesus becomes a life raft that Dimi must hold onto and remain in as waters churn in the inevitable (and proverbial) storms of life. So, what is my part in all of this? I must try daily, slowly by slowly, to lift the veils from my mind, repent of my sins with regularity, read my guidebook, and glorify Him, Who even saw fit to create me. Merely being satisfied with passing doesn't make one a good student, though you technically have graduated. A good student should *want* to work hard, help others, and make the most of this short life she's been given. For me to do anything requires my belief in Him, Who created all possible to begin with! Not surprisingly, as these thoughts were stirring in me, I came upon, or rather, God pointed me to the following definition of faith from Hebrews 11:1 and 3. It defined what I had prayed for but didn't know how to say: "Now faith is the assurance of things hoped for, the conviction of things not seen...By faith, we understand that the worlds were prepared by the word of God, so that what is seen was not made out of things which are visible." I felt compelled to find a way to express my gratitude to God because I didn't want Him to think I was content to have placed my faith in Him and I remain sitting on my laurels. I will wait with breathless anticipation to see how God intends to use me; so far, it has been with teaching.

Gentle reader, should you come to have faith in Jesus, don't be surprised if doubts, misgivings, and misunderstandings pop up and repeat themselves within you; after all, you are an inquisitive being, and Satan is on-call nonstop to trip you up. It's not like you *don't* believe when you question; however, if old wounds, scars, or scabs can be picked at, maybe, just maybe, he'll get you to become unhinged and feel dejected. Like the old hymn, "I Know He Heard My Prayer," says, "The enemy had said to me that my faith in God was dead, and if the way was rough, He did not care (that The Savior did not care)… Thank the Lord it is not true; He thrills me through and through. I know the Savior heard my prayer…" So, it is without reservation or shame that I share with you now, just a little over three years after I made the initial classroom analogy above, the following short staccato of questions that persisted around this quandary. Are you familiar with the question, "If you want something done right, you have to do it yourself"? Perhaps that's how God saw it, that, in spite of "the tutor" (Gal. 3:24), the Law, we people just kept on blowing it left and right. Therefore, He sent Jesus down here (yet of His own volition) at the right time. Do you think God is as irritated as a parent who says to his errant child, "Don't make me come down after you!"? I mean, I know God knew it was coming to all this anyway, but we are so inept that it seems we couldn't *not* need help to look beyond ourselves. Should I feel gratitude for that which I couldn't and can't *ever* get covered, except by being passed and graduated, though I fail every quiz? Flash forward with me to a recent visit of Mark's to see how *he* responded to my school analogy that I came up with to discern better what God was thinking in coming down here. I again remind you that it wasn't just spiritual beans and business that brought us together. Sitting around the kitchen table over a cup of coffee, we would first catch up on life, but I'm sure he came to expect certain themes would crop up. He always treated them seriously, no matter how many times or angles they presented themselves to him. Thus, Mark addressed the two classroom analogies I made whereby I was trying yet again to help myself understand how I could pass and be accepted by God based on what seemed to me like a lie. When Mark and I were face-to-face, I gave a real-life, recent example of a very bright boy in one of my classes who permitted an inferior student to copy off him. I said I feel like that fraud who has passed because of my proximity to and borrowing from Jesus. Mark responded to me and softly said, "This is not the right analogy." He explained that in no way could I ever even *comprehend* God's exam; therefore, Jesus already got my final grade in the course recorded for me! There is nothing I can do; there is no test to take or perform; I can only gratefully accept and acknowledge this act. Mark's answer blew me away in scope, gentleness, and perfection!

The second analogy I made is the one I use in my Russian 1 class all the time. To show them their level of advancement made in language acquisition, I stand with my back against the wall — our starting point — and take a 1-inch step forward and away from the wall to indicate the tiny progress the first-year student has made toward full fluency. Then I take a full step forward from *that* mark to demonstrate what progress the second-year student has made. I make even smaller scooches forward to show how infinitesimally slow progress can be. My students invariably want to know where *I* stand on this spectrum, and I stride forward across the room to only a few steps from what I determine as native-level fluency, which is on the other side of the room. As would be the norm, I demonstrated this to Mark at my kitchen table with a bottle of water, crackers, and a pencil to serve as models and props. Mark said that just because a second or first-year student doesn't know how to speak another language fluently, *God would not hold it against him if Jesus spoke on behalf of him.* In other words, I know that I am that first or second-year student, and God knows my deficiencies and my inability to *ever* speak fluently like a native, but *He loves me anyway*, and, by the way, Jesus *gladly* speaks on my behalf! In less than five minutes, Mark cleared up my flawed or incomplete analogies I had been repeatedly attempting to use to help me understand why and how Jesus could cover our sin. No longer did I feel like an imposture just holding onto His coattails. I don't know how Mark does it, but time and time again, I am bowled away with immense relief with how he speaks my language and unties my tangled mental knots, which allows the flow of faith to proceed again, free and unimpeded. *God knows everything about me and loves me right where I am.* Accepting His gift doesn't make me a fraud; He knows exactly who I am and is still pleased that I chose to say, "Yes!" to His Son, now both my Brother and Savior. God is not like some peeved parent who is exasperated or irritated. That said, our waywardness, stubborn pride, incorrigibleness, and lack of reverence *can* bring about the need for wrath, which God uses to get our attention to remind us that there *is* a standard to which we should *aspire*. Retribution or redress does not occur in a cause-effect and immediate tense or as some swift punishment by *our* bar.

Thank heavens! *That's* what forbearance is all about: God's patience and perfectcding up my scheduled program depicting my first toddling year of faith.

5.30 THE BLOOD OF FAMILY VERSUS THE BLOOD OF CHRIST

Regarding dealing with tensions within one's family relations, I recalled a couple of passages in the New Testament that I'd read many times before becoming a Christian, but only *now* could really appreciate. One had to do with Jesus saying, "I did not come to bring peace, but a sword. [35] For I came to SET ... A DAUGHTER AGAINST HER MOTHER; [36] and A MAN'S ENEMIES WILL BE THE MEMBERS OF HIS HOUSEHOLD" (from Matthew 10:34–36). Reading this now felt like some sort of premonition because I *was* experiencing this very situation with my mother, except that she wasn't fighting so much as quietly distancing herself from me, and I didn't know what to do with this empty, awkward air. Another situation dealing with determining who your family is *as an adult* is when you've settled into an *identity* (not personality) that may not accord with how you were raised as a child; Jesus dealt with this, too. After Jesus left his hometown, having received a lukewarm welcome and many treating Him as one of no account (or having lost his mind), I observe that Jesus picks Himself up and treats His friends and followers more like family than His own relatives. Why? Except for His Mother, who, I imagine, couldn't just up and leave her life, all of his homeboys placed Jesus in a box of what a Nazarene carpenter was *supposed* to look like; therefore, in their obtuseness, they missed out on Who He really was and rejected Him. I know full well that I am some sort of weird, white sheep in my family now, and in making this choice to be a Christian, I am going against the grain. I find this phenomenon all the more interesting because our mothers are typically the spiritual inculcators, that is, those who shape our morals and formulate our religious outlook. Perhaps because of this, we tend to judge our mothers more harshly or stringently later on in life when we reevaluate their choices. Though I think this is unfair and not right, at the time, I was no exception. I think I resented missing out on potential decades of knowing Him, and perhaps thusly, I could have avoided some unpleasantries in my life. That said, I now know He has been preparing me every step of the way and is glad I walked *His* way. As a young Christian, however, I took umbrage with my mother for what I saw as neglect in providing us with any sort of religious framework. In fact, it was just the opposites: we were taught that religion was like a buffet: you picked and chose what pleased you. Really?!? Would you let your child go up to an all-you-can-eat food bar and fix his plate? He'd come back with desserts only! As children, we were told that we could choose for ourselves that which we wanted *when we grew up*. I would later tell others that I believed choosing not to choose is a total copout. Over and over, we were told (and felt relieved) that *our* mom wasn't going to shove religion down our throats like it was castor oil or to make us go to church. Choosing a framework where you do whatever you feel that brings you contentment and theoretical harmony with others in reality defaults to what amounts to saying *anything goes*. I had no single standard, let alone Jesus, to serve as a model, platform, or standard by which to guide my life; the result would be to live a life of self-justification and self-satisfaction in my relative goodness. Such freedom my parents provided, ironically, thankfully, and ultimately, led me to Him. Of course, my mother justified her lack of faith in Jesus as Messiah and overall rejection of Christianity because of its adherents' exacting judgment and *lack* of love. Then there was the rational to be confronted. Some may have deduced that I needed a sense of security or placating because I could not face or accept the stark fact that there is *nothing* to come after we die; this is it. *Finito kaput*.

Add to this that I also knew I would be looked at in the manner in which *I* had previously viewed many Christians: one who lacked intellectual fortitude and moral rectitude; one who had abandoned critical thinking; one who eschewed science, fact, and basic logic; one had deluded himself with platitudes; and most of all, one who had adopted a stance of judgment, as if he had become life's umpire. Sure, there were a few good ones out there, but, by and large, Christians were not particularly humanitarian. All this I now know not to be gospel, and so I keep my energies and mind focused and conclude that I am not here to please my family, but to serve my Lord, and in so doing, I will help my neighbor. My neighbor is any- and everyone. Oh, I got it alright, and as thought I knew the worst of how Christians could be perceived, this made me all the more aware of the need to represent positively and compassionately, but my emerging Christian self did not act that way in the beginning. Being young in the faith, which I *still am*, I openly admit that my approach to my family (and others) was so wrong. In my earliest days post-conversion, I was argumentative, adamant, defensive, skeptical, or just plain old silently miffed when I spoke to unbelievers who were nonplussed, unphased, recalcitrant, or dismissive of what I had to say about Jesus. My affect was not effective for one desiring to portray Him. I also think that part of my frothiness or peculiar verve came about because I became increasingly aware of what seemed like a blink of time left in my life for me to share Him. After all, here I was at fifty, just getting started! Now here I was, one of *them*, so I was ready to put up my dukes and show the world I wasn't like the rest of them in the way they'd thought. More and more, I cut to the chase and got down to brass tacks. If *Jesus* could suffer at the hands of uppity church folks, to the point of death even, thank you very much, the *least* I could do would be to tough it out, march on, and *not* be such a one! It's Jesus who is to be pitied here for what His *bride* has done to His reputation (the comparison is made in Eph. 5:23). I can now say that the obvious and best way to witness is not through my mouth but through my "walk" (Eph. 5:15), and such needs to be done in love and with patience. The constant Christian should effuse a joy, a gladness, that something, that *je ne sais quoi*, emanating from inside which is independent of life circumstances, a state that says *all is well*. A close Christian friend of mine at the gym is always looking for opportunities to sprinkle Scripture in his conversations; this inspired me to memorize Scripture to do so as well. In short, *you've got to love people exactly where they are* and let this love of His draw them to Him through you and the Holy Spirit. We are also told to know when to *let go*. After all, Jesus told His Disciples, "Whoever does not receive you, nor heed your words, as you go out of that house or that city, *shake the dust off your feet*" (Matthew 10:14, emphasis mine). Even Jesus couldn't get the attention of some of the very people who said they believed in Him, first of all, because they admittedly didn't know what was going on and couldn't picture past His being just a Jewish Messiah. Secondly, then like today, in being short-sited, materially-focused, and living life by the *carpe diem* outlook, others "did not honor Him as God or give thanks...their foolish heart was darkened. [22] Professing to be wise, they became fools, [23] and exchanged the glory of the incorruptible God for an image …corruptible. [24] Therefore, God gave them over in the lusts of their hearts to impurity" (from Romans 1:21–24). The ones who *did* believe in Jesus were those who experienced His loving touch first-hand; they were society's outcasts, lost sheep, and "the least of these" (Matthew 25:40 NKJV). I think my family would have preferred and could have more readily accepted my being a Christian if the denomination was of the Greek Orthodox flavor. After all, Dimi loves her Greek heritage and appreciates tradition, incense, icons, and other such symbols. Going to the Greek Church made total sense because it satisfied all the emotional and heritage affiliations through the senses, but Mark — who was this guy anyway? And a Southern Baptist church? There are too many other religions out there to single out one as the best, only, or correct one. I'm sure this just seemed like another form of extremism on my part, and my zeal made it look like I had been brainwashed. It's just that I am acutely aware that I *am* one of the "lost sheep" or "lost coins" (from Luke 12), and I eagerly pledge allegiance to Him, seek to avoid the shadows, and look to "walk in the Light [because] the blood of Jesus … cleanses us from all sin" (1 John 1:7). How could I not?

Mere hours after I wrote the very last line above, something in me kept stirring, and then the word "peace" popped into my brain and wouldn't leave, and I knew that He'd have me add one more note to Dimi's concluding line. This, in turn, led to a realization that this little prompting came from beyond me. Why should I complain or be vexed over how I was raised?!? Look at what it led to and which God knew about before I was born. Though a religious foundation may have been missing, my perception of God Himself was not ruined; I did know His love! Therefore, when I set aside all the previously alluring and partial truths and faced Jesus alone, one on one, *just He and I*, it was easier for me to come to Him! Furthermore, as a Christian — yes, even as a layman and a rookie — who is taking her first steps in life with Him, I am *commanded* "if possible, so far as it depends on [me], to be at peace with *all* men" (Romans 12:18, emphasis mine). I don't have the luxury to bellyache about parenting methods or stew over the ways of the world! All I've got is this life to give and do and grow the best I can for Him. I am to quit comparing or even lamenting over what's out there (or not) and get to the task at hand. How? I should be on-call and available for Him to use me in the best way He knows how with what I can offer. And you don't have always have to a lot to make a difference. Of course, this world is a mess! How could it not be? Look who is in micro-charge of this big, bad, and beautiful world: the prince of the power of the air! That sounds like a whole lot of nothing to me.

Since Jesus pierced my heart and mind, no evil act should surprise or jolt me anymore, even though evil in any form is repugnant. Why? At the end of the day, what keeps me stilled and steady? "He Himself is our peace" (Eph. 2:14). No other religious leader makes such a claim. In fact, just out of curiosity, I Googled how many times the word "peace" occurs in the Bible, and I was astonished to read that in the KJV, it is used 429 times! In other words, no matter what happens (all tenses) in this life, no matter how much I long for loved ones to join me in Heaven, I am *not* to participate in any divisive debate. Jesus hopes to get involved in *all* of our affairs — yes, to the point of becoming a wedge within certain relationships. All He does is so that all may come to Him! When all seems lost or if I feel alone or frustrated, I get reminded "the peace of God, which surpasses all comprehension, will guard [my] hearts and [my] mind in Christ Jesus" (Philippians 4:7). How can this be? I know I won't face God at the great white throne of *judgment* (Rev. 20:11 KJV) because Jesus *has already settled my account*. I'll be tenderly and richly talked to by Jesus at the bema seat and shown what all I accomplished for Him. How can this be? He and I both know I have placed my faith and life in Him, lock, stock, and barrel, yes, even when I am momentarily sidetracked or sideways in my thoughts and actions. He'll never *not* be with me as I keep making my way to Him. He already knows it in my baby-steps, in the teetering and the tottering, as I make my way forward, arms outstretched to Him.

5.31 THE DECEIVER, TAKE 2

For some three months, we alternated Sundays, until slowly, but surely, our desire to be fed Biblical truths and our attempts to live out His ways with practicality, humor, and passion through and with this church grew on us, and we started going *every* Sunday. And Sunday nights. And Wednesdays. This was a *huge* change in life and time prioritizing, but we now could not imagine it any other way. There was no real danger of drinking, and we would continue to go to A.A. on an occasional Saturday noon meeting, ever relieved for its "rigorous honesty" and keeping it real in that circle of inviolable trust. Satan would still try to use the Church to distract and dishearten me and create discord in my home. How dastardly of him. Then again, he's been at it for centuries, hardening people's hearts. He even does so to *believers'* hearts such that they become legalistic to the degree that they not only do not demonstrate Christ's love, but they judge people both in and out of the church and often inhibit some from seeking fellowship in church. It's little wonder people leave the church and/or don't even come to it. As an aside, merely *attending* church doesn't indicate one is saved. *Now* I see why Jonathan Edwards spoke with such passion to the "unregenerate" souls in the midst of his congregation! They were in church but out of Christ! It is not by chance then that Christ so wanted me in a church that He found the perfect person to start that conversation about Jesus with Bonnie and me, the experience of which would, in turn, lead to an opening in our hearts and minds to make Jesus our King and God our Father. I would wonder about this more. I asked Mark why in the world God hasn't already gone ahead and destroyed Satan. If God is so jealous, why didn't He spear the Accuser for good?! In fact, why didn't He just take a hoe to the snake in the Garden a long time ago? It's hard enough with our impressive but problematic dual nature doing battle with the plethora of temptations that we all succumb to in one form or another. Though God is the master of the universe and *everything*, Satan is still is "ruler of this world." Though he loses in the end, he still twists our minds and corrupts our hearts for all he's got. He's got nothing personally against *us*; He could care less. Being the supreme nefarious creature that he is, he is on-call to do battle with Jesus. Is permitting Lucifer to wreak havoc on us a form of a double-check system to demonstrate the authenticity of our love? Maybe it's a way to ensure our coming to Him is *completely* freely done. I'm proud to say I *need* Jesus! The truth is, though *we* are not there in that time yet to be, Satan is *already* defeated and corralled in that lake of fire; *we* just haven't arrived at what for God is just right around the bend. We do not operate in God's Mach 20 rate of speed, and even that doesn't even capture His time warp. I discovered a well-known passage that expresses this dimension of timelessness God operates in: "with the Lord one day is like a thousand years, and a thousand years like one day" (2 Peter 3:8). Satan knows his days are numbered, and that's why he works so hard to destroy as many as possible. But the victory *is* ours. In the end, we win. I'm glad Satan won't last eternally in the lives of those who choose Him, that God will snuff him out. I get that Satan is the Biggest Loser, but in my humanness, I wish this infernal "prince" were just a little further away from planet earth and in my backyard. I take that to mean that I must be all the more joyful and vigilant and dependent on God through His Holy Spirit. So, what's a Christian soldier to do operating in the world when she is surrounded and bombarded with the dark side of earthly values that can glitter like gold? My go-to of non-participation might just not be enough for God as silence might be construed as tacit approval of others' evil words and deeds. I don't want the Holy Spirit to think I'm a chicken, but I don't want to start a row either. And then I'm not supposed to judge. I get confused as to what to do! The devil doesn't "get behind" me far enough when I tell him to, and through people and circumstances, he can be such "a stumbling block" (Matthew 16:23). He just ducks underwater for a short while; then, like a turtle coming up for air, he's back at it. You will continue to see that my upcoming batch of questions reflects my burgeoning growth in faith, and though they are not immediately addressed or answered, they *are* eventually. I'm also still learning the lingo, the language of Christians. As a foreign language teacher, I am excited to become increasingly fluent in the words of His land in which I now am dwelling and walking. Can you tell?

5.32 More Questions for Mark

1. If someone who is *not* Christian does good works, like the youngster in the news recently who anonymously raised $30k for local people in need of food or like Bill Gates spending millions upon millions of dollars for philanthropic works, how does God judge this act?
2. What exactly happens to *Christians* after they die? I know some of the things, but what I've heard or read so far is fuzzy. Are we judged by God, by Christ, or by both? Do they divvy us up and split the job of settling who goes where? Are we all evaluated by the quantity and quality of our works done for His Glory? Is there slack given for ignorance? I assume that since Christ's substitutionary punishment has absolved us of *all* of our sins that it would not be necessary to repent for the transgressions that occurred *after* our acceptance of Christ as our Savior, for which we mightn't've yet apologized. Is there a hierarchy in Heaven?? If there is, I will begin to feel that familiar sense of inferiority again. Will I also see my *earthly* father then and there? Can he see me, too? (I need another word besides "see"!) To be honest, even though it sounds nice, I don't think so. Right now, I imagine Heaven to be a full, one-on-one reception of and eternal basking in God's total, undiluted, and pure Love, like bathing in some warm and radiant glow all over and within, and this is He. Am I off-target?
3. I feel consternation over the fact that I know riches will mold and turn to dust and that it doesn't take much arm-twisting for Satan to divert our attention to the material and to our own welfare and satisfaction. Yet at the same time, we find descriptions of Heaven being full of magnificence and splendor, you know, the likes of the "many mansions" (John 14:2 KJV), "streets of gold" (Rev. 21:21 KJV), and all that jazz. Oh, surely, we will be

astonished by all of this and even more, including whom all we will see that we might not have expected and vice versa, that is, those whom we'd be sure we would, but might not! God only knows!

And another thing: if we aren't supposed to be materialistic, why would we have such a draw or pull toward the very things we are to put in second place? After all, God also wants us to relish and enjoy what He made for us! Nonetheless, we will not be sensate in the afterlife, regardless of where we wind up. Maybe such descriptions of Heaven are used to show the value, and worth God puts into absolutely everything He does and makes and that Heaven is no exception, that it isn't going to be a cave or stark monastic cell. Still, it doesn't seem right for me to expect any reward! Shouldn't all my service be done *pro bono* for Him anyway?!? Whatever "crown is waiting for me" (2 Timothy 4:8 TLB) which I earned in life for introducing someone to Him, am I then to lay at the feet of Jesus? Would such a gift indicate that God was pleased enough to pay me like this? Isn't this more like a grand nod of recognition? Ought I not then of my own free (posthumous) will turn around and give any crown right back to Jesus? Aren't we to be Christ-like because *it's the least we could do* for the gift of life from God, not to mention His suffering and dying in our stead that made restoration and reunification
possible?

These are such the questions His daughter had for Her Heavenly Father.

5.33 To Be a Christian Woman

You know, it's interesting that I take no issue with Scripture regarding women being told to submit to their husbands. Submission does *not* mean inferiority, no matter how much mere man likes to wield his authority! And if the husband's task in the order of things is to protect and defend *to the point of death* his family, all the while respecting his wife, taking a second but *co-equal* spot is the least women could do. Too many chefs in the kitchen mean no meal gets prepared. Man is physically stronger, but so what? That's no big deal; woman usually bears more suffering in life anyway. I also get that God sent down a *Son* and not a Daughter because men held (and hold) higher *socio-political* status in this world; therefore, people would be more attentive to His heed and calling and *not* because God views women as less worthy. Women are *also* made in His image! No matter how much wrong is done to you such that you feel and may have been victimized, Jesus takes all of your past and gives you a new future. You are no victim then. Speaking of which, I also take issue with the case of Eve being blamed for all the world's woes, like some Christian version of Pandora. I mean, if two of your sons followed in the wicked ways of your third child, the one who initiated and provoked the wrong-doing, the one who enticed or convinced the two to partake of the crime, would you punish anyone more than the other? No. Eve was seduced by Satan, but *Adam willingly followed*. What kind of leadership was *that*? And then Adam had the gall to blame God indirectly for giving him Eve to begin with! He could and should have said, "No!" to her! The bottom line is that they *both* disobeyed; *both* were expelled from Eden. Do women suffer more in childbirth than other female mammals? I don't know. It is clear to me that, as mothers and leaders of children at home for the predominant amount of time, women are the principle instillers of spiritual values and religious foundations in them, so why are they asked to be silent or are disallowed to minister in the church? It is *man* that's not fair, not God! There's an angle taken in the movie *Son of God* that may not be immediately noticed, but for me, it was immense: Mary Magdalene is depicted as traveling *alongside* the original twelve;

she was just one of them. I love Jesus for being like that, that is, *so* inclusive. The Son of God showed liberality, compassion, and regard, *particularly* for women at a time when women were chattel, property, and without a voice in society. We, too, are your neighbors. I'll return to this focus later, but in the meantime, here came forth another batch or two of questions in year one of my sanctification. I'd never seen or experienced the likes of this before!

5.34 Selected Points on James and Questions about Judging

The book of Jesus' half-brother, James, gives us so much wisdom of practical value, one being that we are to control our speech — our "tongue" (James 3:5) — and language. I love it when he rhetorically asks, "Can a fig tree, my brethren, produce olives, or a vine produce figs? Nor can salt water produce fresh" (3.12). Like many, I need so much help in this area, especially as I can wield my words to be a sharp weapon. The stakes are high if I don't shift my ways and re-align them to Christ's, perfectly done or not. Here's James' either-or argument: "Anyone who chooses to be a friend of the world becomes an enemy of God" (James 4:4). I certainly have friends and family in the world, and I am full of faults and have *so* far to go. I can't just push people away if they irritate me. I'm sure it would pain the Holy Spirit in me to say or do nothing if I encounter wrong. What then to do? Not wanting to grieve the Holy Spirit, what's this Christian foot soldier to do operating in the world when she is surrounded and bombarded by earthly people and values when she herself must confess, "I am chief [of sinners]" (1 Tim. 1:15 KJV)? The quick answer is that Paul says that we are *not* to judge the world: that's on God, but we *are* to call out our brothers and sisters *with gentleness* if we observe ways incongruous to how He would have us live. I should expect and hope for the same as well but mind those who are biblically accurate and not just well-intended, not to mention those who don't really know me. Mark would frequently advise us to "eat the fish but spit out the bones." A.A. would say, "Take what you can and leave the rest." Both offer sage advice. This may eliminate many people's say-so, but it doesn't mean to turn a blind eye! Reprimanding is no different than steering a ship. The bottom line for me right now is I'm not supposed to judge.

To that end, James asks, "Who are you to judge your neighbor?" (4:12). Later in 5:9, we find, "Don't grumble against each one another," yet 5:20 says, "He who *turns* a sinner from the error of his way will save his soul from death and will cover a multitude of sins" (emphasis mine). How is this "turning" to take place if about half the time *I* act like a sinner? What could this possibly look like in one as young as I? What exactly is my obligation? How can I not look like a Miss Goody-Two-Shoes? I don't ever want to turn into some sanctimonious and bitter church lady people want to avoid! How do I do tow the line for Him, albeit, of course, imperfectly, but not be two-faced? Three years later, I would write a poem about feeling troubled about feeling like a hypocrite, which in the original Greek, I found out means "to be an actor, to play what one was not." Here is that poem:

> I don't plan on bein' a hypocrite, and I don't wanna be a fake.
> There's a price to pay when you lie; it's you yourself you forsake.
> God gives all one life to live,
> And it's in this state we are held captive.
> So, when I fear I'm losing face,
> I turn duplicitous, don't wanna leave a trace.
> Hiding self is what some do to avoid deep internal groans,
> 'Cause none wants to shame or blame or to be cast out all alone.
> There's also no sense or clout to think one's "chosen" or a Pharisee,
> 'Cause Jesus cuts us to the quick and scolds, "Woe to you and me!"
> There's no hiding parts of who I am; I know He really cares,
> So, I run and bare my soul to Him — He's washed away my errs.
> Satan dares to taunt and accuse me even when I'm intent at church,
> He attempts to pervert the word, so I'm stuck inside some lurch.
> I thank God for your awareness and your deep and keener sense;
> The points you preach are rich and dense and to the spirit, intense.
> You ask if you were too hard on us; with your assessment, sir,
> I do, for sure, concur:

We must be authentic in all we do and let nothing be a blur.
There's naught to gain by being a fraud; for this, He'll not applaud,
Just be plain and pure and true and real.
He made us thus, knows all we think and dream and feel.
It's when I'm weak, I know He's strong,
There's no feeling lost or left behind - He's got me all along.
So, I run on up to get down on my knees (it's Him I seek to please),
To pray, I let pretense and ego go so that He can surely shine.
My heart beats strong and glad for all to witness Him divine.
What a journey! Such a task! What an *honor* to be His!

5.35 RAPTURE, RELATIONSHIP, AND REPENTANCE QS

These questions keep popping up, and I want to understand all of them! Right now. When I put them to Bonnie, I often get agitated because either her seeming stock phrases or go-to rote replies do not address my questions, or else she gets off-balance herself, which is the *last* thing I want. Therefore, I am incredibly grateful for being able to turn to Mark. This morning while I was reading in Thessalonians and praying, I got to the part about the Rapture, and I got so confused. The questions poured out of me, like liquid dominos. These that follow are like many you have read previously; only now, I shift in my seat and peer into the netherworld of death. It would take some time and *lots* of help before they got cleared up. Do know that each question (or topic) was more like a splinter in my finger or a pebble in my shoe; they were not "stumbling blocks" (Matthew 18:7) to my actual faith.

1. Will Jesus gather up the dead who believed in Him and *then* collect the living believers and whoosh them all up to Heaven?
2. I thought that my salvation was "sealed" and that my soul will be transported to Heaven when I die (to await the re-conjoining of my body as is described in Revelation). Is this not so? Will I in my entirety go to Heaven when I die, or will I be in some holding tank down under in my grave, dormant and waiting in my ambient state of death?
3. Is my dual nature of body and spirit severed, cleft, or broken apart when I die? In other words, will my saved soul go straight to Heaven upon my death, and only in the case of the Rapture would Christ come back for my dead body? This doesn't make sense to me.
4. If I'm just figuratively "sleeping" in my grave (body *and* soul) and waiting for Jesus to gather us believers at the Rapture, does this mean that I will not experience eternal

life until the Rapture occurs? Does it mean I won't see Jesus' face right when I die? In other words, is it all just nothingness until the Rapture? I think I need to stay away from feel-good, well-intended, but incorrect pop culture literature that tries to paint Heaven as a Norman Rockwell picture of some family reunion. At the same time, I can't believe that Jesus would keep me waiting for Him in the grave after a lifetime of my believing that He paid for my restitution such that I would receive eternal life! I need help here! I would return to this point sooner rather than later.

5. This leads me to my next plight, and I'm a little shy to tell you, gentle reader. Do you remember when I told you that I saw Christ at my window and I could hardly wait to get to Him and that He seared my soul with the in-rushing Holy Spirit at the moment of my accepting that He *also* died for me? Well, I haven't really seen Jesus in that way since then. Such a thought process is clearly the mark of an immature believer. I mean — and daily this occurs — I am *so* aware when the Holy Spirit nudges me, prompts me, directs me to do God's will. I *am* getting more in tune when God puts people, places, and events in my path for me to grow from, be moved by, or take part in for His glory. My imagining or sighting of Christ Jesus now occurs when I pray, particularly early in the morning. I visualize myself seated next to Him, leaning fully *on* Him; I can feel the fabric of His tunic and sense His strength and calm under my head and cheek as I rest on His shoulder; sometimes, it is His chest. At other times I imagine holding His hand when I'm driving, like I used to my father's when he was alive. But when I *pray*, it always starts out to *God* because God is the one who made me and has the plan for my life. When I envision Christ dying for me, I just can't imagine Him concurrently as my friend, like some buddy!! Therefore, frequently, I do not feel like I've actually got this all-important and sacrosanct *personal* relationship with Jesus!! Should it

be that I think of the indwelling Holy Spirit as Jesus?!? Earlier, in my erroneous thinking, I believed that God was too busy and distant to bother with me. In a similar vein, I feel ambivalence now with Christ because I can't fathom this dead/living Man as my "friend" even though I *do* unreservedly accept Christ as my Savior. What a mess I am! Furthermore, I know He favors children and those with a child-like heart; I don't feel like I am such a one. It doesn't seem like I have a *relationship* with my Savior, even *with* my faith quiveringly new and so full of hope. What to do?! I admit I am troubled by the fact that even though I love Jesus' personality (as depicted well in *Son of God*) and appreciate His emotions and humor (as rendered in *Jesus Christ Superstar*), I do not yet feel as *connected* to Him as I do to God the Father or even the Holy Spirit. Of *course*, I love Him! I just don't know *how* to love and *be* loved by Him. I am *very* disappointed in myself and feel like I'm missing the boat or the clue-train again. Yes, I realize that this situation has arisen because, as with many, I can't truly fathom a triune nature, but the three are *also* distinct even within their unity, right? Bonnie says when I talk to one, I talk to all. My *mind* knows this, but now I want to feel Christ like I do the Holy Spirit — a miracle for me, for sure — *and* the certainty of God. Is it really like the motto from *The Three Musketeers*' motto, "All for one, one for all," whereby I receive three-in-one and oughtn't even to try to look at or appreciate each of these "ones" one at a time while I ponder and pray?

6. And finally, to wrap up this batch of questions, some more thoughts on repentance: I know repentance is an essential, nay, *obligatory* part of claiming one's salvation, just as accepting and having faith that Jesus — "the same yesterday, today, and forever" (Hebrews 13:8) — died for me and took on the just wrath of God for my sins. Then why does it *feel* so inadequate to merely say, "I repent of my sins"?? Confession should be *daily*, perhaps even

hourly, right? Feeling sorry for my sinning can't be the same thing as repentance, can it?? Regret is not remorse! When I confess to God, I feel sorrowful, distressed even, but knowing I'm forever flawed, I can be like the "dog that returns to its vomit" (Proverbs 26:11). I am still worldly because I live in the flesh. I still and will probably always suffer from the effects of pride (including my desire to be right). I am so quick to lose my patience. I readily admit that repentance hasn't satisfactorily produced in me a turning over of a new leaf in a bonafide sense, but I *am* working at it, slow and steady as she goes.

I've got to breathe now and say it's going to take time. I do believe that those habits and ways contrary to Him, those that are the most long-established or entrenched in me, *will* get dislodged, become desiccated, or disentangled from the new me, but it certainly won't happen overnight! This notwithstanding, some flaws and wrongful mindsets can and do vanish instantaneously upon my recognizing them as such! What an evolution! What a revolution! To this end, today I taught Alexander Pope's "An Essay on Man" to my seniors, and I found it particularly instructive how Pope explains just where we stand in the balance between heaven and hell. I wrote a translation or paraphrasing of it line by line for them and cite it here for you, too. It's not poetic, but it cuts to the chase as it cuts me to the quick:

Know who *you* truly are, don't try and figure out God;
A person's job is to focus on and understand his fellow man.
It's our fate to be halfway in this in-between land,
Humanity is both smart, but evil *and* simple, yet awesome:
We know too much about life for skeptics to say we don't,
And we've too much feeling to deny or hide them.
We're somewhere in between: we can't make up our minds to *do* or just *be*.
We're in doubt whether we're more like God or just another animal on earth;
We can't make up our minds which means more to us: our mind and thoughts or the pleasures of our bodies;
We are born and *know* we will die someday; we've got great minds, but we make mistakes all the time;

No matter what, we really are ignorant of so much – we can't know everything, no matter how smart we are,
No matter how little or how much we think.
Our thoughts and feelings often get all mixed up which, in turn, confuses us.
We still either deceive ourselves or free ourselves from false ideas;
We were created to know a lot and improve, but also given the free will and lack of perfection to fail;
We're the head of and in control of *so* much in this life, yet we can become helpless ones and victims, too;
We judge the truth yet give errors and lies:
We are God's pride and joy, His fools, and a mystery of this world!

    I will take a look back in my rearview mirror before continuing to the next step: it has been nearly a full year after my initial letter to Mark and his response back which led to my accepting Christ. I have embarked on a journey of change and of new friendships. Afterward, I not only put forth questions to Mark, I even questioned his motive and intent to remain our friend. I once suggested and wrote that now that he had done his job and I was saved, I guessed that I was good-to-go and that he didn't need to fool with us anymore, wouldn't need to visit us anymore. It was all "mission accomplished" and "*Arrivederci*," baby! At Mark's next visit following this cynical blurb I'd emailed him, he initially showed no reaction to what I'd written or insinuated. Then I asked him point-blank if what I'd wondered was true. He let me know clearly and in no uncertain terms that my words had "seared his soul" because doing such was *not* his intention. He said he *loved* us and would always be friends with us, that he'd visit us when we were old, and that one day when he buried either the one or the other, he'd stand over and speak about us, sharing stories about our friendship. I'd never had *anybody*, friend or family, speak like that to me so boldly and reassuringly of a friendship to last a *lifetime*! I still felt self-conscious that my life-altering change happened relativity quickly through the help of a stranger who now felt as close to me as family! I felt at *greater* ease to talk to him about matters of faith and the essential affairs of my life than I did with friends *or* family! How could this be? I think that as

I was looking at the world no longer with worldly eyes, I sought others like me who had this type of vision. I continued sharing my thoughts via emails to Mark, even if I wasn't sure he read through them all, as there were so many (and many rather lengthy). Plus, they just reflect the average growth of a normal neophyte such as I, that is, the churning, bubbling, and constant thoughts, questions, and passions coalescing Him into my fledgling Christian identity and self. The fact that I *formerly* saw God as distant, inaccessible, and unapproachable because I wasn't needy or pathetic enough had completely changed! I was still amazed at my initial ignorance and errancy in Who the Holy Spirit is. And that I altered my view of the heart to be the citadel of volition, purpose, and intent of my whole being was *spectacular* for me! My next three years' journey is as crucial as this first step because it shows how I continued to mature in my faith walk. The next period of my life that remains to be told would also include both a short, personalized journey of the Footsteps of Paul in Greece and, later, some trouble in paradise for me personally and professionally. In a way, though I am now newly singular-minded in Him, I'm very much still *me*. In fact, by acceding *to* Him, I'm more me than I ever was before. Praise be to Him! I am free of sin (though not of faults). He who took this away now lives through and in me. Oh, I want to make Him proud!

CHAPTER 6:
Year 2, Growing Pains

"We also exult in our tribulations, knowing that tribulation brings about perseverance; and perseverance, proven character; and proven character, hope; and hope does not disappoint, because the love of God has been poured out within our hearts through the Holy Spirit who was given to us.
— Romans 5:3–5

[22] Through the LORD's mercies we are not consumed,
Because His compassions fail not.
[23] They are new every morning;
Great is Your faithfulness.
[24] "The LORD is my portion," says my soul,
"Therefore I hope in Him!"
[25] The LORD is good to those who wait for Him,
To the soul who seeks Him.
— Lamentations 22–25 NKJV

6.1 A Slow but Steady Keel

Now that I have shared with you the backdrop leading up to my salvation and the first baby steps taken after that, I will continue with the next three years of this evolution that led to the birth of wanting to share my testimony this way. You may ask yourself, why should you listen to someone as young as I? Good question! My soul is fresh from salvation — I am young in the faith, just like every expert or pastor out there who has stayed the course was once, too. To date, I have seventeen years of sobriety, but I know I'm a drink away from picking up a white chip. In A.A., the newcomer is particularly valued in the meeting because *we remember what it was like being in his shoes.* Therefore, by analogy, I hope that the callow perspective of this babe in the faith makes Christianity, not to mention going to church, less daunting, elusive, or even repugnant for those who have strayed or taken an extended time out. Perhaps you have a bad taste in your mouth from an unpleasant encounter in church or with a Christian. Perhaps you haven't a thought in the world about Jesus. Maybe Christianity's restrictions and seeming elitism go against your egalitarian values and free spirit. Maybe you, as did I, want to ask, "*Who says* that there is one way to God, that Jesus is His Son *and* the only way to Him, and that Hell is real, etc.?" Could you look to real scholarship and more advanced studies than take my word for it, that is, the veracity and merit of Christianity? Of course, you can, and I hope you do, but this can only occur *after* you have been transfigured by reading the Bible or, at the very least and for starters, the New Testament. As odd as it sounds, a full understanding isn't a prerequisite to saving faith; it's the other way around! Your faith will prompt you to further growth. Although I had read bits and pieces of the Bible when I looked up allusions, I had no desire to read it until *after* I'd fallen in love with Jesus. I know a man, an electrical engineer by trade, who had the opposite experience: the night his mother died, he went to her house to start the process of cleaning it out. As he began going through her things, he came upon his mother's well-worn Bible, and he absent-mindedly opened it up, leafed through a few pages, and then somehow got taken in by it before he was aware.

He settled in and kept on reading; in fact, he never went to bed that night, so engrossed did he become. It's hard to know when he came to, but after that night's experience, he never returned to the Unitarian Church. In the wee morning hour of that night, this giant of a man fell to his knees and cried out to Jesus to save him, something he would share with me later on. Not too many months later, this man moved to California to witness about Him to university students. As you know, Mark gave me Bible very soon after my salvation to help me learn more about Jesus and to grow my faith. (I wasn't ready when I received that Bible back in college.) There are countless apologetic authors, scholars, speakers, and teachers, but if you can relate to any of my experiences put forth here, I hope that any "fruit" I may bear will be through the Holy Spirit's whispers within *your* spirit to pique *your* curiosity as you say, "*Hey, I 'get' this! Yes! That's how I think! Could this work for me, too? Could this be what I've been looking for my whole life and not yet finding what hits the spot?*"

With this thought and hope in mind, I want to share with you the next fledgling steps in my early development as a Christian. The previous chapter was buckshot: you saw raw reactions and theological speculations from all over the map. Here I will laser-like hone in on and analyze specific points that have vexed and moved me. Perhaps as you read this, you will be drawn to find a Bible that's been on some shelf in your house so that you can look up a passage or two that is referenced here. Maybe you'll pull it up on your phone or tablet beside you, a first for you. Except for checking on biblical references for literature classes, that was the case for me! I do not pretend to have any kind of authority over what it means to be a proper Christian, but as a good friend at the gym and brother in Christ pointed out to me, we are *commanded*, not suggested by Christ, to speak of Him to others. There is no qualification, prerequisite, corequisite, or any particular amount of knowledge necessary to speak up about Him, and that is what I want to do. Hopefully, a score or two from now, I will be wiser, but my intent here and now is to write from the perspective of one experiencing these pure moments and discerning the changes taking place in her mind and heart *as they occur*, not from a slightly distorted reflection later on. Like each of the four Gospel writers who recollected their unique time spent with Jesus, yet differing in their chronology and topics of focus, I, here too, record the prominent points of visits I'd had with Mark. I'll include thoughts about the Bible that came from our talks or that spontaneously generated within me. I also started journaling to go back and find answers or reassurance if I so needed. You will also see that I also started to write short poems out of gratitude to Him. Poetry often conveys what can't be said any other way.

6.2 Apologetics Continued

When I first saw the term "apologetics," I thought it had to be a mistake or a bad joke. How could it be that I would need a manual to *apologize* for becoming a Christian? I sure wasn't expecting that! Then I speculated it might be some esoteric branch of Christian theology that took its root from the Greek, like hermeneutics, from Hermes, the messenger god. The Apostle Paul used such a stance to present one airtight argument after another to ignorant Gentiles, disbelieving Jews, and haughty rulers. Upon reading a couple of apologetic books, I became even more hooked in my new faith, stoked because certain Christian concepts that I'd *previously* considered spurious or fictional were proven false and untrue. My faith most assuredly had a rational basis, logical foundation, and historical accuracy on which it was established; this is not to say that the whole of God's purpose can be fathomed or that Jesus can be put on notice or in a box! The Disciple and Apostle Peter said we should always be prepared to defend our faith. I came to learn the hard way that this does *not* mean to search and destroy infidels, to start verbal warfare, or to straighten out those who have zero knowledge or interest in Christianity! I needed to remember that the wheels of motion got formed within disbelieving me first by my responding to the Holy Spirit's nudging me to probe further, which, in my case and out of curiosity, meant to send an email to a pastor I didn't even know. This man could have emailed me a quick answer and called it a day, but he didn't: *he showed up*. He didn't come to visit and start a row, give a lecture, launch a diatribe, threaten hell, or promise me Heaven. He listened intently, shared his own experiences, and explained this and that with wisdom, patience, and humor. The bottom line, he showed me that *he cared*. The proof is always in the pudding. I saw that you couldn't make people see the light, but you *can* make yourself available and approachable by cultivating loving relationships. Friendships lead to building trust, which, in turn, makes it safe to be vulnerable, which can then give rise to a supple soul ready to open up and welcome King Jesus. First off, faith has *got* to originate from something *way* beyond us. I certainly can't or didn't fashion it!

I am *not* one of those who have ever thought that there's nothing out there, that there's no God. There are plenty who are atheist or on-the-fence agnostic. They quip, "Isn't there just empty space out there? I can't *see* Him." For me, it's a no-brainer to accept that something vaster created all of this because a nothingness or void can't generate something. Later, I came to believe that all the "somethings" out there came from not *something*, but *someone*.

Before I became a Christian, I certainly didn't want anyone dictating to me who or what God was, let alone bring Jesus into the picture! I give full credit to my being in A.A. to coming to be receptive enough even to have a calm and sober conversation about Him. In A.A. meetings, any mention of the word "God" had affixed alongside, "as we understood Him," just to leave the door open to interpretation and, ultimately, to let Him at least be nearby the person. Another early pet peeve of mine was the fact that various writers anthropomorphize God and ascribe to Him human features (e.g., God's "voice" or "finger") as well as emotions like "incensed," "full of wrath," "pleased," etc. Not yet even a believer of Christ, this seemed a reduction of His glory. Even more troubling, however, was that this "someone" was a *He*. Most folks don't think about this. God seemed to me *beyond* gender and sex, though very much a Creator and Parent. No, I wasn't one of those who subscribed to the so-called "eternal feminine" or anything like that, but I guess I just had to acquiesce that there is not a pronoun that adequality captures God, so "He" it is. I think the case for folks who have the most challenging time accepting God as their Heavenly "*Father*" can be traced back to their not having a loving *earthly* father. Next, although Jesus is "Lord of lords and King of kings" (Rev. 17:14 NIV), as a man, He started out humbly; in fact, Jesus arrived as a nobody of sorts. He came from the middle of nowhere, born to no one important. If you consider several of his ancestors' reputations, His pedigree wasn't particularly stellar on His mother's side either; plus, His actual bloodline isn't even purely Jewish. And yet, there is no religious leader or founder like Jesus anywhere at any time. Is there any other religious leader out there that *died* for you? Is there any other religious founder that came but to *serve* and love while he was reviled? Who else but He was fully a man, yet concurrently divine *and* still (somehow) living? And come to find out, He has within Him not just *a* soul, but *the* Holy Spirit! Furthermore, the Holy Spirit is also not an *it*, but a personage within the Trinity, too!

No perfect analogy exists to capture what and how the Trinity exists, try though I would to find one! Even if you take three of your identities, you still have not been all three your whole life! God as my loving Father, which is mind-boggling enough, is also omnipotent, omnibenevolent, omniscient, and omnipresent, all beyond the bounds of linear time through which we travel. This isn't some tri-fold Hindu God that is a Creator and Destroyer; it takes no active interest in its creation, let alone salvation. The Greeks modeled the gods after *themselves* and upped the ante of our relationship with them by having mortals try to win favor and curry influence with them through flattery, sacrifice, and bribery. Only in Christianity do you have God *coming down to man* to fill the abstract but very real void He created and purposefully left as such for Himself to abide in should we fix our attention on Him. Nothing else satisfies us for too very long, but you have to be looking beyond today to be thus arrested in awe and find peace in Him, regardless of your circumstances. *He* brings about our joy! Yes, there *are* many paths to *contemplating* God. How could there *not* be? He'll do whatever it takes for us to look *beyond* ourselves, but He ultimately wants us to turn only to *Him*. After all, "the Lord…is a jealous God" (Exodus 34:14 KJV). There is only one route *directly* to Him though. Just read the Gospel of John for that golden nugget. Once you realize God, who is anterior to space and time, created our world and galaxy and cosmos out of *nothing*, then, of *course*, He is capable of sending a *person* to planet earth to demonstrate His profound and perfect love for us. I find no incompatibility with science's takes on creation because physicists and astronomers can only logically contend with the particulars *after* it occurred; therefore, I see little need to explore this further; you can read about this elsewhere. I am no expert. In short, science fills in and figures out so many of the details regarding creation and subsequent developments, but it cannot answer the ultimate *why* or the original *how*. In the meanwhile, I quietly whisper the answer to myself and you: "For He *so* loved the world…" (John 3:16, emphasis mine). Hypothesizing how many days it took to create everything, explaining the carbon dating of fossils, investigating earlier forms of life, justifying the various lapses or inaccurate time frames cited in evolution, and listing what animals were or were not on Noah's ark you'll have to read about in other books. Science fits and figures in the comprehensive framework of what God made, not the other way around; any discovery we make necessitates its already having existed, even if in some form something is yet to be expressed! Of course, there is a particular progression or natural evolution of sorts, but God can introduce things or instigate changes whenever He deems them; this is evidenced by genetic mutations and spontaneous events that occur and have no explanation. Even Darwin conceded to this fact! One can find all sorts of evidence of early life transitioning to what we know to be today, but God would determine at which point He wanted to bring forth humankind. Time frames can be as brief as twenty-four hours or several millennia. Quite frankly, making a judgment call as to what time interval you choose to use as your standard still doesn't answer a ton of things. Creation could easily have transpired in a single day, a week, or millennia; *it doesn't really matter*. Once you accept the stark fact that something, the cosmos and all forms of life in it, can't come *ex nihilio* — out of nothing — everything else, by contrast, seems like child's play, and this also includes miracles like the Virgin birth and the Resurrection, to name two biggies. None of Jesus' miracles were performed gratuitously or for show, as a magician would do. *Everything* He does shows intent, wisdom, and love, though from our vantage point, much in life defies our ability to explain.

To that end, I would launch more and more into studying the Word rather than trying to prove Jesus existed or was divine. Over time, I sought to grow deeper in prayer and Biblical understanding through Christian fellowship, knowing that "iron sharpens iron, so one man sharpens another" (Proverbs 27:17). I was finding the whole of the Bible to be magnificently, breathtakingly, and indefensibly harmonious. The litmus test I use to evaluate whether or not I have (more or less) correctly understood Scripture has three criteria; I learned it from my pastor. The method's acronym is C.A.P. for short, and it stands for (1) context, (2) audience, and (3) purpose. For a more thorough understanding, I would consider the cultural-historical context. What was known or considered appropriate then? Though I know neither ancient Greek nor Hebrew, of course, I appreciate the linguistic dimension. Dealing with the audience at hand, what might the writer have wanted to focus on? If I don't engage the CAP method, I risk cherry-picking and reading with *my* agenda, prejudices, and purposes (i.e., *eisegesis*) rather than what the actual *author* of the text intends (i.e., *exogenesis*). Do I *agree* with *everything* I read? No, or rather, *not exactly*, but I'm not worried because truths and knowledge gained aren't instantaneous or immediate or exhaustive; it's cumulative, organic, and hopefully, ongoing. In short, this in your hands is not another apologetics book, though this topic is still one I find myself drawn to for potential future conversations that could lead to Him. My daily reading of Scripture is my "daily bread" (Matthew 6:11).

6.3 WHO IS SAVED? WHO IS NOT?

One Wednesday night at church, I heard someone assert that the Old Testament figures were saved because they had faith in God who encompasses the whole of the Trinity. Of course, I spoke up and asked *how could they be saved if Christ had not yet been born*? If it is such a big deal to make a personal choice, this wasn't an even option for them. They couldn't have done that; it wasn't possible in those days. To that end, I thought Christ went down to Hades during the three days after His Crucifixion/death and before His Resurrection. Even if we don't know exactly what transpired "down there," He *did* go! In my mind's eye, I can just see the Greek Orthodox icon of Christ's Descent into Hell. He is holding the hands of a beleaguered and grateful-looking Adam and Eve (and by conjugation and extrapolation, all the rest of the faithful Old Testament figures) to take them up to Paradise. He's shown defeating a personified death! Jesus's main task, Job #1, was to eliminate our state of sin; a by-product of His imputation of our sin was the fact that He *also* killed death for all time's sake for everyone who would choose to believe He had the authority to do so and accomplished this. And it was during that very moment of Jesus' physical death and subsuming sin that His Father *had* to look away because He *cannot* look on sin. It's not that He didn't care! It took less than a split-second for Jesus to accomplish the supreme substitution even though it took three days before He arose to tell us "of little faith" (Matthew 8:26 KJV) all about it. "*How do you like me now*?!?" He might have wanted to have said! I now move past my point in showing you how the Old Testament leaders got saved, but I'll return. There's so much to tell you!

Then the discussion of faith came into play, and one of the congregants that evening gently explained to me that *faith was credited to them based on what they believed would happen*. What a relief! I was so grateful to this person! It made sense! I can't tell you how often, when frustrated and impatient from my lack of understanding, I would get further mad at myself for feeling so dependent upon Mark in looking to him to answer my questions. Surely, I would outwear my welcome, and he would leave me in a lurch. I was afraid I'd be left to my own devices, twirling and stewing on questions because he would have had enough of all of this, of my infernal questions. Later, I saw that this *was* a legitimate friendship, not just a teacher-student thing to be concluded in a semester. Not only would he be there for us, but we would be there for him. In a way, though I could hardly have known then, we were simply doing life together. He showed how Jesus came to be personal by being real to us. The slogan at this little church is that it is for "jacked-up" folks; all are welcome to come simply as they are. I recalled back when I was a child, I had a Unitarian poster which I'd pinned up on my bulletin board in my room. In a groovy font, it posed the question, *"Who are you are that you think you can change the world?"* At the time, I felt a sense of futility and powerlessness emanating from its happy letters, yet its scope also allured me. Now I see that change *can* be accomplished, but it can only transpire through a power greater than what I (or anyone) alone held; it *had* to come through this God "as we understand Him." And just how do I understand Him now? He is the one living and eternal God who, yes, is *also* Christ, Who is filled with a Spirit given *to me* through which all things good to be done in the world *are* possible.

6.4 THE HEART, REVISITED

Yesterday Bonnie and I asked each other a series of questions that we anticipated asking Mark. We wanted to see if we could answer them first, and later we would check ourselves to see if we were on the right track based on what Mark might say. I considered our doing so a small sign of progress because it showed that we were trying to develop a sound support system for one another to check for accuracy about what we ought to be internalizing. I can't stress enough how everyday life was changing for us in a pronounced if not dramatic way: the content of many of our conversations, whether or not they *started out* theologically or doctrinally, seemed to gravitate that way. Speaking of which, this inclination to consider things from His perspective put me in a state of readiness to be on the lookout for opportunities to initiate dialogue about Him should they spontaneously present themselves. Case in point: about this time, I was in a doctor's waiting room just minding my own business when I overheard a random conversation next to me, and I inserted myself. It started out like a bad joke; an agnostic and a Catholic were having a quiet discussion about some religious article both had read; this was my opportunity! It was no surprise that they weren't making any headway. The topic happened to be about whether one can know if one is going to Heaven or not; neither contended that they could know with certainty; having this in common produced an odd stalemate. I couldn't *not* speak to this one, so I briefly shared that I had experienced what felt like the Holy Spirit electrically enter me and that I am assured that He'll not only stay with me but that this is my pledge or guarantee that I will be in Heaven. I can know this fact here and now; it's not a guessing or waiting game! The Catholic maintained that he could *not* know whether or not he was saved until the moment of his death when he encounters Jesus and learns from Him. The agnostic sat in silent wonderment; like some incredulous sponge, he seemed eagerly absorbing what was said.

Yesterday I came home exhausted, and I've come to be on the alert that when I get tired, the devil has an easier time having his way with me. For example, when I feel countered, I can get irritable, sarcastic, dismissive, not to mention abnormally laden with doubts. In such a festering state of heightened impatience, I don't, no, can't seem to listen with my heart to truths I know and strive to live out. And speaking of being off my game for this and that, I *still* have a hard time hearing other Christians use the word "heart" because mine is often inconstant, mutable, and reactive. Maybe I should consider (and say) that my *feelings and mood change*; my heart remains steady and constant. Now more than then, when I have a dilemma or situation in life, rather than swirl and get stuck in my head, I head straight for the Bible to see if it can't steer me right and give me a clue or answer. In fact, I start my day *expectant* and ready to read and learn of a response to some prayer I've had or some pearl I imagine to be useful to me somehow. At this time, I happened to be reading Acts, which is where you'll find what happened right after Jesus died and also the phenomenal story of Paul. I found several references to the word "heart" that penetrated my mind in a way I'd not been thinking of before. For example, in Acts 13:22, we find a reference to the O.T. figure of David, who though an adulterer and murderer, was later described as "*a man after His [God's] heart.*" This example tells me that despite committing many transgressions, if a person keeps on loving and trying to grow in God, and his heart fully engaged in what he was doing, God will make any good we do great. In turn, this readiness pleases God and moves Him; therefore, David's coming to God would touch *His* heart! The source of David's inspiration and consolation, the One Who filled his heart's desires to the point that He became his heart's citadel and home base, was God. Life's circumstances and his frailties didn't change this fact; it was David's obedience that paled compared to his love. Later, in Acts 15:8–9, I found this passage: "⁸And God, who knows *the heart*, testified to them giving them the Holy Spirit, just as He also did to us; ⁹and He made no distinction between them and us, *cleansing their hearts by faith*" (emphasis mine). Paul is making an analogy between those at Pentecost who received the Holy Spirit and, much later, other believers — including himself — who received the same Holy Spirit. He worded it as such to indicate that *it is the state of a man's heart* which is the linchpin, the determinant for a readiness to receive Him. *Faith is a function of the heart; it cannot be produced in the mind or outward rote behavior.*

Speaking of the relationship between heart and faith, God makes no distinction between them and us; He looks to and at the state of our heart. It was becoming clear to me that *the heart reveals the purity of our motive.* If our soul is centered on God, He immediately recognizes such and, for lack of a better word, connects Himself — His Spirit — within us through His internal communicator, whom you may better recognize as "the Counselor"(John 14:26 Amplified). We are on a different standing when we side with Him, which frequently puts us at odds with the world that abides by a different standard; its driving force is *self*. That same morning, I kept looking for more on the matter of the heart, and from Acts 28:27, I spied just how important it is to God: "Otherwise, they might see with their eyes, and hear with their ears, and *understand with their heart* and return, and I would heal them" (emphasis mine). In other words, it's much more than through rational means that one perceives God's nature, value, and properties. Just the frequency of the word "heart" in the Bible pointed me to an obvious but far richer meaning than we ascribe to it today. I feel like how I have been viewing and interpreting life itself is changing before my very eyes. The way the world depicts the heart cheapens its value. I can tell that my crusty mantle of cynicism is being eroded, and through its being chipped away, His golden truths are getting solidified in me. My desire to be closer to Him keeps growing. Getter better acquainted with God on *my* part has been a very deliberate and slow process, but the fact of the matter is, I was changing and *being* changed from the inside out. There's no stopping me *and* no end in sight.

6.5 CHRIST'S LITTLE VISIT TO HADES

Though I briefly mentioned that it had been explained to me about those who came *before* Christ and never knew Him, yet they believed there *would* be such a Savior, it didn't take inside me. This topic needed further breakdown, and it came. Yes, I got that Christ victoriously defeated death. How could this be, you ask? He bore the penalty and paid the price for the original sin *plus* all sin *after that*; nobody but God (i.e., Christ) could've done that. God was making good on His proclamation that death would be the penalty for our disobedience, so only another aspect/person of the Godhead, Jesus, could have settled the score for *all* time's sake and reversed that curse. I'm re-reading Hebrews right now, so I'll delve deeper into this topic that hadn't yet got settled. In the notes for Hebrews 9:15, I read that when Christ died, salvation was made possible *retroactively* for those that were under the Old Covenant. I wondered if this is so, then why would Christ go to Hades for those three days while he was dead? What was *that* all about? I wondered if He said anything to Satan in particular while He was down there. Did He tell him that *the gig is up*, that he didn't get to keep those in his underworld like Persephone was by Hades? It's true: Jesus went to Hell during those three days after He was crucified and died, but it was not so much to retrieve the keys as I've seen depicted in Greek icons. Jesus alone conquered death, and Satan never possessed the keys to begin with! Only God has control and power over death, and if there are any keys, they are those Jesus possesses to the Kingdom of Heaven! Another myth busted! That Wednesday evening, another pastor taught instead of Mark, and he happened to repeat that Old Testament (O.T.) men who showed faith in a *future* Messiah *had been saved*. Was it all and only about faith? How could their being saved even be possible? Reflexively, I again thought things were out of sequence because Christ had not yet been born. This pastor talked to us in what seemed like autopilot for him; he matter-of-factly told us that the prophets were "saved by faith" and that righteousness was "credited" to them. At that moment, I figured that this would be like my giving a passing grade to students I hadn't taught, let alone met because they believed I could do such! Later, Mark explained to me that those O.T. figures so fully had faith in the coming of a future Messiah, so wholly believed that there would come a Christ, a savior — one whom they couldn't yet even visualize — that God saved them *by virtue of their looking forward to and anticipating the arrival of the Messiah*. The belief was already in their *hearts*. It's this type of thought process and absolute trust that He rewarded and continues to reward. It's all in a day for Him anyway. Now some 2000 years later, we, too, are saved by that same grace; the difference is we *look back* to the cross and believe what historically happened. It's as if we were there alongside the ones who were eyewitnesses of Him *after* the Resurrection and during the forty days of He mingled among folks *before* his final Ascension. According to 1 Corinthians 15:6, there were more than five hundred people He appeared to, and that's not including the remaining Eleven and Mary Magdalene. Wow! In short, they in the Old Testament *looked forward* in anticipation of the Messiah; some got to see Him with their own eyes in that blink of time. On the other hand, we *hearken back to* the actual event, believe, and are saved. These two time period fits together seamlessly, like the pieces of a puzzle coming together to complete the two lines; Jesus is the center point, the bridge, chronologically and vertically, between man and God. My next question would have to do with why did we *have* to die for our disobedience. What was God thinking in doing *that*?

6.6 ADAM AND EVE BROUGHT DEATH?!?

I honestly didn't understand the connection between death and sin. I decided to talk directly to God. Here is a record of the way I spoke to Him:

> Do you mean to tell me that Adam and Eve would never have died had they never sinned? This notion doesn't make any sense to me! I know that salvation and being saved is only something You can do for us through Christ. But doesn't that make sanctification our responsibility? I understand that our loving debt to Him is an ongoing process and one never to be completed. James talks about faith without works being "dead." Is our whole life about making our efforts for You more evident and more frequent?

Questioning about the relationship between death and sin just blew me away! I thought that, surely, normal life processes like birth and death and the cycle of life continued in the Garden of Eden. How could I have imagined that there was no death there? But — and here's where I got blown away — just as the laws of physics and logic are suspended when we think about experiencing eternal life with Christ in Heaven after we die, God, of course, created a state of perfection in the Garden of Eden. There were no factors present to contribute to aging and decay. And by perfection, I mean no sorrow, no pain, no decay, etc. When Adam and Eve chose to transgress God's one solitary rule, duped by the lie that they'd be better off if they had one more thing — *His* degree of knowledge — this set off a chain of events and trying circumstances we *still* see being played out in our lives today. Just turn on the news if you don't believe me. Of course, these two felt shame and remorse that they tried to cover, but I'll bet they'd do it again if He hit the restart button. Knowing that they had sinned and that they could not cover up their guilt, God went ahead and took care of that, too: He killed the first animal on the spot, right then and there, the skin of which they used that literally and figuratively to cover themselves. From then on, for the next 4000 to 5000 years, our capacity to conceal ourselves would be inadequate until the time in which Jesus Christ came and took on the actual punishment due us through taking the hit and dying in our stead, that is, shedding His blood for us. I have actually imagined myself either sitting at the foot of the cross looking up at Christ or being the fellow crucified prisoner looking over at Him and who, at the last minute, verbalized his belief in Him. I picture myself saying to Jesus, "Yes, Jesus, I *do* believe you and *in* you, that you would do this for me, yes, even if I were the only person in the world. You're *that* kind of man. You are *so* my Lord and Savior!" I could relate to the (believing) prisoner crucified alongside Christ! I, too, came to Him relatively late in life; therefore, I took confidence that just as Christ assures this man, I can hear Him say to *me*, "Truly I say to you, today you shall be with Me in Paradise" (Luke 23:43). Often, right after I've made peace within myself about better understanding one member of the Trinity, my mind will roll over and consider another topic.

If I think about the fact that God is eternal and that He decided to create a *finite* cosmos and also conceive of a future life/existence for us mortal believers such that we could enjoy fellowship with Him *eternally*, I am thunderstruck. The sole requirement for being united with Him for all eternity — and that we which cannot bring about on our own — formerly had me speculating whether we were set up for doom and failure. Now I view our part in coming to Him through our submission as humanity's first step in developing a moral conscience. The environment God created for us abound in beauty and absolute freedom; His world for us was not a sterile lab. In these conditions, the character of man would either blossom and grow or begin to rot. If we had not done what He knew we would do — break with Him, then we would have stayed static in *our* characterization and never matured in our relationship with Him. We were doomed *and* damned. It seems to me He did *not* intend for us to remain adorable infants forever, a state in which we couldn't know God as well as when we'd acquired more experience. Mothers may cherish their babies, but they crave grown-up time, too! Maybe God wanted us to know Him as grateful and eager ones who come to Him of their own volition. The die was cast, and the decline began; our savageness and further lawlessness were an inevitable process of our growing up! Sure, there have been moments of clarity in us; this would occur when a few imperfect women and men believed without seeing in some vastly brighter future. His original Garden of perfection is unattainable, or, better to say, is impossible to reclaim *on our own*, but thinking macro-cosmically, He would have us return to Him in His own time when we were readied. How patient He was all the while and still is! Adam and Eve were those infants in new diapers. Much of what people view with dismay in the Old Testament, where we witness His spankings of us, from *His* perspective, must be like a Father viewing His child in the terrible twos. Over and over, in one form or another, we said "*No!*" or "*Mine!*" to our Father and Creator. Contrary to popular opinion, God showed great restraint or forbearance in His smiting us for this and that. Every now and again, some humble person would pop up in history ready to do His will and say, "Yes," to Him; his or her choice included a leap of faith and not one following convention. We see this with Noah's building of the ark in preparation for the unforeseen following cataclysmic, had-it-up-to-here-with-them Flood.

Next, the adolescent years of humanity's history aren't much better: that's the stage when one breaks away from one's parents even more brazenly and begins idolizing all that is seemingly hip and cool in a state of stubborn pride. All the while and through the leadership of a few, we as a mass moved slowly but inexorably to a point and place of readiness for us to witness Him come here Himself and show us all what's what, that is, *why* we're here and *in Whom* we should seek. Again, we see examples of this time and again throughout the Old Testament. He even provided a rule book for us, His own Top Ten list, a primer for His willful teenagers until such a time that we *also* needed to be made aware that even those with clout and power couldn't master His rules and that rule-following wasn't the point anyway! Psyche! It's not sacrificing He wants, but obedience, respect, and compassion; all of these are functions of faith. And so, when He saw that we were of age and at a time of His choosing, He came. To contemplate God deciding the moment ripe for His Son to come in the flesh, what with his vast superiority, yet choosing to lead a humble life and lean into punishment due *us*, all so we were enabled to hit the reset button and have God to forgive us and we to reunite with Him, *mind-blowing* in scope! Most didn't believe then; many do not now. Just when you think there's been no change in the world as far as His progress of growing us goes, consider the fact that it took nearly three hundred years for there even to exist a physical church, and now Christianity is all over the world! From our vantage point, progress is painfully slow, unapparent even, but we don't even know the tip of the top of the iceberg. Only when we shift our axis to revolve our *raison d'être* around Him can the hope for goodness and improvement occur. This is a one-person-at-a-time operation. Regardless, as we march (or fumble) ahead, we believers are told of an impending end leading to an eternity of a still more vast, incomprehensible, and glorious state.

What does it mean to gain eternal life? Does it happen like the cicada that leaves its casing behind, or, better, the caterpillar's transformation to a butterfly? Some might ask, who would *want* to live eternally? If you think about life on just a *physical* level, the law of conservation of mass tells us that *matter* can neither be created nor destroyed, so oughtn't the same hold true for *energy*, that is, our *spirit*? No, this energy will go not to inhabit some new life like a zombie-spirit on the loose looking for a home to occupy. I in no way believe that one's energy, soul, essence, or self transmigrates or reincarnates into another life form or type of personage. Your final cause-effect destination is based on the answer choice you make in this life, namely, one in particular, which is *"Do you know Jesus?"* That question is pregnant meaning and holds eternal consequences. Here's my translation for the blind: "Do you know where you come from?" "Do you know who's your daddy'?" "Don't you want to be with the one who made *you*, made *all* of this, in absolute and supreme *love*?" Previously, I had no way of knowing *how* to answer this, let alone *what* it meant; in fact, I felt affronted by this seeming impertinent question. I was close-minded to my core. Thank goodness, He found a crack of openness still yet in me. I got it such that now, I enthusiastically cheer, "Yes!" to God, to *Jesus*, the Son of God, equal to but different than His Father. When people hear the word "Son," they think He is somehow hierarchically lower than the Father. Still, while He was with us, His subordination was only a temporary, volunteer job, so we ought to give greater latitude to these words here: He is equal in might. Jesus pre-existed right along with God the whole time before He became our Christ. He is the only one of the three that became tangible and real for us, even if only for thirty-three short years and a mere three years of that being devoted to His ministry. Now *that's* productive! God may be the Creator and our Father, but only Jesus is our Messiah, our Christ. And the power of infinitude contained within His human self would be sufficient for *all* time's sake to be able to subsume, absorb, or eradicate sin that keeps us from being back square with our maker. No other man, let alone a religious leader, possesses divinity as part of his essential self; none else of the Trinity took on flesh: He is unique and dear in this omnipotent role. *That's* how He can be equal to His father: God created all life, and Christ died for all to make it possible for us to have eternal life and a sustained connection with the three-in-one Trinity.

Speaking of eternity, we don't have to wait for death to ascertain a sense of eternity now and then, here and now; this reality gives me pause and hope. In fact, I have experienced a kind of contact with or nod of acknowledgment from Him, which I know full well comes from beyond me myself. Sometimes in the quietude and privacy of the still morning hours when I pray with all I've got and frequently when I read the Bible, an inner glow or veritable *stirring* comes over me, like a sense of affirmation or encouragement. This feeling is not from me; it's as if confirmation is sent at that moment to jog my mind. In that split second, I feel as though I've been shot in the heart — in a good and sweet way, though. I know I've been touched or reached out to through the means of my Bible study or prayer from God Himself. It is a physical experience in the form of an overcharged, soulful feeling. This experience does not occur daily, nor is it something that can be anticipated or produced. How can this be, you ask? I have God's Spirit in me, the very one that was in Christ! Now I understand why Jesus said something to the effect that it was in our best interest that He leaves. While He was in the flesh and here among us as a *man*, Jesus could only be in *one* place at a time. However, His Spirit, whom He sent to us after He ascended, is *not* bound by time, corporeality, or space! The Holy Spirit — *as* spirit — *can* be in *all* those who believe *everywhere*, regardless of when or where they live! The supernatural step in faith I took, which resulted in the inhabitation or indwelling of His Spirit — He Who is the proof and guarantee of Jesus always being with me — is not one that I bring to another, let alone produce for myself. (And by the way, the Holy Spirit is a "He" for the same reason God is a "He"; we have to roll with it because no other fitting pronoun exists.) Our individualized ownership of such help and power is the very same one that Jesus Christ had in life. The Apostle Paul eloquently described just what the Holy Spirit is to us believers when he penned the following: "*We have this treasure in earthen vessels* so that the surpassing greatness of the power will be of God and not from ourselves" (2 Cor. 4:7, emphasis mine). We believers get linked to the Trinity!! When I divined this bond, I wanted to shout from the mountaintops or "go tell it on the mountain"!

Oh, this metaphysical possession is not easily explained. That morning in my devotional, I read I ought not to give wisdom to fools, scoffers, cynics, and those who don't believe in Him. I am to *expect* that "[I] will be hated by everyone because of [Christ]" (Matthew 10:22 NIV). It's no different today than centuries ago, yet hopefully, I can still represent and attract a few through love in the way He comes out in me. This often proves difficult for me because there is also a desire to share Christ's Word. Knowing the consequences of refusing Him, I find it especially hard for me to hold back with those who are my dearest ones. Mark said he understood because he, too, knew that some of his close ones would be in Hell for rejecting Him. The longing to share my experience of coming to Jesus and growing in faith with skeptics such as I was once *compels* me to express myself in this way. I must pace myself and start with people exactly where they are, just as Mark did with me. I cannot be too pushy or alienate with words that leave them in a lurch. Over the past year or so, I have come to know that any change in a person will come based upon the Holy Spirit's prompting and "attraction — *not* promotion," as is said in A.A. I must witness to folks through the way I live my life, a visible expression of faith. Actions always speak louder than words, though His word tops them all. I have never given my testimony other than through this my contemporaneous writing to you now. I wonder as I write this, will I ever do missionary work? I have no idea, but I'm propelled and compelled to complete this testimony so that even if one person reads this and takes that step in faith, bound for glory, it'll be worth it!

What do you think about this for yourself? Maybe you'll let me know! It's odd how the promises of A.A. are coming to fruition in my life now as a Christian. God, too, has many Promises. Next, I'd peek into the death of Jesus, His promise-keeper.

6.7 The Torn Veil

As if the crucifixion of an innocent man who showed Himself to be of the same stuff of God proved Himself to be the Son of God wasn't enough, another amazing fact occurred at His point of death. When Christ said, "It is finished," He meant that His job here, which was both to show us the way to live *and* to atone for our sins, He completed and accomplished. *They* didn't kill *Him*, He didn't die as a result of the crucifixion itself (or else it would have taken longer), and He didn't commit suicide. He expired; that is, He gave up His life through the means of His voluntary, willful, and sacrificial death, horrific though the method of punishment was. The solar eclipse that occurred, enveloping all in a blanket of frightful darkness, reflected God's not being able to look on the sum of (or any) sin, let alone to see His Son taking it in such a manner. Jesus, the man, felt forsaken and momentarily abandoned by His father. However, He as God knew for us to be reunited with Him, this crowning act of exquisite, agonizing, and self-sacrificial love was the only way. I could think of it as my earthly father jumping out in front of a moving vehicle to push me aside so I wouldn't get hit, but the difference is, I don't *know* if he would risk death to save my life. Christ most assuredly *did*. Lest we think this was just another day back in Jerusalem, God put on quite the show to frame His horrific death. A cataclysmic earthquake of such force and magnitude occurred that the dark and heavy veil in the Temple of Jerusalem was literally torn away. What a curtain call! Its purpose was to separate the priests from the common man, that is, analogously God from man. The fact that the thick veil was tattered symbolized the high priest's status of being the only one who could right the matter with God for man — an act that had to be performed annually — was *nullified*. Now it would be possible for ordinary people to have *direct* access to God! From then on, the potentiality for having a relationship with God would come about through man's *own* high priest on high: Christ! God made this unveiling earth-shatteringly apparent! The dividing line was gone! No wonder the powers-that-be were furious. I shared my understanding of this with my friend at the gym, Rick. He informed me that this veil separating the clergy from the layman in the temple was a woven tapestry, and it was incredibly dense, so much so that for it to be "rent" was a miracle in and of itself.

I made a mental connection between the torn veil and the reestablishing of such by man as evidenced by the formal hierarchy within the Catholic clergy and even the iconostasis in the Orthodox Church, which is a construct that physically separates the priests from the clergy. Jesus' death tore away the barrier so we could access Him for *ourselves*; it was *man* who tacked back up a makeshift wall! That said, since no layperson in those early days could read, let alone attend a church until around the third century, I can understand and appreciate the need for establishing some parameters in those early days, even if such started out to help ensure the church's survival and to foster an understanding of what He did and who He was. Man being man, he came to view his own rules and construct on par with God's. Even today, associations of various branches of Christianity create their own contemporary commandments via bi-laws and such, as if God needs their remixed input, and often they present a harsher and more rigid legalism than God ever put out, ofttimes unintentionally made odious by not displaying His love. The early elders appreciated the fact that people need guidance and care, but if Christ truly moves a person, he or she will naturally and of his own accord keep hungering for the Word and seek the truths they reveal. All I can say is that I'm glad I was born *after* Gutenberg invented the printing press in the mid-1400s so I can read for myself what all He wants to tell me! I understand that sanctification will be lifelong; I am but a rough draft of what I'm becoming, and I hope my thirst for His word remains unquenched. More and more, I would want to be around others with the same hankering for Him as I.

6.8 God's Looking Away at Calvary:
Another Glimpse of Just Who Jesus Is

When the time came to meet with Mark again, I checked with him about ideas that'd been percolating in me regarding the moment of Christ's death. I sought to know if I was on the right path. I asked him if God turned away when Jesus was on the cross because He could not stand to look on His Son suffering, or was God the Father there the whole time observing and watching the just punishment for humankind rightfully taking place? The answer Mark confirmed to me was that at that moment, He *had* to turn away because, in His holiness, He could and cannot look on sin in any form, even as it was being absolved and conclusively capitulated. That was all on Jesus. When Jesus was receiving the punishment that was due us and not Him, He chose to bear it; unfortunately, there was no other way. He asked. Though at that moment His Father acceded to what He foreknew would take place, that is, that there was no way for us to get out of punishment due, He who is Holy and Perfect could not witness the clod of our mass sin subsumed onto that which is the same essence as Himself. He could not watch His Son take it in the teeth, His flesh until it — sin — was eradicated. (And by the way, such punishment had to take place because God is good to His word; if He would have let us off the hook, He wouldn't be the perfection of Who He said He is.) Did God turn away when Jesus was suffering on the cross? Mark answered me quickly and definitively, "*Absolutely*. God can't look at or on sin; He sees us as redeemed and robed when we choose to believe in His Son." God allowed this horrifying punishment committed by vile men to take place with His Son, both He and Jesus, knowing all the while it was for *us*. Talk about Love! And Jesus came here expressly to accomplish it *though it wasn't initially even His idea*! Talk about obedience! Next, I began to fester over the nature of sin itself, which got us off-track and awry to start with.

I want to tell you that the reference to the actual word "sin" really used to chap me when I heard it. I would say to myself, "That sounds *so* negative and pessimistic! Why even talk of sin? I can't be all *that* bad! I haven't murdered anyone, and I *try* to live right. Doesn't effort count?" Now, however, the more closely I examine my thoughts, actions, and intents, I recognize and acknowledge that I am often motivated by self-gain, self-aggrandizement, or self-preservation; this in and of itself *is* sinful! Plus, pan or play it out, and such thoughts which revolve around self lead to more sin actualized! I realize this is how *all* wrongdoing starts: the capacity to initiate wrongdoing at any time shows me that "sin" is, indeed, the perfect word for what we *all* possess. Every child, every innocent babe has this sin *potential*; it's all a matter of degree in *how* it gets expressed, yet the black-and-white, stark fact of our possessing sin remains. I wondered, is my salvation a lie? Can't He also see that I'm *still* imperfect? That I still stink? Can't He see through the murder of His Son to realize I'm no different? But that *can't* be because I am *not* the same! I *want* to be different; I desire to change for the better for Him, and what I seek in life has also changed. My being saved doesn't make me perfect, like shaking the Etch-a-Sketch tablet back to blank, but it *does* shift the arc of my life's outcome and, hopefully, my ability to produce fruit for Him. Was Jesus like some Bounty Quicker-Picker-Upper paper towel in how He absorbed all that sin for infinitude? Well, that's just what can happen when you are part of the triune God when you are God in the flesh. He Who is eternal *can* take on and blot out an unlimited amount of sin from people for all time's sake, just like Adam started the ball rolling. I kept finding the answers to my questions. Sometimes this would happen *after* I'd already read a particular passage once before — but upon a *subsequent* reading, I'd arrive at just the response I was seeking. Here is one such example that I came upon in 1 Corinthians 15: 20–22 (emphasis mine) regarding how sin (and death) arrived and then got gone: "[20]But now Christ has been raised from the dead, the first fruits of those who are asleep.[21]For since by a man came death, by a man also came the resurrection of the dead. [22]*For as in Adam all die, so also in Christ, all will be made alive.*" God was looking *way* ahead, past the world in its infancy, past my own youth and folly, to a magnificent reunion in our future. How was Jesus as a *man* able to accomplish this?

    Though Jesus was *born*, how He got here is not the same as how we come to be. Jesus was *begotten*, not physically *conceived* in the manner those in God's creation are; therefore, He did not acquire or incur sin like we who are the progeny of Adam and Eve do. Jesus had nothing, no blemish, no impediment — no sin — to prevent Him from being perfect *and* seamlessly connected to God. Of course, this is so because, after all, He alone is incarnate, that is, God in the flesh. That said, while Jesus was here, He *did* have to limit His powers, but on occasion and in His perfect timing, we *do* get glimpses and evidence of His omniscience and omnipotence. For those who believe this is child's play, it's so obvious; for those who think Jesus was some super-nice guy with a great message, the difference He possessed is still not discernable. It was and still is hard for many to believe because He *appears* to be just a man even though He did and said plenty to indicate otherwise. He alone made it possible for our own impeding, ugly sin to be eradicated; our part in this equation is to believe and accept this profound gift of love. If this fact, let alone offering, is hard to accept, I think such is so because we all deal with real and frail people just like ourselves who have never really gone out of their way, never really sacrificed, let alone *died* for us! That's just a bit much, right? Such a demonstration of love seems incomprehensible, and that alone should show you that this sacrificial and precious love came from God, not man, yet also while God *was* man. When I think about Christ dying on the cross and suffering for me, my mind goes to a line from a song that Bonnie often sings, "Am I somebody worth dying for?" and I can't seem to answer that this could be true! Then I proceed and consider that because God very much creates with will and intentionality, He made me, too — on and with purpose. Mark reminds me that "I am fearfully and wonderfully made" (Psalm 139:14) and that I exist because He put "wove me in my mother's womb" (Psalm 139:13). This means He knew me from before the time I was born or even conceived by my parents. I am no accident because *He does not and cannot make mistakes.* I am His from the start, so, of course, I am worth *dying* for! And so, in grateful acknowledgment of His taking the hit for me, I say in turn that Christ is worth *living* for!

    My pre-Christian mind *used* to say, "I never asked for Your sacrifice. I never asked You to die for me, and I certainly don't want your guilt trip." As Patty Smith would sing in her 1975 hit, "Gloria,"

> Jesus died for somebody's sins but not mine...
> My sins my own
> They belong to me, me
> People say, "beware!"
> But I don't care
> The words are just
> Rules and regulations to me...

By her first line above alone, I think Patty Smith felt small, passed-over, and unloved. Because she felt excluded, she projected her hurt onto God and tried to look tough, like it didn't matter to her, as if she was a big girl and owned her own sin. I get her. I agree that my sins are my own, but that I *can* and *do* sin originated before me, so dealing with sin — not even my own — is *not* something that can begin and end with *me*. Despite her protestations and attempts at reverse psychology, *that* she writes about her angst shows she *is* hurt and that she very much *does* care! Her reference to "the words," indicates that she has not yet been touched by *Him*, only words of the men from the church she finds disappointingly reductive and regulatory. It's a copout to focus on and reject *man's* rules and codes; go to the *source*. "Go to *Jesus*," I would tell Patty Smith if I could. The thing is, I now understand and *do* care. I didn't *not* care before; I was just too hurt or sideways in my thinking to see straight. What if the whole reason for my existence is to recognize that my *life* comes *from* Him; like it or not, I am His! My future depends upon my response to His pinnacle offer of love. We get obsessed with death because deep down, we *want* to think that all of this *isn't* the end, that we matter *that* much, but we can't accomplish our ultimate *destiny*, let alone execute bigger dreams and goals into being without outside help. In not fathoming this, unbelievers call it quits before they even get started knowing Him! I'm not talking about your desires or aspects of your identity, but your calling, in whatever form and shape that turns out to be during your life. Way back when, some twenty-five years ago, when I was a college student visiting that big Baptist Church with my best buds, what I didn't understand then, which slew me, was the notion that *self must die*. I now realized this as fundamental truth: *I owe my life to Him who died for me*. I can't estimate the value of my existence without factoring in that from Whom I came. It's not a closed system; John Donne was right! "No man is an island!" Even if

I didn't *ask* Him to die for me, *He did so anyway*! I'm sure He hoped I would choose to believe this fact, believe *Him*. Seemingly impossible, over the ages, *billions* of people also share this personal intimacy with Him as does little ol', formerly unbelieving me.

From the moment of my salvation, not only did the desire to get to know Him more fully and richly transpire but also, I began to wonder what His unique purpose might be for me. Being brought into union with Christ changes the course and tempo of one's life. Through a new patience, readiness, and expectancy, I quietly wait for God to radically transform me into that which He would have me be or do during my sanctification. All the while, *I put one foot in front of the other for Him*, feeling free and already victorious. Mark says that we are to pray "bold and specific," that He can do anything in accordance with His will. I now do. And I see that I'm *not* so small, last in line, irrelevant, needy, or pathetic enough to qualify for receiving His affections and attention. It is *because* I have been blessed in a multitude of ways that He involves Himself in my life *all the more* and loves me, too. I can do much for Him, much for *others*. I got this confirmed when I read a couple of passages of Scripture (Matthew 25:23 and 29) that resonate with me. "[23]You were faithful with a few things, I will put you in charge of many things. . . [29] "For to everyone who has, *more* shall be given, and he will have an abundance…" His love ought to galvanize within me such that I can put my gifts, energy, resources, and talents to work for Him. Why? I *do* matter to Him!

I wish I could go back and tell my old self He has always been concerned with me; this is partly why I write this to you now! Earlier, I would have said that the very advent of man sounded like a setup: it seemed like we were created just to be doomed to fail, that is, "born but to die," as Alexander Pope put it. When I became liberal enough to receive Him, it didn't take long to know all my protestations and "what if's" were but my attempt to reduce God and His plans down to my size and capacity of comprehension. Probably the best Biblical metaphor that made sense to me as to what I am vis-a-vis to God regarding His power and scope is of the potter to the clay, an analogy found in both the Old and New Testaments. In other words, *this is God's showboat*, and He can do as He wants. Don't worry; He may be inscrutable, but He is not capricious or of an unpredictable or miserly nature. Why? He is perfect, and His character is one of *extravagant* Love, whether or not it gets expressed as *you* might see fit. Anyway, what do we know from where we stand? A lot, yet not much. Even if you take the astonishing discoveries made by brilliant geniuses, you still have to admit that our *capacity* to figure out x, y, or z was provided by a source past our fathoming.

I will share one more of the many expressions of the theme of man's stunning lack of omniscience, despite his keen and curious mind. Isaiah intends not one scintilla of condescension towards man when he reports the following: "[8]'For My thoughts are not your thoughts, Nor are your ways My ways,' declares the LORD.[9] 'For *as* the heavens are higher than the earth, So are My ways higher than your ways, And My thoughts than your thoughts'" (Isaiah 55:8–9). Please do not misconstrue my words and think I'm some gung-ho, anti-science proponent who loathes man's attempts to fathom the mysteries of this world. Heavens, no! You couldn't pay me to go back to the Middle (a.k.a. Dark) Ages where ignorance, brutality, and superstition were at the helm. Reason and logic are not to be eschewed or construed as somehow evil! I don't avoid immunizations, and I wouldn't think twice about having a blood transfusion. Why? God knows all, but as we are made in His image, we are, in fact, His best work: He gave us the brain we have to *use*. I knew an elderly man in A.A. who liked to say that "God may have put the worms in the ground for the birds to eat, but He didn't place them up in the nest!" My father was a man of science, and we children all had instilled in us a powerful sense of wonder for the world. We never missed an episode of *Mutual of Omaha's Wild Kingdom*. My father watched Jacques Cousteau like some men tuned into football, and my mother is still a fierce conservationist. To contemplate and appreciate the vast beauty of Nature, not to mention to speculate how the various disciplines like chemistry or biology explained the world around us, was par for the course. Later as an adult, I would become even more fascinated by genetics and neurology, even if from the superficial level of mere curiosity as a layman. In short, I consider myself a passionate rationalist who happens to be overflowing with faith. I am overcharged with respect for Him *and* acknowledge the limitations of our intellectual faculties, which, nonetheless, were expressly created for us prudently *and* excitedly to *use*. At the same time, some folks may wonder about the actual goodness of such a powerful Father who instilled in us His likeness of reason and freedom when in certain epochs of history, it can seem as if He has been cruel or exacting. If the harshness or wrath you encounter in the Old Testament vexes or frightens you, consider the *thousands* of years of *our* ignoring, denying, spurning, or disobeying Him as well as the brutality and heinous acts of violence we still commit against our fellow man daily. Wouldn't *you* be mad if your children did nothing but ignore you and beat each other up? As a parent, what would *you* do? When I look at it from this angle, I'm amazed at the term I learned called God's "forbearance." In His omnipotence, God gets to choose how and when we pay the price for our collective folly and brutality! There's no futility in this, let alone softening the blow.

Panning out way past the Garden of Eden to today, we are still allured and enamored by the magnitude of our power to create (and its inverse, to destroy), and, oh, we make much of ourselves. Such songs of sirens are hardly mythological and no less deadly if we think we can go toe-to-toe with either our Creator (or, come to think of it, the Archfiend) without ramifications. It seems to me that the most extreme example of this type of braggadocio is displayed when countries engage in an arms race, as if they were titans merely arm-wrestling; God knows they'll both topple in the end. The archetype of the creator is evident in many popularized movies based on literature, including *Frankenstein*, *Pinocchio*, or even *My Fair Lady*. If you notice, though, something always goes awry. In short, God doesn't mind me asking questions all day long, even if I know His ways are impossible to understand. I suppose if I had a god I could figure out, what would be the point in worshipping him? Just when I feel like a gnat's wing, insignificant and worthless, such that I can't even *whisper* to my Maker, here comes Jesus right beside me to lift and call me, "Daughter," to love me, and to set things back on track. I *am* tracking! How do I know? My moral compass and heart's direction have changed toward Him, like some weather vane pointing due north now, and I have begun a life unimagined before. My spirit is contained in my body, this physical frame, or "tent" (2 Cor. 5:1 CEV), as Paul puts it. When I expire, my soul's destination is based on my choice here in life; there's no second chance when I'm dead. Therefore, I cling to that Person of the Trinity, my sweet Jesus, who is the one and only one Who makes it possible to experience eternal life and love with such a gracious Father. Life in Christ is not a free pass to a life free of problems, however; that's for sure.

6.9 SATAN ON-CALL 24-7

Before I became a Christian, I didn't give the Devil any more credit than I would have a cartoon character like the Tasmanian devil; just even using the word "Devil" or "Satan" sounded like rhetoric from the Middle Ages or the Puritan period. In today's world, it might be a televangelist we'd inadvertently hear who would use him as a manipulative tactic on vulnerable folks to open their coffers. Scaring children with threats of Hell or the devil "comin' to git ya" might be a method parents might use to stamp out undesired behaviors. However, when I stepped over and took that leap of faith, one of the first things that Mark warned me repeatedly was that, first off, the Devil is very much real; he is a creation of God like everything else, and *he lies*. In fact, I should *expect* him to be double-trouble and on double-duty now that I'd switched camps. No matter what he says or does, I am to remember that to his core, he is a liar. And secondly, he is a "thief, [who] comes only to steal and kill and destroy" your joy and, in the end, to forever divorce us from God (John 10:10). The diction John uses to inform us of the Devil's insidious intent was somewhat familiar to me. After all, in A.A. we say that *alcohol* is "cunning, baffling, and powerful" and that we must "H.A.L.T." before we drink, which means we should figure out if we are hungry, angry, lonely, or tired to be less likely to succumb. My line of thought now leads to the consequences of my actions and decisions on an eternal scale. I couldn't help recall with bittersweet sorrow the anguishing, internal debate the atheist Ivan deliberated on with the Devil in Dostoevsky's *The Brothers Karamazov* I'd read over two decades ago. Whereas Ivan succumbed to despair and accepted the Devil's brilliant argument as true, which then led him to commit suicide, I decided to *fight*. Even if it meant to text or email Mark at every turn for answers to my questions, all my what-abouts, what-ifs, and whys, I persisted. However, at some point, I had to lay down my pen and say to myself that I can't know all answers. The more I looked, the more I saw thousands and thousands of questions just like mine were out there with answers and explanations to help make the fullness of one's understanding more complete. However,

Mark understood me so well and always knew just what to say to peel back another layer of some truth. Rather than experiencing new revelations as a brand-new believer, Bonnie would be coming *back* to her faith. This process took a jackhammer to chip away at the high mortar wall of self-protection, behind which was the painful truth: she felt unacceptable to and unloveable by God. But back to the Devil: I'm *not* saying *he* stirred up questions in me to provoke, challenge, or cease believing in Him. That was a done deal! I wasn't looking for a reason to pounce on or catch Him in the wrong or some inconsistency so I could quit! Seeking His wisdom with clarity was just an expression of my hunger to know Him all the better. The more I got into Christ, the more the Devil tried to flip all my old arrogance, mockery, and incredulousness back onto me. He tried to deceive me into thinking that I was in a phase or a funk and that my metamorphosis in Christ was temporary or misguided. I began to visualize him as a U.F.C. opponent trying to knock me off-kilter, lose my center of gravity, or send me reeling off into orbit. I came to learn that Satan still has my number. He puffs up my conceit and reliance on rationalism, stirs up ire with my family members, and knocks the wind out of the sails out of my spirit such that I sulk about in a mire of self-pity. He uses mockery to foil my goal of glorifying Him in some wholesome and joyful way. Often, evil starts out looking cool, and I have so often taken this bait, hook, line, and sinker! That said, I *am* getting better at recognizing his methods before I get derailed; he always goes for what's easiest to set me off. Before I became a Christian, I assigned to my seniors C.S. Lewis' *The Screwtape Letters* so that I could re-read it. Gentle reader, you've *got* to read it! We are sitting ducks! I'm not about to give the Devil more credit than he is due, but this modality of dualistic thinking, that is, the clash between good and evil, is all too real. Satan *is* lurking around every corner, and though he's not diddly-squat to God, he proves by many ways and means that he is the most formidable enemy of my life. I also remind myself that Satan is merely a creation, too, made by Him; he is the worst of the worst, the nadir of ego wishing to be equal to God; he never died for anyone; he seeks to kill in any way possible: body, soul, or both. I see Satan every bit as calm, cool, collected, and brilliant in the manner Al Pacino plays him in *The Devil's Advocate*. In my mind's eye, I imagine Satan's constant attempts to harass and annoy me like the scary scene depicted in *The Sorcerer's Apprentice*, where Mickey Mouse has to hack the mop, but it just comes back to life, generating many more with it, dozens even, marching toward him aggressively. Satan in his perpetual motion and being on-the-go is just like those angry monkeys from *The Wizard of Oz*, flying in to get Dorothy "and her little dog, too." Yet for me, these devilish emissaries never actually get me, so the fear and dread of it happening, of getting caught, is just a hare's breath away, and the sense of inevitable demise can be debilitating, crushing, and terrifying. How could this way of thinking come to my mind? Why in the world was I not aware of this before? I told Rick at the gym yesterday that I was sick and tired of the devil picking on me and trying to get me angry, agitated, upset, or flustered. Nonplussed, Rick responded, "Well, *of course*, Satan is working hard on you! Before your salvation, there was no conflict. You were on his side, you were in his corner, but now that you are following Christ, he is doing his very best to get you off guard, to deceive you, to do anything and everything to keep you from being full-minded in and serving Christ." *Non-believers don't feel this struggle* because he's already got them in the bag, so to speak; they are preoccupied, deluded, or absent-minded and, resultantly, are not lost to him. Satan *did* lose me; therefore, I am often under attack to bring me back. Rick said for me to look at Bonnie this past year as further proof of the Devil's trying to keep us immobilized for being of use to *his* enemy. I had not thought of it like this before. Bonnie has so much to give and so much goodness in her heart that the Devil used his old bag of tricks to keep her chock-full of self-doubt. Just when she was trying her hardest to please Him is right when Satan pushed back through his whispers of old false lies to her to keep her neutralized for Him. But it doesn't work in the long run. Bonnie is full of the Holy Spirit, so much so that she can't stop playing her guitar and singing, can't stop praying and praising Him, and can't stop her desire to serve those who are downtrodden and hurting. She is that prayer warrior you've heard tell of, though she'd never mention or acknowledge it herself; she might even tell you the times that she found it difficult to pray. Seeing that level of such unconscious goodness scares me because sometimes I think when a person is so fully, so completely *ready* for the Lord — which is *not* to say one *wants* to be done with life — that that's just when He might choose to take that person. I *know* I don't know what I'm talking about, but last night, in the middle of the night, she told me she woke up with extreme chest pains. I went cold and got frightened, speculating that God already knew that she was ready enough such that He might use this opportunity to take her right then and there. I came to a calm through a quiet sigh of trust that, in the end, *everything really would be alright*. The end of the story for each of us is already known: it's no spoiler to say that the Devil will ultimately lose, even if it feels like a billion years from now. We are told by the Apostle Peter, in effect, to chill out: "with the Lord, one day is like a thousand years, and a thousand years like one day" (2 Peter 3:8). I must live in the knowledge that the loser will lose; it's just the catching up and watching it unfold for us one day to know that this is so. I'm sure He'll tell us all about it then. In the meanwhile, He would develop in me, oh, so slowly, that elusive virtue of patience. What He already knows will occur brought me briefly back to pondering providential design.

6.10 Predestiny No More

A full year after Mark started coming to visit, I thought I'd made my peace with it, yet speculations about predestiny trickled back to me. Earlier I didn't know how to contend with what seemed a preponderant amount of evidence to support that *because of* God's omniscience and omnipotence, predestiny *is* real. The more I discovered references — too numerous to count — in the New Testament, which refers us back to the Old Testament, it became clear to me that the N.T. is a continuation and the fulfillment of prophecy in the Old Testament. I was just catching up to what millions have already known. We also have further proof that the unfolding of all events leads full circle back to Him Who started it all to begin with. I used to think that His foreknowledge was equivalent to His foreordination of events. However, this time, I factored in the freedom He provisioned us with that negates any such possibility of predestiny! Then, for insurance, he permits Satan to coax us to do otherwise, so the decision for the good is all the more authentic. Even though *He* knows how events and situations in life all turn out, this is *not* to say He *causes* or makes us participate or this and that to occur; things will transpire one way or another to bring about *that which He desires*. It has happened before; I can bank on God doing so in the future. I can count on Him! He'll ultimately be able to make everything come out to the *very* good! In spite of the fact that much of what we see is madness, mayhem, misfortune, and unspeakable tragedy, there is more to the story than what is befalling us. Jesus may have said, "It is finished," but *we aren't done*. In my coin-toss, I still conclude and say, "No," to predestiny. Why? I now look to John 3:15 (KJV), "*Whosoever* believeth in Him…" That's *me*! Jesus isn't available only to the so-called "elect"; that term isn't even biblical. God isn't so elitist or so esoteric as to be inaccessible (though inscrutable); after all, we are *all* His creation, but it's on me to reach out to the very source that created us and also beckoned *me* to seek *Him*. Such will, force, wisdom, and intentionality speak to a Personhood of the most exquisite and magnificent sort. However, He also has different aspects to His singular essence, which would also be, by extension, *persons*, as we see obviously in His Son and perceive of in His Holy Spirit. Once I realized that His plan flows organically, commencing itself to the results He intends but does not *make* happen, I viewed history (and my life) not so much as a chronological countdown but a vast swath of heavy rubber mat rolling out. In this way, He concurrently sees our past, present, and future *all at once*. God's omniscience must for Him be like watching the whole movie of our lives, of humanity's history, in one big moment, not scene-by-scene, frame-by-frame. He already knows the full outcome that is in His vast plan, but the unfolding of it, the second-by-second occurrences in it, all the ecstasies and agonies of we who live in this imperfect, stained, and yet achingly beautiful world, become *our* experience and *not* some done deal with a foregone conclusion. We evolve into the sum of all our freely-made choices adding up towards *His* end, whether or not we see it at the time or like it. The momentous decision to live in faith in Christ is a game-changer and a show-stopper. When I exercise the will I've been born with, the more I see that how matters turn out are not dependent upon predestiny or random chance. I am a participating free-agent, and like some lesson in perspective, my life's temporal setting is an endless stretch of the present tense; my exit point is death. He made me free within His realm: empowered yet limited, proud yet humbled — that's who we are and were made to be by God; therefore, I say, "Predestiny no more, and *I choose Him.*"

How do I know that I know that Christianity is legit *and* that I'm saved, you ask? My daily reading of the Bible had the double effect of adding credibility unto itself when I consider its overall construction. I mean, what are the chances that a book written over the span of fifteen hundred years could synthesize the thoughts and experiences of forty very different and imperfect authors, all of whom speak to the glory of God? And it's usually those who catapulted from nothing to something! Could such a tome have been achieved by mere chance or random coincidence? Of course, not!. When God speaks, men and women listen, and some who hear take note and scribe; He edits from afar. There's no other way to explain its holistic unity and integrity. I'm certainly not adding anything to the Bible, but I'm here to tell you that He has provided me with the impulse, insights, stamina, and direction utilizing the thoughts that enter my head as I write this volume for

Him (and you)! Why is it that many people still don't believe in Christ or choose another path like Buddhism, Islam, agnosticism, or secular humanism? I don't know. Did God pick a handful of people to come to believe? Had He appointed me to eternal life and not many of my loved ones? Why? I don't know, and it's certainly not all done. Mark helped me and started by saying that this is a common philosophical debate; there is no clear-cut answer to why some get it, and some don't. I knew from a year ago that Mark does not hold the position that God predestines everything. Mark posited that although God is omniscient and already knows what will happen in the future — including whether or not we "make it" to Heaven — this does not preclude Him from being intimately involved in the present moments of our lives. He does everything He possibly can to shape circumstances to make it possible for us to *choose* to accept His Son. Plus, He is in all places at all times, so He's on-call to help us through His Spirit. Therefore, though He may already know the outcome, it has *not* been already pre-set by Him. He doesn't use his omnipotence to force decisions upon us or to send us purposefully to Hell; that is impossible, as it would go against His benevolent nature! Jesus died for everyone; therefore, ideally, anyone can be part of the so-called "elect" *if* he or she decides to embrace Him. God does not play Duck, Duck, Duck, Goose!

Mark added another layer to the argument, hammering one more nail in the coffin of the position promoting predestiny. Mark said that people often use predestiny as a copout to say that they couldn't reach someone, as if Heaven isn't in the cards for such a one. If you say everything is predetermined, it takes the pressure off a person to do what he's *supposed* to do: witness and lend a helping hand! Our God-given task is to share our stories with authentic love and to lead people to Christ. Mark also added that he had never talked to anybody poor who believed in predestiny. The rich could misconstrue that their wealth is a sign that God has blessed them especially, which would mean that the opposite would hold true: if you are financially poor, you were not blessed by God and, therefore, that you were probably *not* one of the chosen. This argument does not hold water with God; He loves us too much to leave us where we are without putting up a row. In considering predestiny as applied to me, you may ask, how did *I* come to believe? *Some* might say that living in the part of the country where

I do, in the buckle of the Bible belt, that it, Christianity, took, that the bathwater finally seeped into my pores. Since I couldn't beat 'em, I joined 'em. However, this was *not* the case because left to my thought processes, free spirit, formative raising, and devices, I *should* have remained a theist at best or an agnostic at worst! Yet somehow, I didn't settle and never stopped searching. He already had me found before I found Him. I did nothing in particular; there was no Eightfold Path *I* followed and no Ben Franklin method for achieving moral perfection *I* mimicked. Quite frankly, I think it was simply a gift, the gift of faith, and it is a gift I *chose* to receive — He didn't make me receive His gift of grace — although no one *I* knew could see this present. My life changed because my heart was moved.

6.11 MELTING MY HARD HEART TOWARD THE WORD "HEART"

Mark once remarked to me one time that *"the mind follows where the heart wants to go"* and that *"the mind justifies what the heart wants to do."* Was he implying that we lived by what our heart dictates? His respect for the heart had the effect of making a crack regarding my prejudice against the heart, strange as that sounds coming from one full of zest. He kept using that word over and over, and though coming from him, it didn't get old, its frequent use was foreign to me. In fact, for some time, I'd been avidly noticing that Christians have their own perspective of viewing *everything*, not to mention nomenclature, and I was searching to find a mental bridge to process these new thoughts as they entered my brain, especially when I didn't yet understand all the jargon. In particular, I really wanted to understand more accurately what it meant when Christians say that they've *"given the hearts"* to Jesus. In the Bible, you will encounter the use of the word "heart" all over the place, and a prime example is with David, who was both a warrior and a king, and yet he was a deeply flawed man. He is one such person in particular that the more I learned about him, the better I understood the import of the heart. Even though he was an adulterer and murderer, it didn't mean he didn't give God his best. His past did not define his future or what he meant to God! By the way, David lived large and with courage and generosity, and even when he was in sorrow or trouble, David showed God he was grateful; therefore, he is uniquely described as "a man after God's own heart" (Acts 13:22). Little by little, I began to see the heart not as merely the citadel of my emotions but the only means by which I would transform my life, and this is just everything! My rational mind is not exempt from the heart's decision-making function; in fact, it is the heart that takes the lead through its commitment potential and helps co-make decisions that color my whole life. Though my mind seeks, grasps, and just eats up His Word that reveals God's impulse, this experience, in turn, stirs my heart and shakes me to my core. After all, if God *is* love, then you can't get a stronger emotion than that, and when it comes right down to it, barring a few physical necessities, that's all we really crave and seek in life anyway! In fact, I am *commanded* to love the Lord with "all my heart, soul, strength, and mind" (Mark 12:30). It is a package deal; He wants *all* of me. Can't *you* tell when someone isn't into it, whatever it may be? This indicates his heart isn't present, though the person perfunctorily may do the task at hand with his mind engaged. I had another *Wizard of Oz* moment: Dorothy was at her best when surrounded by *all* her friends, that is, the scarecrow (her brain), the tin man (her heart), and the lion (her courage). Only when *using* them all can you *have* it all and truly come *home*. If "home is where the heart is," *then my home is now with Jesus*. He has been with me faithfully and without fail as I take His hand and walk through life. To reject the heart is to say I choose black and white; His world is in color! I have to tell you that increasingly I came to experience moments when particular words of realization — like some micro epiphany — would come out of my mouth, but not of my own volition. Do you understand? It was like I was momentarily possessed; some call it being "in the Spirit." I know it sounds weird! I would not take credit for these utterances of truths because they came to me from the Holy Spirit. This phenomenon most often occurs in the quiet hours of the morning as I read my Bible, but it can also happen in some unintended evangelistic moment I find myself in with another person. That, too, has been odd and yet also inspiring for me. The Holy Spirit also steps in when I'm at my wit's end and cannot find a way to explain this or that about Him, and then somehow the right words tumble out of their own accord. God takes great an interest in our motivation, our intentions, and purity of thought, all of which can best be rendered by that word, "heart." So, not only was I gifted with receiving answers through Scripture, the uncanny timing of which convinces me that His revelations *are* intended for me, but I then begin to look at life differently and how *He* evaluates events and priorities. Like other believers, I would often see that that which is esteemed by the world runs counter or contradictory to His righteous ways. The world looks *out* while He sees *in*. The saying, "It's what's on the *inside* that counts," *must* have origc He knows all of my innermost thoughts and feelings, spoken or not, like *no* one else; therefore, He knows of my heart's being into Him as well as my mind's being captivated by Him. My renaissance towards the *heart* had the consequence of bringing about a more robust accountability in me than was present before.

6.12 Exploring Big Scary Words Like "Judgment" and "Repentance" (Again)

Saying *"Yes"* to Jesus was the first and immediate step that launched me into a new direction in my life and a novel way of *thinking*. However, it would take my body — that is, my actions, habits, behaviors, and speech — time to change. Salvation means redemption and deliverance from sin as far as God is concerned, but to grapple with that new positioning down here on planet earth in my *own* life means that I've now stepped on to the Yellow Brick Road. Salvation does not prevent my making mistakes or sin, so what is God's view of me *after* my salvation even when I still flounder and flail? Earlier I thought that though He cannot *look on* wrong, yet He *is* aware of it. Mark once told me, "God chooses to forget to remember my past" and that I should do the same for others. The moment I accepted Christ was when I became a *child* of God, not merely His *creation*. My full and steady steam ahead is what He urges me to do. Since Jesus wiped away both sins and will my future tears, the trial is over, and the jury is not hung. After I turned over my new leaf, God won't judge me; Jesus already took my sentencing. I used to imagine God's Big and Bad Day of Judgment like having to wait in a long line at customer service, all to meet up with a cranky worker that you *know* is going to give you a hard time for the defective item you're bringing (which, in this case, is yourself). That's a puerile analogy, but I would still miss it. Thank you, Jesus! It seemed too good to be true, impossible even. My judgment and punishment took place 2,000 years ago! It would take some time to wrap my mind around this. Instead, we Christians will be judged or evaluated by *Christ* at the so-called "bema seat" What then do we do with our God-given talents *after* our salvation? God grows us and tests us with little things first, and when we can fulfill these, He gives us more significant challenges and opportunities to serve, develop in, and glorify Him. No other religion involves one so engagingly, significantly, positively, intimately, outwardly, and eternally. Yes, wisdom and peace *can* be gained through a process of self-actualization found in other theologies, but the effect of the outward and astonishing, all-encompassing Love He demonstrated and continues to show is incomparable. He *is* alive! No one else died for me, so how could I not want to give back to Him? There's no pain or trouble or inconvenience I could go through for Him that could compare to what He in love did for me. I want to please Him! Though I *did* repent at the moment of salvation, to be honest, I did not realize what this in practical actuality meant.

Therefore, one of the first questions that issued forth within me was, "Well, what exactly does repentance look like?" What about those things I did which I don't even have an awareness or recollection of, let alone control over? Mark said that, in essence, repentance means "to turn away." To repent of my sins doesn't mean I must go up and play out the entire Rolodex of my life, listing this or that! How could I?! It would never end! There are sins of <u>c</u>ommission, those I've done on purpose, and those of <u>o</u>mission, those things I didn't know were wrong. I felt overwhelmed!! There's no way I'll ever get this taken care of! Am I a fraud for repenting when I couldn't possibly get the job done?! Then I realized, *of course*, He knows all of my wrongdoings over the entirety of my whole life, not just those from zero to now. The deal is that from here on out and <u>every day</u>, we must confess our sins before the Lord and ask for His forgiveness and mercy. Jesus' mercies are fresh and available every day! He is so faithful! Plus, He's going to use every aspect of me — the good, the bad, and the ugly — if I am obedient and willing to draw others to Him. At the moment of salvation, it is on me to do a daily accounting. In other words, though I've been given a new set of unbreakable dishes, I still have to wash them as long as I use them. The fact that I can't comprehend such a kind of love it took to reconcile us is because, as Mark told me, <u>I had never been loved like that before</u>! Furthermore, to truly change, that is, to repent, involves not only His forgiveness of my sins but also my need to forgive others <u>as well as myself</u>. Initially, I huffed and puffed and exclaimed that this was not possible! It was not my place to do so! Mark said that he knew that most people found this extremely difficult but that it *must* be done because only then will a person be capable of further growth. To forgive oneself is the ultimate acknowledgment and ownership of the fact we are weak and imperfect and in desperate need of Christ. We can't keep carrying guilt and harboring resentment because these shackles prevent us from loving others; we are wearing not rose-colored glasses but blinders! When one is lost in sin — including being held hostage by *memory* — one gets laden with the burden of shame and guilt that keep piling up over the course of one's life. If we don't release our hurts and let transgressions go through *forgiveness*, the weight of hate will feel like dragging around heavy luggage behind us. (Mark demonstrated this to us one Sunday by lugging up a huge suitcase on stage as a prop to make this point.)

When we come to Him, His forgiveness is enough for all time's sake; when we repent at the moment of salvation, God forgives us. He doesn't decline or refuse. Still, in our realization that we will never be perfect, Jesus provides mercy, like currency, and it's ready and available for us every day. Christ can help me to forgive myself because if God can and did, I need to do so, too. And then, of course, I am to grow from the teachable moment and *ideally* not repeat it.

It is incumbent upon me to do this if I am going to do and be all He intends for me from here on out. It behooves me to do what I learned in A.A.: "*Let go and let God*," in other words, abandon ego and release guilt. This counter-intuitive requisite to forgive *self* becomes a necessary act, which, in turn and over time, can make it more likely — though not always easy — to forgive *others*. Though forgiven, your imperfectness *should keep you humble*. Christ's humility in you is demonstrated by how kind you are to others, *especially* those from whom you have nothing to gain. When I saw someone in the midst of some difficulty, I began to say things like, "There but for the grace of God go I," which purportedly the sixteenth-century preacher and martyr, John Bradford, uttered as he watched a group of prisoners going to their execution. Even the Apostle Paul, formerly a vehement persecutor of the new followers of Christ, said of himself, "...I am the least of the apostles and not fit to be called an apostle because I persecuted the church of God. But by the grace of God, I am what I am, and His grace toward me did not prove vain..." (1 Cor. 9–10). After salvation, repentance involves a daily acknowledgment of our imperfections or sins, which weighs us down and impedes us from growing in Christ the way we are *designed*. I think of it like taking a shower every day. It's nothing to feel guilty about, just something that is necessary; we oughtn't to put clean garments on a dirty body. We aren't fooling anyone, least of all, God, but He has much in store for us to experience for Him than idling in neutral. And by the way, living in these imperfect, fragile, but glorious "temples" (1 Cor. 6:19) now is not to be confused with the perfect heavenly bodies we will have in the future. I will continue to tell you about these inner, ah-ha moments as I reached out to my friend and pastor when questions came and I needed assurance or clarification. It was still foreign for me to feel so different, and I began to wonder *why me*? What about *others*?

6.13 The Holy Spirit and More

I began wondering about the duration and manner in which the Holy Spirit reckons with unsaved people. What does the invitation look like in other lost people, specifically those who aren't aware that there could be such a reckoning, convicting, or prompting? I am not sure what the Holy Spirit's calling or urging entails. I mean, is it just the pounding of your heart that lets you know that you need to come to the Lord? Is the Holy Spirit outside waiting and hovering until you call Christ to enter into your being? For me, it was an overwhelming attraction to Christ, of desperately and euphorically (and finally) wanting Him in my life; I felt my heartbeat so strongly out of joy, pounding in anticipation and excitement, like a racehorse at the gate. I did *not* come prompted by the inner burning of the fear of impending damnation should I choose to recoil or reject. Does *everyone* seek God or something greater than oneself, which could very well lead to Christ? What if a wrong turn is made, the Holy Spirit's prompting is misread, and another religion is chosen?!? Can He also just nudge you quietly, like a whisper? How long will He wait and try? I'm finding myself lamenting for so many people not seeing that God makes Himself known in every minute of every day, let alone their viewing Jesus as some other prophet. As an aside, I also want to tell you that I had another gift of insight that has made God less vast and more intimate for me. Instead of focusing on the vast universe and me being just one in several billions of people, I now see how infinitesimally detailed and hyper-focused God is, which, yes, includes knowing the "number of hairs on my head"(Luke 12:7). Each person matters! That said, I don't know what it would take before the Holy Spirit throws in the towel for prolonged ignoring on the part of some individual. This seems to be the case for any number of my family members. If it were not for His timing *and* my miraculous reception, I could have declined or missed out altogether. I am just grateful that I heard and listened to Mark's sermon over a year ago that got the ball rolling. It was as if he was God's archer and the bow of His Word pierced my mind as well as my heart. Bull's-eye!

Speaking of being struck by His arrow, which contains the marrow of His truth, I've just made up a list of three types of people who are the most likely to resist or reject Christianity. Why would I do this? The very ones I hope may be intrigued enough to pick up and read this testimony of wonder may also unknowingly avail themselves the opportunity for the Holy Spirit to work on another readied heart: *theirs*! Who are these, and is there hope?

1. What about the person of another faith, especially one in a more homogeneous society as in Japan or a predominately Muslim country? It seems much easier to go to an economically-deprived locale and offer rice and beans and a helping hand than to one higher on the rung of Maslow's hierarchy of needs. I used to wonder why more evangelism wasn't done here in the States or in Europe, where unbelief is, quite frankly, *rampant*. The answer is that if we are to go into all the world, then technically, the west has already been exposed to Him, so there's no excuse, if you will; that rejection would be on those individuals. What about places like Greece and Russia, so steeped in honoring a millennially-old tradition but don't hold dear the "personal relationship" sacrosanct to Protestants? Though obviously Christian, Catholics have long dominated the exposure of and introduction to Christ in the southern hemisphere, but indigenous peoples there often corrupt or debase Christianity with the resulting creation of an amalgam that gets infused with their leftover vestiges of paganism and animism. In my estimation, Catholics get diverted by Mary, modern-day miracles, and relics. Add to that the (blasphemous) notion that the Pope is some sort of intercessor for humanity; we also find a veritable pantheon in their church administration with Jesus at the utmost helm.

2. What about the non-committed person, content to just "be good"? I believe that everyone seeks a greater connectedness to something vaster in life at one time or another, whether we call it called God or something else. And by and large, I think *we all want to make a*

difference in this world. I have seen the expressed desire to do so time and time again in the college admissions essays I assign my students. For many, their TV set is on, but the channel is not turned to the station that brings Him into clear view. I do not think it is by happenstance that we each seek and dream for more than is before our eyes; it is obvious God tries to draw people to Him by any means necessary. Some places may be less conducive to providing a come-to-Jesus moment, and some life happenings can cause dreams and hopes to wilt or be crushed. I think that when we are down-and-out is just where we can find Him waiting for us. Though it is not my place to confirm, I do not, cannot believe that the naïve, ignorant, infantile, or those not exposed in a meaningful way will be held accountable for *unwittingly* rejecting Him. Nonetheless, I must stress that should the conditions arise such that the Holy Spirit is trying to draw a person to Him and that person desists, ignores, rebuffs, or outright rejects Him and says, "No," with finality, you don't know but that this might be the last chance. This isn't a threat; it's just reality. Why would He hang around where He's unwanted? I feel overwhelmingly grateful He kept trying with me such that I came to Him. Perhaps it is because inside, I unwittingly remained in a state ready "to work out my salvation with fear and trembling" (Philippians 2:12). The next type of unsaved person, in my estimation, is *not* actually unsaved, but he thinks he is, so he stays away from church and Jesus. He needs a morale boost of encouragement.

3. The backslider is the prodigal son of type person who at one point was, indeed, saved, but he or she has succumbed to life's travails, pressures, and temptations to the point that he thinks he is no longer worthy of God's love and that all that has transpired is unforgivable, so much so that he thinks of himself as somehow de-saved and unsaved. It comforts me to know that when a person's salvation is sealed, it is a surety. God can't undo

this or change His mind because that would negate His perfection or somehow make the contract bi-lateral as if we could somehow renegotiate our salvation. For Him to change His mind would mean He made a mistake in selecting us; this is impossible. It's a fact, Jack, that "once saved, always saved," but you might enter Heaven a saved old man but an infant in your walk. Still yet, there should be *some* sort of evidence to show you're on the path with Him. Quickly or slowly, sparingly or overwhelmingly, your life ought to look different than it did before; otherwise, it's not that God can change His mind or take back your salvation, but that you might not have been saved to begin with. There may be only a scintilla of growth; hopefully, warm and sound encouragement is fanning the flames! Making that call about whether or not one is saved can be a perilous place for those who would like to judge harshly or speak for God Almighty (and many do); we must step away from this ledge! This is *not* our call! No one is qualified to make this determination because we can't see into the future, let alone into someone's core, to know what rebound or growth may be in store! Plus, not all change is executed in the same way, let alone at the same rate. Only God knows how this gets played out in each of us! Many a Pharisee will undoubtedly be surprised.

4. I save the best for last, and that is the desist, theist, agnostic, or atheist. Another subset of this would be the completely disinterested, not religious, and unexposed person; pop-culture and secular humanism all the way for them, baby! Yet these folks, too, are searching and yearning *for what they know not.* Try as they might to attain the elusive satisfaction they seek, they often fill the God-shaped hole with things and stuff and clout (and bigger, better, and newer versions of this and that), be it art and music, sports and entertainment, or politics and travel. There is nothing wrong with these areas in and of themselves; they just miss their mark when it comes to

authentic soul-satisfaction and an eternal connection to the one-and-only who both made and loves us. Frankly, I have the least to say *in writing* to this group because this category needs the most love and tenderizing by the Holy Spirit. There is nothing *I* can write to convince such a one of Him; if religion or Jesus is brought up, they're usually in a way to quickly retreat or go down under in silence. Therefore, should this describe you, I will pray without ceasing that you have contact with a kind Christian *who can show you the love of Christ.* I pray you are open-minded and receptive, such that the Holy Spirit can work His wonders for you to "come as you are," as the song goes.

I should also like to comment on two groups of people in crisis as far as their connection with Jesus is concerned. One hasn't sealed the deal, and the other has broken away with a frightening finality. First, consider the person that has been in church his whole life has been doing life with Christians, yet he has *never had an encounter with Christ*, let alone made a public testimony. Is he called upon to do so as well? Yes! Are you saved just because you go to church or have been raised by Christians? No! Is it even necessary for people to be born again and *outwardly* affirm their faith? Indubitably! In his famous sermon, "Sinners of an Angry God," Jonathan Edwards preaches to those very people, those who are "unregenerate," who fully consider themselves Christians. By his fiery imagery of God holding back what was due them, you would have thought he was talking to heathens! He wasn't! How is a person's heart to be stirred if, by proxy, association, or familial ties, he already *presumes* that he's going to Heaven? This is one place where focusing on the *personal* relationship comes into powerful play. Later I would have problems with this notion of a personal relationship aspect, but for now, I'll make the analogy that you don't get to go to the destination just because you're on the bus. Heaven is not a place that you get to with a free ticket you've acquired from your family. You have to get out and walk to Him yourself! Denominations aside, all church rites and sacraments cast away, the common denominator obligates and necessitates the person enthusiastically and openly say, "Yes," to Christ for all he or she is worth, as if the whole world were watching because God surely is. It's your salvation for the taking, not passively receiving. And secondly, a darker turn can be taken when a bonafide Christian has overtly and intentionally turned his back on God. This is an uncommon plight, and, again, I am not referring to one who, once saved, apparently does little to nothing in his walk with Christ.

I recall feeling anxiety-stricken when I first learned the word, "apostate," which means *one who rejects God*: I hoped that hadn't been the case with me. Apostasy is a Greek word that means "a standing away or withdrawing" and refers to the person who was steeped in faith and possesses full knowledge of Christ, that is, the mature believer, and he has somehow come to reject Christ. Once we accept Him, He assures and promises us, "I will never leave you nor forsake you" (Hebrews 13:5 NKJV). Such a final divorce or complete severance would be the result of *our* doing. Should this rare occasion where a Christian came to such an utter falling away to render him no longer a believer, now *this* could be grounds for expulsion. And thus, the bittersweet notion of what it means to "*grieve*" the Holy Spirit would come into play here. He mourns with and for God when we reject, refuse, or no longer acknowledge Jesus as our Lord and Savior. When He knows our "No" is final, we unknowingly are left to howl alone in the turpitude of the world's wilderness. God is gladdened when anyone comes to Him at *any* stage of their earthly life! Keep in mind that the reckoning, that is, the prodding and stirring of what I know now to be the Holy Spirit coming around to prompt one to "get a move on, little doggie" does *not* last forever. If I would have repeated my rejection of God to the point of slamming the door shut on Him, then I would have been left to play out my life according to the direction of my own will and ego. That's different than Jesus refusing to forgive me. *He doesn't do that*! I'm so relieved and grateful that I never outright said, "No." I'd always been searching, and I genuinely believe that this condition is the norm, regardless of the person's background. Upon my *really* coming to salvation, I desired to have another, yes, my third, but final just-right baptism. That was to happen later.

As I look back over my mode of expression, it occurs to me that it might seem as if I have been brainwashed. Well then, so be it; I'll happily admit it. In fact, it's more than my brain that's been washed. Ha! I can also say the search and angst and vacillating are over, too.

To make more comprehensible for myself just what the "free" gift of grace is that I didn't ask for, I remember coming up with an analogy that my rational teacher brain could use as a means of understanding what His gift of grace meant. It would take more than once for this analogy to work. It goes like this: it is my hope and intent for everyone to pass my class, but in reality, this is not possible or feasible due to mitigating circumstances or a lack of motivation and effort. No one ever achieves a 100% average (without extra credit), just as no one will ever become perfect. And though grades do indicate some level of mastery of the material, we all know it is one's attitude and work ethic that proves key to success. When I have students who hover between passing and failing *and* I know they have done all they can to pass but still can't cut the mustard, I will sacrifice (i.e., circumvent) the system and make it such that they pass because I know that the greater good for them will be to graduate and go out in the world. Does this involve suffering on my part? Not really. Therefore, please know that this analogy is mediocre at best; I'm only trying to convey the notion of *grace extended without asking or deserving*. In short, God not only wants us to pass, but He took the impossible final exam *for* us! I get that now. Jesus' sufferings and punishment demonstrate what we deserve for our transgressions, something that *at first* seemed to be an unnecessary and unpleasant focus on the negative or morbid, but when I got past my disgust and exasperation, I owned it, and, in agony and despair, really focused on what He did for me. Even if He said, "Yes," to His Father, how can we not weep for Him? I would hope that I would have been more like Peter, who though initially weak, became so strong for Him. Meanwhile, having accepted Him, I felt an overwhelming desire to make it known and to celebrate my identification with Him, to show my diploma of passing the course, so to speak.

6.14 Reconsidering Baptism, Take 3

I have to tell you that the whole baptism thing festered inside me for quite some time. Here I had this certificate of authenticity from the Orthodox Church, obtained at a time of which I had no recollection, then, not even a decade ago, I'd taken the plunge again, yes, one made in faith, but mainly still in innocence. I now felt rather ridiculous desiring to have yet *another* one, like some silly girl crying wolf. Embarrassed and shy about pursuing a third go-round, the third charm of finally getting it right, I felt ill-at-ease and tentative about asking Mark to help me do this. I had already sent him a picture of when I got baptized at the Field in the Forest in 2004, as if I were trying to prove I was good-to-go because I had my badge of membership. That said, and as I've told you, it seemed to me that *this* baptism might just be legitimate. Although at the time, I wanted to confirm that I knew and accepted what Jesus Christ did for <u>all</u>, which, yes, including *me*, I did not fully understand everything I'd signed up for. It's like when someone speaks a foreign language and you want *so* much to understand him or her, you say, "Yes," even though not all is comprehended. For example, my notion of repenting had to do with quitting drinking. And it was only a few months ago that I understood what it means to ask Christ in my *heart*. Recall, if you will, my erroneous, if not comical, assumption of Who the Holy Spirit is. *Can* the Holy Spirit in-dwell you if you don't know Who this Holy Ghost is? I don't know. All I knew was that I chose *Jesus* as my Lord and Savior. I was tagging along and hanging by a thread, hoping I was one of the "whosoevers" that Jesus saved, but now it felt different. This longing to consecrate my moment of "Eureka, I finally got it right!" did not wane or leave me. However, not thinking that Jesus minded because I knew that *He* knew it took, I did not press the baptism issue. Instead, I put a lid on it, put the matter on hold, and played it cool rather than bring up what seemed to me by now something not necessary, just *desired* on my part. I was pretty sure Jesus would understand. After all, baptism is *not* a precursor or requirement for salvation even though it *is* an important expression of one's symbolic resurrection into a new life, from the "death" of my old self into a new life in Christ. This hallmark means I *identify* myself with Him! Indeed, Jesus modeled it for us. It is only natural for us to desire this marker, this visible affinity! I, too, craved doing so now to show that it was (finally) for real! That 2004 baptism felt more like a dress rehearsal for a wedding, not because my groom wasn't there, but because I didn't take myself seriously in the equation — I was just some girl who said, "Yes," to *marriage*. I thought it was the real deal, but I had not yet walked the aisle to meet my groom! Now that I knew good and well what I was doing, I very much wanted God to know that I *am* washed anew and to say before a little piece of the world that *I am His*! I talked myself down by saying, *of course*, He is already aware of my acceptance; therefore, I prayed and left it in God's hands as to if, when, and where my baptism might take place again. In the meanwhile, I let it go. Life moved on, and as I grew in Him, the questions kept on coming.

6.15 Why Did God Make Man?

I woke up with another "Why?" question for Mark, which I had no doubt he would be able to answer. Why in the world did God make humankind? He doesn't *need* us, and He certainly isn't lonely! After all, God is already in perfect union *and* communion with His Son and the Holy Spirit. Gentle reader, perhaps you will correctly answer that He made us *out of Love*. Yes, although He is entirely sufficient unto Himself because His very essence is one of love, He created us to live *and* partake of Him, *if* we so chose! As magnanimous, magnificent, and infinitely loving as He is, what kind of God would keep all that love to Himself and hidden from all?!? That wouldn't make sense! First, we have to get over the hurdle of dealing with the fact that we can't *see* Him, that He is not sensate. To know *of* Him can lead to knowing *Him*. He *intends* for us to feel sure we are loved by Him, as all He does is with this ardent intention. This, in turn, ought to bring about reverence for, not to mention gratitude to Him for *all that is*. If we are made in and by His Love with the express purpose to glorify Him through expressing the faith He gifted us, then you might wonder what part do we play? What do we bring to the table? The answer is *nothing*, and that's the point. The old hymn, "Rock of Ages," confesses my condition: *"Nothing in my hand I bring/Simply to thy cross I cling."* That said, I also know life is not a marionette show! Yes, even though we are His creation, He chooses *not* to controls the strings of our love and the choices we make. In fact, there are no strings attached to His love; it is free! One may acquire a pet for companionship, and adults beget children and take pleasure in their being "from their loins," yet both seem to be, in a sense, *acquisitions*. We are not merely products for God. I loved Mark's explanation of our being God's "workmanship" (Ephesians 2:10), that each of us who is His is a "poem"; this moved and inspired me. But *why* would God gift *me* (or anyone) with the capacity for faith? Why did *I* have a desire to seek Him to begin with? Doesn't *everybody*? I don't know. As far as I was concerned, the answer is that God expressly made man to show His love and reflect His glory. I think our coming to be His is all about the relationship we *get* to have with Him because His love cannot be contained! His Holy Spirit testifies this to us! Love is an active (transitive) verb *and* outward act, a noun. As we come to do all we can to reflect this His love to others so they, too, may know of His majesty, God is pleased, and in this way, we bring Him glory. *That's* the circle of love with Him! Jesus is in this circle so God can look on us, we who way back when we were wayward. We have the most incredible opportunity to receive and experience this love through knowing Him (and not merely knowing *about* Him). *That's* why God created us! His Love generates more love to be taken and given. For Him to create us (and everything) indicates a will and desire for us to know, acknowledge, *and* become a part of what we came from: the love of God. When I see moments of beauty, it's like God is saying, "Look at *me*! *I* did this!" Experiencing God in a relationship completes the bond as well as our search for the Big Why. The sweet Apostle John elaborates on this love in detail in 1 John 4:7–16, and I will share a portion because I find the answer as to *why we are here* and what happens when we come to know it. He couldn't *not* make us; it's in His nature. I underlined those lines that speak to this topic.

> [7] Beloved, let us love one another, for <u>love is from God</u>; and everyone who loves is born of God and knows God. [8] The one who does not love does not know God, for God is love. [9] By this the love of God was manifested in us, that God has sent His only begotten Son into the world so that we might live through Him. [10] In this is love, <u>not that we loved God, but that He loved us</u> and sent His Son *to be* the propitiation for our sins. [11] Beloved, <u>if God so loved us, we also ought to love one another</u>. [12] <u>No one has seen God at any time; if we love one another, God abides in us, and His love is perfected in us</u>. . . . [15] Whoever confesses that Jesus is the Son of God, God abides in him, and he in God. [16] We have come to know and have believed the love which God has for us. **God is love**, and *the one who abides in love abides in God, and God abides in him.*

Even though God already has communion within and among the triune because He *is* Love, He can't *not* love that which He created, can't reject or *not* desire a loving relationship, *especially* with us who are made in His likeness. I see! Realizing this fact, in turn, makes me not only grateful for my life, but it generates a new desire to share "the love of God [which] has been *poured* out within [my] heart" (Romans 5:5, emphasis mine). The next logical question is just how is one to share this love? The answer I already know is contained in "the second greatest commandment" Jesus spoke, which is that we are to *"love one another*, even as I have loved you... *By this, all men will know that you are My disciples* (John 13:34–35, emphasis mine). This charge of His goes way beyond and trumps the Golden Rule in that the love we show is not reserved just for "others," but for our enemies and ones challenging to bear, too. Such love ultimately points us back to *Christ* who is our model for prodigal love. At this point in my journey, my attention riveted back to the most mysterious one in the Trinity: The Holy Spirit.

6.16 HOLY GHOST PONDERINGS, TAKE 1 OF MANY

What exactly does the Holy Spirit (a.k.a. Holy Ghost) *do* in communion with Christ and God in Heaven? I know they are all three unified into a whole as well as separate and distinct. Indeed, I am acutely aware of the Holy Spirit (HS) dwelling within me as evidence of the living God. But what could He possibly do with God and Jesus? Is He the silent partner? Is the Holy Spirit just energy between Jesus and God? I mean, when Christ as a man was down here on earth, He probably was so charged with the Holy Spirit that it had to have been overwhelming for Him, like He had some incredible Energizer Bunny inside Him. And yet now that Jesus is back in Heaven sitting right beside His Father, is the Holy Ghost necessary or vital between them in their communion together? Or is it that the Holy Spirit is slipped and seared within each of us Christians as proof and as a means to ready guidance for God's promptings inside us? Is He the residual gift that Jesus Christ bestowed upon me when I accepted him? Does the Holy Spirit in me go back to God, or is it only that God can understand or communicate with me *because* He, the Holy Spirit, lives in me? I just can't stop thinking about the presence of the Holy Spirit within me, and I'm so thankful. He is the best gift *ever*!!!

Heretofore, through Andrei Rublëv's icon of the Holy Trinity, I could visualize God the Father, the Son, and the Holy Spirit as separate and distinct, yet in equal communion with one other. They are seated and turned toward each other while they were having their own private Holy Eucharist. It didn't take too long before I asked Mark point-blank about what the Holy Spirit did, how he functioned vis-à-vis the Father and the Son up in Heaven. Rick, my Christian friend and personal Christian counselor at the gym, referred me to Acts to investigate more about the Holy Spirit. The next time I saw him, Mark, on the other hand, drew a triangle on a sheet of paper whereby God was *inside* the triangle. At the three points constituting the triangle, he indicated that the *Father* in God pointed to His *Son*, Jesus, Who then pointed to the *Holy Spirit*, and the Holy Spirit, in turn, pointed back to God the Father. And these arrows were fluid in that they went back and forth depending upon the need. What Mark explained to me is engraved in my mind: when I accepted Christ, yes, the split second I invited Him in (after He'd been waiting for me), at that moment when I reached out and rushed towards Him, *this* was the moment Christ secured my salvation. He then subsequently and immediately sent, placed, and endowed me with the Holy Spirit of God, Whom He, too, possesses. Therefore, in my alliance and allegiance, I became spiritually connected to this triangular equation by having been implanted with the very Spirit of God. However, having the in-dwelling, living Holy Spirit of God within me does *not* mean, as some might say, that I can charge the Holy Spirit to do what *I* believe (and pray that God deems) or wish needs to be done. That said, the power of positive thinking related to the Holy Spirit's supernatural ability within me *is* limitless.

I want to speak a bit more on what it means *not* to accept Jesus and, therefore, *not* have the Holy Spirit take hold of you. A <u>non</u>-believer does not ingest or speak such a foreign language; it makes no sense to him; further, he does not contemplate or concern himself with a day of final reckoning. I never did! When you are of the world, you stay focused on secular values and more mundane markers for success and failure and evaluate yourself accordingly. The buck stops here. *If* you believe in God, you may think of God as Santa or like a genie to do your bidding should you nod your head or pray hard enough. You may also view God as a parent who either isn't watching or hasn't caught you in the act (or thought) of doing wrong. If nothing big and bad is done to you, then you must be good-to-go, you tell yourself. *Au contraire, mon frère*! God sees all. That said, God is also certainly not the "*git you*" type to sizzle his stern finger and send you, His child, to Hell right there on the spot if you do this or that. What Jesus has provided us *believers* with is a guarantee, a deposit, if you will, that we are *not* left alone in this beautiful wasteland we take for granted. During His resurrected state, Jesus looked ahead past those forty days and knew what would take place at what we call "Pentecost." He proclaimed to His followers something to the effect that He would send to *us one greater than He*, meaning the Holy Spirit, He whose debut had not yet occurred! It's sublime to consider that the actual Spirit of God would be sent down to dwell within Christian believers! Of course, "It" — *He* — is greater, and in a sense, more powerful than Jesus because having accomplished His mission here on planet earth, Jesus is back up in Heaven. Now it is the Holy Spirit (HS) down here and *everywhere* within *all* of us believers until Jesus comes back or we go to Heaven! Therefore, that Holy Trinity depiction that I have long looked at for decades now, where the Holy Spirit is way up there in communion with God and Jesus, fails to render what I have experienced, that is, the HS has also proceeded right on into me!! Of course, Christ is at the right side of God in Heaven right now, and the Holy Spirit is present and accounted for there, too; they three are living and guiding and directing us believers *through the means of* the Holy Spirit. Don't worry — Jesus is ever at hand, too, and God assuredly knows when you speak to Him! The HS's unique aspect is that He is the one and same Spirit Jesus had in Him, Who then comes to be with us, we who have accepted Jesus Christ. How do we know Jesus had the Holy Spirit? It became evidenced and witnessed at the advent of His ministry, specifically, at His baptism. There and then, the Holy Spirit came upon Him, endowing within Him the spectacular divine power to do what He came and chose to do in the next three years of His ministry. God even spoke to this! It's no wonder that right after that, Jesus went straight to the desert for forty days and let Satan try to tempt him. He had just been supremely equipped! Though He experienced and felt exactly what *we* would have, that is, exhausted, hungry, and desiccated, Satan didn't have a prayer with Jesus, all the more so because the Holy Spirit was in and with Him.

Thus, to say that the Holy Spirit is just another guy up there talking between Jesus and God or some energy between the two of them is vastly inadequate. He has a separate and distinct *function* yet is inseparable from the other two in His *essence*. The Holy Spirit isn't "up there" in distinction. He emanates from God within *me* just as He did with *Jesus* (except *so* much more powerfully in Jesus' mortal frame). He's indivisible, from them in Heaven, and when I'm in Heaven, and I meet my Maker and my Savior, I'll witness and be in the presence of all three. There'll be no separation from the Holy Spirit in me then either as I'll be at Home with Them. To think of Him up there, buzzing back and forth between Father and Son, would be irrational and flawed; He is one unto Himself *and* Themself, if such a pronoun could exist. You can read what the Bible says He is to us; depending on the translation, the diction varies only slightly. You will learn He is called such names as "Helper," "Comforter," "Teacher," "Advisor," "Advocate," and "Intercessor." They all come from the Greek word, *"Paracletos." Before* we come to Christ, the Holy Spirit is sent on a special mission from God to nudge, beckon, and draw us to His Son, often over and over and in *so* many ways and different moments, all so that we might come to accept Christ as our Messiah. Then and only then does the Holy Spirit shift from outside to inside us to become a sublime aspect of us. The Holy Spirit points *me* back to Christ. If I hadn't accepted Christ's sacrificial gift for me, it would be the same as if I had rejected God Himself. After all, Luke 10:16 records Jesus saying, "the one who rejects you rejects Me; *and he who rejects Me rejects the One who sent Me"* (emphasis mine). You realize just how high the stakes are when you read in Matthew of Jesus warning us that "whoever denies Me before men, I will also deny him before My Father who is in Heaven" (Matthew 10:33). Being saved, though powerfully moving, is much more than an emotional experience or academic alignment! What does the Holy Spirit do after salvation? What does this look like? Does the Holy Spirit speak to me every single time that I pray? No, He does not. Sometimes He does, but I'm just not listening. Often, I sense and hear Him when I am in a state of *receptivity* — usually in solitude or quietude — and a readiness to let me in on what He desires for me. His directives or thoughts come to me through ideas and even spoken words, which I know I certainly did not come up with on my own. I'm not that astute, let alone sweet! Not infrequently, His messages center on forgiveness and being bold in Him. He whispers to me that I am to model myself after King Jesus, Who, though *past* royalty, "did not come to be served, but to serve" (Matthew 20:28). After I got saved, I remember one time going back to my office and looking up with new eyes at the familiar Holy Trinity icon (which all this time, Bonnie had thought were three robed *women*), and I realized that I now had *direct* access to all three, the one and only triune God! The link was complete, dots connected. How inspirational to be so inspired!

6.17 Some More Thoughts on the Holy Spirit

My prayer time in the morning just seems to be inching longer and longer, and I don't know what to do because I also know I need to keep physically rested. It's just that I crave the Word. I used to get up at 6:25, now I've backed it up to 6:00, and that's not enough time! I'd continue to carve back more and more time for Him as time went by. I couldn't not. And yes, I well realize that neither my spiritual condition nor my rate of growth as a believer is based on how early I rise to study and pray, and I get no kudos for what I need to do anyway; I'm just reporting the change in my daily regimen. This morning I'd like to talk a little more about the Holy Spirit since Mark came to see us this past Tuesday. Love is a two-way street. And, as the Seals and Croft 1976 hit, "Get Closer," goes, "Darling, if you want me to be closer to you, get closer to me!" It is an amazing phenomenon to have His Holy Spirit dwelling within your corporeal self as you also become quite aware of this new and divine aspect within you. The Holy Spirit gives me a direct link to Jesus, Who is not only *for* me; in a sense, He stands right *beside* me. God may seem above and beyond, but really, He is never far from me. You may ask again, does the Holy Spirit speak to me every single, solitary time that I now pray? No, He does not. Often, this occurs when I have the readiness or some sort of prepared involuntary willingness to let me in on what He desires for me, which is then communicated via ideas, sensations, and directives I ascertain. The channel is often clear, and the signal is strong when my ego and volition get out of the way; then I am receptive to His communication which flows or outpours spontaneously. At such a moment, I *know* that the results or answers come from the Holy Spirit, He Who links me to Jesus, Who, in turn, is one with God. God is the infinite beginning and the endless ending, just like Christ is the Alpha and the Omega: He always is, always was, and always will be. I look back for a minute and re-read what I've written, and I think, wow, what a change! I know my former self might consider that I've bought into this Christianity, but I knew such a cynical stance could only betoken some ignorance or blindness. I honestly and frankly can't tell you how or why it happened to me! My becoming a Christian is *not* due to the fact that "I couldn't beat them, so I joined them." That makes no sense; anyway, had I done so while remaining opposed, I'd be a fraud, and there's no way you can *really* fake being a Christian. God knows a fraud when He sees one. I'll confess to you, though, being a Christian can also bring you grief, a sense of aloneness, feeling out-of-step in the so-called "real world" that doesn't operate by His ways; many will misunderstand you and the turn you've taken. And yet, this is no cult I'm in; no other religion has made such a positive impact on individuals *worldwide*. I feel it and know it of myself, too! Denominations aside, the fact that Christianity is *so* widespread and longstanding and is accepted as the way of *truth* held dear by billions is not the same thing as something being popular or *en vogue* for a season, let alone a century or two. To tell you the God's truth, I've never felt so on point in all my life, and I'll be in it for longer than a minute.

Another question that popped up when I was seeking greater clarity about the Holy Spirit was *what is the difference between the Holy Spirit and my conscience*, my inner Jiminy Cricket, as it were? One's conscience deals with moral matters concerning right and wrong, about what one would call an inherent barometer for fairness and righteousness. Conscience is our moral compass and has us asking questions like, "Is it right to do this? Is it wrong to do that? Is it fair to do this as regards my behavior?" Mark clarified and explained that the Holy Spirit impacts me more profoundly in that He may come to me at a moment of a crisis through a paradoxical or nonsensical message in and for my life. For example, Mark said if I were moved to stop teaching before my official retirement time to teach at a Christian school, that would make no sense. That would not be logical because it would involve taking a risk and placing all my faith in God, which we often are asked to do, *especially* when it goes against the grain of the world. Mark confirmed now *that* it would be the Holy Spirit moving me to do something. The invitations to do what *God* wants us to do may not make sense from where we stand right here and now, but from my experience, His exquisite and uncanny timing is His calling card. That said, if we continue to sense inner urgings, promptings, and thoughts beckoning us, then, at the very least, we need to investigate, if not pursue them, despite the seeming lack of sense. Most of all, we should *pray*! When we *do* launch out and start working towards the goal that God has placed in our hearts, the Holy Spirit cheers us on. Not only that, but we will sense what the Apostle Paul did in his obedience doing his missionary work: both enthusiasm and "the peace of God which surpasses all understanding" (Philippians 4:7). Paul's verbal encouragement rings as true today as if he were standing right beside us: "*I am confident* of this very thing, that He who began a good work in you *will perfect it* until the day of Christ Jesus" (Philippians 1:6, emphasis mine). Despite this, if I have done something wrong, the Holy Spirit can urge or prompt me to repent. I am to put to death, to mortify my wrongdoings. (The HS is "*grieved*" when we reject Him, and this is like turning your back on Jesus *and* saying "No" to His Father.) Many of our malpractices — selfish thoughts and harmful actions — are hard to eradicate because we've been stuck in or done them for so long that they don't *feel* wrong. We've got to undo what has become second nature, and that can take time. They can be like icebergs. Some will take a seeming lifetime to break, but God is the titanic coursing through your life. *He loves us where and as we are*; after all, do remember that He made us! You can tell when the behavior starts to change because you will startle yourself by your new and involuntary stance towards doing it. The older way will begin to feel foreign or contrary to what you *now* hold true. What's hard for me may be easy for you and vice versa. So, repentance is *also* something that the Holy Spirit reckons within, beckons us to try, and helps us when we do! You may also find that doing the new and *greater* good won't come automatically or readily. Take a peek at the Beatitudes from Jesus' Sermon on the Mount, and you will likely find that to esteem and respect *His* "blessed" ones might challenge you. There's no judgment here! Just keep practicing!

And where there is already love, goodness, and purity in your actions, the Holy Spirit isn't in the business of changing these. I was beginning to understand that the Holy Spirit, my own best Teacher and Counselor, is and will *always* be there to help me as I go through life. It's a *promise*! The Holy Spirit can *use* my conscience, but *He* is not *it*. Conscience is not involved in the business of changing my character or maturing me for Him; this is what the Holy Spirit does. Conscience works in the specific moments of ethical or moral decision-making. Unless we have a physiological abnormality or aberration in the brain, *everybody* is born with a conscience, the innate ability to distinguish right from wrong. Not everybody has the indwelling Holy Spirit. I don't want to make the case seem elitist whatsoever. *Everybody* has an opportunity to receive Christ, and it seems odd for me to be talking about this because less than two years ago, these words wouldn't *ever* have come out of my mouth. Now I see why it is vital to surround yourself with other Christians — not exclusively mind you, but for strength, fortification, and encouragement! As the Holy Spirit works on improving your character and usefulness for Him, it's not like He changes your soul into someone else; it's still *you* in there! Our *soul* is what makes us *who* we are; it is our core identity, the unique personhood that God created us to be, whether we are dead or alive. A *spirit* is never existent by itself. We *are* our souls. Our spirit is the immaterial but animated aspect of ourselves that is drawn to and can connect with God (through His Spirit), but a spirit is *not* our identity's essential self; this, again, is the soul. When we choose to follow Christ, our *spirit* — not our conscience — joins with His Spirit. (And may I say here that I'm glad I don't refer to His Spirit as a *Ghost*!) I hope that makes sense! Next, I would have a crisis that dealt not so much with faith but with a misunderstanding I came to have regarding the Holy Spirit, and it nearly broke my heart.

6.18 HOLY SPIRIT ANGST CONTINUED

Like any other day, I was reading my Oswald Chambers' devotional (which I do every morning *after* studying the Bible and *before* I pray), but the October 22 entry gave me more than pause. Its message proceeded to slay me, not just during the moment I read it, but, like a thorn, it got stuck and hurt me with each day it stayed; I just couldn't figure it out or pray it away. I was well aware that "the author of confusion" (1 Cor. 14:33 NKJV) was trying to mess with my mojo where the Holy Spirit was concerned. I also know Oswald Chambers' *My Utmost for His Highest* is in no way the Bible; one has to be careful when reading devotionals. I admire Chambers because his stance and tone are rather stern and hardcore in a way that I find both challenging and beneficial in his running from sugar-coated or "feel-good" platitudes. So, here's the particular passage I read that got corroded inside me to the point where I felt abandoned by God and pained even to pray to Him:

> "God witnesses to Himself, He cannot witness to you, but He witnesses instantly to His own nature in you... The Spirit of God witnesses to the redemption of Our Lord, He does not witness to anything else; He cannot witness to our reason...
> The Spirit witnesses only to His own nature..."

I took it to mean that God doesn't want to or can't bring Himself to talk to us directly, that He has to have His own middle man, that being, the Holy Spirit (HS) that Christ gifted us when we asked Him into our hearts. In other words, despite my salvation, it sounded like God *still* sees me as revolting and unlovable. In fact, He can't even *look* at me. Is this true?!? I only just recently came to think that Jesus could and would personally speak to me, let alone hear me! After all, I *have* given myself full force (or as much as can be expected in an old youngster like myself) to Him, and as a result, I also felt overwhelmingly grateful to receive His Holy Spirit! I crave and value Him *because* I love Jesus. Bottom line, this passage above made me feel so incredibly unworthy, such that, despite my being endowed with His indwelling Holy Spirit,

I saw it that God *still* isn't personally vested in me. And here I thought I had a *direct* thing with Him! Is it that He could not be bothered with the likes of me, His "daughter" even *now*?! Perish the thought! I must be too remedial or too fleshly for Him to bother or fool with *directly*, so, He sends an envoy, a spy, or a diplomat of sorts to check up on me and report back to Himself. I felt rejected afresh! It's just His H.S. inside me to Whom He will say what He wants to say, *not* to me! Oh, I see how it is! I would tell myself that I don't matter, that I'm just another loser human who, lucky for me, chose Him. In short, though I also did know that God loves me, loved me enough to send His Son to die for me, I felt like God had abandoned me in His refusal to "witness to" me. I even got to the point of wondering why there had to be a Trinity anyway. Why couldn't it just be God and the Son?? Then I really *could* have access to God on my own and all for myself. Why the "Middle Man"? After all, I *had* full-on accepted Him (and *not* just for the free pass), *knew* my salvation is sealed, and *sensed* that the Holy Spirit was placed in me. Did I still believe in God even though I was anguished? Of course! No take-backs here! But when I read Chambers' stance, I began to question why there even had to be a Holy Spirit living with me; why couldn't it be God Himself inside my spirit? Why couldn't it just be the two of them so that I truly could have direct contact with God? It hurt unbelievably to be given the Holy Spirit as a gift for sealing my salvation, then, come to find out, He is like God's pace-maker and that He, God, can't or won't even talk to me. Chambers made it seem more like a built-in intercom system exists between God and the Holy Spirit, and they report back and forth to one other. I was an *incidental*. Absolutely stuck and in agony, I continued to pray hard about this for almost two weeks, sometimes literally going from weeping in prayer to crying in the shower. I felt like my heart was breaking. I share this with you to show you the process of *trying* to fathom the Trinity, which didn't start as something I understood readily, naturally, or even accurately. I know I can't ever, but that didn't stop my mind from working it out. It had to be ingested slowly, and then, like cud, I had to spit it to chew on it again, all to let it settle in another stomach.

Of course, there will be errors and misunderstanding this early on, and Satan had a field-day tripping me up and agitating me nearly beyond consolation or until Mark could clear things up for me. I was almost ready to stomp on my Chambers' devotional or throw it out!

When Mark did come for a visit, I was finally able to choke out what was troubling me. His first reaction was an observation: "You are reading this *not* because you seek a theologian's clarification or a pastor's evangelism, but this is a real person's process of getting deeper in the Word from sheer enthusiasm and a propelling desire. Don't despair, Dimi! We will get this figured out!" he exclaimed. I was sick at heart because I had fallen in love with the Holy Spirit Whom Jesus delivered to and in me. Having read that "*God cannot witness to you, cannot witness to our reason,*" it just seemed like the Holy Spirit was something that Santa left, like a consolation prize, a go-between *for God*. He wasn't there for me but for God, who still couldn't look at me. The HS was not *my* gift, but rather *His* device. I felt like Christ went *back* to the North Pole, and because I stink so bad, neither He nor His Father will talk to me, but through his security camera and system, He can and will check on me. So, even if I am washed in the blood of Christ, I'm still just an adopted stepchild, and we all know that stepchildren and adopted children are often not as loved as much is the real deal, just an add-on. Good grief!! *This* is the voice of Satan and how he tells me lies to destroy my faith and joy! Can you tell?!? Recognizing this type of talk as Satan's voice helped me leap out of this quagmire and see what's really what! I sound like an impertinent ingrate, like I don't realize that I have part of the Trinity living within me! That is so not so! I *do* crave God with all my heart! At this point, I instinctively knew I had had it all wrong; I just couldn't get my knot untied.

Here's how Mark explained it to me. Mark made the analogy that even when he was gone from the office, his wishes or directives he made known to his secretary. Her job is to convey them to those who call the church asking for him. But his secretary isn't he! And the Holy Spirit isn't God. Wrong! The lapse in logic is caught! The Holy Spirit *is* a part of the united, indivisible, unified, and whole Trinity, thus the term "triune." Such is *not* the same as three beings working at the same place and same time *or* one person with three identities. The Holy Ghost knows the will of the Father, but He is not the Father, yet *I cannot separate them like I might something <u>down here</u>*. To talk to one *is* to talk to the other! Regardless of the different aspects, there is only one God, so, in a sense, of course, God is also in me because His Spirit is in me; in this respect, it's a two-in-one. I also know that the Father can't literally be "down here" with me. Such was *Jesus'* role to do so; He is expressly God incarnate, that is, "in the flesh." Jesus is back up with His Father, but He still loves me! God isn't using the Holy Spirit because He can't stand me! It's just the opposite!! So that I can *always* be connected to Him, His Holy Spirit *resides* in me; the Holy Spirit's job is to indwell (implying He is alive), help, teach, and counsel, like a built-in, personal life coach. God so wants this for me that He also gave me His very own Spirit to be with my spirit!! His own Son died to deliver Him to me!

I also came up with a couple of simple food analogies to unravel the Holy Spirit's role that didn't exclude me from God. I started with me being the marshmallow in an open-face S'more. I hoped for the Holy Spirit to be the warmed chocolate bar that melts and adheres to the marshmallow and the graham cracker. In this analogy, God, the graham cracker, would be inseparable from me, the white fluff, because I was adhered to Him through the warmed chocolate bar. I was the marshmallow, the most fragile part, and the H.S., the chocolate in between, melting me to God, us all together. I meant no disrespect, and I don't mean to be cavalier or trivial or ridiculous. I just really needed to know that God hears me and is not communicating with me via the Holy Spirit because I am unworthy and not beloved by Him. I think that this connection I have with the Holy Spirit *has* to be God's way of talking to me; after all, as Mark later kept stressing, *He and His Spirit are one.* I get one and both and all three. Perhaps then it also could be construed that the H.S. is like being gifted with the middle of an Oreo cookie, like a disk that God swiftly, perfectly, and sweetly settled inside of me. I know that the Trinity is a three-*for*-one, one-*by*-three, like the *original* Three Musketeers, "all for one and one for all." To recap, all I knew was that after I read Oswald Chambers, I felt like I wasn't good enough, that God wants little pieces of Himself everywhere, and that I didn't matter in the vast scheme of things, which was the same way I had felt *before* I became a Christian! If I lay everything at the cross and God forgave and adopted me, why would He then use His Holy Spirit to communicate with me? I well know we aren't perfect, but for me, Chambers made it seem like God *only* talks to the Holy Spirit within Himself, who then interfaces with *us*, like He's got some Pope on standby. I told myself to *stop* before I'd make myself sick anymore. Oh, I missed my Holy Spirit!! That's the day I came very close to burning Chambers' devotional, which Satan had used to lead my mind to corrupted thoughts and agony. You now know that I got this all cleared up and successfully got past this hurdle, but not that day or week. Meanwhile, perhaps because I was *so* near the starting point of my path, I would turn to His beginning for us, and more questions started flowing.

6.19 Ponderings on the First Couple, Death, and the Implications for Today

One other point I couldn't make any headway on had to do with the fact that I came to learn that before the Fall, there had not been any death in the Garden of Eden. How could this be? I mean, I know that we were pure, but there's no way that we couldn't have died! Maybe we were like redwood trees that are capable of living for centuries. After all, even after the Fall, most of those mentioned in the Old Testament lived for centuries; I think Nebuchadnezzar lived almost 1000 years! And so, if that were the case, that is, if Adam and Eve had not have messed up, maybe they could've lived for easily over 1000 years, but I just couldn't accept as fact that it would've been an *eternal* life. Surely, we had to be dealing in a different time zone or alternate way of measuring time. I mean, after all, *would* God, who is eternal and incomprehensible, give us the inception of life as we know it, then make His creation as eternal as He? What kind of living thing in the world has a definite beginning but no end?? It is not problematic for me to accept that *God* is infinite and eternal: He is u̲n̲created, n̲o̲t̲-material, and n̲o̲t̲ bound by time or space as *we* know it; He is the broadest expansion of what Love is and does as expressed in and through Himself, but that which and who all are tangible, living, existent, and made — Adam, Eve, *et al.* — *surely* would have a natural expiration date or some termination point. I couldn't help but continue to consider that *death* most certainly would have been a normal part of life, even if such back then was prolonged. And then, the thought came to me that if Jesus gives us *back* the chance to have *ongoing* fellowship by accepting His offer, to the degree that we are offered *eternal* life with Him *after* we die, maybe, just maybe, it means that we indeed had *it* — ongoing life — *before* the Fall. In fact, it must not have been hyped-up talk when God said to Adam and Eve, "From the tree of the knowledge of good and evil you shall not eat, *for in the day that you eat from it you will surely die*" (Genesis 2:17, emphasis mine). So, life originally didn't cease! God meant that *literally*!

And if God could bring matter to life to begin with, surely, it follows that He can keep it going perpetually. Then that moment came when man crossed the line and disobeyed, and He then followed through and kept His word. Millennia later, we can read about Paul's reminding us that our state of fallibility, which led to decay and death, *can* be righted again: "For the wages of sin is death, but the gift of God is eternal life in Christ Jesus our Lord" (Romans 6:23 NIV). Before the Fall, God had no reason to cause us to experience death; indeed, He loved the fellowship He had with Adam. He established a simple, cause-effect contract of sorts with Adam and Eve with a clause about obedience. Once I saw that God was true to His word, that is, when He instigated the punishment of death as a result of their insubordination, I began to wonder if this could also have brought about the collateral damage of life getting shorter. Why? Our now tainted moral and physical system would have kept increasing in concentration (and expression) with every generation down the line. Man's lifespan diminished gradually over the ages. Maybe the reason why people lived for such a long time in the early Old Testament days is that they were that much closer to the original pair who were designed *not* to expire. Anyway, in contrast to today, with the earth was less peopled then, God allotted greater longevity for much-needed procreation.

The long and the short of it is that now the only way to be reunited with God is through Christ. Either way, our *souls* are going to live on after we physically expire; it's our call where *we* choose to spend it. How do I know this is so? My sweet Holy Spirit is the "pledge" (2 Cor. 5:5) that God will "never leave me; never will He forsake me" (from Heb. 13:5 NIV), which would include *past* the point of my death! Later, much later, the same will hold true for our *physical* selves, which is sometimes called our "earthly tent" (2 Cor. 5:1). Just look at Jesus: He is the sneak preview to our main event! Who but He, one fully man but also fully God, could go back to His eternal state alongside the Father after He proved His identity to us through the Resurrection and Ascension?! Meanwhile, the whole of humankind has the same fundamental flaws and impulses as existed when Adam and Eve made the first wrong turn and veered us off course, and we have proceeded to head further south from there. So-called civilized and advanced nations are capable of even more dire devastation and destruction than primitive societies, whose bare and brutal impulses resulted in far fewer people dying. Modern cases in point include our poisoning the planet with seeming reckless abandon and our capacity to murder multitudes with the press of a trigger or a button. Now that I had come to realize that life was never intended to end in death, I began to wonder more about the fractured state of how people, specifically men and women, treated one another.

Once I got past death, I turned my attention to God's bonus afflictions for Adam and Eve, which came about because God's *original* hierarchy of power established was not adhered to. Then men and women did not relate to each other down here as they should have. Adam spurned his role as the leader of his "suitable helper" (Gen. 2:18), Eve, at the tree. You can find bumper stickers that proclaim, "Eve Was Framed." I say this is malarkey! Rather than bear at least some responsibility, Adam even indirectly blames God for giving him a woman to begin with for this to have happened! Make no mistake: Adam was right there, silently alongside Eve; therefore, he *also* was duped by the Devil. In fact, he *especially* blew it by failing to be the spiritual leader he was intended to be by letting his companion believe the lie. Adam participated in sin with Eve by succumbing to the temptation of thinking God was somehow holding back on them. Satan merely planted seeds of doubt in their minds regarding God's character and word. Doubting may be natural, but it can also be deadly, depending on whom you're dealing with. The devil didn't "make them do it" any more than God was "mean" afterward; oh, we did wrong by Him. His expulsion of the two led to Adam's subsequent resentment of Eve and self-pity before God. This brokenness panned out to the battle of the sexes we witness today. The carnage man commits when he takes the woman by violence or by force is a perverted assertion of power, which, unfortunately, he relinquished when he failed miserably in the Garden. Still, we must remind ourselves that we are *both* made in God's image, so we shouldn't just accept violence passively as somehow acceptable or inevitable without a fight to stand up for *a better version of ourselves*. And just as Christ "nourished and cherished the church, because we are members of His body" (from Ephesians 5:29), aren't both believing men and women as members of the church also then charged to act the same way toward *one another*?

In effect, in Christ, we are made *equal* by being the *same* positionally to Him, even if the role is expressed *differently*. Somehow, down here, "different" gets translated into "less than" as far as women are concerned. Just as God's Chosen People, the Israelites, rejected the Gentiles because they were considered inferior or even savages, sometimes I think that man views woman as somehow second-best because she was created second in God's sequence. Therefore, she is to be looked down on as lesser. Posh! Being made second is not second-best to God! Then added to this plight is her unique God-given "curse" during childbirth, which seems to degrade women further as person *and* mother. As an asterisk, though, consider the phenomenal charge of women in motherhood. It is predominately (though not exclusively) *she* who becomes the spiritual benefactress to her children; it is she who is the one who most often and more readily leads her children to Christ. This role alone of woman's motherhood is, in fact, a monumental, if not partially redeeming and sacred charge. Though I'm sure he did not intend the compliment he gave in a biblical sense, still, Walt Whitman said, "I say there is nothing greater than the mother of men." God never had in mind for women to be deemed inferior or unworthy; there is no such pyramid in God's view of humanity. Just look at *Jesus'* treatment of women! Talk about revolutionary and liberated in His thinking and actions! Jesus came to speak to the sick and afflicted, the pariahs, the outcasts, and the so-called lowly of society — and this *would have included women*. It would seem that in observing God's inclusion, if not elevation of women to the degree that He did in *Jesus'* life, men ought to realize that their female counterparts are no less than they. And yet, men make jokes about women and say all sorts of demeaning, derisive, and derogatory things, as if there's nothing worse in this world than being a woman. Even in the Jewish prayer book, we can find one prayer that says, "Blessed are you O God, King of the Universe, Who has not made me... a goy, a slave, and a woman." *Oy vey!* Just as the Jews became arrogant about being the Chosen People to the point that they rejected *the* Messiah, men misconstrue their place within God's hierarchy and use it to justify marginalizing, belittling, and hurting "bone of [his] bones, and flesh of [his] flesh" (Genesis 2:23). How can man receive Christ without subsequently trying to become Christ-like? Jesus modeled a new prototype of strength: leading through serving and showing mercy over what we consider just. Indeed, man is charged to protect woman, even to the point of death. Women, too, should be amazed and respectful of this type of security system. Love is always at its best symbiotic and focused on the *other* person!

Let's further examine Jesus' treatment of one woman in particular. No one can deny there was something special in the relationship between Mary Magdalene and Jesus. First off, of course, I do *not* mean it was carnal or physical; it's just that at the time, no man would ever have considered the possibility for a man and woman to be friends. Though Jesus is reported to have cast demons out of her — which, for all we know, means He cured her of some sort of depression — we also know that she was a woman of means. Being financially independent may place her as being middle-aged and likely of a more mature and ready mindset to be receptive to Jesus' astonishingly egalitarian message. She may even have provided some financial support for Him and His crew when they were making their rounds. And let's not overlook the fact that it was she and a few other women — *not* men (except for the Disciple John) — who did not duck and run. They were present and accounted for at His crucifixion. It was not a man, but Mary Magdalene who first saw the resurrected Christ. He counted on *her* to do as He said and go tell those dejected Disciples that He had risen! During His ministry, Jesus, in effect, told Martha to "chill" about her sister, Mary, for not cleaning up as she ought, that is, not doing her woman's work. Instead, she chose to listen to Him, and *He commended* her for it; indeed, He said, "Mary has chosen what is *better*" (Luke 10:42 NIV, emphasis mine). That she could even sit among the men was unheard of! And what about the unnamed woman who anointed Jesus with perfume before His death? Everybody gave her (and Him) a hard time for this washing, let alone the extravagant expense of the perfume, but, of course, Jesus knew what was right even though it was not the norm. In fact, Jesus admonished his wealthy host: "I entered into thine house, thou gavest me no water for my feet: but she hath washed my feet with tears and wiped them with the hairs of her head… this woman hath anointed my feet with ointment…Her sins, which are many, are forgiven; for *she loved much*" (taken from Luke 7:44–47 KJV, emphasis mine). It was her love that Jesus accentuated. Jesus also prevented the murder of another woman by shaming the men casting stones at her and pointing out *their* hypocrisy.

Next, there's Jesus' private encounter with a lower-ranked and unmarried Samaritan woman at a well who was living with a man, and he wasn't her first by far. For Jesus to even talk to her was breaking social *and* gender rank and file. That He didn't berate her in His questioning, but instead He told her that there was "better water" for her to "drink," shows groundbreaking compassion (and teaching) without compromising His standard. There are many more such instances, and these here I've cited are out of order, but my focus is on Jesus', thereby God's, treatment of women in contrast to that of man's. I also can't neglect Paul, who, though some, in my opinion, wrongly say he was misogynistic, chose first a *woman* to baptize, and he wasn't even likely to baptize anyway. Her name was Lydia, and she is considered by many to be the first person baptized in Europe. An independent businesswoman of wealth and means, Lydia also had many women who frequented her house, so Paul's visiting her allowed many women to hear of Christ. Little did I know then that just a year later, I would visit the very place where Lydia lived. I should like to add that even when Paul does appear to admonish or belittle women, it is due to a particular circumstance that needs addressing and in a specific place he's visiting. Paul is *not* categorically speaking against *all* women! I could go on, but this little greatest-hits package speaks to the fact that half the world's population ought not to be discounted or rejected based on what people pick and choose from the Bible. God's primary and overarching theme for *everyone* is love and mercy. I next turn for a moment back to my salvation and a new identity.

6.20 MALFUNCTION JUNCTION:
Just What Is Salvation Supposed to Look Like?

I felt the Holy Spirit with me again when I wondered about what had happened to the "old me" after salvation, especially because I had no forethought of asking Jesus to die for me. And now I wondered, is my life now even my own? I concluded that, *no*, it isn't. I know I have my *identity*, and I'm going through this life as Dimi Christakis, but because I decided that I *do* want Jesus in my life. I *did* ask Him into my heart — into the very *core* of who I am, so much so that I *try* to turn away from those things that distract me or damage my character — I'm no longer just Dimi Christakis, living willy-nilly and merely for myself. So, back when I stated, "I didn't *ask* Him to die for me," I realize God could have replied, "Well, I also didn't *have* to have *you* be born, but I *did* conceive of you. In fact, I have a specific purpose for your life, and *because* you decided to accept my Son, your life is now Mine, and I will live in you." How awesome is that?! The Creator of the universe chose to have me be a part of life in His world. How could I question His plans for creation and what all He has in store for us, *including* saving us? Even if I hadn't readily wanted to accept this at the onset, I was very aware I was walking in faith, floating on cloud nine, and wanting to continue doing so. To think that I exist merely because my parents conceived me has me subsequently living autonomously and in a vast disconnect, like some astronaut cut loose in outer space. It would be as if to assume that *I* am the center of the universe in my life, including knowing my origin, determining my purpose, and realizing it's all but to cease at death. If that's the case, then I am no different than a creature like a lizard, but I *know* I'm more than that by my consciousness of my mortality. If I reject God or spurn His offer of salvation, I am, in effect, saying that I am the agent that brought myself into being and that I have no link with any outside entity or creative force. In short, I divorce myself from God! I am not that powerful or self-sustaining. *Of course*, I believe in something vaster that created everything — and a *personal* force at that — one we affectionately call "Abba," which means something like "revered Daddy." God created the world with purpose, and I am a part of that. This fact renders a sense of breathless wonder in me!! Therefore, if God through His boundless and bountiful love chooses to send Himself down by way of a (seeming) mere man — His own Son — to save us because we were not acting righteously, that is, in a manner worthy or respectful of our Creator, *He can do that*! Whether or not I accept this fact *or* Him is on me, but it doesn't negate or change Him!

And as a final aside, why do I refer to God as *He* and not "it"? Everything about the creation of this cosmos, of life — of you and me — speaks to volition, personality, intentionality, brilliance, creativity, and a desire to show love. An "it" would not have had the care to have created us with our intent desire to need or feel love, let alone the capacity to experience the full range of emotions and depth of experiences that we do in life. Contemplating life's origins with no consideration of God is reduced to academic branches like anthropology or archaeology. Though fascinating and informative, these spheres of thought are never complete or exhaustive in their provision of answers, let alone beauty, especially when dealing with the "Big Why." I am in no position to be so defiant and or contrary as to retort, "No thanks, I reject you who made me," to Him who is saying, "Let me love you." For Him to have to come down here in person would indicate that we *do* mean the world to Him — that we *matter* — and that we *were* and *are* in desperate need of intervention and rehabilitation. Remember, He did not *need* us; anyway, the Trinity *is* its own happy, little family. We are *so* far from perfect that it would take an act of God to fix what we only make vain attempts to do through self-improvement. Is anyone so perfect, so complete in knowledge, so without fault or blemish that she or he could not stand real detoxing by having Him wipe our slates clean? Again? Regardless of whether or not I *asked* Him to *save* me, it was *His* choice, and He chose in the affirmative. His intention was always to deliver grace, the proof of His love. And what better way to show Love than through a *person*? I also did not *have* to ask Him because *He already did*! As absurd as it sounds, neither did I ask Him for *life*; He chose and created me *first*! My decision to go past being a tiny part of "the world He so loved" (John 3:16) to pursuing a relationship with Him makes me proud and glad to my bones!

I feel like I'm in Heaven already for being Glory-bound! I turn back to the conclusion of mending my broken heart through Mark's visiting me to help with my misnomer regarding the precious Holy Spirit.

6.21 SUBJECT:
Holy Spirit Deconstructed

When Mark came to visit the next afternoon, it had been well over a week since I began feeling troubled about thinking that God was not able to have anything to do with me. This state-of-mind flipped back on itself such that I believed that the Holy Spirit was no longer a treasure, but God's go-between, like He Himself couldn't stand to talk to me! A week doesn't sound long, but I was in agony, and as Mark passed by me going down the aisle in church on Sunday, he could tell so just by glancing at my dejected state. He stopped for a second to check on me and then assured me we'd meet and get all this straightened out. I could barely talk. When we worked out a time convenient to all, the first thing Mark did was to read that particular day from Chamber's devotional which had gotten me so off-point. I knew he intended to deconstruct what was written for me to understand what Chambers *really* meant, but I felt like I was barely hanging on. I sure hoped he could. Mark said that Chambers intended to convey that *it is a natural tendency for people to bargain with God*, but *God cannot negotiate with people*. In effect, Chambers insisted that God can only offer that which comes from Himself, which is Jesus; therefore, He also can only give testimony to or commune with that which is of His Own Nature, His Holy Spirit. The Holy Spirit fully comprehends the mind of God; we do not and cannot. Isaiah 55:9 tells us that the Lord declares that "as the heavens are higher than the earth, so are My ways higher than your ways and My thoughts than your thoughts." Try as we might (and often think we do), we cannot fully appreciate all He's got going on. This is *not* meant to be an insult to us, but even if it were possible for God to try to explain this or that, it would not only reduce or confine Him. Anyway, we couldn't handle it; there's just too much He figures in. That's probably just one reason why we can't see a single second, let alone a decade ahead in the future. Mark told me that Chambers was trying to stress that God gave us His Son, and *that's just going to have to do*; He's got nothing else — got no other proof, gift, or sign of His eternal love and grace other than the supreme sacrifice of Jesus, the Resurrected Christ. God can only testify or refer back to His Son and what He accomplished on the cross for us. And that just happens to be *everything*: a chance for full atonement, restoration, and eternal life! If that's not good enough, then *nothing* is! The fact that somebody could, would, and did die for me — died for *my* transgressions — is something only God could do. The very potency of such a deed of His is proof that I will get all the help I'll need, though I will not be able to understand all of what He's orchestrating at the moment, including His not revealing all the why's. Answers come in God's timing and not in my bemoaning for such in the moments up until then. I can't even determine which circumstances, known and unknown, are being worked into (or out of) my own life. His provision to help me through it all is through His Holy Spirit, but *it's still God* doing it. He is still here with me, and the Holy Spirit is the unique proof of such. It is on us to be attentive and responsive to His Spirit, just as Jesus did, only perfectly, in His day, too. Therefore, both Father and Son have made it possible for me to have access to them by implanting the Holy Spirit in me. How could I not be overwhelmed with gratitude for that?! He's thought of everything! When I accepted one, I get all three; God doesn't refuse me or reject me, but by God's unique nature, there *will* be things the Holy Spirit gets which I *can't* because of my being in the flesh. That's okay! Through His Holy Spirit, God determines when, where, and in what proportion I apperceive His living touch, nod, insight, prod, or rebuke. Mark had still more to add to help me out with this devotional entry.

When things go awry and people get down and out, Mark says all people at one time or another bargain with God. Even the atheist will say, "Show me this, show me that, prove to me x, y, and z (on his terms and conditions), and *then* I'll believe." That isn't how faith comes — not through logic, proofs, and effort — but through an open, receptive wonder. In short, it's *not* that God didn't want to talk to me *or* that the Holy Spirit somehow became cheapened by no longer being the awesome gift Jesus bestowed upon me, but rather He, the Spirit, is <u>also</u> the *agent* through whom God communicates with me. His Holy Spirit is ever-aware of what's going on with me because "He [the Spirit] intercedes for the saints [me] according to the will of God" (Romans 8:27). The Holy Spirit is who I thought He was *and more*! I am that saint! There is no reduction of who the Holy Spirit is due to my erroneously thinking that God had been avoiding me. I now perceived an expansion of the Holy Spirit: He not only supports me, but He concurrently apprehends God's intelligence and just how His will is to be implicated in my life. I became overwhelmed in that moment of growing clarity, yet I told Mark that I wasn't entirely sure what the role of God's Holy Spirit was; I didn't want to lose this understanding! Bonnie keeps telling me that they're all One, yet I also knew there are three unique and separate aspects! Mark carefully clarified and said that the Holy Spirit is *God's* Spirit and that He possesses all of the best emotions and hopes of God, including His patience, grace, mercy, unfailing love, and all the support and tenderness I could ever hope for in this life! Jesus promised that us that "the Helper, the Holy Spirit, whom the Father will send in My name, ... will teach you all things and bring to your remembrance all that I said to you... Do not let your heart be troubled, nor let it be fearful" (John 14:26–27). Since God is "far greater" (v. 29) than Jesus, we can trust Him. What Jesus said then is just as valid and applicable to each of us today. I, too, have the Holy Spirit, the same one Who mystically arrived and endowed Himself within those in the Upper Room at Pentecost. The very second the Holy Spirit swooped in me, God's wondrous love came in to stay, to teach, to prompt, to love, and to perpetually restore me through Him by His Spirit. My name is also in *His* Book of Life. Mark then proceeded to tell me even more about the Holy Spirit.

Mark explained that before we get saved, the Holy Spirit draws us, beckons us so that we *can* come to accept and know that which Christ did for us, but *we* (must) choose to accept (or not). It was all about Jesus at my salvation, so when I finally got cleared up who the Holy Spirit is, this became a anther cause for another celebration. To use the term "Holy *Ghost*" doesn't especially capture Him because He is *not* a ghost, though He most assuredly *is* holy. To say "*Spirit*" evokes all the rich tenderness that God possesses. Mark gave me two analogies to better understand Who the Spirit is and how He (the Holy Spirit) is differentiated from God's will. The first was that when he, as a pastor, is preparing for the Sunday service, he provides the music director with <u>a list</u> of what he intends to talk about so he can request this and that type of song. That would be like God's will or God's plan, intentions, or directives given. On the other hand, he said if he directly walked up to the music minister and said *with enthusiasm* that he really wanted him to work in "Amazing Grace" because it was going to enhance what he's preaching on, he has presented his will *through his spirit*, that is, communicated his ideas *with his emotions and passion*. I then asked Mark about the workings of the Trinity and where *I* fit into all this, if at all. In my tragic misunderstanding of Oswald Chambers, I, in effect, had covered up the Holy Spirit. I asked Mark why communication could *only* be from God to Jesus and from Jesus to God in their perfect self-contained unit. "Why did there even *have* to *be* a Holy Spirit?" I asked. He said there *has* to be the Holy Spirit because He *is* a part of them, too! When I asked Mark point-blank, "What in the world do you say to someone who doesn't know what the Holy Spirit is?!?" Initially, he didn't answer me right away. And then I think it just came to him, his second analogy, and he answered me with a question: "Don't you know that you still have *your father's spirit* living in you? Don't you have *his* tendencies, *his* energy, *his* emotions, *his* way of preparing food? I've never met your father, but I know his spirit lives in you." He then said that when we have God's Spirit, we get and have *all* those good and tender and sweet qualities of God living in *us*. Jesus had the Spirit of God in full force operating in and through Him. He sure needed it for what He was preparing for! It's not just God's will or directives that come to us, but, oh, we have His passion, mercy, and grace rolled up and given to us and which is always accessible to us through His Spirit. The Holy Spirit knows the depths of the will of the Father; I do not. When I do not have the words to pray, the Holy Spirit speaks on my behalf as He "intercedes for us with groanings too deep for words" (Romans 8:28) right back up to God. At that moment, I became overwhelmed with relief and joy, nearly as much as when I said, "Yes," to Jesus because I understood exactly who the caretaker of my soul, the Holy Spirit, is! He's not just some unknown, invisible part of the Trinity; He has become *the* most important thing inside me; He, too, is proof of God's living love. Later on, I would memorize Romans 8:27–28 because it (for me) best renders this connection between God and me through the Holy Spirit; there is nothing in Scripture that indicates an exclusion of me or a reduction of the Spirit. God desires for the Holy Spirit to have my back because at the same time, He, God, is checking on me *non-stop*! Just wow! His is such a mighty and double-barreled love!

I hope to continue to peel away more layers of the onion so that my Father gets a bit clearer to me each time. In the process, I supplant my will for His as massaged and enabled through His Holy Spirit. Accepting Him doesn't lead to a diminution, reduction, or displacement of my energy, personality, and soul, but a soaring inflation of it! As I become more obedient to Him and feel the encouragement of His Spirit, the compunction of His correction, the stirring of His power for *goodness'* sake, it will be easier, yes, more natural to do His Will. For example, when I quit drinking, my thinking got clearer. I'm sure the old dipsomaniac's underlying desires within me still exist, but over time, I disallowed them any indulgence. Now that I've accepted Jesus, the Spirit of God is in me, so I hope my understanding of Him and His wisdom will grow, but even more, that my readiness to *do* for Him will increase. It takes time, practice, and release for the Spirit of God to harness Dimi's will and bridle her self-centered desires. Of course, my personality and natural traits will still be there, but I pray they will be subordinate to my Father's Will. This time, Mark turned the tables and rhetorically asked me, "How do you know *the Father*?" As I can't see God Himself, His full nature is made evident in His Son. His actions backed up His words. Mark immediately thought of his own daughter to demonstrate how people could evaluate how *he* is as a father: look and see how his daughter acts, and this will tell you a lot about him. And then Mark said the most amazing thing: "Whenever you're in doubt or whenever you don't know what God is doing, err on the side of His sweetness." As a caveat, Mark warned me that the more I seek Him, the harder the Devil will work to abduct my joy and peace in Christ. He looks for overt weaknesses I display through what I do or say. Unlike God, Satan cannot read my mind! Satan's sole job is to pervert God's truths and make me doubt His pure and good motives. There's nothing new here; he is *so* passé! Toward the end of our visit, we momentarily returned to the painful topic generated by that Oct. 22 entry in Oswald Chamber's *My Utmost for His Highest* so that Mark would make sure that if I reread it, I would realize that all is well. By saying God cannot "witness" to me, Chambers *wasn't* saying that God, in effect, uses His Holy Spirit just to reach us; it's that *He can only commune with one who is the same nature as Himself.* All I had to do was think about an adult arguing with a teenager to realize the futility in God's justifying His actions with us. The Holy Spirit's job is to point us back to *Jesus*. Chambers was implying that *God would counter His very nature, His perfection, if He argued with the likes of us or argued with us on our level*; that would go against the definition of who and what He is! If He did, we of the flesh might misconstrue our *own* thoughts as coming from *Him*! Perish the thought! Mark said, for example, that he would not argue with someone who demanded he give proof that he was ordained or claim he's a good father. "Look at the church; look at my daughter," he told me he'd say. Mark said, "God gave us His all, His only Son to die for us such that we could be set right with God. God sees Christ's blood on us, and He has been satisfied." The crux of this is that the launching pad for my life to take-off in the right direction was made possible when Jesus agreed to come down here to serve and love on us. His supreme act of obedience took the hit for the whole of humanity for its disobedience. It's all the more poignant to realize that Jesus arrived here of His own free will and out of love for His Father, but coming down here was *not* His idea, not His brainchild; it was His *Father's*! God gave us all He's got. No matter how weak, unworthy — or conversely, capable — we may feel, Jesus assures us, "My grace is sufficient for you" (2 Cor. 12:9). Jesus' grace is just what was needed to make the ultimate family reunion possible! Could *you* accept His gift of grace? *Have* you? I finally did! I'll now tell you how I came to stand before this ultimate giver, God.

I then pondered what it might mean *not* to know what God's will is. Next, it was Bonnie who corrected me, and she said, "Dimi, we *do* know what God's will for us is: it is to spread His Word and message and to share the good news of Jesus Christ." Mark immediately nodded to this. Being human and alive, we still sin, but we desire to grow and be sanctified. I felt so relieved, so blessed, and so grateful that I was trembling. Mark then remarked that I was "overthinking" God, to which I replied, "Well, what do *you* do when somebody tells you *you're* overthinking, Mark?" He wasn't admonishing me; it was just that I needed to know that *I can't intellectualize or rationalize God*. He doesn't fit in a box or some neat definition, and even on our best days, we are clueless, but He still loves us in a measure and to a degree like no one else. To abandon myself to Him fully and completely through my faith in Him, yes, even "faith the size of a mustard seed" (Matthew 17:20) is what it's all about. I *have* come to Him "like little children" (Matthew 18:3 NIV), full of abandon, freedom, wonder, trust, and love, and it's where I want to stay and what I am trying to do even as I yearn to learn more about Him. Just when I got something figured out, another situation would present itself such that I realized how far I'd yet to go. Next, it would be a proverb that would hit me square between the eyes.

6.22 Arrogant Hearts and All Those Hearts That are Not His

In Proverbs 16:5, I read that "everyone who is arrogant in heart is an abomination to the LORD; be assured, he will not go unpunished" (ESV). I guess I'm in trouble then. This makes me feel like I'm a fraud. How can it be that I am *really* a Christian? My heart is not naturally soft and supple; my knee-jerk, gut reaction is typically not to give. I can be impatient, hypercritical, prideful, inflexible, and, like everyone else, hypocritical. And though one gift of mine may be having a way with words, I can and often do misuse this ability on purpose. As is the case with Bonnie, it is not yet my first impulse to deal with my fears through prayer and supplication; rather, I confess that I prefer to stonewall, run, hide, or bristle in paranoid self-protection. Resultantly and unfortunately, I often can't shore up Bonnie or encourage others with my otherwise usual buoyancy if I happen to be in a tizzy over religious matters or if I feel frazzled with myself; instead, I can get all the more strident or harsh. Agh! The proverb above forecasts that for such willful and persistent disobedience, I will "not go unpunished." So which trumps: covered in the blood or falling through the gaps? Good works or faith? Maybe it's *both* whereby faith will generate good works if I get out of the way. Personality, energy, and spirit given to me by God I divest in what I am purposed to do, that is, teach. Sometimes I even wish I could expand that role and become a life coach and morale booster to individuals in *other* venues! What I teach is secondary to *how* I teach. Speaking of children and teaching, it happens to be Christmas time at this writing, and I just went to my very first Nativity concert. Seeing a real infant stand in as baby Jesus here had me recollecting back on the Band-Aid colored Christ-child in the Nativity Scene that my mom made fun of as we passed by in our beige Plymouth Fury station wagon around what was called "church circle." Fast-forward to Bonnie and me sitting in the sanctuary. As we watch the play, we lament that some of *our* youngest family members have had *no* exposure to Jesus (or *any* religion, other than a little statue of Buddha), and we can't do diddlysquat about it, so it seems. I'm torn and conflicted where my family is concerned because I know how they think about Christians, recoiling or freezing up at the mention of His name, and now I *am* one. I crave to represent Him and still be the authentic me to them! I don't want to hide my faith, but I don't want to sit back passively and feel the loud silence of disapproval or bewilderment. How am I supposed to be in front of non-believers when I'm just a baby in the faith myself, still drinking "milk" (1 Corinthians 3:2)? Aren't I supposed to "be *strong* in the Lord and in the strength of *His* might" (Ephesians 6:10, emphasis mine)? What does this look like?

At this early juncture, I did *not* argue with non-Christians about the fact that the *only* way to God is through Jesus. At the time, I was still sky-high about coming to a better appreciation of the Holy Spirit! Yet, I cogitated over Jesus' uniqueness. Anyone can concede that man has been seeking concrete proof of what God looks like, starting with cave drawings that attempt to render the unknown, leading toward the time when man depicted God in his image through various mythological gods. Finally, we can see in *Michelangelo's* stunning *Creation* of *Adam* on *the* ceiling of *the* Sistine Chapel, where man painted in God's image. Art aside, we do have proof of Christ being nonpareil in two respects: first, Jesus alone claims the same "*I am*" self-identifications as God. He went so far as to say, "I and the Father are one" (John 10:30). Secondly, we'd come to the point in human history where God forever changed the course of life such that death did not mean the end for those that came to believe in Jesus as the Messiah. I believed, and this faith brought untold courage within me. If the topic of death came up in the literature we read in school, as it did in John Donne's "Death, Be Not Proud," somehow sap flowed into *this* "branch" of His "vine" (John 15:5 NIV), and I didn't keep still or shy away. I explained to my students what was implied by the paradoxical last line, "Death shall be no more; *Death, thou shalt die.*" I acknowledged that while blood sacrifices had been made ever since the dawn of man, whether it was with ancient Mayans or through the Jewish leadership seen in Old Testament, *only Jesus was raised from the dead* and walked among us in His resurrected state. This was no classic myth; it was a *fact*. The Apostle Paul, who had a direct encounter with Him after His Crucifixion, made a stunning argument for the reality of the resurrection: "If the dead are not raised, not even Christ has been raised; and *if Christ has not been raised, your faith is worthless*; you are still in your sins…If we have hoped in Christ in this life only, we of all men most are to be pitied. But now Christ *has* been raised from the dead…" (from 1 Cor. 15:16–20, emphasis mine). This is the clincher that makes Christianity as a religion different than all the others. Plus, no other religious leader died for the world and for me. How is one to *share* this, though?

Even though Jesus and His Holy Spirit were sacrosanct for *me* and I knew God existed, I didn't feel like I could stand in front of other non-Christian believers and have a prayer in staking claim that it was in their best interest to consider Christ. Why? I do concede that there are many religions on the planet, and faith is a process, both collectively and individually speaking. Someone might deduce that *if* there is no singularly correct and absolute answer, then *many* solutions or approaches to understanding life are possible. If that is the case, *all* may be deemed legitimate, and none are errant. How can this be? The favored choice popular with relativists so commonly found today is that (d), all the above holds true. However, I no longer subscribed to the "Que Sera, Sera, Whatever Will Be, Will Be" approach to life! There can only be one truth; it can't vary; otherwise, I could argue that evil isn't wrong as long as it suits *me* regardless of what happens to you and vice versa, which *so* isn't so! Personal choice over if and how to *worship* God then boils down to one's *preference*, which is not the same thing as knowing truth, that is, absolute truth. Choosing and combining this and that from various religions to create your own greatest hits religious package ought not to be akin to picking out what you like at a salad bar. What you end up with is a mishmash crockpot of mutually-excluding and contradictory theorems. One may feel consoled choosing the right path for himself and also even pat himself on the back by saying in a *laissez-faire* manner, "I won't judge your religion if you don't diss mine." Most live by a tit-for-tat approach which implies, "I'll strike you back if you do"; this is why we still have holy wars. Jesus broke the mold here with His call for mercy. You may also have seen a familiar bumper sticker out there which depicts all the major religions' symbols in a neat row such that your mind reads one word: "COEXIST." In a sense, this *sounds* pleasing, but when you consider it more closely, coexistence is both implausible, impossible, and therefore absurd. It is a copout to say *everyone* is correct. If you live by the creed that says, "I do my thing, and you do yours," then what happens when my ways conflict with yours, and you get slighted? This blithe notion goes out the window the moment I hurt or cross you. And in reality, we neither tolerate each other nor reserve judgment! We just don't judge in the right manner to bring about the results *Jesus* would have us do. There are *way* too many logs in eyes out there (Matthew 7:5). Though many answers have a *lot* of wisdom to them, there can only be one correct answer, and only one book claims stake to it. Do I, as a Christian, think disdainfully towards other religions and mythologies? No. Why? Ultimately, many roads *do* head in the general direction of God and get close enough so that He may be sensed. But *only* Jesus said, "I am the way, and the truth, and the life; no one comes to the Father but through Me" (John 14:6). This is emphatic and crystal clear. That Jesus performed miracles only validates and substantiates He is who He says He is. They were needed then, and we can look back on them as proof now. My job as a Christian is to present the facts in a gentle but clear way.

I peer into the spectrum of faith and observe people who *say* they are not "into religion," let alone God; instead, they will reach out to the *material* to quench themselves; this state of acquiring becomes a never-ending and quixotic quest. People from ages hence up to our contemporaries all respond to a primitive religious impulse and attest there is *some* force or energy "out there." In a way, semantics aside, this is faith in its most rudimentary form. Even an atheist who says there is no God *has* to have presupposed a god to say he doesn't exist! The next phase of spiritual development — and one in which many people still settle — is pantheism, polytheism, or transcendentalism. The three monotheistic religions introduced various prophets and sages who reveal brilliant glimpses to a higher and better way. Some came before Christ, some after. The paths of many and varied men, each with his own contribution, leads inexorably to *one* man, the one-and-only God in the flesh, who silenced the din and confusion through His revolution of absolute truth, restorative peace, and astonishing love. In short, "narrow is the gate and difficult is the way which leads to [eternal] life, and there are few who find it" (Matthew 7:14 NKJV). *Why so few*? Of course, there exists a natural inclination to seek God, and there are many alluring and brilliant theories, satisfying postulates, and pearls of wisdom, each of which contains *some* truths. How could they not? I suppose that some might consider it wrong to read or study outside of one's faith, but I myself am fascinated by other countries' values, cultures, history, and ways, so I do not deny myself reading about them. I might do so out of curiosity, *not* as looking for an alternative to my faith! Interest in or tolerance of someone who is *not* Christian is not the same thing as passive acceptance, dabbling, or co-adoption. Successful evangelism can only take place through love, understanding, and personal time and resources invested. There will always be something out there bigger, better, faster, higher, but never a lasting, contenting, or final best.

Christianity is the *only* religion that ties *all* the pieces together, starting with the inception of creation, leading to man's seeking to make sense of the world, and ending with redemption and full restoration. Every biblical account has the stamp of His love marking it. Folks who *don't* choose Christianity don't do so because usually they're not dissatisfied with other spiritual food and have become accustomed to a perpetual yearning, even if they experience occasional bliss. It would be like the person who goes to hot and tasty prepared foods he's been grabbing here and there his whole life because he's never had an amazingly delicious and nutritious home-cooked meal. You don't have to order a seven-course meal to ingest Jesus; He describes Himself to be the most basic and elemental sustenance known to man: "*I am the bread of life.* He who comes to Me shall never hunger, and he who believes in Me shall never thirst" (John 6:35). Speaking for myself, I have finally been satiated and quenched! Even those who are attracted to the peace found in Eastern religions have *no hope beyond this life. Nada.* It's incredible for me to glance back at just a little over eighteen months ago and consider that for almost fifty years, I had been looking for God when, in reality, it is *He who has been right here the whole time and has been pursuing me*! I just finally turned in the right direction! Things cleared up fast then, quicker than I could have imagined. As you know, I thought that the Holy Spirit was Jesus' ghost at the Ascension, that Jesus morphed into a cartoon-like Holy Ghost rising. In my mind's eye, He ascended or floated up into the clouds, like Casper the friendly ghost. When I accepted what Jesus had done not only for humanity but for me personally, He rushed in as quick as lightning with His Holy Spirit to confirm my salvation. The topic of the Holy Spirit vis-à-vis the Trinity would remain somewhat cloudy, but I doggedly continued to strive for a deeper and better understanding. I may be like a yo-yo in my growth and I may go through episodes where I either get stuck or get off-center, but with every passing hurdle, I get stronger. Why? How? "I have boldness and confident access through faith in Him" (Ephesians 3:12 NKJV). The Helper, my tutor, schools me right! I am also beholden to the patience and persistence and the friendship and love of both Mark and Bonnie. The sky's the limit when one sides with Him! Speaking of which, I would now look into the implications for our free will.

6.23 FREE WILL AND EVIL

For some time, I used to think that God set us up to fail so we could know we needed Him. How could it *not* be an eventuality that "curiosity would kill the cat," and we'd continue to make an errant choice as did the original pair? However, now I think that giving us free will in its absolute sense is the only way He could have tested the authenticity of our love. In fact, I think that even if there had not been a tree of knowledge and if there hadn't have been the serpent, it still would've turned out the same for Adam and Eve. It's just the first chapter of His primer on what mature love involves. At times, I've even wondered why God didn't go ahead and annihilate Lucifer to begin with and not expel him down here all but for him to think he could reign. Why didn't He snuff him out? Then I thought to myself, how could He *not* permit — as opposed to *cause* — the possibility of evil within the full spectrum of morality for our wills to encounter so as to *grow*? How could faith *not* have a challenge? The test of whether we choose to come to Him wouldn't be complete in some empty vacuum! It's easiest to come to Him when we have been knocked off our self-made pedestal so as to be in the position to humbly, with hands outstretched and hearts parched, reach out to Him. However, the usual response to calamity and misfortune is, "Why? Why me?" Just when you think *you've* suffered, hopefully, there will come some moment of clarity and sober awareness that what we are undergoing *pales* in comparison to what He did to prove His love for us! He came down here as one of us and died on the cross to show us as proof of His most extreme love. Could it really be that? Even after we were expelled from the Garden of Eden and God had given us the Ten Commandments, Jesus simplified these for us and got them down to Two, which still covered them all. He did this to show us that *no matter how good we got, we still couldn't achieve His standard of perfection, let alone excellence.* This construct is not meant to put us down or discourage us, like some great taunt, let alone to instill a sense of futility. He did such that we might recognize for ourselves that we are to look to *Him* for *all*. At least we were provided a rule book, God's Laws, which you'll find described as "*our tutor* to lead us to Christ" (Galatians 3:24) or "*mirror*" (James 1:23), emphasis mine, by which to evaluate ourselves. How do you know how you look if you don't glance in the mirror to see if this or that is amiss? You might be in denial. Metacognition is nice but hardly effectuating. Oh, we are such slow learners! Is human history just one huge, long lesson-after-lesson to present His awesomeness and our needfulness of Him? Does God like to show-off? Perhaps the fact that God is *not* material might make it easier for Him to love because there's less interference. I mean, for us to be in the *material* world is to be surrounded by His *par excellent* creation, yet this also creates the tendency for us to seek satisfaction in the *physical*. It's only natural, yet what we yearn for remains unattainable. Just listen to the Rolling Stones' 1965 hit with Jagger attesting what he can't get. Thank God for Jesus! My gratitude for Christ got me thinking about what it would be like in Heaven.

6.24 What about Talents and Crowns? What about Heaven?

Now that I have been assured of my salvation — over which I still remain grateful and joyful — and I understand that I will be judged by *Christ* and must give an accounting for what I have done for Him after my salvation, I am in a bit of a quandary over the crowns I hear I am to receive. I always imagined that Heaven would be the destination where I would be after I passed, a realm in which the most supreme and intense love is somehow experienced and in which I would eternally bask. Heaven is where God the Father *and* Jesus live and where I will enjoy direct communion with Jesus as well as other believers before me. Formerly, I used to imagine being with Jesus staring face-to-face at Him and smiling in awe. He would place His hands gently on each side of my face so that I could focus on Him and feel the power of His confidence and undiluted love. Hopefully, He will look happy at me and not be disappointed! Does this image of His loving gaze sound boring or static? Mark recommended that I read a book on Heaven by Randy Alcorn, which also depicts the richness of *ongoing fellowship* with other Christians, both those familiar and ones from ages past, all at our beck and call to engage with. *This* sounds magnificent and stimulating to me! Now that I know my salvation is sealed and that Christ will judge me after I die, this brings on a whole new notion of expectation and, yes, distress to me! I imagine Janet Jackson's song, "What Have You Done for Me Lately"? playing in Heaven's background. Not having gotten saved until a month before I turned fifty, I will probably receive not much more than a tin cup! Contrastingly, think about Paul! It'll be like a whole avalanche of gold crowns for him!

At times, it used to agitate me to think that there will even *be* rewards in Heaven! I mean, I'm not doing it — living the life of a Christian — for a reward, *per se*! I'm trying to mature because I love Him, can't stop craving the Word, and I want to serve Him here, that is, represent, if you will. I'm not doing it for a paycheck in Heaven! If I weren't teaching, I would probably feel futile because at least I know

I'm doing right by Him here. To be sure, intent means everything to me, and I want Jesus to know my motives are pure, that I'm not doing it for accruing crowns, which get returned to the Sender anyway. I worry that when I face Jesus, He might say that I could've done *so* much more, that there will be no crowns for Dimi. It still sounds like judgment; only instead of going to real Hell, I might end up separated from Him because He will be celebrating with His real winners. Then I remember Mark's saying to me, "God is bigger than that" and that "I've never before been loved like the way *He* loves," so I think I'd better flush my hypotheses down the drain. Anyway, all this talk about crowns and rewards has got me stirred up because if we are to love Him, place all our chips of faith in Him, and accept His gracious sacrifice gratefully, then why are we awarded for our works in Heaven? It seems like a double standard, but just now, I recall the words of Martin Luther when I taught American lit.: "Good works do not make a good man, but a good man does good works." This to me says Christ-like actions flow naturally over the course of our lives when our will gets subsumed by His, that is, when we clear the way and let His flow go. The more you think about Jesus, the less you think about yourself. I just want to be His Little Engine That Can...

Then, I came to see that just as there exist differences of expression of faith down here, both quantitatively and qualitatively, then, of course, there should be differentiation up there. The merit of what we do for Him is evaluated case by case and has no earthly comparison for such assessment. In Heaven, there is no competition or jealousy. That said, Jesus' half-brother, James, reminds us that we ought to do all we can for Him. Our aim is not remaining "a forgetful hearer but [becoming] an effectual *doer*; this man will be blessed in what he does (James 1:25, emphasis mine). I wondered what it would look like to be judged by Jesus based on our merits, talents, and gifts *used* from that time forward after our salvation. Would I be evaluated on a sliding scale based on what I did with the rest of my life, or does He judge us by potential utilized for Him over the *whole* of our lives? What if I *still* disappoint Him because of my inadequacies that might slow me down or interfere? Will there be a time-out in Heaven? a cloak-room of shame? a waiting room? a ghetto? I know getting there is as instantaneous as our last exhalation means our first breath in Heaven.

Anyway, there is no such thing as Purgatory; to say otherwise implies Christ's sacrificial death wasn't enough. I think what it will be like when we first face Jesus in Heaven will be that He will review our successes made for Him, kind of like in the classic, *It's a Wonderful Life*, only in reverse. The suicidal George Bailey got to learn about the difference he made in others' lives by seeing what life would have been like if he'd never been born. I hope to be shown that I have made more than a few differences for Him by my life's end and not have revealed many missed opportunities. I also wondered how long I might weep tears of sorrow over those loved ones who will *not* be with me in Heaven, who would instead be in a state of perpetual torment in Hell. That's a hard pill to swallow! I've got to ante up my prayer life to be stronger in Him and *show* love better! Believing in and revealing His love, sweet love leads me to Home, sweet Home.

6.25 HIS WORKMANSHIP, POEMS, AND POINTS

Around this time, something started to flow from me that stemmed from a desire to express my gratitude: I felt compelled to write poems about Christ or what I'd learned about Him. These began to bubble forth in the form of short poems or limericks. Amazingly to me, Mark taught us that the original word for "workmanship" in Greek was "*poiema*," which is obviously where we get the words "poem" and "poetry" from in English. When I read in Ephesians 2:10 that "we are His [God's] *workmanship* created in Christ Jesus for good works which God prepared beforehand so that *we would walk* in them" (emphasis mine), I see that not only am I am a living "poem," but if one of my gifts is writing, then I need to do so. *That's* "walking," too! This "poem" of God's likes to write short poems, which *He* gave me the desire and ability to do, to begin with. That I am moved to write to encourage a man of God, and a friend seems only fitting. Here's a short ditty that captures how I feel:

    I crave the Word and seek to please.
    I try to obey - life knocks me to my knees!
    To move my faith from head to heart
    Is when you say real growth can start.
    To enlarge my faith requires more love than I show,
    So, I'll just keep walking with Him in hopes it'll grow…

I end this chapter with a review of summative thoughts on the Holy Spirit and related aspects that either Mark cleared up or the Holy Spirit helped me figure out.

1. Faith, the capacity to even believe in God, comes directly from God, but it is on us to use and personally believe in Him. If God gave us the capacity to have faith, then if I choose to engage this faith, is it mine? Does He know I accepted His Son for real? I don't want God to think my faith isn't genuine because I didn't have the wherewithal, this faith-capacity, to begin, as if my faith

isn't authentic because it had to be manufactured by Him in the first place. I conclude this by assuaging my inner fears in fuller maturation by saying that God knows me so well. As a matter of fact, He understands me better than anybody, so, of course, He knows it's for real, that my faith is genuine. It's like my thinking I needed to tell Jesus that *I accepted Him* for His *own* sake and sacrifice, *not* because I was trying to avoid Hell. He's not going to keep me hanging or change His mind; that I am sealed means I'm His, and we both know it!

2. The Holy Spirit does not dwell in unbelievers, but it reckons and urges them to come to Christ mysteriously and through His perfect timing. I suppose this pressing happens more times than we are aware. When this occurs and the person is ready to engage his or her faith in the way that God intended, then there is a divine illumination within him. This is the point at which Christ, through His Holy Spirit, comes to dwell in us, and we come to say, "Sayonara," to our old life. Nothing can eclipse this moment in your life.

3. The difference between spirit and soul is that the spirit is the aspect by which we come to have a relationship with Jesus; the soul houses the spirit and is the very essence of our being. If you don't know Jesus, you are spiritually dead (or blind) even though you have a soul because you are very much obviously and physically alive.

4. I have read a lot already about the difference between the Holy Spirit's *conviction* and *condemnation* by Satan. I know Satan will try to pervert and lie to me and especially try to have me wallow in self-pity and that the Holy Spirit wants to instruct, uplift, and correct me, but sometimes they both feel like the same thing!! I don't want my ego to triumph, yet I can't always tell how long the Holy Spirit might be reckoning with me. I have since come to conclude that the correcting provided by the Holy Spirit is pure, innately right, gentle, and persistent. You may not like what He has to say, but you know He's right.

On the other hand, Satan mocks, belittles, condemns, and renders you feeling defeated, deflated, empty, and depressed, regardless of what the situation was that might have prompted his manipulation or accusation. That said, when people undergo unpleasant trials, some might say they're in spiritual warfare and blame Satan when it could be that God is trying to grow them by letting things happen. We get "sifted" (Luke 22:31) to rid us of impurities. As I was soon to learn, *no one* is exempt from sinning, not even mature Christians.

6.26 THE LONE RANGER

A friend of ours from church confessed that the greatest sin *he* had a real problem with was *pride*. Indeed, it is the prime mover of *all* other sins evidenced in both us and in the world. Sin also happens to be one of the negative repercussions from the Fall. I asked this church friend, one I'd consider a mature Christian, "Do you mean to tell me that the Fall can also impact genetics as well?" He said, "Yes! Absolutely everything in life has been adversely impacted. He explained the magnitude: "After Adam and Eve disobeyed and were expelled, everything on every level changed, molecular to moral. For example, in Old Testament times, we were then vegetarian, and I am now carnivorous. Humankind has and will always find a way to be violent; the daily news is a sad testament to this. We are *not* good stewards of our planet, and so, we indirectly die from poisoning our environment, and so on and so forth." The Bible tells us that not only people suffer as a result of the Fall they set in motion, but that *"the whole creation groans and suffers* the pains of childbirth together until now… We …groan within ourselves, waiting eagerly for… redemption" (from Romans 8:22–23, emphasis mine). There's a poem by William Wordsworth I teach that also speaks to how we have let everything go sour because of our lack of care, and I couldn't agree more! He wrote that "the world is too much with us… Getting and spending, we lay waste our powers…We have given our hearts away…For this, for everything, we are out of tune; it moves us not." Our little church's manifesto would be that we are all "jacked up"; nonetheless, Pastor Mark stressed that it is inadequate to be content or resigned to *stay* that way. At times, despite my enthusiasm, I, too, can feel stuck, like my wheels are spinning and my engine is running idle. What would Jesus say to me? I believe with all my heart what He'd say to me would be the same as what He said to His Disciples: "Follow me" (Matthew 4:19). Satan will still attack my mind and molest my thoughts. I want to trust the path I've chosen in Him, and I know one can't ever earn salvation! Salvation is not a precursor to or a guarantee of a life lived out in perfect righteousness or holiness, but it *is* the first step towards that direction. There is no panacea for moral ails down

Connecting the Dots...

here, but we are privy to knowing the end of His story: it *doesn't* end, and it will be more beautiful than I can imagine!

As I round the end of the second year after a year of primal growth in Christ, I tell you I just can't stop my testimony here for you (and Him). Why? To restate my purpose in writing to you, though there can be only one turning point in choosing to believe in Him, I want you to see what this looks like in the steps of a toddler learning to walk. You have plenty of access to those who are far wiser and more experienced than I, but it's one of those "if I can do it, so can you" pats-on-the-back of encouragement that stirs me to continue sharing with you. Ultimately, though this is hardly His Word, this follower of the King of kings wants you to see what's around the next bend of this journey and looking back, I notice how my crossing one bridge after another has led to this purposed path of my life. Come with me as I follow Him by reading on to the upcoming chapter, the next year of what it has been like growing in my faith since being justified.

CHAPTER 7:
Year 3, Becoming Fruitful

"Make every effort to supplement your faith with virtue, and virtue with knowledge, and knowledge with self-control, and self-control with steadfastness, and steadfastness with godliness, and godliness with brotherly affection, and brotherly affection with love. For if these qualities are yours and are increasing, they keep you from being ineffective or unfruitful in the knowledge of our Lord Jesus Christ."

— 2 Peter 1:5–8

"In view of your participation in the gospel from the first day until now. For I am confident of this very thing, that *He who began a good work in you will perfect it* until the day of Christ Jesus."

— Philippians 1:5–6, emphasis mine

7.1 More Whys? and How Comes?

My yearning to understand Christ more thoroughly continued. I was "making every effort" to "supplement my [burgeoning] faith" through seeking answers to questions that came of their own accord. I prayed that I was making what felt like tiny strides in my inner character as well as becoming outwardly "fruitful in the knowledge of" Jesus; this was a stuttering, stumbling, and messy affair. The impetus for writing you has not only been to reveal how another unlikely candidate and older disbeliever became a Christian but to show the transformative moments after my turning point. The story doesn't end here; it begins, and as I became more enthusiastic about my faith, I felt compelled to share it; this wasn't something I set out to do! My thought process was that if I can use rationalism to reach the reasoning unbeliever, release my enthusiasm to attract the Greek, speak Russian to connect with a Russian, use the teacher within to communicate to students, or relate my experiences of feeling disenfranchised to draw those who have been hurt *and* if the Holy Spirit partners up and draws such a one to Christ, I'll do it!! I would continue to read and study His Word daily, keep on asking Mark questions, seek his guidance (rather than information), get involved in my church, and, when in doubt or beset with challenges, pray with all I've got. I did all of the above with "self-control and steadfastness." In this early stage, when I hadn't the foggiest idea about how to pray, let alone sustain this conversation without being beset with other rushing thoughts, I somehow steadied the keel within me. Here and now, I will share with you this next year of yearning to grow, starting with a fresh batch of topics, questions, and answers.

What now? What am I supposed to do with this power pack of faith? As I indicated before, I feel the immensity of an urge and propelling commitment to share Him, and my secret fear is that I will not be able to deliver or, like Peter, I might deny Him at some critical point. I feel like I don't yet have the necessary heart which possesses "godliness" and "brotherly affection." I began to ask myself how I could demonstrate, nay, even prove my faith was the real deal; after all, it felt like it was coming out of my pores, and I wanted to use it effectively. New believers desire to know what their calling is or what God wants them to do. He doesn't merely want you to read the Bible. He wants you to show love to other people. It's a matter of the power of attraction. Much of what I observe around me looks like Satan doing his best to ruin everything through his powers of seduction. How can Jesus (let alone I) break through to those who content themselves with the mundane or the trivial, the shiny and new, or the latest and greatest, to the point they think there is little else out there but consumption, acquisition, and entertainment? It's a merry-go-round of a cornucopia *ad nauseam* and an outlook of *carpe diem*. What about those trapped within their minds listening to negative self-talk, which they are convinced is the gospel? What about those aching to confess and feel hopeless about their future? What about those who need a second or thirty-second chance and not finding hope, think all is for naught? Would these my questions never end? None of them are asked in the vein of trying to challenge or stump God, as if there was some deal-breaker out there that would have me turn back. I was filling in my crayon book of pictures I sought to bring more fully to life. I know I'll never know but a whisper of a fragment of His big picture, but I think He doesn't mind my looking up at Him inquisitively and affectionately, pulling at His trousers to ask, "Abba," about this and that. I'm both humbled and grateful for God declaring, "For My thoughts are not your thoughts, nor are your ways My ways. For as the heavens are higher than the earth, so are My ways higher than your ways and My thoughts than your thoughts" (Isaiah 55:8-9). His ways are obviously higher than Satan's, too, he who is always trying to sack the quarterback inside me. Speaking of Satan vexing people, sometimes he taunts, and I worry that I am more like a Pharisee than the contrite and humble tax collector. I'm glad I've only just begun!

7.2 Why do I Keep on Acting Like a Pharisee?

Admittedly, I have had my own set of rules that I think are the right ones to live by for *moi*; I don't consider the way the masses live to be a standard to emulate; in fact, what they do and how they live I often purposefully reject. Not only do I judge, but I am also critical-minded, a state of thinking that comes naturally from much observation of ones in my youth. Then I cultivated it as a part of my being an English teacher, the profession that scrutinizes and looks for flaws to bring clarity. All this is to say I know that I don't have the luxury of such discrimination anymore. Thank goodness, I've got some time left for me to turn to and lean on Him and come to live more lovingly and holily. I don't want to be some mean, old biddy, or cranky crone! I am assured that every Christian feels how I have been feeling now and then, and yes, of course, I will sometimes falter and fail when Jesus asks me to do something. I won't always live up to what I want to either. It is also a good start to recognize that we do not always see people — especially those reviling or practicably invisible to us — as God does, but we can begin by saying, "I haven't walked a mile in her shoes." Saying this to yourself *really* helps halt judgment in its tracks! Try it out! In those valleys, when I can't sleep at night and just can't get some wrong-doing I've done off my mind, to the point that I get convicted to make that change and do so, then the next time I get stronger, and change comes more easily. It's like I make a confession in the quiet of the night, and there He is, listening and nodding. The more stubborn the difficulty, like some resentment I'm nursing *or* like some fault that I justify, is acceptable (probably because I like it), the longer it takes to let go of it permanently. It's in these times of weakness when my worst faults are on display (or are glaring to me, though hidden to you), I need to make the first baby step made in the right direction, however small, and the next time I do so, it will be easier. Such a child I am! Conversely, if you continue to waver, dismiss, or choose not to believe *or* if you persist in indulging in bad habits and attitudes, *this* mindset will strengthen itself and flex the negative until the wrong becomes your right! Wrong-doing never starts out as an act that we initially don't fret over, but, unfortunately, it takes little time for the inch we give to become a mile of our getting stuck in sin like quicksand, whatever the ungodly thing it is. This notion hearkens within me a lesser-known quote by Thoreau that speaks to the process of degradation and moral decline: "After the first blush of sin comes its *indifference*; and from immoral it becomes, as it were, *unmoral*, and *not quite unnecessary* to that life which we have made." Living in a world that operates in the grey of relativity, where right and wrong are can flip on a dime depending on one's perspective (and often, finances), I see the desperate need to establish a moral and ethical center of gravity based on Him and His way. I respond to Thoreau's admonition above as the Apostle Paul might have: "*May it never be!*"

7.3 Faith as a Gift

Why and how did *I* come to have faith? Why has this not (yet) happened to other members of my family? I know it's a matter of free will to decide to claim faith in Him and what He did, but if faith is a gift of grace and mercy that has bestowed upon me, am I actually choosing? The whole idea of *limited atonement* is Calvinist. If "limited" does entail "whosoever," then this puts a whole new expanded spin on "limited." God wants *everybody* to be saved! God's love *is* vast enough, and Jesus' blood comprehensive and *more* than enough to take care of everybody. If God is love and He is both perfect and infinite, then there is assuredly enough for everybody. God will reckon with each person many times in his life, but the person has to be open or receptive to these promptings. The Lord came many times to Pharaoh to let Moses and his people go, but after numerous times of his wavering and declining, God finally "hardened their heart" (John 12:40). Perhaps for those believers who try to reach out and are not successful, the time is not right. Neither God nor Jesus gives demand performances or delivers on a dime by your decree. God blinds the minds of the unbelieving. It's not a matter that they *can't* be redeemed, but the ways of the world have impeded or dissuaded them, and they're hooked on artificial bait. Yes, I have come to observe and know we believe with our hearts differently than we do with our minds.

I used to ask before, "Why would Jesus die for *me*?" Now I see that I belong to and came from my Father, the Creator of *everything*, then, of *course*, He can easily come down and (not so easily) die for me in my state, so that I might know the love that He has for me. The 1978 hit, "Reunited and It Feels So Good," croons with new meaning. God doesn't just intend to love and leave me! He also intends to develop the gifts He gave me via a calling that speaks to me and which will ultimately bring Him glory. Callings can change over the course of one's life too. I find that *as* I am writing, certain thoughts and words do not seem like they come from me or of my own accord! Only God can bring about an action or change in one so intimate, so personal, and yet universally useful at the same time. He knows what has happened to me and continues to help transform me such that my faith produces much for Him. Any other way other than letting you or me choose Him of our own free will would have been fraudulent or sham-like, like some marionette show presenting us loving Him because *He said so*. God lets our life play out and allows us to choose to love Him (or not) for our love and faith to be real and authentic. It's *got* to be real! Such freedom means that we can also choose wrong, and evil also produces its own ripple effect with far-reaching consequences. In short, God cannot contradict Himself or His character. If we say "No" to Him and "Yes" to sin, that is on us, however it pans out in our life. We ought not to put God on trial when things go wrong in the world; after all, the *world* has been "passing away" ever since the Garden of Eden (1 John 2:17). It hasn't stopped and won't until His return. In a way, He stacked the deck against Himself, almost handicapped Himself by letting Satan distract and confuse us by seducing us with more than our senses need in order to be gratified. He makes double, triple sure we want Him, but we have to look past all the beautiful enticements, beckoning distractions and irrelevancies, those sundry sirens of song, as well as beyond the pains and troubles we endure to see through to Him, even in our hobbling, prideful state. Hopefully, we will have people we have brought to Him who also came to believe. It seems that the sheer variety of believers provides unending opportunities for making breakthroughs that can lead to salvation. Much to my surprise, I have come a long way in that I really do desire to promote Him, only in a much different manner than I have experienced in my past. I now briefly turn to the challenge of facing the masses with whom to connect.

7.4 WHY ARE THERE DIFFERENT RACES?

How can I make headway when I may have little in common with others, or honestly, when I get exasperated even when I don't want to? Often, I don't feel qualified when I feel different myself. For this heading, I probably should have asked, why are there different *nationalities*? Though full of pride in my heritage, I also held a negative self-concept because I would never be a "pure" Greek; I have cruelly dubbed myself a "half-breed." I know — it's my hang-up. I get exasperated with Americans who forget or barely know their heritage (if at all), even though I accede that America is *supposed* to be the melting pot or mixed salad and that part of *our* cultural identity hope in the future and not dwell on the past. The diasporic experience of my father's side is a topic for another book; my journey to Him is for you now. Speaking for myself, however, I *have* craved to know my Greek grandparents' traditions and ways from days from even further past. It seems that they have been replaced with values and means that do not last, satisfy, or nourish. When I shared all this at one of Mark's visits, he countered me and said that he was glad that a Greek and an American got together so that he could meet somebody like me exposed to some different cultures. Obviously, being interested in cultures is important to me, so much so that I am aware that it can be a marvel for some to meet the likes of me, a mixed bag of miscellany.

God populates the earth with various peoples, like some *Benetton* advertisement, so that there may be many opportunities and keys to open hearts. I'm going to have to get over the issue of nationality or race; plus, no one is a pure anything anywhere when you get right down to it! Focusing on differences can get reduced further to the point where someone looks for irrelevances and downright absurd differences. Dr. Seuss teaches against –isms in his book, *The Sneetches*. Outer appearance, type, and possessions come and go; love must transcend. Anyway, there's still nothing wrong with taking great pride in one's cultural heritage; that is not the same as racism. When it's all said and done, there is only one human race. We are to view others *as God sees us*, but in some cases — no matter where we live in the world — this takes time to overcome because we may have had negative experiences with a few that we project onto the whole; we may have learned prejudice from our elders. Often, we are barraged with images of negative stereotypes in the media. When it comes right down to it, though, I have *also* been that stranger you didn't know or might not want to have known from Adam. When you dare to come and sit across me at my kitchen table and maybe even befriend me, you might come to notice the spark of what God sees (and made) in me, and, hopefully, *I will in you, too*; then we can get past our differences to become one in Him, through Him, and for Him. *V-i-c-t-o-r-y*! Thoughts of my purpose here and now naturally gravitate to the future of what it will be like *then and there*.

7.5 What's It Gonna Be Like When I Die?

Just when I carved out an understanding of one thing, I began to speculate on another question, like what happens to us after we die. This topic would not get fully addressed until later on. I remember my wonderment began right after I had finished reading 2 Corinthians. I had difficulty understanding what eternal life entailed and especially what our new glorified body would look like. All I could imagine was that our energy or essential self would continue to be with God in an intense, intimate, and absolute way that doesn't exist now and all of which is beyond our current scope. Though we can't discern this state, I still assume we will be drenched in His love and saturated in His light. That said, it's hard for me to conceive that I would have any interactions *per se* with anybody else. And a *glorified* body?!? What is *that*? It's *way* beyond our grasp at this point. Will I really see Bonnie and my other brothers and sisters in Christ, but not my familial ones? This is the million-dollar question. I told Mark that maybe being in Heaven with Jesus will be like a parent holding her infant close and adoringly; Mark said he thought it would be boring just sitting there. We had a laugh over that. Maybe it's like a great big party where everybody is communing and conjoining with hearty conviviality. Think back to when Jesus was making wine, giving bread, and doing a lot of really relational interacting with people. *That* should be our sneak preview! After all, Jesus is the living body of God Himself. If that's what God is like, then maybe that's what Heaven will be like us when we are there. "Oh, it's going to be better than we ever could've imagined!" Mark exclaimed. He went on to explain that no one *makes* another lose the opportunity to be with or choose Jesus. Even Judas had a chance to have changed his mind. At the Last Supper, when Christ spoke to Judas and said something to the effect for him to go and do what he needed to do, that could've been an opportunity for Judas to have turned around. He didn't *have* to do what he did; no one forced him. In fact, we also know that he had great remorse *after* he did so. Mark said he bet Jesus hoped that Judas would have changed his mind. I also wondered if the Holy Spirit who indwells my living soul *now* will *also* still be within me after I die. And if so, what would be His purpose *then*, as I will be in the direct presence of my Father and Christ? I was hoping the seal wouldn't be broken and that He would still reside in me in Heaven! I have faith He will, but in what capacity would He be such for me then? Why, the whole confluence of the Big Three for me might change in that sphere. On the other hand, I could also see that this seeming nit-picking question might turn out to be a moot point because I'd be with the Triune all at once. I kept trying to unravel, juggle, and clutch in my grasp the *Hims* of the Trinity! *Lord*!

7.6 Temptation for Jesus and Re-Gifting

Just when I thought I was getting somewhere with the Trinity, it folded back on itself in my mind, and my understanding collapsed, and the sense of it was gone. Most of the time, I had less trouble accepting Christ's full divinity — His witnessed Resurrection dispels all doubts within me — than I did His also being fully a man, replete with a dynamic range of feelings, passions, and pains. Therefore, when I thought about Him in the desert, I also couldn't imagine that there would've been *any* kind of temptation for Him, you know, with He being God and all. I mean, I *know* He was hungry and thirsty out in the desert, but would the empty promises that Satan uttered *really* have been enough to lure Him away from His Father? No way, José! It doesn't seem like there would even have been a flicker of a thought or doubt in Him. Of course, with Jesus being one with His Father, there is no way that He could sin, but the fact that He was out there in the desert for forty days of fasting indeed *put Him in a physically compromised state.* Maybe this is all that is meant. He wasn't *morally* tempted, but He got to know how hard it is for us in our weakened state. When I'm hungry and tired, I'm hardly at my best, emotionally speaking! When I am running on empty, I say and do thoughtless, stupid, or mean things. We will never know the mind of Jesus at this time, but we do know He would have been at His most vulnerable at this point. Jesus could not have sinned, but He would most certainly have felt physically weak and depleted, as He was also fully human. Though He did not succumb to the offers of relief and power by Satan, He had to get to know precisely what we in the flesh feel so He could stand perfectly in our stead at the cross. How else could taking our place, this complete and voluntary exchange, occur if He weren't like us? I wonder what it is like to limit oneself and one's power to the degree that He intentionally did. It would probably have been like living among a bunch of ten-year-olds and keeping mum about this and that which they needn't know or couldn't take. While He was living in the flesh, he was able to fully sympathize with how *we* feel, yet He never compromised His character or mission.

    This topic of temptation led me to another question which I was able to answer for myself reasonably quickly. If God sent and used His Son to take the punishment due us to reconcile us to Him, wouldn't it be like if I re-gifted a present and gave it to someone else? In other words, is Jesus' sacrificial present devalued since *I* didn't purchase, pay the price, or take the licks due *me* for my lifetime of wrongdoings? Maybe I needed help with the fundamental idea of a gift with no strings attached. How can it be that I need merely and freely take this profound and precious gift? It is I who feels compelled to attach a string the likes of giving myself right back to Him! Jesus' sacrifice for us, that is, taking the punishment due us to satisfy the parent in God who cannot *not* discipline us for our transgressions, is *not* a re-gifting of His Son's supreme expression of love to me. As unimaginable or odd as it sounds, He *wanted* to die for me. Even though He was sent, He still had to agree, had to sign up and say, "Yes," to His Father; because of their perfect union, it could have been no other way. Therefore, it is *not* that God is "using" Jesus as an indirect method of gifting us with reconciliation; it's because, being incorporeal, He can't do the job Himself. He, as God the Father, has a *different* role. It's like I write the letter, but the postman delivers the letter. His Son, totally equal in stature, is the only one who could choose to leave His Father temporarily to reset the balance between us fair and square and once and for all humanity's stained state such that we could even come back to Him. It's more like *the present chose to come to us*, but we have to take the gift in our hands to know the awesomeness of the present *and* the one who sent it. Jesus chose to die for me because both He and, by full extension, His Father — now *my* Father — loved me so much that He died for me two thousand years ago. It might as well have been yesterday because it's no different, and time certainly hasn't changed people's basic impulses. This is *not* a re-gifting; it is the primary gift of pure love to be able to rejoin my Father in Heaven. Christ's death is God's first fruits to us! I had previously made a false analogy of the rich man hiring a substitute during the Civil War, so that he wouldn't have to fight and risk death.

This is not a valid analogy because in the situation with Jesus, Jesus did it for *free*, and He did it *willingly*. He was not sought out or bought out or forced; He volunteered!

7.7 Large in My Smallness

I also wanted to share another minor epiphany I had regarding God's use of me. I've been so used to thinking and saying that I'm so small and God is so far away. Well, I'm in 2 Samuel right now, and when God chose a little nobody of a shepherd boy, David, to kill Goliath, I realized that I'm nothing but a little shepherd girl who also faces many Goliaths. One does not have to start out a warrior or king for God to use him or her. If God can do that with David or Sarah or Mary or Paul and countless other ordinary folks, God can do much with me. So, it's not that I'm so small but that God is so big and can wrap His expansive, loving arms around me and expend me as long as I have breath in my lungs and say "Yes" to Him. God and Jesus do *not* push or force their way; they do but beckon. Emily Dickinson personified death in a manner that for me applies to God: "His Civility." One of my very favorite memories of my father is of him enthusiastically calling for young me to jump out in the deep end and come to him out in the water. I couldn't wait to leap into his open arms! The desire to rush to Jesus was much the same; it will always be just a second ago in my heart that this happened as I keep following Him along, like a baby duck after its mamma, like a starving man hungry for His manna.

7.8 What Now? Another Look at Jesus within the Trinity

If you want to figure out the will of God for you as a Christian, then you only need to recall that God is living inside you; therefore, you always have direct access to Him. Psalm 37 paraphrased says something to the effect that if we seek the will of God, then the will of God will unite with and then become our will. Once you have salvation, then the Holy Spirit, the one who knows the will of God, takes up permanent residence in you. With God dwelling inside me, it's a matter of continually watching for Him to manifest Himself, whether in Scripture or through events, people, and life. Such situations that arise may turn out to be not mere chance coincidences but proof that He is with you or that that moment was brought about for you to witness Him. When you seek the will of God, you may also crave seeing His love being made manifest all the more and vice versa. After all, as Mark pointed out, Jesus' love points back to and demonstrates His God's wondrous mercy and vast will. Again, I come back to the intertwined and indivisible flow: all three refer to and back forth to each other fluidly, organically. If you love Jesus, then you will love the Father because the Father created the Son for our sake. The Son has the Holy Spirit dwelling in Him just as we believers also have His Spirit in us the moment we accept Christ's mercy. Despite our desire and valiant attempts to do right, all the while knowing that we can't be perfect due to persistent misuse of free will, God must've said, "Well, bless their hearts!" I'm sure Jesus would've rolled His eyes in exasperation a *lot* if He were just a touch more like us. Instead, I think He probably *sighed* more than we're aware; we do know He wept (John 11:35 NIV). We also witness His righteous indignation at the Temple, which they'd basically turned into a market. Father *and* Son probably winced in pain or even clenched their fists at all our tomfoolery and senseless cruelty. God foreplanned a time in human history to manifest that which had been *anticipated* through the faith of those alive centuries ago and which is now trusted by us today *looking back* to this pinnacle moment in human history: the advent of Jesus at the cross. Did you know Emanuel means "God is with us"? Nowadays, I love uttering His titles, like "King," "Lord," and "Messiah," which comes from the Hebrew word "Mashiach," better known as "Christ" from the Greek word "Christos," meaning "anointed one" or "chosen one." By the way, my own surname has its roots in Him, too! Did you notice? So cool!!

When I wake up every morning, even if I'm tired, I still make a beeline for my Bible because I can't get my fill of reading His Word. Plus, when you pray, you need to be a little bit quiet, too, so that God or the Holy Spirit can have a chance to talk to you. For me, when I hear from God, it feels like He stirs my silence with small tremors of exultation, moving affirmation, or conviction of what He intends to convey to me. The best way to describe this sensation of His communication is through the *faintly perceptible stirrings in my heart* I get while I'm reading that I cannot produce of my own accord. They feel like itsy-bitsy cheers or confirmations or tiny tugs about this or that. Sometimes the words leap off the page and hit me square between the eyes because the concept is so spot-on, novel, or striking in its truth. Such moving experiences neither happen daily nor on command.

Sometimes different passages I have been reading seem to miraculously line up for a double-dose of a message that I sense that I am supposed to know, and I am keenly aware of His involvement. I try to ask less, be thankful for more, and really listen to Him. I also know it is okay to make requests in His name. I think He likes our dependence; it shows trust. If you get frustrated over your wandering or busy mind, that's simply because praying is new for you; you must develop a tender self-discipline and wait it out. The flow of communication will mystically and organically come. It'll grow to become a conversation between you and God, but you know you are His. Of course, things come up or happen which can divert your energies. He's still there; still, He should get your first fruits.

I love that Jesus hiked up mountains to get away from folks to pray all through the night. He did so for *hours* at a stretch! God will not show up when I'm pouting and demanding; He loves a meek, mild, and gentle stance. Anyway, He's never *not* with me because His Spirit and I are joined at the heart, and mine's on fire. He's already there with me and ever-ready for my prayers. And "where two or more have gathered in His name" (Matthew 18:20), it's a *guarantee* He's with us! There's another reason to worship in church! I also believe that although God *hears* the prayers of all, He especially *listens* intently to the prayers of a believer. We've got home-court advantage because the Holy Spirit is interceding on our behalf. That may sound harsh or preferential, but He probably thinks it stinks when a person turns his back on Him.

How do I *know* I'm saved and not duped by the Devil? Though Satan is temporarily the "ruler of this world" (John 12:31) and the "prince of the power of the air" (Ephesians 2:2), he cannot be my father because I *crave* reading and studying God's Word and because I can't get enough of talking about Christ! If it's possible to say so, it's like I'm lovestruck for Him. People who are Christian have God as their Heavenly Father, not Satan, and their actions and choices reflect this. I wouldn't want to engage with my Father the way I do if I *weren't* saved. That wouldn't make sense. I'm also *not* going through life obliviously, and there's nothing out there that seduces or induces me to sell my soul to have it all. Oh, I can lose my temper, not to mention my cool, but I'm not losing my salvation. The very thought of dabbling with evil in the forms that used to intoxicate me now brings about terror and the music that accompanies the shark in the movie *Jaws*. What propels me to want to do more with my life is that I want to please Him and do as He would have me do! If I *had* remained in the world, my focus would be on satisfying myself, all the while rationalizing about my relative goodness compared to others and unknowingly succumbing to Satan's tailor-made seductions for me to sinning, ultimately leading to self-destruction. I don't mean to be dramatic: demise comes in all forms and shapes: everything from abuse, neglect, or hatred. We all know a thousand more.

What you already love can become better. For example, I enjoy traveling very much, but now I have a greater appreciation and enjoyment of it as a gift from my Father; I am not taking quixotic adventures to find some pot of gold. I now want to *share Him as I travel!* Could there be even more in store? It would have been easy for me to have kept reading *man's* thoughts and not have delved in His Word. After all, Greeks love philosophy, that is, man's wisdom. To be fair, I don't see anything wrong with studying various religious systems! It's just that now I am aware of their limited and incomplete scope, no matter how brilliantly conceived or what points have been introduced. For the ultimate tie-breaker that shifts the weight of God's Word to eternal significance, my go-to of proof comes from Matthew 7:13–14. He tells us to "enter through the narrow gate; for *the gate is wide and the way is broad that leads to destruction*, and there are many who enter through it. For the gate is small and *the way is narrow that leads to life*, and there are few who find it" (emphasis mine). Whew! I'm beyond glad and grateful I *did* find it! What that others I know would! Jesus' singularly announcing of Himself, "I am the way" (John 14:6), which contrasts sharply with the varied and, yes, attractive paths to a higher power. Such ideals as compassion, peace, enlightenment, bliss, nirvana, and the like may be brilliant and contain pleasing pillars of truths, but *none* of them speak to a personal love, a sacrificial love, and an eternal and ongoing relationship with a *living* God who is love. All religions can't be right; that would make right not correct anymore because these multiple rights will invariably conflict with one another by the plain fact of being different. There has *got* to be a standard, and there is. Who *else* says, "*I am* the way, the truth, and the life?" (John 14:6, emphasis mine). Only Jesus! (And, by the way, there's also plenty of evidence to prove He wasn't deranged, deluded, or insane.) Jesus doesn't use the indefinite article and modestly utter of Himself, "*a* truth, *a* way, *a* life"! Only God, who also contains Jesus, says of Himself, "I am who I am" (Exodus 3:14)! Sometimes when I can't unravel or unpack something I've learned, I permit myself to let it go because there will never be a time when I have it anywhere near all figured out this side of Heaven. I'm still grateful I was open to Him; so many people I know who reject His divinity do so because they follow what they can wrap their minds around or acquire what they can in this world, and such seems enough. This is not my experience.

God did not create various philosophies and religions for us to have a bunch of choices to come to Him, scintillating and valuable in their own right, might though they may be. All ideas but one come from *man's* intellect. Why are there so many religions out there anyway? God built into and fashioned within us a deep desire, a need to know Him. Many have accepted alternate answers to be able to satisfy the question as to why we are here or who/what made us. Each has his own life's path to find the way, but it is not a given that he will. All roads *can* lead to Him *if* one doesn't get stuck in a dead-end or cul-de-sac! My brain flipped back to Walt Whitman's words, "Not I, nor anyone else can travel that road for you. You must travel it by yourself." How right! You can't force anyone to move from making castles in a sandbox to the castle itself. When you consider other religious leaders, prophets, or elders, please keep in mind that only Christ claims Godhood. He alone died for us, and only Jesus performed miracles — suspended (not altered or masked) the very laws of nature — to verify His authoritative rank. When I think about the moment in time that made my salvation possible and fast-forward to today, I get dizzied. It is as if the Crucifixion were just yesterday afternoon or that I was there in the Upper Room with Him! An important way to recreate this sense of union with Him is to worship corporately in His church, which is also called His "*bride*," wayward though she may be at times. Of course, man's institution of the church is *far* from perfect, but that it is not what I might hope for or has disappointed me ought not to stop, prevent, or inhibit me from praising and worshipping *"the groom"*! Not seeing the splendid forest for a rotten tree would be a crying shame. Though I did so for half my life, I no longer will; I can't *not* attend church even if I might smart from moments of frustration or painful actions taken by uncharitable but well-intended members with whom I disagree. That would be like throwing the baby in the manger away with the bathwater!! If I get temporarily tripped up about something in church, I've got to put on my rain-gear and don the attitude I learned long ago from a couple of mottos from A.A.: "Take what you need and leave the rest," and it's all about "principles over personalities." Mark, too, would advise me to "eat the fish, but spit out the bones." This is not always easy, but I might be one such "personality" for another, too! A little later on, personal sacrifice related to Christ would become more than an academic topic for me, as you shall see.

When I try to imagine the event of the Crucifixion, where and when He took the excruciating hit for me, I gradually began to flip the idea of sacrifice around in my mind such that I wondered what it would look like for me to lay down my life and desires for Him. Could I? That day back in college when I ran out of the Baptist church I'd visited when I heard preached that I would "have to die" and "lose yourself," I now understood!! Less of me equals more of Him, and the best way to show Him is through the uniqueness He created in me. Christ lives in me, so I am set free to be more of me, the me I was designed and meant to live out! It's just that now I recognize it's all about *Him*! We never get satisfied in this life with any sense of permanence if we think that it's all about *us*, beguiling and natural though this is! Salvation initiates one's lifetime journey of sanctification, that is, being set apart to become more and more devoted to living and being like Him. This is a challenge like no other; in fact, it is impossible, but how could I not try? I'm here, aren't I? And hopefully, as in my years of building up sobriety, whereby maturation, wisdom, and trying for selflessness come "sometimes quickly, sometimes slowly," I will not feed selfishness but try to grow my God-given talents for Him for *His* glory. I am waiting for the day when, as that A.A. describes it, "self-seeking will slip away"! This *so* hasn't happened yet! In spite of everything I've gone through and done, I am told that I am "fearfully and wonderfully made" (Psalm 139:14), so even if there is a crisis of faith or a moment that temporarily blocks my understanding, this teacher prays to Him with head and heart, "Teach me to do Your will" (Psalm 143:10). Everyone seeks the holy grail of perfection or happiness in some form or fashion. The Chosen People surely did. The Jewish people of His day were astonished that Jesus proclaimed that He came from the Father; He certainly didn't act like it from their perspective. He was way too inclusive for this elitist group! Oh, how they missed the boat! These people may have had the credentials that they were from Abraham (in other words, not illegitimate), but Jesus informed them the mic-dropping news that "today this Scripture is fulfilled" (Luke 4:21). In other words, He, the Messiah, has arrived. He didn't fit their bill then any more than He does for many today. But again, I ask you, who but He introduced such a radical concept and extreme expression of mercy and grace? Vengeance, justice, retaliation, and retribution *still* feel more natural to our fleshy selves! In class, I used to try to capture just how underwhelmed Jesus' fellow Jews were by telling my students to imagine *their* senior class president announcing a brand-new policy that he'd *also* like to represent *freshmen* and kids from *another* school. He would have been heckled, and they would have jeered, "You're not our guy!" Same idea, but different scale. My students understood and were not a little amazed. Before Jesus' time, folks had always and only known that you were to get what you deserved, not realizing that *everyone* falls short of God's standard. Anyway, following a bunch of rules isn't really the point: sure, obedience-training *is* a part, but discipline and sacrifices are made in order to *lead us to be more loving toward others like He is*! Meanwhile, I persisted in looking past the present of my life.

It's not a cop-out or sign of weakness to remind myself in *I've only just begun* in this new life that won't end when I die. "Who would want to live eternally?" you might ask. "Ashes to ashes and dust to dust" still hold true, but your *spirit* can't be terminated. In a sense, it's relocated, but not to a place of neutrality. It's Heaven or Hell, baby. Speaking of Hell, I used to not even believe in the Devil. Threatening time eternal in a lake of fire and presenting foul depictions of the Devil we've all seen in horror movies just seemed like Scare Tactic #1 for behavior modification. "Poppycock!' I would say. I can now clearly see that this is precisely what Satan wants: for us to outsmart ourselves into a lull of self-satisfaction! If we don't think that hell or the devil exists, we are also likely to disbelieve in God and the reality of impending judgment. If he can stall us long enough so that we miss out and don't contend with the choice-of-our-lifetime, then he's got us in the corner pocket. Then we become a lame *and* sitting duck, ignorant or obtuse to what's in store for us if we either say nothing or "No" to God: eternal and anguishing separation from Him. Now *that's* Hell! In short, let me assure you that the Devil is not a figment of your (or Hollywood's) imagination, something that's not a real creation, or some force with no punch! Before I get on my high horse or any soapbox, let me cut myself off at the knees. I am no scholar, pastor, theologian, or expert by any stretch of the imagination! Let me remind you that you are witnessing in my messy growth and, perhaps, annoying enthusiasm, a chomping at the bit to share Him with you even while I'm in my infancy. Is there anything big enough in *your* life to transport you, to prompt you to an evangelizing action? Such an event or occurrence hadn't yet for me until now. I would receive advice to harness and channel this savage and radical love. Life would provide me with more lessons soon enough to add depth and grit to my maturation.

7.9 Feeling Frustrated and Learning Forgiveness

At about this time, Mark challenged and called me out on my own judgmental and arrogant tendencies. I had started to vocalize faultfinding with some personalities in the church and even with church life itself. He wanted to know why I had taken a turn of being critical-minded or impatient. I had gotten myself all worked up again and became uncharacteristically pessimistic because I thought the Church wasn't maturing fast enough or doing more things in ways *I* thought it should. I was also frustrated with myself for not taking a greater part in church development. I started to focus on the differences or even (what I thought of as) small-mindedness in the people I saw and heard around me from this modest rural community. Mark asked, "Well, what do you think about *Paul?*" By taking me to task about one biblical person in particular who has been criticized for exclusivity, I knew Mark was testing me. Why did Mark jump to Paul in particular? Mark knew I had become captivated by Paul, and he was aware that I was in the middle of studying his letters for the first time. They are dripping with stunning logic, passion, and a keen and unique display of faith. Still, there are those who fault him for being litigious and even misogynistic. Regarding Mark's insinuation that if I was disappointed by church members, then what might I think about Mr. Paul, I quickly replied, "Oh, I can forgive Paul — he's just an old Jew!" What I meant was, Saul-turned-Paul was by training, birthright, pedigree, and faith, a *supreme* rule-follower, so how could he not still occasionally display vestiges of his old way of thinking even in his new fidelity to Christ? Mark immediately jumped on my reply as his launching point. He raised his eyebrows and said, "That's *exactly* how *you* need to think about people you believe misunderstand or missay things!!" I took this to mean good-intentioned and zealous church members that get to splitting hairs or categorizing those who they think are or are not "in," as if God checks in with *them* about who gets saved. Judgment is *God's* job; only He sees our hearts and knows us fully. In short, I, too, ought not to expect people in the church to act perfectly. *I* surely don't!! The Church does not yet behave in the manner I see that Jesus asks us to, so as I hope for patience and love from others, I need to extend grace and patience toward my brothers and sisters in the church, both here and at large! Who am I to condemn anybody on active route to Him? I can't make fun of churches or churchgoers; that puts me on even footing with the very ones with whom I find fault!! When I become like them, albeit in a different appearance, I become my own worst enemy! Come high water, *I must be the change I want to see in others*! I then remember that Satan will never stop trying to "steal, kill, or destroy" (John 10:10 KJV) me by any means possible. Never. That's the Liar's job. He will satisfy himself with neutralizing us, too. Mark gave real examples where this is so, even for him, some twenty-five years a Christian. He then said that each of us is either "approaching, going through, or leaving a storm." It is in those times I've got to try to be extra close to God. Finally, there will always be Scripturally ignorant people. Always. There are *still* Pharisees and legalists. If I can overlook or forgive Paul for being so, Mark said that I need to forgive other people in Church today, too. After all, Jesus forgave and loves me. At the end of his visit, Mark looked me dead-on and intently into my eyes, and he hit me with a blow-dart of truth: "*You are full of self-pity right now.*" I took it in and looked back at him in shame, my tears hot, full, and burning, pooling up in the corners of my eyes, and I said, "I absolutely loathe self-pity." He replied softly, "I know..." Then he said, "I am your friend, and I would want you to tell me that." I told him that his coming to visit was "like burping a baby." He also said that he loved me and was proud of me. Wanting to please Christ would have interesting consequences for my life's priorities, and that included the people chose to be with

7.10 No Honor in the Hometown

My putting church before my family has been noticed. Yes, of course, I love my family, but I crave Christian fellowship and learning more about Christ. There's so much I have to bridle my tongue over. I don't want to shut up *or* to be a turn-off in my passion for Christ. Nobody wants to hang around a radical or someone with a one-track mind; you can't talk to them. I've also learned that it's not safe to talk about religion in most places. Yet I know my purpose in some form or fashion is to be His ambassador. I want to grow up and shine for Him, but it's so challenging with those I know who *don't* believe in Christ's divinity. Their stance is, "Yes, to God, but Christ — eh, not so much." (My heart is beating fast now.) It's not so much that *I* am unaccepted, as much as this new part of me is a source of consternation or curiosity. It's as if I had discovered the joys of pro-football and wanted to engage with others who could care less about sports in general. Again, I get that! I think an underlying source of resistance or reluctance for non-Christians to talk about Jesus is that Christians believe they've got the corner market on understanding the big why's and how's. On top of that, so many Christians have a reputation as being judgmental and hypocritical. Religion is supposed to be *personal*, so much so that I need to approach all with respect and caution. Anyway, why would I venture into others' beliefs that are none of my business? The unspoken rule in this land of the free and home of the brave is that one is not supposed to talk about religion or politics because it can lead to heated arguments; therefore, Christians often default to neutrality, play it safe, and keep mum. I'm not wired like that, so I can feel stuck and unprepared, as if I'm an alien, muzzled and contained. And so, I pray the following: "*God, help me. Help me to love people and not fall in mind-traps, like the Devil's minefield of despair or futility.*" Breaking through to non-believers won't, can't happen overnight. It took me *decades* to come to Him! I pray I do not alienate or give up on my family or that I become the cause for wrangling among them. I've been slapped on the wrist more than once for bringing Him up with non-believing family members, especially their children, even if it was these kids who brought up the topic with me. I have come home early from a visit with my family of origin expressly to attend church, but while leaving town to do so, I concurrently felt dissatisfied because I want so much more with and for my family! I have looked up online and attended a church that looked to be a good match for me to attend while visiting, and I'm glad I did. Even before becoming a Christian, I would leave early so I could make it back in time to go to my home A.A. group on Sunday morning, but this was done privately and for self-preservation's sake. It's not that I felt *they* were missing out or that I somehow needed to *share* that with them. I suppose it is good that my devotion and love for Christ are being noticed. I must be loving and patient because even without uttering His name and until such a time is right that I can and do bring Him up, I can still impact others through their (unknowingly) seeing Him in me. Dealing with unresolved issues from the past can muck up my walk and representation, so I have to find a *new* way — *His* way— to deal with people from my past, especially family. I don't want to get gnarly and tangled-up or let past ways interfere with the present and future. I am the one who is showing my family Christ, and rather than give some unsolicited monologue or lecture, I need only to *love my family unconditionally*. I mustn't wrangle with words; I *have* to learn to let go of old grudges, past hurts, and Pavlovian responses. If I can only let my love for Christ shine, even while thinking that I'm not getting through or maybe even because it feels so difficult, like I'm banging my head on a very familiar wall, Christ is doing His best work through me to influence the ones I love so much. What more likely way are they to come to know the love of Jesus, heart wide-open, than through me? It might take years; it might take an instant; that's God's call. The chance to talk about did come up, and it happened, of course, on Easter.

7.11 Kyrie Eleison! Lord, Have Mercy!

Speaking of visiting family, when I was visiting my brother this past Easter, for some reason, I got up at 6:30 and went straight down to the kitchen and knelt on the cold tile kitchen floor. Facing the sunrise, I started praying intently because up to then, I had pretty much decided that I wasn't going to attend any church there unless it was the Greek Church and only if Stephen wanted to go, too. I wasn't going to press the matter. I was in the middle of letting the situation go and praying to God that things could go the way *He* wanted. I was also weeping because things were certainly not going the way *I'd* had hoped they would; I felt defeated. About an hour later, Bonnie came down and said, "I *do* want to go to church, you know, that one we looked up online, at the 9:15 service." A few minutes after that, my brother, Stephen, and his seven-year-old daughter, Cindy, had gotten up, and I told him we had decided to stay and attend a contemporary, non-denominational church in town after all. I think Stephen was a bit surprised, and right then, for the *second* time, Cindy asked him if they could go to church, too. Stephen again did not answer her. So, Bonnie and I left for that Church of Grace we'd looked up online to be able to worship that morning. After the service was over, I texted Stephen that we were on our way home, and he texted me right back and asked, "How would you like to go to the Greek Church??" Without hesitation, I enthusiastically answered, "Absolutely!!" By the time we got home ten minutes later, Stephen, Cindy, and Vincent were coming downstairs; I didn't even go past the front door to go inside; we piled up in his minivan and headed straight to the local Greek Orthodox Church. Bonnie stayed behind because she said "she wasn't Greek,' but later, she told me she wanted to give me some time alone with them. As we were driving there and I was telling my brother about the service we'd just come from, Vincent burst out laughing in the back seat because he heard me use the word "nondenominational," and it sounded to him like something from his math class.

As I was relating to Stephen all about this church, and I made it a point to appeal to him by focusing on the fact that the congregation seemed to be educated and that the pastor's focus was on proving that the Bible was more than just a historical or some inspirational book. Their pastor had said that the Bible had merit and meaning for our lives today; in fact, this young pastor went over arguments proving the Bible's credibility and veracity. He used familiar books as props to make his point that we need the Bible as a life manual as much as we would turn to the encyclopedia for general knowledge, a car owner's manual for figuring out how our car runs, and a phone book for acquiring contact information. He stated that the Bible is *the* singular book that both gives wisdom *and* offers the means to salvation, but it is unlike any other book in that it possesses more than mere information. Reading it will engage you in a manner heretofore not experienced. How could it not be considering its Author? To prove its historicity, reliability, and merit, this pastor then made comparison-contrasts to other books we rely on without a thought. He also referenced a Christian theology book, one whose title I was totally captivated by: *I Don't Have Enough Faith To Be an Atheist*. Just as we pulled into the Greek Church's parking lot, I finished up telling my brother about being at this service. I said that they even had a station up front for you to light a candle in remembrance of someone or for you to make a special prayer.

At this local and very small Greek Church which our father had attended, my nephew, Vincent, walked right up to the front like he owned the place, and we sat in the second row together; after he dropped Cindy off in the children's room, Stephen joined us. I quietly whispered jokingly to Stephen that I used to bar-hop, now here I was church-hopping. I have to tell you that in the Greek Church, the stand-to-sit ratio is pretty much the opposite of what it is in the Protestant Church. Vincent had questions in church about this or that icon, and I would always answer every question he had the best that I could and in a manner appealing to one his age. Toward the end of the service, they offered communion, and Vincent said he wanted to take communion, and I asked, "Do you understand why?" And he said (or mouthed), "Yes, that the bread is Christ's body and the wine represents His blood." In reality, I know he was fascinated by the small silver spoon with the long handle and the crimson velvet napkin held by the priest so you wouldn't drop anything as he asked for your word of honor that you'd prepared yourself for communion. Their communion compound is made up of warm, homemade bread that has been mixed and mashed with a thimbleful of wine, all contained in one large vessel. This couldn't be more opposite to the hermetically-sealed, tiny, plastic container containing grape juice and a clean, crisp wafer separate you find provided in Protestant churches. So, I went up with Vincent and took communion first, and then he followed suit. I hoped that the impact of what we were doing would be more than mimicked form for him one day.

Meanwhile, as I was sitting with Stephen, I could tell he was getting a bit anxious because he realized that there was to be an extra service tacked-on to the regular service. Stephen was feeling antsy and trapped. You have to know that attending the Greek Orthodox Church (*especially* if on an infrequent basis) is like being in an endurance contest; time stands still. We both love the sound of the deep male cantors' voices joining in unison with the parishioners' when it's time to sing, "Lord, Have Mercy" (as you're praying for yourself, "And how!!"). Anyway, I found myself quietly defining for Stephen the Greek terminology for what Protestants refer to as sins of "omission" and "commission." On our way home, I also informed Stephen about two guys in particular he did not know about but had heard mentioned today: Joseph of Arimathea and Nicodemus. I started to explain to Stephen about the burial of Christ and why it was such a big deal to bury Him in the first place (as opposed to letting the dogs eat the corpse in some ditch). The Jewish leaders were upset because it gave the opportunity for there to even be a resurrected body and the fulfillment of prophecy, not to mention trouble for them, in that such would lower *their* status. Anyway, as I was saying all this, Stephen up and asked me, "Who *is* Pontius Pilate anyway?" He had been silent, taking it all in, yet the day before, when I was telling him about going up to Boston and hearing the sermon proclaiming, "We are all 'Pontius Pilates' if we turned our back on suffering Christians," he said nothing. I didn't look or act shocked or anything because, after all, I hadn't known who the Holy Spirit was until a couple of years ago. I told Stephen all about Pontius Pilate, that he knew he was condemning an innocent man, that he was all about job security and self-protection, and that the Jews were upset because Jesus said of Himself that He was the Son of God. And then, encouraged by his reception and curiosity, I went on to say how awesome it was the Jesus chose to first reveal Himself in His resurrected form to Mary Magdalene, a woman. He told her to run ahead and tell the boys, that He'd be there soon, and then He went in and showed Himself to them, ate with them, and then sweetly hung around with them and others for forty days. There were eyewitnesses to the fact that He was there in His new state and resurrected form. My brother was like a sponge, it seemed.

The conversation then turned to John, the only man and Disciple of Jesus among the group of women at the foot of the cross, so Stephen then asked me, "Do you mean John the Baptist?" I softly shook my head and proceeded to explain who this John was, that later, he became the last Apostle standing, that all the rest were killed defending their faith, and that he died an elderly man exiled to the Greek island of Patmos. A few years later, I would show this place to my brother in person. And then I began to get excited to share with Stephen who John the Baptist was, since it was Stephen who brought him up. I started out with the special moment just before he was even born. It's fantastic to imagine how John's mother, Elizabeth, while pregnant with him, felt her belly stir the moment her cousin, Mary, pregnant with Jesus, came walking into the house to visit her. Even little John somehow prenatally knew and got excited by His Messiah being nearby in the next womb! I had turned to face Stephen in the front passenger seat of his van, and I guess Vincent was taking it all in the seat behind us; I hadn't even thought about Vincent being behind me. Then I got to the part when Jesus was ready to begin His ministry at the age of thirty, and He asked John the Baptist to baptize Him. This was the historic marker where John followed orders to "make straight the way of the Lord" (John 1:23); John was so influential, he had to clarify for folks that "I baptize in water, *but* among you stands One. . . the thong of whose sandal I am not worthy to untie" (from John 1:26–27). In anticipation of his question, I rhetorically asked Stephen, "Now, why do you think *Jesus* would get baptized? *He* certainly didn't need saving. This act was to serve as a model for us." And all of a sudden and out of nowhere, Vincent burst out from the back seat, "*I* want to get baptized!!" I whipped around, my face all happy, and I asked him,

"That's awesome, but what does that mean, 'to get baptized'??" And he says, "It means I believe in Jesus!" You can imagine that I about jumped out of my skin and skyrocketed to the moon, and I so exclaimed to him, "Did you know that Jesus died for *you*?!" And I emphasize the word "you," and he said, "Yes!" And he repeated those words," Jesus died for *me*!" like he knew it to be a truth that he had just taken in. I'm *so* glad I recorded this in writing then because it's now hard to believe it actually occurred. And again, Vincent asked, "Can I get baptized??" I turned back around and just looked at Stephen wide-eyed, and Stephen said nothing for the third time that day, but at least he was smiling. There is no way I saw this situation that just happened coming! I'm telling you, if there'd been even a puddle outside, I would've stopped the van for him! To add to this, not even two years earlier, when somehow our conversation turned to the movie, *The Godfather*, Vincent asked me what a "godfather" was. When I explained it to him, his reflexive and immediate response to me was, "Well, then I guess *you're* my godmother!" Though I just smiled broadly at him, you could have knocked me over with a feather; I was sky high in joy. However, his brother, Robert, though less talkative, possessed the still-waters-run-deep temperament. He also had a sound and thoughtful character which is often more receptive to such meaningful talks, and I yearned for the day when I could have such with him if invited. This love I felt for them both was equally powerful, though my relationship with each was different.

After that moment, I shifted the conversation to reassure Stephen that I was not abandoning my heritage by not going to the Greek Church! Protestantism helped me realize that my *emotional* attachment to the Greek Orthodox Church has *nothing* to do with Christ in me. Who would I be kidding by saying the Greek Church did it for me *religiously*? Being in the Greek Church is wonderful for my being aware of the millennial continuity of this Church and the constancy of its service, liturgy, and it's just *being there*, day in and year out, etc. No Protestant Church can compare here! However, I told Stephen point-blank that I did not sense Jesus with me in the Greek Church, just a bunch of familiar-looking, swarthy Greeks, endearing (and enduring) Byzantine icons, pleasing incense, and narcotizing intones, all of which made me feel warm and connected, like I belonged, but in an emotional and familial way. My focus had now shifted to *Jesus*, not to all that was a part of the church, pleasing though it may be, and that included the service being spoke and sung in Greek, the priest's bells, candles, the iconostasis, and history which oozes from this church, new though the building may be. I told Stephen that everything here is done by rote memory and formulaically counted, including how many times to swing the (frankincense, of course) incense censer, which I *loved*. When we got home, my brother grilled chops, and I made Lebanese coleslaw; these moments had passed, but later I told Stephen if Vincent ever really wanted to get baptized, to please let me be his godmother, and he agreed. That may be the twelfth of never, but in a way, it felt it was *so* close to happening today. I realize that things happen in their own time and way, and I know that this is just one small story, but it was a significant moment because at least it was a start, although now it's a faded memory.

Bonnie said we were being good role models and quiet examples for even going to church that morning. I'm excited inside that my family had this particular Easter experience and that they may have been positively impacted, even if in a small way. My mind began to grasp at and fathom God's bigger picture. In particular, I marveled at how masterfully and with intentionality He weaves events, people, and circumstances together for His good purpose. I was beginning to see that retrospect or my hindsight of recognizing God's cause and effect of events lining up hardly matched my understanding of what was going on in the moment. Later, I would begin to try to read into seemingly disconnected, odd occurrences and wonder what God might have in store for them in the future. The result is not a fixed or sure thing. However, in terms of matters of faith, I still toss the coin in favor of free will trumping predestiny. His complete foreknowledge of what is to be, including who gets saved, is *not* the same thing as causation. It also occurred to me that if God dwells in eternity, a dimension incomprehensible to humans, all actions and circumstances transpire in some perpetual present; therefore, the way we view sequencing and the cause-effect of events is not applicable to God's involvement in the flow of life. I am one of the Elect not because God foreordained it, but because in the perfect moment He gave me, I gladly took it.

7.12 LOOKING FORWARD TO GREECE IN A NEW WAY

As the school year wound up, I looked back at what had been now just over two years of slow-mo, but cataclysmic change within me. I could only wonder what the future would look like. Though it goes beyond the scope of this writing to speak of my summer travels, both leading students abroad for roughly a couple of weeks in June, not to mention sojourns of my own, I am compelled to speak about this upcoming summer's seven-week trip to Greece. Sometime well over a year ago, I must have been telling Mark about Greece, a topic near and dear to my heart, so much so that I can't recall the specific moment when the idea of having Mark going there, too, came up and took. Bonnie, however, did duly note and remembered. For Mark to be in Greece seemed so natural; his personality and emotional outlook were not dissimilar to that of the Greek temperament. I'm sure I must've indulged in this vision with him frequently because I just knew he would absolutely love it there, that it would be pleasing to his free spirit and optimistic and joyful nature. Why, we could bring to the history of Paul's mission work to life! Plus, it's hard to get me to stop talking about Greece! I do recall late that previous summer talking with Mark about what it must have been like for Paul, the greatest missionary who ever lived, to travel through *Greece*. In my exuberance, I exclaimed that I wished *I* could show Mark Greece, that it would be *so* great; he would love it! His light and free spirit got caught up in the wonderment of imagining being there and walking among ruins, surrounded by the azure Mediterranean waters, breathing in the dry air fragranced by ancient pine trees, hearing the sound of crickets contentedly chirping, feeling the heat of the sun penetrate all the way through to the soles of one's feet, and seeing what Paul must have seen and felt. He said enthusiastically that he would *love* to see Greece together and that I would be just the person to go with. It would be perfect! And let's not forget Ephesus, where the ancient structures have been frozen in time and remain so incredibly intact, that one wouldn't be surprised to see the locals from that time start walking about. And to be exiled on Patmos, ah, let that be *my* fate! I told Mark that you could walk through the cave-like structure where John wrote the Revelation of Christ! Then to start talking about tasty Greek food would mean I would next probably pass right on out. From that slender thread of hope and joy contemplating this possibility to making it actually happen, started with a "Yes." Bonnie later reminded Mark, "Dimi believed you when you said you would like to go with us!" This was to become a dream come true.

Nonetheless, there was something in me that would not let me believe it, that Mark would really go to Greece, yet when it looked like it could be, meaning that he was all in, I turned on all of my powers of planning with the intensity of a laser beam, not stopping and working in all free moments until our itinerary was complete and contacts and arrangements had been set in place. All this was back in October of 2014 when I hammered out our flight plans, made hotel reservations, and scheduled individual tours in various parts of Greece that specialized in "Tours of Paul," including Thessaloniki, Athens, and Corinth as well as neighboring areas pertinent to Paul. Mark asked if his co-pastor could go on this "vision" trip. Of course, I acceded and proceeded with all our plans and reservations until they were finalized by Thanksgiving. Fast-forward to now, the end of May, when Bonnie and I were getting ready for our seven-week stay in Greece, one week of which would be spent with Mark and Thomas. Neither of them had ever been, as they said, "across the pond" to Europe before. Admittedly, we were a motley crew: these two men, our pastors, both with families of their own, were twenty years younger than Bonnie and I, so although technically they were our church elders, it was almost like being with our sons or brothers. Every day we saw the major sites planned, but spontaneity transformed the moments of each day and brought the trip to life in a way I hadn't expected. The morning of their arrival, my heart beat fast with such joy. The day of being able to share Greece with the person who was greatly responsible for leading me to my salvation had finally arrived! I could hardly wait to show them both the many of the places that they had read about and only imagined. Not only that, I had no way of knowing then how much I would become good friends with the other pastor, Thomas, who would so be taken by seeing what Paul had done Greece that a desire to do mission work in that country was birthed within him on this trip! He would lead subsequent mission and vision tours to Greece for the church himself. Following is a skeletal version of the itinerary planned; I will flesh out this out vision quest trip for you afterward.

GREECE 2015:
A Focus on the Apostle Paul's Mission Work

Wed., June 24: Mark/Thomas arrive in Athens
- Walk all around the <u>Agora</u> where Paul observed hundreds of statues dedicated to gods and then spoke with the Athenian Stoics and Epicureans
- Walk up to <u>Mars Hill</u> where Paul delivered his famous sermon in the year 49 AD to the Greeks

Thursday, June 25: Day trip/private tour to ruins in <u>Ancient Corinth</u> - 50 mi west of Athens, where Paul lived and preached for 1 ½ years

Friday, June 26: Depart from the port of Piraeus to head out to the Greek islands on the Aegean

Sat., June 27: Land in Kusadasi, Turkey:
- Excursion to <u>Ancient Ephesus</u>
- Excursion: House of the Virgin, Mary's last dwelling (under John's care)
- Commence next to <u>Patmos Island</u> that same day
- Excursion to <u>St. John's Monastery and Grotto of the Apocalypse</u>

Sunday, June 28: Heraklion, Crete
- Excursion to Minoan Palace of Knossos, considered Europe's first civilization

Monday morning, June 29: The Saints Day of the Apostles Peter and Paul
- Arrive and disembark from the port of Piraeus and take a cab directly to Athens airport for flight to Thessaloniki
- Explore important sites in <u>Thessaloniki</u> associated w/ Paul, including the Old Town, <u>Jewish Quarter</u>, and <u>Berea</u>

Tuesday, July 30: Full day private <u>Philippi</u> tour (~ 100 mi east of Thessaloniki)
- <u>The ancient biblical site of Philippi</u> (including the jail where Paul stayed)
- <u>Lydia's Baptismal</u>

- Kavala (or <u>Neapolis</u> as written in the N.T.), then leave for an evening flight back to Athens

Wednesday, July 1: Mark and Thomas depart for the States

7.13 Greeks in Greece and Their Faith

This is the entry I wrote and sent just *before* Mark and Thomas arrived in Greece; Bonnie and I had already been there well over three weeks. For the most part, my journaling that summer had to do with my observations of Greece and Greeks. Though I read and studied my Bible daily, I felt happy, free, and light as I always did when in Greece. Bonnie and I listened to online sermons every Sunday to make it more like home. Here is the journal entry I emailed to several people the day before Mark and Thomas met us for our week focused on the Apostle Paul's travels in Greece. Mark probably read it on the plane ride over. I include it for you in full because this entry is on Greeks as pertains to their faith of the "ages of ages," infused with my fresh and new perspective.

> It's no secret to anyone that I'm very proud of my Greek heritage. Though I'm picking up more vocabulary while I'm here, I am inspired to want to take Greek lessons someday in the not-too-distant future. I can't get enough of learning about this culture and the ways of both modern and ancient Greeks, but now that I'm also an ambassador of my faith, how can I best serve and represent Him in a way that's a right fit for me? I find myself in a position that has been rather disconcerting for me to reckon: how could I come to Greece, a country that has been a Christian nation for over 2000 years, not even really changing since Christ's time, and wonder and hope and even attempt to talk to people about Jesus? Have I done so yet? A couple of times, but super indirectly. At this point, I honestly have no desire to bring about Protestant churches here, but I do have a burgeoning wish to talk to people about what it means to have Christ living in one's heart, accessible and humble, and yet so empowering. From the outside looking in, it would seem absurd to think about approaching a Greek about changing

his form of Christianity. After all, *their* church has never changed or propagated into subtypes. Greeks are baptized not even six months after they're born. The community centers around their church; it is the one constant in their lives from the cradle to the grave. But when you do a reality check and really talk to people under fifty, there are just as many disillusioned people with the Church there as there are in the States. Still, it is a constant, and one to which the family belongs. Mine did not belong, so I am not qualified to speak to what life is like while growing up Orthodox. I have been a close and adoring observer — still close, but no cigar. Many say it is corrupt, outdated, and money-grubbing. I have a not-too-distant relative living in a village who is a priest, and he is very much a man of God, full of joy and in possession of a keen mind. He is a vibrant and beloved member of his village, so I am not by any stretch making sweeping generalities fact for everywhere! I'm just making an observation that churches here in Greece, by and large, are *not* filled with the young. This cannot bode well for the future, and I crave for so much more in Greece, Russia, *and* the States! When it comes right down to it, there are *many* Greeks who don't focus that much on *Jesus*. Now, they'll attend church on the major holidays, and they know the sacraments, songs, and the *Orthodox* way to cross themselves (right to left with your first three fingers touching as you circulate from forehead to chest, right shoulder to left, then softly touch your heart in closing), but the desire to grow in *Him* isn't a thought. We have many nominal Christians here in the States who would bristle at the thought that some would say that they have a superficial, got-the-t-shirt faith. In fact, a couple of times when I ventured to mention the word, "God," to a Greek, I've heard everything from "I don't believe" to the *laissez-faire* take that "there are *many* approaches and ways to God," yes, even here in Greece. I wasn't expecting this! For example, I met a lawyer on a train on my way to Meteora who said that nobody has a right to say anything about how one is to believe. She said that since God had made her dyslexic and thus made her suffer while

she was in school, He couldn't be a good God. I tried to tell her that God can just as well use her weakness to strengthen her as well as to enable her to glorify Him. He made her just the way He wanted her to be; she was awesome just the way she was, dyslexic and all. And for sure,
she was a bird, a free spirit that He created, albeit not choosing to be His for feeling broken and hurt. It was no dice for her and a sigh for me.
On my previous trip to Greece in 2011, I recalled a relative of mine saying that she didn't particularly like the church and didn't attend church, except for Easter. The prevailing feeling here seems to be that the church is corrupt and has lots of money but is not particularly humanitarian, let alone merciful. In mock anger, this person told me that she was "mad" at those Greek monks from Macedonia — Cyril and Methodius — for not giving the Russians the Greek alphabet *as it was written*. With her hands upheld in the air indicating her questioning stance, she rather melodramatically asked me, "Why did they have to change it? Why?" I told her that to spread the word of Christ more effectively, these two Greek monks chose to get the know these Slavic people first, and upon getting a feel for the language and people they lived among, then they chose to introduce a written alphabet with sounded familiar to the language already spoken. They also realized they needed to add half a dozen new sibilant sounds that they heard spoken; therefore, they modified and custom-adapted the Greek alphabet for the Russians so they could read the Gospel. Eyebrows raised, head tilted back, and eyelids closed in her desire to refuse this fact, she said, "I don't care about the word of Christ!" This exclaim was followed up with that grandly dismissive gesture Greeks have whereby they waive their hand backward beside their face as if sweeping aside some pesky unpleasantry or nonsense. She counter-argued that if Cyril and Methodius had just stuck to the Greek alphabet, she surmised that "Nowadays we could have had so many more Greek-speaking people in the world!!" It is not that she didn't so much care about Jesus;

He just wasn't even a thought. It is quite clear that Greeks are not missionary-minded people. In contrast to evangelical Christians, Greeks think more like, "You are free to believe what you want! I won't dictate to you how to believe in Christ!" I really relish this freedom-of-thought mentality; having such can make you want to develop your faith in Him and make it all the more real because the desire to do so comes from within you. I'm so glad I've got this mindset of the heart for Him!

The Great Commission of "Go!" is a hardly an imperative the Greeks observe. A stolid mindset which has retained the church's first forms and essential messages promulgated, those which the Orthodox Church has jealously guarded and preserved for centuries, is not looking to invite those who don't know Him in the manner or to the degree *evangelical* Protestants or Catholics do. Oh, no! They look *in*, not out; neither do they suppose they have the right or duty to correct another Christian's mindset either. Plus, in reality, and when it's all said and done, it seems like most Greeks care more about the prestige and glory that is *Greece*. They've got all they need right there! Who needs new-fangled missionaries from a country whose culture and values are such a mish-mash, hodge-podge, anything-goes mess anyway? To be honest, at the time, I didn't know how the mass of Greeks felt about their church or their faith as it interplayed within the context of their everyday daily lives. All I understood was that beneath any protestations, Byzantine Orthodoxy was automatic, reflexive, and etched deep in their bones, whether they liked it or not or believed it or not. I don't see their outlook as being one fixated on a personal relationship with Christ. At the time, though, I didn't mind. Part of me also says, "Who am I to question another person's 'correctness' of faith?" Bonnie, ever the balanced one, made a good counterpoint that morning: one's getting baptized at birth bears no correlation to one's faith and level of personal involvedness with Christ. Being such a one, I agreed wholeheartedly. She explained that the common denominator between all Protestant churches is that, regardless of our differences, we all believe that the most crucial moment in one's Christian life is not baptism at infancy, but the decision to turn one's life over to Christ. You are not saved just because you are baptized as a baby; it happens the moment when you of sound mind, pure heart, and an age of accountability commit your life to Christ and turn away from the other stuff; the journey only begins then. Now *that* is worthy of baptism!

However, there are many other ideas and important historical points that I have learned and read about the Orthodox Church that I still find worthy of consideration to understanding Orthodox Christians. For example, icons were *crucial* for an illiterate people who were being introduced to Christianity in the first centuries after Christ. They provided a visual aid to usher in Biblical figures. I myself do not believe in the veneration of icons; for me, faith is a direct deposit made from me to Jesus alone, and the same holds true for my reception of His love and intentions for me. Reading the Bible for oneself for the Greek masses wouldn't be an option until some 1500 years later when the printing press made the Word accessible to all. And that's right about the time when the Reformation period began, so in contrast to Orthodox Christians, Protestants have enjoyed a relative ease in their access to the Bible. Most do not appreciate this fact! Therefore, one believer comes from a reading culture of modernity, the other, a listening and observing one of antiquity. Diametric opposites they are, but both Protestantism and Orthodoxy recognize the role of Jesus as the sole mediator between man and God. I am no Greek gnostic, meaning I don't put a primacy of esoteric knowledge over the material or consider that the denial of the physical world or ascetic practices can lead to a superior spiritual life! Anyway, God made both spirit *and* matter, so I celebrate *both*! One's motive is everything, and not doing this or that, including how one prays or renounces worldly ways, could be construed as another kind of work that is motivated by pride and/or false humility.

Here in Greece, I see a disconnect between the traditional and medieval church and ordinary Greeks' everyday life in the modern world. As a Greek among Greeks, one is automatically and certifiably born into this elitist club of sorts to which everyone naturally belongs because they're all Greek Orthodox. Choice of a denomination isn't a reality, let alone an option; therefore, it isn't even a thought. There's only one flavor: the *best* one because it was the *first*. Only the Orthodox Church hasn't perceptively shifted its ways or fundamental stance since it came into existence. There is no such newfangled idea as "church shopping" or finding a church that seems to be a "good fit" for you. Such an outlook what be preposterous or unthinkable because it focuses on personal satisfaction, yet in being *so* orthodox, the Orthodox Church can seem as distant as if it were still stuck and frozen in time, like some old wooly mammoth.

To their core, Greeks, both in and out of the church, are much more *group*-oriented than westerners, and its basis is religious. This mentality stems from a term called *koinonia*, a transliterated form of the *Greek* word, κοινωνία, which means "joint participation, fellowship, and community." A consequence for the church is that there is a low likelihood of anyone restructuring or revamp it since the church's job as a unifier (in Christ) has been undisputed; there is no contest. In the fast-paced and interconnected world of today, from youth to middle-aged, instead, we find quiet declarations of discontent in the Greek Church as evidenced by low attendance. While for some, the Orthodox Church provides a sense of security, constancy, holiness, purity, and moral stability, but it has also become unresponsive, out-of-touch, and impersonal to the point that, much to many a yiayia's chagrin or woe, it has become irrelevant among the young. In not seeking revitalization or trying hard to retain young and middle-aged adults, there exists the risk of a practicable collapse. Attending the Orthodox Church *does* move me; therefore, this state pains me. Following tradition, partaking of what it provides for one's senses *and* spirit, and being communally involved in rituals that have lasted through the ages is *not*, however, evidence of an active faith.

As in Greece, people in the United States are put off by hypocrisy and holier-than-thou smugness seen in ostentatious church members. But if there is a disagreement in doctrinal stance or position toward even a simple matter, in the States, a denomination can branch off and splinter into another subdivision of the branch of Protestantism. There are *thousands* of these offshoots. It's a tradition that started with Protestantism itself breaking away from the Catholic Church. There exists that kind of freedom! Whether you live in America, which has the Protestant Church as its dominant form of Christianity (with Catholicism a close second), or whether you reside in Greece, where you have the bedrock of the Greek Orthodox Church, neither institution has been particularly successful at being a headquarters for Jesus Christ, and by that, I mean a place that attracts people to *Him*. This may be controversial to say, and I wish it weren't the case. The evidence for my claim is that there has been a decline in church attendance from *both* denominations over the past fifty years. It does not have to stay this way! Does this mean the world is winning and Jesus is losing? Heavens, no! That isn't possible; we already know how the end is going to turn out, but in the meantime, it's on all of us believers to show Christ as real, relevant, and necessary for us *today*. His victory is for all time's sake!! The rub is, how are we to overcome our differences and keep our focus on the cross? United we stand and divided we falter. There is also a part of me that chides myself about making remarks about the Orthodox Church. Who am I kidding anyway?!? Except to light a candle in churches for my father, I only go there once a year for Easter. I am no expert or authority on Orthodoxy, and quite frankly, the same could be said of my assessments of Protestantism *a la* American style. However, I *do* have a unique vantage point and knowledge of *both* that few possess. Plus, miraculously and joyfully, I *have* found and am part of a little church that I've made home where there exists a piercing light through thick fog and thin air for me to follow Him. Meanwhile, while I am here in Greece and feeling the Greek in me happily bask in the sunshine and just *breathe*, I just wanted to share more in-depth thoughts and impressions that have come to me. Thus, in commenting to several of my friends my opinions and observations via this email, I also inadvertently prepared Mark and Thomas for the world they were getting ready to enter in their coming to witness Paul's path for themselves.

7.14 FOLLOWING THE FOOTSTEPS OF PAUL:
One Week with Mark, Thomas, Bonnie and Me in Greece

Athens, Greece

During the week we four were in Greece, I did not journal or write. With all major plans fixed and now set in motion, at times, we felt free enough free to fly by the seat of our pants and at others, the luxury to linger and saturate ourselves in a particular place. After the boys arrived, they desperately needed a nap, so Bonnie and I went out and let them catch a few hours of shut-eye before we got them up, and after that, we went and had our first Greek meal together. It was nothing fancy or out of the norm, but they closed their eyes as they ate their little plates of heaven, making happy sounds as they devoured their sizzling souvlaki on warmed pita, slathered with tzatziki sauce, thick home fries, and on the side, a Greek salad with a generous hunk of feta. Jesus would've loved it, too. We four eating together would be the norm, and dinner was always later on in the evening. Then we trekked through the Agora where Paul walked through on his way up to nearby Mars Hill, or "Ἄρειος Πάγος," that is, "Areopagus," as it is called in Greek, to make his famous sermon to the Greeks. Athens then was, more or less, a college town and not the metropolis it is today. Truth be told, the Greeks of that time were in one of their lower periods of philosophy; the likes of geniuses like Socrates, Aristotle, and Plato had degenerated into the Stoics and Epicureans, the former eschewing the material and the latter indulging in precisely that, just in polar opposite expression. Paul didn't make any headway with these curious but arrogant, intellectual Greeks who probably only let him speak to the crowd because they were interested in who this new "god" of his, the Holy Spirit, he had talked about was. As we four walked through and looked at statue after statue, temple after temple, we could feel what it must have been like for Paul to walk there as well: awe and yet frustration mounting with each step at how much they'd missed the mark with all this idolizing! Why, Paul even found a statue to an unknown god, just in case they'd missed one to venerate and from which to make a last request, as if the offering of prayers was some spiritual *quid quo pro*: I venerate the god, and he or she helps me out. After Mark and Thomas climbed the huge and severe steps made slippery-smooth from years of wear up to the high and broad level area of Mars Hill, we all made our way over to its edge. From there, we looked out past the panorama of the Agora, which was in our immediate foreground, to the Acropolis behind us, and to all of sprawling Athens with its seven historical hills hemming us in all around. Mark and Thomas would have me record the first of three videos to show the church later on. When we came back down to the bottom of Mars Hill and before we went over and up to the Acropolis, at its base, on the foundation, you'll find on a very large bronze plaque engraved in Greek the famous passage from Acts 17:22–31. Here Paul addresses the Greeks and gently reproves them for their misplaced focus on the temporal instead of looking to that which created all. Mark slowly read it aloud in Greek, and I helped fill in a few gaps of pronunciation where needed. Though you could look up this passage for yourselves, I feel like sharing about half of it with you right now so you can read it. I took the liberty of italicizing what struck me as particularly powerful and still applicable. Why? I am amazed at the validity of Paul's ancient statement; it still holds its water and rings true today. We *still* worship idols and are fanatics of things made with our own hands — our little-g gods — no matter how many times and ways God reminds us we are not! Incidentally, in Greek, Mars Hill is translated as "War Hill"; the English used the Roman word for the god of war, "Mars," instead of the Greek word, "Ares." We all engage in spiritual warfare at various points in our life. Here's that excerpt:

> [22] So Paul stood in the midst of the Areopagus and said, "Men of Athens, I observe that *you are very religious in all respects.*
> [23] For while I was passing through and examining the objects of your worship, I also found an altar with this inscription, 'TO AN UNKNOWN GOD.' Therefore, what you worship in ignorance, this I proclaim to you. [24] *The God who made the world and all things in it, since He is Lord of heaven and earth,*

does not dwell in temples made with hands; [25] nor is He served by human hands, as though He needed anything, since He Himself gives to all people life and breath and all things; [26] and He made from one man every nation of mankind to live on all the face of the earth, having determined their appointed times and the boundaries of their habitation, [27] that *they would seek God, if perhaps they might grope for Him and find Him, though He is not far from each one of us*; [28] for in Him we live and move and exist, as even some of your own poets have said, 'For we also are His children'…"(from Acts 17:22–28).

Right from the start, Thomas took to Greece like a duck to water he'd never known and fell in love with it. For both Mark and Thomas, there was just so much there to stun the imagination and one's sense of beauty and knowledge of biblical history; plus, they were transported through time and space in this land, the landscape of which in many ways remained largely unchanged since the time of Christ. They thoroughly enjoyed being in the moment that connected them to the past. Every place we would go on in our pre-arranged, small-group tours, Thomas would absorb every word the guide would say, while Mark, usually several feet away from us, might be found gazing around or in the distance one moment or down on his haunches lost in thought the next, perhaps with his hand touching the cool marble or tiles, transported by his imagination to vistas back in time. Each day seemed fuller than the last, and we joked about how many means of transportation we'd taken; I think we got up to twelve at one count. Our first side trip was to go down to Corinth, a two-hour drive south of Athens into the Peloponnesus.

Corinth:

The next day I had us scheduled to go to Corinth. The van was ready for us bright and early and right in front of the hotel. The guide, a young woman, hurriedly made her way up the street to us because she was late. She looked at our group of four and asked, "Where's your priest?" Mark lighted up and said he guessed that was he. She was expecting a typical Greek priest with a beard halfway down his chest, donned in an obligatory black robe, and probably three times her age. Well, there is nothing priestly-like looking about Mark: relatively young and always with a ready and warm smile and open countenance, he did not fit the stereotype of someone who'd lead a somber and contemplative life. In fact, black hair slicked-back and deeply tanned; he has actually been asked if he was ever a Columbian gang lord. In short, looks-wise, he fit in here with Greeks. Mark is the epitome of the people-person, and his way, which could win you over, was through his disarming charm, quick wit, and sincere interest that he took in you with no judgment or agenda. In short, he simply loves people. He affectionately dubbed our guide "Lina of Troy," and though she was packed with information because she was young and more personable, Mark started evangelizing to her by subtly asking general questions about her life and interests. He never came on being pushy about Jesus. Sometimes where the occasion suited itself, he might sprinkle in an apt Biblical story, told with humor or animation, or he would tell her this and that about our church. It was touching to see her try and maintain her professional composure while Mark got under her skin and made her laugh. Both Mark and Thomas were impressed that our guides were so highly educated. Both of our guides held a degree in archeology and possessed extensive academic knowledge of the gospels, yet it was apparent that neither took a personal interest in Jesus. Thus, Mark and Thomas were also disappointed at seeing such vast knowledge having no bearing on our guides' faith; there simply was none. For a country with a vast history that counts in the millennia, the historical Jesus provides yet another chapter of man's worshipping *something*; this one was called Christianity which arose after an epoch of philosophy, and before that, mythology. Christianity emerged as an inevitability of sorts, organically springing up from the sediment of what preceded it. Nothing seemed to touch the guides personally; after all, it was Greek history they were sharing, and a passage or two from the Bible to correlate was just another type of evidence.

As a result, these two contemporary American men of God standing right where Paul had walked were facing much the same disbelief as he, in spite of all the proof around them, and they became dismayed and incredulous. Their brains were on fire to think of a way to "reach these Greeks"; I stood by and felt the weight of centuries of tradition and silently pondered their naiveté and bewilderment. Yet there was no surprise in their being inspired to missionary dreams here: after all, these men were in the prime of their life, Thomas, 32, and Mark, 36.

They aspired to convert Greeks who were steeped in the rich historical Christianity, yet who were hardly regular attenders, let alone ones who showed interest in cultivating faith. To be Greek is to be Orthodox; to be Orthodox is to be Greek, but neither means you are a practicing real-deal believer, let alone a possessor of the personal relationship with Christ. Such — if it exists — is not only supremely private but, to be frank, becomes passé for them because they have long since been baptized. You always see lots of children under ten-years-old playing outside the church courtyard every night, mothers and grandmothers looking on lovingly, as if its vicinity was a family playground of sorts. It's sweet and so wholesome; therefore, I would imagine that the falling away happens in the teen years. Outside looking in, Mark and Thomas observed that, for the most part, that is, for regular working-aged Greeks, the church is no longer viable. That you can spot lots of widows, elderly folks, those who are poor, young couples with their children take communion, or a flurry of folks celebrating major church events does not translate to a thriving church, let alone indicate the authenticity of one's faith. In Greece, less than 5% are Protestant; that should give you an idea of the loyalty and fidelity of Greeks being orthodox to their Orthodox Church. Therefore, it would seem that the odds are stacked against the evangelical Protestant shifting the populace's stance on Christ or their church. That said, I was such a one who desired for my fellow Greeks to get up close and personal with Jesus and set their eyes on Scripture, not icons. The stark, almost naked buildings and friendly, casual atmosphere you witness in American Protestant churches (or megaliths) differ vastly from the Greek person's associations with the hallowed and serious atmosphere in their church and its ancient Byzantine architecture. Furthermore, the Jesus-as-my-friend approach, not to mention the curiosity and seeming fixation over whether one is "saved" or "knows" Jesus makes no sense to the Greek. Why would this be up for discussion or query? It would seem impertinent at most and odd at the least. Though gregarious and bright, Greek people are xenophobic and resistant to changing their church, even though they would be the first to admit that the church is "not for them" because "the priests are corrupt," etc. A secular Greek will gladly go to church if she knows of a pleasant priest who is personable, friendly, and humble. Though still very democratic in their outlook and passionate about philosophy and politics, Greeks remain much more reserved and eastern in their religiosity. Even though attendance is not high, at least it is not nearly as bad as in Western Europe like Germany or England, where atheism is openly and unabashedly the norm for many between the ages of twenty and sixty. Greeks are so full of freedom in their soul, they would tell you to "believe *what* you want and *how* you want," but never prod, inquire about, let alone inspect another's faith! For Mark and Thomas, the stakes for not knowing Jesus personally are too great to be wrong, that is, to remain in a church where faith is inadvertently apathetic. But I digress.

Thomas felt a spark of interest in doing mission work here, and within three days, Mark, ever the visionary, noted through his accurate observation that "one way to reach Greeks is to go to their cafés. *That's* where the Greeks are and like to hang out!" he exclaimed. When they got back to the States, Thomas, still on fire, scoured online for pastors serving in Greece, including opportunities to do mission work. He not only found Protestant, a.k.a. "Evangelical" churches that were thriving there, but he also made enough contacts to be able to come back the next two summers. He also organized and led smaller groups from our church to visit local Greek Protestant churches, one of which was nestled in a neighborhood in Athens close to where my cousin lives. A year and a half later, Mark and Thomas on their own would visit a refugee camp in northern Greece, bloated with Syrian refugees who were being attended to by Greek Protestant enclaves. In short, a new beginning and connections were made.

Wherever we were on our tour, be it on Mars Hill or in Corinth, after our guide finished her presentation on the history and archeology associated with the biblical facts, Thomas would then and there complete the picture by reading relevant Scripture. This was how we rolled. And while you are among the ruins of Corinth, your mind naturally fills in the details surrounding these columns and still-intact temples to create the complete picture. In a sweep of your gaze, you mentally assemble the great temple and the vast compound alongside and imagine what it looked when it was thriving. Over here was the market where people would gather, sell their wares, come to gossip and socialize, as well as to worship. Portions of the Gospel relevant to Paul's mission work in Greece came to life in this real context. Even where Paul was given a difficult time or ran off, there we would also read Scripture from our Bibles or on nearby engraved marble plaques written in Greek that put it all together. Compared to the college town of Athens, Corinth was a bustling cosmopolitan city with various nationalities, ways of life, and outlooks represented. We would *expect* there to be hedonism and debauchery in this dynamic city; in fact, at the time, there existed the thought that to achieve religious ecstasy, one could accomplish this through carnal means. Looking up, jutting high in the near distance, you can see Acro-Corinth, a mountaintop that served as more like a red-light district of its day, albeit one used in the name of reaching a state of mystical high through union with temple prostitutes. After looking all around what was essential to us in the Corinth of the Bible, we made our way to an unassuming small bay, the port of Cenchreae, where Paul would have launched out to head to Ephesus. I took a picture of Mark and Thomas there, both having waded knee-high in this bay and looking out at the same spot in the distance, as if they were craning to catch a glimpse of Paul on his way sailing to Ephesus where he would spend his next three years. They were mesmerized. Mark then invited our guide, Lina of Troy, and our bus driver to eat with us at the place she had chosen for lunch. Unbeknownst to Mark, this not the norm; usually, the Greeks guides sat at their own table, smoking, texting, drinking coffee, or quietly talking among themselves or with the restaurant owners, but not typically eating or hanging out with the clients. However, we six thoroughly enjoying each other's company, so we ate to our hearts' content and shared this incredible food on this beautiful day, laughing easily among one another as we took turns talking about family or whatever, reveling in what all we'd taken in and done together. Every meal we ate, with or without Greeks, was communal, joyful, and primal. Next on our itinerary would be Ephesus.

Ephesus, Turkey:

When we arrived in Turkey early the next morning to board the school bus that would take us to ancient Ephesus, we immediately sensed we were in another world and dimension, as if time had stood still in this Arabia of sorts. We saw clusters of women in burkas and groups of even huskier and bearded men on their haunches discussing matters in a circle, and there was many a minaret in the close distance.

Our tour there first started out with a brief stopover to see the humble abode of what amounted to a shrine of a room where Jesus' mother, Mary, was alleged to have spent her last days and was tended to by John. Our primary focus in Turkey, which we had been greatly anticipating, came next. We were all let off at the top of Ephesus to make our way down through the main thoroughfare into its heart, along which were skeletal shops. It was like going through a long hall inside of a mall as you head to its center. Then it ended and opened up to the main square where all the people would gather. A library was straight ahead of us; personal apartments were to the back and left, and there was also a brothel across from the massive library, which was straight ahead. (They had thought of everything!) I'm telling you, these structures hardly look like ruins! They were so perfectly intact that it was as if they had been rebuilt, but there's no way one could replicate this. A few steps off and to the right side was an open area designated for toilet seating, where, as in Corinth or Philippi, the men would gather to sit, chat with one another, and use the bathroom all in one fell swoop. In a more open area, just beyond and off to the side, were the actual fields where Paul would have set up a stand for his tent-wares and used as a home base for his evangelizing. Ephesus was the NYC of its day, and the Temple of Artemis (a.k.a., Diana) was one of the seven wonders of the ancient world, so to have interfered with anything dealing with the worship thereof, including associated commerce, would have spelled trouble. That's exactly what happened to Paul, who, again, during his three years there, rained on their parade (and thriving business) by steadily telling them that they were missing the clue train as to whom they should worship. We had a total of an hour and a half there. Ninety minutes, period. I thought Mark and Thomas were going to jump out of their skin; they could have spent ninety *hours* lingering and searching every square inch of that place! So, what did they do? They ditched the tour about mid-way and double back-tracked to where Paul would have established himself a place to work and teach and videoed themselves there for the church. Then they scampered up to the colossal amphitheater where Paul would have been placed on trial for challenging the status quo. What got Paul in hot water was his success in persuading a considerable number of people *not* to go all out for the goddess Artemis. He proclaimed that "gods made with hands are no gods at all" (Acts 19:26) and also that "the temple of the great goddess Artemis was to be regarded as worthless" (Acts 19:27). The whole city was enraged; therefore, Paul's disciples prudently and successfully prevented him from entering this amphitheater to defend himself against the mob. Thank goodness, the chaos during the assembly was quelled, and the case dismissed on the technicality of there being "no real cause for [the commotion]" (Acts 19:40). In great part, this was proclaimed to avoid an all-out riot. If the Jews had wanted to press charges, well then, they could go through proper legal channels. The whole of this dramatic account is found in Acts 19. I video-recorded Mark and Thomas there, too. It was like being in fast motion, yet I could see their minds clinging to and memorizing every detail and nuance of being there, a place to which they knew they weren't soon, if ever, to return. Afterward, we did the obligatory tour of the silk factory, complete with flying carpets being snapped overhead as they were rolled out on display for the flock of tourists. We watched in wonderment as we sipped our hot tea. By this point, we were all were just giddy; the whole of what all we'd seen that day seemed so surreal.

Patmos:

Skipping ahead to that afternoon, dizzy and overwhelmed by the immensity of appreciating what we all had just seen in Ephesus, we now landed on the small Greek island of Patmos, an island far off in the archipelago of Dodecanese islands where the Apostle John had been banished from Ephesus. Here he spent the remainder of his life and wrote what is known in Greek as ἀποκάλυψις —the "Apocalypses" — or translated into English more familiarly as the Book of Revelation. Originally dubbed by Jesus as one of the "Sons of Thunder" (Mark 3:17), John became known more familiarly as "the disciple whom Jesus loved" (John 21:7). Incidentally, John is the only apostle that did not die an untimely death (that is, he was not *murdered* for his affiliations with Christ); in fact, he is reported to have died on Patmos at the age of 93 or 94. Again, we made our way in the packed-like-sardines bus up to the top where St. John's Monastery was situated and adjoined to the side where was the actual grotto of the Apostle John. This tour had gained a lot more popularity from when I had last been there in 2010 with a group of students. Inside the tiny chapel adjoining the cave, there now stood on guard a cross priest who peered disdainfully with his arms crossed, ready to pounce on some misstep taken by one among the group of tourists there. Mark and Thomas got tickled at him for being so gruff, and Bonnie and I were disappointed for them being herded there. What is remarkable is that while you are inside the grotto and all is still and quiet, you can see the three-pronged crack (in the form of a cross, of course), which, according to legend, dramatically occurred when a shockingly white-headed Jesus appeared and spoke to a very stunned John. In reality, the crack is likely to have been caused by an earthquake, but, hey, I wasn't there, and I didn't see or hear what John did, and I'll bet it *was* a cataclysmic experience to have Jesus Himself talk to him in the manner and appearance He did! Anyway, it is God who would have been the cause of the earthquake, which gave rise to the vision to begin with! Thank God that John wrote what he did and as instructed, though it may be obtuse in its symbolism for us to decipher today. For all Christians, this last chapter of the Bible unveils and gives us a glimpse into our future, light years past "happily ever after," and into an eternality face-to-face with God. While we four were there in the grotto, Mark peered out of the eye-slit sliver of the window in that cave into the bright blue sky pouring in and out onto the shimmering Aegean Sea. I could tell he was being transported through the lens of his imagination to the time and place of John's being here. Meanwhile, we moved along from inside that tiny cave, packed in tight with the other tourists through to the monastery's mini-museum to exit. All were on overload from having experienced being in John's tiny cave. Yet there was no love lost there where it was stifling, so, making our way outside, Mark and Thomas sat on a low stone wall to wait for the bus. They looked out at and were mesmerized by the turquoise sea and this small island, a great expanse visible from where we were situated on high. We could take in the whole of the island with one panoramic glance. Bonnie and I were enveloped by a peace there, with the warm winds of the pines blowing over us; breathing in deeply, we were all grateful and so in the moment.

I now fast-forward to our disembarkation from the ship at 6:00 a.m. when we arrived back in Athens. My taxi-driver friend, Panos, shuttled us directly to the airport where we were to fly directly to Thessaloniki in northern Greece, arriving at noon. As we waited and had a minute to collect ourselves in the airport, we sat passing the time checking our phones and sipping cups of strong Greek coffee.

Thessaloniki:

When we arrived in Thessaloniki and retrieved our baggage from the tiny turnstile, overflowing with tumbling suitcases and a throng of people grabbing their bags, we met another guide, Marie, and the driver of our van. Marie had that unique, copper-colored hair Greek women get when they try to cover black with red, and she was very different from Lina of Troy. Although young like Lina, Marie seemed more sophisticated, cultured, and professional. Lina of Troy was easier to become friends with, although she was initially professionally cool, too. Marie was one of those Greeks who is rather snobbish towards other Greeks, as, by and large, the mass of them seemed unthinking cretins to her. She lived with her boyfriend and held no compunction about it, and though she'd been baptized, she, too, had no apparent faith in, let alone, stirrings about Christ. That said, I took to her because she, like I, was also one of three sisters, and I liked to make her laugh. Her biblical knowledge was full, but strictly academic, and again, I noticed the wonderment in Thomas and Mark over these people's lack of faith, especially considering where we were and the evidence all around them. Like other educated guides there, the common outlook is that they believe that Christianity is just another chronological offshoot or expression of humankind's perpetual quest to make sense of and find meaning in life. There was nothing remarkable about yet another religion coming about. Greek gods and temples gave way and got refined to Jesus and churches, which were literally built atop the very foundations of these old temples. You can still see this! That said, they readily accede that Christianity was a major occurrence within the historical and thematic progression of man reaching to God in that it inversed this direction. Yet from these Greek guides, you will hear no *personal* acknowledgment of the resurrection other than it is something their grandmothers believe in, and such gives rise to the time of year they everyone comes home to attend church. It almost seems like these guides view Christianity as an extension of Greek mythology: part II, the saga continues. The immensity of what Christianity evidences for humanity seems lost on them, but I should concede here that perhaps this is because they are taught to maintain their professional objectivity and aloofness so as not to offend anyone. However, we outright asked them what their take on all this was, and it became clear to us that for the most part, these Greek guides with ring-side seats to Paul's missionary work had not come to genuine faith in that which their education and vocation evidenced to be genuine.

TOUR OF THESSALONIKI AND VERIA (BERIA):

On our first day, we were scheduled to have the city tour of Thessaloniki and then visit Veria (spelled "Beria" in the N.T.). I want to mention that our itinerary was *not* in the order Paul and Silas (then Timothy) saw Greece; we did it backward. I enjoy picturing what it must have been like for Paul to have had a such a particular missionary vision that differed from his intended plan. The change of plans came from "a man of Macedonia standing [and] beseeching him and saying, 'Come over to Macedonia' and help us'" (Acts 16:9 RSV). Instead of going east as he'd originally intended, he heeded this angel and sailed from Troas to a place called Neapolis, which the Greeks call Kavala, and from there, to Philippi, a Roman colony. Here Paul baptized a European, a wealthy woman named Lydia who was a "seller of purple goods" (Acts 16:14 ESV). Though not mentioned at length in the New Testament, Lydia's story became quite dear to me. Selling fabric to royalty and the wealthy, she was, for sure, a respected businesswoman with a thriving enterprise, and she would have had quite a few employees. She was already a believer in the Good News, and for Paul to visit and stay with her while in the area gives credence to this fact. Did you know that she is considered the first person to be baptized in Europe? Like Jesus, Paul wasn't one to do a lot of baptizing, but he baptized Lydia, which is all the more remarkable because she was a woman. It's no surprise that women in general at that time held low social status. Evidently, Paul respected her and valued what she was doing for and in Christ. The river where she was baptized just outside of Philippi has become memorialized and is situated in a lovely and intimate setting. It is almost like a small park, and it beckons baptism to many who visit it. There will be more on this place later, too. While in Philippi, Paul got annoyed with a slave girl who kept following him around while he was preaching there; she announced that he was a "servant of the Most High God" (Acts 16:17). Not able to shoo her away, he charged her "spirits" to come out of her, which, by so doing, would've resulted in no money earned by this portentous girl and, thus, no income gained for her masters. This situation led to Paul and Silas being "beaten with rods" (Acts 16:22) and thrown in jail. That night, these men sang praise songs in the jailhouse! Miraculously, though not surprisingly, an earthquake occurred during that very night, bursting the tiny jail open, yet Paul assured the jailer he had no intention of fleeing, which, in turn, so moved this man, he asked to be baptized! Because Paul was a Roman citizen, the two were released the very next day when he pulled rank through reminding them about the technicality of his citizenship, which entitled him to have received a fair trial *before* his "unfortunate incarceration." From there, Paul left for Thessaloniki, but after teaching about Jesus in the local synagogues for only a couple of weeks, the local Jews got jealous, and they chased him out of town. Then he went to nearby Veria, whose people were more educated and receptive to him. Yet the Jews from Thessaloniki followed him there too, so Paul then headed on down to Athens, and from there, to Corinth, then over to Ephesus, etc. Okay, that was my quick take on Paul's mission work in Greece as taken from the book of Acts. I must make a particular note to the Christian reader who might be reading this and wondering why in the world why I'm summarizing parts of Acts. For those who aren't at all familiar with Paul, let alone know of the missionary work he accomplished in Greece, I am compelled to synthesize what we now *saw* with what he then *did* to impress upon the reader the purpose, value, and intersection of our travels with Scripture.

Our manner of seeing what Paul accomplished was not diminished one iota by not observing where Paul traversed in his chronological order. Furthermore, to *really* be there, driving, seeing, walking, touching, learning, and feeling all of this which was related to Paul and Christ had been compounding in us with each day that passed, and the case was even more so in northern Greece. These final two days were particularly packed full of our seeing sites related to Paul's journey. There would be fewer purely Greek cultural highlights woven in. That said, right after we first arrived and checked into our hotel in Thessaloniki, we had lunch at an outdoor café across the street and then took our drive around and stopping at significant historical spots in Thessaloniki. As a Greek city, Thessaloniki has an entirely different atmosphere than Athens; it seems more European and cosmopolitan, and though "Greek-old," as I liked to put it, there are fewer ruins about. Both Mark and Thomas liked it there a lot; the pace wasn't as frenetic as Athens or overrun with tourists from all over the world. It was Beria (pronounced "Veria" in Greek). However, we had a special treat that day because we got to go to the old Jewish Quarter, and in general, this particular area was much greener than any place we'd been. Marie was brimming with information about how everything we witnessed was related to Paul, and I was pleased by this for us. Alongside this hamlet of the Jewish Quarter, a broad river meandered, gurgling audibly from just beyond the narrow and deserted streets we were exploring. Marie was a harder nut to crack for Mark, meaning it took more effort and humor for her to speak to us more personably than professionally. I believe this was because she took no interest in religion; it seemed like this was just another tour with Americans. I came to see all encounters for him turned into opportunities to evangelize, but first came cracking the façade of formality, and each person was different. You have to study, listen, learn, and let them feel *liked* first, and then you must have no expectation of a preconceived idea of an outcome because nothing is on you; all is on how God and the magic of the moment. Mark is a natural people-person and is curious about how people tick and what rocks their world; I can relate. As time went by and conversations flowed more freely, she smiled and laughed more easily with us; maybe my being Greek didn't hurt either. Mark was incredulousness over her seeming indifference and blasé response to a question he asked her, which I'm sure, he has asked *himself* many a time: "Don't you want *more* for your life? Isn't there more to life than cafés, friends and family, and going to work?" to which she calmly and confidently replied, "No." I wondered to myself if this wasn't the way most people thought and went through life. That evening, famished from another full day of ingesting Paul's world, the four of us feasted out-of-doors in a corner pocket of Thessaloniki where a cluster of excellent tavernas was, just down from where our hotel was situated, and we partook of a smörgåsbord of delicacies. The whole area of small alleys with quaint cafés hither and yon seemed like a "set for a European city," Thomas observed happily. Mark was on fire, walking fast as he was intently focused on a vision that had come to him; he dreamed out loud of how he could "reach these Greeks." I, too, was infected by his enthusiasm and also longed for this to occur. We ambled back after dinner that evening, talking and laughing easily among ourselves. The next day in Philippi would be our last full day in Greece together before the boys caught a red-eye flight back to the States the following morning. Bonnie and I ourselves would spend another three weeks in Greece afterward.

Philippi, Lydia's Baptismal, and Neapolis (Kavala):

This last day started bright and early because it was a good two-and-a-half-hour drive from Thessaloniki to ancient Philippi. When we got to the amphitheater in Philippi where Paul probably spoke — a smaller one compared to those in Athens — we were amazed to spy a trap door on the stage floor through which lions and wild animals would have entered to devour their human prey. Such was done for the entertainment of the wealthy Roman spectators. After all, the Romans were some of the most advanced and ruthless torturers in the ancient world. Mark went into gladiator mode, his eyes wide open, looking about the empty stage, imagining the various beasts coming out for their terrible feast. From there, the five of us made our way to the Agora or open-air market. Marie explained about this and that in this vast area which was systematically and extensively organized. The Agora served not only as a market, but within its environs, it also held a court, hotel (i.e., rooms for rent), a specific spot where one could hear public announcements or speeches made, a communal toilet zone, and a worship center. Unlike Athens, this part of Philippi was all on flat ground, sprawled way out. And just as we made our way around the corner to its largest open area, what should we see tucked in, smaller than we might've expected, but the very jail in which Paul was kept! It amounted to four dirt walls, chain-linked off so you couldn't go into the 10' by10' area below. We spotted a small and unassuming sign attached to this primitive fence simply labeled "Prison of St. Paul" in both Greek and English. Speaking of which, what are the chances that today, June 29th, our last day following the "Footsteps of Paul," would be the very day for celebrating Saints Peter and Paul?! I videotaped Mark and Thomas for our church there at its entrance, and I found it curious that Marie, who had walked way past this point to smoke, came back to where we were, interested to hear what all Mark was saying. After he finished recording and noticing her hesitant but evident fascination, Mark took the opportunity to walk and talk with her alone and chat about why he would have recorded this moment. At this point, just beyond the confines of the Agora, the ancient world blurred with the present when we heard a small flock of sheep pass nearby, bleating, their bells gently jingling.

At the termination point of the Agora, we came to a portion of ground that had a protective carp to cover and preserve a tiled floor of intricate mosaics being excavated and restored. On a portion of this flooring, you could see that Paul had signed his name using teeny tiles. Mark got down on his haunches to gently touch the individual tiles, and then he put his whole palm on the floor. We still had another site to see nearby, so we made a quick pit stop for water and snacks at the little store by the entrance so we'd be fortified for our next stop, the place where Lydia was baptized. It was situated very close to Philippi's archeological site and just about ten miles outside of Kavala. When we arrived there to a place technically called the village of Lydia, also out in the green countryside and just beyond the church called Saint Lydia's Baptistery, we heard the waters of the river before we came to gaze upon it. So clean and pristine, so peaceful and serene, there could be no more perfect place for Lydia — or anyone — to have been baptized! Narrow, platformed seating was set up along both sides of the river for a span of about twenty yards or so, and a little bridge made in the shape of a cross traversed the river; the place was idyllic for a small river baptism. Behind were erected some bleachers. A man of few words, but clearly in awe, Thomas drank in the feel and import of this setting: the small church nearby was built to be a commemorative marker just up and past the stream. Who wouldn't want to take such an opportunity for baptism? The gently gurgling waters and the lush green setting brought to life a few lines from Acts he'd read, no doubt a hundred times before. For the third time that day, Thomas read pertinent Scripture to us that corresponded to the setting. He could not have known then that he would come back to this very spot one year later with a group of twelve from our church and baptize two women right here. His desire to share Paul's vision work in Greece and do mission work was launched by the Holy Spirit working in him on this trip! Talk about full circle! After all, we'd seen these past two days, we four just sat and reflected quietly and contentedly, lingering there a bit longer. Then we went inside Lydia's church, where should one prefer, he could have a more formal baptism in this small but unique and ornate Orthodox Church. There was a mosaic of Paul's missionary travels on the entry floor, like a gigantic game of Candyland.

By that time, it well into early afternoon, and we were famished, so we drove to nearby Kavala (a.k.a., Neapolis in the Bible) to have some lunch. The port of Kavala was also quite picturesque and pleasingly simple. Marie and our driver had wanted to drop us off at the row of restaurants on the harbor, but Mark told me to ask them where they ate to see if we couldn't all eat together. They were readily open to the idea and took us back a few streets to a taverna where we had someone the best over-the-pit grilled meat anywhere. By now, we were happy and familiar with each other, and there was much laughter as we talked easily among ourselves. At this point, our tour was officially finished, but since we had a little extra time, they wondered if it was okay and asked us if we might want to spend time at a local beach nearby before driving back to the airport in Thessaloniki. Of course, we did! We drank iced Greek coffee with our new friends and chatted and laughed together under an umbrellaed table where we all sat and gazed out at the Aegean Sea. It turned out to be a particularly stirring day for me.

And that is the long and the short of our trip to Greece and traveling along the Footsteps of Paul. Exhausted, spent, but deeply content, we waited for a torrential downpour to end in Thessaloniki before our flight could take off; then, we landed in Athens and grabbed a final bite to eat around the corner from our hotel. As we stood eating our savory gyros, we each caught a glimpse of the Acropolis up in the distance, lit up and haloed by a full moon. Though late, we took a quick stroll in the Plaka and were among the many tourists and Athenians still out as the night was alive, the atmosphere so vibrant! Soon though, we made our way back out to our hotel and hit the sack. We said our goodbyes early the next morning as my taxi-driver friend, Panos, drove them to the airport. I wouldn't write another journal entry related to religion for the rest of the summer, but it was during this chapter that the bookend and long-awaited expression of my faith occurred in the world of Paul two thousand years ago, which merged and vividly came to life with my dear friends. Bonnie and I both love Greece so much; it is where our perspective on what's truly important in life gets restored, and now this stance expanded to include our journey of growing faith.

I wrote a short poem to captures the yearning, the compulsion, and mission that comes from *beyond* me and transcends who I *thought* I was, to who I desired yet to be for Him:

Though the Holy Ghost magnificently did come upon me, oh, so big and full,
There has since arisen a longing, a loneliness, and a constant tugging pull.
In this yearning, I crave to have Him over-the-top me fill,
So, I must relinquish all unessential, egocentric, in short, I must me myself kill.
And no, it is not suicide or self-slaughter
When I do for Him what I ought'er.
The flesh has many enticing and powerful ways all of us to seduce.
For me, it deals with identity and ego, but in the end, I must the following deduce:
That God doesn't think me a weak even though I'm just half-Greek,
And should the day come when I'm truly able and fluent,
Why, this tent must be struck, needs still be rent for all of His sublime content.
Yet I also know that He made us each unique;
Because of this fact, my curiosity is always piqued.
All that the world can see in me, this unparalleled jumble of yearning,
I will never not hope to share, in ways befitting His desire to grow and keep me burning.
Wholeness comes from using gifts for Him He does richly bestow,
And so, I seek at every turn to somehow authentically grow:
I teach, read, speak, bound about, and write.
And hopefully, He'll use this woman in some way to show His glory, love, and might.

7.15 PRAYING TO JESUS:
How Am I To Abide in Him When I Still "Don't Know How to Love Him"?

A couple of times since I had come back from Greece, I noticed that I was experiencing hesitation and difficulty in praying expressly to *Jesus*. Now that He has infused me with the Holy Spirit, I confess that, in my immaturity, I miss the Jesus beckoning me at my window. As God is my Heavenly Father and Creator of the universe, *He* has always been my first go-to person of the Trinity when I pray, but then afterward, I have felt increasingly like I'm leaving Jesus out. Perhaps it is because I tend to go directly to the top first. And therefore, since God is the source of all life and everything in existence, then it seems as if God should also be the source of the second person in the Trinity, His Son, who came down here. *That is not so*! God can't be the source of His Son if they both — nay, all three — have existed in unity for eternity! It says in Genesis "we" when things were being made. Jesus *must* be equal in absolutely every way to and with the Father. Otherwise, God would not be *one* triune; He would be polytheistic! As Paul was want to say, "*May it never be*!" All this to say that when I pray to Jesus, instinctively and reflexively, I feel like I should be praying to God, but now as I pray to God, having been gifted with his whole Holy Spirit by Jesus, I don't want to leave Jesus out of the equation! I needed help. I feel like I'm making goulash! I just want to get it right! I suppose that as long as I am receptive and attentive to Jesus, these fuzzy distinctions of the Trinity, of the Triune God, will diminish. Just as it took me well over a year to comprehend and appreciate who the Holy Spirit is, now I'm doing the same with Christ. Don't worry! This is not a faith thing but a matter of getting my focus right! Now that I've been gifted with His Holy Spirit, I don't want to leave Jesus out. When others pray, do they pray to God or Jesus? Is it kind of like having a holy huddle with the two at the top? Does one talk to them concurrently, turning his head back-and-forth gently between the Father and the Son as they speak to him through the Holy Spirit, feeling those stirrings, promptings, and waves of love from that still, small voice within? My summative conclusion is I should think of it like this: God is *above* me, Jesus came to be *beside* me, and the Holy Spirit lives *in* me! Because I didn't grow up learning songs like "Jesus Loves Me" or "What a Friend We Have in Jesus," I thought I wasn't as intimately connected to Him as other folks except when I reflect on the pivotal moment of my salvation.

To that end, I have to say that it is difficult for me to think of Jesus as my buddy, "friend," or the like because it seems *so* disrespectful! Neither do I look at the trinity as some icon in my head or unapproachable Great Oz behind a curtain either. The veil was torn! Jesus taught us how to pray, and sometimes even in the gym, while I'm running around the track, I will say the Lord's Prayer, repeating each line until I have stressed each word in that line with mindfulness. It was also true that I am falling more in love with Jesus as I read His words and get to know Him better. I picked up on His verbal irony (and sometimes even sarcasm), appreciated His humor, and am blown away by His paradoxes, parables, and portents. Nonetheless, I didn't yet feel at ease in knowing how to pray to Him. I don't want the moment of my joy-filled recollection of salvation to be just that, a static memory. A simple act of faith, such as touching the hem of His garment (Matthew 9:20), is how it all started for me. If you take an inch, He'll give more than a mile!! After an oh-so-brief thirty-three years here, Jesus is back up there at the right hand of His Father. I also appreciate what the Holy Spirit does, Who he is, and am beyond thankful for Him. Not a day goes by that I don't think about this and say prayers of great gratitude! I get vexed with myself because I can get blocked in my prayer stance towards Jesus; it can overwhelm me to consider what He did and then endured. When I think about my prayer life, I also then wonder about *Jesus'* prayer life was like. It must have been incredibly intense but also, oh, so sweet! I would keep trying to seek what God had in store for me around the bend, including finding peace in prayer.

7.16 What Was It Like for Jesus as Man To Pray?

Though He did so frequently and at length, I wonder if it was ever difficult for Jesus to pray when He would go up to the mountain. It probably was a relief to get away from the rush of crowds and an uncomprehending group of the guys He chose to be His friends and so much more. Sometimes I mused over whether Christ and His Father had a particular discussion which led to Jesus agreeing to come here and live among us in mortal flesh, knowing all the while that His appointed task would entail dying a horrible death for us. I know that we are all given free will, but I wonder if that extended to Jesus while He was a man as well. Of course, Jesus already knew what He was going to do when He came here; therefore, He wouldn't *not* do what He came to do when that perhaps even dreaded hour arrived. It may have been His Father's idea, but Jesus was *that* obedient! He wasn't forced or cajoled. He was already all in and didn't or couldn't change His mind (because He's perfect). Without Jesus, reconciliation with God, our Father and Creator, and restitution would still not be possible. Occasionally it seemed to me like Christ had no will, choice, or voice in the matter. Did He really choose or even *want* to die for us? He was sweating blood in the Garden just the night before, for Heaven's sake! I remind myself He's not a mere man but God in the flesh, but still, crucifixion makes dying an agony. Yes, He agreed to accept His Father's wrath on our behalf, so I don't think there could've been any other way for punishment *long* overdue to be exacted, so in this way, I think He knew deep inside there wasn't a choice for *us* in our standing. We could never make things right on our own. God's plans and Jesus' arrival converged at the climax of the cross, where emerged the junction from the Old to the New Testaments, and thanks to Jesus, His Father's plan for a reunion was fulfilled. No more time out! Initially, I wondered which came first, God's idea or Jesus' agreement, but this way of thinking was replaced by my recognizing the concurrence of God's forbearance *and* Jesus' readiness to resolve our matter. And not only that, He came in humility and expressly sought out those who *weren't* at the top, weren't the mighty, and weren't even considered worthy! Though I read every morning, it's never enough.

The more and I study His word, the more I long for Him, yet also the more I see the world as the same as it was 2,000 years ago. God *had* to be dramatically overt in the early days; we were so rebellious, incorrigible, or "stiff-necked" (from Exodus, Chs. 32–34 KJV). Has there been any real change or progress made since then? We seem the same, but Christians live around the globe. So-called progress is not made on a straight upward arc but in undulating cyclical waves. Growth for Him seems small and slow; still, it has been sure and steady! We can be so daft and in such desperate need! Look at me! It took fifty years, but the moment of my acceptance happened quickly. It wasn't like I needed convincing or deep studying for my actual *becoming* a Christian to happen! This experience was unlike any other I had ever had in my life; I had had an epiphany in mind and soul. A comprehensive understanding is not jettisoned alongside when one becomes a Christian: fact upon fact and truth upon truth compound with interest inside you over time. If one were the prerequisite to another, few would become Christian. The degree comes first, then the education follows; it's to last a lifetime! And in this way, it was no wonder I was desperate to get my prayer life right with Jesus! It wouldn't come by my forcing it or thinking I could get Christ fully. Oswald Chamber says, "Faith is not an intellectual understanding; faith is a *deliberate commitment* to the Person of Jesus Christ, even when I can't see the way ahead." And what more honorable and right thing than for me to be in concurrent awe and wonderment as I was falling deeper in love with Jesus? What would Jesus want me to do regarding my prayer life? Does He want me to talk to Him throughout the day? Is God cool with that? I'm hoping Jesus will be patient with me until I can speak to Him as readily and directly as I have been to His Father. It took Mark's coming to visit to help me get that one step past stuck.

7.17 How to Bring My Prayer Life to Life

Next, it had gotten to the point that for *weeks* now, when I prayed, I kept feeling an overwhelming sadness over the suffering that Jesus went through for me. I couldn't stop hurting about this, even to the point of crying when I even thought of Him. When I told Mark about this, he compared Christ's "passion" – the Latin word for "suffering" — to a mother going through birthing pains for her infant. The pangs and pain are instantly displaced and forgotten when afterward, she becomes consumed with the all-powerful love she has for her child. Though I have not experienced childbirth myself, I have witnessed it, so I've seen this switch from pain and hurt to love and joy in the blink of a push. Therefore, just as a mother passes the pains of delivery, Jesus doesn't hold it against me for that which He endured! It was necessary for my birth to take place! Christ has a consuming love for me, too. I was grateful for this watershed moment impacting my prayer life! Another part of my life hurt my prayer with Jesus; this situation involved how I represented Jesus when He was brought up in regular conversation.

To be honest, I had been feeling shame before Christ because in my dealings in the world — especially with those I was close with — I was finding that even the word "Jesus" could be a turn-off. It made me feel like *I* denied Him when I put a deliberate lid on a conversation by not even mentioning His name. At the same time, and considering where I was in my Christian walk, I *do* try to represent Him the best I can. The grace I received is not dependent on longevity or differentiated by maturity. Plus, you can't intentionally put on some spiritual cloak (or voice) without coming off as a fake. Most of the time, people neither need nor some Bible verse recited at them, just an arm around their shoulder and knowing that you're there for them is what's in order. They won't usually benefit from a verse unless it is preceded or accompanied by tender, loving care. If you do so without considering the person's plight, then the focus shifts to your verse memorization rather than the need of their heart. Timing and sensitivity are everything here; the son of man, Jesus, who knew just what we felt, knew this. When you cry out, He will be there for you *both*.

I'm also aware of some Christians' off-putting exclusivity, and I smart for others' resentment of this. Still, truth is not relative or negotiable; otherwise, the truth would cease to be the truth: it would just be an opinion. Truth for God can only mean such in the absolute sense; there is no gray with God. Only one man lived a perfect life of love, obedience, and sacrificial goodness. Jesus Himself announced, "I am the way, and the truth, and the life; no one comes to the Father but through Me" (John 14:6). No other person has made this claim. As you have seen, over the years, I have done a lot of broad reading about various major religions, and, for example, when you look at Buddhism and Hinduism, there is no acknowledgment of *any* God. Islam is riddled with inaccuracies; they deny that Jesus even died on a cross. The non-Christian looks to the founder of a religion or philosophy he becomes enamored by in order to pursue a higher state, but somehow, it escapes him to seek to *the maker* of life itself, of everything, and us all. And this maker tries in infinite ways to show us His love, yes, even while we groan and fumble in the dark. Only Jesus, He who is singularly and uniquely God incarnate, authoritatively proclaimed, "I am the Light of the world; he who follows Me will not walk in the darkness but will have the Light of life" (John 8:12). When it's all said and done, yes, though there *are* many ways *to contemplate* God and there *are* many well-intended and interesting God-oriented *men*, there are *not* many ways to *God*. Therefore, all other religions now appear to me to be valiant attempts to reach God, to figure out what He seeks, and/or to appease or please Him. That's a strikeout. Aside from Christianity, all — bar none — invariably take a wrong turn and posit that *works and deeds* bring us closer to God, to perfection, or the like. Even the atheist who purports not to believe in God, in effect, makes a god of himself, and though perhaps he has achieved success by the world's standards and may be as sharp as a tack, you will not have to look too far or for long to find evidence in his life that proves he is hardly noble or his philanthropy fully expansive and evinced. Why, even the benign and ubiquitous Golden Rule proves to be off-center: "*Do* unto others…" The focus here, too, is on *doing*, when the very problem with humankind is his very *being*! How can we "do" good for any sustained period of time when we are laden with insidious selfishness? Paul wryly quipped, "There is none righteous, not even one" (Romans 3:10). We cannot be so glib, fanciful, or light-hearted to think otherwise!

I return to focusing on the intimate circles of my own life, where those nearest and dearest to me gravitate towards transcendental notions of God, such that if and when I bring up my faith, there is heard a deafening silence. They clam up and go under; this topic is avoided; the case is closed. I feel as if my hand has been figuratively slapped the moment I am aware of their awkwardness, disappointment, aloofness, or incredulousness when I confess my allegiance to Christ, like *I'm* the crazy one who has gone off the deep end or something. My inability to pursue, let alone break through to them has made me feel ashamed before Him at the time, and thus, for this reason, too, I have had trouble praying to Him. (At the time, I was not taking into account that only the Holy Spirit can prick a person's readiness to believe.) So, I would go to the top, to God, the Creator of everything — my Heavenly Father. Invariably, I do come full circle because God leads me straight back to Jesus who invited me to Himself and Them in the first place. I can get stuck in wanting to straight up and candidly just talk *to* Him, yet I also desire to be appropriately reverent toward and respectful *of* Him; the two didn't seem to align. How did God speak to and resolve this quandary within me? A resolution came about through a song, a new one for me but a classic for others. This song captured my longing and wanting to be closer to Him in prayer; it's called "Blessed Assurance." So, after all, as the song says, *"This is my story, this is my song, /Praising my Savior all the day long..."* Praising is the ticket! Surely, my technical difficulties are no different than what others have experienced. If I feel overwhelmed or in momentary doubt or stuck in idle, *I make the executive decision that I will simply try and talk to Him, anytime, anywhere, no matter what.* Direct is just how He wants me to be with Him. I'm confident that He loves it when I make an effort and attempt to pray, all the more so since I do so without fail now. The spigot is on! God won't take offense; to talk to Jesus *is* to talk to God because He's present there just as sure as His Spirit now resides in me. In our limited humanness, to multi-task means to divide one's attention; it ain't like that for any of *Them*! God and Jesus, that is, Father and Son, may be different in aspect or identity, but not in essence or substance, so it's a win-win, Yes-Yes, whether I pray to the one or the other! And, oh, when I *praise* Jesus and *thank* God for everything — yes, the good *and* the bad, I turn my attention away from self-pity and bask in His full richness, all the while growing my faith! Thank you, Jesus, for this moment!

7.18 MORE QUESTIONS:

Where Did God Go after the Fall? Why Was There A Fall?

One month later, not only had I not been able to find online the answers to some of my previous questions, but several more issues came swimming into my kenning. Would these questions bubbling up ever stop? Would I ever be done with them? They certainly were not meant as a challenge or deal-breaker in keeping my faith! It's just that the more I read the Good News, the more questions came to my mind of their own accord. How could they not? As far as knowing Christ goes, I was in catch-up mode! Are my questions unique? Hardly! Is this process I'm going through significant? I think so, in fact, so much so, that it gave rise to my writing so *you* can know of the critical moments *after* salvation, those where faith is being exercised like a new muscle, gaining strength and new sinew that hadn't even existed before! And what is the point of all this learning and churning? Certainly not for my edification. God isn't spinning out riddles to stump me or anyone. Over the sorting, sifting, writing, questioning, *and* experiencing new joys, it came to me to *share* this journey, this traversing into becoming a more mature Christian. And so, as I continue to share the evolution of my interior revolution, you'll see "something old, something new, something borrowed, something now true blue" in me; I have been forever changed, newly imbued. Speaking of new, I'd next try to make sense of early man's monumental evolution and progress, however infernally slow.

The time frame when God's actual presence became known, felt, and enjoyed was as short-lived as a child is an infant. Consider the moments when Adam was talking directly with God in the Garden before there was even any need for a Savior. Could he still talk to God *after* his colossal folly? Was man put in a semi-permanent time-out until the Flood, then another spell of such until Christ? It's not like Jesus comes down in God's week two to save the pair. After Adam and Eve are expelled from the Garden of Eden, did God literally *and* figuratively withdraw from the world to go back to Heaven to wait until it is time for the New Heaven to join the New Earth? Does this mean He is in another realm or dimension we call "Heaven"? Did He leave us to our vices in our mussed-up land of sin? It seems like He only contacted the few, the not-so-proud, and the far-from-perfect to take us to the next level He would intend for us. (If He did choose those who were mighty or haughty, He made it such that life could break them to re-make them.) Did Adam and Eve leave, and did God stay behind in the Garden? Do you think Adam *missed* talking to God? Do you think Adam realized the immensity of his foolishness? I'll bet he did! And though it would have been marvelous, heavenly, to have heard God "walking in the garden in the cool of the day" (Genesis 3:8), by then, God already knew what wrong the pair would do. I see now that though there is a chronology to the Bible, in a sense, it doesn't matter that it was Adam and Eve; *any* person would have done the same thing in their place. We don't get to blame them because we, too, willfully *still* do wrong. Daily. It's not just a congenital defect. We are all active participants in sin. Did I have this right? How can we be agitated over *their* disobedience and the subsequent guilt by association we share with them when I misuse the *same* free will God gave *me*? We are they, and we would have done the same thing; we do so now! Help, however, was always on the way.

Anyway, to have let them stay in the Garden would have meant remaining in a suspended infancy of sorts, and love isn't tested that way; one can't grow in a static or fixed environment. That God gave man freedom also means He already knew that we were going to be disobedient to Him. The ball had to get rolling, so to speak, for us to begin this expedition of faith, growth, and submission, all to culminate in His astounding, unmerited mercy. Jesus took quite the hit for *millennia* of willful disobedience. It's no wonder God was so strong-armed in those early days. Just as the individual must grow to a state of accountability, humanity had to progress through the terrible twos, then to ugly-duckling adolescence, past the rebellious teen years, centuries upon centuries later, to a time when there existed a thread of readiness within us to engage in faith. Then and now, I think the point is to keep growing and always come back to Him. That said, even with His exasperation demonstrated with the Flood, God continued to show restraint or forbearance. In some ways, though we are not as barbaric and primitive in our approach to violence, evil seems expressed in even more pervasive and pernicious ways. The presence of wrong in the world has gone from a little bit of bad yeast in humanity's dough to loaves of fully-baked, toxic bread everywhere. "Water, water everywhere, and *not a drop to drink*," writes Samuel Taylor Coleridge. Before such despairing thoughts of the inevitability of sin and suffering in man suffocate me, I then force myself to *think it through* and know that all roads lead to Jesus coming here. This is *so* not the end! He is our great Physician, our Teacher, and

our Redeemer. That I can and do see the inevitability of Christ coming here *is* a gift for which I am incredibly grateful. Seeking to know Him evermore, I hatched another batch of topics for consideration that had been brewing in my brain, compelling my heart forward. Here they are:

7.19 Q'S FROM ALL OVER THE MAP

1. In Matthew 25:15, what does it mean that a man is given talents "each according to his own ability"? Is this referring to money or to a person's innate talents? Could it mean both? I thought stewardship means recognizing one's God-given talent and not wasting time and life by not using it for Him. If my primary gift is, for example, teaching, and that is my vocation, how will that look when I no longer have that job? I also need to feel productive, and I find it both difficult and dissatisfying just to chill. Even the word "retirement" sounds like a death sentence. After all, the origin of this word means "to retreat"! Could writing also be considered a way of serving God? And in a similar vein, I now find myself evaluating myself and others differently concerning how we express our portioned spiritual gifts listed in Romans 12:7, and this has been especially the case with how I view Bonnie. For example, I see that Bonnie possesses the gifts of mercy and giving, which, frankly, seem to be my two weakest areas, and therefore, I am in awe. With faith growing drop-by-drop, inch-by-inch, Bonnie and I have also been able to relinquish some golden calves and take up new means to help those in need, be it children in Haiti or those in dire straits as serviced by our church's disaster team. As for myself, I weave in His Word, subtly or not so subtly, where I can, even at school. I pray for Him to use me and for me to be receptive to the moments He avails.
2. I realize that I have to be extremely careful in how I share my faith. In so doing, it feels like I am trying to hit the on and off switch at the same time, and I get static. Do you think He's upset with me when I choose silence at times? Am I being like Peter denying Him when I choose not to talk about Jesus with nonbelievers? To be honest, it is

hard for me to talk about Jesus because my view of Him and knowing how to talk about Him shifts. What do I mean by this? Of course, He is my Savior, but that is not what I mean. I do not think of Jesus as my buddy, friend, or the like, but I also don't look at Him as some sort of distant, mystical icon. He is the Messiah, King, and my Man all rolled into one. I visualize Him walking beside me wherever I go, no matter what I'm doing. Sometimes I imagine holding His hand like I used to love to do with my father, and sometimes I visualize my head resting on His chest; sometimes, I kiss His cheek. By now, yes, I do know that if I talk to one (God), I'm also talking to the other (Christ). Occasionally, if I make the sign of the cross — up, down, right, left, and then touch my heart — I say the following: "My Father is infinitely *above* and *below*; Jesus is to the *right and left* of me wherever I go, and the Holy Spirit is alive and well *within me*." Psalm 103:12 solidifies my symbolism and expresses His scope: "As far as the east is from the west, so far has He removed our transgressions from us."

In short, my prayers to *Jesus* — and Him alone — encompass the all-for-one, three-in-one Triune, the singular Trinity. I just *let it be* and choose not to fret if one day I talk to God and the next day, Jesus. Neither minds as they are of one accord. And speaking of which, I contemplated just how the Word fits in with God. The Apostle John tells us, "In the beginning was the Word, and the Word was with God, and the Word was God" (John 1:1). Does the Word, His *logos*, the essence or will of God come alive or animate when we read it? Yes! I indeed experience this! "Logos" — or λόγος in Greek — to the Greek means so much more than the lexeme, "word"! It involves His wisdom, prescience, *and* sovereignty. As you read the Bible, regardless of the writer or book, you sense God's volition and love expressed intently for us as He is the author of both it and us. Then, as I was making my way through Proverbs, I found that "The LORD *by wisdom* founded the earth" (3:19, emphasis mine). I pondered over the word, "wisdom," too, something so dear to those early Greeks. Evidently, *it* has been in the mix since time immemorial too. How could it not? This time, I sought *Godly* wisdom through dialogue and relationships with other Christians and not ferreting it out in the world.

7.20 Iron Sharpening Iron:
Original Sin Revisited

Though Bonnie and I had very different backgrounds, experiences, gifts, and outlooks, we helped each other out where the other faltered or had questions. Were we grateful to have a mentor, guide, teacher, and friend in Mark, perhaps even beyond being our pastor, especially when we didn't understand ideas in the Bible or at those times when Satan got us off-kilter? Absolutely! Yet over time, with patience and tenderness, Bonnie and I more and more began to be able to talk through questions and insecurities for ourselves. Our support of and for each other would contribute to growth. In fact, I learned that this mutual helping of one another was an example of "iron sharpening iron" (Proverbs 27:17), which refers to the fact that we are to receive a gentle reproof from as well as to give encouragement to a fellow Christian when we falter or fall. This can also pertain to another Christian help me develop a more accurate understanding of biblical principles or occurrences. Even though we were hardly "sharp," still we could serve to "sharpen" each other! Case in point, Bonnie helped me understand the nature of Original Sin this morning.

It still vexed me in those days when I considered that and how Adam and Eve's wrongdoing got passed on, as if sin was akin to dimples or some dreadful congenital disease we inherited from our parents. What Bonnie explained to me was that we had been living in a perfect state, then we *chose* to believe Satan's lie so that *we could be like God*. In taking a bite of that beautiful bait, through that decision, we, His creatures *and* the world in which we would inhabit were forever tainted, poisoned, and irrevocably altered. The crucible contained a new compound. We chose our wants over God's one singular command; we were disobedient. We couldn't even do *one thing* right! With the transgression, we disqualified ourselves and could no longer stay in the Garden of Eden, the home base of perfection. The immense gravity of this act was demonstrated by their new shame: they tried to hide from God — a laughable thought! What God gave us — our free will — man used to try to place himself *on the same level as* God, which is exactly what Lucifer did. Being *made* in God's image is not the same as *being* He! Our waywardness resulted in the perversion and misuse of our gift of freedom; we ran amok. God couldn't *not* give us this liberty with which to choose to obey Him *and* to love Him. We *had* to be t-totally free in our thinking; otherwise, we would've amounted to being His puppet on a string. I had had it wrong. Love wouldn't be genuine if we were His marionettes! I'd rather be His slave! Sin is *not* passed on like hair type or eye color. Sin is a state of *complete* transmogrification or, as Bonnie put it, a "pollution," a going-to-pot that Adam and Eve initiated. It can't cease with mere and mortal man, so it still taints *our* relationship with God. He *had* to banish us; otherwise, acceptance would mean tolerance sin, and then He would not be He. Thank God for Jesus!

We continued in this discussion. Today we still blindly, though sometimes even gladly, take up our folly daily. Everybody has this sin because no one uses his free will perfectly, law or not, intentions righteous or not. And merit is not based on the grading system of A through F; there is no extra credit, no class curve; it's pass or fail! There is *only* perfection with God. Then I asked Bonnie, "But what about the Law?" To which she responded, "If you can be obedient to the law 100% perfectly, go for it; then you are eligible." God got so mad that He wanted to wipe everybody out, so Bonnie said that we are actually *the offspring of Noah*. And even though God let everyone perish except for Noah and his family, sin persisted because we still chose to worship the own gods of our own making. In short, sin is not so much in our physical or genetic DNA as it is in our moral code, fiber, or constitution, which *also* originated from God. It's like a birth defect *we* caused. Sin spoils something very dear inside us, and if we had not been born with free will, we wouldn't have had the capacity to choose to recognize God, let alone love back, the way the prodigal son finally does of his biding father. The Apostle Paul helped us both play it through here. He tells us, "[12]*through one man sin entered into the world*…[and] [15] by the transgression of the one the many died, [yet] much more did the grace of God and *the gift by the grace of the one Man, Jesus Christ, abound to the many*" (from Romans 5:12 and 15, emphasis mine). The Law came about in between. Think about it like a married woman having a child from an adulterous relationship. That *child* is forever affected by the sin of the mother. Just look at that airy sprite Pearl from her mother, Hester Prynne, both characters from the novel, *The Scarlet Letter*. She was ostracized for her mother's sin, yet she, too, was wayward, spiteful, and uncontrollable. In her precocity, she knew the deal and intuited the Reverend Dimmesdale was special and was somehow connected to her. Indeed, when the parents and their child held hands, "the three formed an electric chain." I share that link with everyone, like it or them or not! Sin is not a *literal* birth defect; it is the mutator of our whole moral system. No, Eve was not "framed," as some feminists quip. It's not Adam's fault he turned out to be a poor leader. This is *not* about the doing of a man or a woman, but *disobedience*, pure and simple. By the way, this systemic sinfulness (or, if you prefer, *lack of moral perfection*, if the word "sin" is yet unpalatable to you) is *not* the same as the reference to Exodus about the sins of the father visiting the son. I think *this* means that the ramifications of parental mismanagement can and do spin out for generations, but God is not expressly punishing *the kids*. If and when we follow our parents' example, we become culpable or responsible for our wrongdoings. It's just a shame about those behavioral patterns where we have the cards stacked against us, and we all do. Out of pity, loving mercy, and necessity, Jesus took onto Himself in one fell swoop the punishment due to us. Everything then and there at Golgotha got reset in a way more comprehensive than the Flood could ever wash the world. This kind of intent and intense love is incomprehensible because we are incapable of doing the like; we are one three-dimensional to His being beyond any measure, no perturbation intended. Only a scantling few of us turn out to be able to sacrifice our lives, but any such act, though so appreciated, does not change the course of humanity. Following is a recorded snippet of a conversation Bonnie and I had one Saturday morning that captures our contending with the subject of man's plighted state:

> **Dimi:** If it was Eve who was originally the weaker one, I wonder why God didn't make another human being that was as perfect or complete as Adam was. I wonder why he had to take a *rib* from Adam and create Eve from him. Maybe if He would've made another person all from scratch, then that weakness would not have had in it a potential propensity for

weakness. Do you think that Adam would have disobeyed God had he remained alone?

Bonnie: Pretty much, yeah, I do. I don't know that he wanted to be God. I think Satan just deceived Eve into thinking that she could also have His wisdom if she ate the fruit. That sounded pretty good to her, and she might have thought God was holding out on them, like He was denying them or something. Being human, we make bad decisions with our free will.

Dimi: But we didn't start out that way; evidently, there were a few years of complete submission and obedience and perfect fellowship.

Bonnie: Haha, ha, probably not for long. Yeah, I don't know how long it was before Satan came.

Dimi: I'll bet he was in the bushes the whole time. Nah, I suppose that he was not even hiding because he had no shame — he's all ego, you know.

Bonnie: True, he was just hanging out and waiting for the right moment. Hook, line, and sinker, we took the bait.

7.21 POISONED DARTS AND TRAPS TO TRIP THIS "WHOSOEVER"

By now, I know that just as surely as alcohol was once "cunning, baffling, and powerful" to me, I have become most aware that Satan wants to crush and hush my joy in Christ. One of his most potent weapons to squelch me is through the lies he tells. He's *still* at it! Surely, the way I respond to those lies factors in, too. For example, when I find myself defeated and deflated, I can easily feel that all is for naught or that everything I do is futile. Clearly, I have a perception problem. Also, during those moments when I think I've been treated unfairly or slighted, I can feel wronged, and this can turn into me turning sour and dour on a dime! Self-pity is such a loathsome thing! The cure for self-pity is not to forcibly minimize the whole situation away or to think how much better off you have it than other folks, as in, "after all...," which is just inducing guilt in yourself. You must give yourself a little shake and remind yourself of the spectacular power of Him Who now dwells in you. Inside every Clark Kent is a Superman! He wants to use me throughout my life, so I am *not* unimportant to Him! In fact, I am on call for Him. Together we are unstoppable! This is what is meant by "I can do all things through Christ who strengthens me" (Philippians 4:13 KJV). What a beautiful symbiosis! I am still a work in progress because sanctification is ongoing; the rate and quality of such growth are mainly on me.

Meanwhile, Satan custom-designs traps to stall, prevent, or reroute our energies designated for Him; if we remain unaware of this fact, there's no battle. Satan's got you in the bag, so to speak. This is why when one becomes a Christian, the battle for your mind is made evident to you, and sometimes his onslaught can be fierce. Whether the struggle comes from within or is launched from without, the new Christian quickly becomes hyperaware of the ways and means Satan uses to have him stumble or falter that previously he was oblivious to. Satan doesn't *have* to battle the person who already lives by and for the world. A person who gets his affirmation, esteem, and value from the world struggles from that introspective psychological struggle, that is, until or unless he feels inexplicable empty. Until then, Satan needs to do no further tempting; he's on cruise control headed south with this lost soul. This person thinks of himself as "cool" or even superior when really, he is driving blind, not seeing where he's ultimately headed. As one who now sides with Jesus, I have experienced Satan violating my private time reading the Bible; sometimes, he twists up passages, and they turn into mini wrecks in my brain! One difficult passage that has evaded me is "narrow is the gate and difficult is the way which leads to life, and there are few who find it" (Matthew 7:14 NKJV). Oh, if I'm not careful, I can get stuck here for a long time thinking I'm *not* one of the "few"! I take some comfort knowing even my King and Savior had to contend with Satan in His Temptations. That said, do not ever think *you* are stalwart enough to go up against him without relying on Jesus in such situations! On the other hand, I certainly don't want to give Satan one bit of credit where credit is not due! Unlike God, *Satan cannot read your mind or be present in all the moments of your life*! I will share a few of my internalized put-downs because if/when you also come to Him, you too may be careened with negative thoughts that you don't understand how or why they occur to you. I can sometimes fixate on my small-minded, regulated, routine, and uncourageous life. I can feel like T.S. Eliot's Prufrock when he says, "I have measured out my life with coffee spoons." What all can I do in my life to glorify Him? I think to myself, "I'm not fooling anyone." I'm crimson-covered rubbish; the Holy Spirit dwells within a big fat zero. I may be an adopted daughter, but if I'm not in the mindset or heart-ready to live and do for Him, I become like nothing. There's *got* to be more I can do for Him. Satan can paralyze me with what *seems* like real truths right now. I was ashamed of writing about how little time each day I spend with the Lord, daily though it may be. Big whoopee. Why should I get a pat on the back for doing what I'm *supposed* to do anyway? I've taken no *real* risks for Him. I have not begun tithing, and I have led no one to Christ. I know I have spiritual gifts, and I am using them, but I often replay ingrained tapes from childhood that whatever I do will never be enough. I am so glad that God's got this regardless of whether I even exist or not. For someone else, he might instill fear. I don't want to give him any more credit where none is due. Satam *is* lazy, and he uses tried and true traps that work on *you*; you must make yourself aware of them. For example, as one with a naturally encouraging spirit, Satan's method on me has been to discourage me. He also uses persons to distract or destroy you when he's behind them the whole time.

You may ask me now, how do you get past this battle for the brain? First comes recognition. I find that if I *turn the page* — sometimes if I *go outside* or keep *moving forward*, as hard as it may be to get started at such times, the moment *does* pass. I also give myself a good talking to and remind myself that there's absolutely *nothing* that can keep Him from me. Paul comprehensively delineated what these "things" constitute: "neither death, nor life, nor angels, nor principalities, nor things present, nor things to come, nor powers,[39] nor height, nor depth, nor any other created thing [that] will be able to separate us from the love of God, which is in Christ Jesus our Lord" (Romans 8:38–39). I also don't stir the pot and keep strife or negativity alive by verbalizing these things aloud unless there's a solid Christian friend nearby who can help lend me a helping hand. A back-and-forth, push-and-pull, tug-of-war, or yo-yo sort of life regarding who you are and what you do is a sure sign that you're in the process of shifting your allegiance to Him. After all, you've uprooted yourself and moved the foundation of your "tent"! As a young Christian, you may feel threatened and unsure, but you must turn your focus on *Him* with blinders on, full steam ahead. You may feel invincible, but you are not, even if Christ wins in the end. Maybe other young Christians never doubt or have fears or feel deflated, but I'm just relating my own experience with you. I also would *pray* to get unstuck. Invariably, I come around. Jesus gives me a pep talk of bolstering truth, and it looks something like this: If I get sucked into a spiritual paralysis not only of questioning but of doubting my salvation, I remind myself that it doesn't matter what anybody says. I will *not* place my stock and faith in *man*; I put it squarely in *Jesus*. And then I'll trust Him with my heart, that is, *all* of me. *He will not fail me!!* Even Mark would proclaim to me, "Now listen to me, sister, get your head up and shoulders back and be encouraged. *You are a daughter of the King!!*" Then somehow, I back away from the edge of despair because I am acrophobic, and *I run* to my rock, my Redeemer.

So, back to efficacy: in short, God doesn't make anyone useless; plus, He has built-in bumpers, measures, or safeguards against such evil that would tarnish our character if we would only heed

His help; first, though, He's got to be *in* us. Deep inside, we all crave meaning in life and a union with that which set our life in motion. If I'm not in the mindset of Him and get tangled or bent up in ire, that's on me not to cower or get distracted! "Keep your eyes on the prize," I say to myself! And it's also not my job to fix, let alone to save anyone else! I suit up for Christ and *let Him have His way with me*, whomever I may come to impact. Part of suiting up involves daily reading His Word and praying; it's not a *have*-to thing, but a *get*-to and a *want*-to! No, just because praying becomes part of your daily routine, this is not to say that it is rote or ritualistic. He knows the difference! Your prayer life ought not to amount to recitation or formulaic counting of this and that! He likes it when I spend time with Him, earnestly and respectfully talk to Him, and encounter Him by reading His Word. After all, the way I recognize Him more in life is by getting to know Him better. I'm sure He knows I'm just starting! From day one, ground zero, it is evident to me that He has been drawing me to Him. Can you see this, too? I've no doubt that should you look back over your life, you, too, can connect the dots of *your* life and watch them lead straight to God who made you and Jesus who saved you, all wrapped up in love. The completion of the circle beginning and ending with Him occurs when you accede to Him. If you ever wonder if, in the Garden of Gethsemane, Jesus might have had second thoughts about dying for us, as it is apparent that He was anxiety-stricken over his impending torture, the answer is "No." He didn't grow up all but to say, "Just kidding. They're not worth it. I'm having second thoughts about all of this." It's not *that* but *how* He was to die that was killing Him before the Romans actually did so. (Plus, His Father would be momentarily MIA from the scene of *this* crime.) The "cup" referred to in Matthew 26 has to do with Jesus asking His Father if there was another means by which He could accomplish His Father's will. As a man, Jesus wouldn't have wanted to have felt that horrific suffering! His divinity meant that He knew what was coming ahead! When it's all said and done, the manger leads us straight to the cross through His obedience! My being troubled by someone — Jesus — *dying* for me leads me back to the realization that, as Mark puts it, I've "never been loved like this." All this free mercy is new and overwhelming to me. Right at my heels and as I stand with arms outstretched to Him in this blossom of love and burst of faith over His staggering gift of fierce love, I find Satan, sneaking and lurking like a pygmy in the bush, shooting poisoned darts in my temples, saying "It ain't so! He doesn't want you!" Agh! Such is a day in the life of an early believer. It's maddening and futile for me to do anything but cling to Christ. And though I am covered by what Christ did and am no longer viewed as a sinner, *I* know *He* knows I still sin. Of course, I do! I'm alive! If I'm at my wit's end, I hearken upon His words that pacify, fortify, and uplift: "the peace of God, which surpasses all comprehension, will guard your hearts and your minds in Christ Jesus" (Philippians 4:7). And He said, "*will*," not "might"! Therefore, I continue to take tiny steps in obedience as well. Faith sure ain't a feeling!!

Another aspect of my trying to grow in Christ involved dealing with the notion of initial illegibility, that is, the million-dollar dilemma of whether any and everyone can be *and remain* the "whosoever" Christ proclaims in John 3:15. What then to do when, just a few pages past the four Gospels, one encounters Paul's admonition that some [believers] will *not* see the kingdom of Heaven if they stay in situations not optimal for the Christian life? Can one disqualify one's own saved status? Does lack of perfection in one's walk lead to some inadvertent apostasy? Can you of your own accord undo and flip your status as "whosoever" to "not now or ever"? Yes, I know that Jesus died for our sins, but what is one to do when Paul asks in Romans 6:1–2, but "what shall we say then? Are we to continue in sin so that grace may increase? May it never be!" Just how is "sin" determined or defined? Is it man or God that makes the list by which we abide? Is it by our law, His Commandments, both of these, or more? In one of his exhortations, Paul concludes that to continue to breach what God would have us do and merely live for *self* would lead to or indicate one's *not* being able to "inherit the kingdom of heaven" (1 Cor. 6:9). This is not a little troubling. No one can live up to this standard! It can be difficult for *anyone* to reconcile these seeming conflicting stances between Jesus and Paul. I think many Christians get diverted from their primary purpose, and instead of focusing on what they *can* still yet *do*, which is *serve*, they derail themselves and harp on what we *can't* do, which is to become perfect. No, of course, just because our sins are covered and we are saved doesn't mean we have a license to do wrong! Good grief! Paul's declaration above was *not* meant to counter, disqualify, or negate Jesus' invitation; he just didn't want folks to sit on their laurels of salvation and remain unmoved by Him. I believe if Paul were around today, he would tell us to "get up and *go*, just *do* for *Christ*!" It's a matter of both personal choice *and* life's timing that can turn around whatever hampering situation you're in that keeps you from doing and being your best for Christ. Nothing you do can sever the tie you've made with Him. We are assured of this because "He Himself said, 'I WILL NEVER DESERT YOU, NOR WILL I EVER FORSAKE YOU'" (Hebrews 13:5).

All that to say, and here I quote my friend Mark: "the Christian life isn't just difficult; it's impossible!" What Christian doesn't know this of and for himself daily? *All* fall short of His standard. So, bottom line, just how "narrow" is the path? I then wonder to myself, "How would Jesus weigh in"? If a person who has accepted Jesus but doesn't "produce fruit" and makes no apparent changes, will he still make it to Heaven? Upon his death, might he hear the dreaded words from Jesus, "I never knew you; DEPART FROM ME, YOU WHO PRACTICE LAWLESSNESS" (Matthew 7:23)? I think Jesus knows the difference between a nominal Christian who said, "Yes," but without heart and mind engaged. We humans can't know this difference though we often think we can; only He does! The simple answer to whether or not you're Heaven-bound by coming to Jesus to begin with is that, "Yes," you are in! Jesus knows we're not perfect, and even though we do wrong, this isn't the same thing as "practicing lawlessness." Amazingly, it was Paul who confessed that he had an affliction or some unnamed problem *that wouldn't leave him*, and yet Jesus assured him that "My grace is sufficient for you, for power is perfected in weakness" (2 Cor. 12:9). Only someone like Jesus could utter such a paradox and scoop us up in love when we come to Him on our scuffed knees. And, oh, the most ordinary day in Heaven will be better than any best day in Hell. Know that Satan will never stop trying to dissuade and discourage you, even if he has to twist up piecemeal threads of Scripture in such a way that you miss the spirit of the breadth and depth of God's message for us. That would be missing the forest for the trees! The goal of the "author of confusion" is to "kill, steal, and destroy" us (John 10:10), but my God and my Savior will always have the last word.

How does Jesus help me get off the ground and back on my feet? We need to fasten our attention on nothing and no one but Christ for our salvation *and* restoration. That "no one" includes Paul, a few well-intended neighbors, and many a preacher who spouts isolated biblical passages like a hit-and-run technique, albeit even for the greater good. To ask about what might disqualify a saved person from his salvation is to give credence to the loaded question and engage in a no-win logical fallacy where *either way, you lose*. If someone proclaims that a person who has accepted Christ but *appears* unchanged or unmoved is not nor was ever saved, he would, in essence, be calling Jesus a liar, as if to say His grace *wasn't* sufficient. God will not abandon a person who has knowingly decided to put his faith in Christ! Such a decision trumps whatever imperfect residual behaviors remain! That said, if you never grow in your walk and remain as you were from day one, surely that indicates a slight and superficial nod to Jesus. It's as though once you've completed your Sunday school lessons or have moved on to the conventional markers of success like job, home, and family, you're "good-to-go," or else you say in passing, you have "been there and done that." Let me tell you that Jesus will be sighing over *you*. The truth is such a person never really took steps in his sanctification; therefore, no matter how old she or he is chronologically, this adult remains an infant in faith. He is still in spiritual diapers! Oh, I pray, may this never be the case for me!

There are no take-backs with Jesus; one who is saved can't be <u>un</u>saved or <u>de</u>-saved, as it were. It's a done deal. On the other hand, if you tell the new believer that there is nothing wrong with remaining unchanged, you placate and discourage that person from growing in faith and character. The person should desire change for Him, even if there remains a struggle for the rest of his life. *All* believers experience this in one way or another and at one season or another! It's just that the difficulties either lessen or shift to more subtle ones such that you aren't hacking away at glaring sins but buffing out minor scratches. And since all sins are equally abhorrent in the eyes of God and there's no gray and everyone sins, who am I or anyone to pick and choose and make a hierarchy of sin?!? Certainly, no one! If a person is saved and gets baptized in youth and then blatantly remains in carnality throughout his adulthood, with sinning rife and alive, only after he dies will that person shed many a tear when Jesus shows him all he neglected to do and all of the opprtunities he missed to glorify Him. This predicament is between that person and Jesus. On the other hand, as a believer, I *do* have a right *and* a responsibility to find a way to tactfully and caringly correct such a one. After all, we are told, "Brothers and sisters, if someone is caught in a sin, you who live by the Spirit should restore that person gently. But watch yourselves, or you also may be tempted" (Galatians 6:1 NIV). In my opinion, I would *really* have to know, understand, and love this person to be able to help "restore" him. The cautionary caveat means that if I'm not careful, I could be tempted to be as judgmental as a Pharisee without having examined and removed my own sin! Plus, the Holy Spirit and the individual's state of readiness are part of this matrix, too!

Paul's warnings *are* still valid and applicable today, but we must look to the environment and conditions he observed first-hand to appreciate his slant or focus. If Paul were alive today, his list undoubtedly would be longer! What is the bottom-line, common denominator flaw upon which Paul hits again and again? When one chooses self over God with reckless abandon, divorces her body from spirit with disregard for both, and maligns her neighbor and herself for a moment's satisfaction, that is tantamount to disrespecting the creation and Creator. Whose job is it to inspect, inform, and reprove the Christian youngster or potential convert from straying or indulging in harmful behaviors? Perhaps a loved one can help, but if the correction is given in a spirit of hate, condemnation, or even condescending pity, then nothing is likely to be accomplished. Honestly, no person is completely qualified to do so, as we all fall short. Therefore, we also ought to forgive others' trespasses against us just as we seek such grace and compassion for ourselves. Yes, this is a messy affair, but Jesus certainly thought we were worth it. Drop the condemnation, and you can be a part of the change for the good you might not ever fully come to see. There's *another* exercise for your faith! Again, Scripture and God through Christ alone — not Paul or any other renowned theologian or popular pastor — always provide the final and definitive answer as to how to redress another. When it's all said and done, Christ Himself errs on the side of *mercy* such that when a sinner — saved or not — comes into an awareness of just what being "saved" entails, changes for him will come *in the manner and timing King Jesus intended.* How could it be any other way? (Do remember that we can't predict the arrival of a sinner's salvation because we can't see into the future, so we who believe must always try to be full of hope and not send mixed messages.) Everything about Him exudes unmerited and free mercy, radical grace, and authentic love. There's no one like Him. Still yet, there's no *guarantee* that a saved person will "*bear fruit* in keeping with repentance" (Matthew 3:8, emphasis mine). You may come to see that person go through circumstances that are designed to make him more appreciative of, dependent on, or enthused about growing in God. Such challenges ought not to be looked at like spiritual warfare but fitness training! Regardless of whether or not one discernibly grows in sanctification, the bottom line is that Jesus doesn't and won't change His mind about that person if he's been saved. "Once saved, always saved," is how I've heard it said. Following is the passage that *guarantees* salvation is secured. Paul wrote it, and he ought to know; he was a "wretched man" himself (Romans 7:24). "I am convinced that neither death, nor life, nor angels, nor principalities, nor things present, nor things to come, nor powers, nor height, nor depth, nor any other created thing, *will be able to separate us from the love of God, which is in Christ Jesus our Lord*" (Romans 8:38–39, emphasis mine). Once you put your faith in Jesus, "it is finished" (John 19:30) for you, too, meaning His mission of reconciliation *then* became accomplished in you *now*, so it's then a done deal. Signed, sealed, delivered, you're His! His very Spirit is placed in you; therefore, you are eternally connected to Him. Nothing and no one has the power to divorce, negate, or deny you of being the child of his or her Heavenly Father. All that to say, for me personally, I hope and pray that with the time I have left that I can be useful and available to what all He needs me to do and be such that He might say, "Brava!" to me later on. I want to make Him proud and do Him right!

Should one feel downcast, discouraged, disqualified, disappointed, or impatient, there is another way to bolster one's faith. When I get the blues, I know it's just a matter of time before I come upon a biblical phrase or utterance that hits the spot and soothes my being troubled about something I don't *yet* understand in a passage or wording of the Bible. As I said before, lingering and saturating oneself in the Bible leads to a supernatural experience or dynamism between God and you!

I am told to "cast all my anxiety on Him because *He cares for me*" (1 Peter 5:7). Before I was a Christian, there was a restlessness, a yearning, and a stirring in me I could only *temporarily* satisfy. Afterward, in my earliest growing pains and when I was trying to make up for lost time, I not only wrestled with understanding the role of the Holy Spirit, including just how sealed I was, but I got sidetracked with a new language. I was both fascinated and overwhelmed by words like "eschatology," "propitiation," "hermeneutics," and "imputing." Good heavens! If I was at the gym and ran into my friend Rick, I would catch him up on the latest this or that in my walk or a particular passage I either had gotten hung up on or fallen in love with. He would reassure me by quoting Biblical passages, and this was one, in particular, he'd say to me numerous times: "Take My yoke upon you and learn from Me, for I am gentle and humble in heart, and YOU WILL FIND REST FOR YOUR SOULS" (Matthew 11:29). If I got agitated over (momentary) misunderstandings, I was like a bloodhound on a search for the truth, *His* truth. The wasn't *Who Wants To Be A Millionaire*, with my options being Ask the Audience, Phone a Friend, and 50-50. No! I wanted to get it *right*. I'd quickly write down my questions and check in with other believers that I was sure were more mature than I. Then I would cling to Jesus in prayer in my mind and rest on His assurance that "Peace I leave with you; My peace I give to you; *not as the world gives* do I give to you. *Do not let your heart be troubled*, nor let it be fearful" (John 14:7, emphasis mine).

Focusing so long and hard on the nature of sin impedes us from actively serving the Lord because our eyes can get stuck on our navel. The flip side of feeling stuck in sin is trying to jump from one happy moment to the next, looking for the next spiritual high. That is just as erroneous, not that there's anything wrong with pursuing happiness. However, Americans tend to have their priorities skewed. John MacArthur said, "Spiritual joy is not an attitude dependent on chance or circumstance. It is the deep and abiding confidence that regardless of one's circumstances in life, all is well between the believer and the Lord." Mark shared this quote with us one Wednesday evening to express that as we go through life, we should discern between short-lived moments of happiness and not confuse this with the more abiding joy in the Lord. He intended this discernment between the two to encourage us when we might be going through painful times or feeling frustrated with ourselves. Living for Him daily, intentionally trying to be more like Him, and relying on Him will naturally and of its own accord change a person *from the inside out* in the manner and rate *He* intends. Knowing this should help fortify one and keep him from the doldrums or the blues, which I mentioned earlier. A young Christian's evolution might not look like what man could anticipate, let alone prefer. After all, we are "*His* workmanship" (Eph. 2:10, emphasis mine). Maturation that lasts comes gradually; the metamorphosis then becomes beautiful. I wrote this ditty to express my condition *and* aspiration:

> That I surrender not all but some
> Can make me feel like whitewashed scum.
> Lord, I pray that my faith grows into deeds
> Such that I bear fruit and for Him plant eternal seeds...

7.22 Well, My Soul and Body!

As a new Christian, the internal operations and changes I have made have been clunky but discernible, and I take comfort by what I read in the Bible where we are shown how arduous and frustrating it can feel inside to struggle between the way we *were* to the state of how we *are*; oh, how our fallibilities and limitations persist. Paul wrote at length with precision and accuracy the struggle between the flesh and spirit we Christians face daily; the two are inextricably connected, as if you were dragging around a dead animal behind you, but you hope to lessen this load as you trek through life. Why do I qualify and say "we Christians"? Sure, any person may differentiate good from bad, but unless he is saved and made unsullied in his innermost self, this self-perception of being new, yet existent in the old frame and not wanting to remain as such, just isn't present. You will feel as if you are fresh and clean but walking around in filthy rags (even if designer brand). In my mind's eye, I had a cartoon-like South Park episode going on which graphically displays the fight between the new Dimi and her old tendencies and habits, that is, His morals against my moods. I have become a living oxymoron, a walking contradiction of terms because I desire to abide in goodness and unselfishness and to please Him, yet I can't deliver perfectly or consistently. Why? There are sinful ways we enjoy; pride in all its many splendid forms shines like a flare. Oh, sure, we may be outstanding in *some* areas that may come readily, and in others, we're back to square zero; we falter so. I initially (and erroneously) had the impression that Paul was playing the victim card in the midst of his introspection, that it wasn't his fault, but rather it was that sin made him do wrong to begin with. However, this most assuredly is *not* a case of Greek dualism! Paul knows our bodies are not all evil any more than our minds are purely good; we in body and spirit are a beautiful, flawed, and fragile fusion, yes, still made in His image. Furthermore, early on, Paul established that "sin dwells in me"; it is *still* a part of his system. Why? As *a Christian*, his inner self *has* been made pure and clean and new, but it is still housed in his body, his flesh, which has *yet* to be redeemed. There *was no such conflict* before he got saved! Therefore, he is frustrated and can feel stuck. There is no freedom and no chance for receiving loving help as we go through our lives but through Christ. He is the only one qualified to take away the bad; He did, and He'll do the same for our bodies in the future.

Meanwhile, thanks to the Holy Spirit, we *can* have a fighting chance to improve as we go through our lives. Who wouldn't be grateful for this?! Because some of you who are reading this may not have cracked open a Bible, I'm going to go straight to the horse's mouth and share with you a famous passage that details the inner struggle Christians face. It's a schizophrenic kind of life here because we can get torn in two directions; both claim us, but only Jesus gets us. The following comes from Paul's letter to the Romans (Romans 7:15–25, emphasis mine). I suggest you read it aloud; I'm sure you'll find you recognize yourself, and it should leave you humble. None are exempt.

> [15] For *what I am doing, I do not understand*; for I am not practicing what I would like to do, but I am doing the very thing I hate. [16] But if I do the very thing I do not want to do, I agree with the Law, confessing that the Law is good. [17] So now, no longer am I the one doing it, but *sin which dwells in me*. [18] For I know that nothing good dwells in me, that is, in my flesh; for the willing is present in me, but the doing of the good is not. [19] *For the good that I want, I do not do, but I practice the very evil that I do not want.* [20] But if I am doing the very thing I do not want, *I am no longer the one doing it, but sin which dwells in me*. [21] I find then the principle that evil is present in me, the one who wants to do good. [22] For I joyfully concur with the law of God in the inner man, [23] *but I see a different law in the members of my body, waging war against the law of my mind* and making me a prisoner of the law of sin which is in my members. [24] Wretched man that I am! *Who will set me free from the body of this death?* [25] *Thanks be to God through Jesus Christ our Lord!* So then, on the one hand, I with my mind am serving the law of God, but on the other, with my flesh the law of sin."

As a born-again Christian, I try to reflect in critical self-evaluation. What is *my* sin? Well, to be honest, what "crime" have I *not* committed? The Law can still be a "tutor" (Gal. 3:24 NKJV) of sorts, though I have come to Christ. When I look at His Top Ten list, I've done ALL of them (and many numerous times) in some respect, and if I get judgmental or too exacting of *others*, Jesus charges me to forgive others "up to seventy times" (Matthew 18:22). He certainly did this, yes, died for all, including those very ones who reviled Him! I used to think I was not all that bad until I realized I'd violated all of the Commandments, even if to a small degree or in a figurative sense! Here is what that looks like. I freely confess that I have (1) put plenty of gods before God in my life, gods of worldly success, education, work habits, and financial security; (2) made an idol of pride in vocation, intellectual pursuits, health habits, and Greek heritage; (3) taken the Lord's name in vain too many times to count; (4) not kept the Sabbath day holy, let alone devoted my life to God for the most of my life; (5) harbored bitterness and resentment toward my mother with an unforgiving and critical spirit and disrespected my father, sometimes treating him like a fool or ogre; (6) in my heart I have murdered and used poisoned words of gall to purposefully hurt others and kill their spirit; (7) committed adultery by having had many an intimate but superficial and loveless encounter with no commitment intended *or* went beyond the bounds of respecting who belonged to whom; (8) stolen and still have to fight the old thief within, and this also includes taking chips off another person's character by talking about him; (9) lied *about* others to their detriment and lied *to* others seeking self-preservation or self-promotion; and (10) coveted not so many material things in life, but the attention and affection others have received that I believed I was due. Have I renounced and repented of all of these? As loudly as I can shout from the top of my lungs, I exclaim, "*Yes!! Yes!! Yes!*" These guideposts show me that I can't do it alone, that I can't pull myself up by my bootstraps in self-sufficiency, and that I can't act or think righteously anywhere near 100% of the time. So, just why would I look to and place *Jesus* above any other religious leader way out there? Only *He* came *to* us expressly *for* us and so obviously and uniquely *loves* us. Through the perfection of His gift I freely (and finally) chose to take, God made it such that He "put His law *in my mind* and wrote *it on my heart*" (Hebrews 8:10 as applied to me). In short, there is only one way, one perfect example, and one man whom I long for; He just happens to be God's one and only Son.

Connecting the Dots...

You may ask, "*Now* what is to be *done?*" Jesus may have said, "It is finished," but I have become that proverbial "work in progress." To put a bow on what post-salvation sanctification looks like, I want to share some signs of such in me for you. First, *I thirst* for His Word, read and study it daily, and I desire for it to be expressed in my life. (By the way, daily devotionals should not take the place of the Bible!) Secondly, *I pray daily* (and behind closed doors) without following form or rote script, which includes taking, as A.A. puts it, "a moral inventory" as best I can. Next, *I get involved* in and *attend church* with regularity and frequency. In short, I care, I give, and I am engaged! Is there room for growth? Always! My teaching has also changed in that I do not shy away from discussing with relish Biblical allusions. I am generous and specific in my encouragement of others. In fact, I love doing this! My relationships with my family members are changing, oh, so slowly from my trying not to fall into old and faulty response patterns and loving each exactly where he or she is in life. Though I have plenty of frustrations at work beyond the classroom, I know I am living out my gift and my calling. I am getting better at recognizing former tried and true methods Satan uses to get me off-kilter. Life ain't perfect, but I've got "salt in [me]" (Mark 9:50 KJV). I am both a light and His "workmanship" (Ephesians 2:10), a veritable poem with a purpose of eternal significance. God knows I still do wrong, but He also now remembers my sin no more, period, end of story. He *chooses* to forget my past and anticipates a brighter future! Thank you, Jesus!

7.23 Big Wheels Keep on Turning

Believe it or not, less than two months later, several more questions cropped up. They may be similar to ones you have thought of, so here they are:

1. What I am *to Christ*, or more precisely, what will He "look like" in me? I never thought of my having faith in Christ as a "work." Though we are gifted with the inborn capacity for faith (and seeking Him), isn't it ultimately *on us* to choose to accept or reject Him? In other words, which is stronger, our free will or the vacuum He created within us to seek Him to *begin* with, in which case, it seems that for those who *do* choose Him, they do so because it is an inevitability and therefore *not* a choice. I need God to know and Christ to believe that my faith is real and authentic, not just that I used what was already provisioned

   within me to seek Him! This is similar to my previous desire for Jesus to know that I fully said, "Yes," to Him, that I did not do so because I was motivated to get the "fire insurance policy," as I've heard some say. My faith in Christ is based on the fact that I fell in love with Him, and the zeal, gratitude, and attraction that persists reflect my desire to grow in and for Him. How could He really know that *I choose Him, too*, and that my saying, "Yes," to Him isn't some predestined winning of the cosmic lottery!?! I didn't want to be a victim of circumstance, even if it were to the *good*! A time came when I could finally ask Mark directly just how faith is both a gift from God and yet something I must activate.

2. And alongside this quandary, I found 1 Thess. 5:23 puzzling because Paul refers to "spirit and soul and body," but MacArthur's study notes say we are *dual*-natured.

What's the deal? Is it two or three natures we possess? Then to add insult to injury (or query), I find that Satan seems to like to taunt me especially in church. He tells me I merely want book knowledge of Christ and/or that I don't necessarily even need to attend church. This isn't true! And speaking of the devil, how does one tell the difference between conviction and his agitations?

3. What is the original wording in Greek for "*fear* of the Lord" (Proverbs 9:10)? To be honest, I have a particular disdain for those who go through life wearing mud-colored glasses of guilt, fear, and shame. This mentality particularly pervasive around me (especially among women) in the south. This *can't* be how Jesus operates! Greeks certainly aren't a fearful people, so the original word must include other nuances that are not captured in English. I certainly don't want to be in an anxious mindset, for example, when I wonder what happens to me the split second after I die.

4. How am I to act around those who don't know Christ (let alone give Him the time of day), but *are* ones *I* love *and* pray for them to know Him? I suppose I must be the face of Christ for them until they meet Christ Him for themselves. How else will they be drawn to Him unless an enthusiastic follower shows them His love? I can't seem to get this right! In fact, I confess that I have shifted to a protective, even defensive stance vis-à-vis my family with regards to church and matters in Christ. It's like I've got (or put) a chip on my shoulders before they've said anything because I have readied myself for what I *think* they'll say. Selfishly, I don't want to experience criticism, rejection, or incredulousness, even if only unspoken (but still loud and clear to me), but I surely might. And yes, I know, that's *nothing* compared to what He did for me. I really don't mean or want to put the cart before the horse and anticipate what might happen. I want to be bold and joyful for Him in front of others, not corrective or strident! If and when I do have the opportunity to

respond to some topic of faith, I usually get silence or the ubiquitous nodding and the "that's nice" smile in return to something I might have said. I don't want my Lord to think I'm ashamed of Him, but I don't know how to broach the topic of Christ. What's wrong with me that I am both so insecure and protective of this treasure? I seem to have *no* trouble talking about Him in class when the occasion calls for it, as in when I explain some allusion.

The solution to this is two-fold: until a person comes to Christ, that person will be hostile to Him. It's all over the Bible worded in so many ways. My job is not to judge anyone for this. How in the world could *I* ever do so, considering I had dread and suspicion of pushy Christians just a short time ago?! Another question I invariably get — and one that I am reluctant to bring up — is of what denomination is the church I attend. People seek to conveniently categorize what they think they know about this or that denomination. Again, in ignorance, I have done this, too! I know judgment is on the near horizon when, upon hearing the denomination, people mentally refer to the tiny file drawer of associations and stereotypes as to how they think the revealed denomination behaves, and then they judge accordingly, often in some negative capacity, as if they are prophetic. I don't want for the little church that I've found and have come to love to be reduced or diminished by any "ah-ha" or "uh-oh" looks. For me, this church I attend, though a Protestant-based denomination, is beyond classification; our pastor's exuberant and yet intimate preaching is fully biblically-based, and its members are not pretentious. We are as real as rain. Therefore, any defensiveness, suspiciousness, or even slight hostility on my part (in anticipating judgment) should be whiffed out. If someone asks me about the church I attend, including the denominational flavor, etc., I should be glad for *any* interest or dialogue! Knowing this helps generate patience within me I once needed from other Christians. My charge is simply to *love people* throughout my life *as they are* and *where they are*, and should the Holy Spirit prick them, His salvific grace very well could transpire within them. To that end and to tell you the truth, I think the saddest moment in the New Testament (from the fifth chapter of the Gospel of Mark) occurs when Jesus has just exorcised a bunch of demons out of what was probably a schizophrenic man. In sending those evil spirits into a herd of pigs, the local townsfolk became so resentful about their material loss that they missed the miraculous transformation in the healed man of their community. In fact, they even told Jesus to *leave*, and *He did*! I am *so* relieved that I didn't tell Jesus to leave by saying, "No." One has no idea if he emphatically keeps on rejecting Him, just how often or long — or even *if*— Jesus will wait or return to invite him to partake of His grace. And thus, grateful to be His Christian soldier, I march on.

    I crave the Word and seek to please.
    I try to obey - life knocks me to my knees!
    To move my faith from head to heart
    Is when you say real growth can start.
    To enlarge my faith requires more love than I show,
    So, I'll just keep walking with Him in hopes it'll grow...

7.24 A Word about His Word and Evangelism

This chapter may seem a little out of place, so please look at it as a local commercial break from my sponsor, God. I want to add a layer of credibility to my little *magnum opus* for the reader who wants to know just why the Bible is so great; obviously, I refer to it a ton in here! I ask you, my reader: what other text in the world contains sixty-six books written by some forty people over 1,500 years to be composed, all the while progressively fulfilling itself historically, from old to new, beginning to endless end? People's *perceptions* of the Bible along the way are time-dependent, but the *Bible's principles* are timeless and true. Before I was a Christian, of course, I never cracked open the "Good Book" except to look up an allusion here or there for class, whereas now if I miss reading even a day, I feel like something is missing, and I can get off-center. When Mark first gave me my Bible, I didn't know where to begin; I was overwhelmed! He suggested Philippians, and so that's where and how I got started. I also added a proverb a day for each day of the month because there are thirty-one in all. It goes beyond the scope of this book to prove the reliability of the Bible — there are entire books devoted to just that — but suffice it to say, I believe that the entirety of the Bible is God-breathed and authored, inerrant, and perfect, including all phenomena and events recorded. Topics like life after death and creation, which that I *used* to believe were contradictory, conflicting, or unknowable, I now see as very much possible. I don't let the details trip me up. That doesn't mean I think we can ever have it all figured out, nor am I suggesting we shouldn't learn as much as we can. We *should!* The most intelligent genius may contribute to the body of knowledge now, but nearing the mind of God will occur on the twelfth of never. Anyway, we're all expiring; we just don't know when the clock runs out. Furthermore, intelligence is no predictor of *character*, and *that* becomes our legacy.

Upon hearing that the writers of the Bible were "inspired," I used to roll my eyes, that is, until I opened my mind and gave their arguments a chance. I have personally experienced words figuratively coming out of me and seemingly jumping onto the sheet of their own accord and not of my reflection or volition! So, in a sense, I really can't take credit for that which did not originate within me! The fact that the Bible was composed and that there are various translations from which to choose naturally leads one to ask, "Which one is right for me?" I need to add that, contrary to popular opinion, the King James translation of 1611 is *not* the gospel of Gospels; many other translations in English make His word accessible while remaining true to the original language, be it Greek or Hebrew! Next, does the version you choose go by the literal letter or by the spirit of the author? As a teacher of languages, the precision and accuracy of a word's meaning are extremely important to me; therefore, it is of vital concern to get as close to the meaning, the *spirit* of the *original* word's denotation *and* connotation, that is, *if* such a word *also* possesses a figurative meaning or symbolic application. I do *not* stay fixated on the literal meaning of a word (translated into English) if it misses the mark for what all else might have been intended in its original language for the audience of the day. Case in point: the one word "love" in English has *four* words in Greek, each with its precise shade and nuance, depending upon the context given. I want to respect this.

Another angle to examine would be not so much the vocabulary but the intended *audience*; respecting this can help me appreciate the author's tone taken towards them, as in the case of Paul with the Corinthian Greeks of *his* day. Furthermore, we have words in modern English that do not correspond to what might have been used in ancient Judea; new words get invented all the time. I suppose many people might not care to examine so closely. When I know this to be the case, I pretty much smile and stick to something that doesn't need deciphering or unpacking, but I always seek to relay the truth of a matter when I notice a well-intended but mistaken opinion. I am often that person still; I just know where to look for clarity or help. There are also plenty of outside texts that can explain seeming anomalies, inconsistencies, contradictions, or inaccuracies; indeed, some of what is worded in the versions of the Bible does merit further examination for a more thorough understanding. In fact, as we scratch beneath the surface of the text and dive deeper, it's to be expected that there can be vigorous discussions on both vocabulary and interpretation. Still, none should dissuade from reading the Bible, or worse, cause one to fall away from believing at all! God is not in the business of defending Himself to us; we can never out-know God! The most important takeaway point here, however, is that, thankfully, expertise is not a prerequisite to a saving grace and faith in Him. I want to stress that faith, which is the *capacity* to even believe in God, comes directly from God, and it comes first. *Then* comes the desire to learn and act out your faith in real life; it's not the other way around.

Next, I had to decide whether or not to *believe* Him and *in* Him solely and personally for *myself*. I could not just *accept* a blanket package deal that applies to all. When I did so earlier, I had no compulsion to go further because I took in *facts* but had no sustaining *faith*. It's not so much that I don't get why faith isn't distributed evenly; maybe it is. Our focus and choice are paramount; I'm not a believer because I know He did what He did for *everyone* but because I know He did so expressly for *me*. We are not *all* covered unless *each* of us, one at a time, come to accept and believe in Him. Ephesians 2:8 tell us "for by grace [we] have been saved through faith; and that not of [ourselves], it is the gift of God." That God gave me my faith made me feel like my faith wasn't authentic because He brought it about in the first place. The point here is that God knows our tendency to take credit for our faith (or anything, for that matter), and doing so would shift the focus back to *self*, so He makes a provision for this faith capacity to come from *Him*. I just opened my mind and heart to Him, and the rest came on its own.

With all of this detail concerning the nature of faith, you may wonder how I ever got off the ground. Becoming a Christian is *not* about studying some new philosophy; it is about embarking on a life-altering journey whereby you know that *you are never alone*, and though you can't *see* Him, you are with the uniquely *living* God. I now want to distinguish between my *formerly* being His loved *creation*, His "creatures," to transforming into a beloved *child* of His, that is, a son or daughter. How can this be? The Holy Spirit does *not* dwell in nonbelievers, but He does mysteriously reckon and urge them to come to Christ when the time is right. When this happens, that is, when the person in full readiness decides to engage his faith by believing that Jesus is the Christ and is his loving Messiah, then there is an extraordinary illumination that occurs within. At this moment, Christ instantaneously ushers within us the Holy Spirit to dwell in us, and we, in turn, come to say goodbye to our old life. As you've seen, this is the beginning of the life of a person — of me —as "a new creature; the old things passed away; behold, new things have come" (2 Cor. 5:17).

7.25 What the Sheol?

When I'm fuzzy or seeking help, I first try to check with Mark regarding the accuracy of my take of select points on which I've become fixated (or stuck). I have since come to hope to be able to share with others should the occasion arise. Do I ever look online for answers? Of course, I do, and some of the sources that have become my go-to for biblically sound answers include *Got Questions, Blue Letter Bible,* and *Bible Hub*. These are the ones I pursue after reading the detailed commentaries at the bottom of the margin in the *MacArthur Study Bible* that Mark gave me. Later, I would buy a book of commentary solely devoted to the New Testament; in fact, there exist volumes upon volumes for each of the individual books within, too. A final comment I want to make here deals with my previous question about the difference between the spirit and the soul. The spirit is the aspect by which we come to have a relationship with Jesus; the soul houses the spirit and is the very essence of our being, our core selves. If one doesn't know Jesus, one is *spiritually* dead even though he or she possesses a soul and is very much *physically* alive and animated with that soul. In other words, the soul is the person's unique self or essence, and the spirit is that aspect of us which lives forever; it profoundly longs for union with the eternality of God. I wake up every morning glad to be His, and I feel no different than the blind beggar mentioned in the Gospel of John Ch. 9 who, upon hearing Jesus say, "I am the one," gained sight through Jesus' anointing of him. Just how one is to *share* that faith and *talk about* Jesus would be yet mystifying. I'd get one such lesson soon enough.

Yesterday in church, another of our pastors, Todd, gave an introduction to Christianity 101, that being, what exactly it is that Christians believe. For someone who has lived in the church his whole life, it was apparent to me that Todd had little idea how to approach those who have *not* done so. He started by saying that a man well into his 70s and on his deathbed asked for him, Todd, to "come and explain Jesus to him." But after doing so, Todd was sadly bewildered as to why this man did not accept Him. When a well-intentioned Christian goes up to a non-Christian and asks "if he has invited Jesus into his heart," it sounds like a kind of response one might say to the Avon lady calling! The assumption that the non-Christian picks up on is if one does not do so, he is headed for Hell, which makes the whole encounter a complete turnoff! I know it was like this for me for decades. You can't just pour Jesus down someone's throat like medicine to a child even if you know they're sick, and you try to be gracious and caring. Others go all out and hurl God out like rice thrown at a wedding. Then again, who knows? Maybe seine fishing *can* be effective in catching new fish. Some stand on street corners and condemn like Jesus never did. Todd proceeded to explain the Trinity as being like the three possible states of water: the fluid form of water is God; vapor serves as the Holy Spirit; solid ice becomes Christ. For me, this analogy misses the mark by looking at attributes or states rather than relationships. Except for Jesus, the former we cannot know; the latter then becomes the key. I can get so frustrated with *how* a message is conveyed because my desire to share Him and have Him grow in me is huge. More than anything in life, I want Him to come out of (and into) everything I say and do and feel. Then again, I suppose every Christian craves this. I wish to tell *so* many people I know and love that Jesus Christ is different from every other religious leader, let alone man. I had a Christian student privately remark to me once in glee, "Hey, Ms. C.! Just look at how the world over keeps time! The center of chronological relativity we use began with the birth of Christ — not anyone else! B.C. sure doesn't stand for Before Confucius!" In other words, you don't tell someone the year you were born by using the Chinese or Jewish calendar, let alone through any other dating system. Christ's birth next leads me inevitably to the topic of death. This topic is also tied to my question about the difference between the spirit and the soul.

Having recently witnessed the brother of my good friend and neighbor die, I again find myself wondering what happens to us the moment after we die. It now seemed to me that we do not go to Heaven right after we die. How could we? Isn't it that we are "asleep" in Sheol? Yes, the physical body decomposes, and the soul (that is, our earthly identity) desists, but our *spirit* is sleeping, or rather, is waiting in dormancy until the Rapture comes. This event refers to when Jesus gathers *first* those who died believing in Him and *then* the other living believers. At the Final Judgment before God, I will *not* be among those who *don't* believe in Him; instead, I, along with the rest of the other *believers,* will be at the bema seat justifying my service (or lack thereof) to Jesus. This is the time when the crowns come, that is, *if* there are any crowns to come at all (which, in turn, we ought to give right back to Him). From my current minute perspective, that seems like such a crazy-long time from now. And our glorified state of newness comes yet after this! So, is it that after I die, I will be alongside my brothers and sisters in Christ from Thessaloniki in Sheol like a waiting room? Why do people even say we're going to Heaven after we die when it's probably an eventuality but not an immediate thing? No! This can't be right!

In the early stage of becoming a Christian, a neophyte, for sure, I began to wonder: are we *really* in the presence of Jesus after we die? That's what *Paul* says happens right after we die (2 Cor. 5:8); we are *alive* but not *living* as we are *now*. It doesn't *seem* like it, but I'm sure banking on it! I know God's eschatological sequence and timetable are beyond my imagination, but right now, for me to imagine being dead sounds awfully lonely or like I'll be in a void of nothingness. I mean, the Holy Spirit won't even be with me when I'm dead because my God is a living God, and I won't exist even to be dwelt in anymore. I won't even be a thought after I die. I would have to wait until Mark could clear up my muddled mess of misunderstanding, this maze of my mistaken mind. I knew that I was way off and wrong on this point, but I didn't know how to get it righted. I'm telling you this not to confuse you but to show you that a lack of accuracy or discernment can be common in one's toddler stage as His child.

7.26 THE MIND AND MORBID MATTERS:
from Dualism to a More Perfect Union

At this point, I need to interrupt myself for a moment and clarify about what more I have recently learned about the division between the *body* and the *spirit*, a position that had me feeling discombobulated. The ancient Greek belief called Gnosticism sees not only a rift between the two, but that the spirit is *superior* to the body. Such a way of thinking can lead to an elitism of the spirit, whereby one views the body as separate, base, and inferior, and this bisection, in turn, can lead to our excusing what we do with our bodies because it wasn't the "real" us. The non-Christian will indulge his (body's) desires and appetites while remaining unconcerned about their impact on his *total* self, including his spirit and character. For example, if you indulge in sex in a moment of lust, there will not come about the satisfaction you crave; you will keep seeking for more because the heart and soul are left wanting, but you don't know this in the thrill of the moment. More than any other partaking, it is sex that is uniquely and so holistically involving; that is why the stakes are incredibly high and the imperative all the greater for one to maintain purity until one finds another to cherish and love with *full* measure. Your body is not meant to engage in sex like it's a sport or fast-food meal. We Christians do *not* say the spirit is better than the body (or vice versa); the Gnostic differentiates between the two to assure himself that at least the spirit will go on forever. Unlike the Greeks, Christ never said or paid greater homage to the spirit at the expense of the body. Even the resurrected Jesus challenged Thomas to touch Him on His wounded hands and side; what had happened to Him was very real!

Furthermore, God is pleased with our taking delight in the world He gave us! He does not consider our physical bodies as inferior or second-rate; without our frame, how could we partake of the life He gave us *and* house His Spirit? Through the actions taken by the members of our bodies, we glorify Him, and in so doing, we sense through our inner joy evidence that He loves us. The world itself is also proof positive of the awesomeness, the splendor of His love for us. And it takes our bodies to enjoy it, so our bodies are not evil. When the non-Christian takes care of his body, it is for the sake of his health, longevity, or appearance; this is no longer the case for me! Accordingly, I came to memorize a verse capturing what I thought I owed Him in homage to my physical ability to partake of life. While running around the track, I'd recite: "Do you not know that your body is a temple of the Holy Spirit who is in you, whom you have from God, and that you are not your own? For you have been bought with a price: therefore, glorify God in your body" (1 Corinthians 6:19–20). Asceticism is not the means by which to acquire holiness; self-denial, self-discipline, and self-improvement in and of themselves will not lead you to a closer relationship with God; and avoidance of those who irritate or vex you will not generate godliness. And by the way, fasting or sacrificing *for Jesus* is a different matter altogether. We do this intently and *in private* to have a burst of focus on Him, perhaps because we have some special request or need we want to make known in prayer. Fasting not only refers to food, but it can refer to time and resources as well. It is not meant to last forever, but it *does* involve an imposition, inconvenience, hardship, or cost. One ought to sacrifice and offer such up as "first fruits" (Leviticus 2:12) for Him in a designated manner and time frame. Yes, go up into the mountains and *pray and fast* but do come back down and imitate Jesus!. Love on the unlovable; after all, am I not that one to others? In this area, I needed so much help!

Here I now pick back up where I left off in my contemplating what happens to us after we die; I will share with you a necessary correction to which I came. In contemplating what happens the split second after we die, I initially had read into what happened at the Rapture incorrectly. Mark pointed out a passage to me, which informs us that "therefore we also have as our ambition, *whether at home or absent, to be pleasing to Him* (2 Cor. 5:9). I had erroneously thought that being dead would be kind of like we were asleep in both body *and* soul until Christ took us up. Up to then, we would be in Sheol or use the Greek word, Hades, just "*sleeping*," but if this were the case, how is it that I could still be loved by God and know it in this soporific state? And what about the Holy Spirit dwelling in me? How did *that* work? I am assured that our eternal life with God commences the second we die; there is *no* separation from Him even with my dead *body* lying in the cold ground. Are my body *and* soul both waiting for the Rapture? No! My spirit will be with Him. Body-soul reunification happens *much* later, and then, all will be better than the perfect we can only imagine now. I read the best depiction of what to expect: "to be absent from the body [is to] to be at home with the Lord" (2 Cor. 5:8). This is immediate! I had previously understood it wrong! I am not down there, body and soul, in the ground; only my fleshly corpse is! To die is to gain eternal life with Him on the spot, instantaneously. When I once told Mark that I would be satisfied to be a pleasing memory to God until He saw fit to raise me, Mark said that He did not need to be with me *in person* to feel or to know my presence. Once I am figuratively lying asleep in His arms, *He doesn't love me any less than when I was alive and awake*! Mark said when we're in Heaven, we don't have to do or to perform; we can just bask in being with God. All this business of my being in the presence of the Lord when I die may very well transpire *before* the Rapture. What I had misunderstood was that I thought that I — *including* my spirit— would be in the grave *until* then! The Thessalonians were waiting for His Big Return, and they were worried that their dead relatives would miss out; therefore, Paul reassured them that the dead *would* be raised *before* they, the remaining ones alive, would join Christ in Heaven. My physical, corporeal "tent" (2 Cor. 5 CEV) will go back to the earth as ashes and dust, but my soul will live forever. I now understand that in death, I am so much more than just a memory of me to God. Because I have accepted Him, I will be in His presence in Paradise.

Mark said that there are different levels in Heaven and Hell and that they have to do with the chronology of events and whether one is saved. I can hardly wait to go back to reading about Heaven. In any event, Mark also added that those folks who end up receiving at the last hour, even though saved, do not have the depth of faith as fully developed or richly expressed as one who came to Him earlier. What that I was such a one! Mark also warned me to be very careful not to add or insert certain things into the Bible which are not there. Not only had I mixed up what part of me goes where upon my decease, but also the whole sequence of God's chronology I had gotten out of order. I thought that when I died, my essence would be transported then and there at the bema seat, with me facing Jesus reviewing all I'd done for Him, both the known and unknown. That is *not* the case! That comes *so* much later! When I *do* face Christ at the Bema seat, He'll not only evaluate all I've done to glorify God, but He'll show me my missed opportunities. I will also become aware of those who would *not* be with me there in Paradise. I could only imagine how this would make *me* weep. I am assured that "He'll wipe every tear away" (Rev. 21:4). Anyway, who could be sad for long being around Jesus?! And when it comes time to being at the bema seat before Jesus, may I state for the record, I surely don't want to be the person who has so little to show for how he represented and served Christ that he got only a single crown. I told Mark it would probably look like a flimsy, cardboard Burger King crown. Mark laughed easily and added, "Yeah, with tattered ends, maybe like a pirate."

I return to my focus on death. This is when I will be sanctified in *full*, when all the residual effects of life's tribulations and despairs get gone. When my light-as-a-dove spirit enters Paradise, I, that is, my spirit will be in the presence of Jesus. Wow!! Justification started one month before I turned fifty, and, God willing, the rest of my life, I'll be trekking in sanctification, no matter how slow, gradual, and progressive is the sloughing off and relinquishing of sin. At the same time, I devote myself more fully to Him. It's like breathing: in with the oxygen; out with the carbon dioxide. I can't imagine what experiencing the whole of the Trinity will be like then! At some indeterminable point after this, when Jesus returns to earth in His magnificent glorified state, He ushers in the apex, the completion of *our* sanctification: *glorification.* Then we will experience *complete* reunification of body, soul, *and* spirit in a supra-real state. (Do you remember that Peter, James, and John got a sneak preview of Jesus' glorified state at the Transfiguration when He must have glowed like a live wire? The depiction of this is still one of my favorite icons.) In all likelihood — and at this rate — I will be dead and gone before the Rapture occurs.

My body, my physical self, my "tent," will be left *here* temporarily, maybe in an urn somewhere; I don't know. God can easily and perfectly rejoin our spirit to our body (in any form it happens to be in) the same as He made man out of clay, to begin with, way back when. Reassembly for Him is no biggie! Even the staggering moment the *final* glorification when *everyone* who is His will not only be glorified, but we will <u>be with *God*</u> in *His* glory. In that future epoch, I will behold "a new heaven and a new earth. And God will dwell among His people, and they shall be His people, and God Himself will be among them, ... *and there will no longer be any death...*" That passage is from Revelation 21:1–4 (emphasis mine); it is the climactic end *and* new beginning all rolled in one. It will be beyond any perfection imaginable. Okay, this is a *lot*. Until that time and for the time being, His Spirit is working on transfiguring me, step by step, little by little, right now until I die. At the moment of my life's final exhalation, I will be in the presence of God, all three-in-one of them! Yes, this means the Holy Spirit, too, who previously had been inside me during my life. If the Holy Spirit dwells in the real me, He sure isn't going to stay down in the ground with my dead *body*; He'll be with my spirit in Heaven. The Holy Spirit is with me *now* as a pledge, a seal, or certificate of God's authenticity that I am His; I am assured that He "will *never* leave [me] nor forsake [me] (Heb. 13:5 KJV, emphasis mine). The Holy Spirit is within me *now* in life, and He will be with me *then* when it's just my spirit alive.

My purpose is not to detail eschatological events; I am no expert! I want you to share my thought process as I search for what I'll come to experience moments after I die; plus, I just *had* to find an easier way to make sense of what I read in Revelation! To that end, I taped two sheets of paper together side-by-side, drew out a long line starting from the point of Jesus' resurrection to the Rapture, then on up to the tree of life in the New Jerusalem. I used various pens and colored pencils to render little drawings of this super-condensed timeline of events foretold along the way. The long and the short of it is that, upon my death, my spirit will *not* be down there still inside my dead body because that would mean that my spirit would *also* be sleeping or ostensibly dead. You can't have a *living* spirit in a *dead* body six feet under! That would be horrible! My spirit won't be "asleep" to be awakened later like some zombie apocalypse! My spirit will *never* die; therefore, at that point of death, *I will be in God's presence*, and "I will know fully [whom I face] just as I also have been fully known [by God the entirety of my life]" (1 Cor. 13:12). When Mark told me that *it's enough to be in His presence*, my mind immediately went to a sweet recollection of my own father, who was happy and content just to be near and with his children! We didn't have to do or say anything; being in each other's closeness was enough! That is such a precious notion to me! As I wrestled with these postmortem events and how I fit in the scheme, I could not have anticipated then that Mark would teach us his congregants about Heaven in a series of his one year later. Then a year after that, he cleared up some misunderstandings regarding Hell. I had never before really considered what it might mean to be eternally separated from God. Little did I also know then just how close-to-home the nearness of death would brush by me with Bonnie finding out she had cancer only a year after this. More on this is yet to come. In the meanwhile, I riveted my attention back to the Holy Spirit.

7.27 How Long Does the Holy Spirit Beckon? How Does He "Grieve"?

Regarding just how long the Holy Spirit reckons with a person and how faith functions in real-time, initially, I was troubled to think that since God gave me the capacity to have faith to begin with. My coming to faith wasn't even of my own doing; therefore, I didn't view my faith as actually legitimate or valid since He provided the means to do so. I wanted God to know I was for real His and for Him! Mark re-explained that, yes, everybody can have faith. The God-space exists within us, but more often than not, we fill it with other things. When the moment is right, it is God that turns on or activates the capacity in us, and only then is it on us to choose Him. God never forces us to say "Yes" to His Son and our Savior, though the ripest opportunity to do so is on His watch. When we do consent, then the Holy Spirit comes in to dwell at that twinkling, and He stays with us. Conversely, if we reject Him at the moment of crisis, at that split second of opportunity when God has turned on our faith receptor, be cognizant that this critical juncture is not sustained indefinitely! A person could be reckoned with in some life circumstance through the Holy Spirit trying to prick the spirit's attention for a single moment or an entire season; at such a time, God's Spirit hovers about him or her then like an invisible cheerleader giving encouragement, as it were. He does so when He detects a readiness, openness, and receptiveness in us, but if we decline, dismiss, or cower, then this particular opportunity may leave forever. Do we notice, heed, or choose to be obedient? You do not know if or when or how the chance may be available to you again! He may or may not check in later; therefore, I say, take it while you can! As sure as I am of anything, this was the case with me! As a caveat, there must exist within you a vulnerability, a suppleness, a readiness, and a curious attraction, too. It cannot be acquired at will or when you are "stiff-necked" in resistance (Acts 7:51). When I look back over my life, I can see that the Holy Spirit *had* been reckoning with me, tilling my mind, and massaging my heart for many years. It's a wonderment to me that He was so patient and waited on me such that my salvation occurred. Somehow, I agreed to an invitation to go to some church to watch a friend's child get baptized. By April 29, the Holy Spirit had already been preparing and create a readiness within me to come to Him. I had been being prepared in ways beyond me for the Holy Spirit to move my softened heart. When I heard Mark's invitation at the end of his sermon, it snapped, and I sprung. If I had declined, dismissed, or turned away when I felt that strong tug, that pull, that drawing in, well, that might've been it! "She's done, baked, hardened, and lost to sin," God might have remarked to Himself. Little would I have known that ignoring or turning away from the Holy Spirit at the moment of His nudging me would "grieve" Him because I would have been rejecting *God* and His Son's sacrifice. This amounts to rejecting the one who even made it possible to be united with God. Jesus even tells us that "I and the Father are one" (John 10:30). Turning away from the Holy Spirit's promptings and stirrings which lead us to God is tantamount to rejecting Christ, and this is the one egregious and unforgivable sin. No wonder we are ordered, "Do not grieve the Holy Spirit of God" (Ephesians 4:30)! I assure you that when I said, "Yes," it was authentic, real, tender, intense, and secured, and God knows this. My acceptance of Him is *not* lessened or cheapened by God's making faith possible to begin with; He knows my motives, thought processes, and the ways of my heart completely and fully, in fact, better than anyone, including me! There's no need for me to fret! He knows my accepting Him was genuine and for His sake only!

Speaking of the Holy Spirit's dealing with me, once He's in there, I next became curious about what exactly He *does* in there, especially when I encounter tribulations. *How* would He communicate, guide, and keep me focused? Would I be able to tell the difference between condemnation and conviction? It seemed to me that the sense of guilt or shame could be attributed to either the Devil or the Holy Spirit; indeed, it could be both! The difference is that *conviction* always leads me to seek Jesus. (I got a real, practically palpable, inner stirring the moment I uttered that.) On the other hand, condemnation will make me feel ashamed, unworthy, and full of negative self-talk that can neutralize me and render me powerless for Him by dimming my focus on Him.

How does this happen? Is guilt automatically self-induced? How does self-criticism within the person get started, and can't it also be for the good? Is it because some of us have metacognition and self-awareness of just how flawed we are, or is it due to the effects of socialization, whereby we learn the behavior we watch and unknowingly imitate what we see in our parents? Could it be due to something more insidious and powerful *outside* us? If self-awareness leads us to an evaluation of things that need improvement or an acknowledgment of limitations and flaws, that is good; if such leads to a figurative self-flogging and self-debasement, this has the mark of Satan on it. Christ builds up and Satan tears down, even though we may perceive things are not going our way in certain moments.

Mark reminded me that Satan is the "enemy" (Matthew 13:39) because he is "the prince of this world" (John 12:31 KJV); in fact, he is on-call 24-7 and "prowls around like a roaring lion, seeking someone to devour" (1 Peter 5:8). Mark warned me that Satan is a formidable opponent and for me not to think I can go up against him *on my own*, that I am no match. His whole purpose is to get and keep one off-kilter, and he has various and sundry ways and means to do this. It seems counter-intuitive, but if you think about it, it makes sense that when you *first* become a Christian, that is, a kindle for Him has been sparked within you such that you become quite star-struck, this is *just* the time when Satan tries to squelch you, dampen your mood, and trip you up. He knows you've changed camps and are working for *his* opponent. Satan wants me *dead* in any capacity, and he'll try hard to cause me "to suffer the slings and arrows of outrageous fortune" (*Hamlet*, III, i.) such that I'm neutralized for Him. He wants my flame to burn out a.s.a.p. As Mark reminded me again, Satan came to "steal, kill, and destroy" us (John 10:10). The Holy Spirit's guidance or even correction never makes me feel down and out for the count. I now clearly see that spiritual warfare is real and not for the faint-hearted or unprepared! How he tries to do so within me looks different than what he does, for example, to Bonnie. His method with me is to deflate my usually buoyant and optimistic spirits; with Bonnie, he launches an attack to get her fearful. He'll get us both derailed if we get fussy with or feel hurt by family. The sense I get, which is a by-product of Satan having his way with me, is when I get agitated with inner taunting that leads to self-pity. I can get stuck in the past by fixating on some wrong, blinded by pride, or resentful of or hateful toward another person I perceive to be a stick in the mud. No, I'm not equating every bad thing or mood that occurs to be from Satan! Life is *fraught* with conflict! If, however, the attitude or action you're engaged in can cause you to stumble for God and misrepresent to the point of getting you to doubt, ignore, or reject Him, *especially* by subtle means, Satan's on it. Before I became a Christian, I was <u>un</u>aware of the spiritual war in the world and his designs on individuals. Indeed, talking about the Devil seemed medieval and ridiculous, but now I see that in many ways, *little has changed.* The battle lines are still the same, except modernity dismisses the titanic conflict of good versus evil. They dismiss such talk as anachronistic, but when primitive dualism meets and embraces pluralism and moral relativity, right and wrong no longer exist. The rules are not in black in what but in shifting shades of grey.

As a Christian, you cannot be smug or complacent and think you are safe just because you are Heaven-bound and know that Satan will ultimately be defeated! Oh, no! Satan will go after his own lost sheep and attempt to rob God of His saved one by putting you back in his back pocket of lost souls, if only temporarily. I have this confidence because Jesus tells us that "I am the good shepherd. The good shepherd lays down his life for the sheep" (John 10:11 NIV). Jesus gives; Satan takes. I can't stress it enough: Satan wants me dead — spiritually and/or physically, and he'll bring it about any way he can: through alcohol abuse or some other addiction; through rancor with non-believers who are dear to me; through cynicism or even sanctimoniousness. (As an aside, may I say how grateful I am to be sober now seventeen years?!) It is important to remember that though Satan is powerful, *he is no match for God*; God made him, too. Satan cannot read my mind and doesn't possess any of the omnis to his identity that God alone does, but still, he is incredibly forceful, lethal, and not to be dismissed. All the same, he is hum-drum predictable in that he will go for our weak spots every time; this we can anticipate *through the Holy Spirit's help.*

For me personally, I am most vulnerable state before Satan when it comes to dealing with my family members. It's with them I have the deepest history, hurts, and memories, both delightful and painful. Can awareness of Satan's provocations, temptations, and trappings help in these moments? Sometimes yes, but often not, as *in our flesh*, blood pressure can spike, feelings get hurt, and self-righteous indignation can flare in a nanosecond. As my walk in Christ grows, the likelihood of getting caught in his traps can and does lessen with time, but it's a bumpy road! Practice, practice, practice makes *improvement*. When one first gets saved, one is gung-ho and hasn't learned how to pace oneself for the long haul; Satan knows this, too, so one shouldn't get impatient with oneself if it feels like progress isn't quick enough or if the high of getting saved isn't sustained in the manner hoped for. Faith is a choice you've got to make over and over again until it develops into a habit of love, as in exercising a spiritual muscle. Obedience to your commitment of *loving Him back* brings you strength as much as if you'd made a deposit in a bank. It is the Holy Spirit who helps you to discern and distinguish condemnation from His conviction so that you can continue to be encouraged and grow in Him, step by step, little by little, as well as by leaps and bounds. Letting go of the pains in the past, often through forgiveness, liberates and lightens your load up for what's ahead.

As I adamantly tell my students time and again to "focus, focus, focus," I say this now to myself regarding Jesus. After all, Jesus is *the* greatest Teacher *I* will ever know; He is the Savior of the world and the Son of God. Wow! I seek to spend the remainder of my days emulating and worshiping Him. My faith is not a duty, and I follow no method; following Him has become my heart's desire. I know it's for real when I experience an inner, bittersweet longing and a yearning to lay my burdens, cares, and weaknesses with complete and relieving abandon at the foot of the cross; after all, it is here where He nullified all sin forever. It's still astonishing that this metamorphosis within me was even instigated. I now cannot imagine life without Him. How does God get our attention? With the child, it is easy: we come into this world with wonderment, joy, and a desire to know the source of it all, though we have no words for this. Then come all the "why?" questions which can only be answered by God. Anyway, He *is* the answer. He comes to us in the form of jolting life events that can drive us to our knees in prayer, yes, even in non-believers. We can also see Him in believers that quietly display His love in unexpected times. He can be discovered during a stillness or a readiness as we search for Him expectantly, persistently, and thoughtfully. He has that light touch! Ah, He showers us with love and shows us in a thousand myriad ways that He loves us and that He cares for us. Now I better fathom that which I had said by unthinking rote before: *"God is love"* (1 John 4:7). Sometimes, His love comes when you least expect it. Four years ago, I was in such a state myself: Yes, I was a reasonably content and happy person, but beneath the surface, I was steeped in a defensiveness where religion was concerned. When I wrote to Mark after that sermon, God knew — though I certainly didn't — that I was standing at a crossroads; I dared to take a chance. I'm so glad I did. It boils down to asking and receiving. I am also grateful that Mark agreed to pursue that which God had nudged in him; such led me to accept my Messiah. Soon after this turning point, it becomes natural to want *others* to come to this state of enlightenment, too. How in the world did this take place within the likes of me? And *why* me anyway? What prevents others from coming to Jesus? This I would next investigate.

I know I can bear witness to Him and evangelize in my own unique and seeming unqualified way. He can and will position me as He needs, but circumstances do exist that make coming to Christ unlikely or quite tricky. I made myself a list of conditions and types or personages, knowing all the while that God can get through to them, too! Here they are: (1) The person who lacks exposure to Christ, be it that he lives in a very remote area of the world or in a country where the culture is steeped in another religion. This scenario can be remedied with missionary work and *sustained* help, but if not, it seems that such a person, like an infant who dies young, cannot be held accountable for what he or she never, ever knew. (2) The carefree person who has so bought into the world's values that promote self that he cannot and does not consider that there exists any other way to live; this is all there is. Jesus isn't even a thought. (3) The person with a hardened heart is one whose pride rules and/or where pain once was birthed and now rankles. He is close-minded to anything he (or man) cannot rationally explain or verifiably prove; therefore, there is no God for him, or if there is, Jesus sure ain't He. Though the burden of proof is actually on *him*, He won't even look at historical facts. He may even say that the Bible is full of "inconsistencies," yet all the while, he has never even looked into it! Such the person becomes one with his own messiah complex. Lack of belief in the merit of faith in God, let alone in Jesus Christ, makes for a person who is spiritually dead in the water, no matter how bright, thoughtful, caring, philanthropic, happy, or witty she or she is.

I also feel compelled to comment on two types of Christians that get stunted in their growth. The first is the nominal Christian, the "Chreaster," one who shows up at church twice a year for Christmas and Easter, but for all intents and purposes, shows no sign of acknowledging God is in the actions of his life. Jesus' own brother said, "Faith, if it has no works, is dead" (James 2:17). In other words, action speaks louder than words; we ought to be able to see it (faith), to believe it (i.e., that it's genuine). This person may have his salvation, but he is still a pauper, spiritually speaking. The second type of Christian who becomes disabled refers to persons who started out in full faith when they were but children but then strayed far, far away from Him and for decades. Going through the proverbial school of hard knocks coupled with bad representation from churches where scare tactics are used regularly can further repel, revolt, alienate, or terrorize the infant in the faith, though she or he may be middle-aged. She won't come back, or if she does, she may quickly exit stage left to avoid the glare of condemnation. What about *them*? When I asked Mark about this, he looked at me, pointed over to Bonnie, and said, "May I present this case to you as my Exhibit A?" What I took that to mean was that although Bonnie had accepted Jesus at the tender age of thirteen, she *continued* to be reckoned with and quietly convicted by the Holy Spirit even after leaving the church. Though she set Him aside, she was, for sure, saved! Life knocked her to the ground, and then she went astray from Him and lived in perpetual doubt for decades, but God kept working on her to come back to Him, this time without fear. Bonnie had unknowingly projected onto God her own feelings of unworthiness as well as others' reproaches and had erroneously concluded that *He* didn't want or love her anymore! Wrong! Bonnie, too, <u>re</u>took the leap of faith and came back in full measure to Him who had never left her to begin with!

This year three of my journey in faith might seem to some of you like a cerebral exercise, an intellectual investigation, or some shiny apple I can't get my fill of (but that one day might lose its luster). I am hardly unique in the lineup of impressive and imperfect people, extraordinary and ordinary folk who have had their foundations rocked to the core such that when the tectonic plates settled, the world as they knew it was changed forever, and they'd have it no other way. Music is probably the best analogy I can make to show you the healing, joy-producing, and transformative power of God and His Son made in me. It's like you finally are in tune with the One who has perfect pitch. For every question I have, there are a hundred others that *you* will have, too. None of them for me has ever been a deal-breaker such that I would reject my found faith; I wanted to share with you the nuts and bolts of what faith growing looks like, that is, in excitedly, zealously, and passionately wanting to get to know, to love and adore Jesus and our Father. A lifetime won't be enough! Earlier, I would have quoted Thoreau's saying, "If you have built castles in the air, your work need not be lost; that is where they should be. Now put the foundations under them." As a Christian, this now translates to, "Let your light shine before men in such a way that they may see your good works and glorify your Father who is in heaven" (Matthew 5:16). Why? Paul advises me to "work out [my] salvation with fear and trembling" (Philippians 2:12). Though the work may be hard and the outcome of impact uncertain, I need to persevere and do my best for Him; He in me anyway! Just when I'd reached what I thought was a tiny level of accomplishment in my growth in Him, my faith as a Christian was to be tested in up-and-coming, real-life challenges and threats, as you shall soon see. Looking back, these growing pains occurred, in part, to steel my faith deep down in my bones, beyond just my mind and heart's captivation.

Chapter 8:
Year 4, "Be Anxious for Nothing" — Philippians 4:6

"Consider it *all* joy, my brethren, when you encounter various trials, knowing that *the testing of your faith produces endurance. And let endurance have its perfect result, so that you may be perfect and complete, lacking in nothing.*"
— James 1:2–4, emphasis mine

"You are from God… Greater is He who is in you than he who is in the world."
— 1 John 4:4-6

8.1 Chapter the Last:
The Rubber Meets the Road

I am now settling into this book's last chapter of testimony, though it is hardly the end of my story. My initial plan was to write about the nuts and bolts of what three years of growth in my faith looks like, warts and all, the chills and thrills, the good, bad, and ugly moments of this Christian odyssey. Originally, I thought I'd stop writing when I finished my third year because it matched up with the number of years in Jesus' ministry. This was not to be. It would be in my fourth year where push came to shove, and my faith was tried out in real life and braced through various trials. Bonnie would encounter a terrifying threat to her very life, and I would experience challenges at the workplace I would never have dreamed I'd have to face. Did God cause these to happen? Of course, not. Were they harder or worse than the norm — whatever that is — than anyone else experiences? Not by a long shot. Were they trivial? Nope. It was my internal coping mechanism and outlook that had radically changed. When you get over, or rather, let go of some of the previous hurt, fear, and anger, such that you turn to Him like you never did previously, and in so doing find yourself alongside new brothers and sisters in Christ, you get to come to see the power of prayer working. Questions still arose this year, but I settled into a steady groove where I made greater strides as time went by. Join me as I show you this last year of queries and quagmires.

Just when I thought I'd settled one cycle of questions, somehow more popped up; at times, they ricocheted off another answered question while I was musing during the day, and at other times, they came to me while I was engaged in my morning Bible study or prayer. That my brain works like a Dyson vacuum cleaner, intently searching for answers so I could scrub my mind free from questions about Jesus or Christianity, is *not* to imply I thought it possible to attain answers to all of my questions! Goodness, no! Anyway, Q & A is not what this all about! I look at my curiosity more like a seeking to fill in the gaps which naturally arise at the early phase of faith. Anyway, I craved feeling saturated with a sense of deep dependence on Jesus, and this partially hitched on being filled with the best knowledge I can of Him. For me now, seeking Him comes from beyond my will; it's just natural. Each person has questions unique to himself, but none are surprising to God. I have mentioned a few of those that are commonly asked, but most of what I share with you deals with my own experiences and evolving thought-processes. Do remember that I am but a neophyte reporting in these moments of my testimonial journey, so, of course, my writings will be rawer and less polished than a more mature Christian; nonetheless, they are real. More and more, I would look to a couple of online sources that seemed in line with how Mark had been teaching me, that is, ones that are biblically sound and not sugar-coated or imbued with any one person's agenda or platform. I will share a few more of these topics in this chapter. Visits with Mark would become more sporadic, quarterly even, and our visits would be more as friends and less as needy children, topics of utmost importance would be taken on. Oh, but we joked and cut up and broke bread too! Sometimes we dealt with hers, sometimes, mine, but usually, it was a beautiful jumbled mess of all of our thoughts. I don't know why questions kept coming up, but they did, and they got more specific than before. For the record, I want to say that they have nothing to do with doubt or lack of faith; they concern areas that continued to absorb my interest. This chapter will reveal such remaining questions, but more vitally, you'll also see more of my purposeful interactions with unbelievers through the litmus test of real-life challenges, including a devastating health issue and a potential loss of livelihood. In short, this year is where the rubber met the road.

8.2 Keeping My Cool while Answering Real Questions about Existence

For starters, there is one area I feel compelled to delve into because of the increasing opportunities I find to witness *incognito* to those unbelievers around me, and more pointedly, to impressionable youth who may not have anyone to whom they can direct their perplexities. No matter how frustrated this teacher may get with her students, I don't have the luxury of not taking their questions in earnest. They don't even know that I am fighting *for* them and fighting for space in their brains! Why? Oh, how easy it is for kids to fill their hearts and minds with what amounts to garbage, which, in turn, can lead to spiritual damage, emotional paralysis, and even physical death. Therefore, I will not shy away from answering challenging questions about life and will do so in love, respect, and honesty. I would venture to guess that two-thirds of my students are *not* Christian, and the most common question dealing with God would come from one of my nephews, Robert. He merely liked a status on Facebook of someone who posted something to the effect that if God is so great and good, why does He allow bad things to happen to good people. In my estimation and in so doing, he was waving a tiny, red flag of attention to be paid. This wasn't new to me. In the classroom, when we are going over some literary work dealing with values ad dilemmas, this is the million-dollar question I get more than any other. Even with my nephew, I had to revisit my answer because I did not feel my first response satisfied him. The answer I gave is worth noting here because I'm not too far out or past his point to understand his sense of frustration and even defiance in exposing apparent contradiction. When you see pain, wrongdoings, and iniquity both worldwide and next-door, how is it that God, who is mighty and allegedly loving, *seems* to do nothing and *appears* not to care? Often, such a question arises in a home either hostile to Christianity or one where questioning is encouraged. The world puts out pictures of Buddha, who appears all hip and peaceful, but the stereotypical one of a rather effeminate-looking Christ looking off into the distance hardly inspires confidence, and then there's the fact that you can't even *see* God. The first word in their supposition, "*if* there is a God," becomes the launching point where I assume a tentative, albeit reluctant nod of acknowledgment that there *is* a God, that there *is* something "out there" in charge of cosmic justice. In my answer, I flip the perspective from ours to God's. I ask them if they believe that they know more than ants do and that if an anthill is somehow knocked down because some monument is being built, would that ant ever understand why his home was being wrecked? I then say that God's ways are beyond our capacity to know the bigger picture of what *He's* got in store. If I can tell that this answer seems like resignation or copout, I follow up by saying that what or whoever made this world is one that is positive, vast, intentional, and loving. The very act of creation could *not* be accomplished by a negative, destructive, and disinterested force, even though we may dislike or anguish over some particular act. I tell the questioner that he was known before he was born, and then I name and say that *God* already knows *all* of the sufferings, joys, and challenges any and every person will experience over his or her life. We live within the context of millions of preceding ripples from the past, most of which we aren't aware of, converging into ours. Lest we forget, we can't even see five minutes into the future to know *what good may come of some bad circumstance.* You may not get to see the effect of such in your lifetime. Moses never saw the Promised Land. Then I stress that being all-good, God never *causes* harm to happen; He is incapable of *doing* bad things. Nevertheless, He will permit mayhem, sickness, or troubles to occur *if* they serve to bring about His grander purpose *later.* A kindergartner will cry if he doesn't get a cookie or if he spills his milk; we are no different than these babes to God. Prophets and leaders look further down the pike. Without the youngster's knowing it, I will sometimes quote a portion of Scripture, such as "God causes *all* things to work together for good to those who love God, to those who are called according to His purpose" (Romans 8:28).

I believe it's a matter of time until any person not only *acknowledges* God but also *loves Him back*, even if he or she *starts out* disinterested, bewildered, or hurt about something *else*. I don't make a habit of making statements like the whole world is evil or that the reason why we people are all so messed up is because Satan continues to have a field day with us. Why? People outside the faith don't want a guilt trip that implies that we collectively are the cause of evil and suffering — especially if they're dealing with some*one* they love who is hurting. They will roll their eyes at what sounds like mumbo-jumbo if you say there are "evil forces" at play in our lives. Jargon about the devil sounds antiquated and puritanical, and such is offensive to unbelievers who prefer socially-accepted, secular terminology found in the annals of psychology. It's all good and well if I "meditate" or study self-help books that are brilliantly written and on the best-seller list, but the moment I mention "*prayer life*" or wanting to heed *biblical* principles, non-believers go silent or start to whisper ridicules. I ought to know; I was one. They aren't ready for this speech or angle because non-believers either think they are already *pretty good*, or, very least, *they're not that all that bad*, certainly not bad enough to deserve misfortune, let alone wind up in Hell! If we ask why bad things happen to good people, then we should also probe why good people get away with doing wrong and don't get caught or receive their due punishment. I mean, haven't *you* gotten away with a lot that you *ought* to have been called on the carpet for but weren't because you didn't get caught? I have, for sure. No one complains about *that*! It is easier to point the finger at people who have gotten in trouble but don't *look* like you, like corrupt politicians, those already in prison, or decadent celebrities who are a few (or many) steps further in their misdeeds. Such a focus on others' ills may fool you into thinking you're somehow better or less evil than they. But wrong is wrong; there is *no difference* to Him, who is perfect. Justice doesn't get served, and perpetrators of vile acts don't get punished in the manner or timetable *we* think is best or right or fair. Punishment doesn't undo the deed. That doesn't mean vindication and justice won't get served! God knows it will! Yes, good folks you know and love *will* experience ill-tidings, and the wicked will seem to get away with murder; I know they will perish, just maybe not today. How can such treachery be? *We live in a fallen world!* We *all* will get knocked down because our playground is booby-trapped with land mines of all sorts, which *we* instigated millennia ago. Nonetheless, His righteous "purpose prevails" (Proverbs 19:21 NIV).

I admit I get a little anxious thinking what an unbelieving adult or youth might make of all I have to say. An important takeaway is that when you share Christ — even if you don't get to talking about Him from the outset — you've *got* to be loving and personable. Why must I concern myself and accommodate them? Well, how else can Jesus get in if I speak in a manner off-putting or they don't feel heard? Honey always works better than vinegar; even Paul adjusted his speech and style to suit the occasion and his audience. It's not so much *what* you say as *how* you say it that can make all the difference in the world. I want *both* to match up for His glory! Being around a rigid, joyless, or bitter person is hardly the ticket for sharing answers and cannot induce another to seek the Good News of Him.

8.3 A Mission Field in My Back Yard

I continue to pray fervently for my unbelieving friends and family, just as Bonnie's grandmother undoubtedly prayed for her for *decades* while Bonnie, in her hurt, became a wayward child and reckless young adult. I'm pretty sure that I had no one praying for me. Though some may be touched, I can't expect for a single lecture, let alone this book, to change a soul on its own; this is the job of the Holy Spirit. Aside from television specials watched and gifts or candy dispensed at Christmas and Easter, if children have no real exposure to Jesus — as was the case for me — for the time being, they are walking through life blind, and other than what the world decrees is acceptable or normal or cool. Actually, they are living without an ulterior aim. (This is not to say they won't have immediate, practical, and life-sustaining goals.) I ache in particular for my nephews because even though they are loved and cherished by their parents, they are being raised in a secular wilderness. I ought to know; I was. Although they've memorized the Boy Scout Motto and can recite the definition of "integrity" (but not "reverence"), they are in the vulnerable years of being exposed to temptations that can further taint their baseline values. I've been there myself. They keep their real thoughts and ponderings on secret lock-down for fear of reprisal or casual dismissal. I can relate. I suspect they romance doing derelict activities. I observe them giggling at someone saying grace, and I shudder as I watch them learn that it's acceptable to laugh at the profane or to watch adult-oriented or unwholesome programming and the like. I was no different. Why do I mention these matters if this book is about *my* spiritual path? Though I have spent time sharing my spiritual transfiguration, a work still in progress, such a change in me has brought about a desire to share that which wasn't in me before by jumpstarting the like in others. No other topic, regardless of how it is dear to me, has propelled me to do the like. How I interact with those family members, friends, and acquaintances must be in a manner that is consistent with my faith because *people watch*, and *every* place is a mission field. In short, a Christian is on-call non-stop. Though a middle-aged lady, I am a young Christian; my messy, imperfect, and flesh-filled passions and feelings often get the best of me. I can bristle with vexation or spout off wicked sarcasm without batting an eye when what I *really* need to do is breathe, turn the page, and let others see Christ in and through me, that is, *His* strength, tenderness, and faithful love, even if in a smile or through a touch of support. In short, I seek to lead others by following Him. The way I've heard it said, some folks in your life are leaves, some who are branches, and some who are roots. Though you can't see the roots and aren't as pretty as the leaves, leaves drop and fall; it's the roots that keep the tree alive. In other words, we are to put people, places, and things in their proper perspective and prioritization. Ultimately, knowledge acquired but not activated is arid, dry, dull, unattractive, futile, wasted, and stale.

At work, where I encounter many beleaguered colleagues, apathetic seniors, sophomoric juniors, or seemingly aloof administrators, I feel set apart to try not to participate in what further dispirits people, even if I sometimes think in the same way myself. When I visit my non-believing family or friends, I know that Christ shining in and through me is what counts the most in life. How empowering to know that "we have this treasure in earthen vessels" (2 Corinthians 4:7). I must try to be patient and wise and loving, never forgetting that "there but for the grace of God, there go I," an oft used quote allegedly stated by the English reformer, John Bradford. Some upcoming sufferings soon will be made known to you, and for the first time while in the midst of them, I would try to understand these ordeals from God's vantage point rather than ask with petulance or angst, "Why me?" Regardless of the progress I've recently made, I still feel and am very aware of the Socratic paradox, which is that "the only thing I know is that *I know nothing.*" Nonetheless, when I read my Bible, I am assured as if Jesus Himself were speaking to me that "what you do not realize now, *you will understand hereafter*" (John 13:7, emphasis mine). It's like when you're in first-grade learning how to add and subtract, and then, a few years later, you are taught how to multiply and divide. Sometime after this, you are introduced to the unknown variable x in algebra. A decade or so later, you might even master calculus, which operates more in symbols and Greek letters than in numbers. Few ever get to the level of understanding astrophysics, but such advanced levels of science only further prove God's genius, thoughtfulness, and purposefulness. At the beginning of your life, you never expect that later on, you might comprehend the likes of higher math, only in this case, the truths apprehended through the means of Christ's "mirror" (1 Corinthians 13:12) as well as the lens of my growing faith, not a calculator or slide rule.

8.4 HOLY SPIRIT, WHERE ART THOU NOW?

Speaking of this "treasure" we have inside us, I continued to mull over and wonder what exactly the Holy Spirit would look like for me when I'm in Heaven with God. I know the Holy Spirit is *with* me now and resides *in* me, but what about when I'm dead, and there's no "me" to indwell? Where will He be relative to my spirit in Heaven *then*? What will be the Spirit be doing when I'm directly facing Jesus? It seems His purpose would shift from helper, comforter, and guide to that of some sort of loving energy from our Father in Heaven. Technically, He cannot continue to indwell, as this will no longer be necessary, let alone possible. I look at Heaven not as a specific locale in time or space, but, for lack of a better word, some sort of dimension beyond my current ability to fathom. God, His Son, and the Holy Spirit all occupy Themselves in this whereabouts, and so do we believers in Jesus Christ who are no longer living and breathing. Back when Christ was living among His Disciples, the Holy Spirit did *not* indwell them. It wasn't until *after* He departed that the Holy Spirit came to encamp these men. I have been hoping the Holy Spirit won't *ever* depart from me, even if He somehow, albeit differently, occupies Dimi's spirit. After all, the Holy Spirit has been just the ticket, the very one who has helped me penetrate a few of God's mysteries and has become the evidence that Christ's unsurpassed love is for real. I know this beyond certainty! I'm sure that the Holy Spirit will still be very much present and accounted for even after I die; after all, they three are one, so, if anything, He will always be in me, but in the metaphysical sense. I somehow and also will be beholding and glorifying the other "Hims" then: Christ and God the Father. In other words, my salvation is secured such that when I go to Heaven, I will not only immediately be in the company of God and Jesus at His right side, I will be in the presence of the one triune. I will be privy to them *all at once* in one big, gestalt-like revelation. It's like instead of just *having* the one Spirit with me as I do right here and now *in* my person, I will *be with* and "face" all three at the same time, which is something I can't yet witness, let alone grasp now! I can always tell when the answer is right because, whether I like it or not, the Holy Spirit gives me a super-charged nudge and a quivering of excitement in my heart. We are locked and loaded!

In further trying to help me better understand the Holy Spirit within the Trinity, Mark made an apt analogy using my father. He told me that during my life, my father had been with me. Now that my father is dead, what I have of him here is the memory of his soul, a recollection of him, but when I die, I will detect him again but in a different manner when I join him in Heaven. This is a pale and frail comparison to what I will experience with God the Father. Once I confessed to Mark that I was scared that the Holy Spirit would leave me or might abandon me if I didn't adequately measure up or mature as a believer, but Mark assured me quickly and quietly that "never ever, ever would the Holy Spirit leave me, not even in death." Hebrews 13:5 says of Jesus that, "He'll never leave nor forsake us"; the original proof of this came about at Pentecost. And now I see that, if anything, to die will be an exponentially rich experience, *way* beyond my imagination or comprehension; there won't be regret because I will be in the presence of all Three-in-One, the Holy Trinity. It's a huge swap-out. As Paul said, "to die is gain" (Philippians 1:21), which is *not* to say that anyone *seeks* to be deceased. When my angst gets quelled, I cannot express the relief and moving joy I experience when I get put back aright in my understanding. I wish school were not in session because He consumes me, and I want to devote much more time to Him. I know that this is the case for millions of believers, but it is all still so fresh for me. I wrote Mark a note of gratitude for spending time with us and getting me back on point with Jesus:

    Just when I'm at wit's utmost end
    From trying to fathom points upon which much depends,
    You come along with your keen mind and touch
    And explain some mystery that's anguished me much.
    And though I question, stew, fret, and wonder,
    Please know it's no doubt, though I often blunder!
    I'm just young and am eager for His milk
    That moves me so that I shun all that's bilk.

Thanks to you, I know His Spirit in me resides,
And when I'm dead and gone, it's with the whole triune I'll abide!
And though for long, Christ I did so sadly spurn,
He waited, turned on my light so that I might to Him turn.
Rushing to Him, I finally exclaimed, "Yes, I do!"
Such that the Holy Spirit sealed my fate and stayed — and now I'm stuck like glue!

A little later on and continuing in this line of thought, I thought about Jesus feeling forlorn on the cross because for a split second and as a real man, He must have felt abandoned in those moments He suffered while taking on the punishment and suffering for our sins. Talk about the weight of the world! When He asked His Father, "Why have you forsaken me?" He did so because he was experiencing the exquisite pain of hanging on a cross in His full humanness, one of the most excruciating forms of torture known. Mark said that for the first time, Christ felt rejection and abandonment by the Father. What, oh, what suffering! Oh, such glory! His death brought about our chance for eternal life. The debt was paid, and our redemption was secured — was once and for all, available to all, but only *for those who would believe*. Other than John and a handful of close women, none of his disciples bore witness to the most significant act of love God showed us. Jesus would use their weakness and doubts to pour on more love later on. I think that would have to be considered on the same grand scale as Creation: life from nothing to life from death. His death was not for naught: millions upon millions of people's lives *have* been changed, in fact, more so by Him than any by other person on the planet. Faith in Him transports us past our heart's ceasing to beat. I used to avoid or raise an eyebrow in doubt if some widely- accepted premise was popular as if its being commonly-liked devalued it. I used to tell myself that the masses have simplified, superficial, or narrow views of life; some are just plain, old wrong. Most of what is in style, vogue, or fashion fades and becomes passé. Not here, though! Not with Jesus. In this increasingly secularized and polarized world, He is all the more relevant and essential. What is popular or the latest cannot be confused with who is profound and universally renowned for *all* time's sake.

My teetering on looking at Christ from this stance led back to my next tottering back to the Holy Spirit, this time in reflecting over the moments leading to salvation.

8.5 BLASPHEMY REVISITED

If the three are one, wouldn't blasphemy towards one be blasphemy to all? I know that Christ died so that I might live, and He lives in me by way of the Holy Spirit. I can't reject one without rejecting them all. I suppose this topic is related to my desire never to have the Holy Spirit depart from me, even in death, a moot point though it may seem here and now. I got to talk to Mark after church, and he answered my question by referring me to Luke 12:10: "And everyone who speaks a word against the Son of Man, it will be forgiven him, but he who blasphemes against the Holy Spirit, it will not be forgiven him." What I think this means is that Jesus says something to the effect that He will forgive us, but you can never disrespect the Holy Spirit. After all, when Jesus went back to Heaven, He didn't abandon us leave us to our own devices without help or aid. We need Him, the Holy Spirit, so we ought *not* to throw under the bus in word or by deed Him who is one with Them *and* inside us here and now! Jesus said, "I will ask the Father, and He will give you another helper who will be with you forever. That [helper] is the Spirit of Truth, whom the world cannot receive because it does not see Him or know Him, but *you know Him because He abides with you and will be in you* (John 14:16–17, emphasis mine). Jesus' Ascension and ten-days later, the special delivery of His Holy Spirit at Pentecost then leads straight to the life-altering affair we experience here and now during the moment of our salvation! The Holy Spirit is a bonafide, built-in support system, a direct link to (and from) the Father and Son for as long as we live! Mark understood what I was saying. He told me that though *we* might cut off ties with Him or even get angry with God or Jesus at some period in our Christian lives, this doesn't mean They'll do likewise with me. The bond between us involves no *quid pro quo* in *any* sense or form! When the Holy Spirit comes to reckon with and beckons one to accept Christ, then, if the time is ripe, our capacity to have faith in Him gets triggered, activated, or stimulated. If one ignores that call, nudge, or inner stirring, if one rejects... Then as I completed Mark's sentence, a shiver went down my spine: *to reject the Holy Spirit would be to reject Jesus, which would be to say "No" to salvation, which is to say "Yes" to death, nothingness, and eternal separation.* Repudiating Jesus is equivalent to rejecting His Father and our Maker. Game over. Straight to jail we go, and I don't mean like in Monopoly! That's worse than biting the hand that feeds you! Looking back, I have had multiple preparatory moments when Jesus was introduced to me, but evidently, the timing wasn't right for me to claim and accept His magnificent grace. The inner switch hadn't been turned on. Though Jesus died for everybody, for all the "whosevers" out there, including me, when God's ordained right timing arrived, Jesus surely knew it, and the Holy Spirit roused that readiness within me and helped a (future) sister out. How could I *not* run to Him like a child, a Daughter, with my whole self a big "YES"? I can't even imagine saying, "No," but I do feel extra blessed because I think it gets harder for people to hear and be open to such an invitation with every passing year.

8.6 SPIRITUAL GIFTS

To be better empowered to serve God, last week in church, we were shown a quick and easy way to assess what our spiritual gifts might be — what our own personal mix is. Thus, we would neither have to wonder nor try to fit a square peg into a round hole and serve at something that was not in alignment with our natures. If you try to force yourself to do that for which you are not suited, even for His name's sake, such will likely lead to frustration and perhaps a desire to quit. Pastor Mark suggested taking a test online, the source of which, I think, is something like *ChurchGrowth.org* to clarify which dominant gifts within us may prove productive for serving and glorifying Him. I did so, and here are my results:

Evangelism	18
Administration	18
Teaching	17
Exhortation	17
Pastor/Shepherd	16
Giving	11
Prophesy	11
Showing Mercy	7
Serving	5

No, I do not know the highest number possible per category, but I can get an idea of the relative scale through Bonnie's results. She scored in the mid-*twenties* in those very areas where I scored the lowest. Her capacity for mercy and serving is off the chain! Where I am weak, she is strong and vice versa. How and why can this be? "God has placed the members, each one of them, in the body, just as He desired" (1 Corinthians 12:18). And may I say that there is no pecking order as to who has which gift, just like all the parts of the body are necessary to have one functioning fully. For me, this thought is best expressed in 1 Corinthians 12:4–6 (ESV): "Now there are varieties of gifts, but the same Spirit; and there are varieties of service, but the same Lord; and there are varieties of activities, but it is the same God who empowers them all in everyone." The more I view the world as a Christian, the more I notice God teaching through irony and paradox, meaning His truths are revealed in unexpected or unconventional means, ways, people, or real-life situations. The Beatitudes presents such in a nutshell. Decades earlier, as a freshman in college, I took an extensive career interest survey test. It was determined and reported that I would be happiest as a college professor, psychiatrist, and — drumroll — a truck driver! Later I would come to see my classroom as my "rig." The online test we recently took was quite lengthy, and the results from there may reveal as much to you about me as my words do here in this book. Surely, my even writing this book — doing so while I'm still in the throes of a time and energy-consuming job like teaching high school — writing to *you*, is a testament to my top four gifts being used for His Name's sake. It was certainly never a part of *my* original plan to do so! Lord, no! Extraordinary living becomes just what fits the bill for Him, and somehow, He makes uniquely serving possible.

Any success we have in bringing people to the Lord is based on two premises: number one, the Holy Spirit must be present, and number two, I must be flexible, open-minded, and kind. I see that I'm in good company; Paul changed and became like this. He didn't compromise his principles, but he availed himself ready to be a go-between betwixt a potential proselyte and Christ Jesus! The following quote conveys what Paul does to realize his aspirations for Him, all the while not becoming a fraud or a two-face: "To the Jews, I became as a Jew so that I might win Jews…; to those who are without law, as without law, though not being without the law of God but under the law of Christ, so that I might win those who are without law. To the weak I became weak, that I might win the weak; *I have become all things to all men, so that I may, by all means, save some*" (1 Corinthians 9:20–22, emphasis mine). I can *relate to this seeming shifting stance, and it is a gift of mine that people find it easy to* open up with me and that my multi-faceted self can connect to many people in various ways. Now my formerly perceived incompleteness — my being half this and half that, neither fully from here nor there — in short, all my insecurities dissolve, and these beautiful and eclectic pieces of myself are made useful, whole, and robust for and in Him. Therefore, these test results (unsurprisingly) corroborate my career choice; it's just that now I renew my focus by doing such from a different perspective and with more vigorous intent.

In that spring and summer, questions and topics still posed themselves as I read His word, albeit they were coming at a slower pace; some were biblical, and others were related to the nature of my relationship with Jesus. I didn't know at the time that I was being prepared for some hardships that would come the next fall, first with Bonnie and then the following spring for me at work.

8.7 WHY DID THE CROWD TURN ON JESUS?

To save time and not bug Mark so much, I now tended to search a few select online sources for the answers to my questions. I've already mentioned some of them, and they cover a host of topics in a detailed, lucid, and biblically-based manner. Sometimes I would ask Bonnie's brother or turn to Rick at the gym, as both men were steeped in His Word and had been actively involved in their church for decades. As we approached Easter, I then began to ponder why the crowd turned on Jesus. Was it a different crowd than those He fed, taught, or healed? He had done so much for so many that I couldn't imagine how Caiaphas and the other leaders would be able to manipulate the crowd into asking Pilate to release Barabbas instead of Jesus! Bonnie's brother told me that both the Jewish leaders and their cohorts were interspersed among the crowd, pushing and promoting the crowd to choose Barabbas. These were the professional demonstrators and agitators of *their* day. From the Jewish elders' point of view, he who equated himself with God was a "blasphemer" (John 10:33). If there were the slightest chance that Jesus was more than a man, the Jewish leaders would have lost clout, credibility, and power; therefore, they turned the pressure up on Pilate, who also had much to lose politically if the people backed Jesus. Not only that, the very ones that celebrated Jesus as He came into Jerusalem thought He would lead them to overthrow the Roman rule. By now, they *had* to have realized that He would *not* be the military or political type of leader they had expected, and in their disappointment, they turned against Him. My friend at the gym, Rick, told me how he understood it was that the crowd which lined along the streets waving palm branches and laying them at Jesus' feet as He rode in town before his Crucifixion had been looking for a king to overtake the Roman government. They wanted to be liberated from Roman tyranny and reclaim their rightful position. However, Jesus did not exercise this type of authority. He knew His mandate was to come and die for humanity. Rick recalled the old gospel song, which, of course, I did not know:

Connecting the Dots...

"He could've called 10,000 Angels..." He could have rescued himself from the crowd, etc., but He *chose* to be the perfect sacrifice.

Then, as per norm, Rick would proceed to recite an appropriate verse; I'll bet he had memorized scores of verses! That day he left me with Matthew 20:28: "The Son of Man did not come to be served, but to serve and to give His life a ransom for many." By frequently quoting Scripture to me, Rick, in turn, motivated *me* to begin memorizing passages of Scripture as well. Before the year was up, I would memorize nine passages I adored. The verses I selected are well-known, but it was another mini-milestone for me. I practiced my memorizations while driving to places, usually to and from work, by making a recording of them on my phone's voice memo and playing them back, line by line, and hitting pause to recite them. I even practiced these Bible quotes on people who'd be willing to listen to them at school, and since then, I still recite them a few times each as I jog around the track at the gym. When I'm in dark moments, I always go to a slow and purposeful reading of the Lord's Prayer, literally focusing on and stressing one *word* at a time. I find other quotes all the time that capture what I'm experiencing in my journey of faith, and I am taken aback at how commonplace the first phase of early growth in Him I've been going through is, unique though it has been to me. I would imagine that by now, you have noticed the seismic shift in my way of thinking such that now my authoritative center of gravity is Scripture, and underpinning this is Jesus Himself. I'm in good company: St. Augustine, circa, mid 400's explained this well: "*Credu ut intelligam,*" which means something to the effect that "*We don't understand to believe; we believe to understand.*" Sometimes when I let it all go, I still imagine running straight to Jesus, and He always smiles at me and welcomes me with open arms. There are no questions then, just love.

8.8 What Motivates the Heart and Another Vision Quest in Greece

Towards the end of the school year, Mark came by for a visit, and I was so happy to see him! Among other things, we talked about the motivation of the heart. I ask Mark about what he meant when he said this past Wednesday night that "to be at peace with sin is to be at war with God." I told him that I certainly didn't hoped to be "at war" with God! Mark said the Holy Spirit is convicting and moving us all the time. God judges our inner motives. He said the reverse of this notion also existed: to be at war with Satan was to be at peace with God. How can you know you are at peace with God? Is it just a feeling? Here, too, we rely upon and become ever more sensitive to the cues of the Holy Spirit. For me, this amounts to my not feeling settled until the thing is right, even if (and especially) if it goes against my wishes. Our secondary pastor, Thomas, was still on fire from our "Footsteps of Paul" vision trip to Greece last year. He decided to replicate in like measure what we'd done the summer before in Greece; only this time, he would be the one to do all the planning and offer a similar trip to a group from our church that June of 2016. This time, Thomas made all the arrangements, checking in now and again about what tours we'd done and whom I'd used as our guide and transportation.

Highlights for me on this trip under Thomas' leadership that I didn't experience in Athens and Corinth last year include the following: Thomas read Scripture and taught us on Mars Hill what Paul had been seeing in Greece at the time. When we were in Corinth, our group hiked to the tippy-top of Acrocorinth, the red-light district of its day, where and when men took part in various religious reveries. Paul got so riled up at those deluded into thinking they'd reached spiritual ecstasy that he wrote particularly forcefully and didactically to the Corinthians about their misguided morals. Acrocorinth is a relatively small area at the apex of a range of mountains there, a configuration of large rocks around what might be the size of a typical backyard. However, the view from up there, which looks out and onto the expanse of water by the bay below and past the whole of Corinth, is simply breathtaking. You feel like you're the king of the mountain. However, hiking up to the very top cost Thomas teaching time down in Corinth, so when we got back to the hotel, our group went up to the second floor of our hotel in the breakfast room, and there he taught all he'd prepared and wanted to say. Most were tired and found themselves nearly snoozing, the air was so warm and still, but I eagerly ate up everything Thomas had to say. Not dissimilar to re-reading the Bible, it turned out that the rest of this short trip brought me fresh insights and better clarity of what I did know.

Another aspect of this trip that was different was that Thomas shifted the focus from educational also to include some missionary exposure. He had located a Protestant Church in Athens for us to visit and hear from its pastor, a Greek who had converted to Protestantism. In Greece, all Protestant Churches are labeled "Evangelical Churches" to remain innocuous and inoffensive to the Orthodox Greeks. Our group went to the church he'd contacted that was widely known for helping the local poor. Even the nearby Greek parish gave them money to help support their coffee house in the garage below the church used to help the Greek homeless population. Visiting here was certainly a highlight for me on this trip because I got to hear from real Greeks how and why they'd come to turn to the Protestant version of Christianity. They told our group that frequently, they had to explain to the local Greeks they were not a "cult," that their core beliefs were *identical*, that they were Christian even though their church didn't look the same as the Orthodox cathedral. Then these Protestant Greeks explained all of the ways that they were reaching out to help the community. I listened to everything they said with rapt attention, somehow gladdened that these Greeks got it, that is, recognized that form does not trump function and you need nothing more than to go straight to Jesus. Clearly, they wanted Him so much that they were willing to risk being ostracized or shunned in a Christian country that was unified by the time-honored bonds of the powerful and pervasive Greek Orthodox Church. Like me, they had let such go.

There is something in my nature that comes alive in Greece and settles into a groove and modality absent in the States. Viscerally and soulfully, I feel at home in my skin. Does that mean I haven't had frustrating times in Greece, waiting in so-called lines, that is, small crowds, or that I haven't felt frustration with their inertia, inefficiency, or what looks to be laziness (primarily in men)? Many Greeks enjoy the spirit of the happy moment; they each have their "1000% best" theories why their country's economy has gone awry and what needs to be done to improve things in the future, both for their country and in life for themselves. As one taxi driver told me when I asked him what he thought about the current economic crisis in Greece, he wryly quipped, "Greece has survived a million years; it is now a slave country once again, but *we will survive*." Greece is full of informed people who love discussing politics, but most people under fifty are cynical and mum about the church. Even though they're all steeped and versed in Orthodox traditions, by and large, it's when people get past fifty that they come to revere the church in a possessive, if not affectionate way. There also exists a kind of Greek arrogance displayed towards those who are *not* Greek. Even within myself, this generates an internalized micro-civil war, which most Americans would find bewildering. And yet I love it here so much! I crave looking into faces like my own, experiencing knee-jerk, similar responses to occurrences in life, and exuding a familiar and inherent optimistic outlook on life. Though I lived across the pond, I felt a powerful pride in possessing a shared history of several millennia with them, and I also had that same desire to discuss matters of import with passion. For me, such now also includes my Lord and Savior. Greeks are an exuberant people; Russians are a suffering one. Both are spiritually very deep people. Heaven help me! The "flesh" in me feels such a natural and powerful, immediate, innate, and loving attraction to Greeks. My soul is *still* drawn to Russia and Russians. The Spirit in me must help train my mind and heart to know that ultimately, regardless of my attractions and biases, I am now "an ambassador for Christ, as though God were making an appeal through me" (2 Corinthians 5:20). I cry out, "*Hosanna!*"

In Thessaloniki, as in Corinth, we had the same tour guide, Marie, whom we'd used the year before when it was just the four of us. I can't tell you how glad both of these two Greek guides were to see me, the "Greek" in the group. They wanted to catch up with me all of what had happened since last year, and I felt closer to each in a short amount of time. I stuck like glue to them, and, for sure, I did to Thomas over many others in the group. While in Thessaloniki, I learned so much more on this trip because I felt familiar enough with Marie to ask her questions about the Orthodox Church. I did this in part so that the rest of our group of East Carolinians could get to know the mind of a typical, young Greek person who considered herself Orthodox by faith, yet, in the same breath, she would say she "didn't really believe" and that she felt "disconnected" from the Church. Wow and wow. The same detachment is present at home! Such a divide is even more challenging to overcome in Greece because of the widespread and longstanding influence of the Greek Church imbued in Greek society and their collective cultural psyche. It's simply unthinkable to change, adapt, or (so-called) progress. That would make no sense and discredit the church if this were done because God's principles as expressed in this church are, by definition, *unchanging, constant, and perfect*. In other words, "if it ain't broke, don't fix it." Anyway, Greeks are just so "Greek," meaning that even though they may feel private frustration or apathy, they're not going to fundamentally challenge the church because it serves the good *and* the whole of their collective nation. By contrast, though also freedom-loving, we Americans are individualistic to an extreme and, as a country, are *not* unified by faith. Ironically, the Church is also just the thing that keeps many Greeks from personally getting to know Christ, thirst for His Word, and live out a life shaped by and for Him. In fact, with the freedom of spirit that only a Greek has, Marie said, "We Greeks do not read the Bible like you. If we want to hear the Bible, we go to Church, and the priest reads to us." Astounding! Amazing! I thought that one lady from our group mentally considered attacking her for saying this, as if our Greek guide was disrespecting the Bible. One must be sensitive to the fact that Greeks do *not* have a history of reading their own Bibles because Christianity had been present there for centuries before people possessed printed copies of the Bible, centuries before they could read the same language the New Testament which, for the most part, was written in Greek! There wasn't the need to read for themselves when they were read to! Plus, a whole layer of subconscious gratitude and respect for those church fathers and elders whose zeal and dedication kept the early Church alive and thriving exists in Greek culture. The typical American doesn't have an *inkling* of this background information, non-essential though it is for being a Christian. We also met a pastor in Beria, who chatted non-stop with me in Greek, as if I understood everything he was saying about his work with refugees in northern Greece. Agh, how I long to be fluent! I'd love to know all that he was doing! A little later on that day, I felt a special bond with two of the women in our group because, in being so moved by Lydia's Baptismal, they asked Thomas and our youth pastor to re-baptize them right then and there in these clear, cool streams. I felt exhilarated for them, and I quietly and joyfully recalled the rapture I experienced one year ago when I got baptized in the Mediterranean Sea off the shore of Kavala. Though more occurred, that's the long and short of this trip. I can say with certainty that the thought of spending more time in Greece and finding a way to help younger Greeks — even one person at a time — reconnect with Jesus grew strong.

8.9 QUESTIONS ABOUT THE BOXES

When we got back from Greece, I continued my dialogue with Thomas about a sermon he had given that dealt with sin and how God views us, the analogy of which he gave I just didn't completely understand. Though I was on vacation, by now, that hardly meant I was taking a break from Jesus. One morning, I was running at the beach and thinking about the interlocking box analogy Thomas made at church. You know the boxes I'm talking about: they are the plastic storage bins at Wal-Mart that can fit inside one another until you're ready to get them out and use them. He had several up on stage by the pulpit to illustrate how Jesus covers our sin. Thomas asserted that God sees us who have accepted Christ as spotless. When I got back from my run, still sweating, I emailed him a question I hoped he'd answer. I informed him that I felt like I am fooling no one, that I am *still* a sinful person. I told him that I felt like I was the smallest black box inside Christ's next-sized box, which would naturally be red with His blood covering me. I ain't fixed! I'm *still* broken! Is God in denial?!? It doesn't always help me to pray and confess, especially when I can feel a sense of futility *after* I've done so. I feel fraudulent because I know full well I will sin again. I pollute the world with myself! I get vexed at the fact that, though I *am* saved, I am in no way pure, and it bothers me to think that God forgives me based on what Jesus did for me; it makes me even more aware that I'm an unrighteous sinner. Perhaps I could offer the following analogy: I must confess every day and wash off my moral scum just as I shower daily. I could appreciate this, for sure. What in life had changed for and within me now that I was a Christian? My stance toward and approach to doing life have altered, and I required realignment again and again. Sanctification is infernally slow! I sin beyond my own volition, yes, even in my dreams! I also know that it can be a waste of time to focus on my flawed state because

I also know for sure that God wants me to *get at it already*, that is, to use the good He gave me. Ultimately, Thomas did answer my question about how God can view me as His spotless child though I am still an imperfect person.

8.10 An Explanation of How and Why My Debt Was Paid

Thomas wasted no time answering me back, and I will now fully recount what he told me. He started by explaining that when Jesus said, "It is finished!" (John 19:30), this word, "finished," actually comes from the Greek word verb, "tetelestai." It was a banker's term used to indicate when someone paid off a debt; it was paid in full and thus was marked with "tetelestai." It was kind of like paying your car off and then receiving your title from the bank. You now officially have what you were paying for. Thomas explained some of the grammatical aspects of words, which both as an English and foreign language teacher, I really appreciated. Thomas said that the verbal perfect tense used indicates a complete act with continual results in the future; in essence, this means you can enjoy the present state of a completed past action. The passive construction means that it was something done to or for you; you are the recipient. The indicative mood is a statement of fact, which screams that this is true. That's quite a bit of thought and theology for one small word. So, to put that all together, Jesus' death on the cross was something He did; it was a completed act in the past that pertains to your present sin. It was paid in full, and His one action is good for the past, present, and future. His taking the wrath upon Himself (which happened in the past) means I can stand in the bright shadow of His righteousness provisioned for me right now and today, and I can stand on and walk in that forever. For me, the passive construction of "it *is finished*" means that I had nothing to do with the forgiveness of my sins and the wrath due to me. The indicative mode underscores that this is true. The hard question for most of us is *not* "Do you believe *in* God?" but "Do you *believe* God?" Often, people ask the same questions over and over, and they get the same response over and again. I think they ask certain questions because they don't believe the answer they get, so they continue to ask. Thomas returned to this new term. He said that "tetelestai" refers to a legal courtroom type of document, but it does not speak about the sinful nature we all still have. As a result of having belief in Christ, Paul tells us that Jesus sent the Holy Spirit to dwell in "jars of clay" (2 Cor. 4:7); we become "a new creation" (2 Cor. 5:17 NKJV) with a new purpose. In other words, your soul and sinful flesh still dwell in the same physical body, but they do so right alongside the brand new (to you) Holy Spirit of God. That's how I can live in the flesh in one minute, and the next, I can live in the Spirit. The Spirit gives us power over sinful flesh through our continued faith and practice, but the flesh's desires often overrule. God doesn't entirely remove the flesh. If He did, then there would be no need for the Holy Spirit.

Thomas finally brought his teaching together with what I'd asked him what he had intended by bringing those storage bins on stage. He said, "You were taken out of sin and sin took out of you in a legal sense, paid in full, and then you were transferred to becoming 'saints in the light' (Colossians 1:12 NKJV). You still have memories, dreams, and desires for the life you once had in our father, Adam." I understood this to mean that the beauty of the Gospel is that God knew that in saving us, we would be in the position to have to make a choice every day to follow Christ or to remain in the flesh. That's not to say God doesn't intend for us to revel in and fully enjoy His world! I am talking about morality here. Thomas declared, "You are not pure, and neither am I, but when God 'sees' me, I am pure because the righteousness that is Christ's has now been imputed, that is, ascribed to me." In a daily sense, we are all dirty, but in this legalist sense, according to God, we are righteous because of Christ. That's why the Christian life all revolves singularly around Christ. There is nothing that I have done for my salvation; it was and still is all about Him. Thomas proceeded to expound on the term "sanctification," with which I was already familiar. He confirmed that, yes, we would never complete such until we got to Heaven, but most people don't even work at it. He told me to consider professional athletes: they operate at a different level than most of us regarding playing their game. Even though we non-athletes call them "great" (e.g., Michael Jordan or Serena Williams), if you ask *them* about their performance, they would answer that they continue to strive every day to become even better! The point is that they work at it to get to the level where they are and still think they're not good enough. Most people expect sanctification to happen to them "like catching a cold or the flu"; it's just going to come to them, but the reality is we have to be diligent just like the professional athlete is perfecting his shot, etc. The challenge is to get up every day and go through life, work, and study to be the best you can be. Thomas then spelled out for me what living out the Christian life looks like. For the Christian, this means "to pray, to seek God, to study his word, to obey the Holy Spirit, to follow his commands, to love the poor, and to do something about injustice, etc." To be theologically correct, I see that we Christians were sinners who have been saved by Jesus Christ and now have a calling from God to carry the Gospel to others as "ambassadors" of Him. Remaining broken and imperfect allows the beauty of the glory of Christ to shine through our imperfections! If we were already complete, then He would have no room to show Himself. So, the curse of our flesh is the very thing that God uses to declare Himself! I was astonished at Thomas's revelation, and I felt so inspired.

Thomas gave me some final points to ponder about "the flesh." In Revelation 20, the Bible says that Satan has been waging war, and at some point, he will be locked away for a thousand years. Here's the question: with demonic activity gone, will sin still exist then? Will there be any enemies of God? Even though Satan will be absent, evil and sin will continue to exist in the world. Just look at what happens when Satan gets released: he immediately and successfully gathers an army for war. Thomas answered his own questions by proclaiming, "There would be no armies available if there weren't sin and evil already still existing within man's heart. Because of my sinful nature, I don't need Satan around to be able to sin; *I do a good enough job without him!*" Therefore, even though God created the world and saw that it was "good" (Genesis 1), sin was introduced into every form of the life. Humanity, Nature — yes, all animal and plant life, right down to the microscopic level, have been damaged and continue to feel the effects of sin. Creation is beautiful, but it also longs for and "groans" (Rom 8:22) redemption and the riddance of evil the same as we people do!

I did have one final, personal suggestion about the boxes: it would be cool to put a little standing camp flashlight inside the smallest box and then turn off all the lights on stage. Then people could see that precious, little light that symbolizes the presence of His Holy Spirit within us. The moment Jesus saves us is when we get that little light, to begin with. Both of these boxes, He and we, are held inside the biggest box of all, God, and He sees our light, His Spirit, through the plastic bin. As the American folk song declares and, I, too sing, "This little light of mine, I'm gonna let it shine!" Mystery solved!

8.11 SOME LIGHT SUMMER READING JULY 2016

Another sign of my growth in Christ was evidenced in the books I chose to read. Formerly, I would have read classic or contemporary *fiction* that delivered richness, pith, or humor. Over the years, admittedly, I have found myself searching up and down aisles in bookstores and not finding anything that sparked my attention. Sure, I loved biographies as well, and that hasn't stopped, but when I became a Christian, not so slowly, and I began gravitating toward *nonfiction* works that would improve my understanding of Jesus. These also included books on spiritual growth, spiritual warfare, apologetics, biblical commentary, and other Christian pilgrims' experiences. I didn't go around talking about it or announcing what I was reading for thinking I might come off looking to be preachy, pushy, close-minded, or fake, like I had it all together. In fact, and in private, I felt like I never ingest enough spiritual bread related to Him. Not only books, but what I chose to watch regarding TV, music, and movies was changing as well. I listened to Christian podcasts and other pastors' sermons on YouTube. I was not becoming a fuddy-duddy; I am just more careful about what I chose to consume mentally. I couldn't help what all came upon the world, but I could where my activities in life were concerned. Did I still love classic rock and soul music from the seventies? Do violin music and Russian composers still move me? Deeply! Did I still crave to hear Greek folk music? Oh, yes, so very much! Now I also happened to have a growing and eclectic Christian playlist, which I would've balked at collecting before.

I won't list all the many books I came to read, but I can share a few, as you have already seen. This summer, I bought a book called *Christianity and Greek Philosophy: Or the Relation between the Spontaneous and Reflective Thought in Greece and the Positive Teachings of Christ and His Apostles*. I've now gone to Greece twice to tour where Paul traveled and served a missionary there. This book explained the Greek philosophical underpinnings pre-dating Christianity to present the argument that it was a natural, a shoo-in, and perfectly ordained timing to introduced the Gospel to the Gentile world of *Greece* in particular. Plus, I also love Greek philosophy, so I was immediately drawn to this book connecting the two spheres. Knowing that Paul was surrounded by lesser Greek philosophers — the Epicureans and Stoics, the former, hedonists who sought personal pleasure, and the latter who pursued self-denial for purification purposes — it is no wonder that the Apostle Paul left Athens feeling underwhelmed and empty-handed. I erroneously thought that "the statue to an unknown God" to which Paul referred meant that the Greeks couldn't find the name for one more god that was out there to cozy up to. I was wrong! Paul recognized in the Greek nature an innate sense and desire to access the divine — *starting* with a recognition of the unknown god. The unknown god represented *the ultimate and unknowable divine*!! This book explained that the earlier (and superior) foundations of Greek philosophy, that is, the ideas from Socrates, (especially) Plato, and Aristotle, lay the groundwork for an intellectual readiness in the Greeks *to be open to Christianity*. They were already seeking that which is beyond and more significant than they knew to exist. This is one of the most complex books that I have ever read, and it is more philosophical than religious, but the two spheres merged in a beautiful synthesis in such a way that made me appreciative of my faith's history and of God's preparing us in such a way. I am so proud that the Greek language became the vehicle for introducing the New Testament to the world! I also learned that these Greek thinkers used precise language and a recondite vocabulary to express the cosmos. Their words would become the perfect vehicle for conveying the Epistles' ideas! In short, before Christ arrived, the best of Greek philosophy fulfilled a preparatory mission for Christianity by paving the way for man to find a better way to live morally and ethically, one that could not have arisen through his own making or conception. It was a message of heretofore-untold redemptive love that came from God Himself.

The other book I devoured that summer was packed with more of what I deep down desired to learn, and I knew I had hit the jackpot just by scanning the table of contents. Mark had recommended a book to me called *Soul Cravings*, and my soul indeed lapped it up like a hungry dog. In fact, this would be one of many books he'd suggest I read. The author, Erwin McManus, goes into great detail about the various needs of the soul and how it longs to be meaningfully engaged, fulfilled, and purposed. He also warns us about what happens when we don't do that which is needed. There is nothing fake, frivolous, or pretentious about this book, and it filled me with a quiet joy and edification as to why Christianity alone is how we can be contented and completed. While we were down in Florida, we checked out the church we went to last summer, where Mark's mentor and hero was preaching. After the sermon, I went up and spoke to this pastor, so glad was I to hear his sermon; he, too, was a man grateful for his faith and on fire for the Lord. To date, I have read well over thirty books related to Christianity in four years and have made five laps of reading and studying the New Testament and a more haphazard one of a goodly portion of the Old. What does this mean? I am passionate for Him, and I hunger for His Word. My next tribulation came because of an issue I had with semantics, in particular, how Jesus could be called my called "friend." Once again, I turned for help to my friend and mentor, Pastor Mark.

8.12 "What a Friend I Have in Jesus!" How Can This Be?!?

I confessed to Mark that I was still having problems with the notion of Jesus being my *friend*. It seems informal, disrespectful, not to mention untrue to call Him — my Lord and Savior — by this familiar term. Even if He is *my* friend, I certainly can't imagine that I could be *His* friend! Technically, I know I'm both His sister and God's daughter, but "friend"? No way, José! How can He be my friend without the friendship being but a one-way street? After all, did I die for Him? Have I ever done anything *for* Him other than believe *in* Him? I certainly have changed because *of* Him, but has my faith brought about the so-called "death" of me? I have memorized that which I now know to be true for myself, and that is "I have been crucified with Christ" (Galatians 2:20). Maybe it is a matter of wording because I'm still me, but I *have* been changed. He is not my *buddy*, but I can imagine him as my teacher, mentor, and the most peaceful and loving man who has ever existed. At the risk of sounding not very spiritual, I would like to add that I believe Jesus must also have had quite a sense of humor. Not only did He speak in parables, but He who broke the mold used paradox, sarcasm, hyperbole, and irony with regularity and gave the powerful leadership what for, rendering them speechless, grumbling, annoyed, unsettled, and ultimately, threatened. Why? He spoke the truth which decimated their prestige and advantage.

Not only did I have trouble with the label "friend," but I still got hung-up on one more aspect of my relationship with Him. When I consider the immensity of what He accomplished for us all then, which includes me here and now, I don't see how my salvation and subsequent friendship could be "personal" when His sacrifice was intended to be *universal*. It seemed to take away from the intimacy and specialness of what He did for me when through His Death, He brought life for billions of others, too. Do I sound jealous, possessive, petty, and unrealistic? I can just hear someone say, "Yep, God can do all of that," that is, be both intimate *and* universal with believers. I was still feeling insignificant in the vast scheme of things, but, I suppose, why shouldn't I? I'm no different than anyone else, even if He knows who I am. I am no better or worse than you. I felt like I just took a number in a waiting room I chose to enter until it was my turn to come up to His counter. Honestly, at this moment, I felt closer to the Holy Spirit and even to God the Father than to Jesus, but two out of three ain't so good in this situation.

I think I may understand why Jesus being my "friend" has been so problematic for me: I have never really had a super-close friend in my life; I guess that means I've never been one to another person either; plus, I sense my ineptitude before Christ. Our family has always been the pack type, and wherever we lived, we were always the outsiders, neither northern nor southern, neither Greek nor American, and those choosing arts over sports, etc. And since my parents' divorce, I see that, when it's all said and done, you really can't even count on family when the chips are down or you're down and out. Friends have come and gone through the scenes and seasons of my life; there have been few constants. So how could this be the case with Christ? How can He be a friend to me when I bring nothing to the table? In my mind, I well know that faith is not works-based, but in my heart, I keep saying, "But still...!" I surely hope that in some measure, I can be one of the ones I've heard tell that "you will know by their fruits" (Matthew 7:16). I have come to know people whose friends have supplanted their family members. Even Jesus ditched his hometown boys and disbelieving family for His own chosen buddies. Therefore, of all of the identities Jesus possesses — Son of God, Redeemer, and Savior, I don't understand how anyone can add the term "Friend" to the mix! If He is a friend, and what He did as my friend is something that friends ought to do for one another, then I am no friend and ought not to have such a friend. To be painfully blunt, I don't think I have the strength to die for a loved one, let alone a stranger or an enemy! That makes me feel like I'm a weak fraud! Yes, I know I'm to die to the world as I grow in Him, but that doesn't happen overnight. So, to hear of Him being a "friend" pains me much. Look how his "friends," His Disciples, acted surrounding the event of His Crucifixion. Thankfully, they dropped everything to be with Him during His ministerial stint, but John withstanding, they were not loyal to Him at the bitter end.

Now I see that how Jesus showed love and grace in yet *another* way: He put stock in the common man to lead the charge of evangelism. *After* the Resurrection and Ascension, they were rekindled and on fire to share Him! How could they not?! They saw and walked among Him again! We, too, are to be like them, but I feel more like His Disciples at the end of His life than when they became His powerhouse Apostles. Why? I avoid conflict and do not readily or promptly counter others' disdain, apathy, or disbelief. I don't even know how to approach folks to start a conversation about Him. Maybe that I am like them ought to give me comfort because Jesus chose the ordinary ones to be His crew. When I look at Mark, I see him loving on people exactly *as and where they are*; they soon know that they can open up and share without fear of reprisal. Love must always be the answer. Always.

Another way to express my predicament about trying to find a way to have this "friendship" or "personal relationship" with Jesus is that even though we are in the same room, He is sitting at the grown-up table, and I am at the children's table. When He came to me at my moment of salvation, that was incredibly intimate, powerful, and beyond any joy that I had ever experienced. I am not ungrateful or disrespectful! Eyes wide open, I am aware of what He chose to do for us and for *me*. I am *not* still looking for the mountain-top high of salvation. Now that I'm am His, He is back at the right hand of the Father, and I am left with the memory of my supernatural encounter with Him, but, He *also* lives in me. Maybe that's the be-all, end-all of the *personal* part, but it can't be! How is it that I am to acquire, let alone maintain a *relationship* with Him? When I pray, I *do* try to address and talk to Jesus, but I feel that ultimately it is *God* who is orchestrating events and listening to my tiny prayers; after all, *He* is the Sovereign One. I don't feel like I really *know* Jesus or that I am in a personal relationship with Him, at least not in the sense of those I've ever had before. One way I can express myself when feeling either moved or troubled is through poetry, and since I felt both in my frustration of trying to comprehend what it meant to have a relationship with Jesus, I wrote the following:

    Close to Jesus, a Poem
    I thought a "relationship" was a two-way street;
    If that's the case, J sits across from an empty seat.

There's nothing that I can bring to Him;
That's so very clear to me.
My faith, love, and fruit sure ain't a thing compared to His grand fee.
Who in the world would call J "Friend," when under pressure, I'd know I'd bend?
He wouldn't want a friend like me,
So, I can't ask Him — don't you see?
Of course, I know He saved me; He came to my very home!!
And it's solely the Holy Spirit that does deep inside me roam.
But Jesus's very own presence, I cannot seem to feel;
I'm uber aware of His Father and know that He's for real!
But now that Jesus is back in Glory at His Father's own right hand,
I'm left with a magnificent story, but a man I cannot understand.
Did He love me, then leave me until I am dead and gone?
But of the three, He's as far from me as some distant shimmering dawn.
Why am I overwhelmed with longing for the man so many call "Friend"?
Bonnie chides me for focusing on the three in one. For her, they add up to one — it's done!
And when Todd compares the three to water, mist, and ice,
It's all I can do to not to roll my eyes and let out a big ol' sigh!
You've helped me fathom the power and flow of the Wholly Holy Ghost,
And of Him, I'm as sure as I am of God, but it's about J that They do boast.
And so, I long and pain for Him shared by many who are far from dim,
Yet like Superstar song does go, I to you must confess,
"I don't know how to love Him," and that leaves me under duress.
So, while others claim He's so Personal,
I'm out wandering in my own infernal cell.

I wrote and shared these thoughts and poem with Mark, but

knowing it would be some time before he could come and visit, so busy was he with the growth and involvement of our church in the community and beyond, I checked in with Bonnie's brother. He responded almost immediately and helped add another layer of understanding to this plight of mine. He told me that he understood my "friend of Jesus" question and had even felt somewhat the same way. It seems a bit flippant to say that the Omniscient, Omnipresent Creator and Sustainer of the universe is our "friend," but even if we don't feel worthy of that being the case, it *is* true. Most people *like* the thought of His being our Friend; only a few consider it disrespectful. Her brother informed me that there are verses that make the case for us being a friend of God. One of the best passages is where Jesus calls *us* His friend for doing what He tells us to. In John 15:13–15 (emphasis mine), Jesus says,

> "Greater love has no one than this, that one lay down his life for his friends. *You are My friends* if you do what I command you. No longer do I call you slaves, for the slave does not know what his master is doing, but *I have called you friends, for all things that I have heard from My Father I have made known to you.*"

This not only applies to the original twelve disciples but for all Christians henceforward! Another verse that is similar in vein is found in James 2:23 (emphasis mine). It says, "... 'AND ABRAHAM BELIEVED GOD, AND IT WAS RECKONED TO HIM AS RIGHTEOUSNESS,' and *he was called the friend of God.*" I think this means that since Jesus is alive and is always with me because I believe in Him, being who He is, He always wants the best for me, and He finds ways to encourage me to do what is right. He is there waiting to help me when I fail or fall, so in *this* respect, I certainly can look on Him as my friend! One Wednesday night right after church, I went up to Mark to see if there wasn't a time we could meet. Knowing what was concerning to me, Mark quickly told me that *I am to bring myself to Jesus*, meaning I must be willing to walk every day with Him and be available for Him. I need not get tripped up; I should be confident today! Nothing has changed between Jesus and me. He is as close as ever! As always, Mark assured me that soon we would untie "all those pesky knots" as soon as we could sit down together. I just don't want to

"Peter" out on Jesus in the meanwhile, so I'll lean on Him and know clarity will come, and my stream can flow all the more fully. Out of gratitude, I wrote about Jesus and how each and all of "Them" were taking care of me. I share it with you now:

> If J is part of G, and He is in charge of all,
> Then J is with me, too — Yahoo! — there cannot be a wall.
> Time, space, and love and gnosis - they all belong to God,
> So as the Father runs the world, the Son hears our every nod.
> It has to be so personal
> As the Son came down for me,
> And though He's back in Heaven, He's also ever-near,
> And as the Spirit assures me, I need not ever fear.
> He died so hard for me back then, and I give to Him me now,
> He's not as far away as I may think; all I have to do is bow.
> Omni-present means He's here, though sight of Him won't do,
> As faith charged up is what it takes for me to see Him true!

Little did I know that one month later, all these speculations, contemplations, and explorations about the nature of my relationship with Him would shift to engaging my faith to the next level. It was one of complete abandon because I didn't know what had just hit me. In need of help, life hit pause on my serious game of *Probe*, and I prayed and placed my trust in Jesus with all I had.

8.13 An "Incidental Finding":
Faith Put to the Test

When calamity or disaster happens, there are co-related events, happenings, and phrases said that become like shards of highlights you recall only in the aftermath. Bonnie's "incidental finding" was one of these. As I indicated at the beginning of this chapter, all that Bonnie and I had come to know in Christ, all that had come to change us from within, would be put to the test this year. By now, Bonnie was volunteering to do as much as she was able for our little church when asked, and that fall, she helped with some fall sprucing up of our campus. Once while helping spray pesticide at a swarm of wasps, she inadvertently inhaled the poison at the very moment a breeze came up and suddenly changed direction such that it came back fully towards her. Instantly, her lungs hurt sharply, and this pain didn't let up by the evening. In fact, later that day, she also began to get a fever; therefore, scared, she took herself to the E.R., and there they conducted some tests and gave her a Benadryl-like medicine. The next day, she followed up with an elderly doctor who told her that she was still "very sick," and he had her admitted to a nearby hospital. Additional testing was done, and she ended up having to stay at the hospital a couple of more days to receive steroidal shots used to kick in her antibiotics. On the last day, as she was checking out, a young doctor excitedly came into the room and told her that they'd found "a mass" in her left lung. He was buoyant and pleased to tell her so because this finding had been initially overlooked and missed before. Then came the whirlwind of the hurry-up-and-wait game as a battery of even more tests were conducted so as to conclude this or that. In the meantime, no one with full authority told her anything conclusively, and she couldn't help but wonder what horrible thing was wrong with her until her worst nightmare was confirmed; all of that checking led to a diagnosis of cancer. To go from being healthy one day to thinking the next she might potentially die left Bonnie and me reeling. As soon as an appointment could be made, Bonnie then went to a pulmonologist. While sitting in the waiting room, feeling shell-shocked and ice-cold numb inside, she was gifted with seeing on this doctor's a large Norman Rockwell-esque painting of a physician pouring over his notes and Jesus standing unseen behind him, guiding his eyes and mind to curative solutions. Bonnie stood up to gaze at this painting, and for the moment, she was calmed. The first reaction to finding out she had the "big C" was one of speechless shock; the next moment, she was saying, "*Now* what?" A kind nurse there told Bonnie gently and in private that "now she would get to see just how strong she was," and then *she prayed* with Bonnie. Initially, Bonnie wanted to tell no one, but within a week, she had told several of her close prayer warriors at church, and only after this did she reveal she had lung cancer to some of her family members. I once told you that Bonnie was a prayer warrior, and now I witnessed the power of Christ come fully charged inside her to bring about quiet confidence that was beyond her own calling. Was her inner strength constant? No. Flannery O'Connor once said, "sickness is a place, … and it's always a place where there's no company, where nobody can follow…" No truer words were spoken, and I felt frustrated at being at the other end of this bottle-neck because I couldn't do anything or fix this. Did I pray? You'd better believe it. Every morning and behind closed doors, I fell on my knees, just Jesus and me; my speculations as to whom I should direct my attention went out the window. People who aren't Christian scoff at what seems like talking to the air or wishful thinking, especially when things aren't going their way; this year would burn away whatever vestiges of that sort of outlook that had existed within me. Why? I, too, now possessed "the confidence which we have before Him that if we ask anything according to His will, *He hears us*" (1 John 5:14, emphasis mine).

    I want to insert an additional word about prayer here. Is praying odd at first? Yes. Does or can your mind drift? Yes. Does God care this occurs? No. If you keep your mind coming back to Him, you will slowly but surely build your concentration capacity to remain in union with your prayer's flow with Him. Think back on a time when your ability to jog a mile might have been nil; practice makes perfect here, too! As the Staple Singers sing, "I may not know how to pray, but He loves it when I try." For years when we read Anne Bradstreet's "Upon the Burning of Our House" in my American lit. class, I taught the students that there are three levels of prayer, starting with the most superficial: making *requests*. The next level is our expressing *gratitude*, and the highest level, *communing*, is when we plainly talk and *especially* listen to Him. I *never* wanted my prayers to be misconstrued by God and have Him think I am making a wish list as if to Santa Claus or that I am negotiating with Him. By now, I felt the same as the one who penned the words in the old gospel song, "Nothing to Him I bring; simply to the cross I cling." I used to be hesitant about asking for things or pleading for intervention from Him. After all, the Lord's Prayer clearly states, "*Thy* will be done"— not mine! I look at prayer differently now: I know He likes it when we come to Him earnestly because it shows we trust in Him to hear our prayers. Any way, if I *don't* ask, Jesus' own brother tells me that "you do not have because you do not ask" (James 4:2 NKJV), so how could I not pray for Bonnie's complete healing? Those of us who believe *are* assured because "God causes *all* things to work together for *good* to those who love [Him]" (from Romans 8:28, emphasis mine). You may ask me what "good" could possibly come from this situation of Bonnie's. We also were wondering this, but all you can do is fall flat on your face and pray with complete abandon in full-on faith; otherwise, fear creeps in, and you feel done for when this is *so* not the case with God. One's faith can sometimes be a moment-by-moment, touch-and-go experience. Does the fact that I pray hard enough mean she will be cured here on planet earth? Not necessarily. Healing might happen only in death when *all* sickness and sorrow is gone. Of course, she doesn't want to leave this life!! Of course, I don't want her to die, even though to do so "would be gain" (Philippians 1:21), as Paul was want to say because he knew he'd be with Christ! Oh, now is when our human selves cry and groan deeply! By now, both Bonnie and I had enough Biblical knowledge in our hearts and minds to know where to turn for helpful truths in Scripture. Plus, we have the Helper living in us who intercedes for us when we don't have the words, don't know how to pray (Romans 8:26). Having faith powerful enough to believe in the power of prayer does not serve as a false security blanket or placebo effect. Having Christ dwell in me empowers me with resolve *and* "the peace of God which surpasses all understanding, [and it] will guard your hearts and minds" (Philippians 4:7 NKJV) even and *especially* when I am weak and helpless. I'm so grateful now that I didn't "grieve" the Holy Spirit, that

Connecting the Dots...

I didn't reject God when Jesus came a-calling and tugged at my heart. He both convicted *and* convinced me to come to Him; no words were needed. Now was just the moment that I clearly see just how much we need Him for *everything*.

8.14 THE POWER OF PRAYER DEMONSTRATED

Speaking of my reluctance to ask for things or actions from God, I remind myself that it is incumbent upon me to do just that! When I pray, I am showing I *do* believe, that I have *faith* that God is in control of all. It's not about my *asking*, but about my *trusting* Him; He loves me and likes it when I come to Him! Bonnie did not resign herself or conclude that God wanted to take her away. She still wanted to live, love, and serve! The Apostle James also quipped, "You ask and do not receive because *you ask with wrong motives...*" (James 4:3). Bonnie's motives were pure when she asserted, "I am not done yet!!" When it's all said and done, it never hurts to ask for more life. Her cancer was diagnosed as being at Stage 2 because it had been found in three of the eleven lymph nodes removed. During a span of four months, Bonnie not only underwent a lobectomy, but she bore four rounds of the strongest chemotherapy on the market for a person under the age of sixty. Yes, there would be quarterly scans for the next two years to observe her closely, and to remain five years clear is still the benchmark to declare oneself cured of cancer, but for here and now, He *had* conquered her cancer! All the same, Satan does a number on you and tries daily to scare you, in this case, by unexpectedly having had you face your mortality. Then you get whiplash in looking back on what you just endured. Good-intentioned Christians will say, "It's a win-win either way!" In other words, either you live and get healed, or you die and get to be with Him; *eventually*, we Christians will all possess a glorified and perfect body. Let me tell you that this is *not* what you want to hear! You still love life and inherently cling to it! God understands this! Satan tries to distress us with anything and through anyone he can, and I remember that Bonnie would even get unnerved or troubled when folks would reflexively say, "I'm going to pray for you." It sure didn't feel like so to her. Why? It seemed to her that these prayers were superficial and not genuine, but a guardian angel and new friend to her told her to "claim them" because when prayers are spoken, even in that split second of intent, God hears them, so they *do* count. Plus, Mark said most people just don't know what to say or do in this situation. Finally, as one who wants to know what to say or do when I hear someone has cancer, I will share and take Bonnie's advice and in her own words:

> I have heard many times over the last several months that most people don't know what to say. First of all, do let that loved one with cancer be aware you are going to pray for them. Maybe you could offer a prayer right then. Hopefully, in the following months, you'll let them know you're still praying for them, even though their outcome is ultimately in God's hands. An occasional note of encouraging Scripture meant *so* much to me, too. In fact, I saved many of them. Some would begin, "I just read this and thought of you." I would read those messages over and over. Often, the days I'd get those messages would be days I might not even feel like responding other than a check or a quick thank you, but they meant the world to me.
>
> Next, don't underestimate the power of a hug!! Hugs gave me added courage. I needed to feel loved. I was trying to trust the Lord, but this can be difficult when you are sick, hurting, and feeling alone. After discovering I would need chemo, a lady I met at the hospital said to me, "Can I give you a hug?" Then she said, "Now you will see how strong you are!" Initially, I thought to myself, "I'm not feeling really strong right now," but over the next few months, her words came back to me, and I felt stronger. You should know that cancer makes one feel so alone. Please don't feel hurt if your loved one says this. Real hugs say, "I care enough to hold you." Great words of wisdom are not required! The day of my surgery just before I was going back, my pastor was going to pray with me, I had him pause for a hug!

Ironically enough, though perhaps not so surprisingly, about halfway through Bonnie's treatments, Mark began an ambitious six-week series in church he had prepared which he entitled "What Heaven Looks Like." During this trying time, I viewed our growth in Christ, including prayer, as analogous to the new birth of a chick: fragments of the old shell cling a bit to the fresh, new chicklet, but flecks drop off bit by bit as the chick goes through its first steps of life. For me, one such "fragment" of the shell that fell off my new and developing self was coming to witness the power of prayer. Prayer also happens to be a two-for-one because when you pray, your faith is grown, too. Answered prayers don't mean you get your way; it means you see how your life unfolds as Jesus would have it for you, all according to God's perfect timing. God is already there at the end of any event you're troubled over! After all, He is sovereign. Bonnie and I began to fit the puzzle pieces together, from our meeting one other, to her moving to South Carolina, to our getting sobered up, to reconsidering church, to beginning a friendship with Mark, to attending church regularly and reading our Bibles avidly, to getting Bonnie's health care moved to South Carolina, and to our praying here and now for God to restore her health. All other insecurities vaporized at this point. Our church family was also praying for her which made us feel closer to them. Bonnie said it best when she said, "This is the loneliest journey" because close ones, even I, cannot appreciate the persistent weakness, nausea, and headaches that take turns nonstop. Bonnie did find humor in her predicament because she was the only person she knew that could gain weight with cancer and on chemo, but it beat the alternative. "Set your mind on things above, not on things on the earth" we read in Colossians 3:2 (NKJV) as we would try to bolster ourselves. Though Bonnie got too weak to read her Bible, she never stopped praying, and we still knew He was very much with each of us through this ordeal. In any event, come mid-February, she completed all of her rounds of chemo, and her oncologist informed her that now cancer-free, she was to "go about the businesses of living." Bonnie told me that she felt like she had been then thrown out of a plane. Still weak and bewildered from the dizzying speed of brushing so close to death, she was supposed to get up and proceed to take up where she had left off after being interrupted, as if nothing had happened. That was an odd moment, too! Still, she said that you tell yourself, "*You're alive...*" And though we all must die one day, all the while knowing we're Heaven-bound, we still cling to life. This experience not only made our friendship stronger, but it contributed to our faith growing by leaps and bounds.

There would be a second spiritual battle after what Bonnie just underwent, but this time, it was custom-designed for me. In the meantime, I had a few more months of grappling with questions I want to share with you, but I can tell you that my questions did start to diminish in frequency and quantity. This year we each and both were on the battlefield. I don't use the term "spiritual warfare" lightly. Just because things aren't going your way or you are encountering everyday struggles, obstacles, inconveniences, or even threats, certainly doesn't mean Satan is trying to trip you up or that in that moment, he has it out for you. Life is teeming with pain as well as joy. If, however, you are trying with all you've got to build your life's walk for Christ more strongly and do Him proud, Satan will go after his old black sheep with fury and abandon. You can count on it, and he'll attack what's dearest to you because you threaten him by being for and joining the other team. Therefore, he will do whatever he can to mess with your Christian mojo, sully your thoughts, and kill your spirit, if not take your very life! God lets this happen because He still and always has your back. If you are steady and sure in your faith in Him, you will come to see that He will see you through. Oh, such grace and mercy! Just as I used to love to hold my father's hand, sometimes while I'm by myself in the car, I imagine doing this, only it is Jesus who next to me, and it is *His* hand extended out and ready for me to take. When I say that Jesus will see you through, I mean that regardless of the outcome we would wish for, things will work out for our best interest considering the whole of our life, and Jesus is there loving us all the while. It's in the moments in between that we must turn to Him for light and love, which are as real as rain. If you come to Him humbly and as you are, with no pretense, He will protect your heart *and* life for eternity. Wow and wow! I now briefly return back to what it means to be up close and personal with Jesus before my battle would ensue.

8.15 MY PERSONAL RELATIONSHIP WITH JESUS DEMYSTIFIED

After ten gratifying weeks of Skyping Greek lessons on Tuesdays with an Athenian man, I was finally in the position to be able to coordinate a time when we could hook up with Mark. After our usual humorous banter and quick catching-up, we settled into our groove and got serious about this and that, be it biblical questions or things going on in life. I reviewed what'd been troubling me, that is, how Jesus, my Lord and Savior, could also be my *friend*; Mark was ready. He would also be able to explain to me what it meant to have a *relationship* with Jesus and just how and why it is *personal*. I was so relieved and grateful! The first analogy Mark made to try to prove I had a relationship with Jesus was this: He said, "*I've* never met your dad. Prove to me that you knew your father and that he existed." I responded, "How about a birth certificate?" He said, "Well, that could be fabricated." He was trying to get me to hone in and say that I did have a personal relationship with my dad, though *other* people might not have seen or met him. All I could do was tell Mark about my father, even though Mark himself had no actual proof that my father ever existed. I think the analogy that he was going for is that although I have never met Jesus and cannot see Him, my relationship with him most definitely exists, and it is both highly personal and real. That analogy proved confusing for me because I have never doubted that I had a real relationship with my *father* or that it was personal. I never doubted Jesus *existed* such that we might be able to have a relationship with Him here and now, either. Mark was trying to get me to see that I most assuredly *could* have a relationship, that is, a nearness or intimacy with *Jesus* in a manner similar to what I had with my father, but this particular analogy was not working because the comparison didn't *feel* the same. The crux of what was troubling me was how a *relationship* could exist with one that isn't in the *flesh*. The adjective "personal" I could more easily understand. Such was not meant in the person-to-person sense of a physical presence or proximity; what I had with Jesus was personal because I possessed an affinity towards and closeness with Him as He is a supremely vital person to me. Each person who knows Jesus has a special and, yes, personal relationship with Him because He has touched and moved the believer in an essential, compelling, and unique way. What *I* have with Jesus will look different than what it might look like for somebody else because each transformation that occurs is specific to that person and with consideration to his or her God-given personality and identity. Optimally, the "He" in me will be expressed through my gifts and talents. Though Mark had moved on to another conversation with Bonnie, I pulled him back to this topic and asked him again what he had meant by bringing my father into the equation. I still didn't get it. Mark said that he was trying to make an analogy by showing me that, in a way, he has come to know my father by the way I talk about him, by seeing the pictures I have of him on the wall, and by my inadvertently imitating him through my mannerisms. To answer his question to me, "How do I know that he really existed as your father?" he explained that *you don't have to actually see that somebody*, in this case, my father, *to know that he or she remains inside me*. The mark of the person of Jesus, too, is evidenced in me! Mark next shifted his argument to explain the term "relationship," but in a different way.

The evidence of my having a relationship with Christ over the past three years is that what I have with Jesus has developed past a mere acquaintance to that of a continual and growing desire to know Him better and more deeply. I cannot deny this fact. Mark said, "You go to church (and more than just on Sundays), you read books, you do everything you can to learn about Christ. In other words, you crave to be fed." He then made a comparison using our relationship with him: who could say that we don't know Mark? I would feel angry if someone denied that Bonnie, Mark, and I were friends, so, analogously, I should feel the same way if I or someone suggested that I didn't have a *relationship* — a *friendship* — with Jesus; it most definitely exists. I have witnessed Jesus come into my life! The day that I saw Jesus at my kitchen window and I invited Him into my heart and life was the day that this relationship became personal; it has been sealed until the day of redemption. You know that it's a relationship because it's *ongoing*. I could easily acknowledge that. I could now see that I have a personal relationship with Jesus because I took that chance and opened myself up to Him. And when I said, "Yes," to Him, it — our relationship — began. Rushing to accept Him was my way of acknowledging that I believed that He could and did shower me with love and His saving grace; *He died for me, too*! This clinched and cinched my eternal connection to Him. I can't break this bond, and, in turn, He will never abandon me. The fact that it's a relationship is so because *it exists and will continue to exist* until the day that I die. The rate and depth of my maturation are, to some degree, dependent on my actively seeking Him daily. Therefore, what I have with Jesus *is* personal because *this particular bond is something just between Jesus and me*. It's a relationship because it is *an ongoing and abiding love* that we have for each other, evidenced by my hunger for Him and through His living in me, hopefully, and optimally witnessed in how I live my life. I'm now ready to cry for joy!

To seal the deal and make sure I understood, Mark went there as only he seems to be able to do and flipped the argument on its head. Mark then asked me why my relationship with Christ *couldn't* be personal, as real as if it existed in the physical respect. If I had been alive at the time of Jesus being alive, couldn't I have met and known Jesus the man, as, after all, He existed as a person in addition to being God? I most certainly *did* have an encounter, albeit a mystical one, with Him when I got saved. To that, I replied, "Well, that at the time, what I had was just an *encounter* with Christ, which did not qualify as a 'relationship.'" Mark then asked me to consider what had happened after and since that moment. I think somewhere deep inside, I had the notion that Jesus would love me and leave me, leave me with the consolation prize of the Holy Spirit in His stead, no disrespect intended. That hurt. It felt like He just swished in and delivered the Holy Spirit inside me and then vanished and was gone. Then Mark started proceeded to ask me a series of questions to prove that Jesus had *not* left me, to which I couldn't help but agree. I came to church with regularity because I yearned for His Word and wisdom. On my own time, I read and studied His Word as well as other books associated with Him. To be sure, many conversations that I was having with my students and other adults have been different, not the least of which was the daily ones I had with Bonnie; these had been *completely* transformed! And ultimately, from a changed mind and heart came not only an altered discourse in me, but other lives have been touched as a result of having seen my attitude, behavior, and action change.

I'm still very much in the flesh and imperfect, but life is getting better all the time, even if "sometimes quickly, sometimes slowly," as A.A. jargon puts it. If *that* doesn't show Jesus is active and manifest in my daily actions, that Jesus *is* in my life, existing and relating to me within my heart and mind, what else *but* a personal relationship could this be called? And this is how Mark was able to demonstrate to me that Jesus is and will continue to be in my life every day. My desire for Him and how He continues to furnish me is proof positive that He loves me and won't leave me. He is with me and beside me. The pinnacle of proofs, the zenith expression of His love given to *each* of us *after* He left life in the flesh is His present-day gifting of His Holy Spirit. What was in Him while He lived is now also in me. It's like I have an inner walkie-talkie of sorts, that is, a direct and immediate access to the will and mind of God which Jesus possessed. I get to enjoy an ongoing rapport, an actual give-and-take with Him. There is no qualifying length of time to indicate or prove you've arrived at some plateau of perfection any more than one can in A.A. The person with one year of sobriety is no better or worse than the person with decades of sobriety. I who have trouble with one sin am no better or worse than you with your sin. We don't get to rank, but it's *so* much bigger than that! I am to do *more* than turn the other cheek, go *beyond* loving my neighbor as myself; I am charged to get over myself. Paul instructs us "with humility of mind [to] regard one another as *more important than yourselves*; [4] do not *merely* look out for your interests, but also for the interests of *others*" (Philippians 2:3–4, emphasis mine). If that doesn't smack of Jesus' sacrificial love and service in a palpable way, I don't know what does! In the case of either the alcoholic alleviating himself of the affliction of wanting to drink or the angst of me as a Christian being concerned over the close connection I am to have with Jesus, my reprieve is contingent upon my daily dependence on and especially obedience to Him. Mark said, "Just *talk* to Him, Dimi!" And so, to help me get my groove on for Jesus, I not only continued to take in the hard lessons of Oswald Chambers, but I would read the daily devotional, *Jesus Calling*, for a jump start to talking directly to

Him. And I took my sweet time with Him. I know that my prayers to Him are true-blue, closer than breath, and as dear as life. He hears me and listens. Increasingly, in the ordinary moments of my life, whether I run, drive, do errands, or am at work, I pause and look up and *do* just talk to Him. Before I became aware, this habit of love took hold of me and became a part of my grain.

This is not to say that I didn't experience a glitch with this concept. Nearly eight months later, Mark was preaching one Sunday morning, and he said that whatever significant encounter we had had with Jesus would pale in comparison to what Simon Peter had with Jesus because he was there with Him. Because of my relatively recent misunderstanding of the concept of my "personal relationship" with Jesus, this wording stung me because, at that moment, I thought that, compared with Peter, I must not really have a personal relationship with Jesus, that I must have been sorely mistaken into wishful thinking. Of course, I know I do not have the historical and literal contact with Him that Peter did. I thought to myself that maybe Mark was trying to make the point that even someone who was there in the flesh with Jesus messed up to the point that he went back to his former life, and yet even then, Jesus found a way to turn Simon Peter into a rock. Even 2000 years out, we are no different and are also called to come forward and tend. We may not have had a home-court advantage as far as historically being there goes, but *we are no different than Peter*. I tremble as I say, yes, I *do* have a personal relationship with Jesus even though I did not see my Lord in the flesh. Mark helped me again as I tentatively reached out to him to stay firm in my faith. He told me that Peter might have had a literal hands-on and eye-to-eye contact with Jesus, but the point he was making in church was that if Peter could go back to his former way of living, then *we can, too*. He was a man who spent three years with Jesus; therefore, his personal relationship story will make ours pale simply because Peter was *there*. We haven't been, but this has nothing to do with salvation! In times of difficulty or when we take our eyes off Jesus, we will go back to what we know, just like Peter did. If Peter can slip, we can, too. Therefore, we must pay attention and continue to be mindful of Him. Mark then reassured me that the enemy tried to strike my heart with fear but that I should not hear because I *do* have a personal relationship with Christ! I thank

God for Mark's encouragement; he comes to my rescue when I got anxious about Jesus.

The other topic that we got cleared up dealt with my reluctance to applying the term "friend" to Jesus. If Jesus is my "friend" and as my friend, He died for me, then I am no "friend" because I am too weak to be able to return the favor; therefore, we have no friendship. He upped the bar so high as to render for me practical meaninglessness to the word, "friend." Mark said, "Well, that is not fair because a friend is somebody, anybody who *cares for you, comes to your aid, and supports you. A friend is someone you can rely on.*" I think what he meant was that you don't *literally* have to die for someone to be his or her friend. That said, there has been a mighty shift because I now have the sense that "it is no longer I who live, but Christ lives in me" (Galatians 2:20). Plus, Jesus is not *just* my friend; He's that and more: He is my Savior. It is not an either/or situation, but a both/and reality! And we would *expect* Him as Savior and the Son of God to take friendship to a whole new stratosphere! *It doesn't lessen or devalue the term "friendship" just because I can't ever do what He did.* I enjoy a friendship with Jesus in that we have a give-and-take relationship that is not contingent upon what I bring to the table but what He did for me, and we both know it. I am the one who relishes realizing this, and I can't stop talking about Him. I confided to Mark that this current confusion reminded me of a little bit of that time a couple of years ago when one of Oswald Chambers' daily devotions had it worded such that the Holy Spirit was the medium through which God communicated to us. Do you remember? It had so pained me that I felt worthless in my not being able to be talked to by Him directly, that He needed a "middle man" of the Holy Spirit. Mark remarked that this was evidence that I had "a very high opinion of myself." Mark said that God's overwhelming knowledge and presence "*had* to be channeled through the Holy Spirit so that I would be able to understand His will." The Holy Spirit was exactly what I needed, and thus, He was gifted to me by God so that I *could* understand Him. "And remember," Mark reminded me, "The Holy Spirit speaks to God on your behalf when you are not able to pray effectively." That was the end of Mark's visit, but the beginning of another moment of clarity bringing me that much closer to Christ by the unraveling of a few words that had tripped me up. When Jesus said, "It is finished,"

God's reunion plan was completed: no longer would anyone have to go through any person or anything to get to Him. However, what I now have with Jesus cannot be finished in me. Our relationship is ongoing; in fact, it will never stop. What remains of my earthly father are lots of incredible memories; my relationship *per se* with him no longer exists because he is dead. With Christ, however, though I've never met Him in the flesh, the relationship that started through my acceptance of Him and His grace will never end as long as I live. Not that I want to rush things, mind you, I will be even closer to Him *after* I die. That is the ticket! When I have these revelations or realizations and get unblocked, my prayer life opens up like a floodgate!! It was like the veil had been torn away for *me*! Yes, I *do* have a real, direct, and ongoing relationship with Jesus. There *is* evidence! It was like Jesus was smack-dab in front of my face! Satan tries to use words as sticks and stones against me, but I have the power of the sword of the Spirit *and* His Word! How could I not *also* exclaim, "if God is for us, who can be against us?" (Romans 8:31 NIV).

8.16 THE GREAT CHASM

During those months, as long as years as Bonnie was battling cancer, it seemed like sickness and the threat of death had moved in, like unwanted tenants. She was doing double-duty, also suffering from the secondary effects of the meds used to treat her cancer, yet she didn't feel like she had a right to complain because they were working. Ironically, Mark had started a series on Heaven, and he opened his first sermon by asking us rhetorically what we thought the first thing we would see after we died was. (Thankfully, Bonnie was too sick to attend.) The answer for me came immediately: in the blink of an eye, just as soon as our physical system shuts off and our senses cease, I am sure that the *essence* of us is <u>there</u>, that is, in Paradise, immediately and instantaneously. Hell has *got* to be beyond distant and separate from those of us in Heaven, but certainly not in any geographical sense that we could render now. In my mind's eye, I can't imagine Hell as being anything but utter darkness where there'll be no contact with anyone, just an endless free-fall of torment and perpetual regret. I have private shudders and fears about having to face death, which I know is a certainty, but dealing with cancer up close and personal right now brings death up in your face. Bonnie told me that she got up in the middle of the night because she couldn't sleep, so when I saw her the next morning asleep on the couch, uncharacteristically lying on her back, her hands on her belly, and with dark circles under her eyes, I felt unhinged. She confided to me later that if this chemo doesn't work, she "can't do it again." I told her to stop and not to go anywhere near that hypothetical time in her brain. Some things I just won't go near even if I know we are both Heaven-bound. Am I weak to think like this? I guess I'm not so wise or brave because I felt like I was tiptoeing on the edge of what felt like doom. You may ask me why I would discuss cancer in the context of my testimony. I'll tell you why. The likelihood of your knowing at least a dozen people, even somewhat close to you, who will die from cancer throughout your life is quite high. And as a Christian, I wanted to be fully vested and available to do and be all I can to bring comfort and love in His name's sake for that person.

As one saying goes, no one gets out of here alive, but I hope to show His love streaming on that person as he or she makes his exit. Stirred by new life and the topic of death intersecting and overlapping, more questions arose within me. I will now share a few of these questions and, later on, the answers to them.

1. 1.Mark had prepared a tremendous amount of information to teach us his congregants about Heaven, and I became particularly intrigued about a verse from an account in Luke that he read to us. By now, you can tell that it sometimes takes no more than one verse, sometimes even a single word that can launch me into vistas of speculation. Here was that verse:

"And besides all this, between you and us there is *a great chasm* fixed, so that *those who wish to come over from here to you will not be able*, and that none may cross over from there to us" (Luke 16:26 (emphasis mine).

Can we *really* see one another from Heaven and Hell? We are told that the rich man sees Lazarus, but does Lazarus see the rich man? I don't understand how the rich man could even see to look up at Lazarus and then be answered by him. This would surely be torturous! I tried to envision what this "great chasm" would look like for those viewing back and forth between Heaven and Hell. Will I be able to see those who didn't make it to Heaven? How long might I weep? Will I be longing for my loved ones who are in Hell? Will they be sick with regret? There's no putting in a good word for anybody when we're dead! I do lament for those close to me who don't know Jesus, especially my family. And by "know," I don't merely mean to "know *of*" Him! To know Him is to love Him, that's for sure! That said, faith can't be forced! It's likely that they'd be exasperated to think I even speculated about such a maligned future for them!

2. When we are in Heaven, I know we will be with Christ, but will we also knowingly be with the Father, or will that be reserved for later on, when we will not only see but also be with Him then in the New Heaven and New Earth? I

still assume the Holy Spirit will be with us in *full* measure in Heaven and not remain how He communicates with us here and now inside our frames. I wonder if I am on the right track.

3. With Bonnie facing the prospect of two years of quarterly scanning for cancer and all this discussion of Heaven in Mark's series, the reality of the brevity of life was feeling all too real. Our local campus' pastor, a kind, prayerful, and well-intentioned man, once asked us, his congregants, "How do you *know* that you *know* [that you're going to Heaven]?" This was the million-dollar question, and it would take a visit from our friend who sometimes felt like a young doctor to put things square again.

Mark visited us a week before Bonnie's last treatment and explained what Scripture meant in giving us a glimpse at those who would be mourning in Heaven for those who hadn't made it and were in perpetual regret and torment. Whether or not we in Heaven can see our loved ones on earth or whether we can discern those even deeper down in Hell, Mark responded by saying that it is not an "either/or," but a "both/and" answer. This means that, yes, there will be grieving in Heaven because the Holy Spirit has the same essence as God, and if the Holy Spirit can grieve, then God also can mourn for those who do not come to Him. Ultimately, however, the outcome will be joyful because we will be focusing on Jesus in Heaven. I am woefully aware that I lack the language to convey the life we'll have beyond the here and now of today, but I'll try. We in Heaven may be aware of what's going on down here. If so, we will surely silently cheer for the good things happening to our loved ones, but we will also be privy to realities that can't be known down here. Why? We will be living outside of chronological time; therefore, what is just around the bend or what may be the purpose of a particular predicament or painful trial someone is undergoing might be already known and understood by those of us in Heaven. There's no *lasting* sorrow or worry when we are in Heaven, just some brief grieving for the anguish of those we love who still suffer our being gone, but in no way, shape, fashion, or form will that *ever* overshadow the immense joy that we will feel in the presence of Jesus! I told Mark that what he'd taught me left me feeling bittersweet: I was relieved for myself, but I felt anxious for those who as of yet chose to remain outside the dotted line. Scripture confirmed what Mark had told me. Revelation 21:14 assures us that Jesus "will wipe away every tear," which means that He will take away our emotional pain. It doesn't mean that we won't experience sadness for our loved ones left behind or even for those in Hell, but we do not get to come back down to earth or visit them in Hades. Despite personalities and TV shows that indicate otherwise, no medium can provide a glimpse into this future. Then Mark quoted something in Hebrews about not throwing away our confidence. Later that day, I went home and found the passage, and I was ecstatic also to discover it related to *another* of God's promises for those who keep their faith in Him by doing His will and following His lead! Yay! Here it is so you can know it, too:

> [35] Therefore, do not throw away your confidence, which has a great reward. [36] For *you have need of endurance*, so that when you have done the will of God, you may receive what was promised… [39] But *we are not of those who shrink back to destruction*, but of those who have faith to the preserving of the soul" (from Hebrews 10:35–36 and 39, emphasis mine).

Whether or not people in Heaven can look down and see us, we down here are not running our race for them. We are not hoping for their approval or listening to their applause. The author of Hebrews also says to keep our focus on where it belongs. We are to "fix our eyes on Jesus, the pioneer and perfecter of faith" (12:2). One way of staying on point is by patiently and persistently concentrating on what matters to Him, as evidenced by what He said and did. It behooves us to wear figurative blinders just like a horse wears his real ones to keep from being distracted or agitated by what's beside or behind him. Satan will try to harass and annoy you, but press in. Therefore, when in doubt, disturbance, or dismay, head for Jesus and your Bible; do not tarry so you will not come undone. And when you're on the other side of your challenge, jump back, join in, and help your brother and your sister out, too! They need your help! Jesus is also called "that blessed hope" (Titus 2:13 KJV), and we should reflect that in our actions as well. I don't mean to say, "Bless your *heart*!" Mark told us once in church to get out and bless others' *lives*! After this caveat about Satan's intentions, Mark was also quick to point out that when the New Heaven and the New Earth come together, there will also be a real lake of fire and sulfur. Nonbelievers will also be cast into this lake. There won't be a thought, a memory, or suspended sadness over this when we get to Heaven. We can still expect to feel some grieving over this, but in no way will it diminish the glory that we will experience in being in the holy presence of Lord Jesus!

8.17 Salvation Signed, Sealed, Delivered

As a result of pondering the rhetorical question, "How do you know that you know?" Bonnie momentarily lapsed into doubting. I was too green to provide the reassurance she needed. It's hard to have "iron sharpen iron" (Proverbs 27:17) when you feel like one of the blind leading the blind! Bonnie desperately needed help dealing with issues about salvation that kept swirling around in her mind. Though not as soon as she might have liked, Mark was always right on time, and only he — though increasingly I, then eventually she for herself — could assuage her fears, doubts, and misgivings. Mark tirelessly, tenderly, and considerately listened to and uplifted her in her times of need. Stricken with cancer, now more than ever was a time she sought assurance, and he always spoke the truth to her, unvarnished and biblical truth. To the point, Mark would help Bonnie to be able to answer for herself the answer to "How does she *know* [that she's saved]?" He used himself as an example. How *he* knows is that "he loves Jesus with all of his heart, soul, mind, and strength, that he has repented and turned away from sin, and that he tries to love and live for Jesus every day." He asserted that Bonnie has done and does all that, too! God is even bigger even than that! Mark said, "When you hear words like those that make up that question, words that make you doubt, as for myself, I go straight to Jesus and cling only to Him and to what He says in Scripture." Just after Bonnie had complimented me on memorizing Scripture, to which I had replied that I was impressed with how many lyrics of Bible songs that she knew, Bonnie said, "Well, that's still not Scripture." I replied that neither are the words that get her tormented. They don't come from Jesus. God doesn't work like that; *torment through fear is not conviction.* Though we can't "do good" our way to Heaven, we believers don't get rejected or pre-kicked out by anything or particular action here. If that were the case, there would probably be only about twenty-five people in Heaven, and *that is not the way God operates.* After all, the second greatest commandment is to love others. If we believe in Him, then whatever sins we've committed, Jesus has it covered. To disqualify yourself would be tantamount to implying that what Jesus did on the cross was not adequate, and this is not the case! Then Mark examined how Jesus treated Nicodemus when he, too, was asking Him questions about salvation. Mark speculated that when Nicodemus asked Jesus about what it means to be "born again," Jesus couldn't help Himself and got a little sarcastic with him. He said something to the effect like, "No, you're not going to go back up to be born out of your mother again." When Nicodemus earnestly wanted to know if he was truly saved, Jesus would not have toyed with him by asking, "How do you know that you know that you know?" Mark told Bonnie "to borrow his faith" if hers faltered, but that *under no uncertain terms should she look for the answer or search for confirmation in the world*, even if the source *seemed* authoritative or religiously legit. She should "always go straight to God." Furthermore, if she was looking for God to show a sign, then he said that, too, is the wrong approach because "signs and wonders can be misconstrued." If you go directly to God, then you have something you can hold on to. Jesus simply said, "Come to me" (Matthew 11:28) and "believe in God, believe also in Me" (John 14:1). Mark said some folks are always going to get picked on more than others because it's people's nature to want to be better than somebody else, like they've got an advantage or edge over others. Mark ended by asking Bonnie pointedly, "Do you really think that God is going to turn you away after you have given yourself to Him? Of course, He's not! You are saved! *Instead of seeking the answer from man, just seek to know God.* When you were looking for this or that confirmation, answer, or sign, stop yourself from and go straight to God; talk to Jesus directly." He won't disappoint or cast you aside because, as Peter affirmed, "He cares for you!" (1 Peter 5:7). One month after her last round of chemotherapy, it was determined that Bonnie was cancer-free. As I was praying hard one morning, I had a vision. Just as the blind man came to be a spokesperson for what Jesus has done for him by bringing back his sight, perhaps everything that Bonnie had undergone and endured to rid herself of cancer, Jesus will use to demonstrate His strength and steadfastness in her. After the removal of her afflicted lobe, Jesus applied the figurative mud — only in this case, His spittle came in the form of chemotherapy — to irradiate cancer.

Like the blind man who saw, she with cleaned lungs could then breathe easily and rest assured of His saving grace for her. Unexpectedly, He used sickness to grow and solidify her faith! I'm telling you, *she can't stop praising Him*! As I type, Bonnie is now singing this old gospel tune called "That Heavenly Home," the lyrics of all of the verses she learned back in the home church of her childhood. She used not to be able to listen to more than one or two such songs; now she's belting this one out. Goodness, gracious, it's such a relief to see Bonnie able to anticipate Jesus telling her, "Well done, good and faithful servant!" (Matthew 25:23 NIV). By the end of our lives, I hope we each can say, "I have fought the good fight" (2 Timothy 4:7). As for now, I, too, am so grateful for her clean bill of health. It's obvious that Jesus had His hand in all of this, including every development leading up to her finding out she had cancer. I marvel at how so many events have turned out or came together for the good regarding her health. It all fits. As I heard one Christian say about dying, "Any way you slice it, it's a win-win. Either way, you have Jesus." We're just glad it came out this way.

8.18 Troubles Brewing at Work and My Being Sifted, Take 1

The very last thing that I shared with Mark at this visit was about a challenge I had just faced at work. It seemed so ridiculous and insignificant to me at the time, but little did I know that Bonnie's cancer would precede the most trying moment I would ever experience in my career. I was a little embarrassed to bring it up with Mark because it meant telling him that I had been reported to a social service entity at work. Here I'd taught twenty-eight years without a blemish on my record, and suddenly, under the helm of the fifth principle I'd worked for, came fire and brimstone the likes of which I'd never experienced. I was caught off guard and asked myself, "How could this have happened?" It would take many prayers and full reliance on Jesus to guide me and prevent me from being defensive or distressed; all the while, my flesh experienced the fight or flight adrenaline rush of cold fear. The predicament happened less than two months after Bonnie rounded the corner of completing her fourth and final cycle of chemotherapy, just when we'd passed the bend into a sense of relief, hope, and normalcy. Now, it was my turn to walk through a landmine; only for me, the hardship came about in my professional life. It all started when a student who had fallen asleep in class told his parent that I had "flicked" him on the head to wake him up. In reality, I had knocked on the corner of his desk as if to ask, "Is anyone home?" I also took his phone up that same day because he was texting in class; this necessitated that his parent come and retrieve it. Not a little miffed by this inconvenience and embarrassment by the wake-up knock, he went home and bent the truth into a fib to his mother, who then proceeded not only to call our school but a higher local authority. Unfortunately, there have been several instances where other administrators failed to immediately report an alleged inappropriate action or misdeed of a teacher to the proper authorities, and such led to litigation pursued. To not have a whiff of a cover-up occur, I was called into an administrator's office to address the situation of this mother's accusation. At the time, as my administrators proceeded to interview me about the matter, I had *no* idea what was happening; I strained even to recollect what had happened in class because it was so unremarkable to me. I was asked to write a statement and yet told not to fret because all this was "just routine." It was the proper course of action to take, and there was "nothing personal" by what was being asked of me. Reeling in disbelief, I felt sideswiped and stupefied, yet I could also appreciate my superior's preemptive tactic. Such was the world we now lived in, and somehow, I'd missed the boat of how we got there. I was used to handling things in my classroom on my own; now, disciplining was to be done in a more ventilated and cooperative fashion. As asked, I submitted my statement, and then all the students in the class were interviewed individually. My case was thrown out the same day it was submitted, so unsubstantiated the claim proved to be. All that said, the parent was still discontent and wanted him moved, and rather than have her make a ruckus at a higher level, that student was quietly and swiftly transferred to another class, where he proceeded to do poorly as well. It seemed to me that the parent won, the child lost, and an unfortunate precedent had been set where the one with the squeaky voice could get his child moved. Bonnie, Mark, and I wagged our heads at just how out of order the world was. Our youth have been spoiled (as in ruined) through a lack of sound parental guidance, godly wisdom, corrective and loving discipline such that we have a nation full of entitled and spiritually-starved children. This matter would foretaste another incident in store for me, one that drove me to my knees. Needless to say, my prayer life went into overdrive. At the end of Mark's visit, we three prayed in the manner that we do: we quietly bow our heads as we stand together side-by-side with Mark in the middle. His arms are wrapped around us as ours are him, and he prays for us.

8.19 What It's Like Being a New Christian and Dimi's Evangelism 101

While all this was going on, I also had stirrings of wondering *what more* I can do for Him in the world. I felt like "Pay It Forward" should somehow become my internalized *status quo*! I don't want to be seen as the new Christian with regular Dimi absent, like I'm somebody who's experienced an invasion of the body snatchers. I may be a sinner, but I am a saved wretch nonetheless! It's so hard to be a Christian because every day, you've been charged to *give up your ego* or self and love on others, even and especially when you don't feel like it. Anyway, the Holy Spirit is there to help you. Practice makes [one closer to] perfect. Normal people in your life need to see that it's still you; all the while, however, you now have this knowledge within you that says, "having been put to death in the flesh, [you have been] made alive in the spirit (1 Peter 3:8). I would go so far as to say that, paradoxically, come what may, the more of yourself that you give to *Him*, the more of yourself you get to be! Unity in and with Christ brings a truer, richer, and happier life than you could have ever imagined. If folks see you as having a false mantle of appearing holier-than-thou and squeaky-clean or that you get squeamish over the regular and imperfect occurrences of life, they'll end up walking on eggshells around you because you can't handle real life. Why, at any moment, they'll think you may spout out the "J" word and may start talking about stuff and in a manner you've never done before. All that being said and without a doubt, *I am and have been changed*!

I just hope it is apparent that it's for the good. I've come to seek opportunities to subtly but assuredly share the Good News, and I pray every day that God can use me in such a way that would bring Him glory. I also pray that He sustains me in challenging situations. I'm now waking up at 5:10 to study the New Testament, pray, and write. Have I got a picture of a cross on the wall? Yep. There's one that was given to Bonnie from Catherine during her first round of chemo that says, "It is well with my soul." I also put up a picture of a painting I bought of Jesus talking to the woman by the well. And if I could find one that I like, I would also love to hang a picture of the sick woman who strove to touch just the hem of Jesus' robe for healing, which she did, and it commenced! I love that story! Jesus even calls her "daughter" (Mark 5:34)! Truth be told, I feel like her sometimes. I also want to tell you that reading Paul blows my mind: his thirteen or so letters are so stunningly logical, thorough, and tender, yet at the same time, they are intent and stern, and all get rolled into one unified message. If you want the real scoop of what life is all about and why you are here, seek Jesus always. You'll get more than you bargained for in His big-picture answers told in the form of analogies and parables. Does that make me a person who is berserk for Jesus? Okay then, yes, I'll own it! Really though, I'm a follower of His, and to follow His lead necessitates my stepping out in faith and meeting others straight on and in that moment. Ready or not, here I come! My litmus test for determining whether something of significance I want to do intently is merely for Dimi or if it's a God thing is to evaluate if my actions and motives are "honorable, right, pure, lovely, of good repute, excellent, and praiseworthy." If they are, why then, I am to "practice these things" (Philippians 4:8–9). In daily living, I've got to focus on loving the person I am called to talk to exactly where he is in life. That person may somehow be like me before I fell in love with Jesus! It is the Holy Spirit's job to reckon with that person in his own time, not mine; a person's salvation is not on me! Jesus is the one that beckons them in His way. I may or may not be the agent He uses in a particular time and space; I can do nothing of my own power. And if I'm not willing to build and invest in real-life relationships that are genuine, I probably won't lead anyone anywhere!! As a teacher, I know this to my core. I must *never* forget how I felt before I became a Christian and was approached by a concerned Christian citizen who didn't know me from Adam but wanted to talk to me. I felt wary, distrustful, and suspicious of the genuineness of their motive, let alone care. I was *en garde* for their judgment and close-mindedness. I didn't want "their" Jesus, let alone a one-way conversation about Him.

Later, I would come to see that *you can't lump all Christians together* any more than any other group of seemingly similar people. We are all are different, whether you're talking about stages of maturity in life or levels in one's walk with Christ! Furthermore, it seems to me that *there is no one prescribed method for coming to Him*. There is no cookie-cutter recipe; the way that somebody comes to believe in Jesus and express it is unique unto to him. It *is* personal! That said, you *do* have to be of the right mindset and attitude to seek and ask, but Jesus is not going to say, "No" when you do. My job as a Christian is to try to live authentically *and* in a manner that hearkens to Jesus's ideals — not the ways of the world. Those who see me should be attracted to Him dwelling in me; that way — *His* way — is seen in how *I* show T.L.C. Ben Franklin said, "None preaches better than the ant, and she says nothing." Still, I hope that God will give me the words to become unique keys for unlocking a hard heart and obdurate mind like I used to have. When the Holy Spirit involves Himself in this reckoning process, it is neither through luck nor by some wagered odd that an unbeliever would take a step toward Him. Faith comes not by chance. Even though we are supposed to share Jesus, you don't know what that moment is going to look like in the moment of opportunity; all I know is that divine appointments come in life's ordinary moments, and you can't force or fake anything. Someone who is affectionate may show Christ's love through kindness or a thoughtful action, even something simple, like a touch of the hand in support. Another person's curiosity may be piqued by a Christian's quiet confidence and humility. On the other hand, a Christian might desire to talk about Jesus or share his testimony, but the timing isn't right. The Holy Spirit might deem another day or time the right one. Tact is tantamount, and often less is more: sometimes the occasion calls for dropping tiny nuggets rather than deliver a truckload.

Accepting Jesus as the Christ is also dependent on a person's suppleness of spirit, ready heart, *and* open-mindedness, and it is my job to aerate and till *before* I plow and seed! Some might view Christianity from a more academic or intellectual standpoint and recognize the universal themes of *sacrifice* and *redemption* as familiar archetypal motifs in human history. I would respond by saying that no other religion in the world connects these two impulses back to Creation itself and then forward to our destiny through one man: Jesus Christ. He provides the bridge between man and God; through His sacrificial love, we have the removal of our transgressions "as far as the east is from the west" (Psalm 103:12). We who seek to evangelize may find ourselves needing to be all things to all people to lead even one to Christ. In other words, barring compromising His standards, I should feel free to do or say what is necessary to get Him across to others. It takes sensitivity, discernment, a light touch, and lots of love; it takes *time* to show you care! What better way to show what Jesus is like than through a friendship started with you. They'll see Him in you first! Jesus will do the rest in His way and timing. When acceptance happens, the initial shift to Christ is swift; other follow-through acts of maturity occur along the bumpy road of life. I surely never thought *I'd* be listening to Christian music or praying for those people who hurt me! Bottom line, Christians are vessels: we don't know how or when we are going to be used, so we should be open to such and be willing when the moment strikes. It's like in basketball when one guy dribbles the ball hard and fast down the court, but it may be the forward he's just passed it to who dunks the ball through the basket and scores! We don't know how it's going to pan out, but God does; He's already there.

I think the deal-breaker for many non-Christians who are caught off guard should they experience conventional, zero-to-one hundred evangelism is when they are asked if they *"know"* Jesus or if they have been *"saved."* Soon after, they'll probably hear that Jesus is the only legitimate way to God. Yes, we well know that Jesus says, "I am '<u>the</u>' — and not merely *a* — way, the truth, and the life" (John 14:6). It seems like an either/or logical fallacy to say that there are only two options: Jesus or bust, and not deciding on Him leads to Hell. That's a lot to stomach if you're not used to contemplating eternal consequences! I used to be repulsed when I witnessed Christians use the threat of Hell, fire, and brimstone to motivate wayward, misguided, ignorant, or so-called lost people through fear into coming to Jesus. You cannot use such a method on the skeptic because he either will bolt and run for cover (in the recesses of his mind), or he will shoot down anything you have to say until such time at which he may be readied! (By the way, "skeptic" is a Greek word, which benignly means "to think" or "to consider.") Anyway, who wants to be accosted with veiled threats or predictions of demise? What's even worse is feeling judgment through non-verbal clues and pomposity as loud as bad perfume. When I feel stuck, confused, bitter, or hurt, I always look squarely to *Jesus* for how I *ought* to act. That may sound like a no-brainer, but ironically, even those who deliver sermons can put Christ in the back pew of their church. If that's the case, you won't feel or see much love! Jesus knew that by the time we get to be adults, we each have a world of hurt unique to us, so though we *need* Him, we often don't *know* it, let alone *want* it. Therefore, if an evangelist tries to witness to someone without first getting to know this person and love on him or her, it isn't likely to take for long. Why would it? Oh, I'm *still* so grateful Mark came to visit after I sent that initial wary email! A friendship was launched, and I got saved! Jesus showed people around Him tender affection so they could *feel* His love. His concern wasn't just for those with physical ailments, but "seeing the people, He felt compassion for them because they were distressed and dispirited" (Matthew 9:36). This points straight to Jesus' gut-level mercy for us who ache inside for emotional relief and love. Who wouldn't turn to and take a chance on Him?

Some of you may point out that Christianity is not unique in forecasting what happens to us after we die in terms of there being a reward and punishment. I well know that identifying destinations for the afterlife is hardly new: primitive people like the ancients believed we went a place after we died, whether it was "Hades" for the Greeks, "Sheol" for the Hebrews, or the "Land of Two Fields" for the Egyptians. Why, practically every religion you can name has its version. The turning point of human history in terms of what can happen to each of us after we die occurred when Jesus Christ resurrected three days after His death. No other religious leader renders a model for how to live a life of compassion, purpose, and love *and* offers us the means to eternal life. He and only He lived up to His claim that He "abolished death" (1 Cor. 15:26); He went to Hades, the mode of dead souls, to take away its "sting" (v. 55), that is, death's painful reality. There were eyewitnesses of Jesus walking about in His supra-human state from the third day until His Ascension around day 40; the laws of physics and nature could not confine Him! How could they when He is One with the One who created all, including designing the laws of life's governance? No matter how you slice it, as a man, Jesus practiced what He preached, and He did so flawlessly and perfectly. He never mistreated anyone at any time; instead, He went out of His way to do life with underdogs and pariahs. Those in need knew they needed

Him. Can you imagine who the lost sheep of today He'd hang out with today?! I'll bet there'll be a great shock at seeing just who "makes it" to Heaven! And like the Pharisees and the Sadducees of Jesus' time, those of wealth and means today condescend to those who don't meet *their* grade, not realizing that they miss the mark of God. He measures us by how we give away, not what we hold dear. When I teach *Hamlet* to my seniors and explore the reasons for Hamlet's contemplating committing suicide, I steer them to look at Hamlet's "dread of something after death, the undiscovered country from which no traveler returns." Fear keeps him treading and trying, but that's not enough to be a well man, let alone or satisfied one. Hamlet was also an arrogant snob, but his hatred for hypocrisy and his commitment to purity of purpose win us over. Through Hamlet, we see that life without faith and hope is a dead-end proposition. What happens after this gloriously messy life ceases is beyond our comprehension or imagination; nonetheless, it *is* real. As Emily Dickinson says of Heaven,

"I never spoke with God, nor visited in heaven.
Yet certain am I of the spot/As if the checks were given."

Where can we learn about this vaster picture? The most powerful tool for evangelism is the Bible. Though the details may not line up seamlessly, the bigger picture which points to redemption *does*, so if you are looking to prove the Bible's reliability based on various *details* lining up just so, you're missing the boat of apprehending His higher truths. Reading the Bible is a supernatural experience. Bona fide truths penetrate your soul *and* mind with subtle force, and you innately know they did not come from man, even if they were written by men. Through my voice here, you can witness what one former non-Christian person's journey looks like, step-by-step *after* she decided to say "Yes" to Jesus. The most important thing I did was to take that chance, that leap of faith. You don't even have to go to church initially; just open up your Bible to some chapter in the New Testament. I suggest you first start with the Gospels because it will help you get acquainted with Jesus. Before you know it, you will go from being curious to craving being around other Christians, so *do* go and find a church, all the while knowing that it is made up of very fallible people just like you, so you must also be patient.

Don't be hard on yourself and don't expect a lot early on, but keep at it slowly, but surely. This is not a fifty-yard-dash but a life-long marathon of a love story that will grow richer and deeper. You will be amazed at moments as you look back; therefore, I also suggest keeping a "claim it" journal that will help you marvel at the circle you've completed, at the dots *you've* connected. You'll not want to stop there! And don't worry about what kind of Bible you get; all English versions are translations of the original Greek and Aramaic anyway. Don't feel you *have* to get the King James translation because you're the old-school type. The King James Version is not the original, let alone the most useful language used anyway! Just go to some bookstore, pick one verse, and *see how you like how it flows for you* as you inspect the various translations. I choose the New American Standard Version because my pastor says that it best captures the original language's meaning in its essence. I used to read a paraphrased version for several years before that. That's okay, too!

When you find yourself a church that you can get plugged into, one that you can see yourself going to with regularity, take this step as well. Slow and steady is the course: you will feel like a tortoise with the heartbeat of a hare. You're reading about such a one who has been at going at it for nearly five years now. Life in other areas didn't stop; it's still *me*, after all. I don't pretend to be an expert, but I want you to know about life *after* the pivotal moment of salvation. Hopefully, if you explore who He is, you may begin to find that past pains and negative or defeatist attitudes you possess you can relinquish. Get out of the rut of your life and still the voices of dismissal in your head, those harpies of negativity, and hear His essential voice of truth. You may experience a hope and joy you never dreamed possible, regardless of how old or young you are. The time to come to Him is never wrong: it is always *now*! My personal prayer for you, my reader, is this: "Be anxious for nothing, but in everything by prayer and supplication with thanksgiving let your requests be made known to God. And the peace of God, which surpasses all comprehension, will guard your hearts and your minds in Christ Jesus." That quote comes from a New Testament Epistle called Philippians 4:6–7. If you have read this far, know it is not an accident that you have stumbled perchance upon this book. As Holden Caulfield says in *The Catcher in the Rye*, "Grab the golden ring!" You'll be amazed by His grace.

I am compelled to repeat that reaching disinterested, dismissive, or damaged people is *much* harder than connecting with those who, like children, have little to no knowledge of Jesus. Why do you think missionaries don't go to Western Europe? The field of unlikely acceptance there is hard ground. Rest assured, pain and pride and prejudice *can* be overcome; the Holy Spirit must be involved for God to actualize the potential. My task is to love folks, warts and all, enough to massage a readiness in them. An interested party will invariably ask you about any or all in the Godhead. As you can tell by now, I love contemplating the Trinity, and the last analogy I'll offer you is a mathematical formula of $1[God] \times 1[Christ] \times 1[Holy\ Spirit] = 1^3$. One cubed is one, each numeral is inseparable from the other and indivisible from the whole, or, as Mark would say, "each one points to the other." When I became a Christian of the Protestant persuasion, my family was bewildered, and quite frankly, I'm sure they would rather have had me identify as Greek Orthodox. At least that way, they could justify my evident need for tradition and stability through the mystical experience of gazing at icons, smelling frankincense, and hearing the ethereal intones of cantors as an expression of my faith. However, that was not the case. All that *is* alluringly powerful, but it ain't Jesus. One perfect man undid sin for all time's sake what one regular man did once (Romans 5:15); that's powerful.

To return to math for a second, one positive number multiplied by a negative number, even if it were as small as $1^{-0.000001}$, is always negative, but one times any number to the positive infinite degree, as in, 1^∞, is always positive forever; it's unreal. This explains why Christ's work on the cross two thousand years ago is good for all subsequent years; the effect of the cross is as potent now as it was then. This fact is captured in Hebrews 13:8: "Christ is the same yesterday, today, and forever." It's probably a sign I'm coming to closing of this my testimony to you because my ratio of texts referenced over the past four and a half years has flipped 180° from relating no Scripture to nearly dripping with Scripture. This afternoon, I heard an old song by England Dan & John Ford Coley from the seventies that was playing on the radio, and it occurred to me that God found a way at that moment to remix its meaning inside me I hadn't thought about before: "Love is the answer. Shine on us all. Set us free. Love is the answer." Since God is love, He is the answer!

Though our visits with Mark became much less frequent and my emails loaded with questions this year started waning, I didn't stop checking in with him. After all, he is my friend who also happens to be my pastor, an indivisibility unto itself. There exists between us a mutual respect for and admiration of one other. I text because I want to share with him on some regular basis normal moments in real life, including both the banal and silly, as well as the ironic or disturbing, and I like to send him notes of encouragement as well. By the way, Bonnie and I still go to A.A. meetings upon occasion, probably about quarterly, and it is always refreshing to hear the raw honesty that comes out "in these rooms." During one particular meeting, I remember that people were sharing how the church had hurt them. Half the people were in pain and anger; the other half had been able to come *back* to the church and gingerly examined how the church and A.A. could fit together. The Doobie Brothers' hit, "Jesus Is Just Alright with Me," is how one fellow explained how he was able to come back to church. This man put the focus on *Jesus* and not on whether or not the church was "accepting" enough or if the preacher's style suited him. "Good man," I thought to myself. Many priests and pastors and the like have done a *lot* of spiritual damage such that folks look for relief in alcohol. People still avoid Jesus because of the big-C Church. One guy said that A.A. was in the business of saving *lives*, while the church was in the business of saving *souls*.

I'm so glad I'm sober and alive, and I am incredibly grateful for my pastor and church. I even had a dream of Jesus reaching through my body, gently taking hold of the back of my lungs to pull me up and forward. It was so cool! At church that Sunday, Mark gave a shocking figure that "only 6% of those who were older than fourteen would ever come to know Christ." This startled me greatly because if it is true, then I am blessed beyond measure for this to have come to be! Now more than ever, I saw that all things leading to my salvation were not by chance. I also felt a little worried and wanted to caution Mark that I hoped that this statistic wouldn't mean he wouldn't try to help other older unbelievers and leave us for dead; we still needed help, too! And so, I wrote him a poem:

An Older Believer
Though I may be one from the single six percent,
Of adults who finally come to Him, ready to be Heaven-bent.
Being such a one myself, I find the need to say
That I hope you never stop helping us come to Him, those of turning grey!
At fifty many come to a crossroads of just some sort or type,
I'm just grateful that all I've found in Him is so much more than hype.
You speak of fresh faith and focusing on our youth,
And as a teacher myself, I applaud you as if you were a sleuth!
Just please remember and do not pass us by beguiled,
There are plenty of us elders who crave to come to Him like a child…

8.20 THE LAST BATCH OF QS FOR THIS BOOK

Over the past couple of months, I did have several questions come seeping up from my morning reading and prayer, ones that I couldn't find the answers to readily in my go-to online sources for an explanation, so I sent them to Mark. They are thematically related to ones I'd asked before, yet they stood out as unique in my mind; these questions were more specific, too. I also knew that the next time we met, they might or might not get answered. That was okay; our getting together was to *share life*, not have some Q & A session. Catching up and getting real with the Holy Spirit guiding our conversation was how our kitchen table talks went and how we rolled. This is my last set; the questions are (finally!) starting to slow way down in frequency, and when they do come up, I can usually navigate reliable sources to find the answers for myself. I am no longer stunted in my daily morning worship, nor do I find that I must write scrolls of questions to Mark. He still is the best person to answer me because he is my friend and knows me and understands how my brain works to find answers. Though I wouldn't record the answers until after I share my final challenge and ordeal with you, here they are:

1. 1. John 5:22 and 27 say, "For not even the Father judges anyone, but He has given all judgment to the Son… and He gave Him authority to execute judgment because He is the Son of Man." I thought Jesus did *not* come to judge, but to *save* us. What's going on here?!?
2. What does it mean in John 15:22 and 15:24 when Jesus says, "If I had not come and spoken to them, they would not have sinned, but now they have no excuse for their sin…" and "If I had not done among them the works which no one else did, they would not have sin…" Why does Jesus say this?!? He cannot mean that since He *did* come that they *do* have sin!! I thought the preceding Ten Commandments that served as our tutor also showed

that we could not do the right thing, let alone doing so perfectly, try though we must!

3. Just as Jesus picked out His disciples, did Jesus really also first select me, rather than I choose to believe in Him? As the Apostle John reports Jesus saying in 15:16 and 19, "You did not choose Me, but I chose you… I chose you out of the world…" Reading the likes of this makes me again feel like something is trying to take away my volition, intent, and ultimate legitimacy, as if I'm a pawn, albeit one for His good purposes. I want Him to know I chose Him, and it's for real! I fervently pray that I can "bear fruit" (Matthew 3:8); it would pain me "to be cast into a fire and burned" (John 15:6) for my lack of productivity for Him! How can I remain His friend if/as I am incapable of doing in a sustained fashion what He commands?!? I am more than motivated; I have become compelled and cannot *not* do what I am fashioned to do (and enjoy doing) for Him. Just about a month and a half after Bonnie's final chemotherapy treatment and two months after a young man in my class falsely accused me of physically waking him up, which led to the investigation which proved my innocence, I faced an even more distressing situation. Equally spurious but more dire, this incident challenged me to the core and rendered me needing to lean on Him with complete abandon once again.

8.21 Dimi's Trials and Tribulations

I had yet another student in another class that same semester, one I had purposefully seated right in front of my podium to help him stay focused because he was doing rather poorly. Still, I frequently found him looking over and snickering with another boy two rows over. I was reading John Keats' "To a Nightingale," and I happened to be focusing on the particular line, *"Now more than ever seems it rich to die,"* and I wanted them to feel its power and beauty. Instead, I heard the giggling of two boys looking at each other and were mentally a million miles away. This was the case only with them; the rest of the class was transfixed by this intense moment. In order not to break the stride of the lecture, I looked over my podium at one of those boys and gently touched him on the cheek for a split second to revert his attention back to me. The look in my eyes said, "Eyes on me. Focus." I didn't miss a beat and kept on reading to my otherwise rapt students. There was nothing unusual about the situation; it was just another day, and the boy quickly got back on task. In a manner of speaking, this line of Keats foreboded what would nearly happen to me figuratively and professionally.

The next day, I realized something was very wrong: this student told me he had gone to an administrator's office about an attendance issue, yet this administrator was not even there. The following day, I preemptively went to the administrator to check in, but she told me that "she could tell me nothing" about the student, which, of course, though legally accurate, this confirmed within me that something was quite awry. I felt like my heart was in an ice-cold vice-grip. On my way back to my department, I ran into another teacher, a Christian woman, who, in fact, was the very one who had observed me just a day after I'd been saved. (In fact, she enthusiastically hugged me upon learning of my salvation.) I immediately shared with her this odd situation. She comforted me and reminded me that, come what may, I needed to keep my focus on relying on Christ for my strength; I knew it was no coincidence that I ran into her, but the situation was far from over. The following day, I was called from class so that two detectives and someone from a local government agency might take a statement from me, but I politely said that I would not do so until I had my attorney present. With nothing to say, I returned to class a few minutes later. Less than ninety minutes after this, when the bell rang to dismiss school, my administrator came to my room to bring me back to her office; I felt like I was walking the plank, trudging along to Chopin's Funeral March; I was sure I was heading to mount the gibbet. On the way to the office, I recited the Lord's Prayer to myself nonstop, like a security-blanket mantra. Upon entering, I met someone from the system from downtown who informed me that effective immediately, I was to be placed on (paid) administrative leave and was then promptly escorted out of the building to my car. I could only quickly gather my necessaries. My colleagues hugged me, and I was admonished for even saying goodbye to them. As we walked down the hall, this administrator asked me if I was "okay enough" to drive myself home because I was visibly shaking involuntarily. I still had not been informed of what exactly I had done to warrant this action, but I knew it was connected to the boy in class who had not been forthcoming with me that day. In bewilderment and desperation from having no one in whom to confide at that moment, I blurted out that day's circumstance to this administrator as we stood by my car. Though completely unsolicited, I left nothing out because I had done no wrong. As we stood together in the parking lot, I suddenly became aware of this gorgeous spring day being so bright and full of sunshine. As it turned out, this administrator tucked away what I'd shared, this inadvertent "confession" of an innocent heart, and said he'd be in touch after he'd heard from his superiors and other authorities to determine if I would be allowed to return to school. I felt like I was losing my mind and having an out-of-body experience, so I texted Mark, first a cryptic note about being put on leave. I hoped to meet with him because I was stunned and felt left for dead. Instead, he would call me while I was attempting to run it out of my system at the gym's outdoor track. All the while, I was looking up at the sky, and I felt my tears lying hot and heavy on my eyelids, making my vision blurry, and I prayed to God. I was in the middle of flooding my brain, supersaturating it with praise music when Mark called me. I kept asking him what God was trying to burn out of me, what impurity or dark stain might He be trying to rid me of in this trial. Mark said it might not be that at all, but that I should trust God to make the truth known in His timing. I also spouted off some angry things as well, but Mark just encouraged me. Nevermore than on this day could I so clearly see the world in two realms: the one where Satan's seduced my students to selfish and desperate acts of self-preservation, which included being untruthful to their parents. In reaction, the parents focused on the child's lament and did not hold their child accountable for his misbehavior in class. I kept fervently praying for God's will to be revealed and that I might be strong in my faith in His realm of grace and mercy.

After coordinating a time all could meet, I met my attorney at a local headquarters to where I was summoned so that I could give my statement to these detectives; it was located somewhere out in the middle of nowhere. It was then and there that I learned of my alleged infraction. It turned out that *another* boy in class, the one with whom the student in front of me had been giggling and getting off-task, reported to my administrator that I had "slapped" this student so hard that it "could be heard across the classroom." Wow! Talk about passive-aggressiveness for being called out; it also wasn't lost on me that with a whopping 30% average, the young reporter had nothing to lose and much to gain in crafting his lie. I went over the whole incident carefully, calmly, even imitating the scene, using my attorney as the student in front of my desk. I felt surprisingly at ease. Mark had already told me earlier not to worry; being blameless, I need not over-prepare because "the Holy Spirit will teach you in that very hour what you ought to say" (Luke 12:12), and this is exactly what happened! Though initially nervous about being there, I maintained my composure as I spoke; after all, no harm was done or intended. Sure enough, the tense and formal tone among us soon became alleviated; after I'd finished relating said event, the detectives became friendly towards me, and we even bantered. Such can only be attributed to God's presence and my innocence. This was all that was to happen that day, and right afterward, my attorney told me that she did not think it would go far. Then Bonnie and I drove downtown, and I enjoyed a pistachio gelato. I walked about feeling oddly liberated but still in a suspended state of limbo, as if in a free-fall. My mood shifted as I took in the warmth and beauty outside; my inner chill from the loss of normalcy in my little world lessened. That day was a day like no other. The next morning, the representative assigned to me told me that he had spoken to the detectives to whom I'd given my statement yesterday, and they told him it went "very well." So now he would (again) gather statements from every student in that class before getting back to me, and the agency with which they'd be dealing had sixty days to close out the case. I was encouraged by his tone and again was struck by the immensity of this situation. My prayer life was on fire right now, and I don't mean just in the asking; I was flat-out on my face. I was walking 1000% in faith and holding onto what, at the time, felt like a thread of hope. While I waited the day after my interview on to a second and third day with no news, I felt my faith in God being stretched, even though I believed the truth would prevail! I also know that there are those who wait two or three *decades* for their answer, and some never find *here* what they seek. Satan knew that one way to try to trip me up would be through my passion and pride, that is, through my work. It had been over a week since this all began, including three days of not being on the job. It felt more like forty days, and that day happened to be Good Friday; it was another glorious day outside. I looked at this as a gift from God to spend time with Bonnie out in my Edenic backyard and work on sprucing up the yard and planting flowers this spring. At one moment, I sat down on the fresh, green grass, tilted my head back, closed my eyes, and felt a pleasant breeze kiss my cheek as the intense sun warmed my face. I was so grateful for that moment and so happy to be with Bonnie, now past her own life-and-death trial! It occurred to both of us independently that God was giving us some time to enjoy His beautiful world. Ever wise, Bonnie reminded me of something Mark had said once, that being, when we pray, God is not going to respond to our prayers and petitions capriciously, cruelly, or unfeelingly. Like the Puritan writer, Mary Rowlandson, who sought answers about a trying situation in her life by locating a parallel event in her Bible, I did likewise. It says that God treats His children with kindness, not malice. I found my hope in Matthew 7:9–10 when Jesus rhetorically asks, "What man is there among you who, when his son asks for a loaf, will give him a stone? Or if he asks for a fish, he will not give him a snake, will he?" That then could apply to me, too! Fresh mercies were in store for me; I just had to wait for them to be dispensed. This predicament also gave me the courage to share my faith more directly with some at work, also a first. I had a couple of exchanges with my colleagues whom I would never have had the courage to attest to before because you're not supposed to talk openly about religion, but now I couldn't imagine not sharing my sustaining faith! One group text included seven of the ones with whom I'm closest there. Though I said nothing about my case and life was to be "business as usual" there, I wanted to encourage them, too. One fellow, believing teacher merely texted me a link to a YouTube song called "Thy Will," and though I had intended to listen to it when she sent it, evidently, I was meant to hear it later in God's perfect timing. My heart was agape and agog at the perfectly apt lyrics, as if God were speaking through this song to me. There's no "as if"; He *was*!

8.22 An Easter Never to Forget

On Good Friday, Bonnie and I went to visit her sister in Georgia, and she, like her sister, had of late come back to the Lord; it was readily apparent in her fresh stance of gratitude. Like me, she had undergone an incredibly stressful time at work, so she told me about a couple of classic gospel songs that she would sing to herself while at work in praise of Him. Ironically, this got her mind off a challenging time when her crass boss seemed to have it out for her. God worked through her to get to me, and He gave me yet another song I realized had a perfect application for what I was enduring in its hand-delivered message. I downloaded it that very day. The day after we returned home, I got dressed to make my annual trek across town to the local Greek Orthodox Church. On my way to the midnight Resurrection service, I blared my new, favorite song in my car, singing along for all I was worth, setting it on repeat to fill myself with Him. That song is called "'Til the Storm Passes by"; it was brand new to me, yet familiar to many an older Southern Baptist. I was tearing up while I sang and drove, feeling weak yet strong, pained yet victorious, not knowing, yet believing that "*'mid the crash of the thunder, Precious Lord, hears my cry, keeps me safe till the storm passes by…*" What exaltation! When I got there, I was already moved! The Easter service at our church the following Sunday morning was incredibly dynamic; in fact, I forgot about everything going on in my little life as Mark transported us in his sermon to the very morning of the Resurrection two thousand years ago. I found myself at the foot of the cross mourning with the few women there and John, stood silently beside Mary Magdalene when she witnessed the risen Jesus and sat with the Disciples as He came in and showed them His wounds, comforting and encouraging them. I even attended one of our church's services *before* I went to the Greek service; so, technically, this was my third Easter service. Later that Easter evening, I spent a relaxed, or should I say, a distracting time of normalcy at the home of my former student and good friend, Catherine. All of her brood — her mother, both of her sisters, and all of their kids and their friends were there. When you're there, it's easy to get lost in their laughter and chaos. When you are in the midst of what feels like a slumber party or family circus in full swing, for this duration, both your troubles and the cares of the world are no longer on center stage. They are like family for me, and we love each other through thick and thin. I still had no resolution to the matter at school, so I was feeling anxious and like my life was on hold. Just two days before, on Good Friday, I was told to check back in with the representative assigned to me on the Tuesday *after* Easter Monday, so I was in the middle of a waiting game. Then unexpectedly, out of nowhere — miracle of miracles — my representative called me that Easter Sunday evening, right when I was in the midst of all this happy chaos. I had to cross the street to find quiet. He told me *I'd been released to come back to school tomorrow,* Monday morning because this case had been dismissed. The charges were found baseless, and the evidence revealed no mal-intent on my part. I nearly dropped the phone and started simultaneously laughing and crying as I just kept repeating over and over, "*Thank you!!*" The person assigned to me was personable, kind, direct, and all the while, authoritative; I would then come to know he was a Christian, too. I had just one remaining move in this grown-up version of Candy Land to finish up, and that would be to meet with my administrator who was to have a consultation with me.

I returned to work the next morning only to be told that we teachers were to go directly to an emergency faculty meeting before our first class met because we'd just had our second suicide that year, and we were to be briefed as to what measures were set in place for grieving students. Again, I was reeling! My big return from being wronged was put in proper perspective by a child whose suffering had gotten so bad that he ended his life. At the end of the meeting, about half a dozen teachers came up and quietly hugged me in acknowledgment that they were glad I'd been vindicated. That was that. I went back to my class without fanfare; I was just glad to be back safe and sound in my classroom. It would be another two and a half weeks before my meeting would take place. Soon after, I also joined my local teachers' union for support, representation, and legal counsel, just in case I'd need help again. I believe God had His hand throughout the whole experience because, as it would turn out, I would need His sustaining guidance yet again for another minor circumstance that arose. I felt like I was in a boxing match, and I didn't know how many rounds there were! My inner questioning went from "*What are you trying to teach me, Lord?*" to a realization and ready acceptance that I was in some block of intense training to instill obedience in me, to further solidify my reliance on Him, and to buff into me a soft shine of a humble heart. I took all it in. When I first got back, I couldn't even look at my superior. Erring on the side of caution to protect the school and all parties concerned, she followed the letter of the law, which had put me in the hot seat. As a result, this situation felt like an attempt to assassinate my character and break my spirit, but I now know it was not; I am teaching in a different environment than the one in which I did over two decades ago. I had continued to pray almost without ceasing over the whole situation until an acceptance and peace of "*come-what-may*" came to me; God took charge of this, too! This stance sustained me until the matter fully resolved itself to the good. Forgiveness did not happen overnight; it took about three months later for it to occur, and then I forgave the whole lot — the boys, their parents, and the administrator — for starting this domino effect that befell me. After this, I began to feel real peace. I didn't want or need to talk about it anymore. For good measure, I chose to forgive myself for any hurt feelings that may have arisen from my end. God knows I asked Him to repair the whole situation, and that included me as well! I did not want to harbor resentment; bitterness is such a heavy load to bear. Now that I'm on the other side of what happened, I wanted to examine how I could grow from this experience to help ensure I was doing my part to keep up with the times of this educational landscape. As I climbed my way out of this mire, there would be more reasons to fall back on my face in prayer. All pain and travails are relative, and I am fully aware that what befell me is hardly of the magnitude of dealing with the likes of an unexpected turn in one's health or a tragic death, but as it affected my professional life, it still smarted nonetheless. Each person's joy and pain are real unto him.

8.23 SELF-SLAUGHTER AT SCHOOL

My administrator canceled the meeting that we were scheduled to have because another student, a senior, had killed himself; he was one I'd taught last semester. His suicide made it the third from our school that year! And the boy had been a Christian! Rage, sorrow, and helplessness clawed at my breast! Could we have seen or prevented it? I felt like shaking my fist at modern-day education, the priorities of which seem so skewed, detached, and uncaring. Running a school now co-involves a near-obsession with collecting data, stats, and measurable growth to the point that we have become diverted from our primary calling and the *human* aspect of our job. Class size needs to be reduced so we can pay attention to subtle clues of the students we teach. A lighter load makes it easier to give the individual attention should additional help be needed. We are *also* called to develop *relationships* while cultivating these young men and women's minds and character. They aren't products to be tweaked to obtain improved results. For us to be successful at teaching, children of *all* ages must sense we *care* for them. Can you tell that the Christian call for community is needed not only in the sports arena but also in the classroom? We who love teaching know this innately and provide this the best we can despite the ever-increasing requirements that impinge upon our time, resources, and energies. The insipid ninety-minute video on "Suicide Prevention" we teachers are mandated to watch every year, alongside the dearth of information provided to the students about this, doesn't help matters. An increasing number of students feel isolated and lonely because they are starving to death for validation, authentic love, consistency, righteousness, and even a way to escape bullying or feelings of futility.

Being hyper-aware of this silent, stabbing pain of theirs has made me feel even more urgent about somehow sharing Christ with them because, as it turned out, I also discovered that there had *also* been three *attempts* this year. With the explosion of violence we have witnessed in our country over the past twenty years or so, these could just as easily have been homicides. In my lecture on existentialism to my seniors, I press in passionately when offering the answer to *take a leap of faith* to overcome anguish and despair. There is a God, and He cares! I do not shy away from being frank in an earnest and respectful way, and I do not shy away from sensitive topics. Indeed, that is half the reason why, for example, I teach *Hamlet*. "To be or not to be" is just another way of asking, "should I live or die." For Shakespeare, "the undiscovered country" of what happens to us after we die is where we go after we expire, that is, to Heaven or Hell. The stakes for the buffet of choices we make in life have *eternal* consequences; those the students make now in high school do not merely impact or prepare them for a future career or other vocational opportunities. We can assume that the characters in *Hamlet* are Catholic, in which case, it was erroneously presumed that if one took his own life, salvation would be forfeited. Suicide — here called "self-slaughter" — would be considered another type of murder, which, as you know, God denounced in His Ten Commandments. Hamlet believed that choosing to live rather than ending the torment meant he wasn't courageous enough to risk going to Hell (by breaking God's law), so his decision to live out his life in anguish meant that conscience "doth make cowards of us all." He'd rather stay in the "hell" of his life than risk going to literal Hell by committing suicide. Even though this is not so, that we *don't* go to hell for being mentally sick enough to kill ourselves, at least it inhibited Hamlet.

Kids today with no belief or faith in God have no breaks or compunction; they seek a quick out from emptiness and pain. It is normal sometimes to feel despair, and one can't see down the pike far enough to know we can find hope in the power of love. Regardless of how much people can disappoint us, Christ Jesus always offers us love. Always. Impetuosity and impatience are marks of immaturity. Everlasting fire is infinitely worse than any torment we feel right now, so how can we not grab hold of the love that can save us now and then? There is no such holding cell or waiting room as the limbo-land abyss of purgatory. You will find no mention of Purgatory in Scripture. Plus, when one *accepts* the love of God through His Son, "*nothing* will be able to separate him from the love of God" (Romans 8:38, emphasis mine). Yes, I have actually said this to students in public high school; for me, there is no separation of God and state. At least they respect my honesty and concern; I hide nothing. Plus, teenagers can whiff out hypocrisy like no other age group; they are developing their moral character right before our eyes. There have *got* to have good and loving role models, people on whom they can count, but it seems this number is diminishing. As a Christian, albeit a young one, and as a veteran teacher, I realize there's not one moment to spare in trying to pour out God's love; He can draw them to the wellspring of His love. You can't get frustrated with kids who don't *seem* to care; spoiling children with material items while withholding love creates a want and a hunger for love that gets substituted with things that never quench. Adults get mad at how much time kids spend on their devices, but they fail to see that *they* are not filling the void that alluring blurbs and shiny images do. The solution starts with our freedom to choose a better way, a life sustained in joy, which does not depend on circumstances. Choosing Jesus is a risk that worked for me. I've never known a love like His before.

When the day and hour finally came that I was to have that final meeting of consultation with a primary administrator, I had the president of the teacher's union accompany me. On the way to the meeting, I repeated in prayer over and over again, "*Be anxious for nothing*, but in everything by prayer and supplication with thanksgiving let your requests be made known to God" (Philippians 4:6, emphasis mine). I then visualized "casting all [my] anxiety on Him…" (1 Peter 5:7), as if I were throwing out a seining net full of these anxieties. Still, I found myself in a cold sweat again. Less than fifteen minutes before that dreaded appointment, some members of a local Baptist Church happened to be to the school to bring goodies to the faculty as it happened to be Teacher Appreciation Week. One of our secretaries brought the group down to our wing because one of their members, a youth pastor, was, as she said, a "particularly good hugger." When they entered our hallway, a group of us believing teachers quietly gathered together in a small circle of prayer with him, and we bowed our heads and held hands as he prayed intently for us. This year's time of woe with three dead students had left a big hole in the hearts of many. He prayed for our strength and leadership, prayed for God's love to be present there at school. I have to admit, just minutes away from my upcoming meeting, I knew that this seemingly ironic moment of receiving such support I could attribute only to God's timing; this was His way of showing out and encouraging me.

Then I met my union rep. Together, we went to the final conference with my administrator, where I was read the "charges" brought against me. This administrator, professionally cool and aloof, chose to believe two of my worst students who had lied in their way of taking vengeance. I had not walked a mile in this administrator's shoes to know that the stakes were too high *not* to submit a report; after all, way too many teachers and administrators had abused their power and had gotten caught doing improper things. My administrator was just following protocol and doing her due diligence. To avoid any heat from above for tolerating a potentially wrongful situation, he reported me. Next, I had a chance to read back my statement to the administrator, and what I wrote was attached to what was read to me. My mind was calm, but my insides were a wreck; the meeting passed, and life went on. Long story short, no harm, no foul. For a period afterward, I went under into a sort of hibernation, telling myself just to bide my time and lay low. I came to feel calmer over time, but withdrawing and withholding aren't true to Him or me. God is not in the business of resignation.

I realize that ultimately, I serve God, not man, but I am also commanded to love others, yes, even my "enemies." I did some serious soul-searching and reflected on this incident not related to teaching. Mark frequently says, "Hurt people hurt people," which is doubly true with desperate students going nowhere fast, academically or personally. Plus, I am very much still living in the flesh! I was sad and mad and hurt intermittently and somehow concurrently. Later that same afternoon, I confided what had happened at work to my friend at the gym, Rick, who is a natural encourager and is always ready to crack a joke to get a smile out of me. His first response to my telling him how my superiors dealt with the situation by suspending me was, "Why, suuuuuure, they did!" Rick was never surprised by evil that is manifested in the world, and in this case, it started with a teenager; after all, the world is filled with unbelievers over whom Satan has clear dominion. The reason Rick wasn't incredulous is that he knows troubles are to be expected, and we must shield ourselves by delving deeper in Him and shining our light all the more brightly. Rick continually quoted Scripture to me, but in this instance, I thought of one for myself to help me make out of the situation at hand, and I shared it with him: "Behold, I send you out as sheep in the midst of wolves; so *be shrewd as serpents and innocent as doves*" (Matthew 10:16, emphasis mine). My spirits *did* rebound, but it took some time. Who could have predicted that over the following year, I would share the burden of disciplining students and check in with my superiors to such a frequent degree that I was recognized for my "flexibility" and "growth"?

Another response to serious life challenges is that I found myself wanting to surround myself with other *Christians* for support. No question. In fact, I hadn't yet told my actual family about any of what had happened because I so sought biblical wisdom and guidance. I now knew I wanted to memorize the Twenty-Third Psalm. The evening after I saw Rick at the gym, I attended the funeral of the student who had most recently taken his life, a young man I'd taught the previous term. He was our school's final suicide victim that year, and for the second time that day, I felt my heart pounding hard as a hammer. When asked in the service if anyone had anything to say, without reason or a thought, I walked right on up there to the podium in God's cloak of confidence. I spoke with words *He* provided to a small sea of people, some of whom were standing for the lack of available seats. There was also a small sea of students sitting on the floor. I spoke to that young man's incredible character, to the fact that he never wavered, never missed a day, despite his not being a stellar student. And I even said that I had the feeling that he was the kind of young man — the strong, silent, John Wayne type — who I knew would have taken a bullet for me. I praised his parents for raising him right, and I assured them that he was *not* gone and that he was much loved. To tell you the truth, these deaths and complaints raining down made me feel like I was in the middle of a real-life Call of Duty or an old Centipede video game. After this funeral, I became so agonized that I wrote a poem to share with students. It didn't feel like it was I who wrote it: I did not doubt that the Holy Spirit directed my pen, and the words flowed. Here is the short message I penned for these young adults:

To all my students:
Though unspeakable tragedy has recently hit our school,
To not discuss and help heal would surely make me a fool.
So, I'd like to take the time right here and now to say,

Dimitria Christakis

That I like all my teachers for you do truly pray,
That all of you will come to live a rich and vibrant life
And that you know you're loved by us through and beyond this strife.

8.24 "Do Not Go Gentle":
More Tribulations

Soon after this incident had transpired, I would yet again be besieged. Satan has a way of instigating pains, and God, in turn, has a way of turning such predicaments on their head for His good; however, such circumstances hardly transpire in the time frame you might wish for. Two days later, I was teaching Dylan Thomas's classic poem, "Do Not Go Gentle into That Good Night," in which the poet encourages his father to "rage" against the "dying light," that is, *fight death*. This poem just happened to be on the schedule for that day, and it was in the students' textbook. In their illogical, immature, and passionate teenage brains, my grieving students twisted this poem to mean that I implied that the student who had committed suicide — their friend — had been a coward, that he had not *fought* his self-destructive impulse. During lunchtime of the day I was teaching Thomas, an administrator came to me and demanded to know what I was teaching. Learning about their complaints of this poem *and* considering the current school climate, I dropped this poem like a hot potato. I wouldn't have hurt their feelings for anything! Even though I did so, the gossip mill was already churning more than I could know. Two hours later, I found out that two boys had made vague and veiled threats on social media towards me. Again, an administrator came outside my room, this time with the security officer. You can imagine I was terrified and wondered what *then* I had done. She assured me I wasn't in trouble, but she was choosing to escort me out of the building "for my safety" until she could sort all this out. She put her arm around my shoulder and said that she was trying to protect me. Incredulous, I felt like I was living in another dimension. If what had happened this semester had occurred five years ago, I would have become cynical and bitter toward my students and harbored rancor toward the administration. Now, however, I was nonplussed, unafraid, and once at the gym, not even fifteen minutes later, I dropped to my knees and prayed *not* for myself but for the suffering students who had complained. The next night at church, for the first time, I also prayed for the administrator who had felt like my trespasser, prayed that God would soften her unbelieving heart, prayed that I might even have an opportunity to witness to her one day. These are changes in me for the better due to my becoming a Christian; for sure, I am putting all my chips into Him who saved me. I hope God can utter, "It is Good," here, too.

Finally, I should like to mention that my *initial* reaction to pain or perceived threats is hardly holy — often, far from it, but I do rebound more quickly than before when I probably would have just gotten further stuck in sin. I am learning that I can't criticize the form of sin others succumb to but to which I don't; the same applies to others toward whatever my deal is. Satan's got my number and knows precisely which buttons to push, so now I concertedly try to look ahead and anticipate the next chess move of his to take my king. I remind myself that God allows these things to happen; He never causes them. There is an intersection where temptations or unwanted and painful situations occur, which God uses to make us stronger, ultimately for His glory. He can transform our pain into His pleasure and heal us, to boot. While I am enduring or persevering for God knows how long, His purpose usually isn't known or made readily apparent. Satan evades our scrutiny, so *God often gets the blame.* Sometimes, the Lord "will be quiet in His love" (Zephaniah 3:17); at other times, He will "roar" (Joel 3:16), but I am here to tell you, He has been present and accounted for with Bonnie in her dire health situation as well as with me at school in my professional predicament. Another famous verse from the Bible I'd memorized that now had real meaning for me was a lengthy passage from the sixth chapter of Ephesians that tells us to put on "the full armor of God," and, whoa, I surely did. A recommendation for how I was to improve my communication with parents was brought to my attention the next fall. Once more, my first reaction was made in the flesh: initially, I was dismissive and defensive, but I rebound more swiftly than the last time and hearkened to Him. I became ready to grow, adapt and receive help in communicating with parents, yet maintain my high standards so that students knew their successes were legit.

How I came to improve my interactions with parents did *not* come from the articles or blogs printed out for me but from Scripture. In every form of correspondence, I would use "pleasant words [which] are a honeycomb, sweet to the soul and healing to the bones" (Proverbs 16:25) — even if I had difficult information to give them.

8.25 ANOTHER GLIMPSE INTO HEAVEN AND A LONGING

Later that evening, as Bonnie and I were driving back home from a friend's an hour and a half away, Bonnie broached the topic of death, and out of nowhere, she asked me, "What do *you* think Heaven will be like?" Almost instantly, it came to me. I told her that we would enter Heaven like blind people, who, having just had a cornea replacement upon entering there, suddenly had sight! We will feel as if we had gone outside for the first time and could not stop looking up at the trees and the sky and all that vibrant color; Heaven will be so beautiful and bright that we will want to cry for joy! We won't want to look at anything else. I think it will be like that. And this is just the beginning! To see Jesus and loved ones obviously will be beyond anything we've experienced or can imagine. We will come to be reunited with our earthly father *and* meet our Heavenly Father. And yet, it is *so* hard fathoming leaving what might seem to be *early* to us. Without saying so, Bonnie was contemplating *her* dying time — not that she was *remotely* ready for it, mind you! After all, she loved life and her friends and family, loved visiting new places and wanted to see "every inch" she could, and desired to keep on serving the Lord and helping those in need, especially her newfound friends in Haiti. Bonnie's need to know that she'd be going to Heaven was *huge*. She also hoped to see her granny and parents. This time, I finally answered her not with exasperation for seeking reassurance for the hundredth time, but with a calm and a cheer I prayed would become a helpful stay for her. I said that the fact that she believes that Jesus is the Son of God, that He died for her and took the punishment due us in our stead, that she turned to the good, and that Jesus' love was sealed by His giving us the Holy Spirit to be our guide and helper evinces for her that she *has* cut the mustard. It *is* going to happen! She *is* bound for glory, headed for Heaven! Jesus loves her and won't leave her! What's done can't be undone! This fact is not dependent on her (or anyone's) opinion or any feeling. I made an analogy about fact versus opinion by saying that sometimes in the morning when I'm getting dressed for work and trying to pick out my blue trousers that are so dark, I argue that they are black. Only when I'm out in the light can I see that they *are* blue. In mental moments of dark doubt, one may not be sure and may mistakenly and erroneously think that the pair of pants he *thought* was black is actually blue. In other words, she can *think* her destiny is black when it is really and truly blue. I point-blank said that having met the criteria, she for sure will one day be in Heaven. Then Bonnie smiled broadly and started singing a contemporary Christian song, "Great Are You Lord," that was particularly poignant for her because of what she'd undergone. In the car, she lifted an arm in praise as she burst out,

"You give life, You are love
You bring light to the darkness
You give hope, You restore
Every heart that is broken
Great are You, Lord!
It's Your breath in our lungs…
So we pour out our praise to You only."

Though every now and again, Bonnie's assurance can be lightly shaken, I know she no longer doubts as she once did, which rendered her "like the surf of the sea, driven and tossed by the wind" (James 1:6). Once again, Oswald Chambers came to my mind in how he defined faith: "Faith is not some weak and pitiful emotion, but a strong and vigorous confidence built on the act that God is holy love." That makes "throwing ourselves with total abandon and confidence upon God" *the* most important act we can ever do in life! At that moment, I recollected back to when I was a young girl, and looking up at my Great Aunt Carrie, and I asked her in the middle of a department store what happened to us after we die. She looked down with her wizened face, with that ever-mischievous twinkle in her eye, put her arthritic hand on my shoulder, and answered me with all seriousness, "We all become a memory to others after we die." I remembered feeling a vague disappointment settle in me which was inconsistent with the look of satisfaction on her sage face. Without the words to justify, let alone know why I felt like I did, I instinctively knew her answer was wrong and nonsense. How could we be born but to die and live but to lose? Now pushing five decades older, I know beyond a shadow of a doubt that this life is *not* the end, that I the right choice regarding how I want to spend the rest of my days here, but my death won't be my demise. There is no sense of disappointment with *this* finding. Why? I now "know the truth, and the truth shall make [me] free" (John 8:32 NKJV). "Eureka," I say!

On our way back home, Bonnie and I looked out the front window and gazed at the tender greenery and awakening land all around us. It felt so good to take in this beautiful spring evening, and I felt a powerful rush of lightness and gratitude for the moment's splendor. One's spirits can quickly get dampened if one ingests too much of what goes on in and to this world; in fact, it can actually become a habitude or outlook to live in the blues. Sometimes I have a longing so powerful for what I think doesn't even exist, like a nostalgia for some truth or intimacy I either can't find, attain, or sustain. No, I'm not talking about the so-called God-shaped hole each of us is born with, but something akin to the Portuguese word, "saudade," which means a longing or a "missingness" for an absent something or someone that one loves. It produces sad and happy feelings together, a pain for missing and a wistfulness for having at least experienced the feeling. Maybe it all boils down to a universal and inchoate recognition of our post-Edenic reality, where deep inside, we know *things just aren't the way they're supposed to be*. By "things," I mean how we treat *all* forms of life, be it our next-door neighbor, a group of people at large, or our planet. The fact that I possess a faith strong and unshakable within me doesn't mean I can't still get to feeling down upon occasion. As the Negro spiritual confides, sometimes I, too, "feel like a motherless child." A Christian pilgrim may feel like this as well; as we disconnect from what we *used* to do and who we *were*, we feel torn from ones we *still* love but with whom we no longer share core values. In sanctification, we go about the business of replacing the negative with positive, godly ways, but we don't throw away people!

Ultimately, we all yearn for everything to get righted again. I am *so* grateful for the Apostle John's vision in the Book of Revelation, where God lets us know how it all turns out in the end for all eternity. If one isn't aware of the role we play in directing that course for ourselves, one might not see the futility or lack of importance in chasing shadows, which are of such little consequence. An apt analogy would be to observe the impact of a lifetime of food choices we ingest on our overall state of health. Cake and chips may please our tongues, but our body needs nutrients. Either you choose to accept Christ as your Messiah, or you don't. In Revelation 21, we discover that there will be the bringing about of absolute and ultimate perfection — not just a redo of what all we wish to have restored right now. God will bring about the union of "a new heaven and new earth," and He will "dwell among" us (taken from Revelation 21:1–3. Amazingly, we'll even get to see His face! The scene of the original crime at the tree of good and evil will rotate to the tree of life. Still, the light we all crave in those dark winter months, the light of ultimate knowledge we seek, and the sheen from moral purity and goodness we desire *are* available for those who choose Him. As Christ announced, "I am the Light of the world; he who follows Me will not walk in the darkness but will have the Light of life" (John 8:12). Fast forward past all the end-of-time events, and we find the presence of light *never-ending*, only this time this state is achieved through God. Since the Father and the Son are one, the Light of the believer's future is God. As a matter of fact, we "will not have need of the light of a lamp nor the light of the sun because the Lord God will illumine them; and they [the Trinity] will reign forever and ever" (Revelation 22:5). Just as I have been connecting the dots of my own life for you here in this book, the more I read the Bible, the more I can connect the dots there, too. It's astonishing! Each of these dots is a music note in the most magnificent symphony ever composed and by a Maestro second to none. I have revisited aspects of my own life and identity them with you here to show you that we each possess a vaster role in His living score.

So, how do I make sure I fit in His vast plan when I can also get absorbed in my personal agenda? How do I tell them apart or marry them together? I used to and still do feel immense pride in my Greek heritage. When I exude the best of what I innately possess — my tendencies, affections, ways, and preferences — which *seem* so Greek to me, the "flesh" in me gravitates towards that source and others like me who have a similar nature. I feel so at home, so *myself*, in Greece and at ease when speaking Russian with a Russian! I don't know how to explain it, but speaking another language brings out another aspect or identity that exists within a person. Yes, I am ecstatic that if I desired,

I have the right to one day make Greece my home, but there is a quiet and newly persistent voice way down inside me that whispers a more profound truth, that being, that my ultimate home is in Heaven. I also intensely love the life that God has brought about and unfolded for me right here in these hills of South Carolina. Opportunity to further serve Him will come where it will — where *He* wills — perhaps even in my own backyard. It's no accident I'm living here right where I am! And even though I can and do falter, grow impatient, or wallow in self-pity, I pick myself up by my bootstraps and turn to prayer more quickly than I did before, all the while knowing that I've got to represent. Why? I now live my life with an awareness that I am an "ambassador for Christ" (2 Corinthians 5:20); people witness God through the likes of me! Bonnie, too, understood exactly what I meant as she'd experienced a slight separation from former friends. She continued to love on her friends and let them know it was still she, Bonnie, but her priorities had values had changed. An appreciation for our roots, culture, and friends remains, but they are appreciated in a new light. After speculating on these endless vistas and imagining how it's gonna be, we came back to earth, and quite famished after that talk, we decided to feast on sushi for dinner that evening.

8.26 Answers from Him

We would visit with Mark once more before the summer began, and I looked back and decided that I wanted to try to answer my questions for myself in case he didn't get to them, and, well, because I just needed to do so. Over four years out, now my questions were not the type that anguished or plagued me regarding my salvation or God's triune nature. After percolating on the questions I'd had from well over a month ago, I'll share with you the answers that the Holy Spirit delivered to me.

1. Yes, of course, Jesus came to offer redemption and to give grace to humanity in an unparalleled way, that is, the forgiveness of sins and substitutionary atonement. That's not all! Here's another co-answer that is equally true: not all will people accept Christ; neither did they then, nor will they now. Ultimately, because Jesus and God are equal, the final judgment involves both of them divvying up this momentous task. There exists only one of two gateways a person upon death stands at: (a) the Great White Throne, where God judges those who are not Christian and condemns those who knew of His Son but outright rejected Him, and (b) the Bema seat, where Jesus evaluates us believers as to what we did for Him to further His kingdom. This also includes exposing both our missed opportunities as well as revealing known and unknown acts of our promoting Him. We receive crowns which, of course, we will exuberantly fling with joy right back at Him, be it one crown or a pile of them. Jesus will also console and comfort us for any loss or regret we might momentarily experience.

2. When Jesus says, "If I hadn't have come, then you wouldn't have sinned," He is *not* saying, "J.k. Ya'll can keep on doing what you're doing. You're cool." Nope. The minute Jesus came here, it became known through the many ways He evidenced that He was the Messiah

and Son of God and that He was here to establish a New Covenant written on "the tablet of our hearts" (Proverbs 7:3). Like they in His day, we, too, can no longer claim innocence or ignorance. We who have heard of Him can't plead the Fifth! We are culpable if we reject Him the same as if we were the ones who condemned and crucified Him! If we Christians are doing our jobs right and going out there to share the Good News, there ought to be fewer folks who are not unaccountable. May *you* be such a one after reading this primer! On the other hand, if you *have* come to know Him and still reject Him, that strike is on you. I implore you not to let past hurts with Christians (or the Church) damage your future with Him!

3. Did Jesus pick me first, or did I choose to accept Him? This question smacks of the topic of predestiny, so I am inclined to seek another both/and solution. First, whether I recognize it at the time or not, my capacity for faith and the desire to know Him who made me is God-given. When I seek, I will find, but in certain crises when, unbeknownst to me, God sees that I need help, the Holy Spirit draws me to Him such that there is an inclination and a tentative curiosity that can blossom oh-so-quickly. It's a harmonious and symbiotic occurrence, but one which He ultimately activates. That being said — here's the "and" part — it is on *me* "to work out my salvation with fear and trembling" (Philippians 2:12). He chose me first, but I still have to say, "Yes," before I can get on with the empowering privilege of serving Him who loves me like no other.

4. Just how long does God reckon with a hardened heart? What happens if one either ignores or rejects God altogether and/or outright says, "No"? What exactly does it mean for God to relinquish us to our sins? You may not use the word "idolatry" in your everyday lexicon, but I think what displeases God more than anything else is when we worship, value, serve, or lust over the creation more than the Creator. Let that sink in because it covers

so much! After all, "the LORD is a jealous God" (Exodus 34:14). Does He ever really give up on us? I think that even though we may get stuck in sin or fettered to matters and things of this world to the point that He may not expend His energies on us in the moment — which for some of us may even last decades — as long as we have breath in our lungs, I do not think He *ever* gives upon us! That's the God we serve! I believe this is why Jesus tells stories of the eleventh-hour worker who gets the same paycheck as everyone else or why several Gospels give the account of the thief who accepted Him as he's being crucified next to Him. That said, if you are seduced by fame, power, or comfort or you have sunk into such apathy and passivity such that you can't see beyond your own nose, God is not going to wait on you to come around to achieve His purposes. He will promote *another* person to do the job that goes toward fulfilling His master plan. Likewise, He can employ a person or a life event to stun, shock, or move you out of your state of bliss, narcissism, ignorance, or inertia. If it sounds like He is using us. If that ruffles your feathers, remember that all of life is *His* showboat. He made all; you made none. I think we should first be grateful that Someone *is* in charge, that all of what happens in life isn't just according to happenstance, randomness, chance, luck (or the lack thereof) cosmic entropy spinning itself out. Secondly, this great omnipotent "Someone" — God — who identifies Himself as "I Am" (Exodus 3:14) is *love incarnate*; His love is so magnificent that it's mind-boggling, heart-stopping, and never-ending. That you exist and *crave* love is living proof. It's all about Him, but He gave and continues to give His all for *you*! After all, who has his own son killed for the benefit of strangers who also hate his boy, all so these people can have a chance for something better? *He* did! Thank you, *Jesus*! An average person continuing on his merry way of a self-focused, self-serving, and self-contented life, one of unacknowledged and unconfessed wrongs, is in danger of desensitizing — "searing" (1 Tim. 4:2) — his conscience to the point that his perspective becomes contorted and he remains lost. He will not see Jesus though he may seem content. What's wrong might get called right, and he may never see the light. The further along one travels on this meandering path, apart from his maker and Savior, it becomes increasingly difficult to turn to Him. But do not fear! Calamity, disaster, and misfortune can bring one to one's knees and break through the hardened heart. It does not follow that if perceived bad things happen to good people, God is mad or sadistic; we just aren't privy to what's taking place at the macrocosmic level, His big picture. Turning away from sin changes your destiny, direction, positioning forever and helps point you to a path for which you were designed. You may not be used to hearing, let alone *using* the word "sin" in your vocabulary, but call it what you will; if you've got a twinkling of self-awareness in you, though you often may be good, you know you are far from perfect. Accepting Christ means that it is no longer *you* who is in control because He lives in you. That does *not* make you a moppet, puppet, or marionette because you *still* have your voice, life, and volition which He gave you. Indeed, you are freer to be who God made you to be when Christ is alive in you. Soon enough, you will not evaluate or estimate your net worth by the world's standards anymore. Oh, you won't change overnight, but people *will* see a difference in you. Hopefully, as you devote yourself to Him and get better at doing life His way, your heart will get softer *and* pulse with new vitality. Through submission and obedience, you will be stronger than you ever thought possible, and all of it comes about through love.

8.27 The Prodigal Son's Older Sister

Speaking of this radical transformation, this regeneration of my system, with every step I take towards the Light, I need to confess to you just how slow progress takes place and just how many more "miles I have to go," as Robert Frost penned. I don't want to give the impression that it has been smooth sailing; there have been and will continue to be thematic problems or issues that may remain such until the bitter end. Feeling frustrated with myself, I once told Mark, "I just can't fix myself, and Jesus is going to take a lifetime!!" I recall his chuckling at that. Looking back in hindsight, I can already see that God converges life circumstances to give us lessons and proof of His involvement; we just may not be noticing. What had my reaction to problems in the workplace, let alone the impetus for asking many of the questions you've read, have in common? Fear and doubt. Of what, you ask? Fear that I am unlovable and doubt that I even matter, that all is for naught. *Would* He answer me? *Is* there a "happily ever after"? My tangled mess is cloaked with a mantle of healthy self-esteem and worldly self-confidence that often points straight to personal pride. And this kind of pride will always lead to conflict until you deconstruct it and grow in Christ, which is what I want, even if sometimes I gnash my teeth along the way. There's a Bible story that speaks to this situation, and boy, howdy, did I find *my* place in it! I know you have heard of the story of the Prodigal Son; it is Jesus' longest parable. At some point in our lives, we become *all* of the characters in this tale: the repentant son, the resentful elder brother, and the rejoicing father. Though the youngest is the central focus, and I, too, have had my wayward moments in life, it is primarily the eldest son in the story to whom I relate. To be honest, I look forward to a time when I can be the father in the story and rejoice with ecstatic jubilation over those I know and love coming to (or back to) the Father. I want to tell you how I came to display the *second* greatest commandment, that is, loving my neighbor, who in this case was my brother. I tell myself daily that "our struggle is not against flesh and blood" (Ephesians 6:12), so it is not even my brother or anyone in particular that's the problem. Satan uses them as props in his schemes to trip, stun, or stop us, and often he blindsides us when things are going well or strikes when we least suspect it. Applying this parable to my life, I had done all the required things the right way to achieve worldly success before becoming a Christian: I earned my degrees, attained a good job, and developed a lifestyle of healthy habits for mind, mood, and body. It wasn't until I met Jesus, took Him in to settle at home in my mind and heart, that I realized just how much I had *yet* to improve within me, though my fate had been secured to the good.

For me to identify with the elder brother of the Prodigal Son is to admit I was full of resentment, envy, and anger. The healing process can only start when I rip off the Band-Aid to expose, debride, and apply a salve of forgiveness to my sins and emotional scars. It is no fault of my brother that he was born the son of my father, a very Greek man who favors the one who bears his name. There is nothing he did to receive the special affection that a mother often feels toward her only son, especially one toward whom she may feel guilt; add to this that he is the youngest and last babe. For years, I experienced cognitive dissonance over feeling both a huge love and protectiveness of my brother and yet deep-seated jealousy and resentment. It has been easier to judge and begrudge my brother than face the sinking sense that I was loved less. Whatever I achieved was never enough to meet my parents' approval and receive enough love to eradicate my warped perception of favoritism. When something happens to spark my righteous indignation or envy, I become a lame duck, and Satan can push me over with his little finger so that I'm back to saying my old mantra: "It's never enough; no matter what I do, it is never good enough! Nothing matters." Not only that, but my overtly trying to conform to His standards such that I erroneously think I may have "arrived" means that I am likely to judge others, particularly those who matter the most to me. Paul reminds me that "in that which you judge another, you condemn yourself; for you who judge practice the same things" (Romans 2:1).

In Matthew 7:3, we find Jesus using hyperbole to jibe us about the necessity of removing piles of garbage from our own side of the street before we attempt to point out a little dirt in other! Satan takes what is familiar, familial, and adored to divert and deflect my attention away from His good. He wants me to note the bad in those most important to me, which makes me ugly to them, and then they can't see Christ in me. Oh, to be cross is just the approach I want to take to "win friends and influence people" for Jesus, said no person ever! So, what's a girl to do? After I get to the point where I can give myself a good talking to and then throw in the towel of self-reliance, I finally listen to the hearkening of the Holy Spirit's convictions. He reminds me I must forgive, forgive family and friends, anybody and everybody, not to mention myself too. I've heard it said that holding on to unforgiveness is "like swallowing poison and expecting the other person to die." We are warned if we do not forgive others, then our Father will not forgive our transgressions (Matthew 6:15). Resentments can weigh you down like lead. Ultimately, whether I have conflict or bitterness that brings angst at work or displeasure with family members, resentment can be so difficult. You may get stuck for a while, but this is necessary to overcome; you do not want to (unknowingly) change your character for the worse, let alone beyond your own recognition by nursing your grievances, no matter how justifiable you think they may be! Mark would later wisely advise me "not to let that grudge turn to bitterness because bitterness is *so* hard to deal with. It is *vital* not to let it even take root!" I realize that the only way to combat one's anger towards another is to admit you have been the source of pain to someone else, too! Over time, I want to get better at the saying, "Seek to understand rather than be understood," if for nothing else than to get a much-needed perspective check. Mark assured me, "God heals our hearts. And sometimes He does it with understanding and sometimes with grace. Either way, life is *way* too short to live with a grudge." I say, "Amen," to that!

That said, resentments tend to fester and rankle longer with family members because the love for them is so much deeper; therefore, the wound takes longer to heal. I know I've been in the wrong so often. I am learning how to apologize in a timelier fashion when I hurt someone's feelings or get impatient or critical and cut them to the quick. And by the way, conviction isn't the same thing as a guilt trip! God doesn't work like that! For me, conviction feels like a compulsion to be true and humble all rolled up in doing the next right thing a.s.a.p. Why, Jesus' own half-brother, James, who undoubtedly came to regret how he treated his brother when He was alive, said that "saltwater cannot produce fresh" (James 3:12). What comes out of my mouth and through my actions won't be right until I'm scoured on the inside. Salvation is so just the beginning! Taking a really good look in the (preferably, magnified) mirror makes it abundantly clear to me, and, therefore, I become acutely aware that "THERE IS NONE RIGHTEOUS, NOT EVEN ONE" (Romans 3:10), starting with me! I continue to struggle to chip away at the stone, to keep working on removing the plaque away from my own heart that impedes the flow of His love coursing through my spiritual veins. I know Lucifer longs to lure me into feeling either all high and mighty or deflated and defeated. Honestly, these traits are just forms of entitlement, which also emanate from pride, which boils down to putting oneself before God. Agh! God doesn't impede or disallow adversity in my life because He is training me to become stronger so that others can see Christ in me. In any event, when it's all said and done, I am better now but not as good as I hope to be then. Improvement can only come through prayer and *tons* of practice of replacing negative behaviors *and* outlooks with righteous ones, all through the strong, invisible guidance of the Holy Spirit and the love of God. As they say, the best offense is a good defense, so you've got to anticipate Satan's using guerrilla warfare on you; he may also try to shoot like a trained sniper. In this case, your bulletproof vest will be the "full armor of God" recounted in the sixth chapter of Ephesians. You have to unlearn to relearn and take it in the chin like Him, your King, as you go about the business of living.

To that end, I hope to have many decades of being an attractive light to not only students and strangers but also, yes, to family. I know I'm on-call all the time and am being closely observed for signs of smugness or hypocrisy, the likes of which frequently are shown in the media and are how Satan conspires to keep people at bay or far away from Him. My former student and current dear friend, Catherine, keenly honed in on precisely what I was concerned about my walk in front of others. She encouraged me by saying, "On the topic of religion and family, I feel like Satan would LOVE if your choosing Jesus meant losing cherished relationships within your family. If he could equate choosing with losing, he'd gain more ground, *so don't let him.*" I do not intend to do so! Later that night, my brother called me, and we had an earnest talk I'd been hoping to have with him, and I did not hide the fact that I was dealing with spiritual warfare. Our talk was rich; I was gentle and really listened to him. The Bible tells me to *"pursue peace with all men"* (Heb. 12:14) and to *"resist the devil, and he will flee from me"* (James 4:7), and I'm here to tell you — praise be to God — this is true! As a closure to this topic here, and, as God — not fate --- would have it, the very next Sunday, Mark preached on Saul's jealousy of David to show us how to combat jealousy and envy in a biblical manner. Mark ended his sermon by promoting the action of *serving others* to get out of yourself. As it turns out, the best way to slay the green-eyed monster within is to leave the scene of the crime and help another in need. I wrote a poem that reflects this difficulty I am trying to overcome:

> Though I do not like to admit or say,
> The green monster sometimes does me assay.
> It boils down to daughter just can't be son,
> Which for us, I assure you, never feels like fun.
> So rather than face the pain of lamenting over what I'm not,
> I'll spurn and chide my brother and treat him like a sot.
> Yet if I continue the pattern where he sees me so often judgie,
> He'll not see Christ's love and I'll remain morally pudgie.
> So, I will do as you did today suggest,
> And remind myself God made us each by His own special behest.
> And when I'm feeling possessed with swift mad jealousy,
> I'd best think on His love for all in order to change my legacy.

8.28 A Fool for Christ Is Nobody's Fool

When I read back over what I've written you, I wonder if you think that I'm one of those people who wear rose-colored glasses. Why, she *can't* be in her right mind; she isn't who she used to be! Paul proclaimed what I can now also say about my Christian core, that is, "*I am what I am*" (1 Corinthians 15:10) for *Him*, so, yes, baby, this is it! Oh, yes, I'll be a fool for Christ if a word or two of mine penetrates someone's brain and entices him or her to turn to Him. By now, you well know that apologetics, the readiness to give a defense of the Bible, is pleasing to me. I don't get how people can be so critical of the Bible and yet have never read it! We don't do the same with other spheres! I'm not going to avoid surgery because I've heard tell that the surgeon takes a scalpel to one ill person yet decides to postpone an operation on the next! I challenge anyone to read the Word of God and not experience its dynamically being "active and sharper than any two-edged sword and piercing as far as the division of soul and spirit…able to judge the thoughts and intentions of the heart" (Hebrews 4:12). Like any profound book, each read reveals new truths depending on where you are in life. Like millions before and after me, I am discovering this *progressively*.

I feel beholden to share a smattering of a few lines from my favorite Proverbs that mostly deal with wisdom; they may appeal to you, too. Hopefully, out of curiosity, you will check them out for yourself. I include the number and verse parenthetically, and all come from the New American Standard (NASB) translation. There are just enough Proverbs to read one every day of the month!

- The fear of the Lord is the beginning of wisdom (9:10).
- Trust in the LORD with all your heart and do not lean on your own understanding (3:5).
- How much better it is to get wisdom than gold! (16:16.)
- Every man's way is right in his own eyes, but the Lord weighs the hearts (21:2).

- Take hold of instruction; do not let go. Guard her, for she is your life (4:13).

Nonetheless, it is of paramount importance to tell you that *knowledge without action is futile*! Paul tells us to "do nothing from selfishness or empty conceit" (Philippians 2:3). What this means is that you can't *ever* think you're better than someone else. How dare you or I get "puffed up" (1 Corinthians 4:6 NKJV) in pride! We've got to give what we get from Christ away, at least, that's what I want to do! I have one final point on this topic about what happens should you decide to test the waters and say, "Yes," to Him. Like starting to play a musical instrument, you must then *practice*, which takes self-discipline. You will not be a Wynton Marsalis just because you have taken up tooting a horn, but *be encouraged*. God really loves it when you try, so keep at it and stick to Him like glue. I love being self-disciplined because it is my way of showing gratitude and obedience to Him. I know I'm nowhere near what He might have me be, so I try not to compare myself with others; His will and ways are unique for each person. Why should you focus on a purpose and place in His scheme? Think big! Your parents may have brought you into this world, but He conceived of you long before you were born. No matter what, you were pre-purposed for splendor, fulfillment, joy and His glory, so much so that He came down here in person to guarantee your eternal life with Him. If this isn't the acme of love, then I don't know what is.